ERASED ❶

KEI SANBE

Translation: Sheldon Drzka
Lettering: Abigail Blackman

BOKU DAKE GA INAI MACHI Volumes 1 and 2
© Kei SANBE 2013.
First published in Japan in 2013 by KADOKAWA CORPORATION, Tokyo.
English translation rights arranged with KADOKAWA CORPORATION, Tokyo through TUTTLE-MORI AGENCY INC., Tokyo.

English translation © 2017 by Yen Press, LLC

Yen Press
1290 Avenue of the Americas
New York, NY 10104

Visit us at yenpress.com
facebook.com/yenpress
twitter.com/yenpress
yenpress.tumblr.com
instagram.com/yenpress

First Yen Press Edition: February 2017

Yen Press is an imprint of Yen Press, LLC.
The Yen Press name and logo are trademarks of Yen Press, LLC.

Library of Congress Control Number: 2016958580

ISBN: 978-0-316-55331-5 (hardcover)

11

WOR

Printed in the United States of America

Page 321
Hirobumi Itou: Japan's first prime minister. Born in 1841, he was assassinated in 1909. Depicted on the ¥1,000 bill from 1963-1984.

Page 323
Souseki Natsume: The most famous and respected novelist of the Meiji era (1868-1912). Considered to be "Japan's Charles Dickens." Depicted on the ¥1,000 bill from 1984-2004.

Rise: As a way of showing respect for the teacher, Japanese students collectively stand, bow, and resume their seats when their teacher enters or exits the classroom.

Page 354
Regional dialects: Japan has a lot of dialects, but when the Japanese move to the Kanto area (which includes Tokyo), where "standard Japanese" is spoken, they tend to hide or downplay their regional accent in order to fit in (as social pressure dictates), usually only letting loose when speaking casually with friends or relatives from the same area. Standard Japanese is taught in schools and used on TV, as well as for all official matters. This is why Satoru (as a child) considered Yuuki's affected standard Japanese manner of speech to sound mature and authoritative.

Page 386
"Pun intended": The pun is that the kanji for the author's surname, Sanbe, are the same characters used for the word "*sanbu*," that is, "part three."

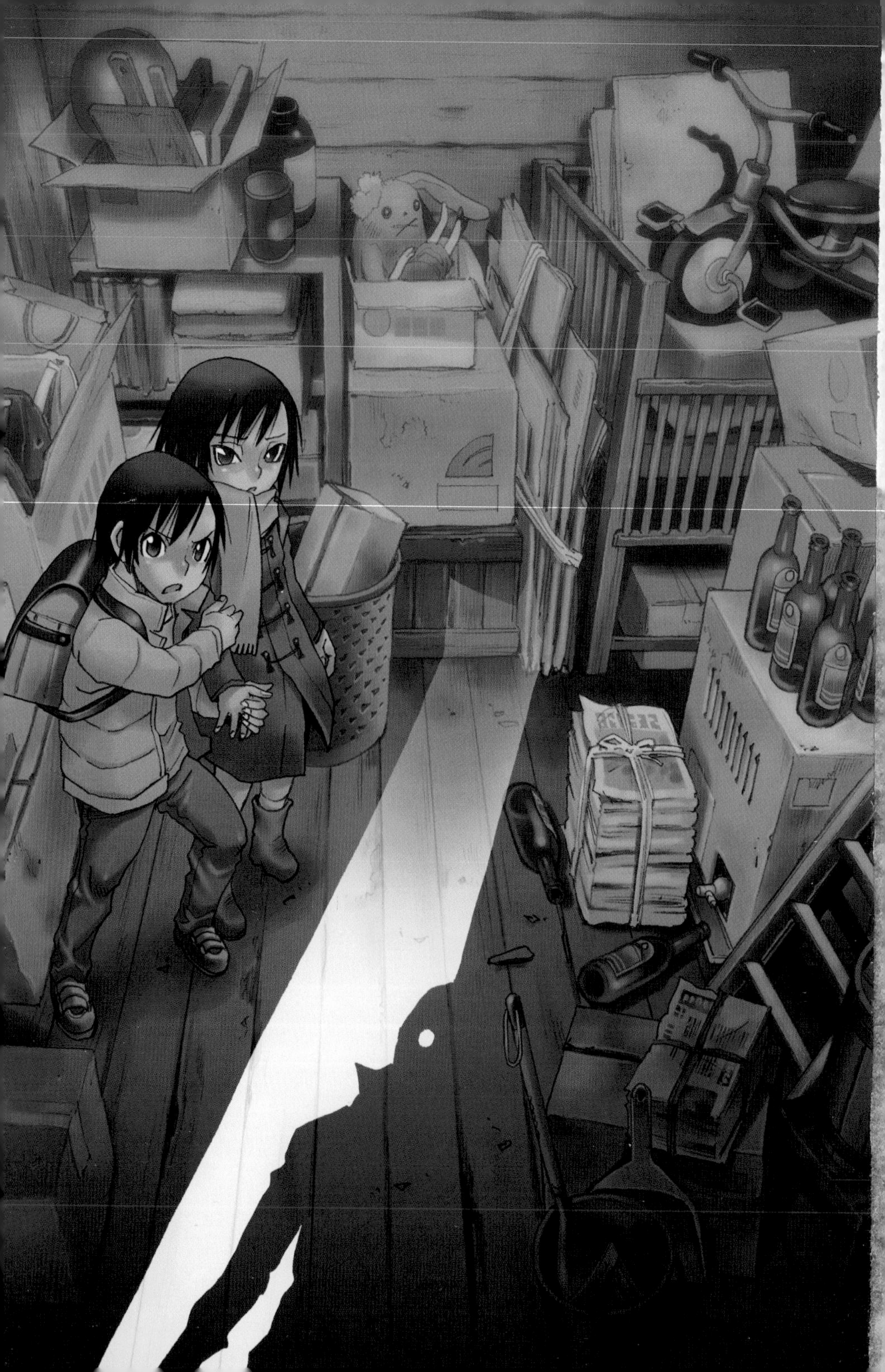

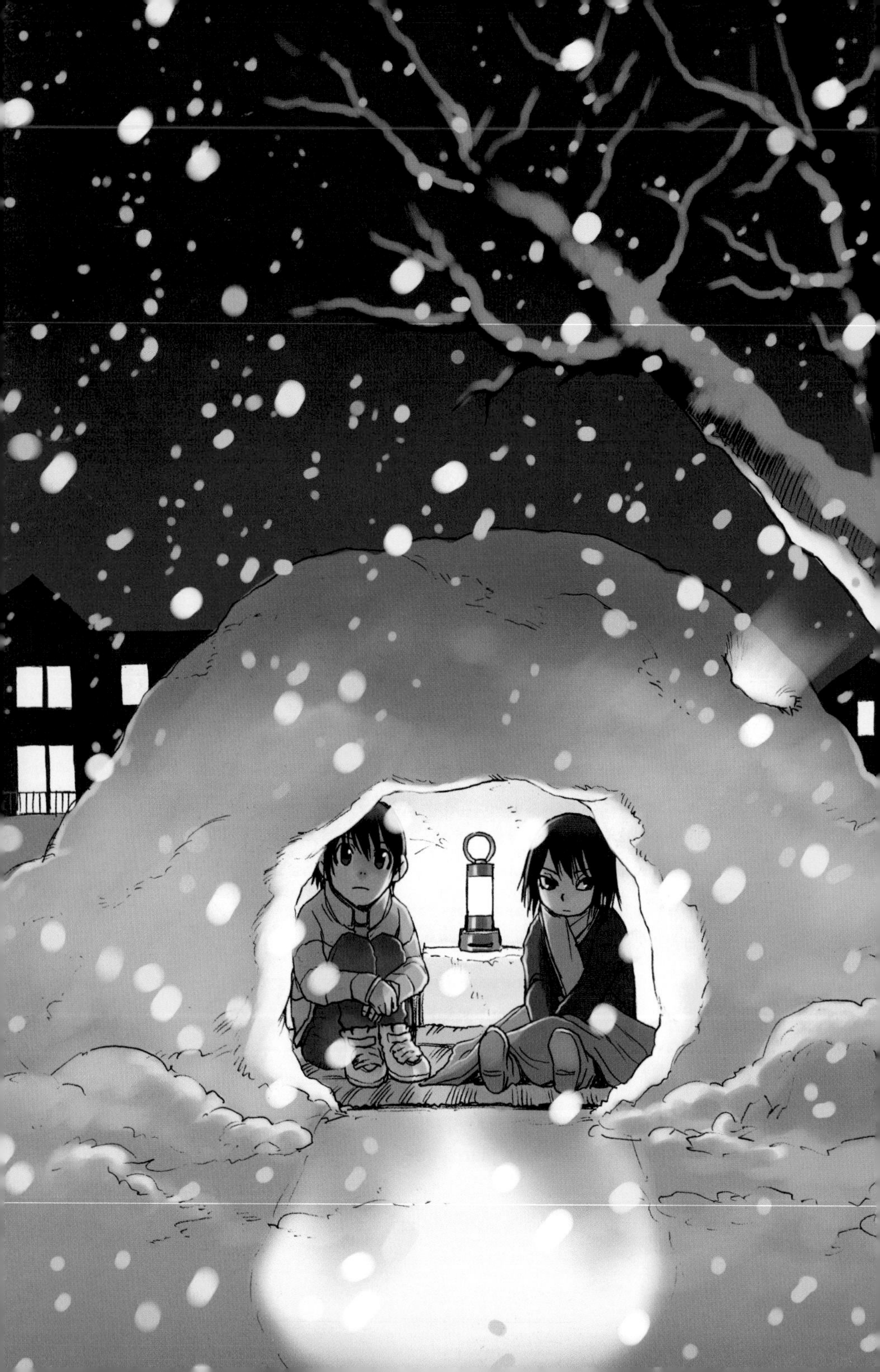

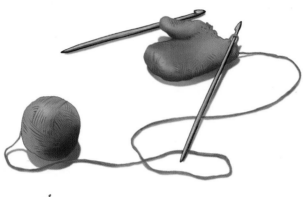

C O N T E N T S

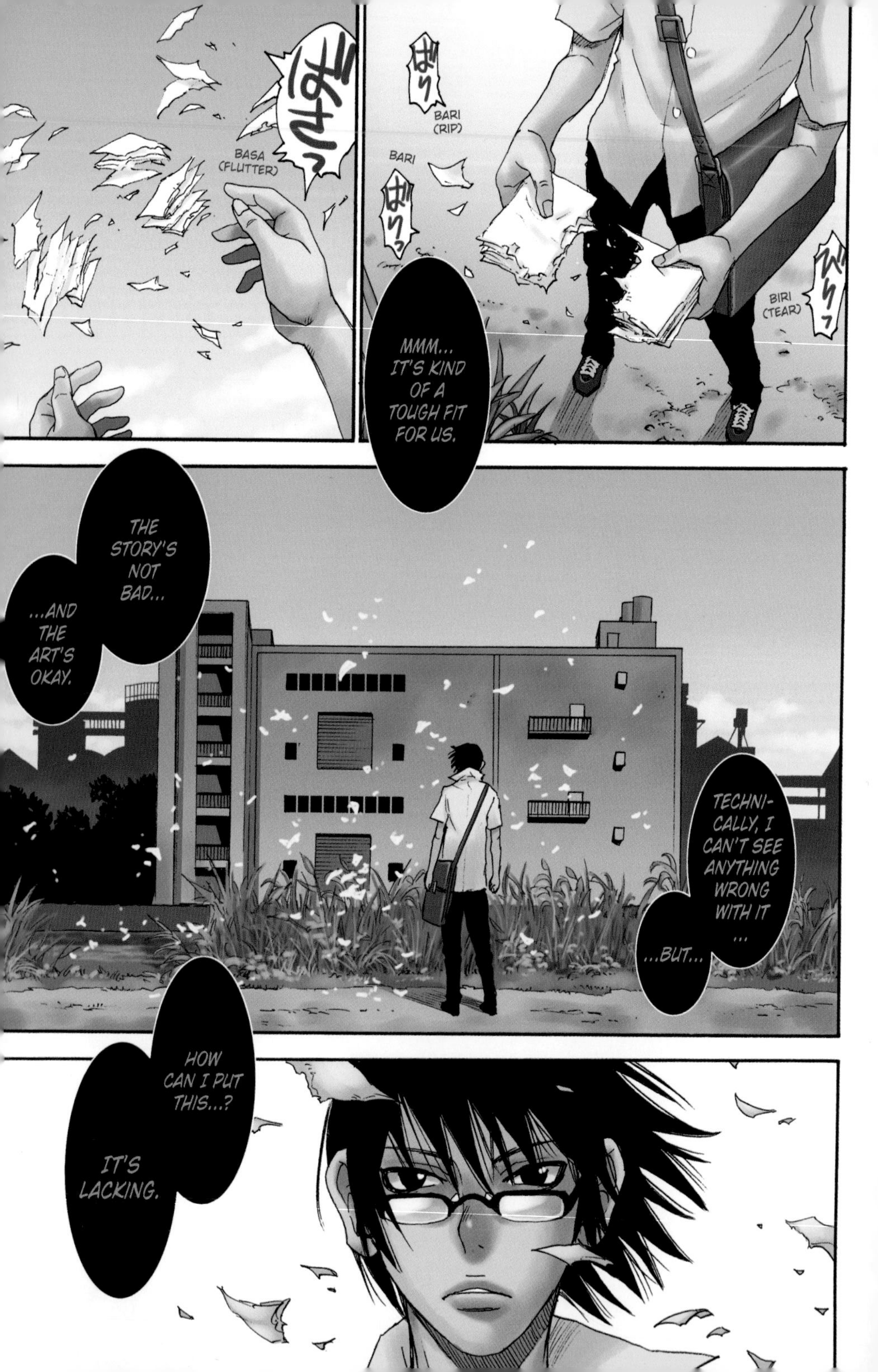

ばり
BARI (RIP)
BARI
ばりっ
びりっ
BIRI (TEAR)
MMM... IT'S KIND OF A TOUGH FIT FOR US.
ばさっ
BASA (FLUTTER)
TECHNI-CALLY, I CAN'T SEE ANYTHING WRONG WITH IT ...
...BUT...
THE STORY'S NOT BAD...
...AND THE ART'S OKAY.
HOW CAN I PUT THIS...?
IT'S LACKING.

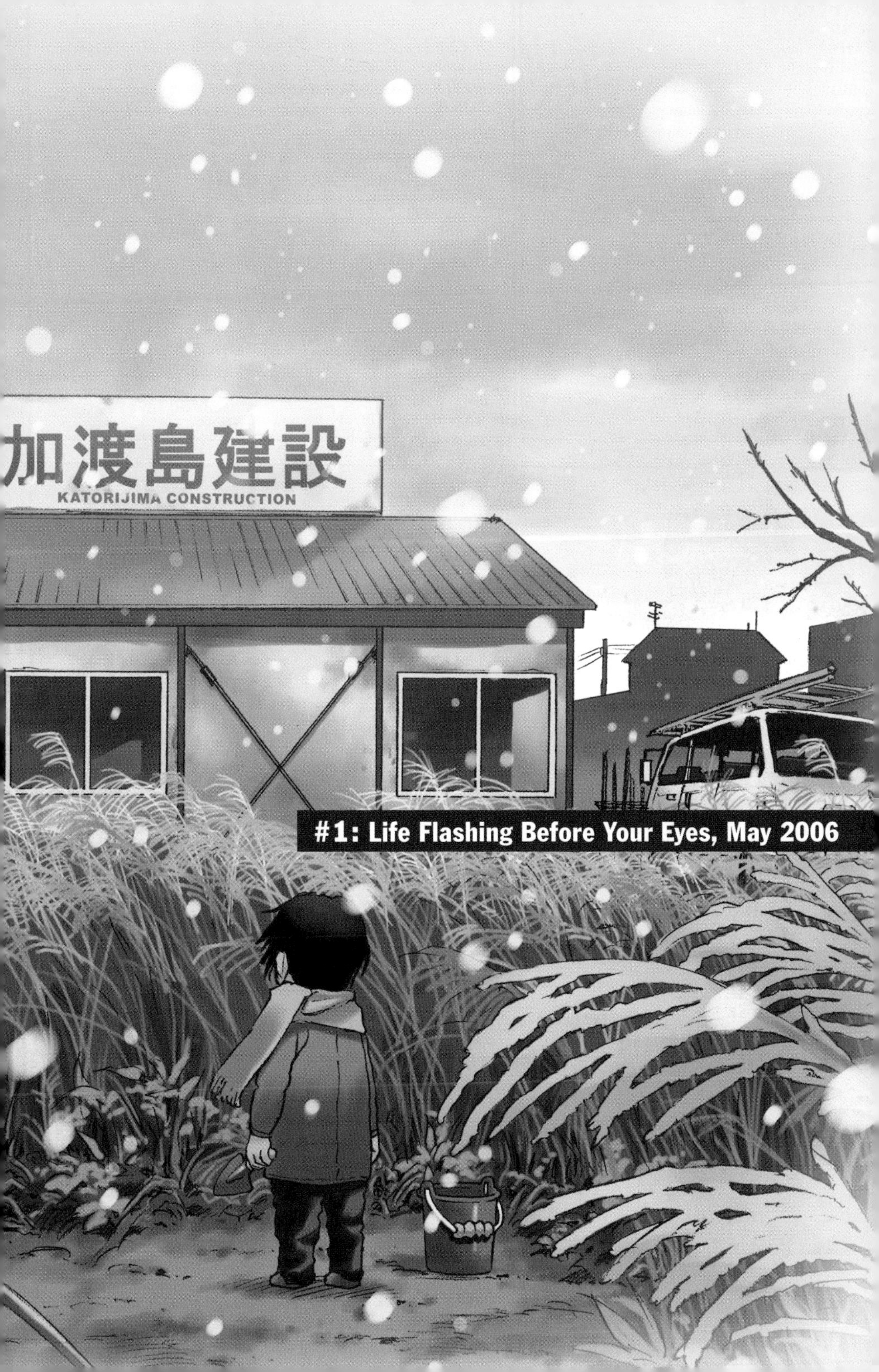
加渡島建設
KATORIJIMA CONSTRUCTION

#1: Life Flashing Before Your Eyes, May 2006

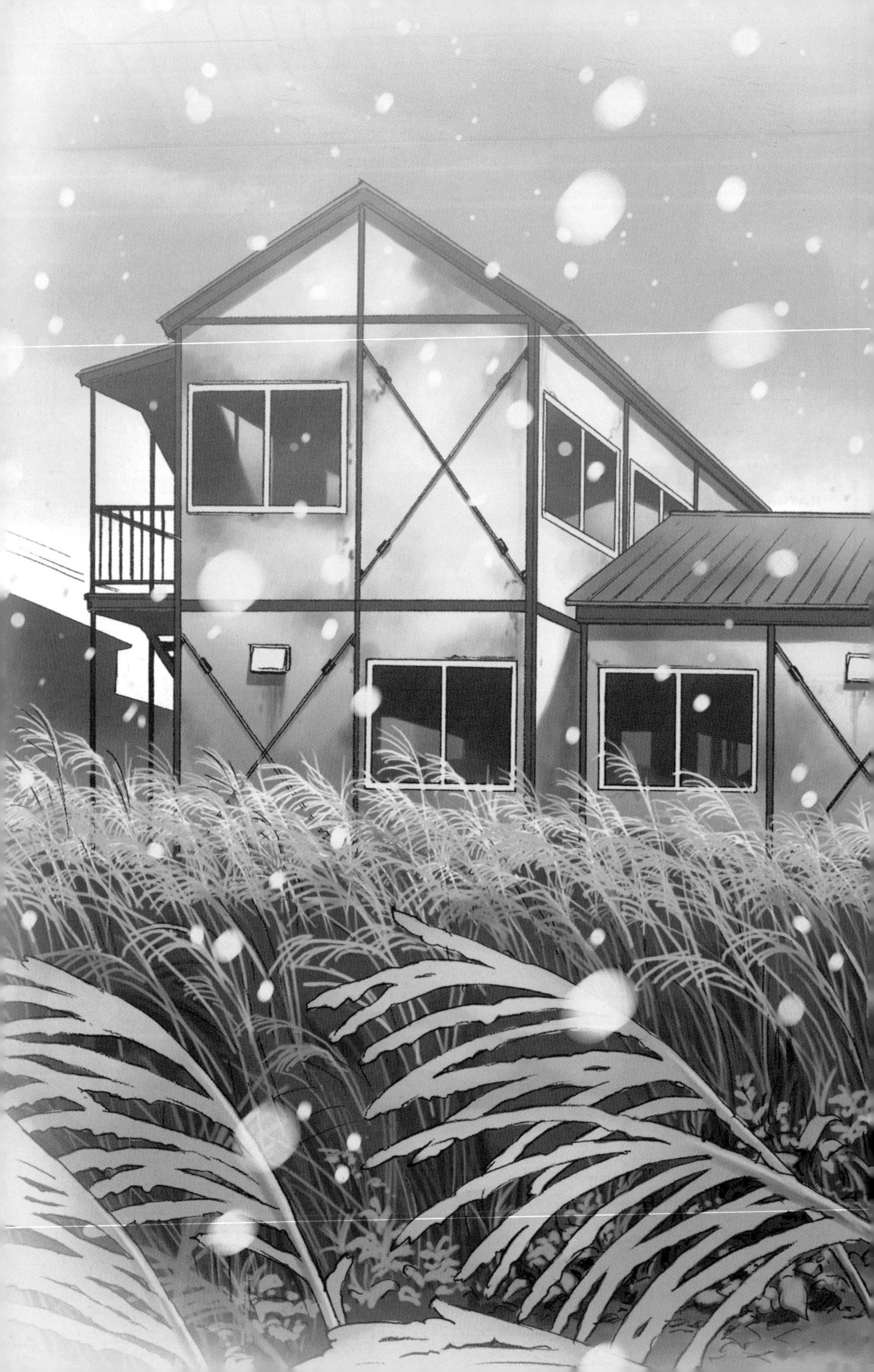

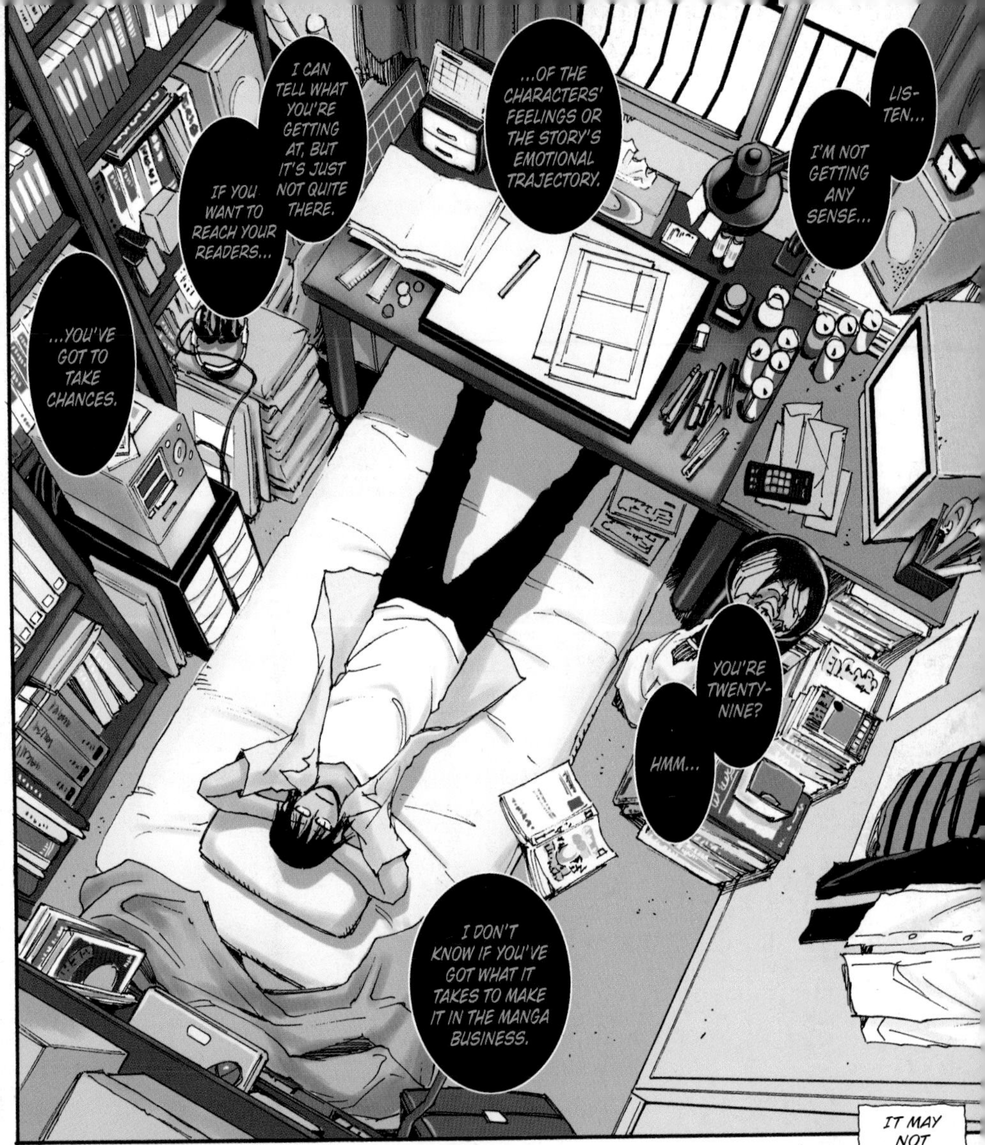
LIS-TEN...
I'M NOT GETTING ANY SENSE...
...OF THE CHARACTERS' FEELINGS OR THE STORY'S EMOTIONAL TRAJECTORY.
I CAN TELL WHAT YOU'RE GETTING AT, BUT IT'S JUST NOT QUITE THERE.
IF YOU WANT TO REACH YOUR READERS...
...YOU'VE GOT TO TAKE CHANCES.
YOU'RE TWENTY-NINE?
HMM...
I DON'T KNOW IF YOU'VE GOT WHAT IT TAKES TO MAKE IT IN THE MANGA BUSINESS.

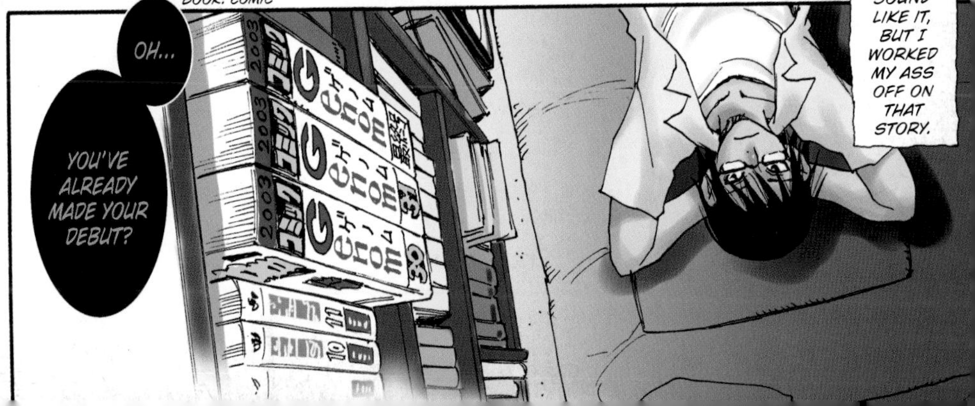
IT MAY NOT SOUND LIKE IT, BUT I WORKED MY ASS OFF ON THAT STORY.
BOOK: COMIC
OH...
YOU'VE ALREADY MADE YOUR DEBUT?

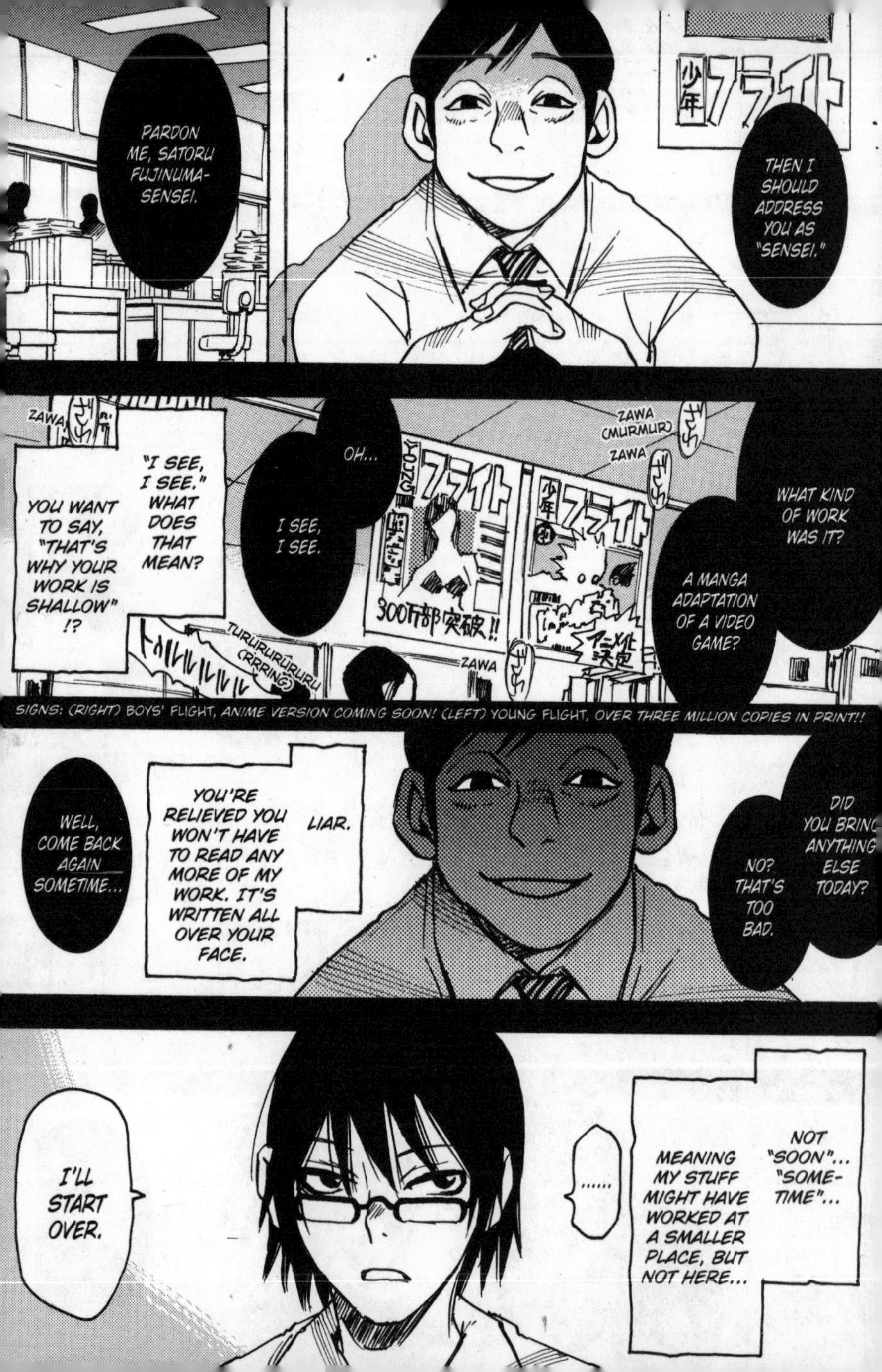
THEN I SHOULD ADDRESS YOU AS "SENSEI."
PARDON ME, SATORU FUJINUMA-SENSEI.
WHAT KIND OF WORK WAS IT?
A MANGA ADAPTATION OF A VIDEO GAME?
ZAWA (MURMUR) ZAWA
ZAWA
OH...
I SEE, I SEE.
"I SEE, I SEE." WHAT DOES THAT MEAN?
YOU WANT TO SAY, "THAT'S WHY YOUR WORK IS SHALLOW"!?
TURURURURURU (RRRING)
ZAWA
SIGNS: (RIGHT) BOYS' FLIGHT, ANIME VERSION COMING SOON! (LEFT) YOUNG FLIGHT, OVER THREE MILLION COPIES IN PRINT!!
DID YOU BRING ANYTHING ELSE TODAY?
NO? THAT'S TOO BAD.
LIAR.
YOU'RE RELIEVED YOU WON'T HAVE TO READ ANY MORE OF MY WORK. IT'S WRITTEN ALL OVER YOUR FACE.
WELL, COME BACK AGAIN SOMETIME...
NOT "SOON"... "SOMETIME"...
MEANING MY STUFF MIGHT HAVE WORKED AT A SMALLER PLACE, BUT NOT HERE...
......
I'LL START OVER.

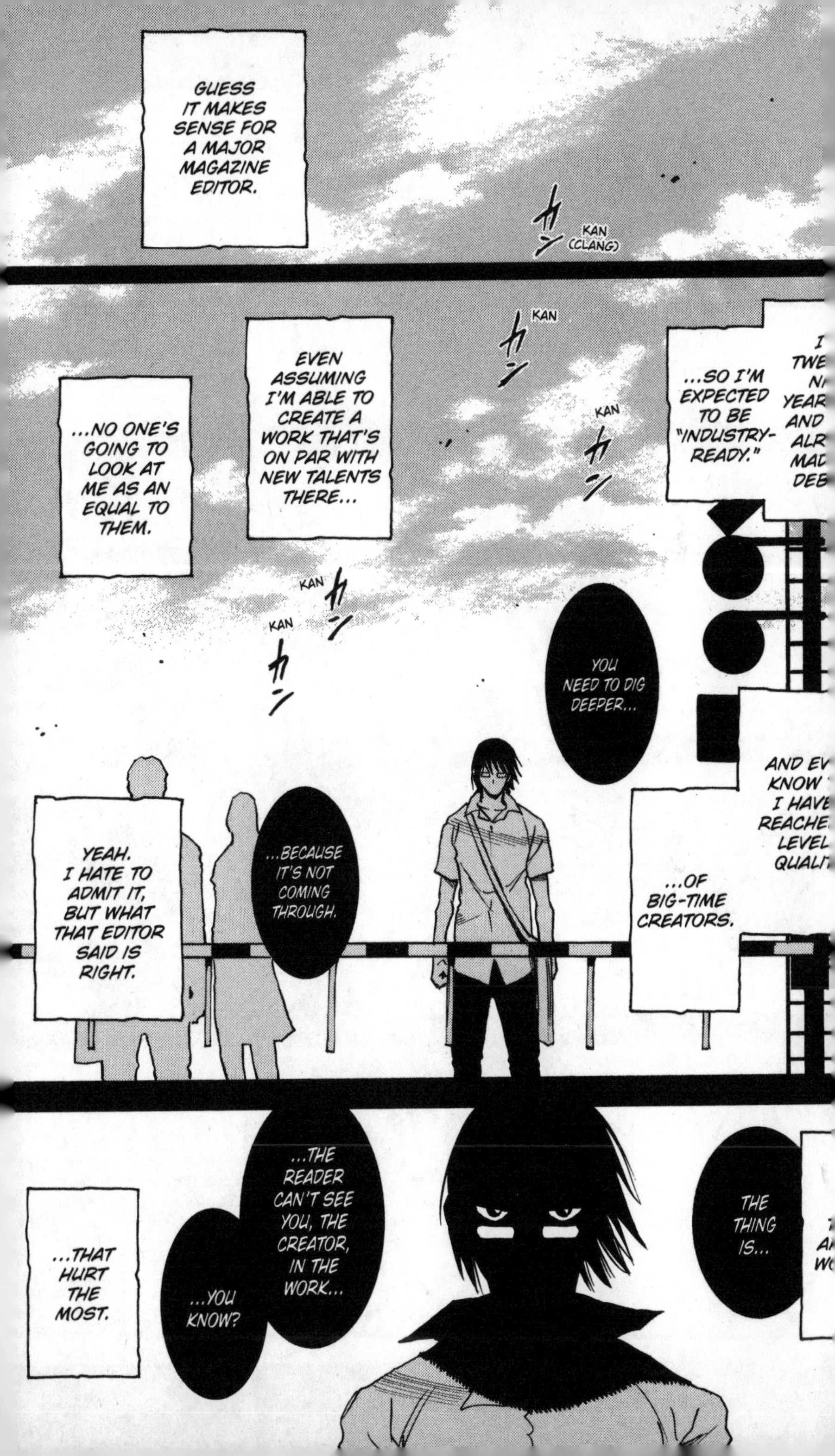
GUESS IT MAKES SENSE FOR A MAJOR MAGAZINE EDITOR.
KAN (CLANG)
I TWE NI YEAR AND ALR MAD DEB
...SO I'M EXPECTED TO BE "INDUSTRY-READY."
KAN
KAN
EVEN ASSUMING I'M ABLE TO CREATE A WORK THAT'S ON PAR WITH NEW TALENTS THERE...
...NO ONE'S GOING TO LOOK AT ME AS AN EQUAL TO THEM.
KAN
KAN
YOU NEED TO DIG DEEPER...
AND EV KNOW I HAVE REACHE LEVEL QUALI
...OF BIG-TIME CREATORS.
...BECAUSE IT'S NOT COMING THROUGH.
YEAH. I HATE TO ADMIT IT, BUT WHAT THAT EDITOR SAID IS RIGHT.
THE THING IS...
...THE READER CAN'T SEE YOU, THE CREATOR, IN THE WORK...
...YOU KNOW?
...THAT HURT THE MOST.

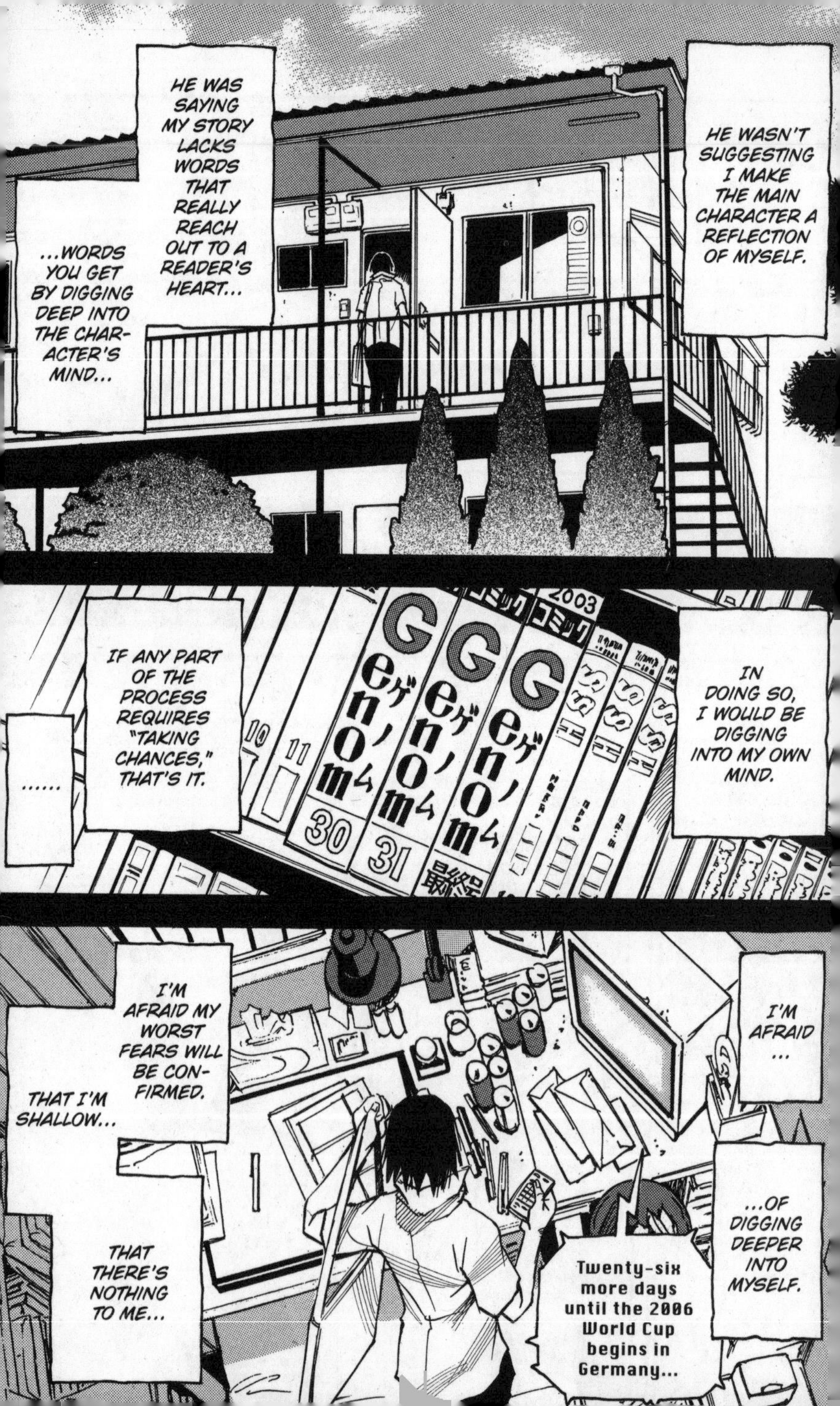
HE WASN'T SUGGESTING I MAKE THE MAIN CHARACTER A REFLECTION OF MYSELF.
HE WAS SAYING MY STORY LACKS WORDS THAT REALLY REACH OUT TO A READER'S HEART...
...WORDS YOU GET BY DIGGING DEEP INTO THE CHAR-ACTER'S MIND...
IN DOING SO, I WOULD BE DIGGING INTO MY OWN MIND.
IF ANY PART OF THE PROCESS REQUIRES "TAKING CHANCES," THAT'S IT.
......
I'M AFRAID...
...OF DIGGING DEEPER INTO MYSELF.
I'M AFRAID MY WORST FEARS WILL BE CON-FIRMED.
THAT I'M SHALLOW...
THAT THERE'S NOTHING TO ME...
Twenty-six more days until the 2006 World Cup begins in Germany...

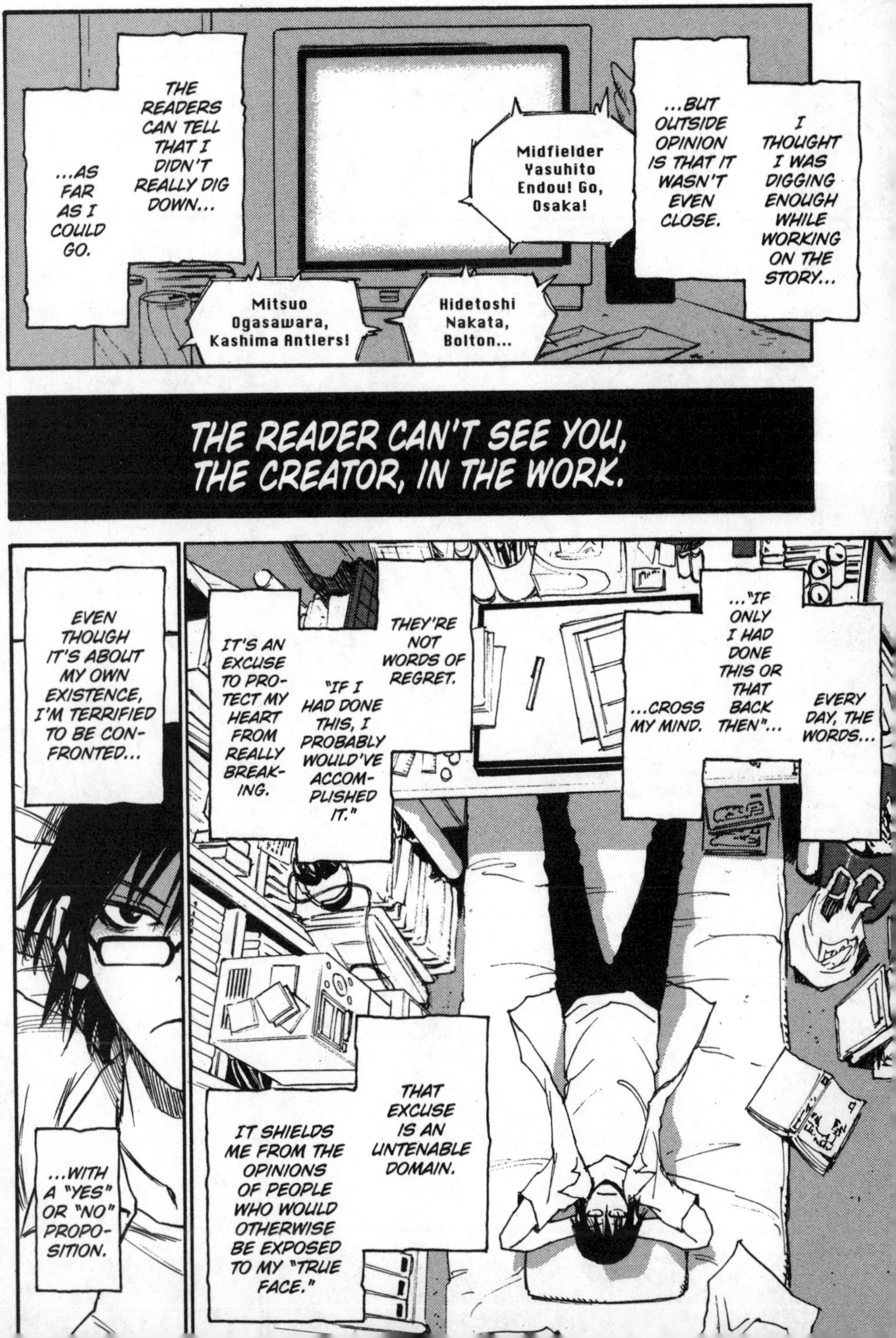
I THOUGHT I WAS DIGGING ENOUGH WHILE WORKING ON THE STORY...
...BUT OUTSIDE OPINION IS THAT IT WASN'T EVEN CLOSE.
Midfielder Yasuhito Endou! Go, Osaka!
Hidetoshi Nakata, Bolton...
Mitsuo Ogasawara, Kashima Antlers!
THE READERS CAN TELL THAT I DIDN'T REALLY DIG DOWN...
...AS FAR AS I COULD GO.
THE READER CAN'T SEE YOU, THE CREATOR, IN THE WORK.
EVERY DAY, THE WORDS...
..."IF ONLY I HAD DONE THIS OR THAT BACK THEN"...
...CROSS MY MIND.
THEY'RE NOT WORDS OF REGRET.
"IF I HAD DONE THIS, I PROBABLY WOULD'VE ACCOMPLISHED IT."
IT'S AN EXCUSE TO PROTECT MY HEART FROM REALLY BREAKING.
THAT EXCUSE IS AN UNTENABLE DOMAIN.
IT SHIELDS ME FROM THE OPINIONS OF PEOPLE WHO WOULD OTHERWISE BE EXPOSED TO MY "TRUE FACE."
EVEN THOUGH IT'S ABOUT MY OWN EXISTENCE, I'M TERRIFIED TO BE CONFRONTED...
...WITH A "YES" OR "NO" PROPOSITION.

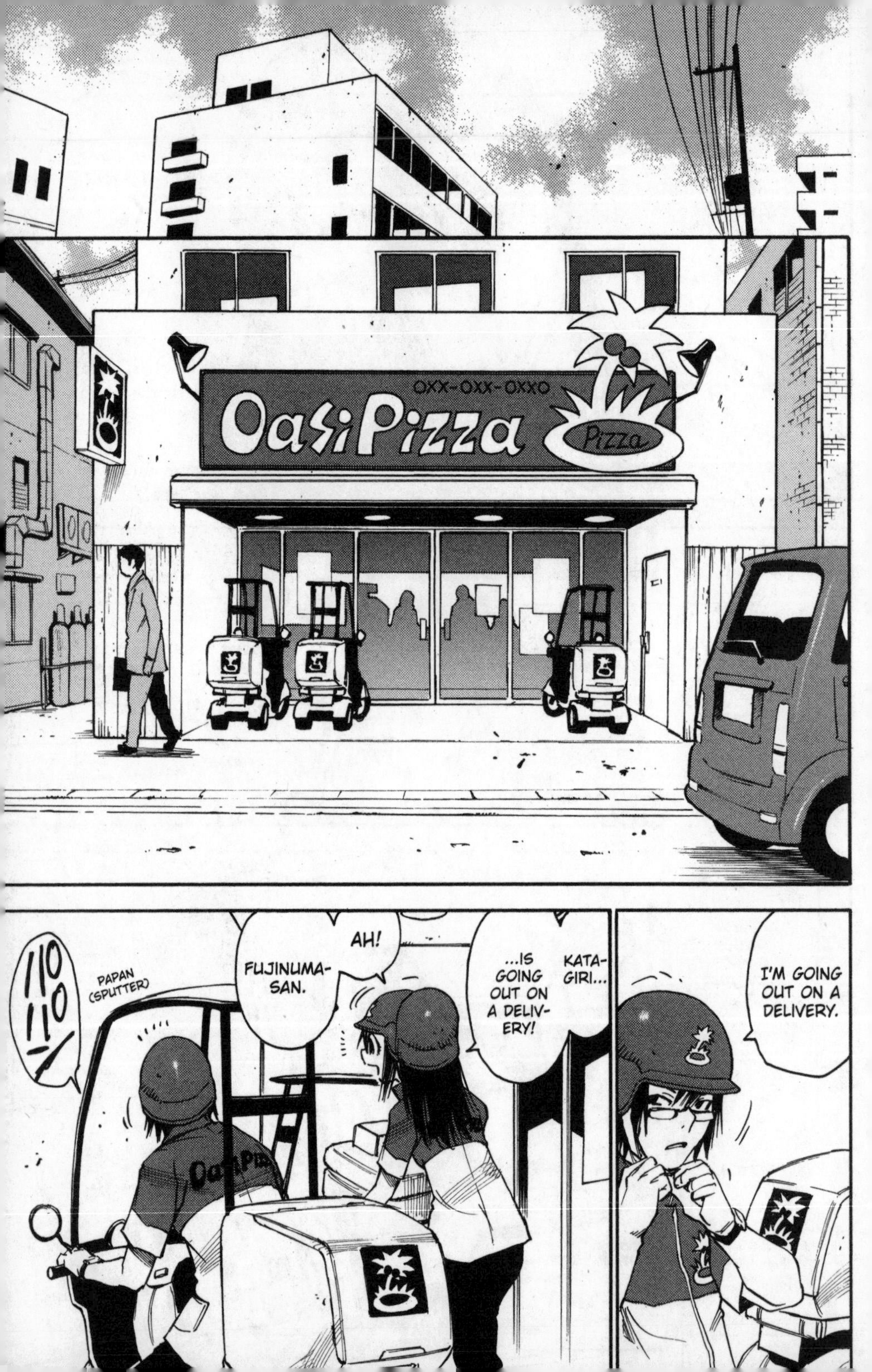
OXX-OXX-OXXO
OasiPizza
Pizza
I'M GOING OUT ON A DELIVERY.
KATA-GIRI...
...IS GOING OUT ON A DELIV-ERY!
AH!
FUJINUMA-SAN.
PAPAN (SPUTTER)

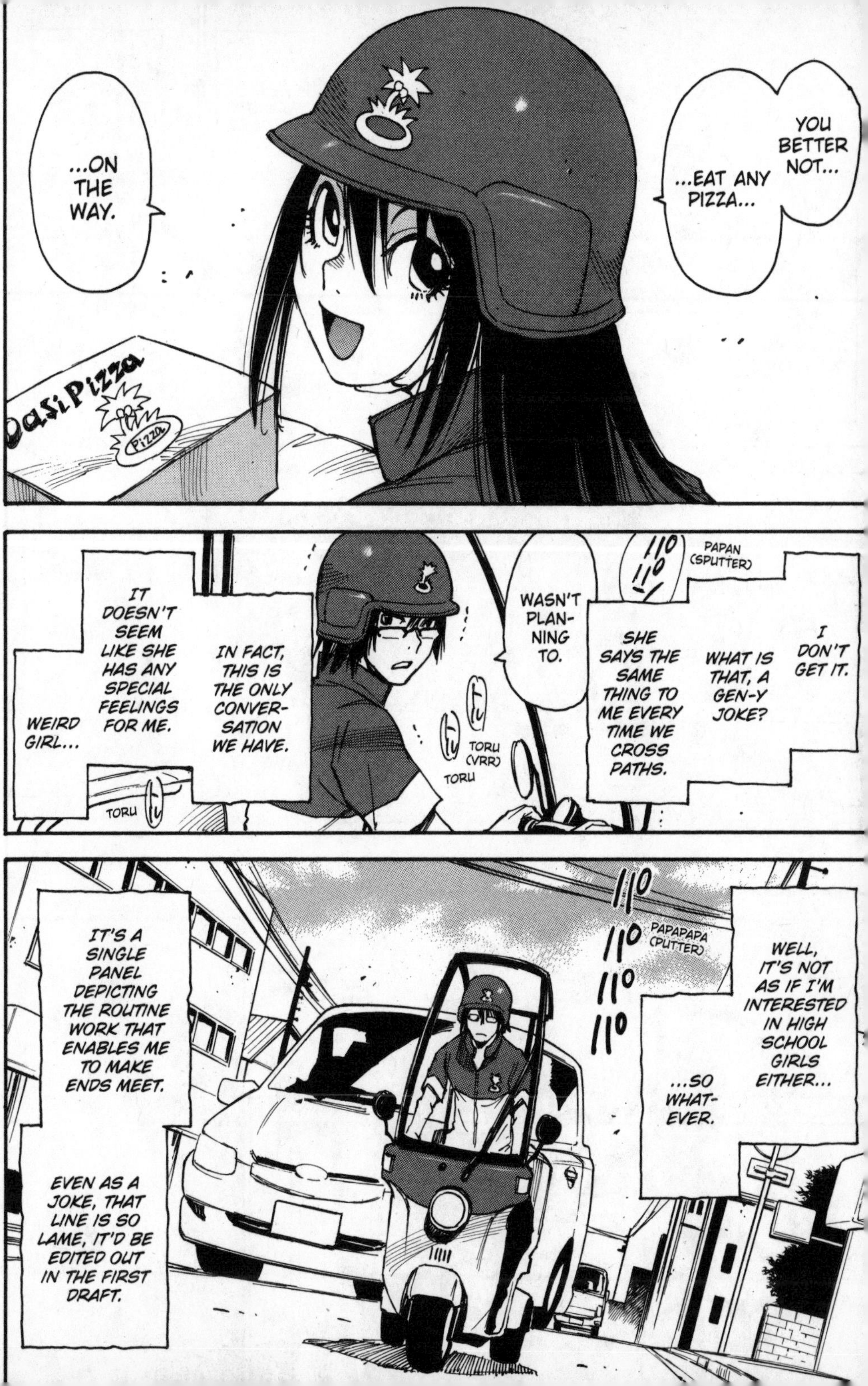
YOU BETTER NOT... ...EAT ANY PIZZA...
...ON THE WAY.
PAPAN (SPUTTER)
I DON'T GET IT.
WHAT IS THAT, A GEN-Y JOKE?
SHE SAYS THE SAME THING TO ME EVERY TIME WE CROSS PATHS.
WASN'T PLAN-NING TO.
TORU (VRR)
TORU
IN FACT, THIS IS THE ONLY CONVER-SATION WE HAVE.
IT DOESN'T SEEM LIKE SHE HAS ANY SPECIAL FEELINGS FOR ME.
WEIRD GIRL...
TORU
PAPAPAPA (PUTTER)
WELL, IT'S NOT AS IF I'M INTERESTED IN HIGH SCHOOL GIRLS EITHER...
...SO WHAT-EVER.
IT'S A SINGLE PANEL DEPICTING THE ROUTINE WORK THAT ENABLES ME TO MAKE ENDS MEET.
EVEN AS A JOKE, THAT LINE IS SO LAME, IT'D BE EDITED OUT IN THE FIRST DRAFT.

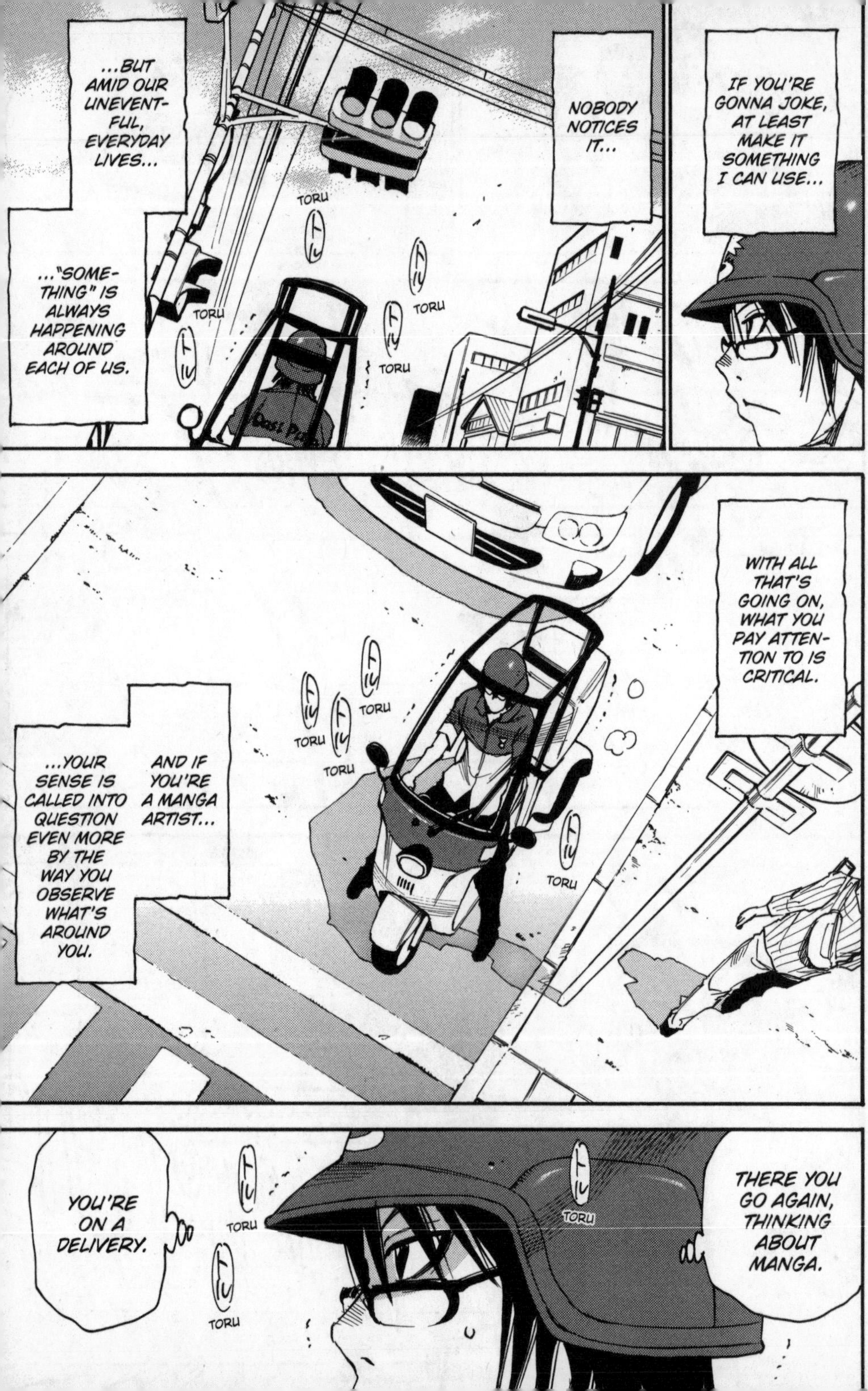
IF YOU'RE GONNA JOKE, AT LEAST MAKE IT SOMETHING I CAN USE...
NOBODY NOTICES IT...
...BUT AMID OUR UNEVENT-FUL, EVERYDAY LIVES...
TORU
TORU
TORU
TORU
...“SOME-THING” IS ALWAYS HAPPENING AROUND EACH OF US.
WITH ALL THAT'S GOING ON, WHAT YOU PAY ATTEN-TION TO IS CRITICAL.
TORU
TORU
TORU
TORU
AND IF YOU'RE A MANGA ARTIST...
...YOUR SENSE IS CALLED INTO QUESTION EVEN MORE BY THE WAY YOU OBSERVE WHAT'S AROUND YOU.
THERE YOU GO AGAIN, THINKING ABOUT MANGA.
TORU
TORU
YOU'RE ON A DELIVERY.
TORU

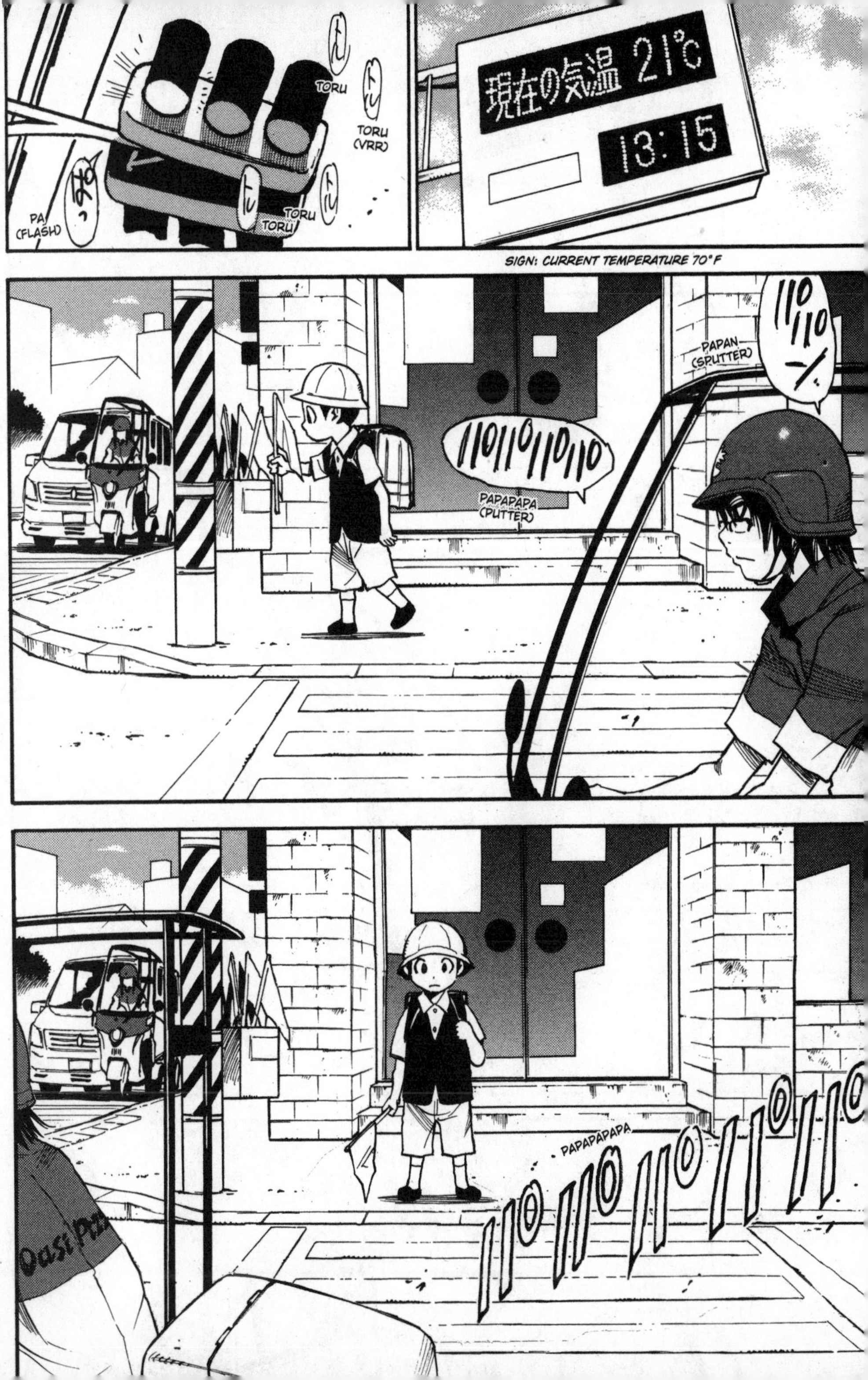

現在の気温 21°C
13:15
SIGN: CURRENT TEMPERATURE 70° F
TORU
TORU (VRR)
TORU
TORU
PA (FLASH)
PAPAN (SPUTTER)
PAPAPAPA (PUTTER)
PAPAPAPAPA

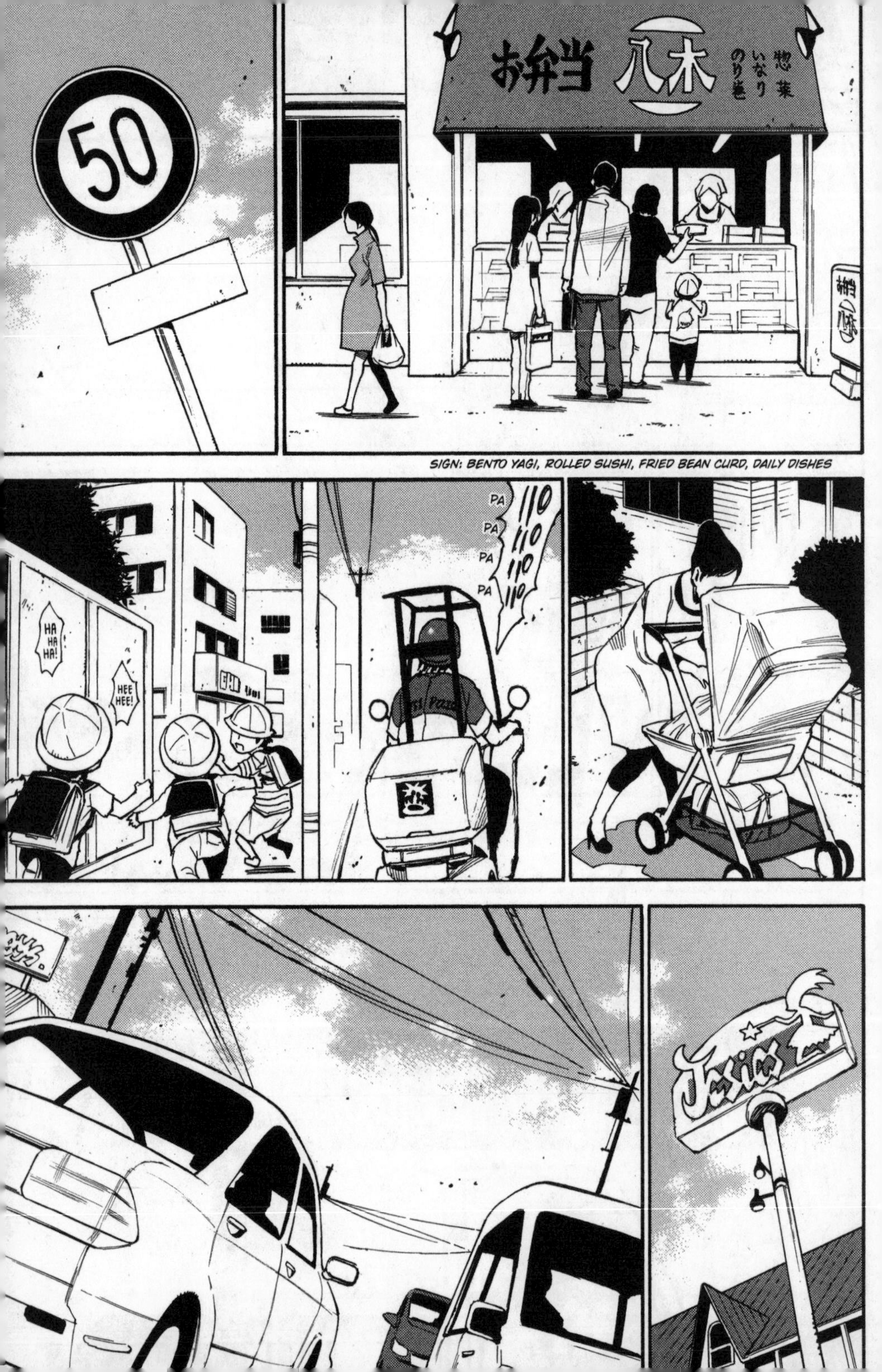
お弁当 八木
惣菜
いなり
のり巻
お弁当 八木
50
SIGN: BENTO YAGI, ROLLED SUSHI, FRIED BEAN CURD, DAILY DISHES
PA PA PA PA
HA HA HA!
HEE HEE!

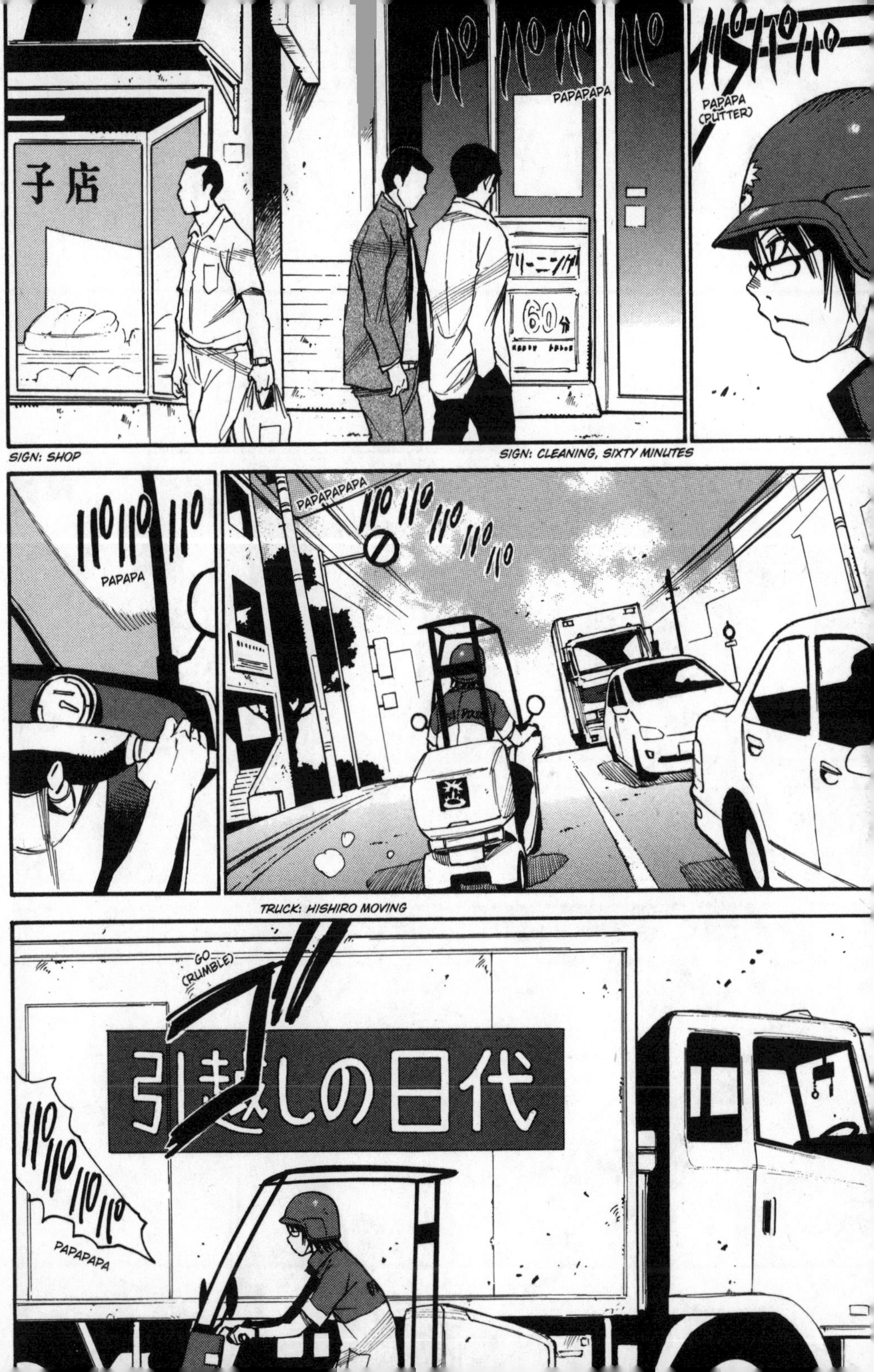
PAPAPA (PUTTER)
PAPAPAPA
クリーニング
60分
子店
SIGN: CLEANING, SIXTY MINUTES
SIGN: SHOP
PAPAPAPAPA
PAPAPA
TRUCK: HISHIRO MOVING
GO (RUMBLE)
引越しの日代
PAPAPAPA

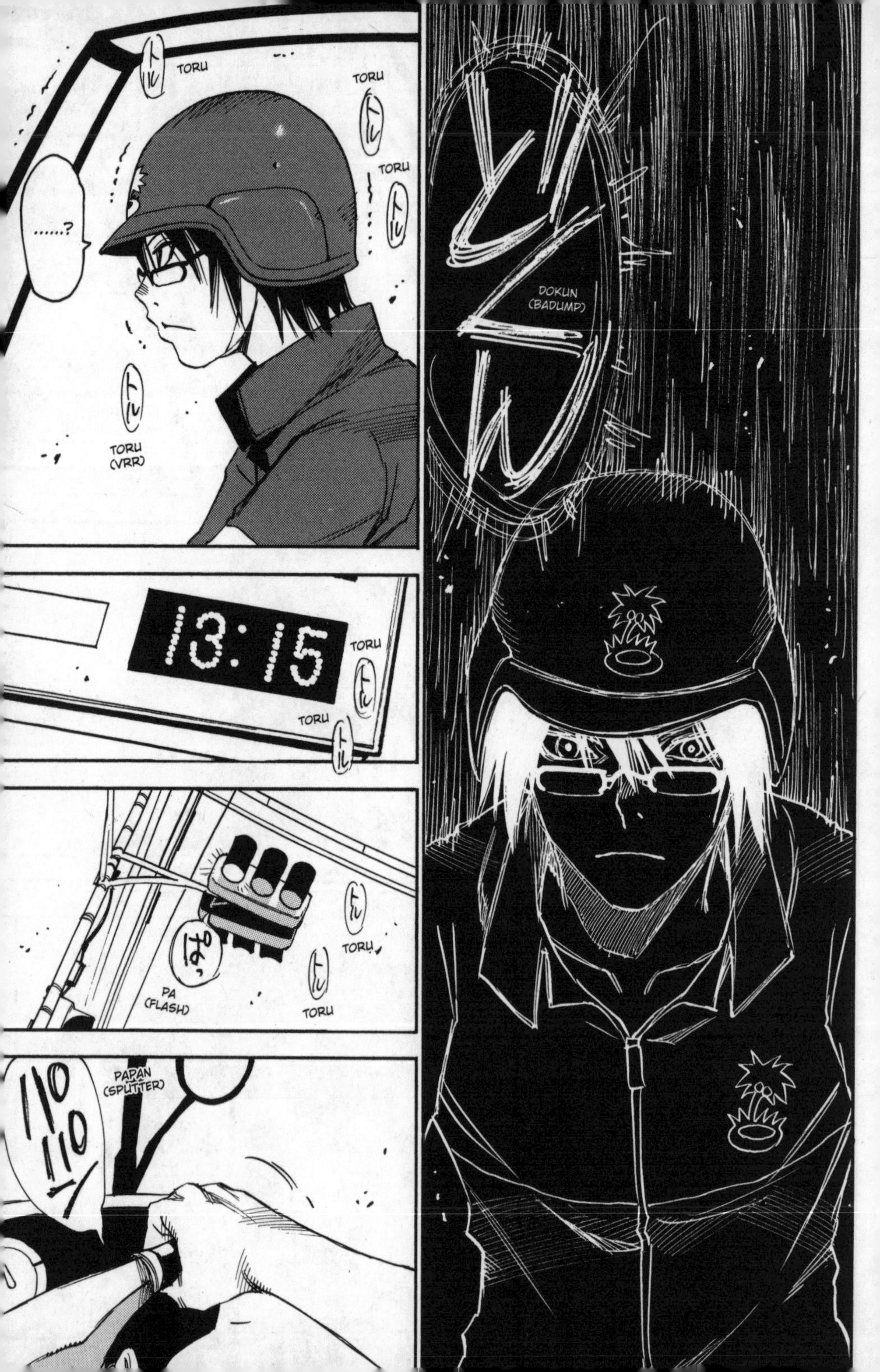

ドクン
DOKUN (BADUMP)
トル
TORU
トル
TORU
トル
TORU
......?
トル
TORU (VRR)
13:15
トル
TORU
トル
TORU
トル
TORU
トル
TORU
ぱっ
PA (FLASH)
PAPAN (SPUTTER)

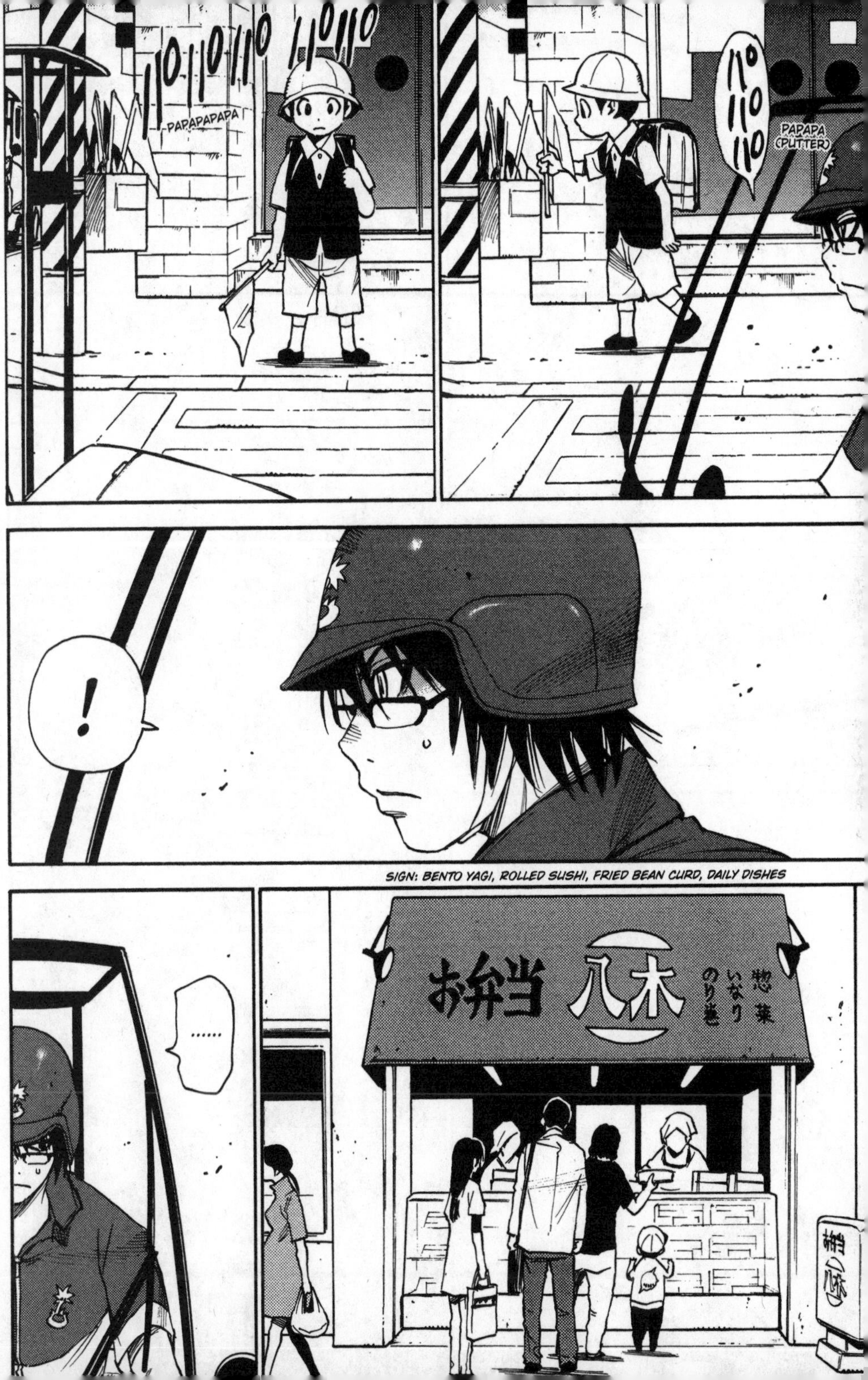
パパパパ
PAPAPA (PUTTER)
PAPAPAPAPA
!
SIGN: BENTO YAGI, ROLLED SUSHI, FRIED BEAN CURD, DAILY DISHES
お弁当
八木
惣菜
いなり
のり巻
......

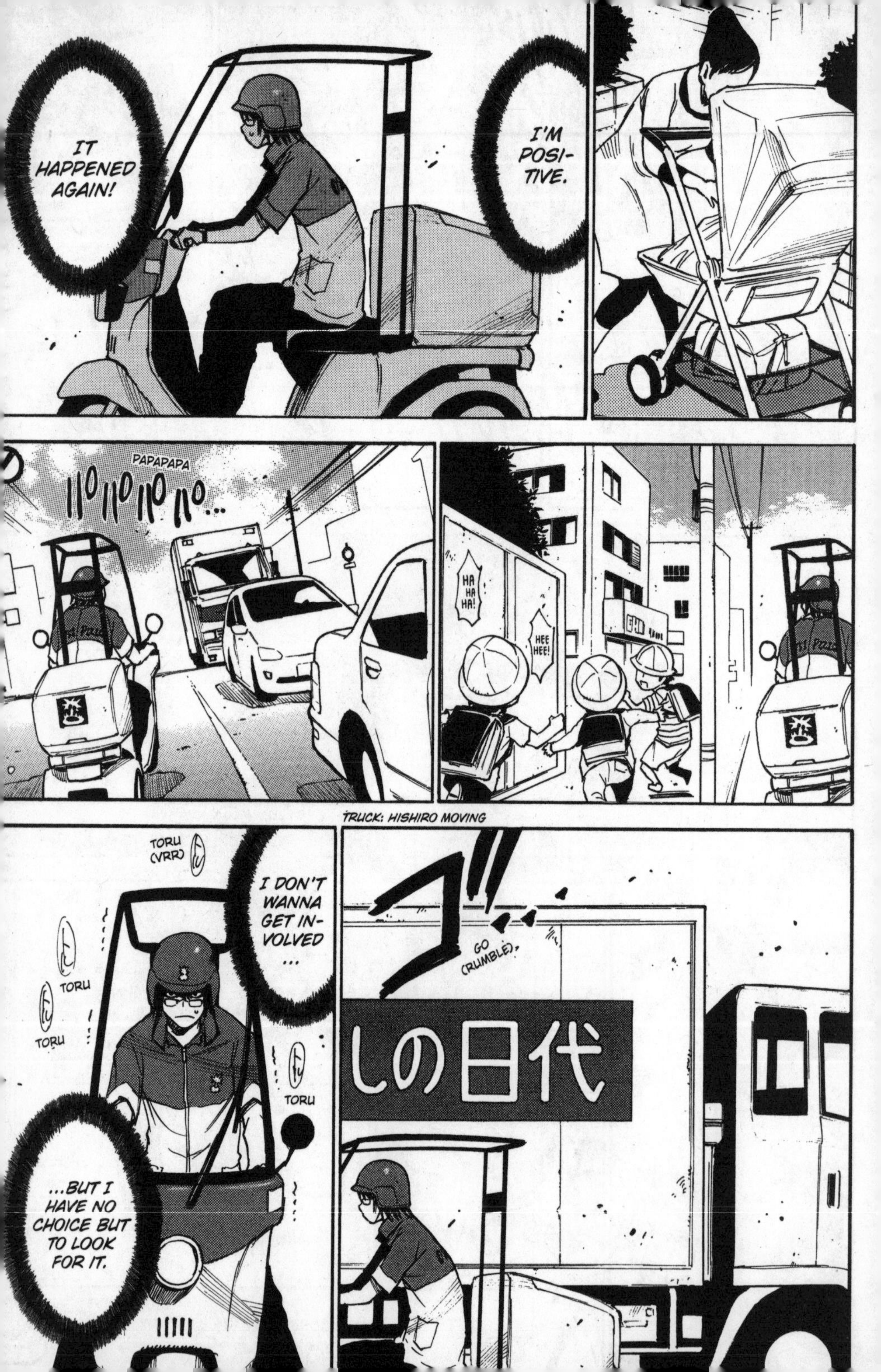
I'M POSI-TIVE.
IT HAPPENED AGAIN!
HA HA HA!
HEE HEE!
PAPAPAPA
TRUCK: HISHIRO MOVING
GO (RUMBLE)
しの日代
TORU (VRR)
I DON'T WANNA GET IN-VOLVED...
TORU
TORU
TORU
...BUT I HAVE NO CHOICE BUT TO LOOK FOR IT.

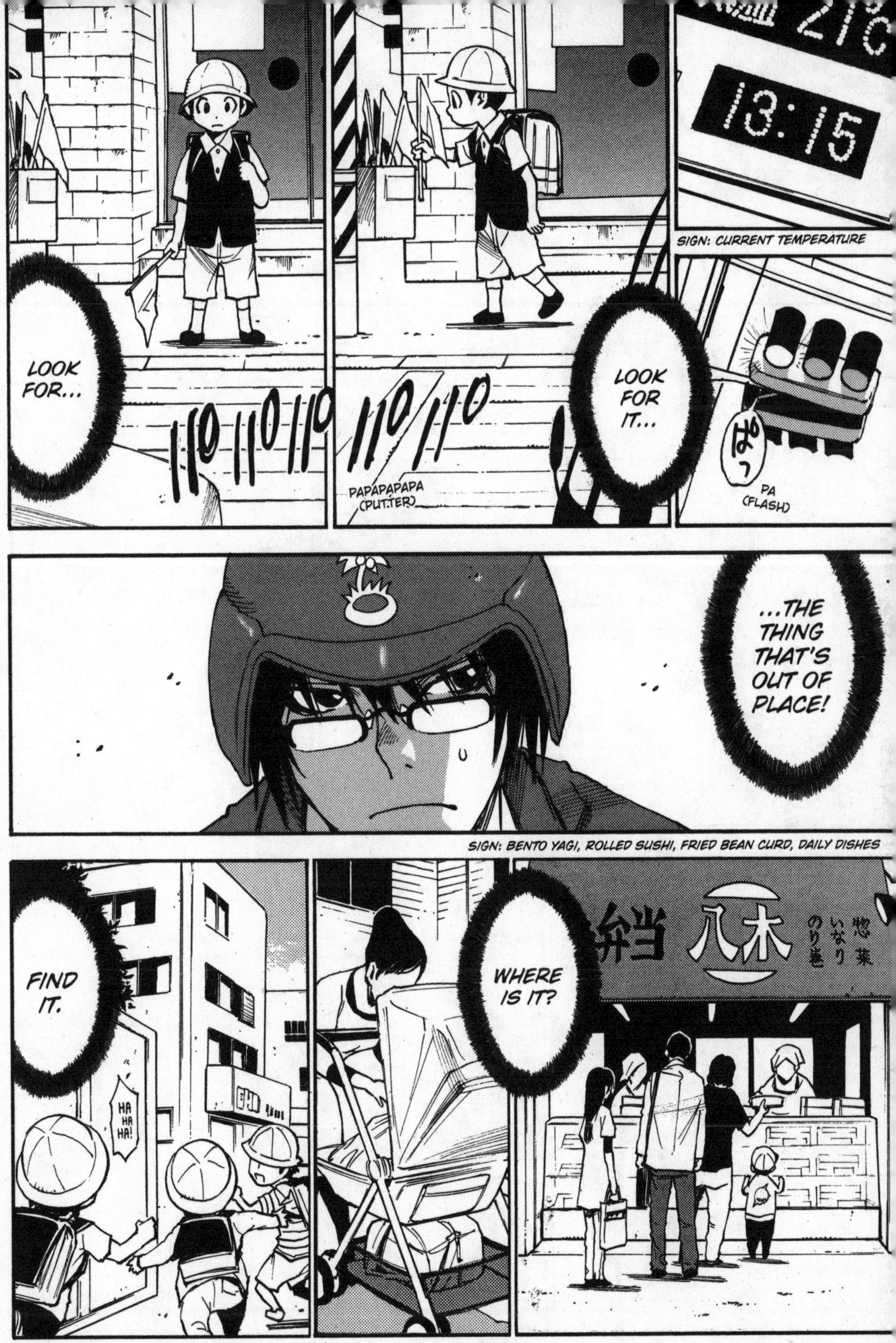
SIGN: CURRENT TEMPERATURE
13:15
ぱっ
PA (FLASH)
LOOK FOR IT...
PAPAPAPAPA (PUTTER)
LOOK FOR...
...THE THING THAT'S OUT OF PLACE!
SIGN: BENTO YAGI, ROLLED SUSHI, FRIED BEAN CURD, DAILY DISHES
弁当 八木
惣菜
いなり
のり巻
WHERE IS IT?
HA HA HA!
FIND IT.

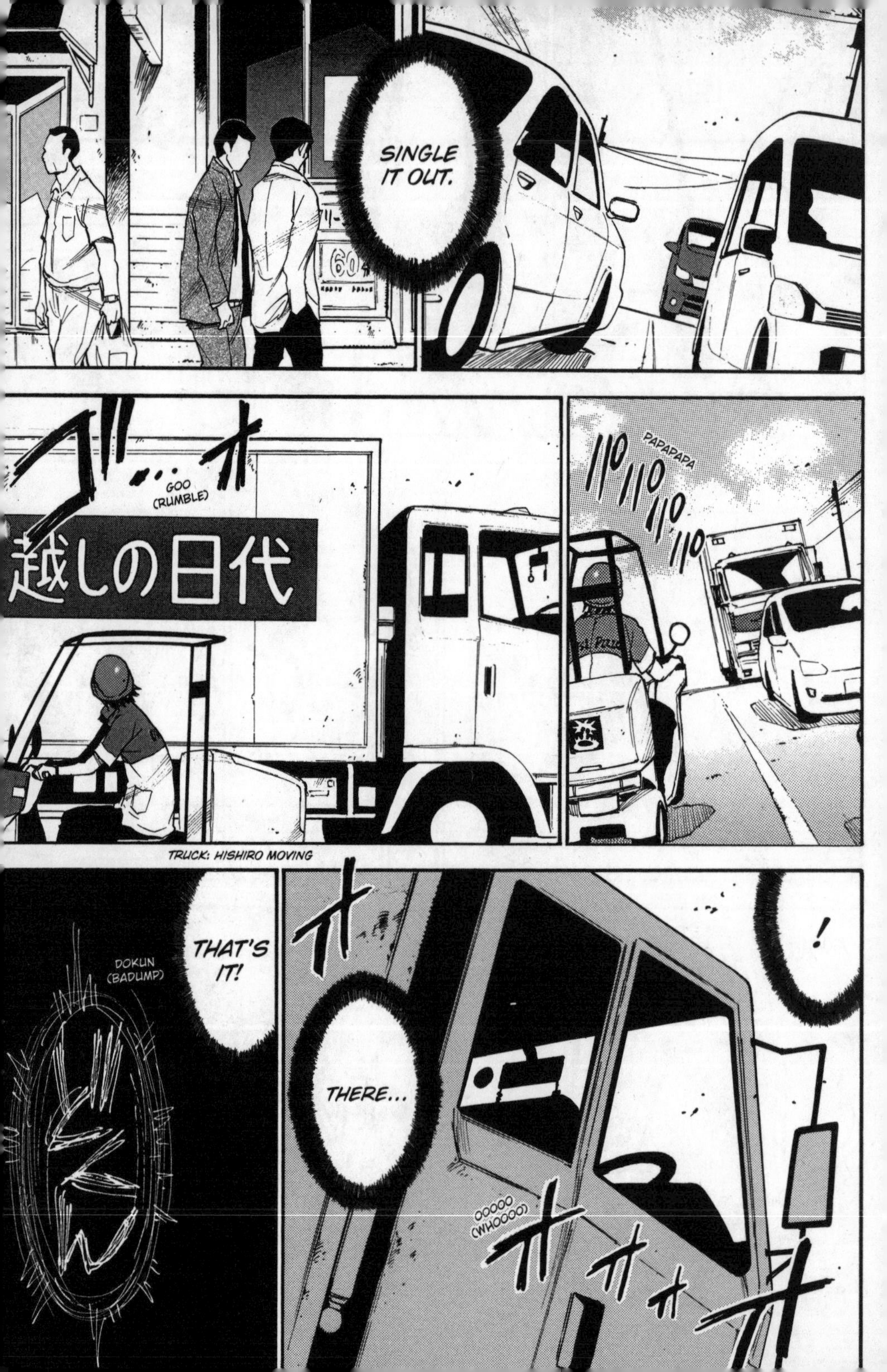
SINGLE IT OUT.
PAPAPAPA
GOO (RUMBLE)
越しの日代
TRUCK: HISHIRO MOVING
!
THERE...
OOOOO (WHOOOOO)
THAT'S IT!
DOKUN (BADUMP)

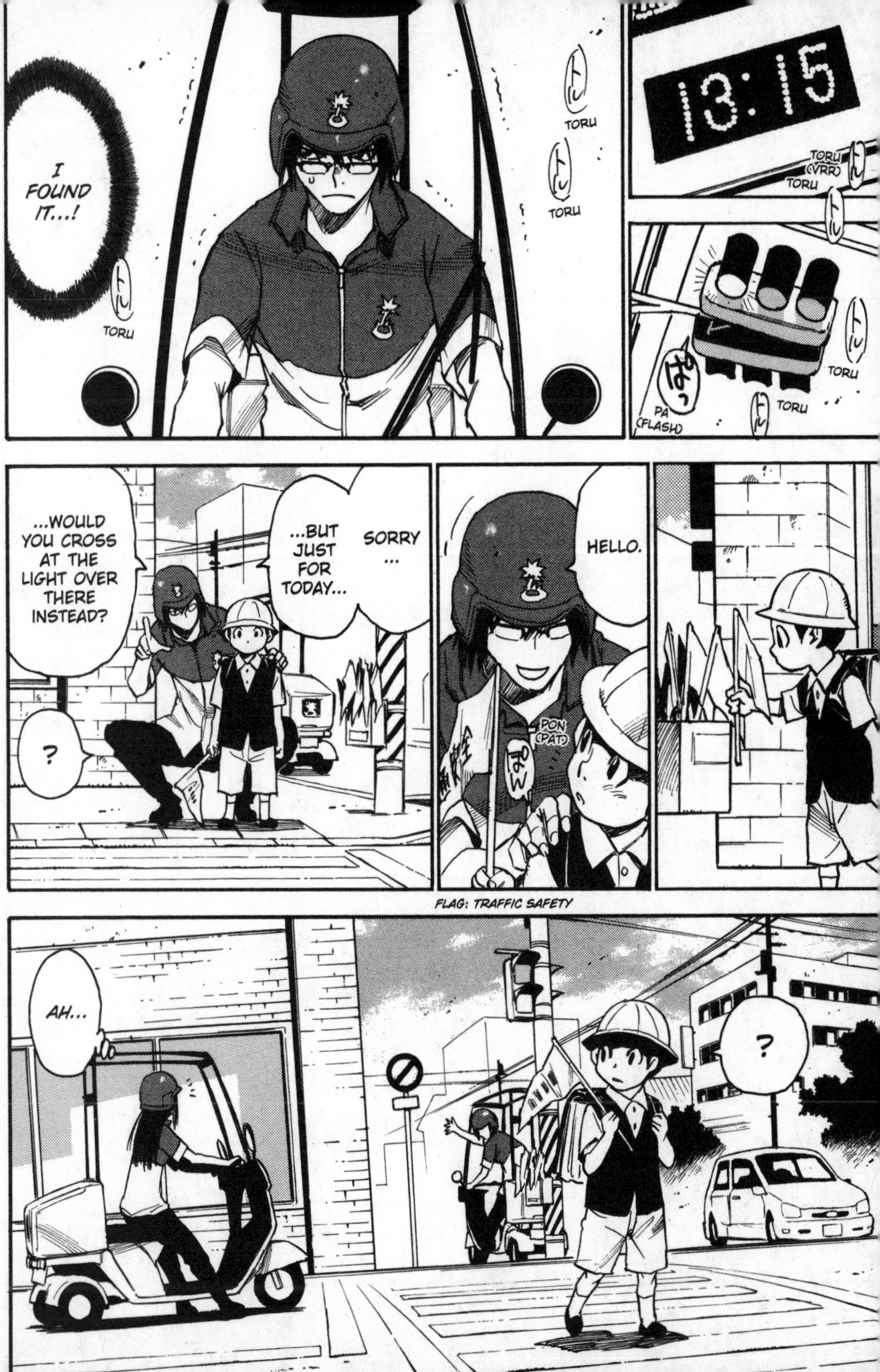
13:15
TORU (VRR)
TORU
TORU
TORU
PA (FLASH)
TORU
TORU
TORU
I FOUND IT...!
TORU
HELLO.
PON (PAT)
SORRY ...
...BUT JUST FOR TODAY...
...WOULD YOU CROSS AT THE LIGHT OVER THERE INSTEAD?
?
FLAG: TRAFFIC SAFETY
?
AH...

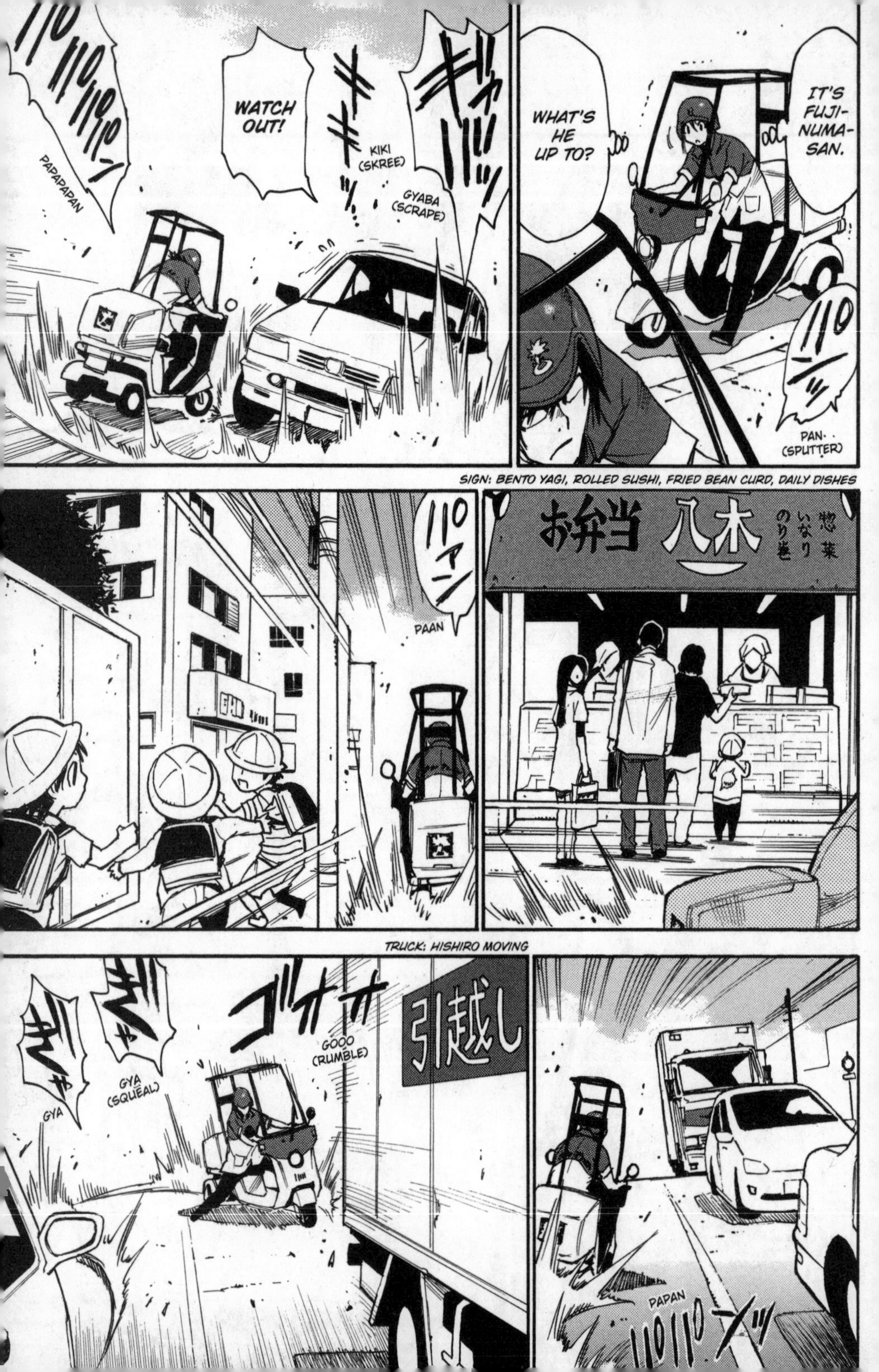
IT'S FUJI-NUMA-SAN.
WHAT'S HE UP TO?
PAN. (SPUTTER)
GYABA (SCRAPE)
KIKI (SKREE)
WATCH OUT!
PAPAPAPAN
SIGN: BENTO YAGI, ROLLED SUSHI, FRIED BEAN CURD, DAILY DISHES
お弁当 八木
惣菜 いなり のり巻
PAAN
TRUCK: HISHIRO MOVING
PAPAN
GOOO (RUMBLE)
引越し
GYA (SQUEAL)
GYA

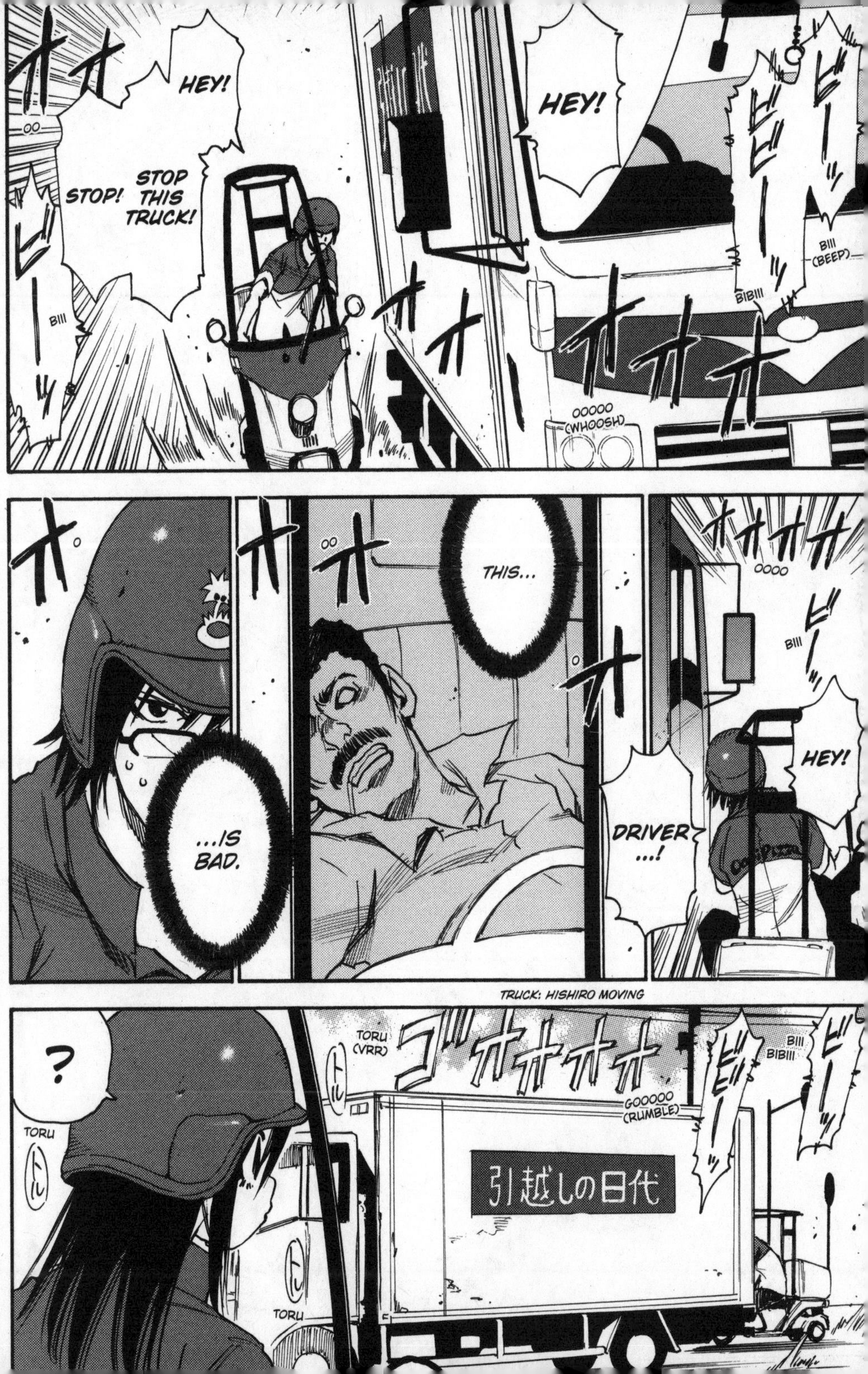
BIII (BEEP)
HEY!
BIBIII
HEY!
OOOOO (WHOOSH)
STOP THIS TRUCK!
STOP!
BIII
OOOO
BIII
HEY!
DRIVER ...!
THIS...
...IS BAD.
TRUCK: HISHIRO MOVING
BIII BIBIII
TORU (VRR)
GOOOOO (RUMBLE)
引越しの日代
TORU
?
TORU

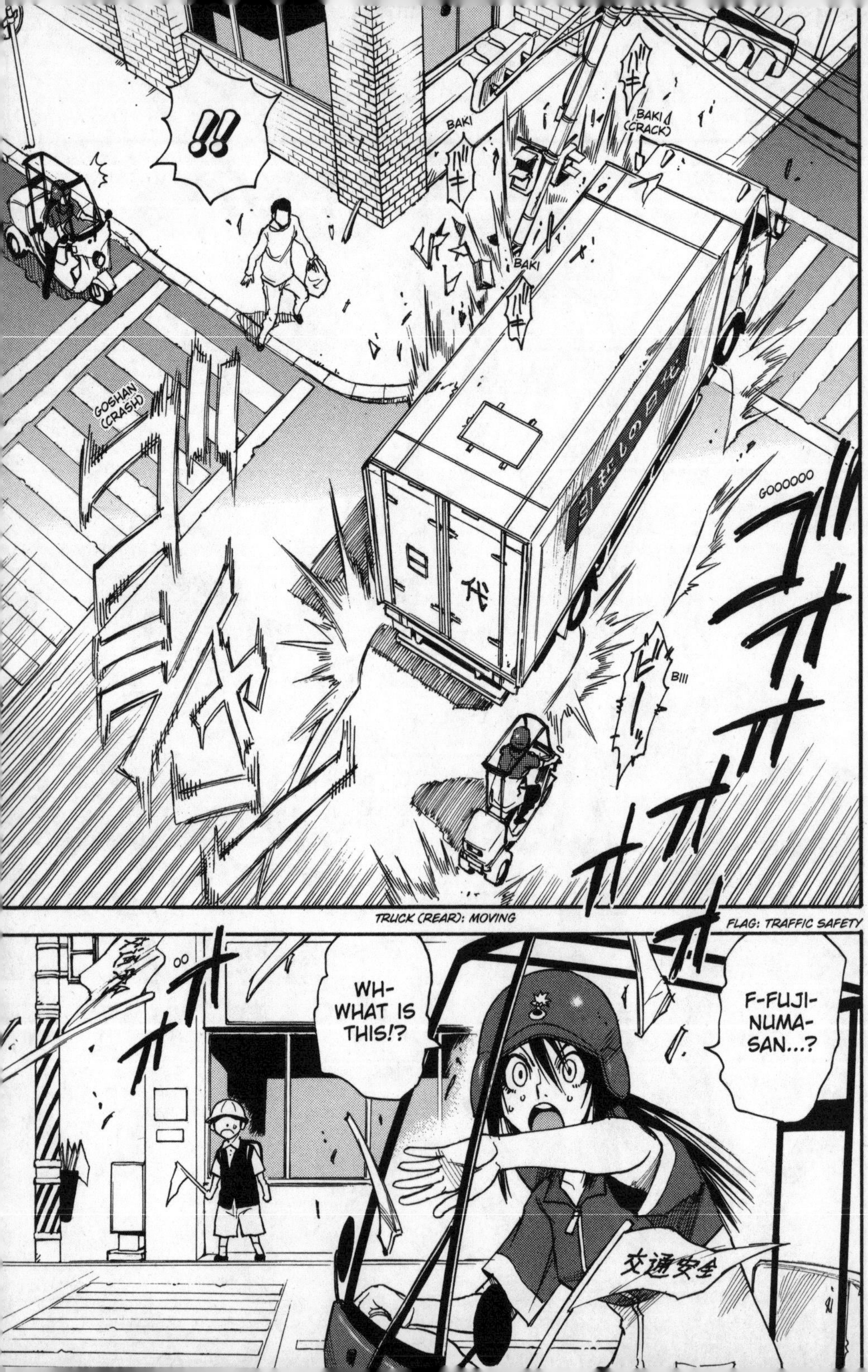
BAKI (CRACK)
BAKI
!!
BAKI
GOOOOOO
BIII
GOSHAN (CRASH)
TRUCK (REAR): MOVING
FLAG: TRAFFIC SAFETY
F-FUJI-NUMA-SAN...?
WH-WHAT IS THIS!?
交通安全

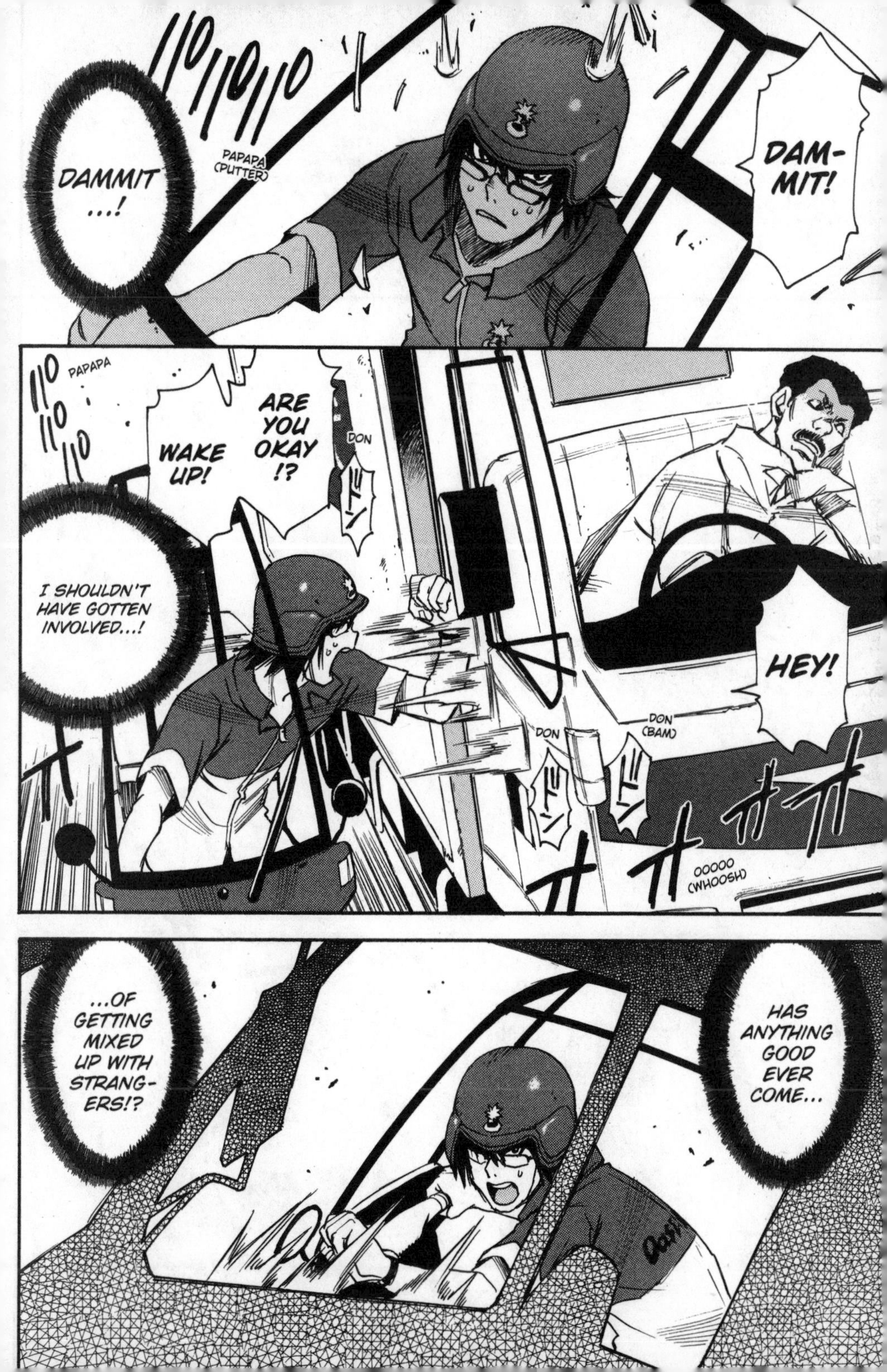
DAM-MIT!
PAPAPA (PUTTER)
DAMMIT ...!
HEY!
DON (BAM)
DON
OOOOO (WHOOSH)
ARE YOU OKAY !?
DON
WAKE UP!
PAPAPA
I SHOULDN'T HAVE GOTTEN INVOLVED...!
HAS ANYTHING GOOD EVER COME...
...OF GETTING MIXED UP WITH STRANG-ERS!?

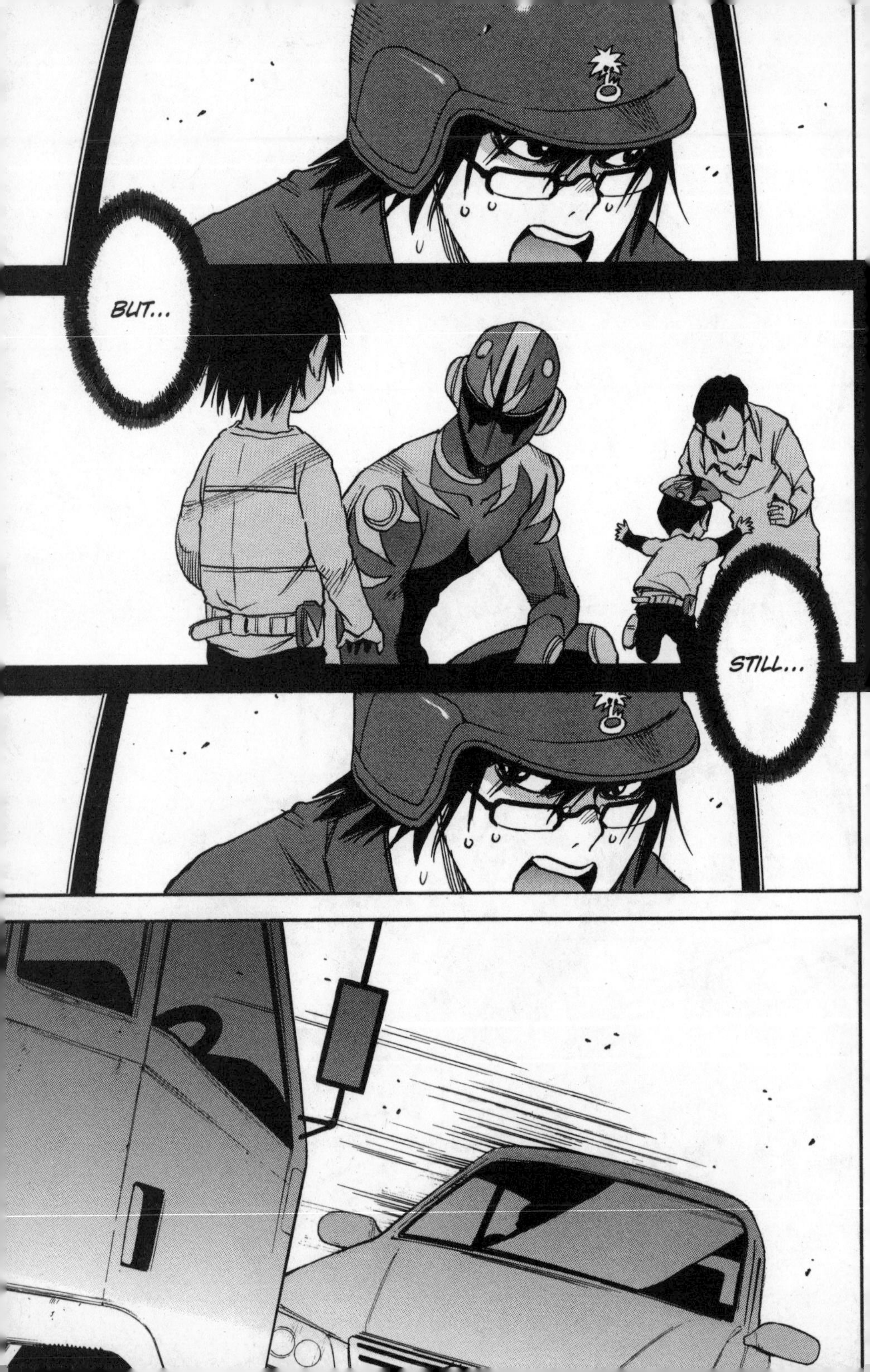
BUT...
STILL...

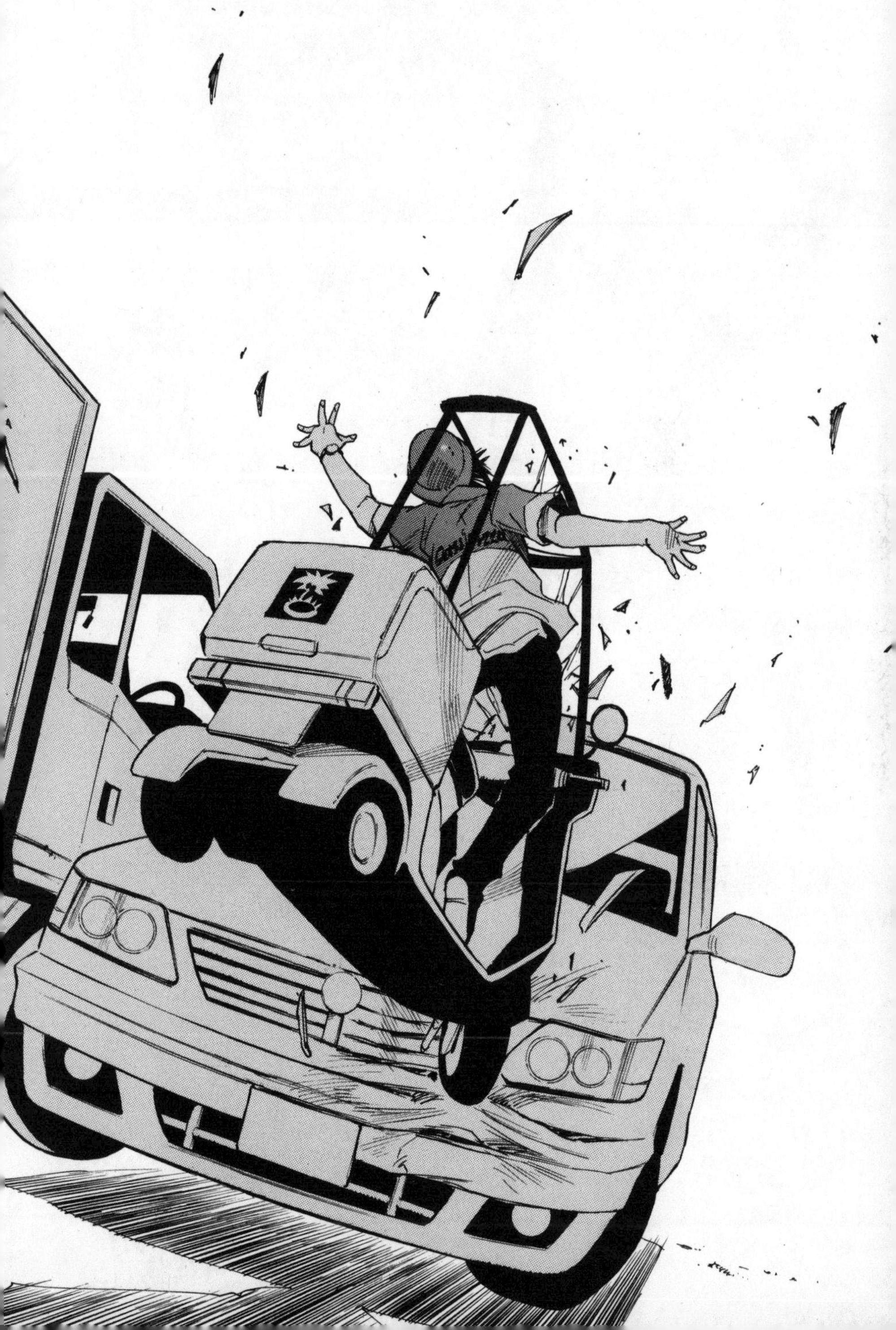

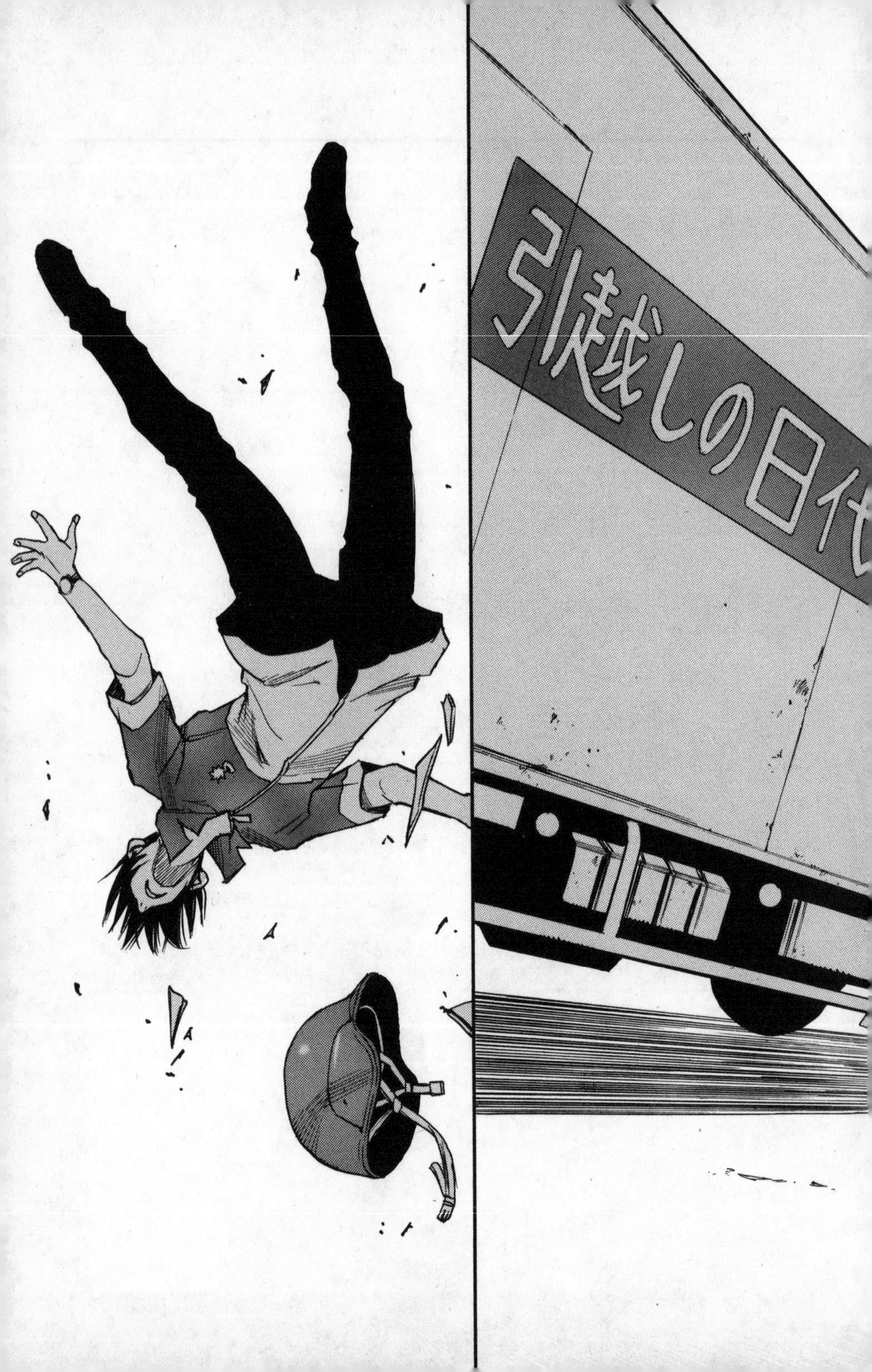

引越しの日

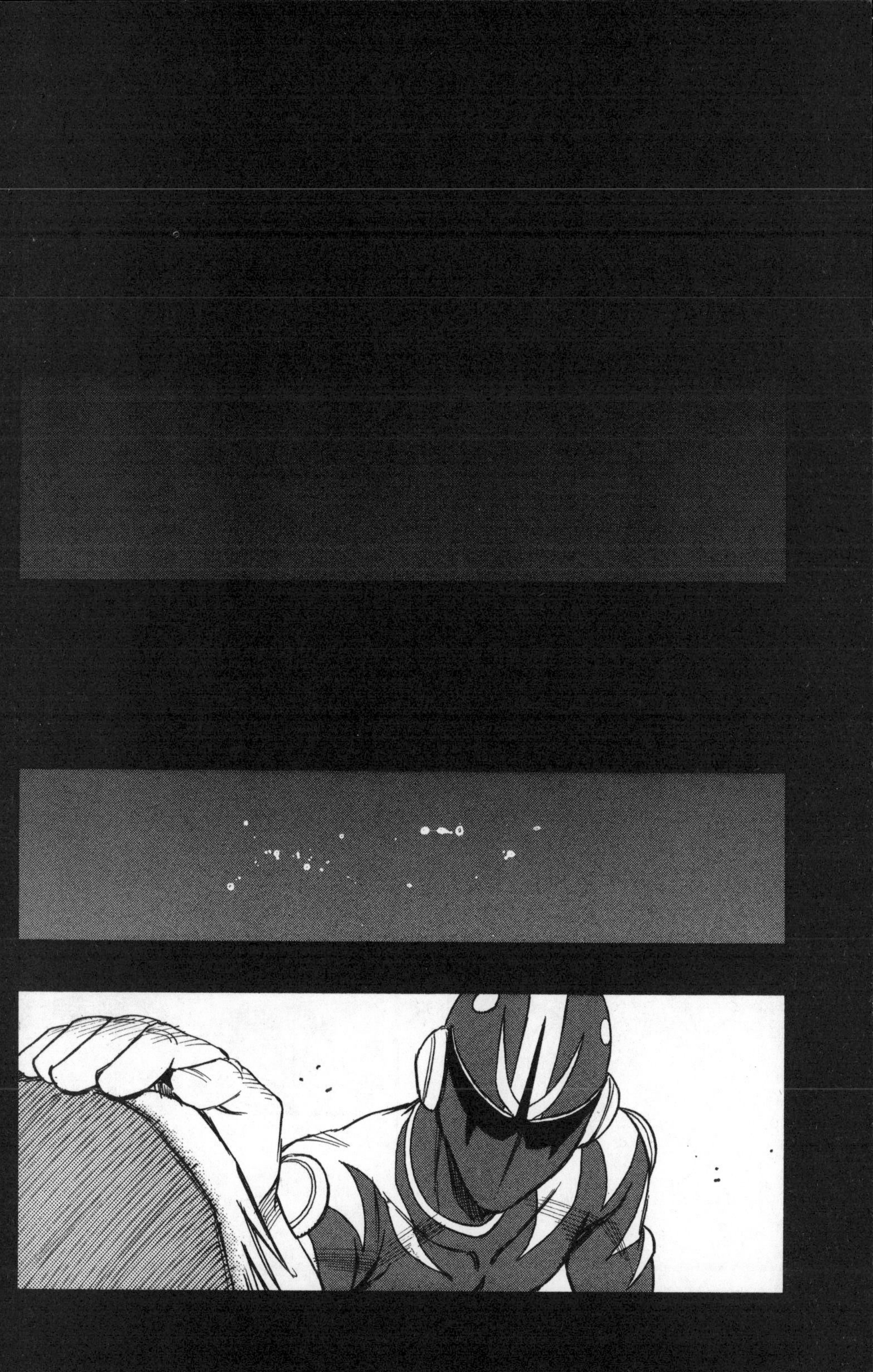

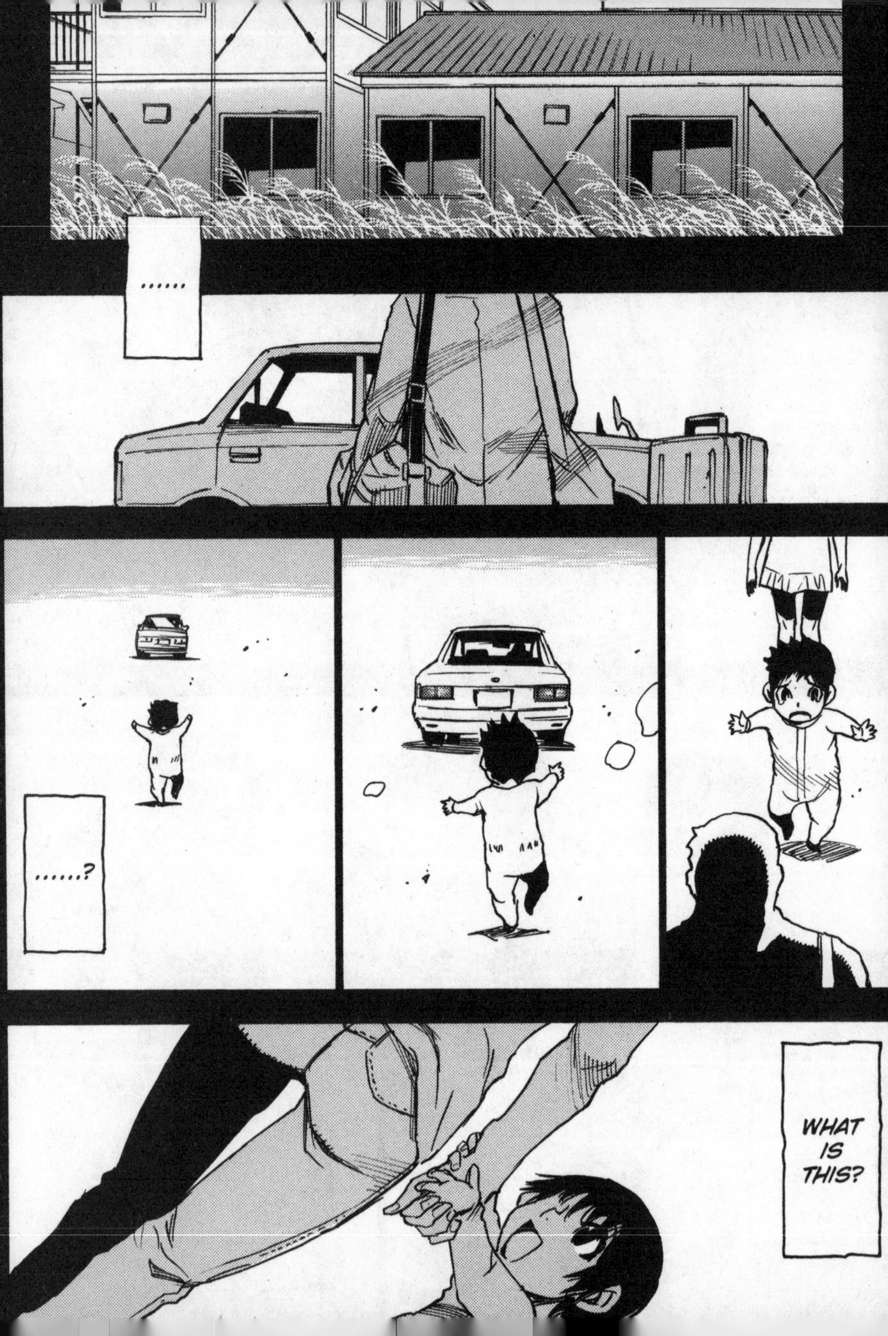
......
......?
WHAT IS THIS?

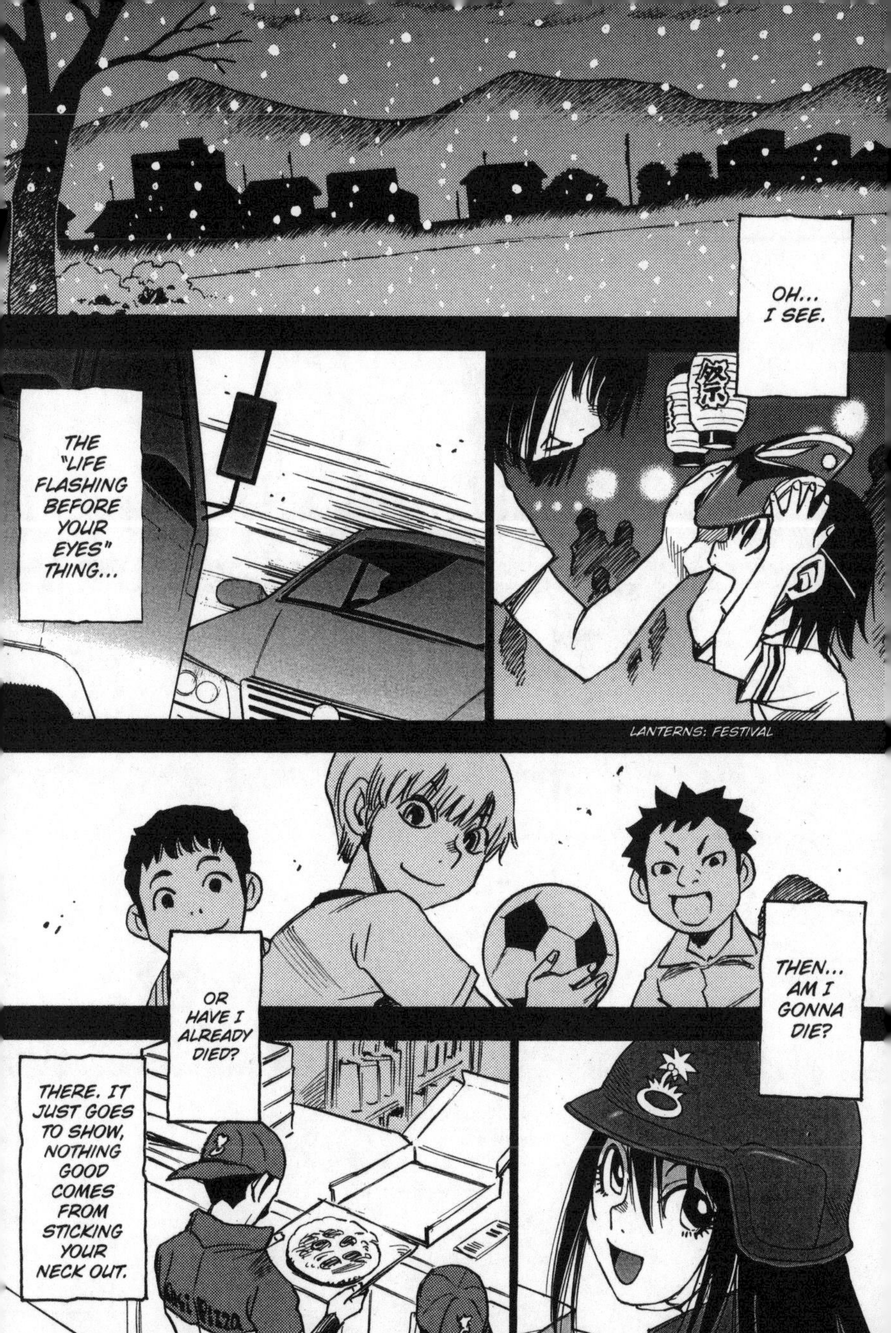
OH... I SEE.
祭
LANTERNS: FESTIVAL
THE "LIFE FLASHING BEFORE YOUR EYES" THING...
THEN... AM I GONNA DIE?
OR HAVE I ALREADY DIED?
THERE. IT JUST GOES TO SHOW, NOTHING GOOD COMES FROM STICKING YOUR NECK OUT.

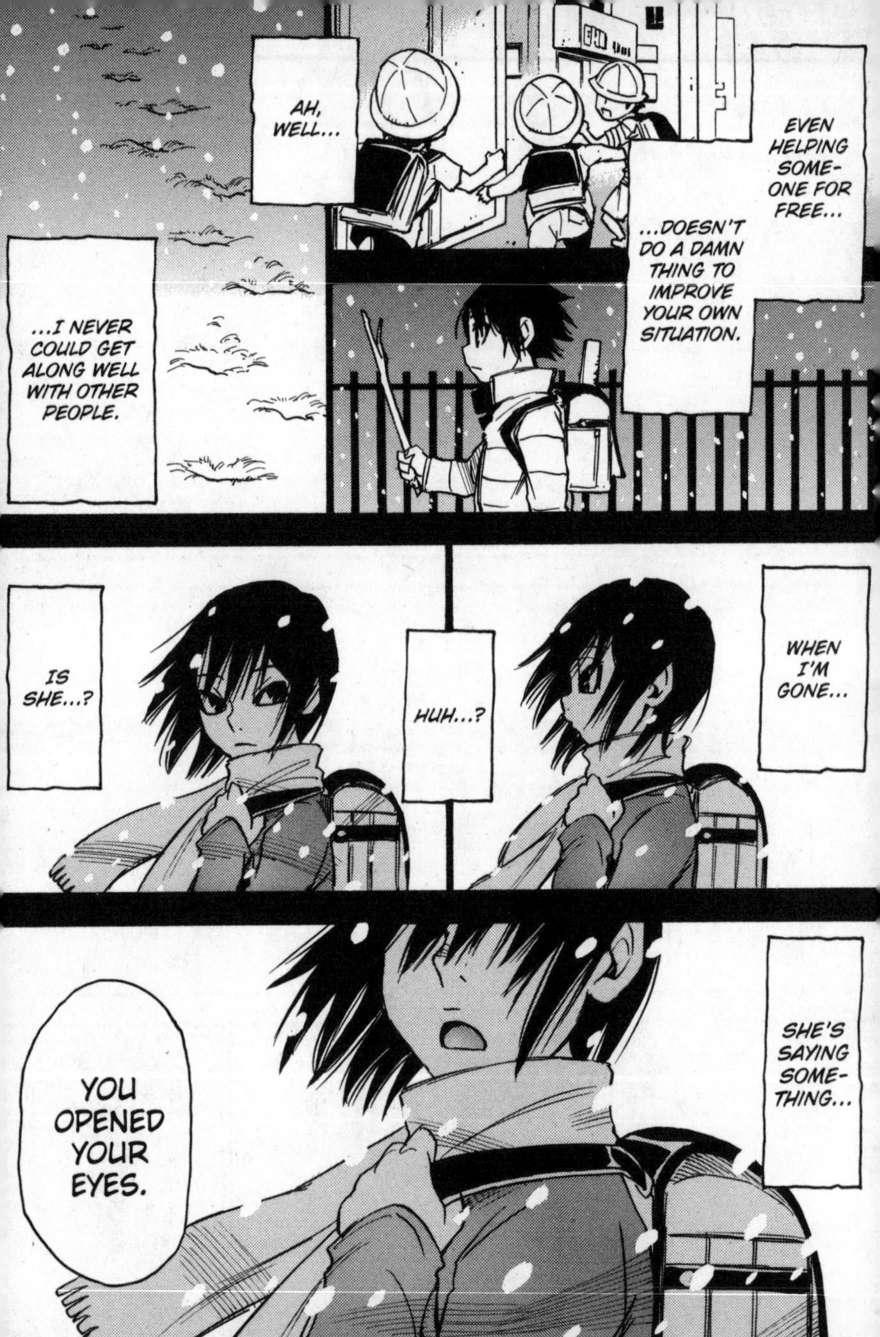
AH, WELL...
EVEN HELPING SOME-ONE FOR FREE...
...DOESN'T DO A DAMN THING TO IMPROVE YOUR OWN SITUATION.
...I NEVER COULD GET ALONG WELL WITH OTHER PEOPLE.
WHEN I'M GONE...
HUH...?
IS SHE...?
SHE'S SAYING SOME-THING...
YOU OPENED YOUR EYES.

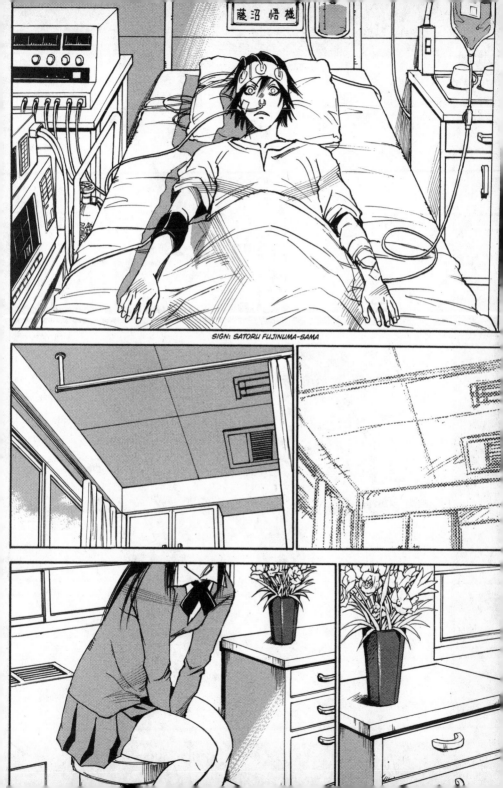

SIGN: SATORU FUJINUMA-SAMA

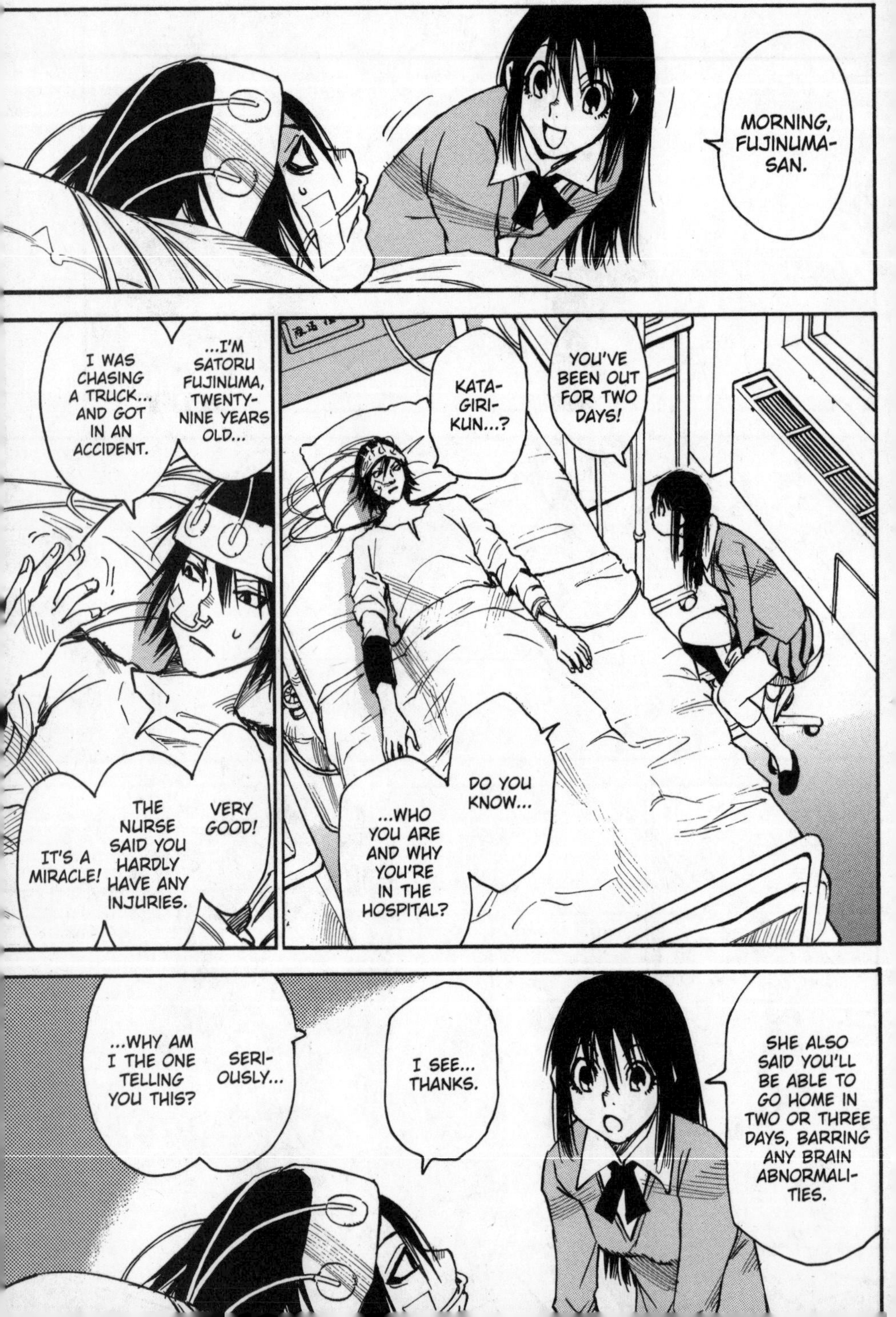
MORNING, FUJINUMA-SAN.
YOU'VE BEEN OUT FOR TWO DAYS!
KATA-GIRI-KUN...?
DO YOU KNOW...
...WHO YOU ARE AND WHY YOU'RE IN THE HOSPITAL?
...I'M SATORU FUJINUMA, TWENTY-NINE YEARS OLD...
I WAS CHASING A TRUCK... AND GOT IN AN ACCIDENT.
VERY GOOD!
THE NURSE SAID YOU HARDLY HAVE ANY INJURIES.
IT'S A MIRACLE!
SHE ALSO SAID YOU'LL BE ABLE TO GO HOME IN TWO OR THREE DAYS, BARRING ANY BRAIN ABNORMALI-TIES.
I SEE... THANKS.
SERI-OUSLY...
...WHY AM I THE ONE TELLING YOU THIS?

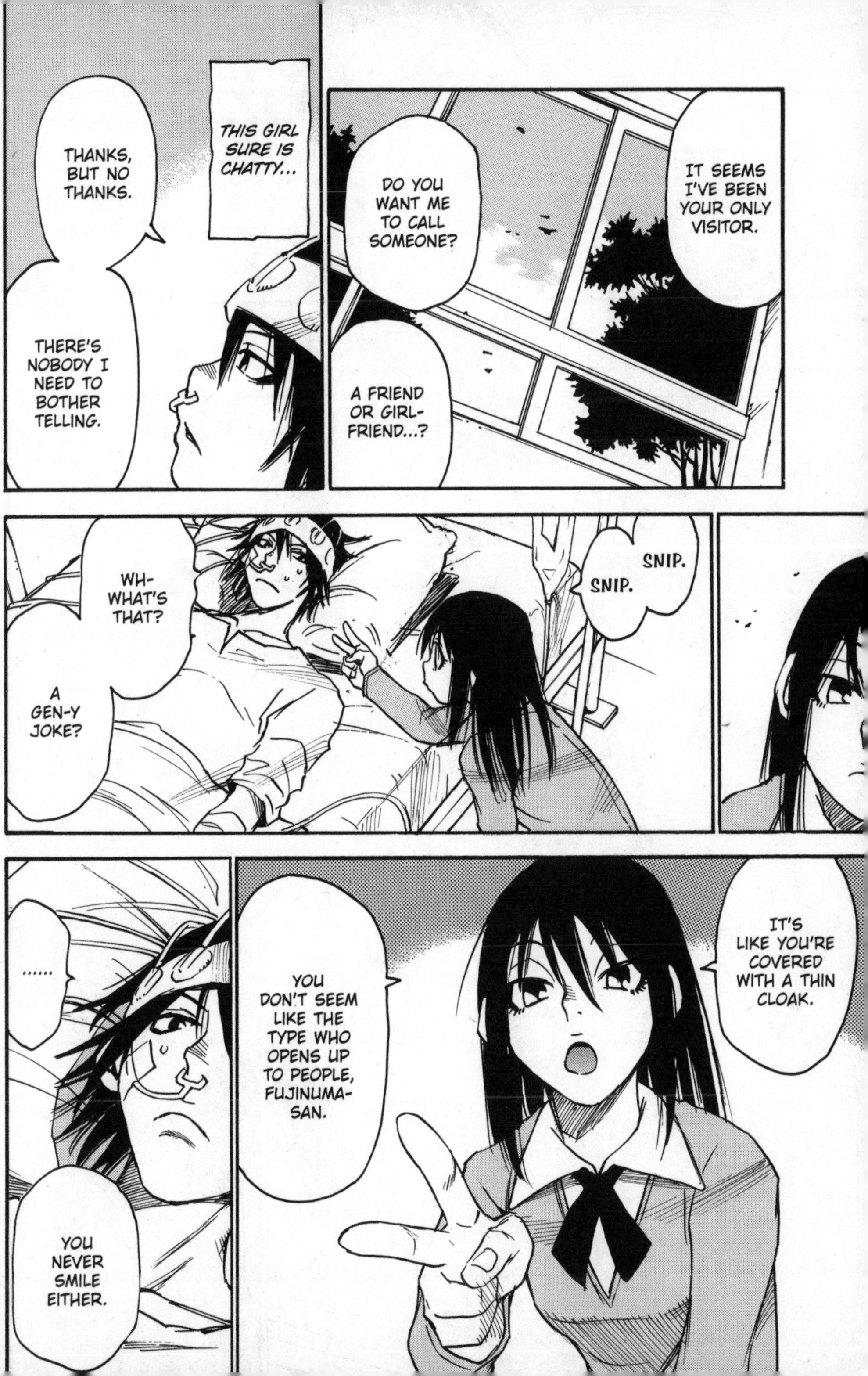
IT SEEMS I'VE BEEN YOUR ONLY VISITOR.
DO YOU WANT ME TO CALL SOMEONE?
A FRIEND OR GIRL-FRIEND...?
THIS GIRL SURE IS CHATTY...
THANKS, BUT NO THANKS.
THERE'S NOBODY I NEED TO BOTHER TELLING.
SNIP.
SNIP.
WH-WHAT'S THAT?
A GEN-Y JOKE?
IT'S LIKE YOU'RE COVERED WITH A THIN CLOAK.
YOU DON'T SEEM LIKE THE TYPE WHO OPENS UP TO PEOPLE, FUJINUMA-SAN.
......
YOU NEVER SMILE EITHER.

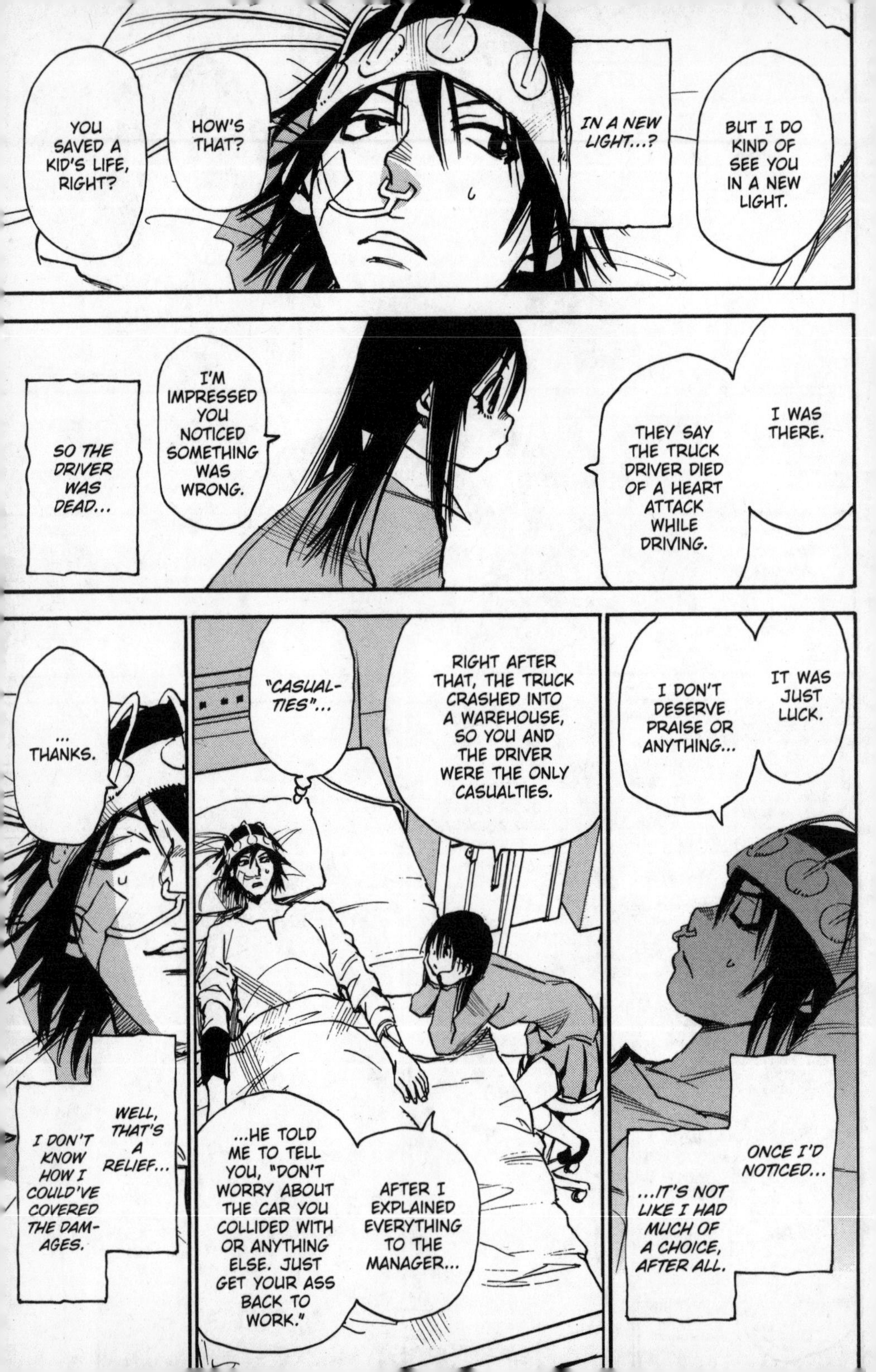
BUT I DO KIND OF SEE YOU IN A NEW LIGHT.
IN A NEW LIGHT...?
HOW'S THAT?
YOU SAVED A KID'S LIFE, RIGHT?
I WAS THERE.
THEY SAY THE TRUCK DRIVER DIED OF A HEART ATTACK WHILE DRIVING.
I'M IMPRESSED YOU NOTICED SOMETHING WAS WRONG.
SO THE DRIVER WAS DEAD...
IT WAS JUST LUCK.
I DON'T DESERVE PRAISE OR ANYTHING...
ONCE I'D NOTICED...
...IT'S NOT LIKE I HAD MUCH OF A CHOICE, AFTER ALL.
RIGHT AFTER THAT, THE TRUCK CRASHED INTO A WAREHOUSE, SO YOU AND THE DRIVER WERE THE ONLY CASUALTIES.
"CASUAL-TIES"...
AFTER I EXPLAINED EVERYTHING TO THE MANAGER...
...HE TOLD ME TO TELL YOU, "DON'T WORRY ABOUT THE CAR YOU COLLIDED WITH OR ANYTHING ELSE. JUST GET YOUR ASS BACK TO WORK."
...THANKS.
WELL, THAT'S A RELIEF...
I DON'T KNOW HOW I COULD'VE COVERED THE DAM-AGES.

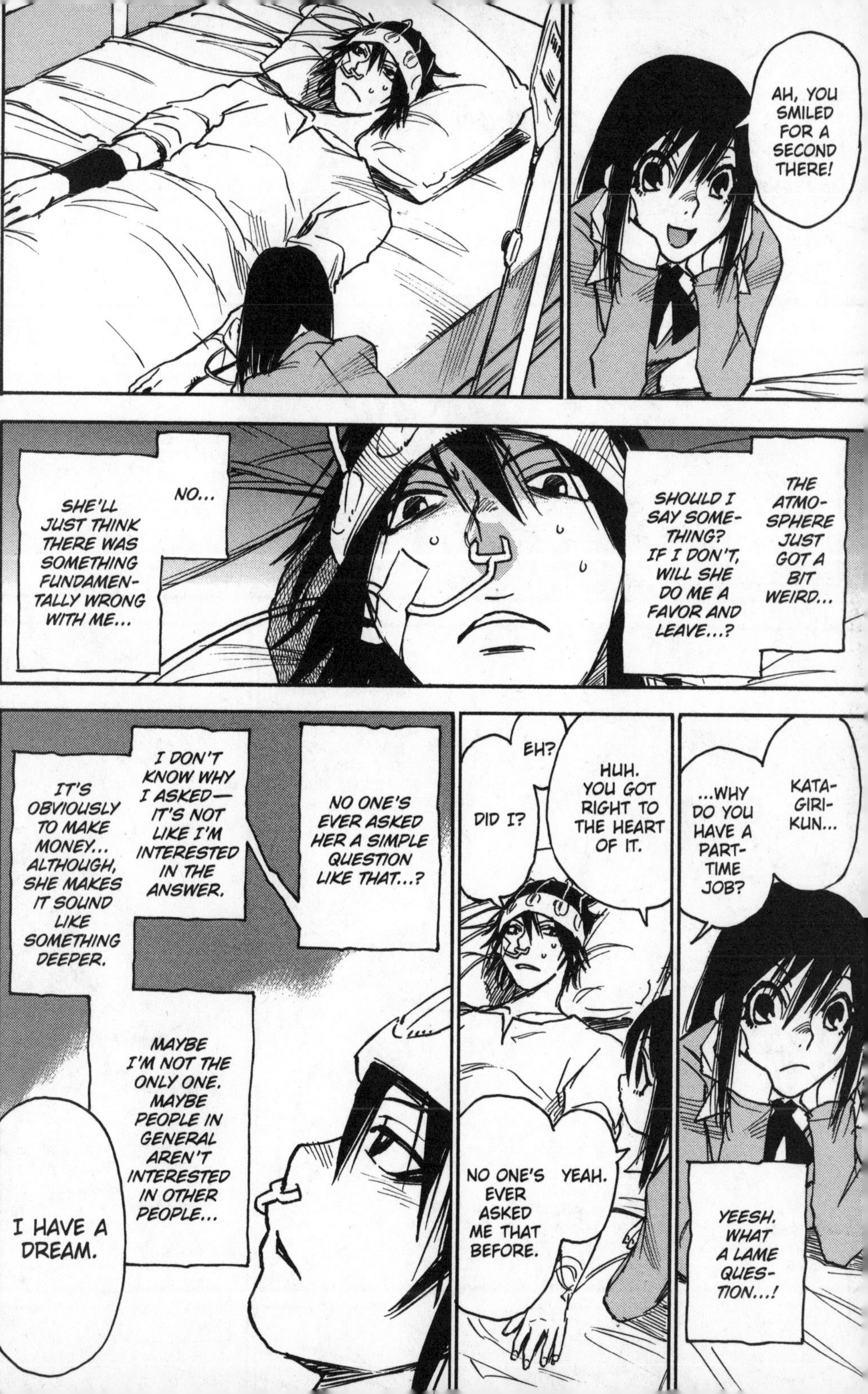
AH, YOU SMILED FOR A SECOND THERE!
THE ATMOSPHERE JUST GOT A BIT WEIRD...
SHOULD I SAY SOMETHING? IF I DON'T, WILL SHE DO ME A FAVOR AND LEAVE...?
NO...
SHE'LL JUST THINK THERE WAS SOMETHING FUNDAMENTALLY WRONG WITH ME...
KATAGIRI-KUN...
...WHY DO YOU HAVE A PART-TIME JOB?
YEESH. WHAT A LAME QUESTION...!
EH?
HUH. YOU GOT RIGHT TO THE HEART OF IT.
DID I?
YEAH.
NO ONE'S EVER ASKED ME THAT BEFORE.
NO ONE'S EVER ASKED HER A SIMPLE QUESTION LIKE THAT...?
I DON'T KNOW WHY I ASKED—IT'S NOT LIKE I'M INTERESTED IN THE ANSWER.
IT'S OBVIOUSLY TO MAKE MONEY... ALTHOUGH, SHE MAKES IT SOUND LIKE SOMETHING DEEPER.
....
MAYBE I'M NOT THE ONLY ONE. MAYBE PEOPLE IN GENERAL AREN'T INTERESTED IN OTHER PEOPLE...
I HAVE A DREAM.

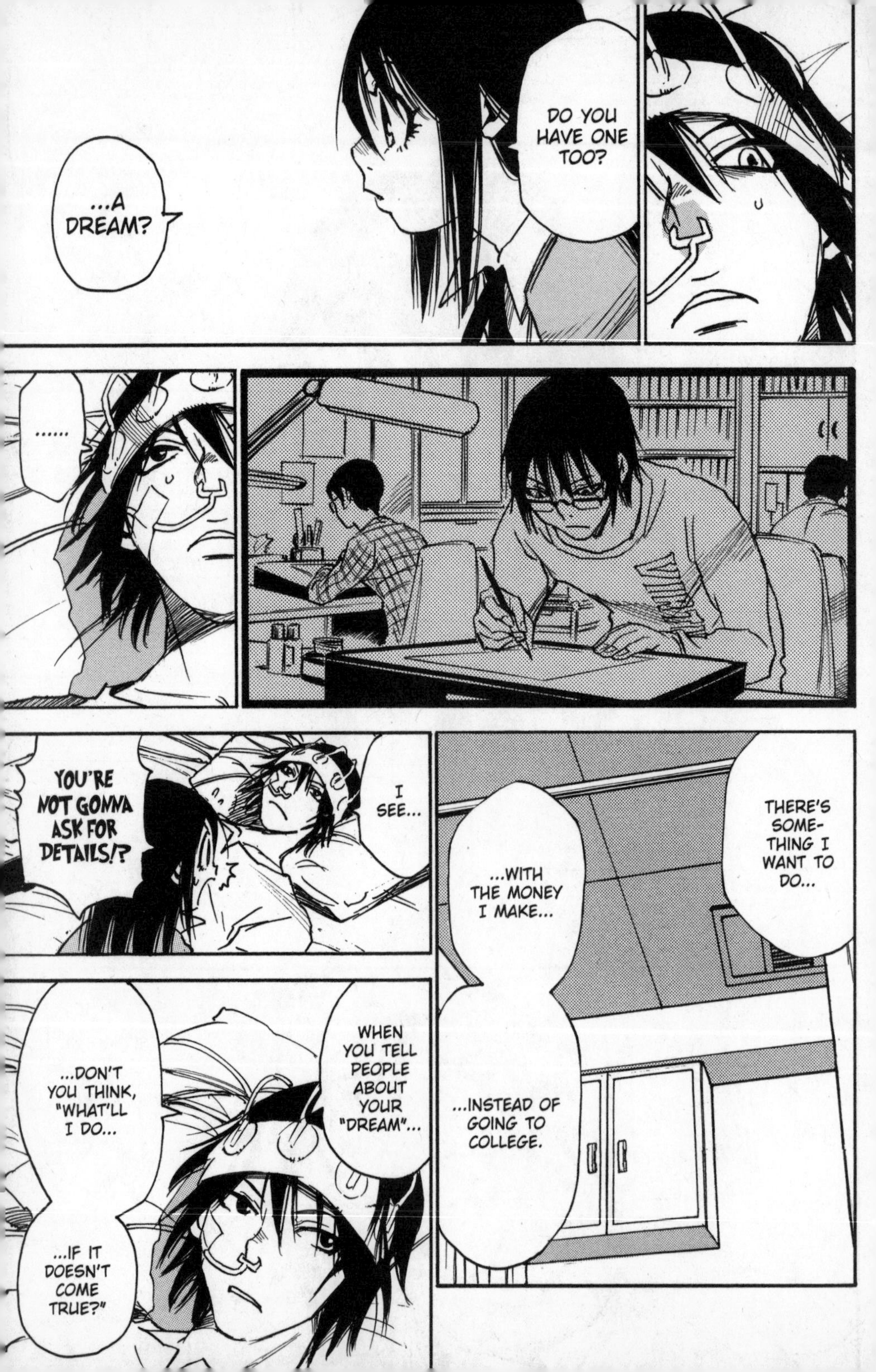
DO YOU HAVE ONE TOO?
...A DREAM?
......
THERE'S SOME-THING I WANT TO DO...
...WITH THE MONEY I MAKE...
...INSTEAD OF GOING TO COLLEGE.
I SEE...
YOU'RE NOT GONNA ASK FOR DETAILS!?
WHEN YOU TELL PEOPLE ABOUT YOUR "DREAM"...
...DON'T YOU THINK, "WHAT'LL I DO...
...IF IT DOESN'T COME TRUE?"

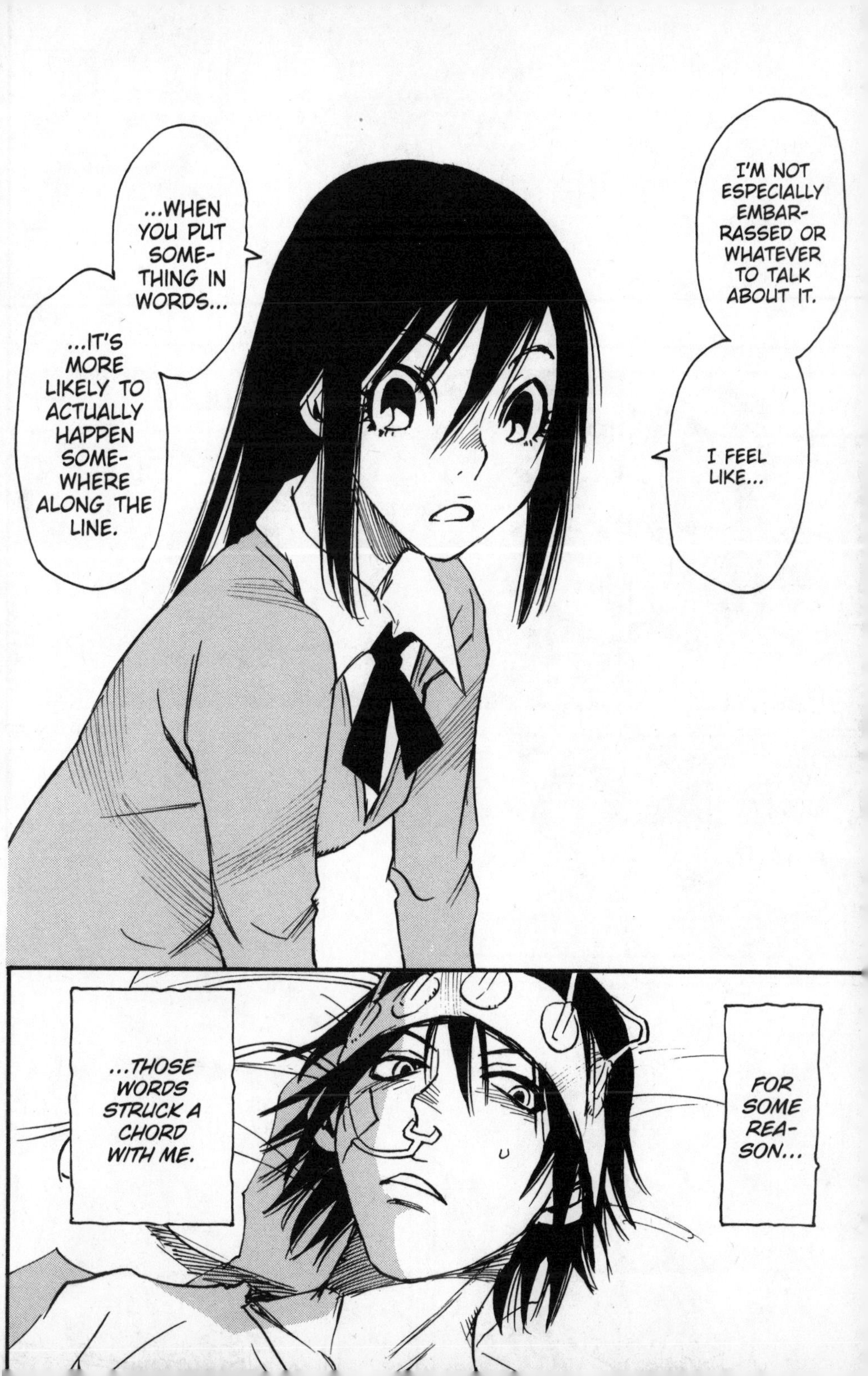
I'M NOT ESPECIALLY EMBARRASSED OR WHATEVER TO TALK ABOUT IT.
I FEEL LIKE...
...WHEN YOU PUT SOMETHING IN WORDS...
...IT'S MORE LIKELY TO ACTUALLY HAPPEN SOMEWHERE ALONG THE LINE.
FOR SOME REASON...
...THOSE WORDS STRUCK A CHORD WITH ME.

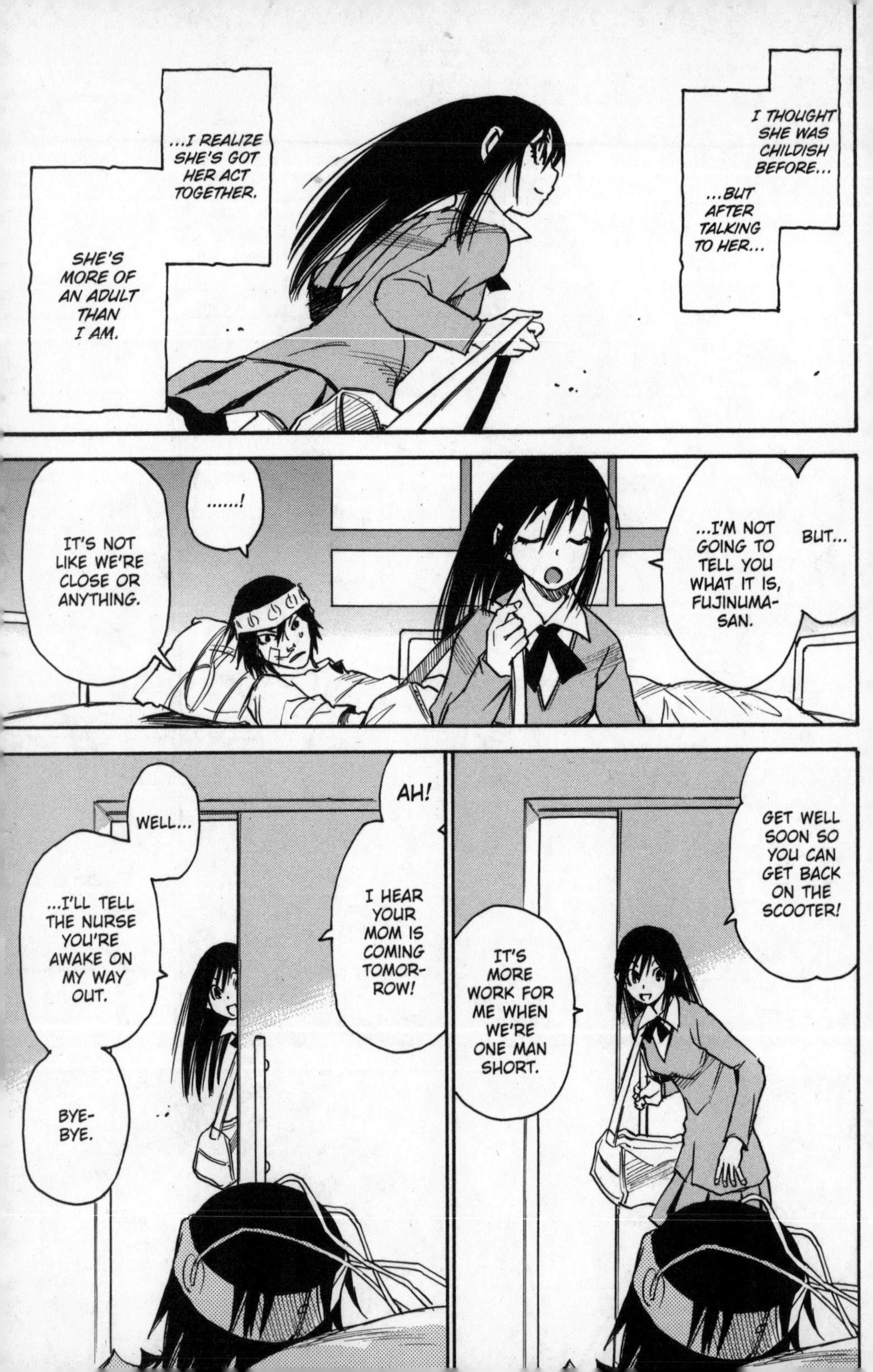
I THOUGHT SHE WAS CHILDISH BEFORE...
...BUT AFTER TALKING TO HER...
...I REALIZE SHE'S GOT HER ACT TOGETHER.
SHE'S MORE OF AN ADULT THAN I AM.
BUT...
...I'M NOT GOING TO TELL YOU WHAT IT IS, FUJINUMA-SAN.
......!
IT'S NOT LIKE WE'RE CLOSE OR ANYTHING.
GET WELL SOON SO YOU CAN GET BACK ON THE SCOOTER!
IT'S MORE WORK FOR ME WHEN WE'RE ONE MAN SHORT.
AH!
I HEAR YOUR MOM IS COMING TOMORROW!
WELL...
...I'LL TELL THE NURSE YOU'RE AWAKE ON MY WAY OUT.
BYE-BYE.

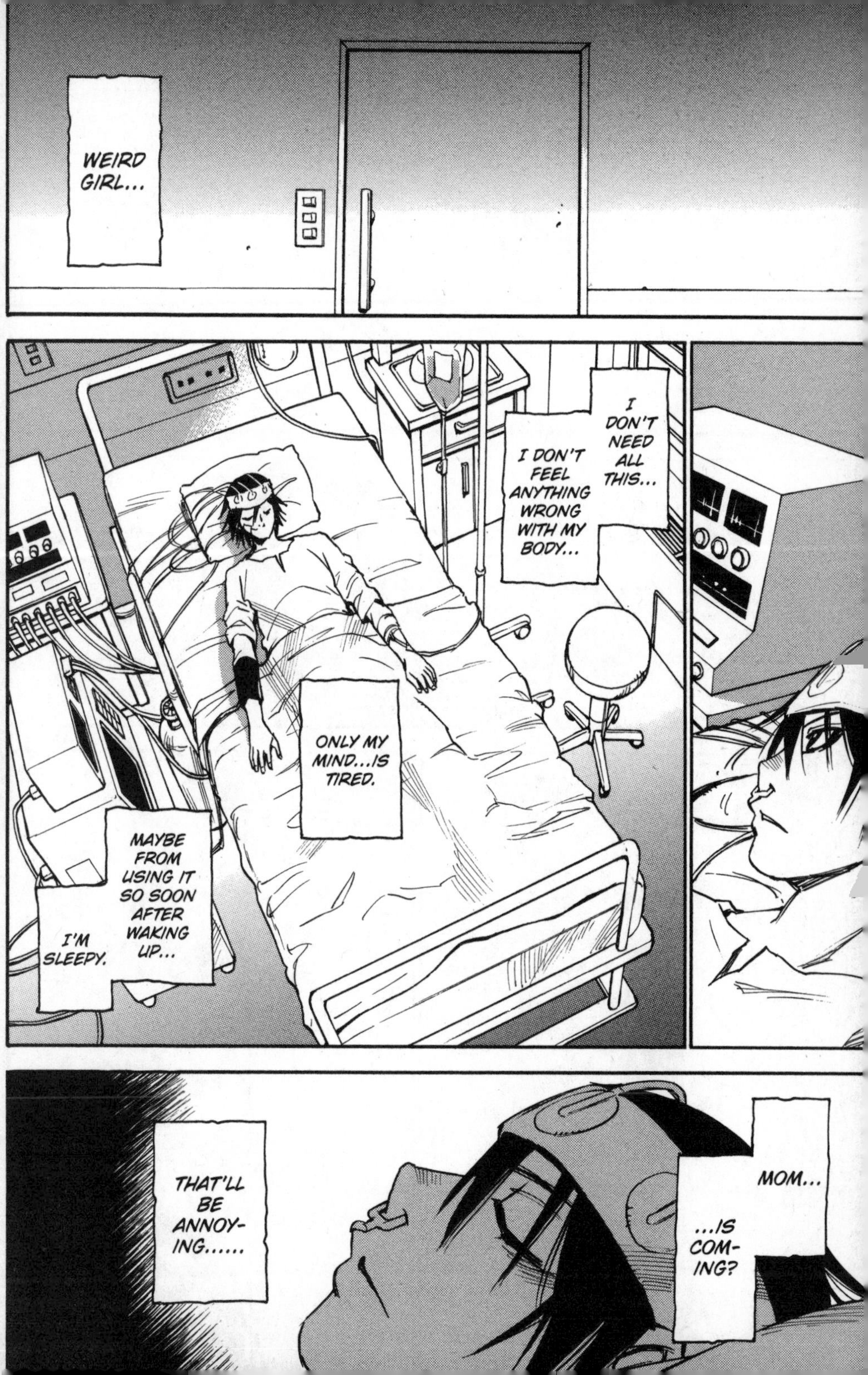
WEIRD GIRL...
I DON'T NEED ALL THIS...
I DON'T FEEL ANYTHING WRONG WITH MY BODY...
ONLY MY MIND...IS TIRED.
MAYBE FROM USING IT SO SOON AFTER WAKING UP...
I'M SLEEPY.
MOM...
...IS COMING?
THAT'LL BE ANNOY-ING......

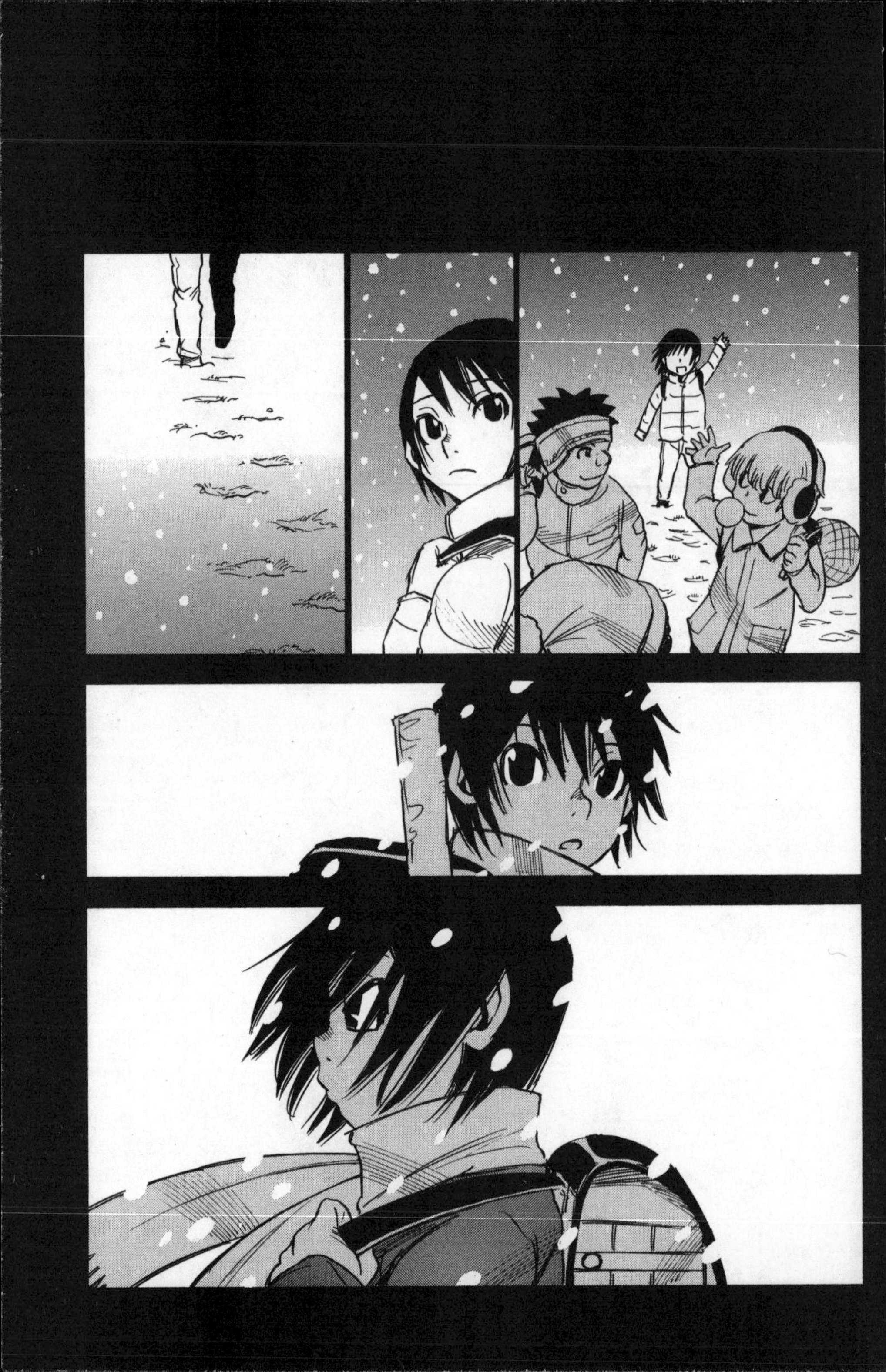

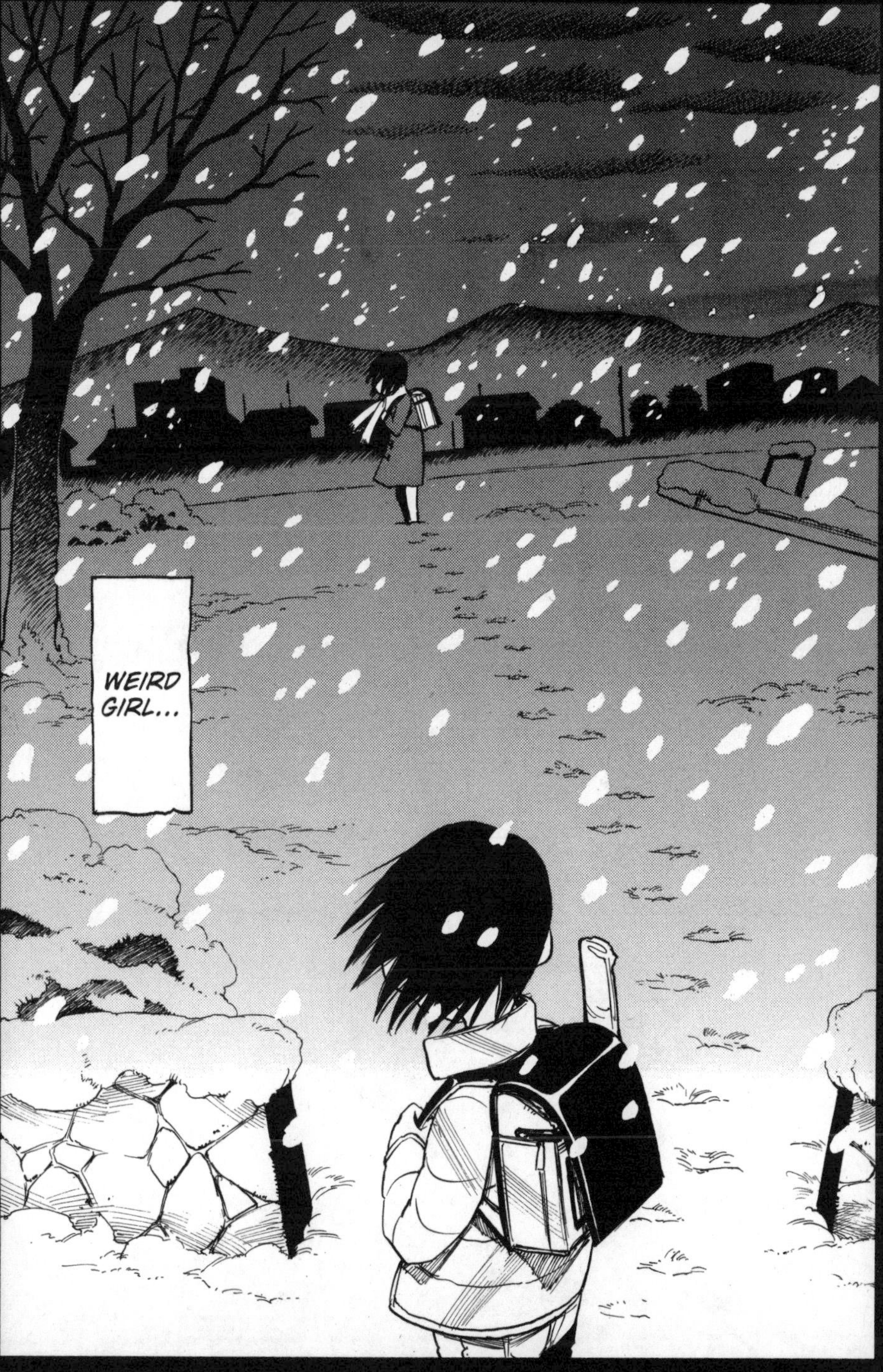
WEIRD GIRL...

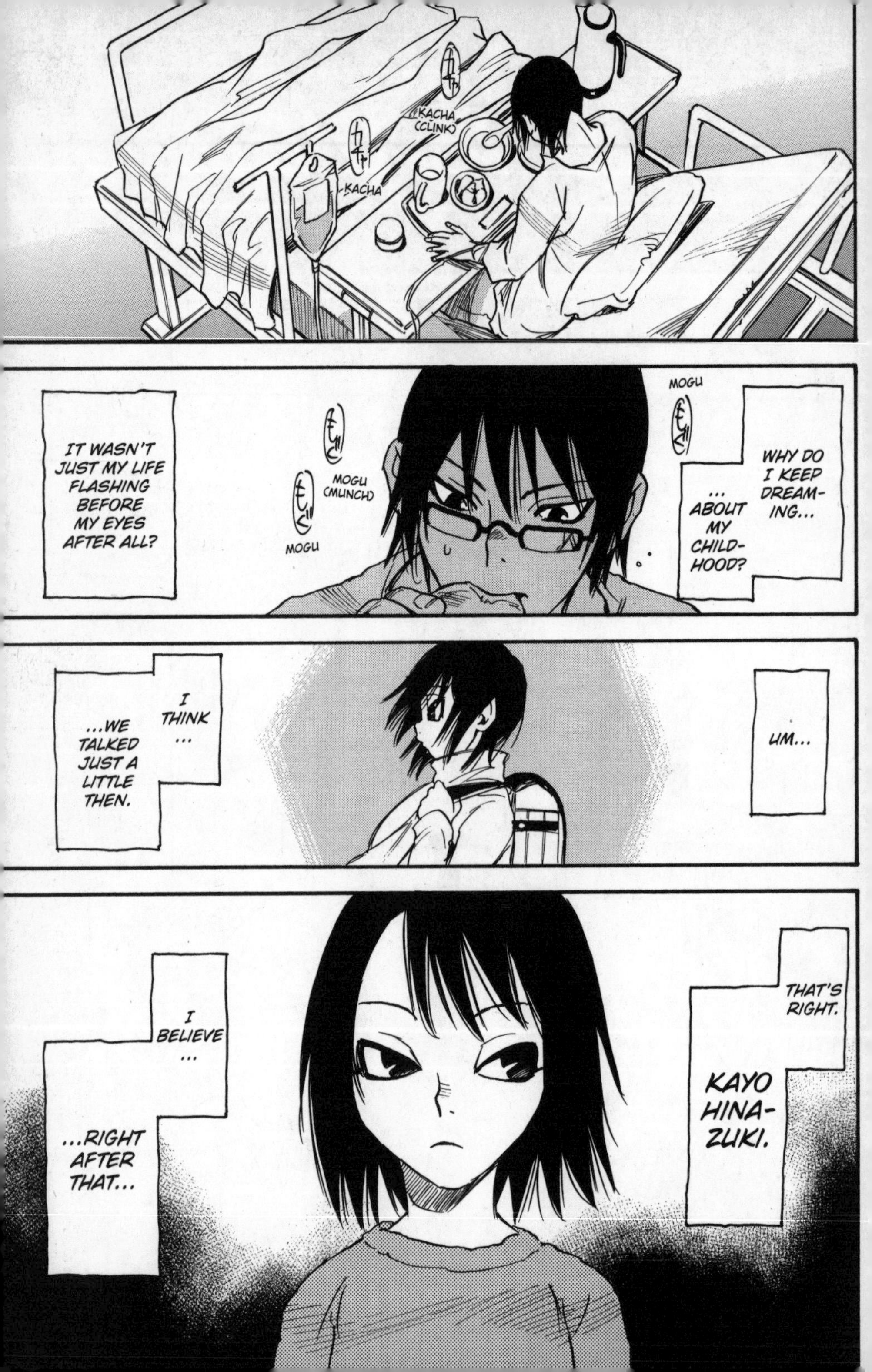
KACHA (CLINK)
-KACHA
WHY DO I KEEP DREAMING...
...ABOUT MY CHILDHOOD?
MOGU
MOGU (MUNCH)
MOGU
IT WASN'T JUST MY LIFE FLASHING BEFORE MY EYES AFTER ALL?
UM...
I THINK...
...WE TALKED JUST A LITTLE THEN.
THAT'S RIGHT.
KAYO HINAZUKI.
I BELIEVE...
...RIGHT AFTER THAT...

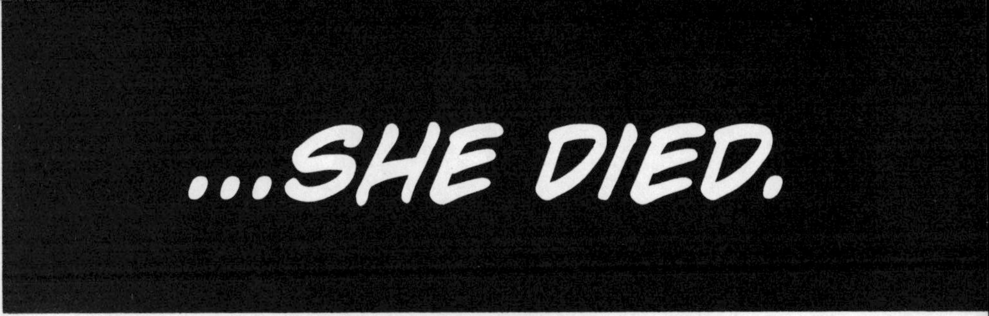
...SHE DIED.

SIGN: PHARMACY

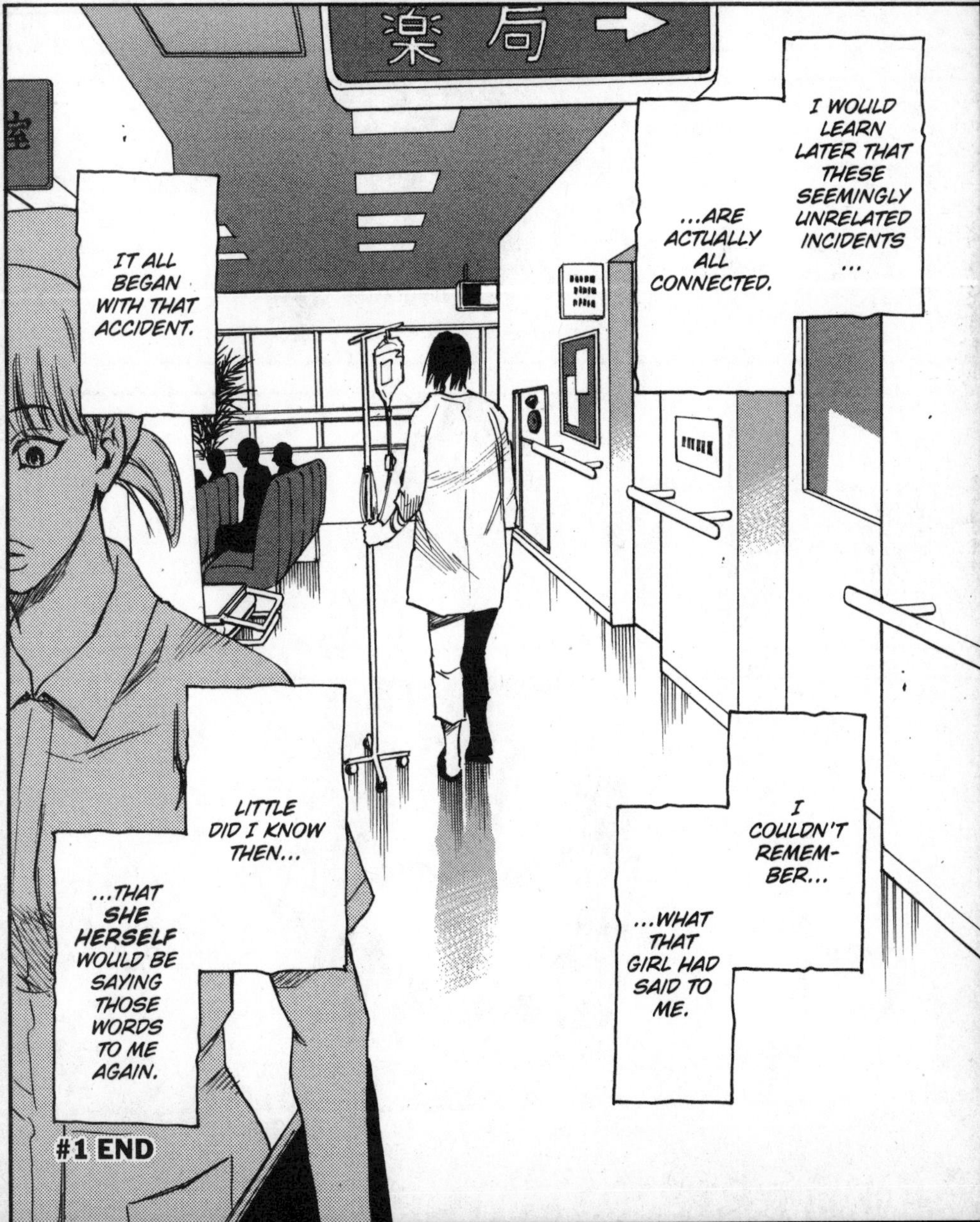
I WOULD LEARN LATER THAT THESE SEEMINGLY UNRELATED INCIDENTS...
...ARE ACTUALLY ALL CONNECTED.
IT ALL BEGAN WITH THAT ACCIDENT.
I COULDN'T REMEMBER...
...WHAT THAT GIRL HAD SAID TO ME.
LITTLE DID I KNOW THEN...
...THAT SHE HERSELF WOULD BE SAYING THOSE WORDS TO ME AGAIN.
#1 END

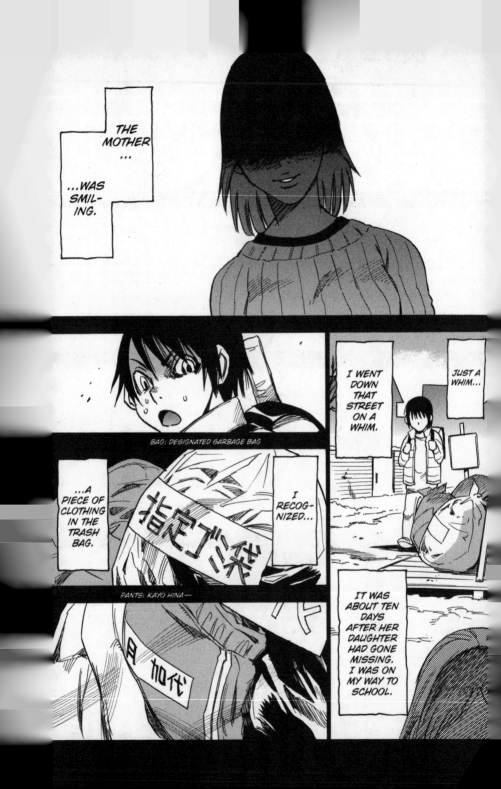

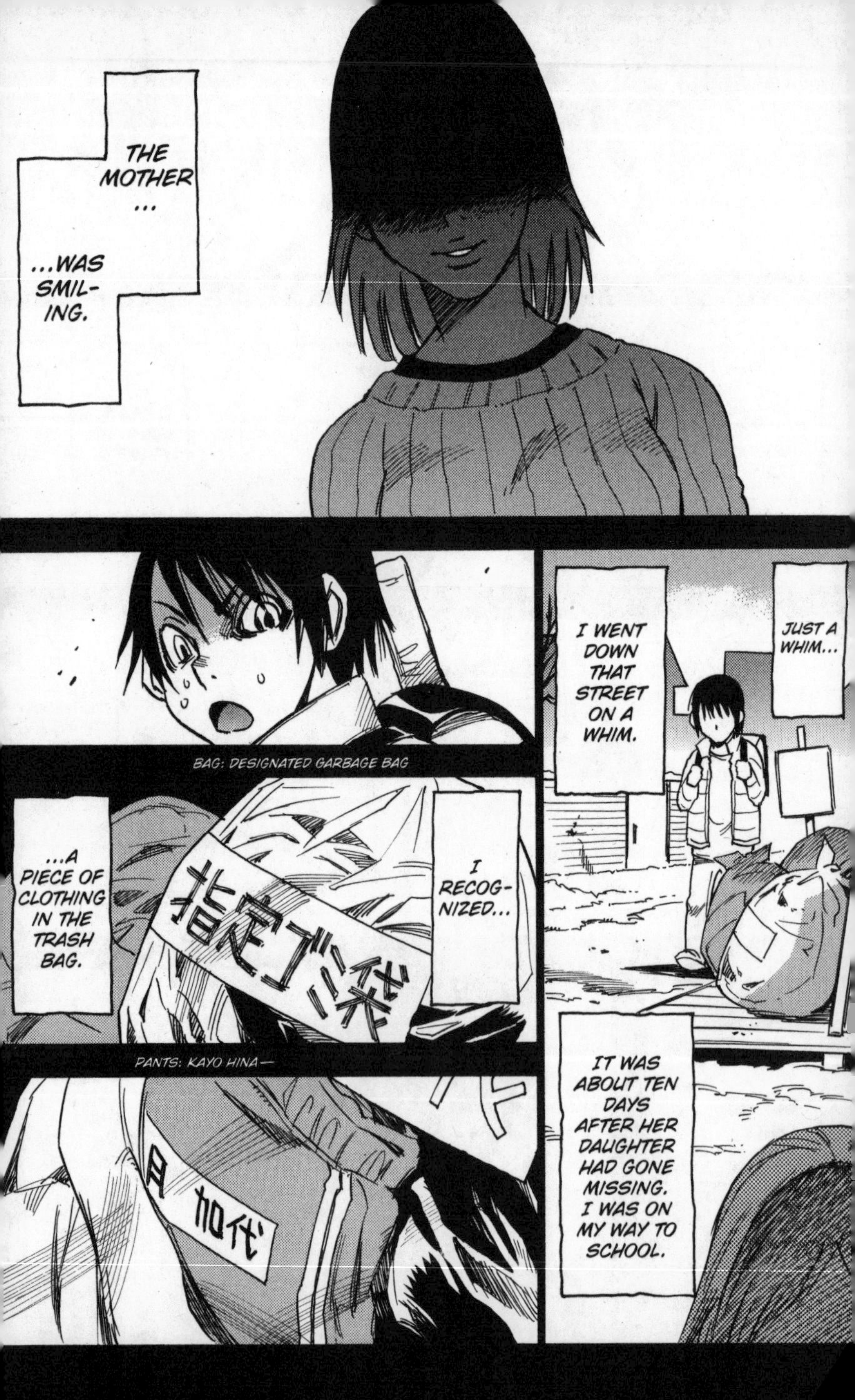
THE MOTHER ...
...WAS SMILING.
JUST A WHIM...
I WENT DOWN THAT STREET ON A WHIM.
IT WAS ABOUT TEN DAYS AFTER HER DAUGHTER HAD GONE MISSING. I WAS ON MY WAY TO SCHOOL.
BAG: DESIGNATED GARBAGE BAG
I RECOGNIZED...
...A PIECE OF CLOTHING IN THE TRASH BAG.
指定ゴミ袋
PANTS: KAYO HINA—

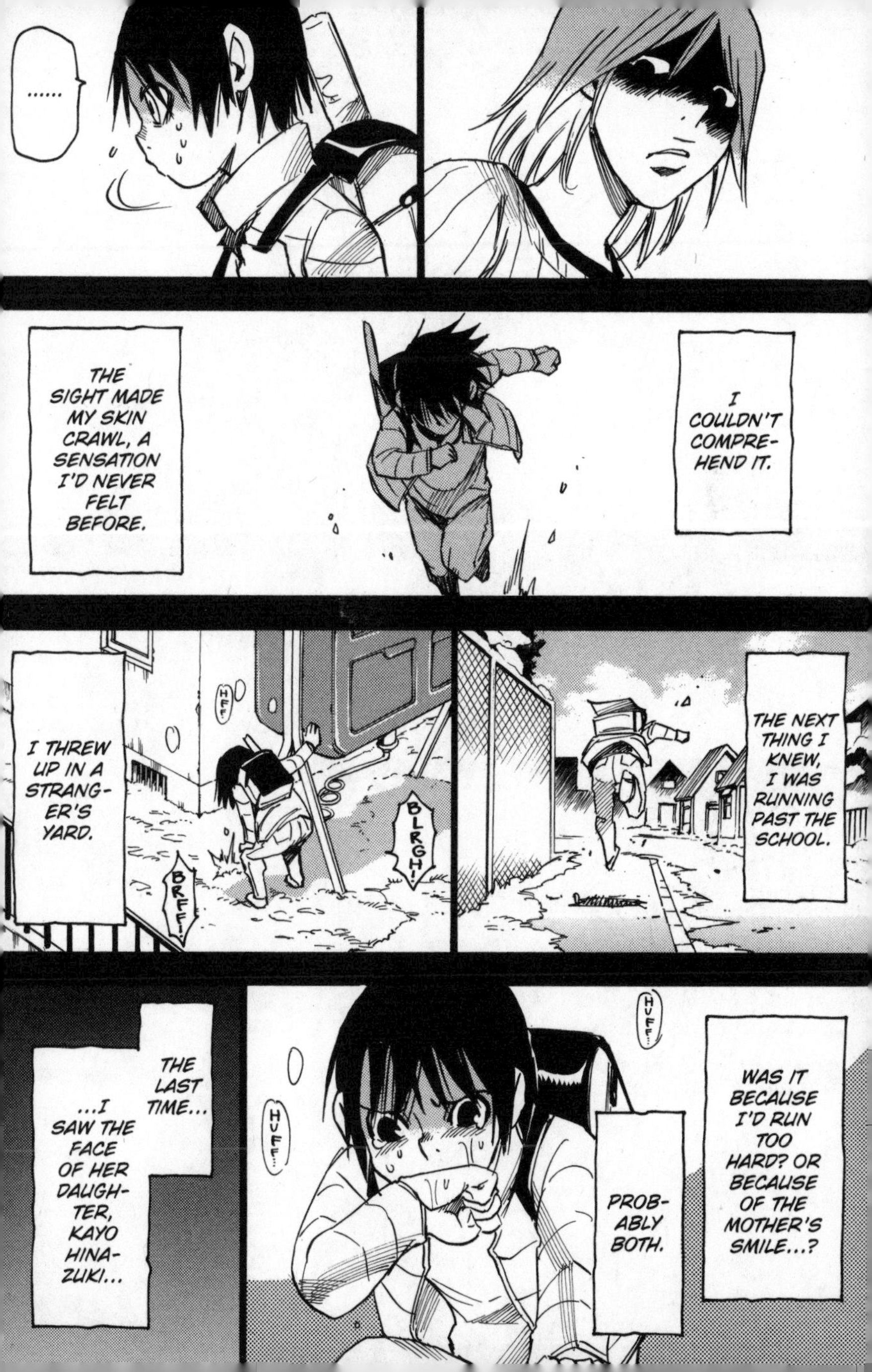
......
I COULDN'T COMPREHEND IT.
THE SIGHT MADE MY SKIN CRAWL, A SENSATION I'D NEVER FELT BEFORE.
THE NEXT THING I KNEW, I WAS RUNNING PAST THE SCHOOL.
I THREW UP IN A STRANGER'S YARD.
HFF
BLRGH!
BRFF!
HUFF...
WAS IT BECAUSE I'D RUN TOO HARD? OR BECAUSE OF THE MOTHER'S SMILE...?
PROBABLY BOTH.
HUFF...
THE LAST TIME...
...I SAW THE FACE OF HER DAUGHTER, KAYO HINAZUKI...

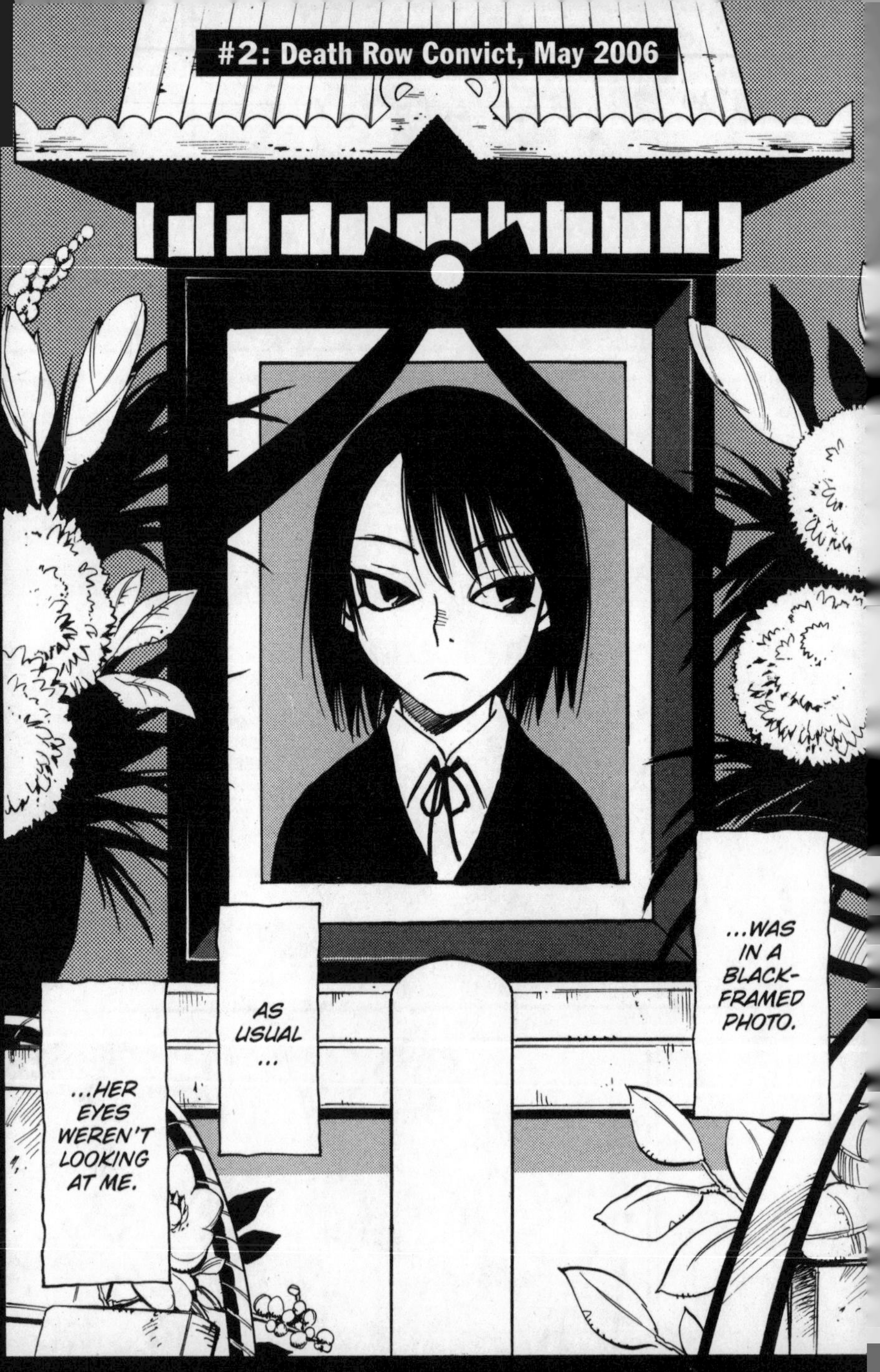
#2: Death Row Convict, May 2006
...WAS IN A BLACK-FRAMED PHOTO.
AS USUAL...
...HER EYES WEREN'T LOOKING AT ME.

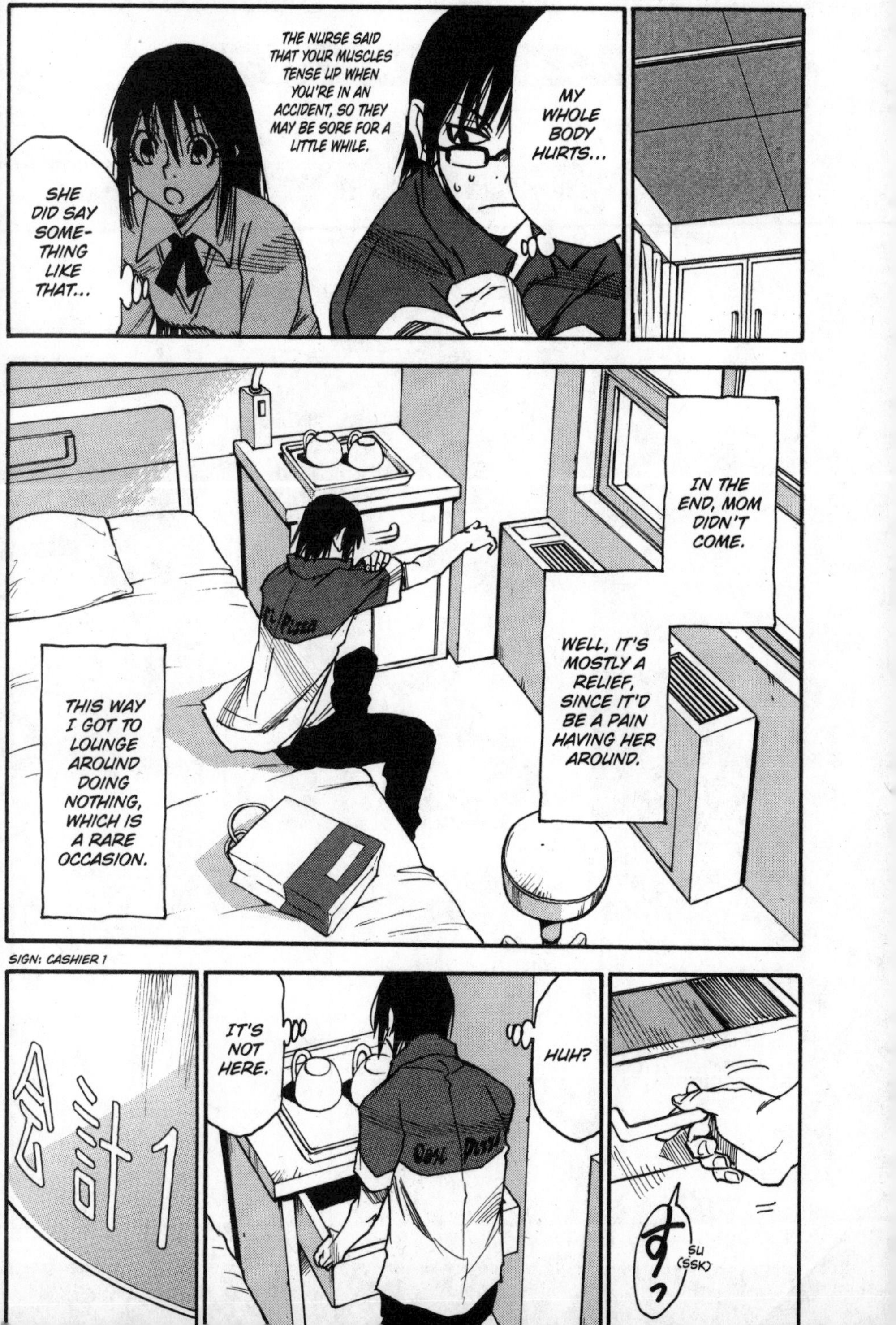
MY WHOLE BODY HURTS...
THE NURSE SAID THAT YOUR MUSCLES TENSE UP WHEN YOU'RE IN AN ACCIDENT, SO THEY MAY BE SORE FOR A LITTLE WHILE.
SHE DID SAY SOME-THING LIKE THAT...
IN THE END, MOM DIDN'T COME.
WELL, IT'S MOSTLY A RELIEF, SINCE IT'D BE A PAIN HAVING HER AROUND.
THIS WAY I GOT TO LOUNGE AROUND DOING NOTHING, WHICH IS A RARE OCCASION.
すっ
SU (SSK)
HUH?
IT'S NOT HERE.
SIGN: CASHIER 1
会計1

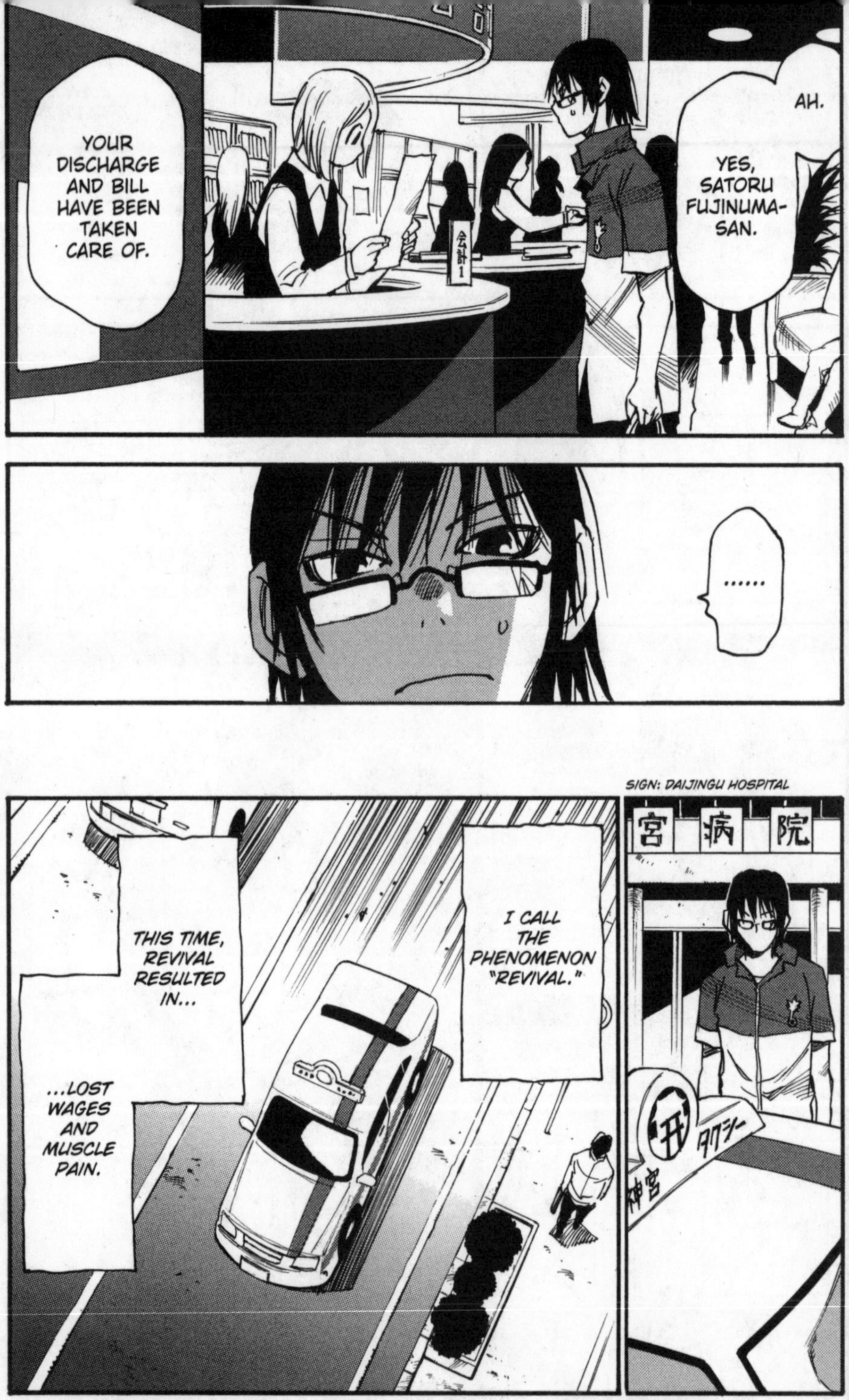
AH.
YES, SATORU FUJINUMA-SAN.
会計1
YOUR DISCHARGE AND BILL HAVE BEEN TAKEN CARE OF.
......
宮病院
タクシー
神宮
I CALL THE PHENOMENON "REVIVAL."
THIS TIME, REVIVAL RESULTED IN...
...LOST WAGES AND MUSCLE PAIN.

SIGN: DAIJINGU HOSPITAL

CAR: DAIJINGU TAXI

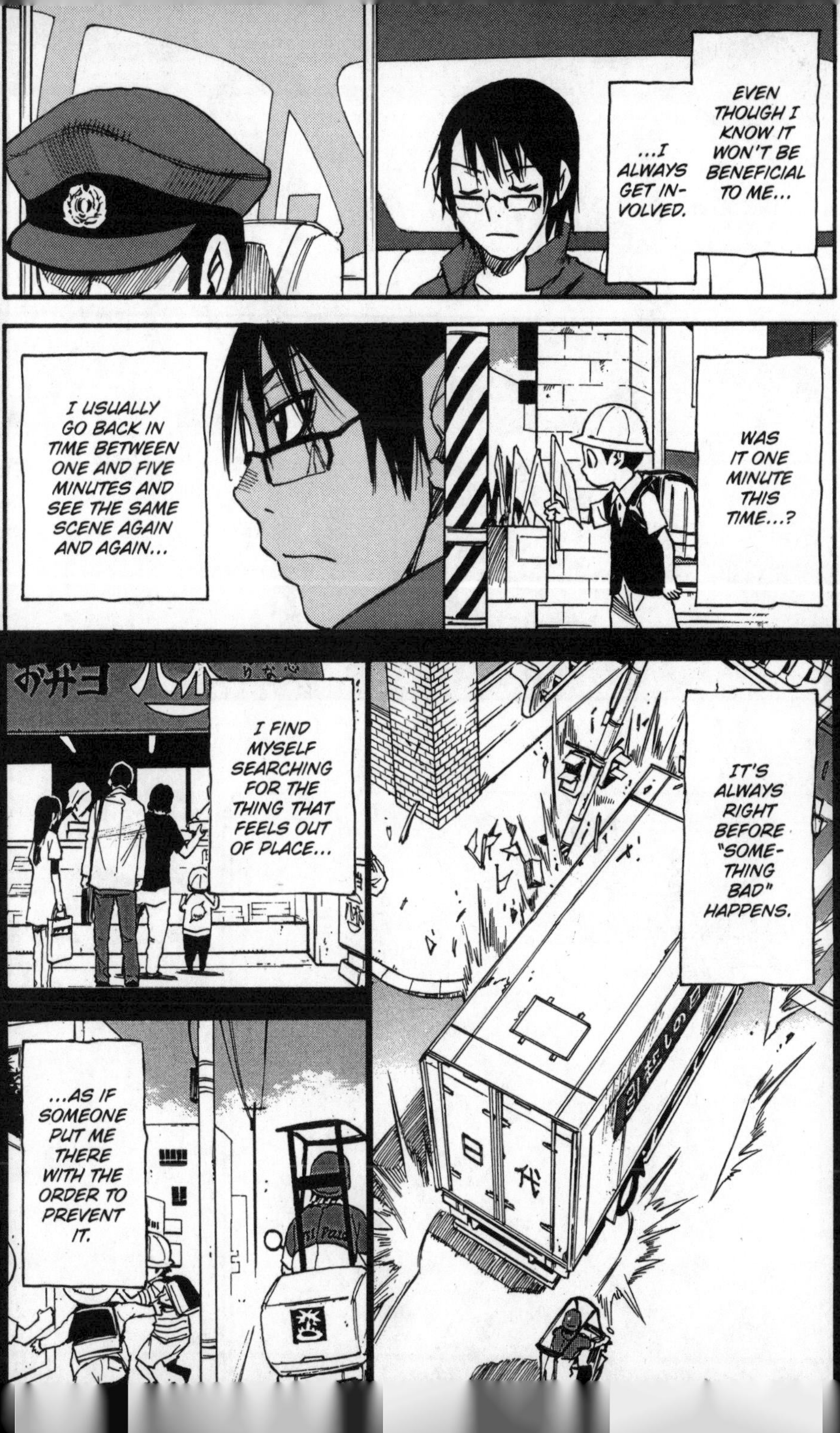
EVEN THOUGH I KNOW IT WON'T BE BENEFICIAL TO ME...
...I ALWAYS GET IN-VOLVED.
WAS IT ONE MINUTE THIS TIME...?
I USUALLY GO BACK IN TIME BETWEEN ONE AND FIVE MINUTES AND SEE THE SAME SCENE AGAIN AND AGAIN...
IT'S ALWAYS RIGHT BEFORE "SOME-THING BAD" HAPPENS.
I FIND MYSELF SEARCHING FOR THE THING THAT FEELS OUT OF PLACE...
...AS IF SOMEONE PUT ME THERE WITH THE ORDER TO PREVENT IT.

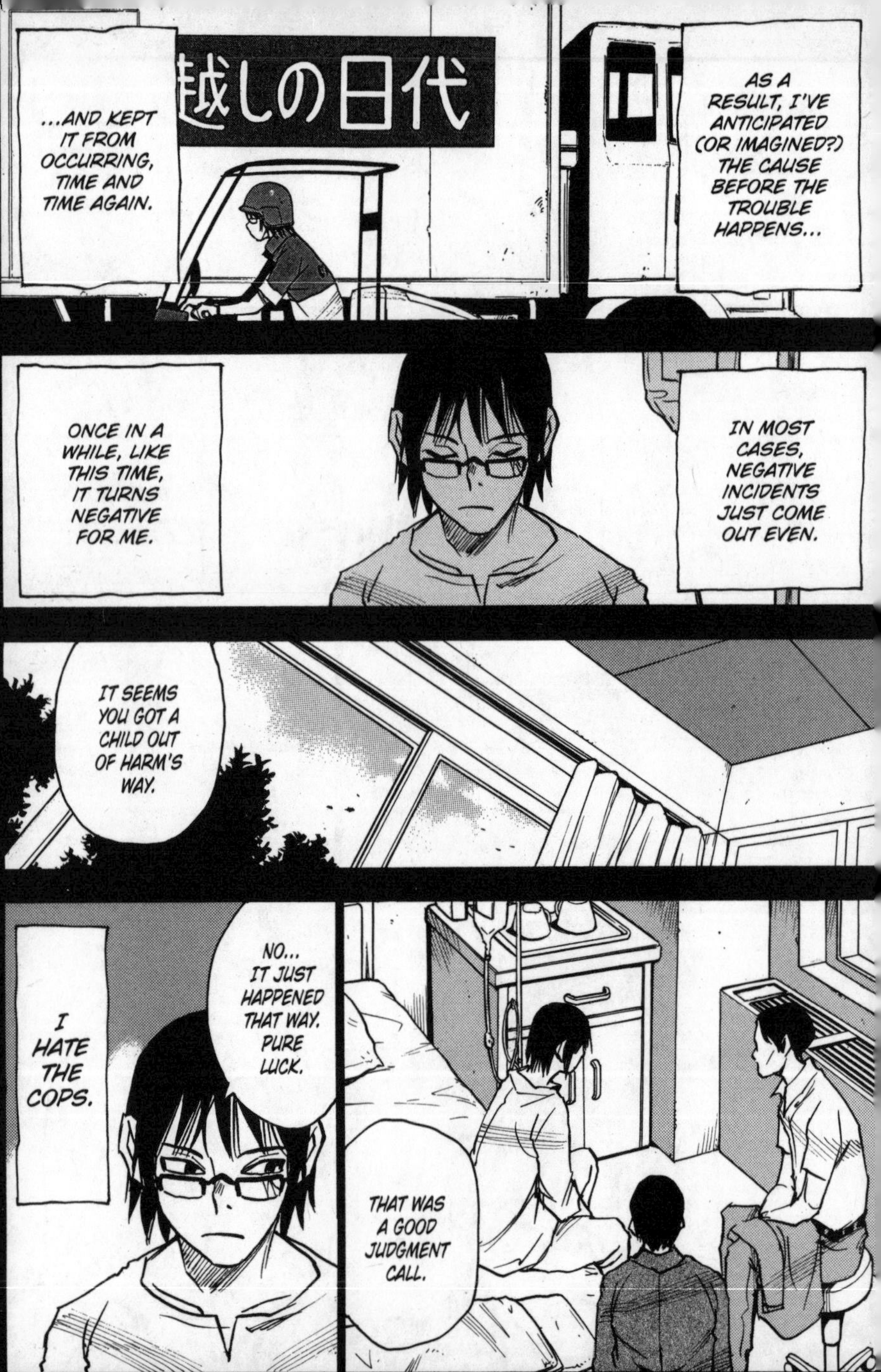
AS A RESULT, I'VE ANTICIPATED (OR IMAGINED?) THE CAUSE BEFORE THE TROUBLE HAPPENS...
越しの日代
...AND KEPT IT FROM OCCURRING, TIME AND TIME AGAIN.
IN MOST CASES, NEGATIVE INCIDENTS JUST COME OUT EVEN.
ONCE IN A WHILE, LIKE THIS TIME, IT TURNS NEGATIVE FOR ME.
IT SEEMS YOU GOT A CHILD OUT OF HARM'S WAY.
THAT WAS A GOOD JUDGMENT CALL.
NO... IT JUST HAPPENED THAT WAY. PURE LUCK.
I HATE THE COPS.

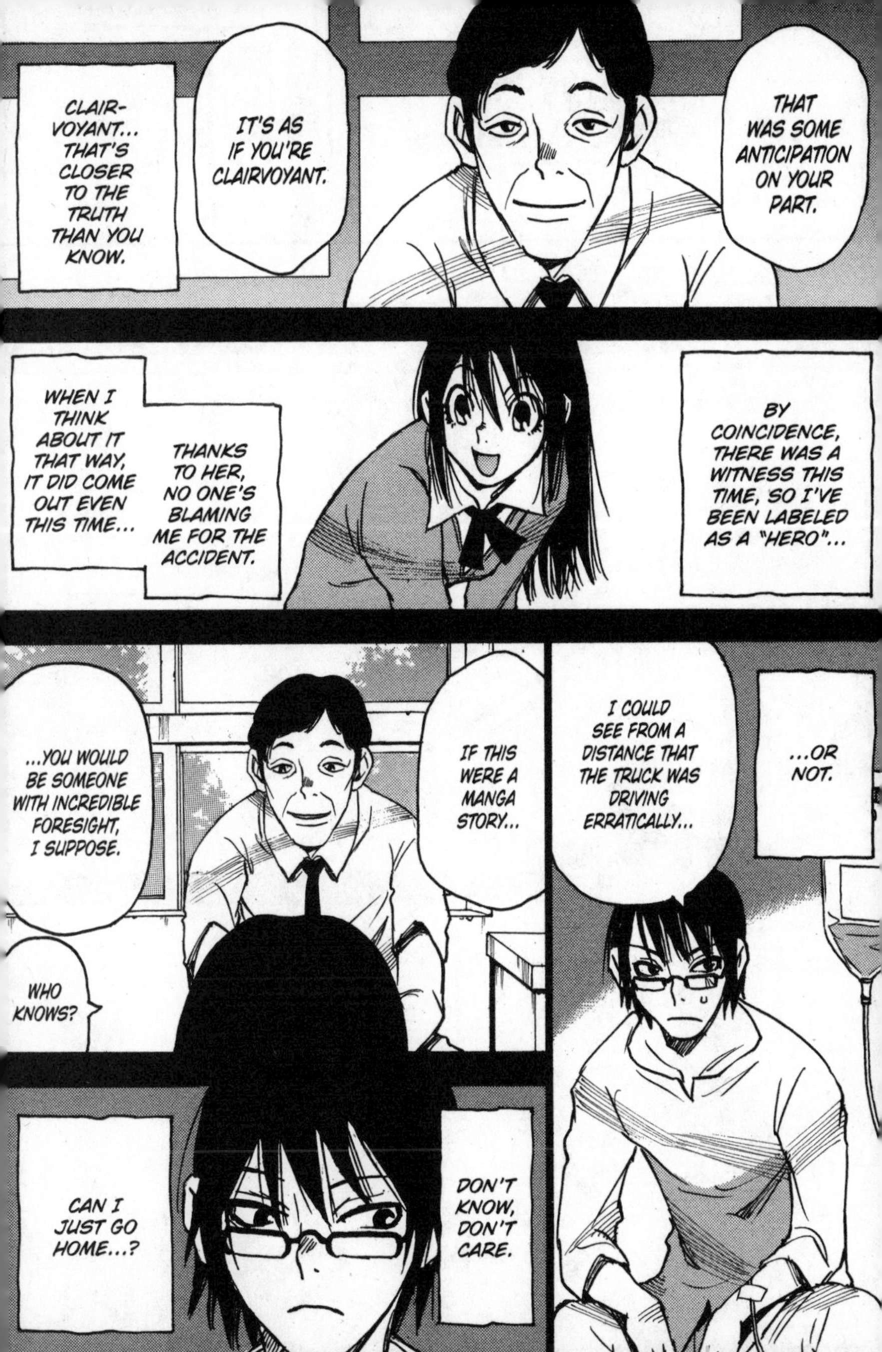
THAT WAS SOME ANTICIPATION ON YOUR PART.
IT'S AS IF YOU'RE CLAIRVOYANT.
CLAIR-VOYANT... THAT'S CLOSER TO THE TRUTH THAN YOU KNOW.
BY COINCIDENCE, THERE WAS A WITNESS THIS TIME, SO I'VE BEEN LABELED AS A "HERO"...
THANKS TO HER, NO ONE'S BLAMING ME FOR THE ACCIDENT.
WHEN I THINK ABOUT IT THAT WAY, IT DID COME OUT EVEN THIS TIME...
I COULD SEE FROM A DISTANCE THAT THE TRUCK WAS DRIVING ERRATICALLY...
...OR NOT.
IF THIS WERE A MANGA STORY...
...YOU WOULD BE SOMEONE WITH INCREDIBLE FORESIGHT, I SUPPOSE.
WHO KNOWS?
DON'T KNOW, DON'T CARE.
CAN I JUST GO HOME...?

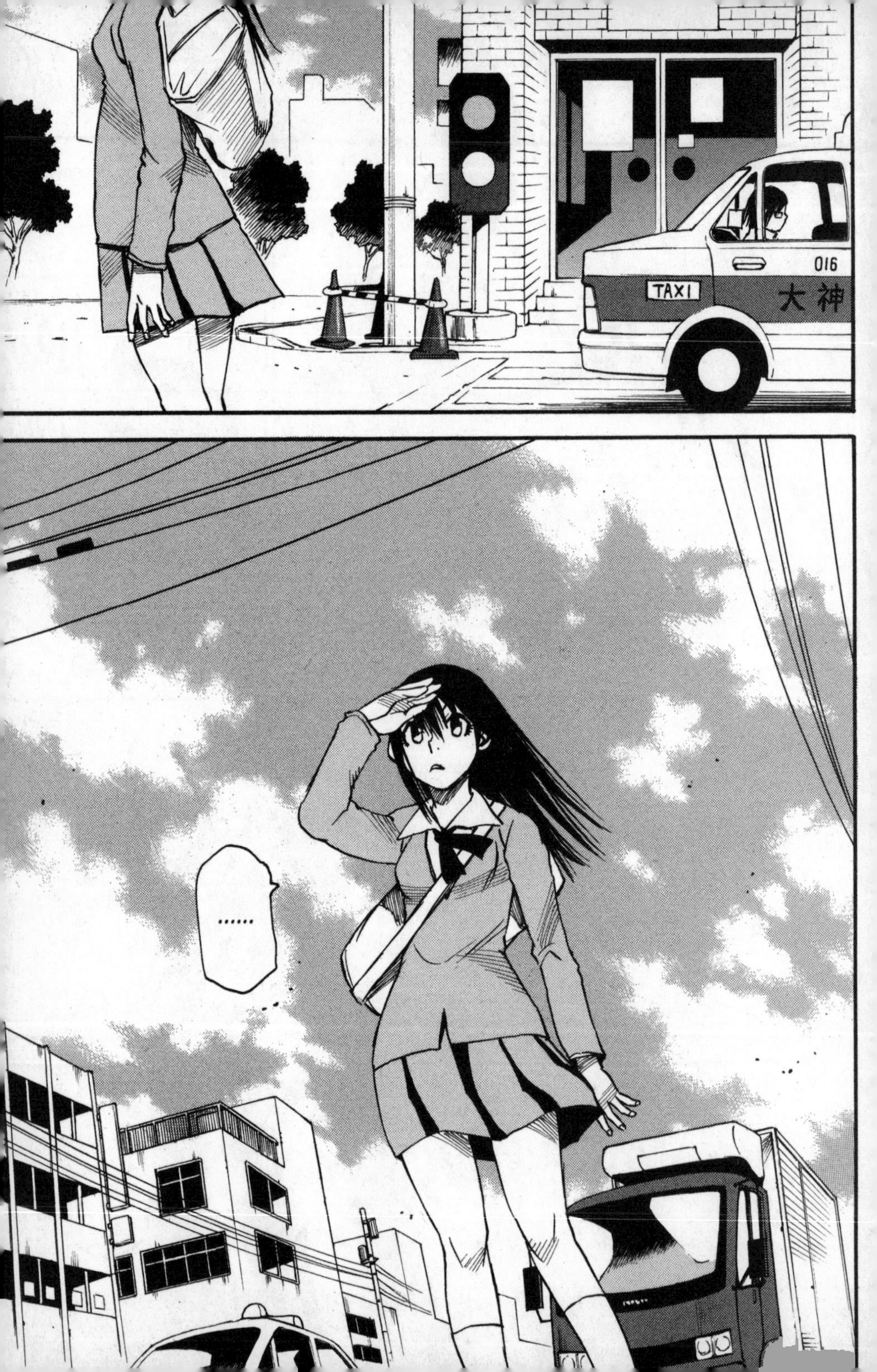
016
TAXI
大神
......

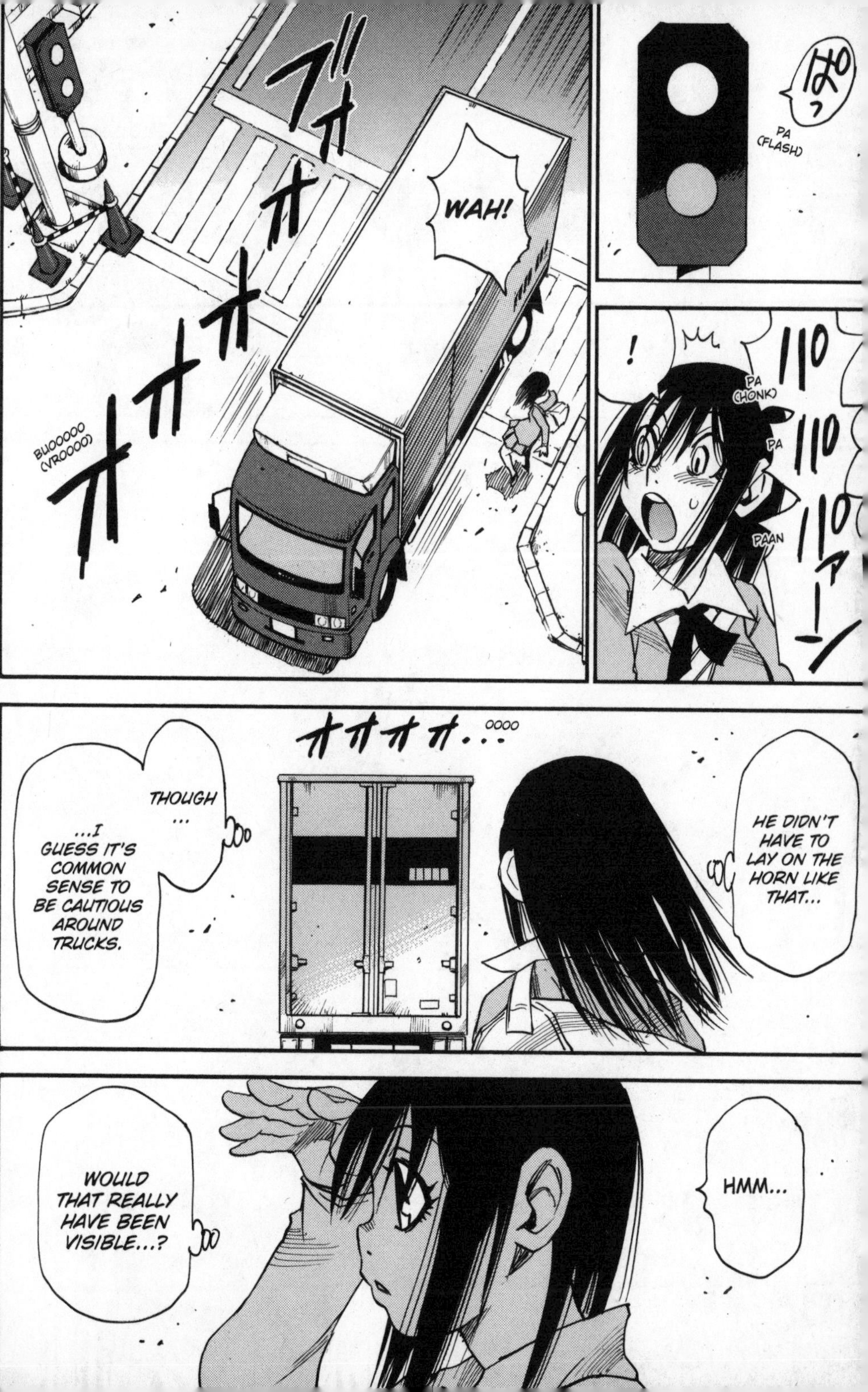
ぱっ
PA (FLASH)
!
PA (HONK)
PA
PAAN
WAH!
BUOOOOO (VROOOO)
オオオオ…OOOO
HE DIDN'T HAVE TO LAY ON THE HORN LIKE THAT...
THOUGH ...
...I GUESS IT'S COMMON SENSE TO BE CAUTIOUS AROUND TRUCKS.
HMM...
WOULD THAT REALLY HAVE BEEN VISIBLE...?

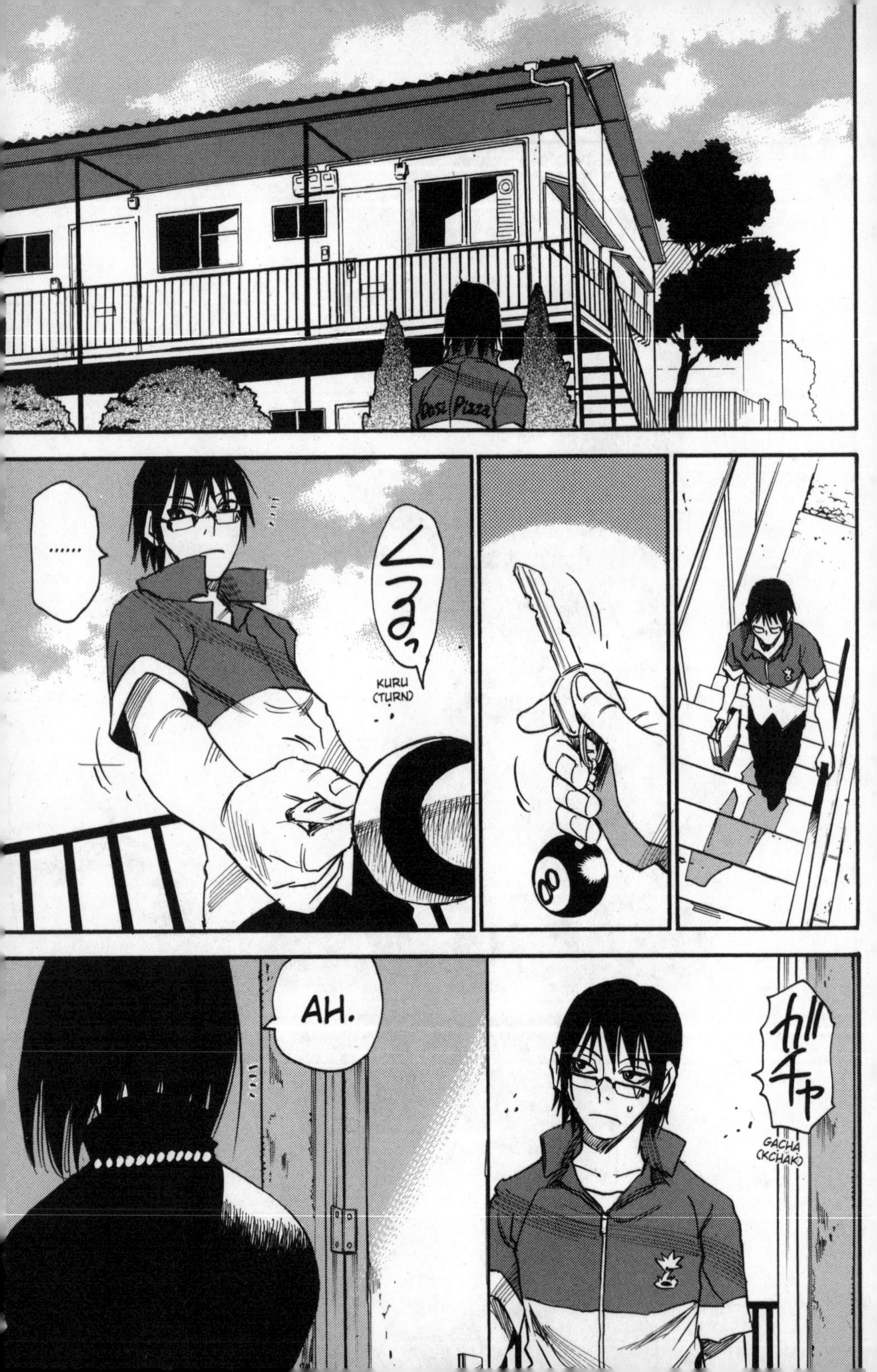
くるっ
KURU (TURN)
......
ガチャ
GACHA (KCHAK)
AH.

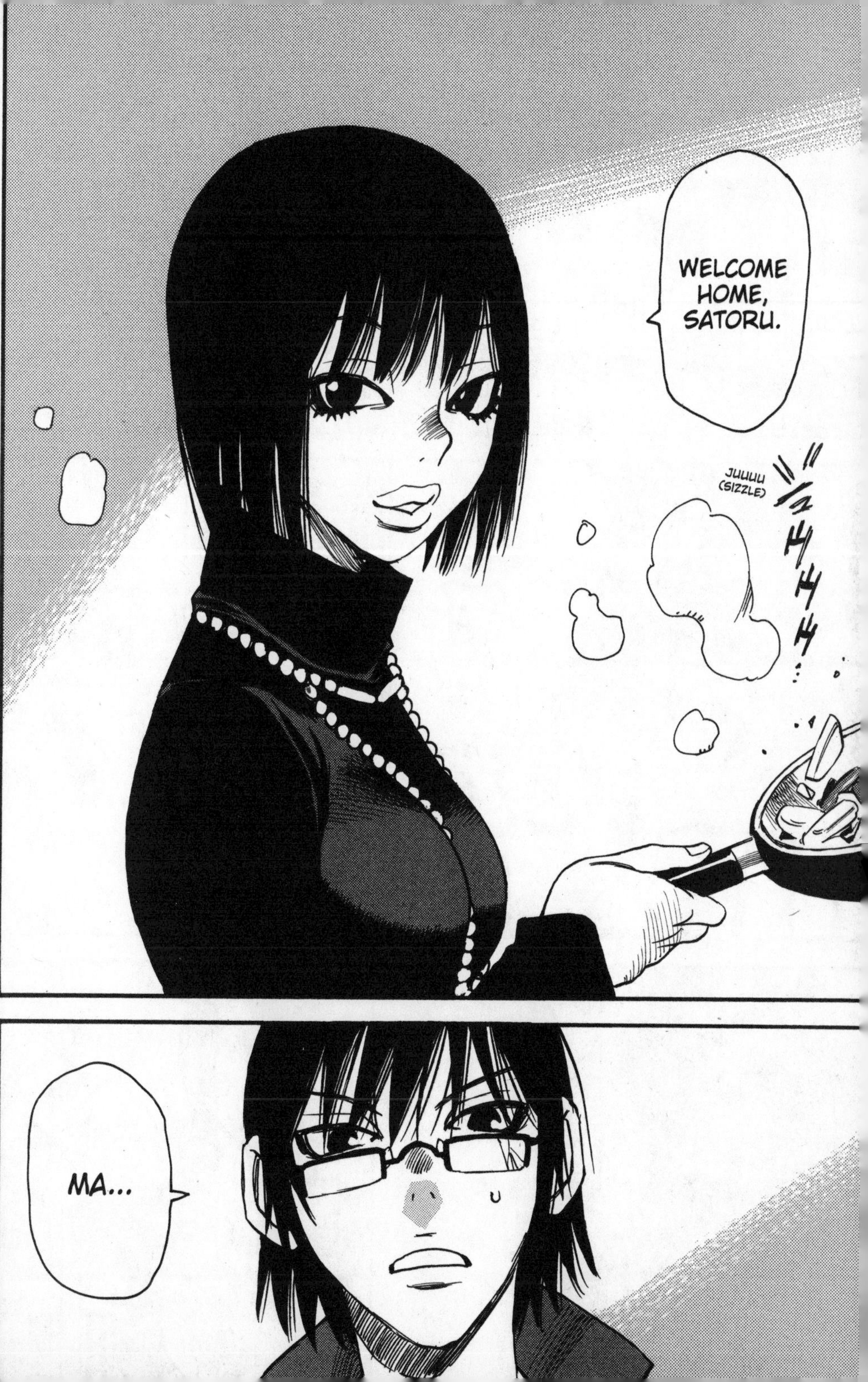
WELCOME HOME, SATORU.
JUUUU (SIZZLE)
MA...

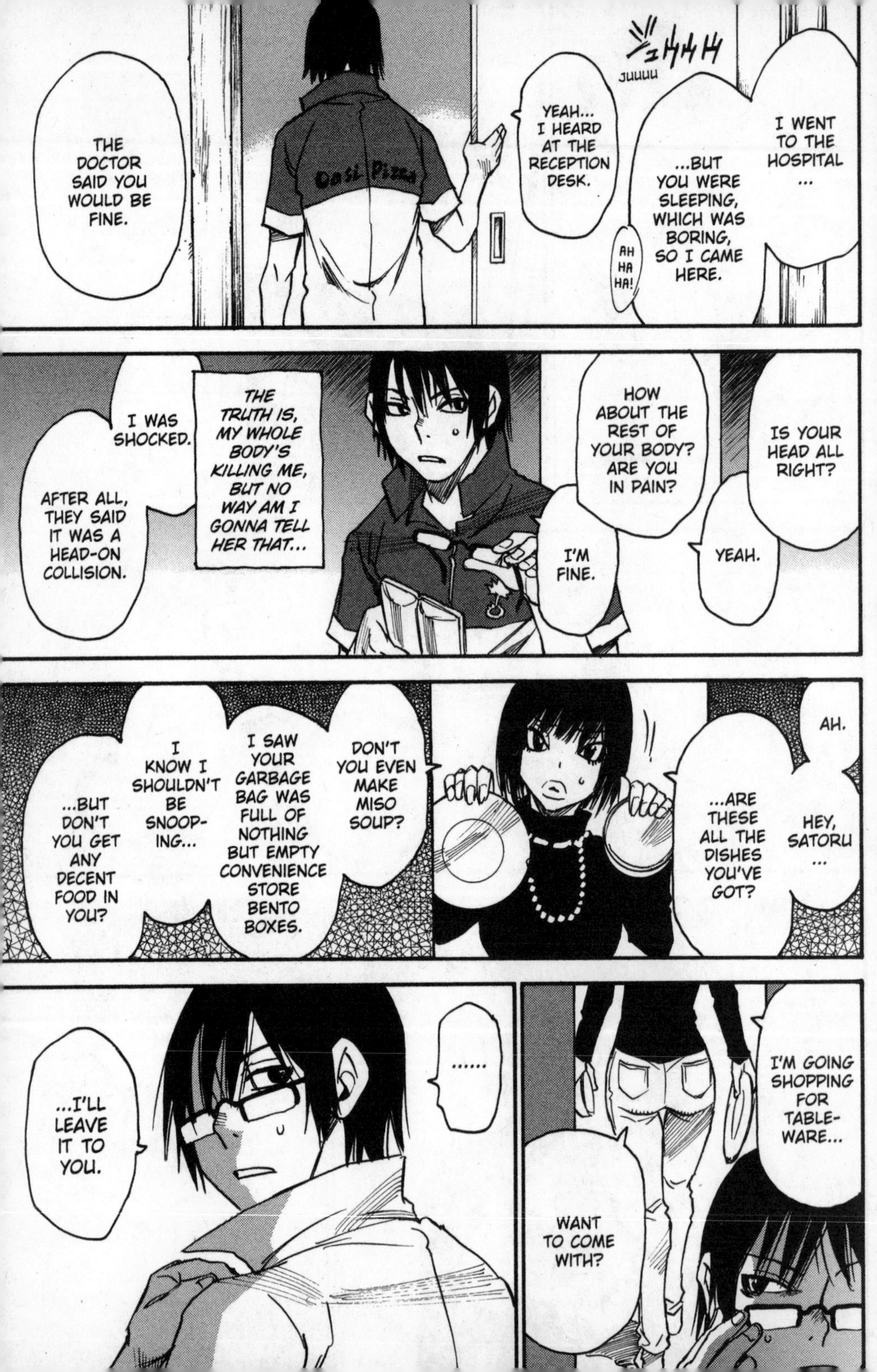
JUUUU
I WENT TO THE HOSPITAL...
...BUT YOU WERE SLEEPING, WHICH WAS BORING, SO I CAME HERE.
AH HA HA!
YEAH... I HEARD AT THE RECEPTION DESK.
THE DOCTOR SAID YOU WOULD BE FINE.
IS YOUR HEAD ALL RIGHT?
YEAH.
HOW ABOUT THE REST OF YOUR BODY? ARE YOU IN PAIN?
I'M FINE.
THE TRUTH IS, MY WHOLE BODY'S KILLING ME, BUT NO WAY AM I GONNA TELL HER THAT...
I WAS SHOCKED.
AFTER ALL, THEY SAID IT WAS A HEAD-ON COLLISION.
HEY, SATORU...
AH.
...ARE THESE ALL THE DISHES YOU'VE GOT?
DON'T YOU EVEN MAKE MISO SOUP?
I SAW YOUR GARBAGE BAG WAS FULL OF NOTHING BUT EMPTY CONVENIENCE STORE BENTO BOXES.
I KNOW I SHOULDN'T BE SNOOP-ING...
...BUT DON'T YOU GET ANY DECENT FOOD IN YOU?
I'M GOING SHOPPING FOR TABLE-WARE...
WANT TO COME WITH?
......
...I'LL LEAVE IT TO YOU.

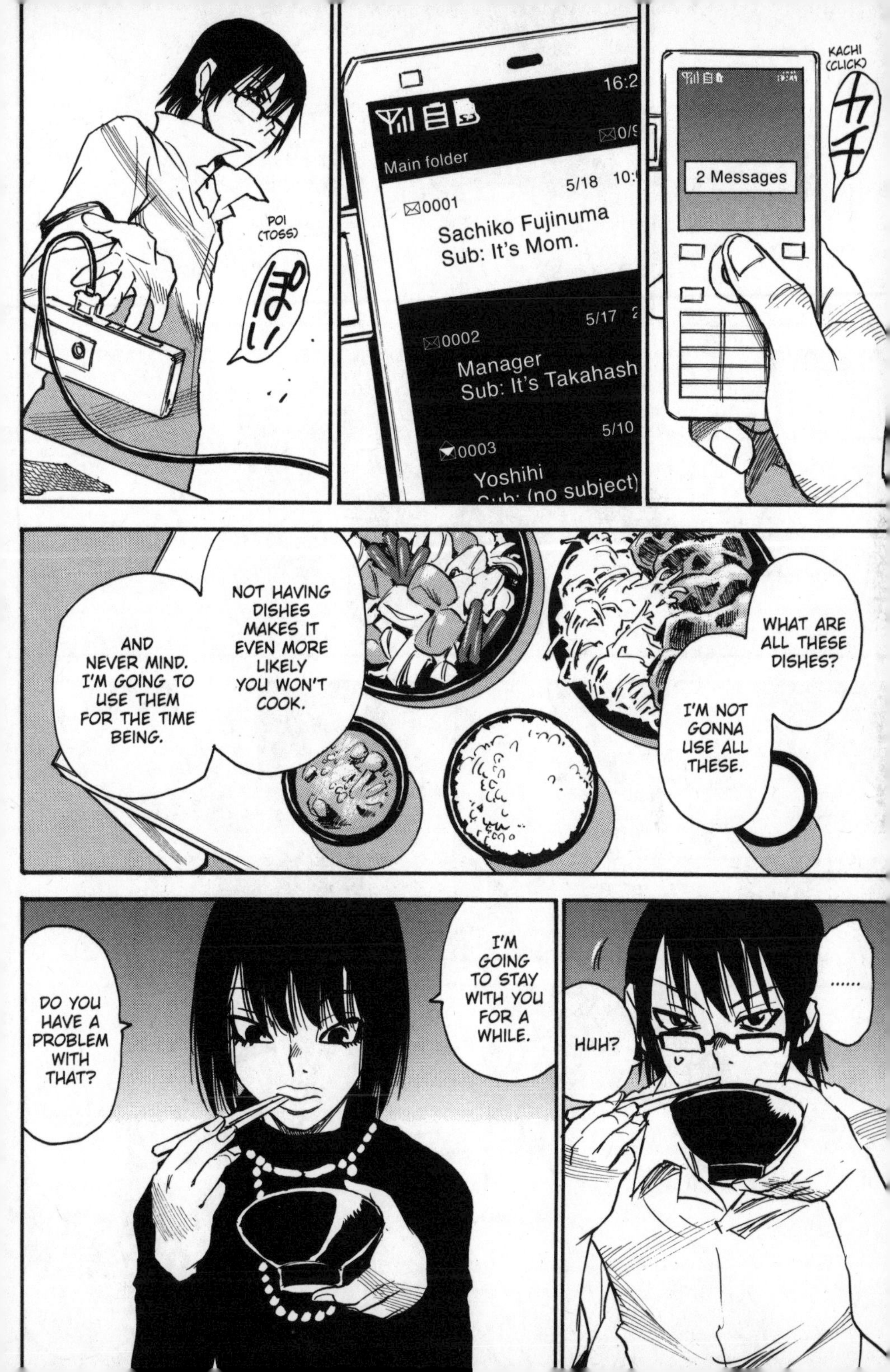
2 Messages
KACHI (CLICK)
カチ
Main folder
5/18
0001
Sachiko Fujinuma
Sub: It's Mom.
5/17
0002
Manager
5/10
0003
Yoshihi
POI (TOSS)
ぽい
WHAT ARE ALL THESE DISHES?
I'M NOT GONNA USE ALL THESE.
NOT HAVING DISHES MAKES IT EVEN MORE LIKELY YOU WON'T COOK.
AND NEVER MIND. I'M GOING TO USE THEM FOR THE TIME BEING.
......
HUH?
I'M GOING TO STAY WITH YOU FOR A WHILE.
DO YOU HAVE A PROBLEM WITH THAT?

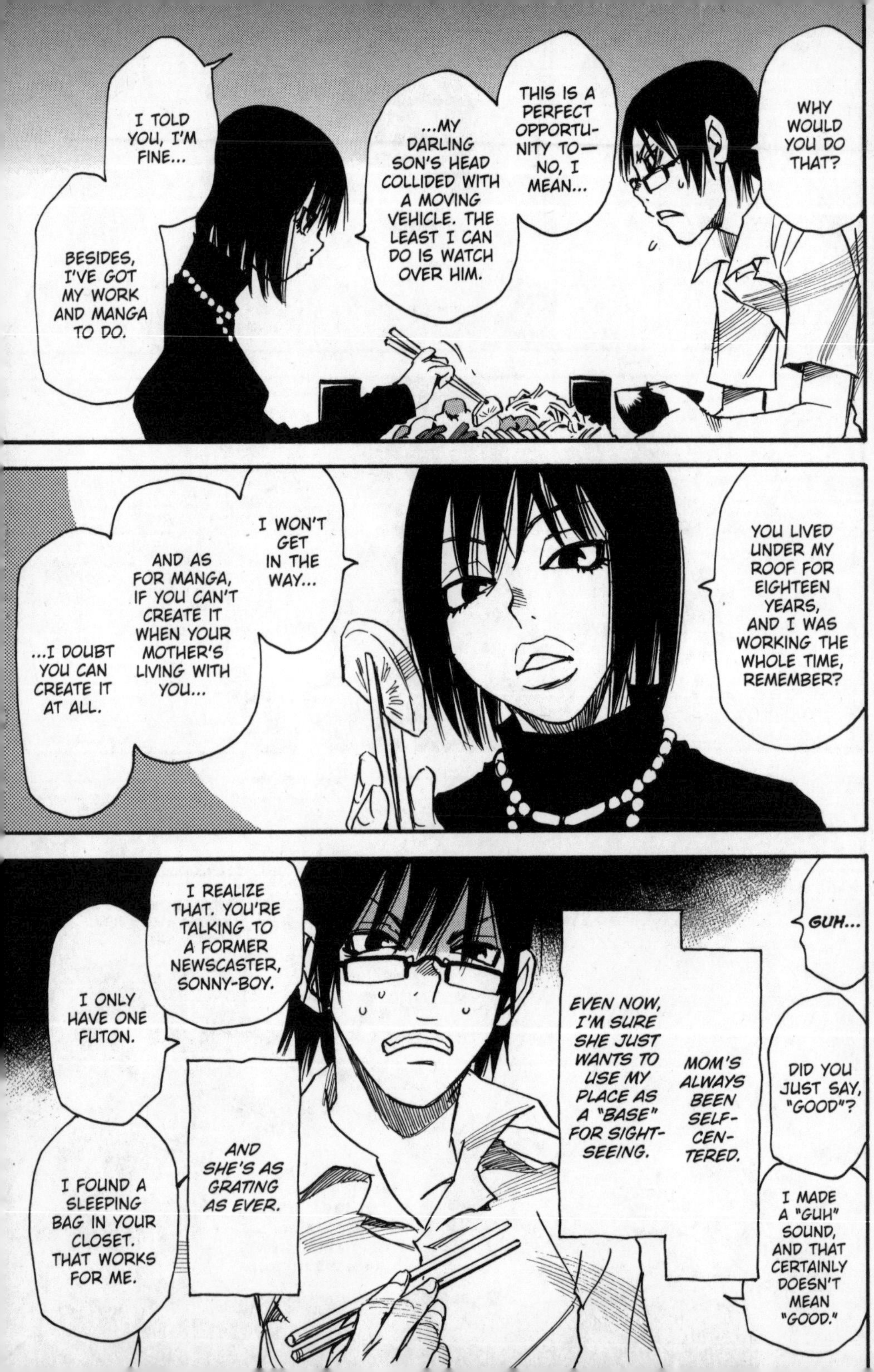
WHY WOULD YOU DO THAT?
THIS IS A PERFECT OPPORTUNITY TO— NO, I MEAN...
...MY DARLING SON'S HEAD COLLIDED WITH A MOVING VEHICLE. THE LEAST I CAN DO IS WATCH OVER HIM.
I TOLD YOU, I'M FINE...
BESIDES, I'VE GOT MY WORK AND MANGA TO DO.
YOU LIVED UNDER MY ROOF FOR EIGHTEEN YEARS, AND I WAS WORKING THE WHOLE TIME, REMEMBER?
I WON'T GET IN THE WAY...
AND AS FOR MANGA, IF YOU CAN'T CREATE IT WHEN YOUR MOTHER'S LIVING WITH YOU...
...I DOUBT YOU CAN CREATE IT AT ALL.
GUH...
DID YOU JUST SAY, "GOOD"?
I MADE A "GUH" SOUND, AND THAT CERTAINLY DOESN'T MEAN "GOOD."
MOM'S ALWAYS BEEN SELF-CENTERED.
EVEN NOW, I'M SURE SHE JUST WANTS TO USE MY PLACE AS A "BASE" FOR SIGHT-SEEING.
I REALIZE THAT. YOU'RE TALKING TO A FORMER NEWSCASTER, SONNY-BOY.
AND SHE'S AS GRATING AS EVER.
I ONLY HAVE ONE FUTON.
I FOUND A SLEEPING BAG IN YOUR CLOSET. THAT WORKS FOR ME.

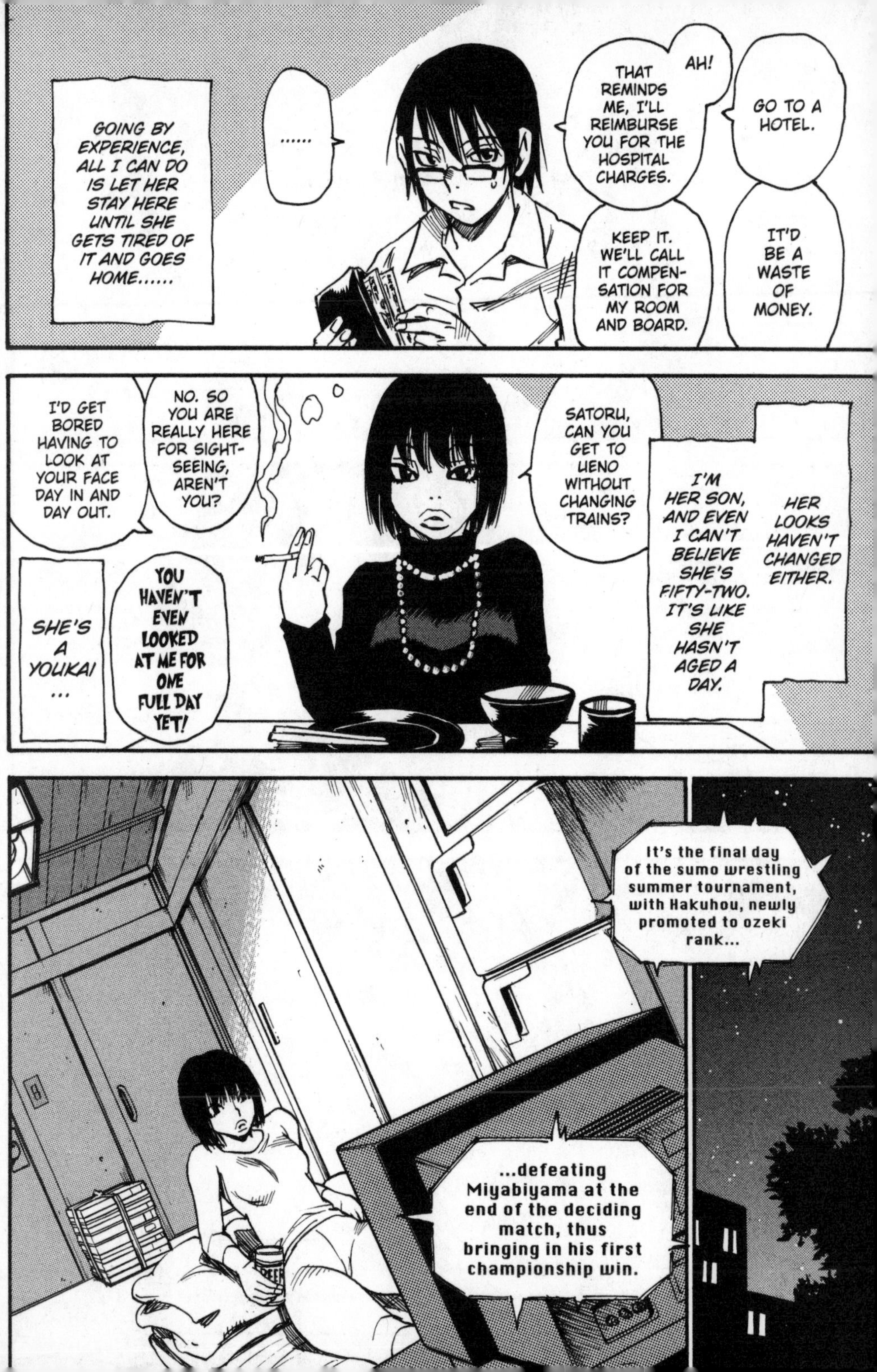
GO TO A HOTEL.
IT'D BE A WASTE OF MONEY.
AH!
THAT REMINDS ME, I'LL REIMBURSE YOU FOR THE HOSPITAL CHARGES.
KEEP IT. WE'LL CALL IT COMPEN-SATION FOR MY ROOM AND BOARD.
......
GOING BY EXPERIENCE, ALL I CAN DO IS LET HER STAY HERE UNTIL SHE GETS TIRED OF IT AND GOES HOME......
HER LOOKS HAVEN'T CHANGED EITHER.
I'M HER SON, AND EVEN I CAN'T BELIEVE SHE'S FIFTY-TWO. IT'S LIKE SHE HASN'T AGED A DAY.
SATORU, CAN YOU GET TO UENO WITHOUT CHANGING TRAINS?
NO. SO YOU ARE REALLY HERE FOR SIGHT-SEEING, AREN'T YOU?
I'D GET BORED HAVING TO LOOK AT YOUR FACE DAY IN AND DAY OUT.
YOU HAVEN'T EVEN LOOKED AT ME FOR ONE FULL DAY YET!
SHE'S A YOUKAI ...
It's the final day of the sumo wrestling summer tournament, with Hakuhou, newly promoted to ozeki rank...
...defeating Miyabiyama at the end of the deciding match, thus bringing in his first championship win.

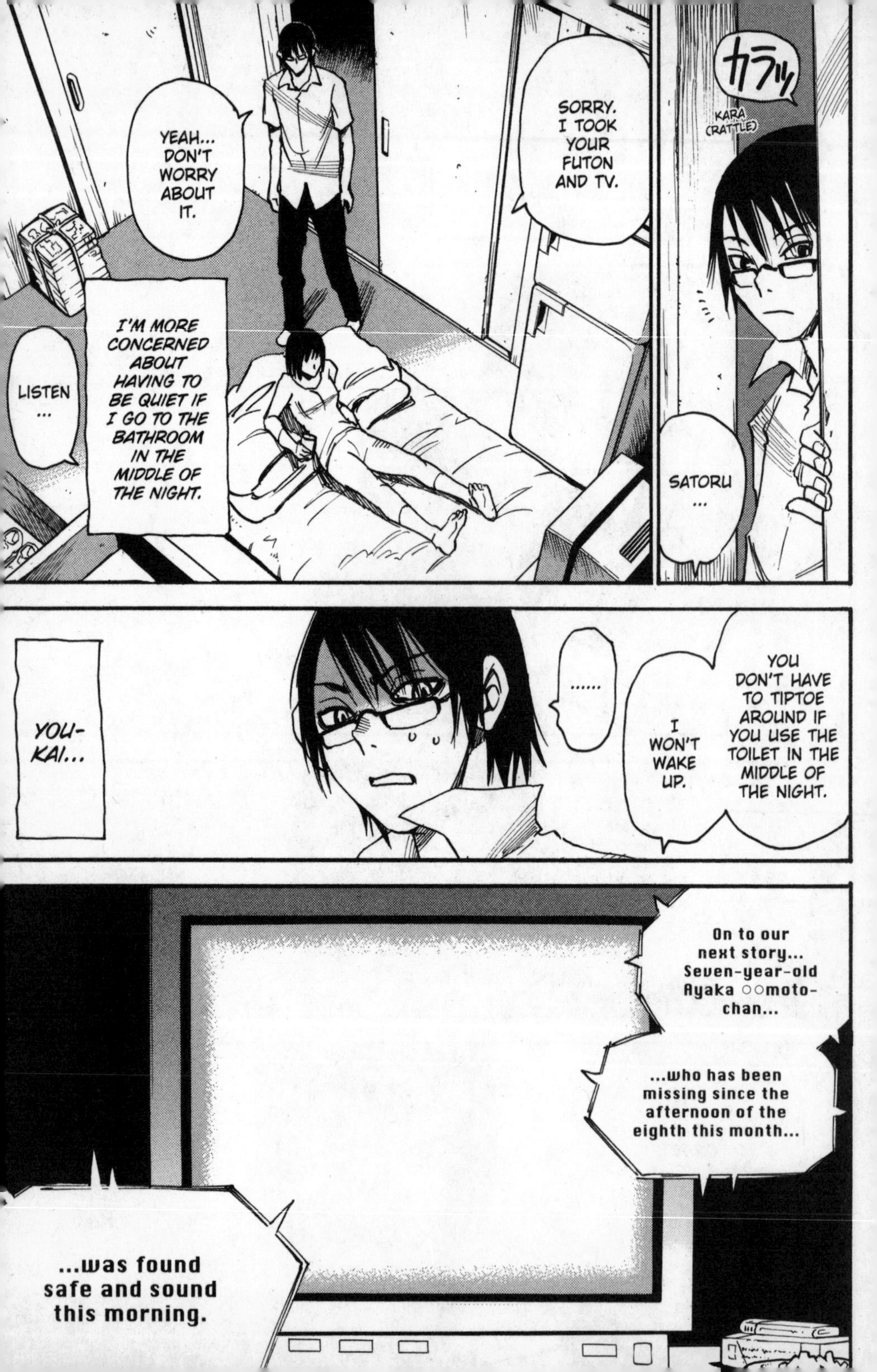
カラッ
KARA (RATTLE)
SATORU ...
SORRY. I TOOK YOUR FUTON AND TV.
YEAH... DON'T WORRY ABOUT IT.
I'M MORE CONCERNED ABOUT HAVING TO BE QUIET IF I GO TO THE BATHROOM IN THE MIDDLE OF THE NIGHT.
LISTEN ...
YOU DON'T HAVE TO TIPTOE AROUND IF YOU USE THE TOILET IN THE MIDDLE OF THE NIGHT.
I WON'T WAKE UP.
......
YOU-KAI...
On to our next story... Seven-year-old Ayaka ○○moto-chan...
...who has been missing since the afternoon of the eighth this month...
...was found safe and sound this morning.

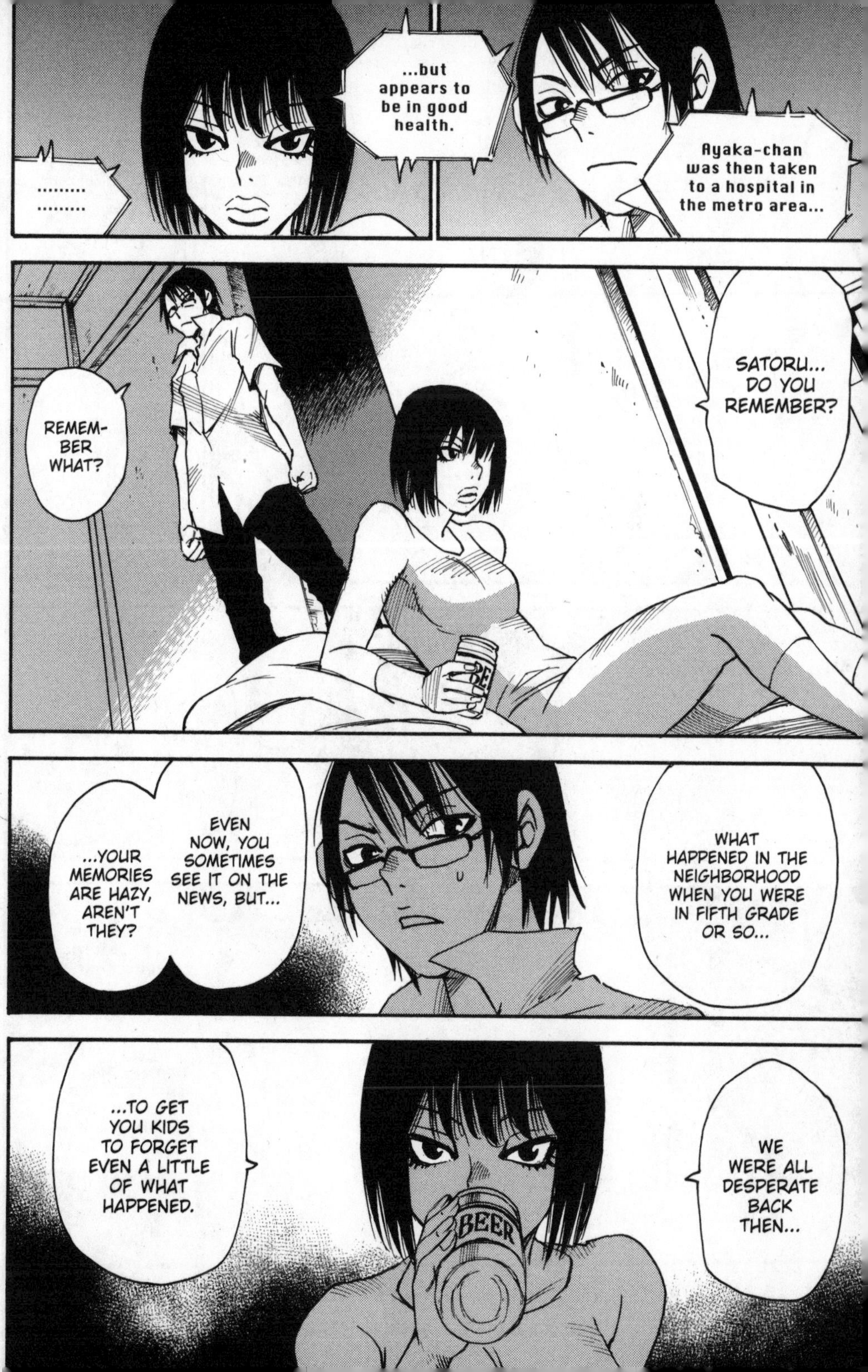
Ayaka-chan was then taken to a hospital in the metro area...
...but appears to be in good health.
....
....
SATORU... DO YOU REMEMBER?
REMEMBER WHAT?
WHAT HAPPENED IN THE NEIGHBORHOOD WHEN YOU WERE IN FIFTH GRADE OR SO...
EVEN NOW, YOU SOMETIMES SEE IT ON THE NEWS, BUT...
...YOUR MEMORIES ARE HAZY, AREN'T THEY?
WE WERE ALL DESPERATE BACK THEN...
BEER
...TO GET YOU KIDS TO FORGET EVEN A LITTLE OF WHAT HAPPENED.

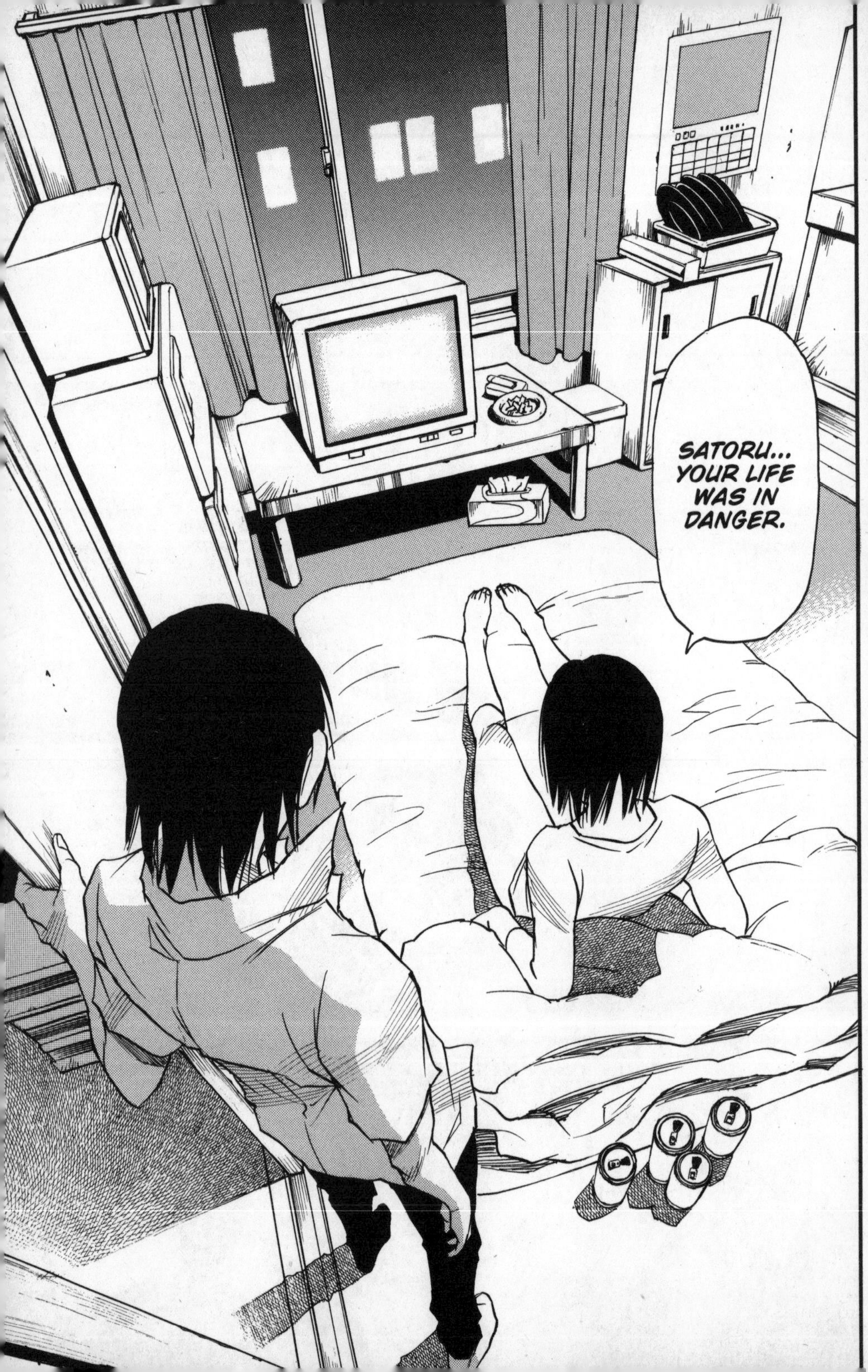
SATORU... YOUR LIFE WAS IN DANGER.

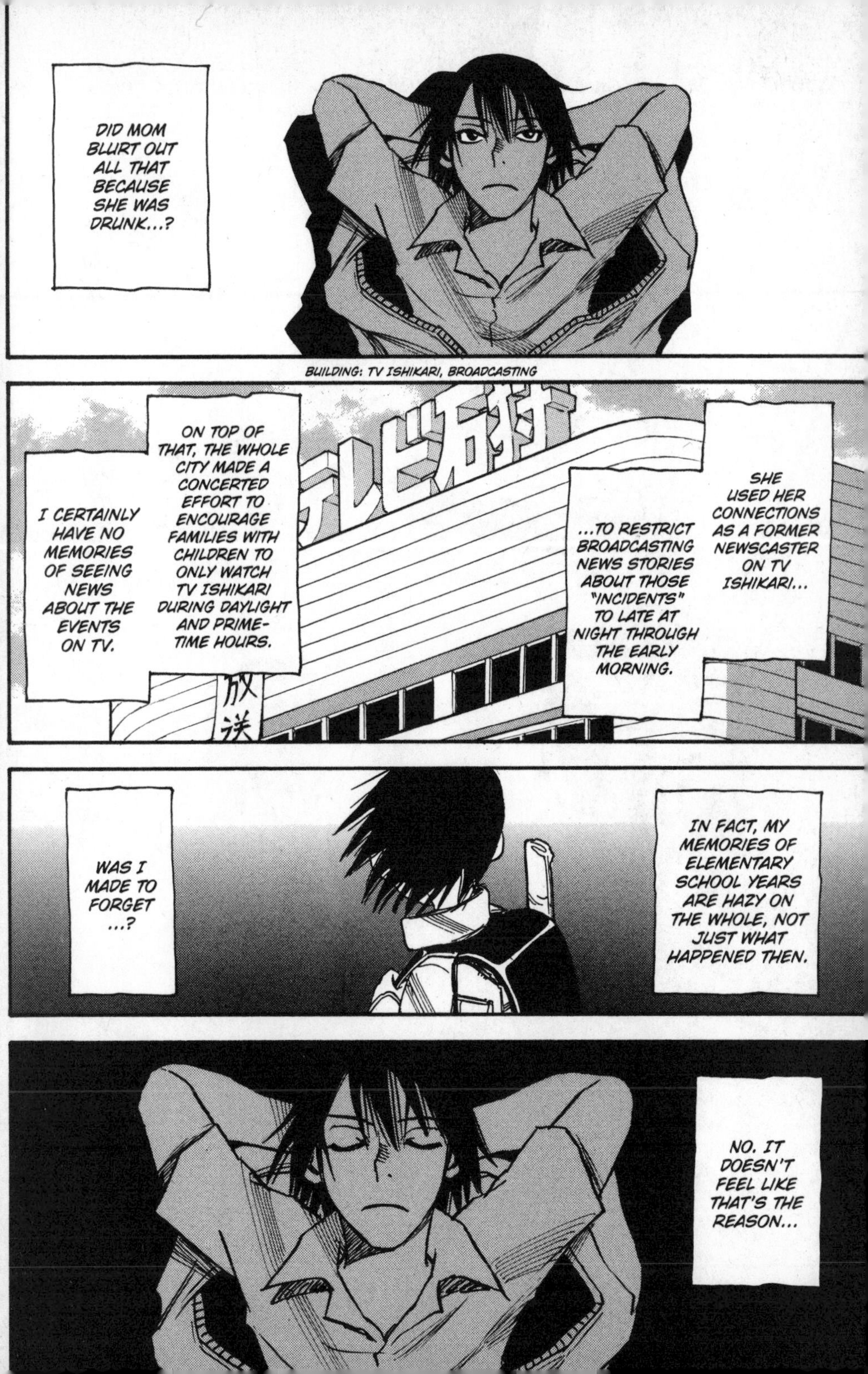
DID MOM BLURT OUT ALL THAT BECAUSE SHE WAS DRUNK...?
BUILDING: TV ISHIKARI, BROADCASTING
テレビ石狩
SHE USED HER CONNECTIONS AS A FORMER NEWSCASTER ON TV ISHIKARI...
...TO RESTRICT BROADCASTING NEWS STORIES ABOUT THOSE "INCIDENTS" TO LATE AT NIGHT THROUGH THE EARLY MORNING.
ON TOP OF THAT, THE WHOLE CITY MADE A CONCERTED EFFORT TO ENCOURAGE FAMILIES WITH CHILDREN TO ONLY WATCH TV ISHIKARI DURING DAYLIGHT AND PRIME-TIME HOURS.
I CERTAINLY HAVE NO MEMORIES OF SEEING NEWS ABOUT THE EVENTS ON TV.
放送
IN FACT, MY MEMORIES OF ELEMENTARY SCHOOL YEARS ARE HAZY ON THE WHOLE, NOT JUST WHAT HAPPENED THEN.
WAS I MADE TO FORGET ...?
NO. IT DOESN'T FEEL LIKE THAT'S THE REASON...

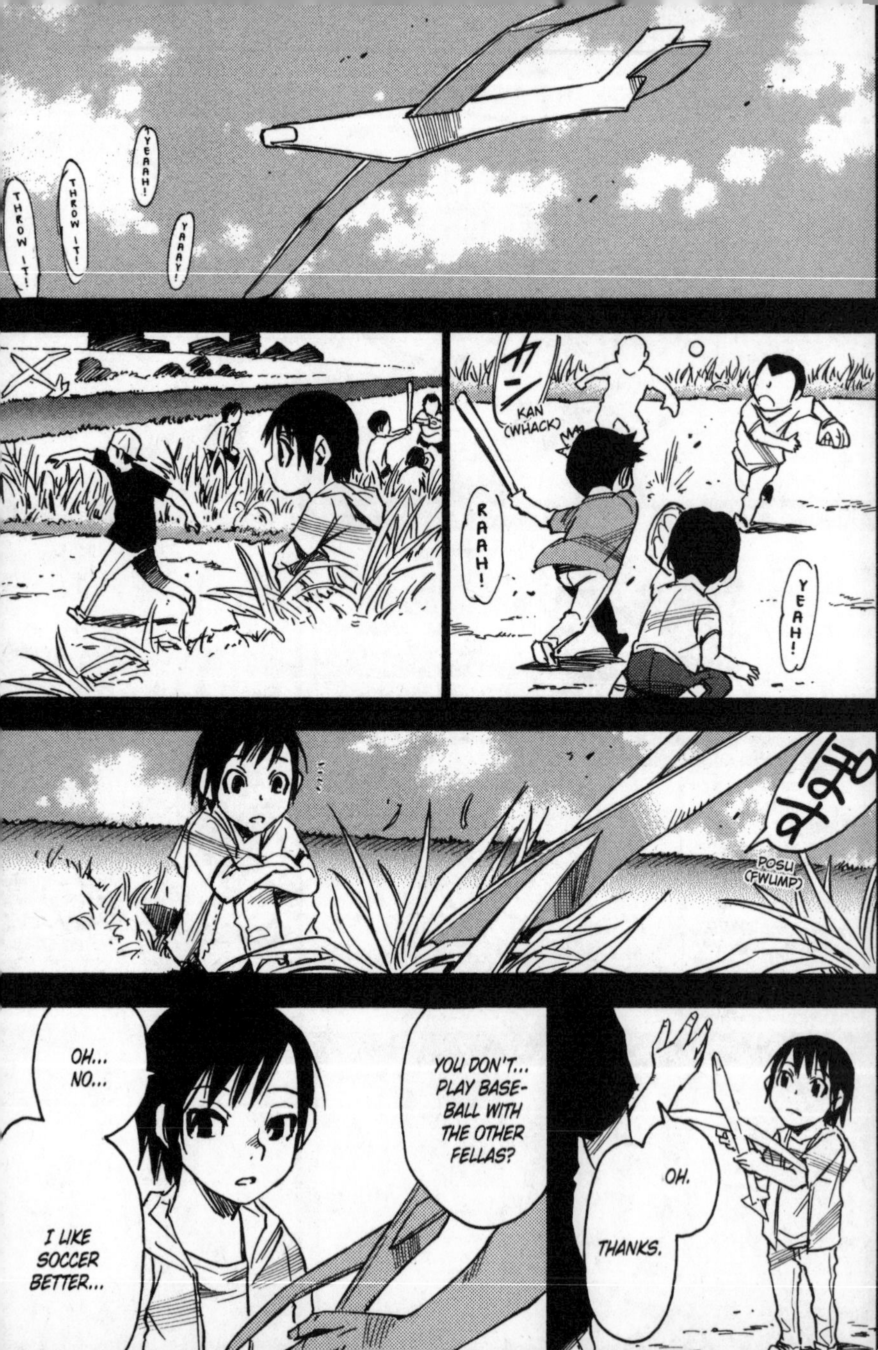

YAAAY!
YEAAH!
THROW IT!
THROW IT!
YEAH!
カン
KAN (WHACK)
RAAAH!
ぽす
POSU (FWUMP)
...
OH.
THANKS.
YOU DON'T... PLAY BASE-BALL WITH THE OTHER FELLAS?
OH... NO...
I LIKE SOCCER BETTER...

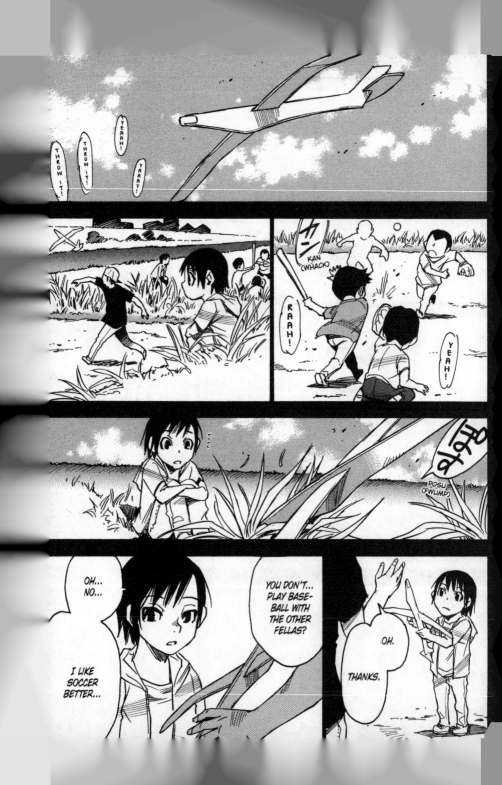

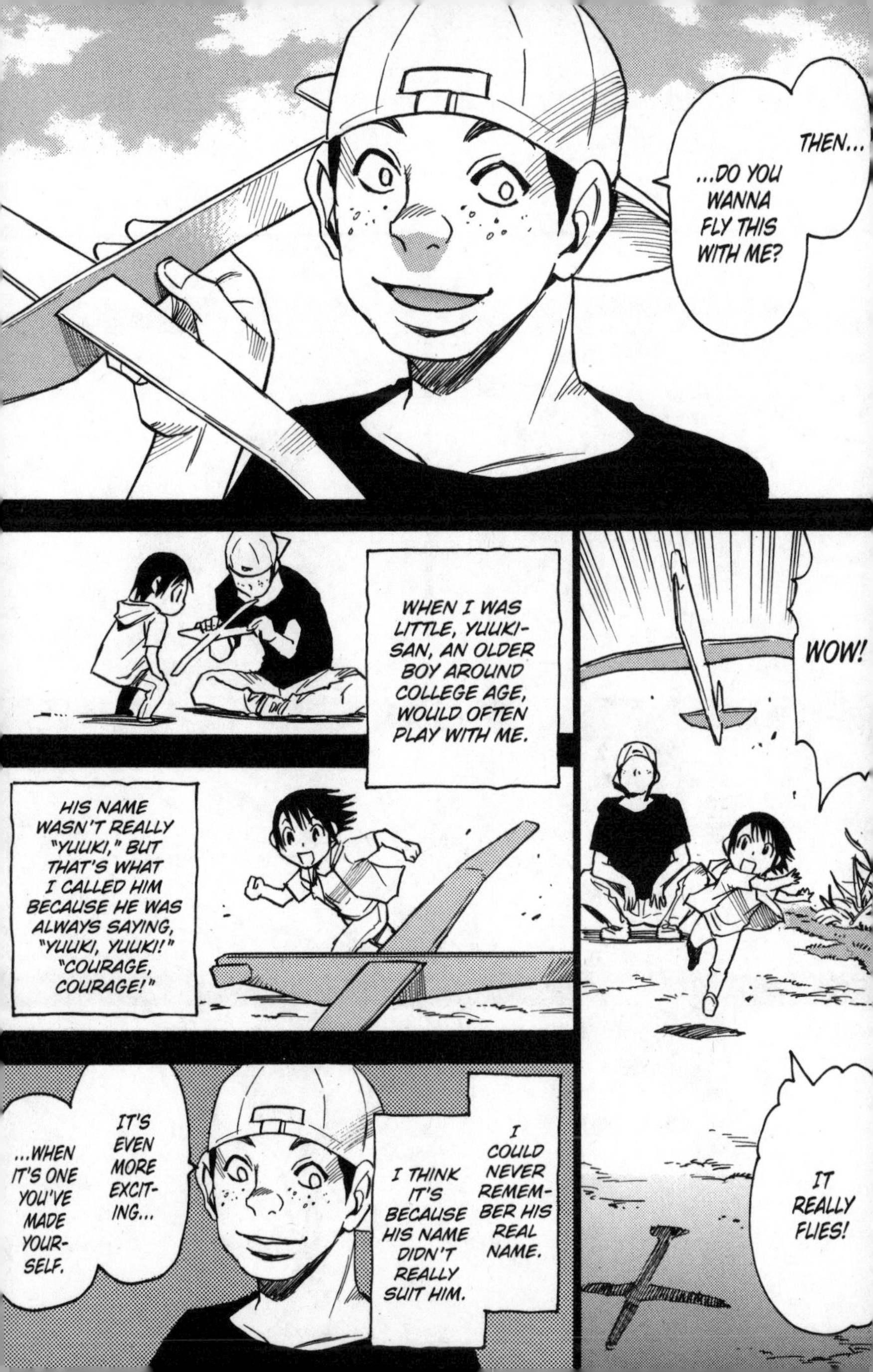
THEN...
...DO YOU WANNA FLY THIS WITH ME?
WOW!
IT REALLY FLIES!
WHEN I WAS LITTLE, YUUKI-SAN, AN OLDER BOY AROUND COLLEGE AGE, WOULD OFTEN PLAY WITH ME.
HIS NAME WASN'T REALLY "YUUKI," BUT THAT'S WHAT I CALLED HIM BECAUSE HE WAS ALWAYS SAYING, "YUUKI, YUUKI!" "COURAGE, COURAGE!"
I COULD NEVER REMEM-BER HIS REAL NAME.
I THINK IT'S BECAUSE HIS NAME DIDN'T REALLY SUIT HIM.
IT'S EVEN MORE EXCIT-ING...
...WHEN IT'S ONE YOU'VE MADE YOUR-SELF.

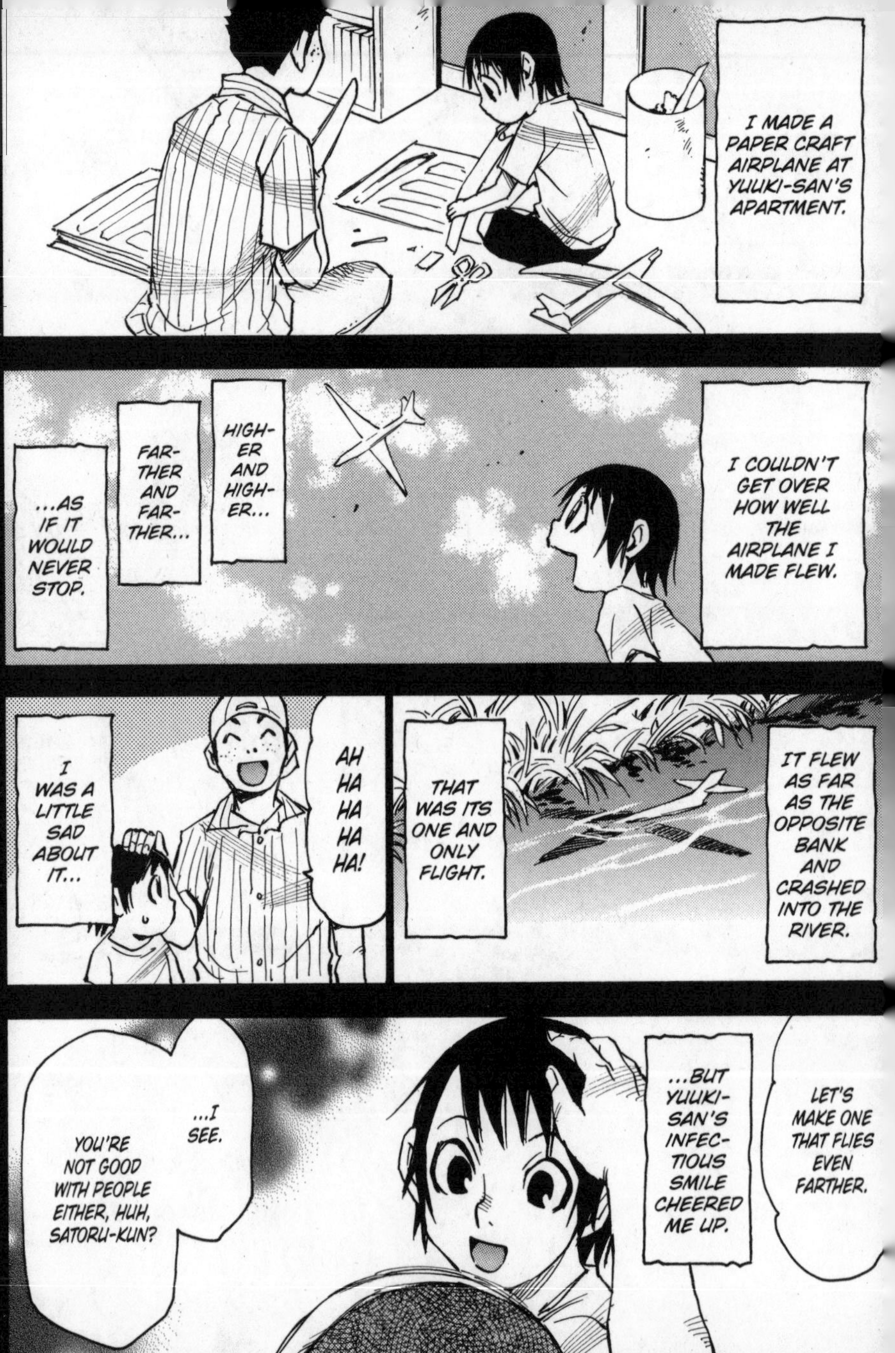
I MADE A PAPER CRAFT AIRPLANE AT YUUKI-SAN'S APARTMENT.
I COULDN'T GET OVER HOW WELL THE AIRPLANE I MADE FLEW.
HIGHER AND HIGHER...
FARTHER AND FARTHER...
...AS IF IT WOULD NEVER STOP.
IT FLEW AS FAR AS THE OPPOSITE BANK AND CRASHED INTO THE RIVER.
THAT WAS ITS ONE AND ONLY FLIGHT.
AH HA HA HA HA!
I WAS A LITTLE SAD ABOUT IT...
LET'S MAKE ONE THAT FLIES EVEN FARTHER.
...BUT YUUKI-SAN'S INFECTIOUS SMILE CHEERED ME UP.
...I SEE.
YOU'RE NOT GOOD WITH PEOPLE EITHER, HUH, SATORU-KUN?

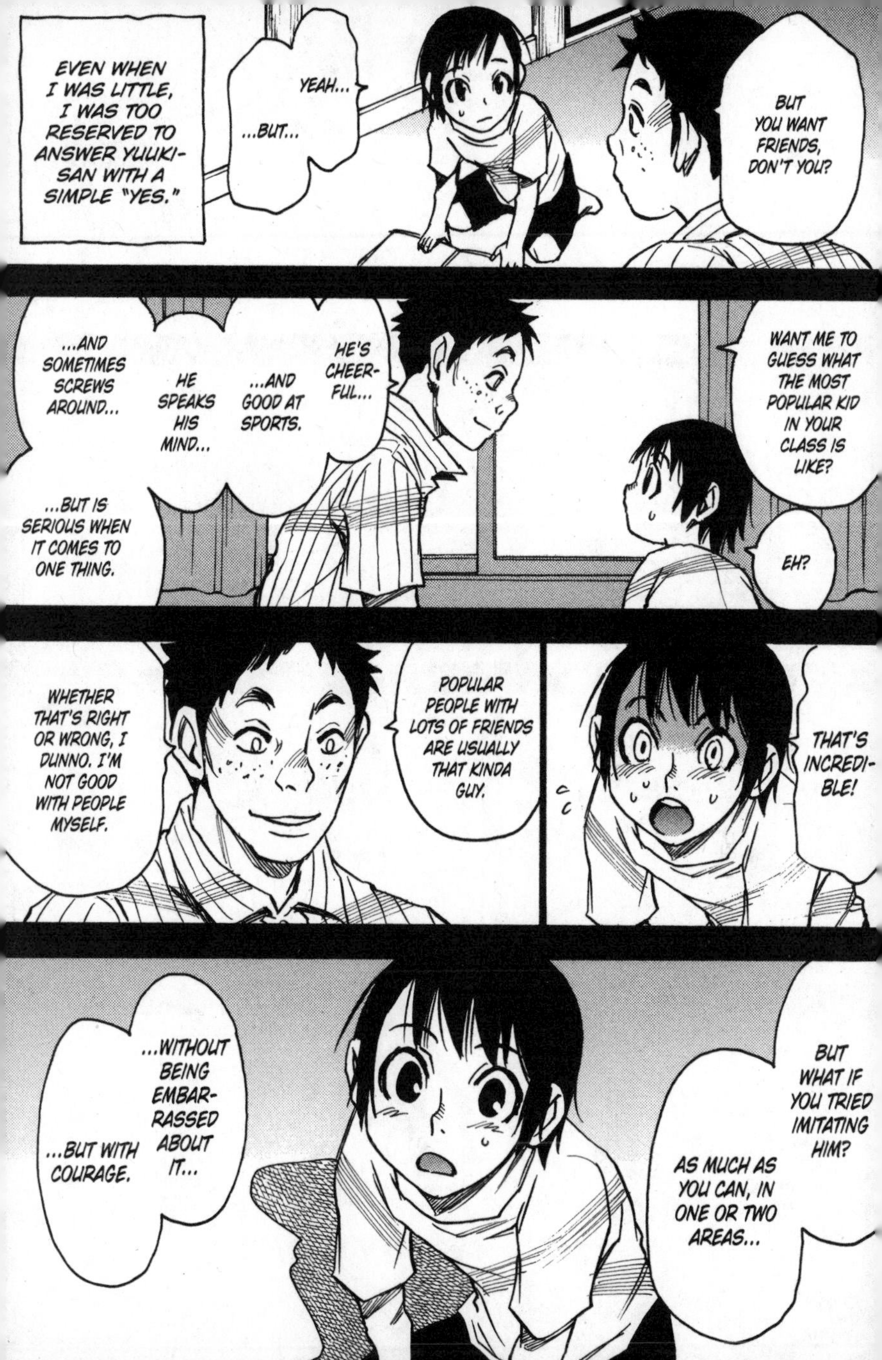
BUT YOU WANT FRIENDS, DON'T YOU?
YEAH... ...BUT...
EVEN WHEN I WAS LITTLE, I WAS TOO RESERVED TO ANSWER YUUKI-SAN WITH A SIMPLE "YES."
WANT ME TO GUESS WHAT THE MOST POPULAR KID IN YOUR CLASS IS LIKE?
EH?
HE'S CHEERFUL...
...AND GOOD AT SPORTS.
HE SPEAKS HIS MIND...
...AND SOMETIMES SCREWS AROUND...
...BUT IS SERIOUS WHEN IT COMES TO ONE THING.
THAT'S INCREDIBLE!
POPULAR PEOPLE WITH LOTS OF FRIENDS ARE USUALLY THAT KINDA GUY.
WHETHER THAT'S RIGHT OR WRONG, I DUNNO. I'M NOT GOOD WITH PEOPLE MYSELF.
BUT WHAT IF YOU TRIED IMITATING HIM?
AS MUCH AS YOU CAN, IN ONE OR TWO AREAS...
...WITHOUT BEING EMBARRASSED ABOUT IT...
...BUT WITH COURAGE.

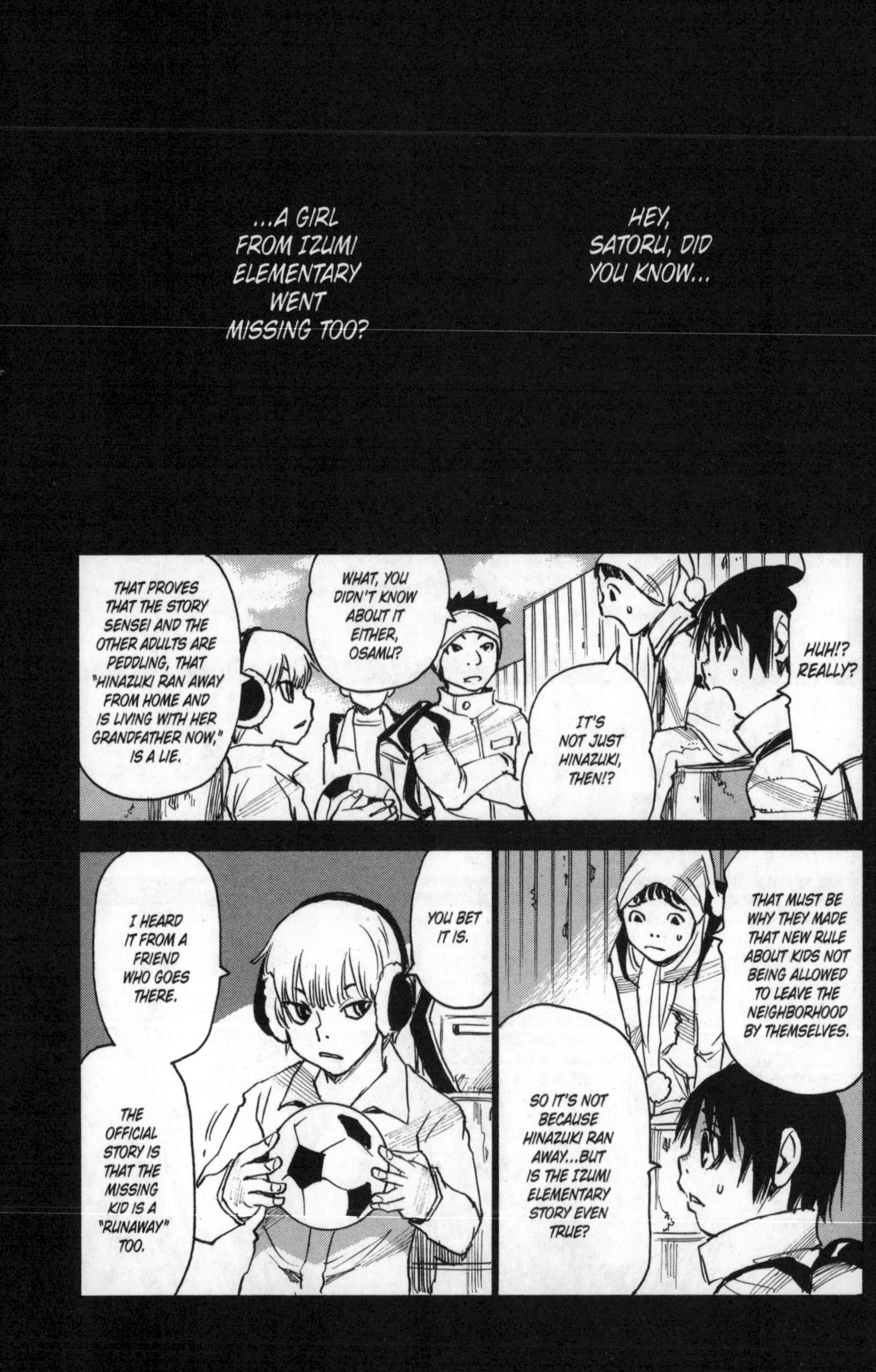
HEY, SATORU, DID YOU KNOW...
...A GIRL FROM IZUMI ELEMENTARY WENT MISSING TOO?
HUH!? REALLY?
IT'S NOT JUST HINAZUKI, THEN!?
WHAT, YOU DIDN'T KNOW ABOUT IT EITHER, OSAMU?
THAT PROVES THAT THE STORY SENSEI AND THE OTHER ADULTS ARE PEDDLING, THAT "HINAZUKI RAN AWAY FROM HOME AND IS LIVING WITH HER GRANDFATHER NOW," IS A LIE.
THAT MUST BE WHY THEY MADE THAT NEW RULE ABOUT KIDS NOT BEING ALLOWED TO LEAVE THE NEIGHBORHOOD BY THEMSELVES.
SO IT'S NOT BECAUSE HINAZUKI RAN AWAY...BUT IS THE IZUMI ELEMENTARY STORY EVEN TRUE?
YOU BET IT IS.
I HEARD IT FROM A FRIEND WHO GOES THERE.
THE OFFICIAL STORY IS THAT THE MISSING KID IS A "RUNAWAY" TOO.

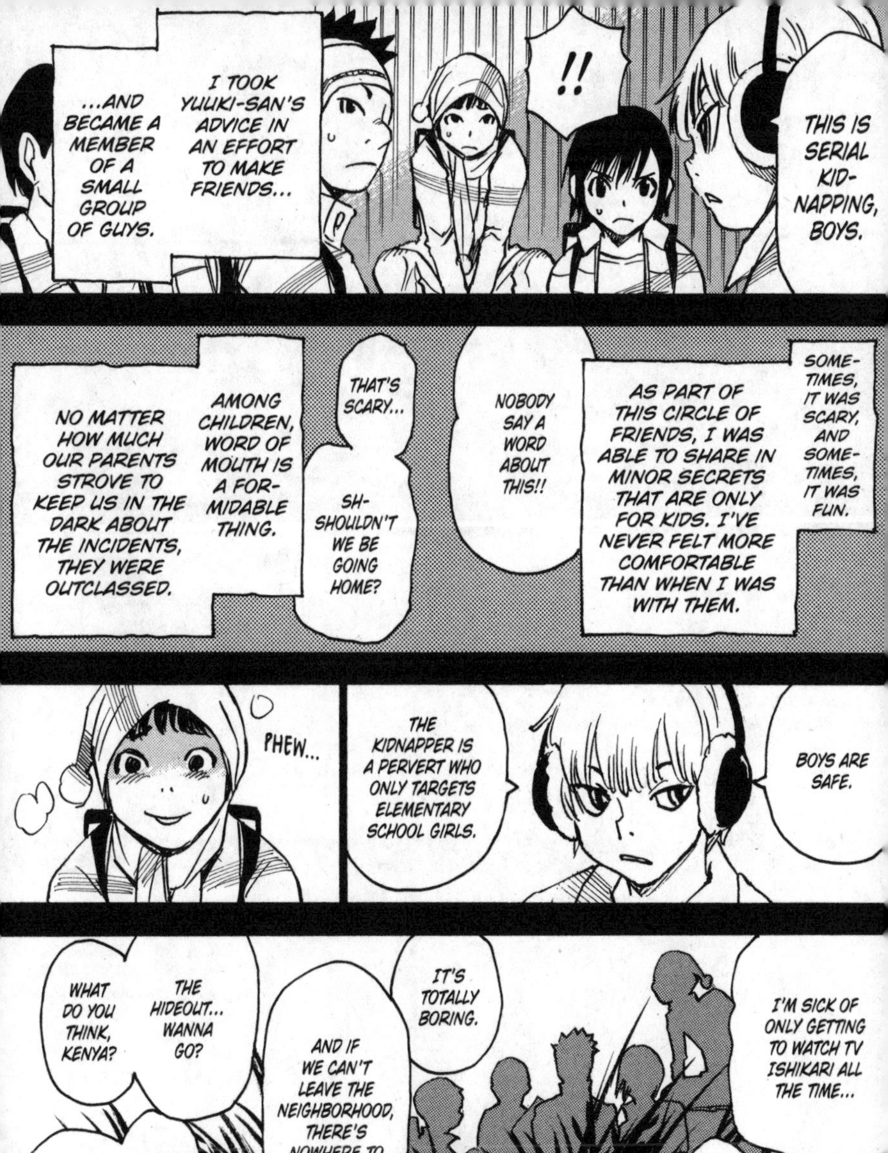
THIS IS SERIAL KID-NAPPING, BOYS.
!!
I TOOK YUUKI-SAN'S ADVICE IN AN EFFORT TO MAKE FRIENDS...
...AND BECAME A MEMBER OF A SMALL GROUP OF GUYS.
SOME-TIMES, IT WAS SCARY, AND SOME-TIMES, IT WAS FUN.
AS PART OF THIS CIRCLE OF FRIENDS, I WAS ABLE TO SHARE IN MINOR SECRETS THAT ARE ONLY FOR KIDS. I'VE NEVER FELT MORE COMFORTABLE THAN WHEN I WAS WITH THEM.
NOBODY SAY A WORD ABOUT THIS!!
THAT'S SCARY...
SH-SHOULDN'T WE BE GOING HOME?
AMONG CHILDREN, WORD OF MOUTH IS A FOR-MIDABLE THING.
NO MATTER HOW MUCH OUR PARENTS STROVE TO KEEP US IN THE DARK ABOUT THE INCIDENTS, THEY WERE OUTCLASSED.
BOYS ARE SAFE.
THE KIDNAPPER IS A PERVERT WHO ONLY TARGETS ELEMENTARY SCHOOL GIRLS.
PHEW...
I'M SICK OF ONLY GETTING TO WATCH TV ISHIKARI ALL THE TIME...
IT'S TOTALLY BORING.
AH, ME TOO.
THEY HARDLY HAVE ANY ANIME OR TOKUSATSU ON.
AND IF WE CAN'T LEAVE THE NEIGHBORHOOD, THERE'S NOWHERE TO PLAY.
THAT INCLUDES OUR HIDEOUT...
THE HIDEOUT... WANNA GO?
WHAT DO YOU THINK, KENYA?
NOT A BAD IDEA.
BESIDES, THE KIDNAPPINGS HAVE NOTHING TO DO WITH US.

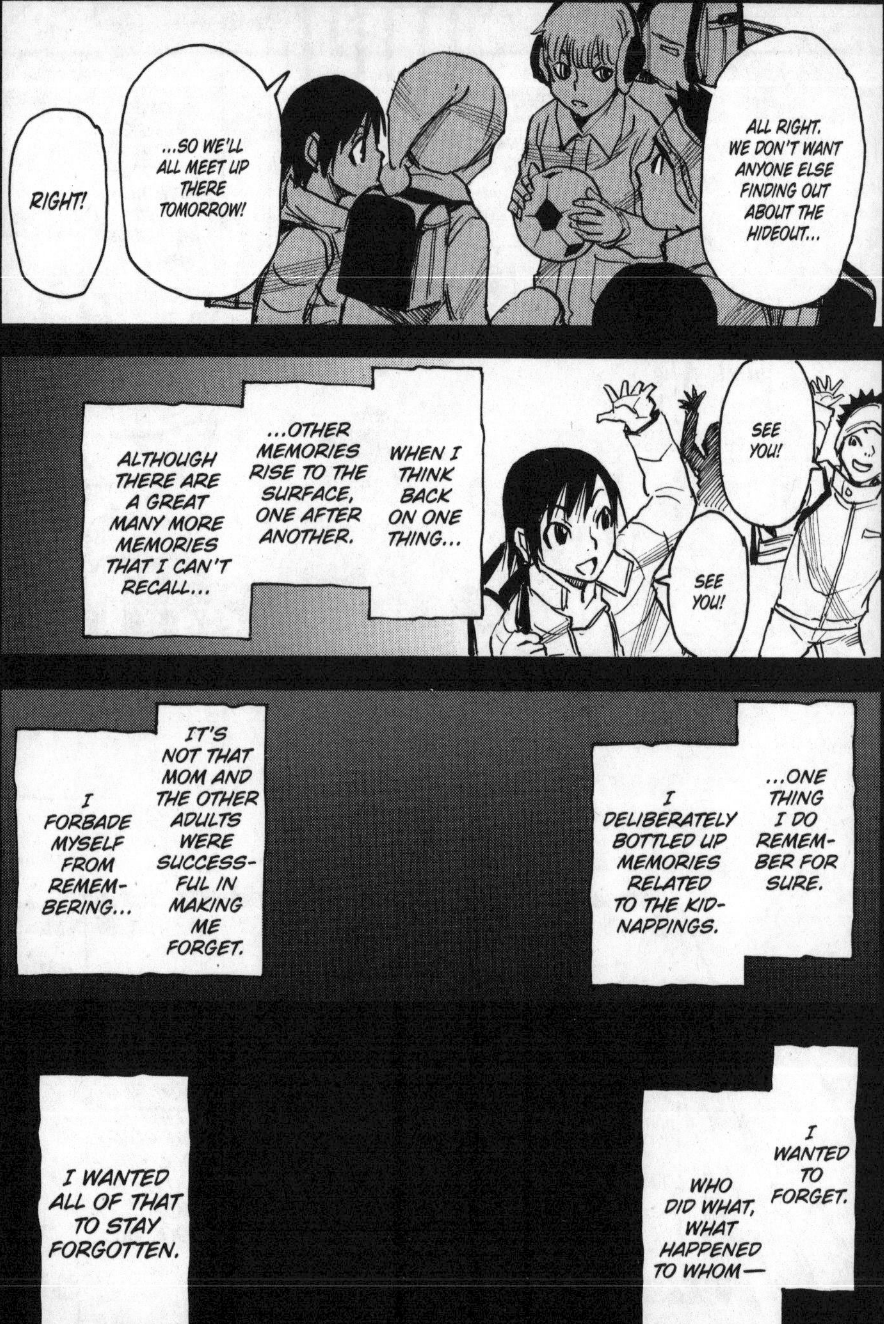
ALL RIGHT. WE DON'T WANT ANYONE ELSE FINDING OUT ABOUT THE HIDEOUT...
...SO WE'LL ALL MEET UP THERE TOMORROW!
RIGHT!
SEE YOU!
SEE YOU!
WHEN I THINK BACK ON ONE THING...
...OTHER MEMORIES RISE TO THE SURFACE, ONE AFTER ANOTHER.
ALTHOUGH THERE ARE A GREAT MANY MORE MEMORIES THAT I CAN'T RECALL...
...ONE THING I DO REMEM-BER FOR SURE.
I DELIBERATELY BOTTLED UP MEMORIES RELATED TO THE KID-NAPPINGS.
IT'S NOT THAT MOM AND THE OTHER ADULTS WERE SUCCESS-FUL IN MAKING ME FORGET.
I FORBADE MYSELF FROM REMEM-BERING...
I WANTED TO FORGET.
WHO DID WHAT, WHAT HAPPENED TO WHOM—
I WANTED ALL OF THAT TO STAY FORGOTTEN.

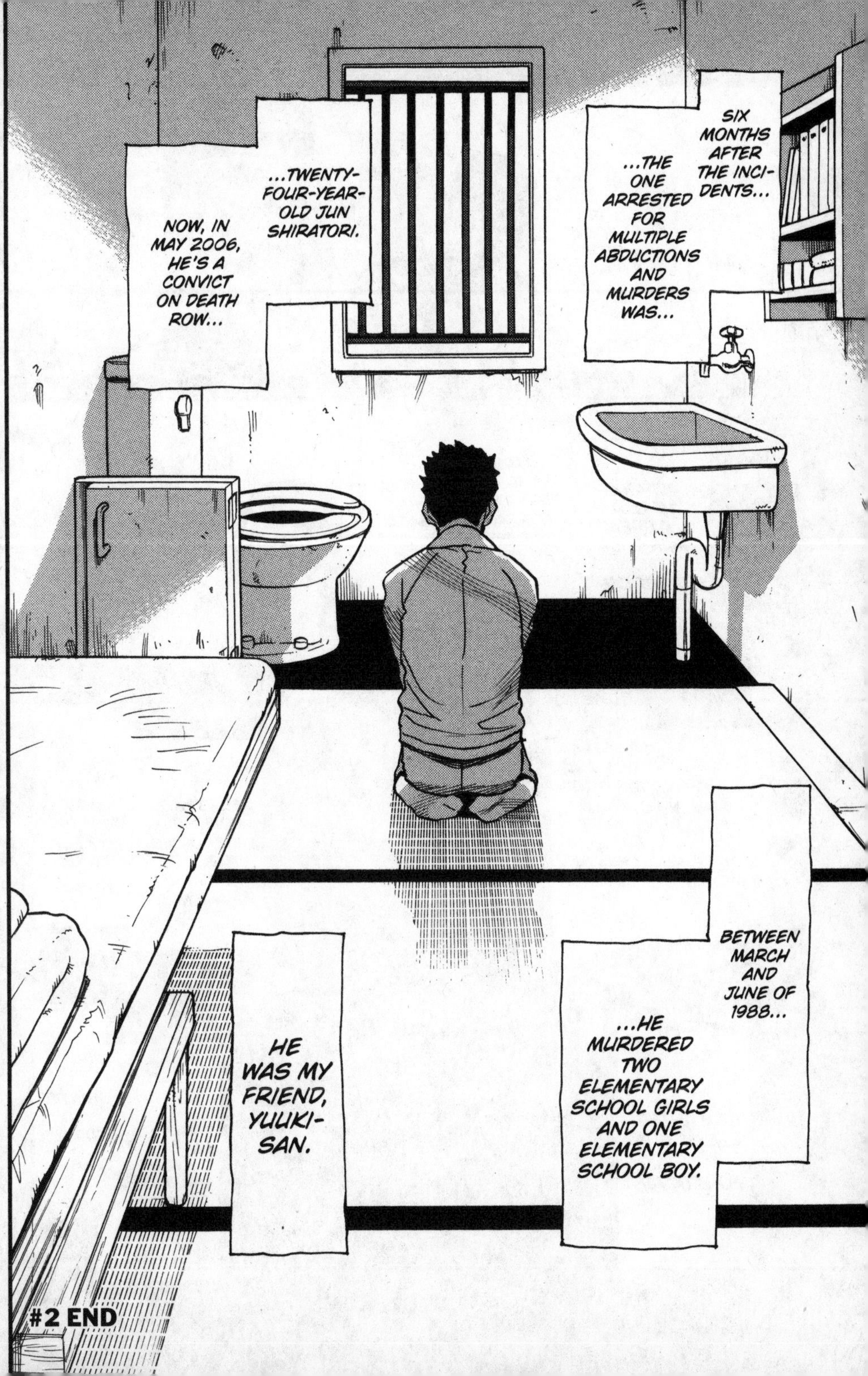
SIX MONTHS AFTER THE INCIDENTS...
...THE ONE ARRESTED FOR MULTIPLE ABDUCTIONS AND MURDERS WAS...
...TWENTY-FOUR-YEAR-OLD JUN SHIRATORI.
NOW, IN MAY 2006, HE'S A CONVICT ON DEATH ROW...
BETWEEN MARCH AND JUNE OF 1988...
...HE MURDERED TWO ELEMENTARY SCHOOL GIRLS AND ONE ELEMENTARY SCHOOL BOY.
HE WAS MY FRIEND, YUUKI-SAN.
#2 END

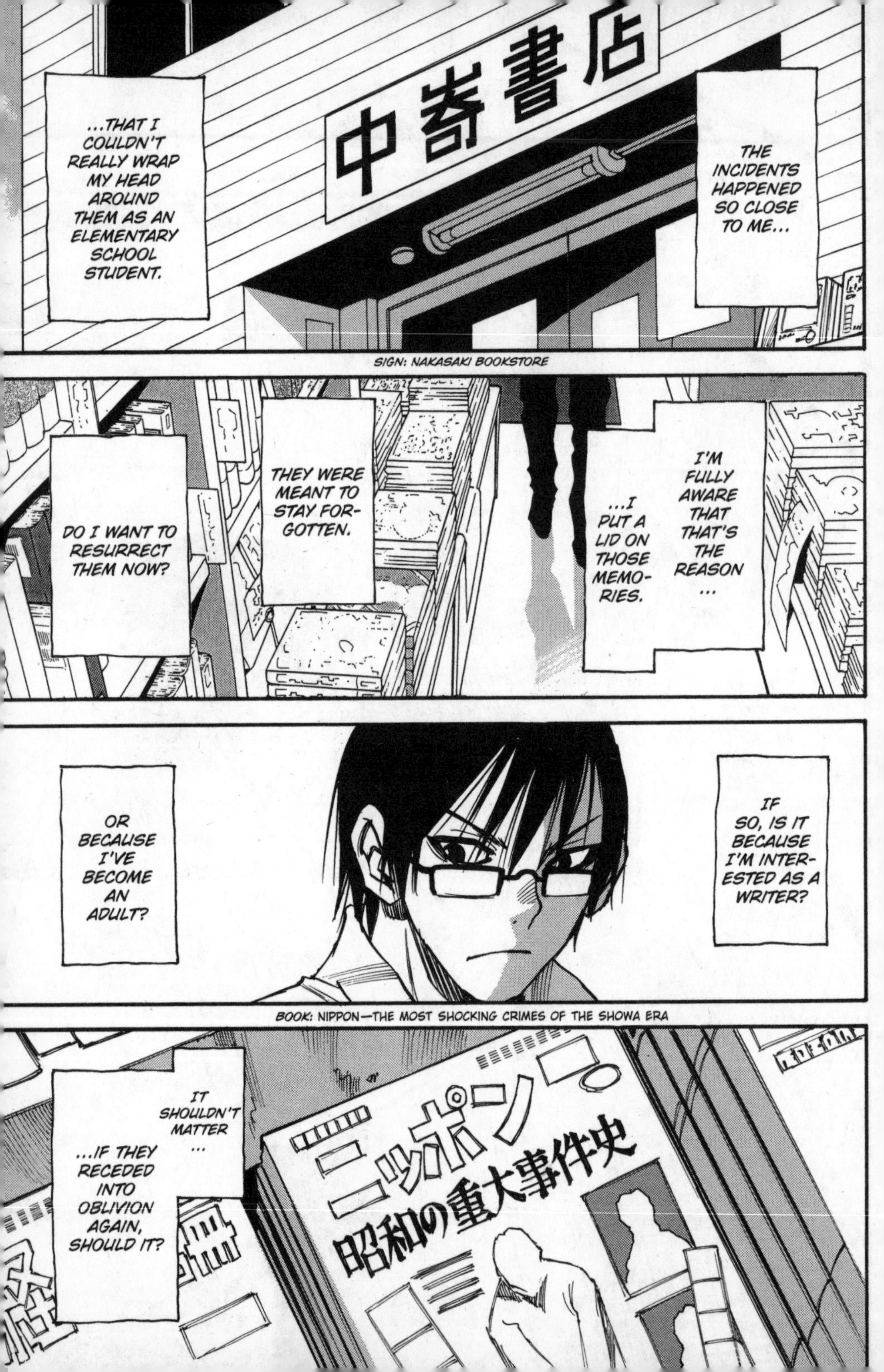
中嵜書店
THE INCIDENTS HAPPENED SO CLOSE TO ME...
...THAT I COULDN'T REALLY WRAP MY HEAD AROUND THEM AS AN ELEMENTARY SCHOOL STUDENT.
SIGN: NAKASAKI BOOKSTORE
I'M FULLY AWARE THAT THAT'S THE REASON...
...I PUT A LID ON THOSE MEMORIES.
THEY WERE MEANT TO STAY FOR-GOTTEN.
DO I WANT TO RESURRECT THEM NOW?
IF SO, IS IT BECAUSE I'M INTER-ESTED AS A WRITER?
OR BECAUSE I'VE BECOME AN ADULT?
BOOK: NIPPON—THE MOST SHOCKING CRIMES OF THE SHOWA ERA
IT SHOULDN'T MATTER...
...IF THEY RECEDED INTO OBLIVION AGAIN, SHOULD IT?
ニッポン
昭和の重大事件史

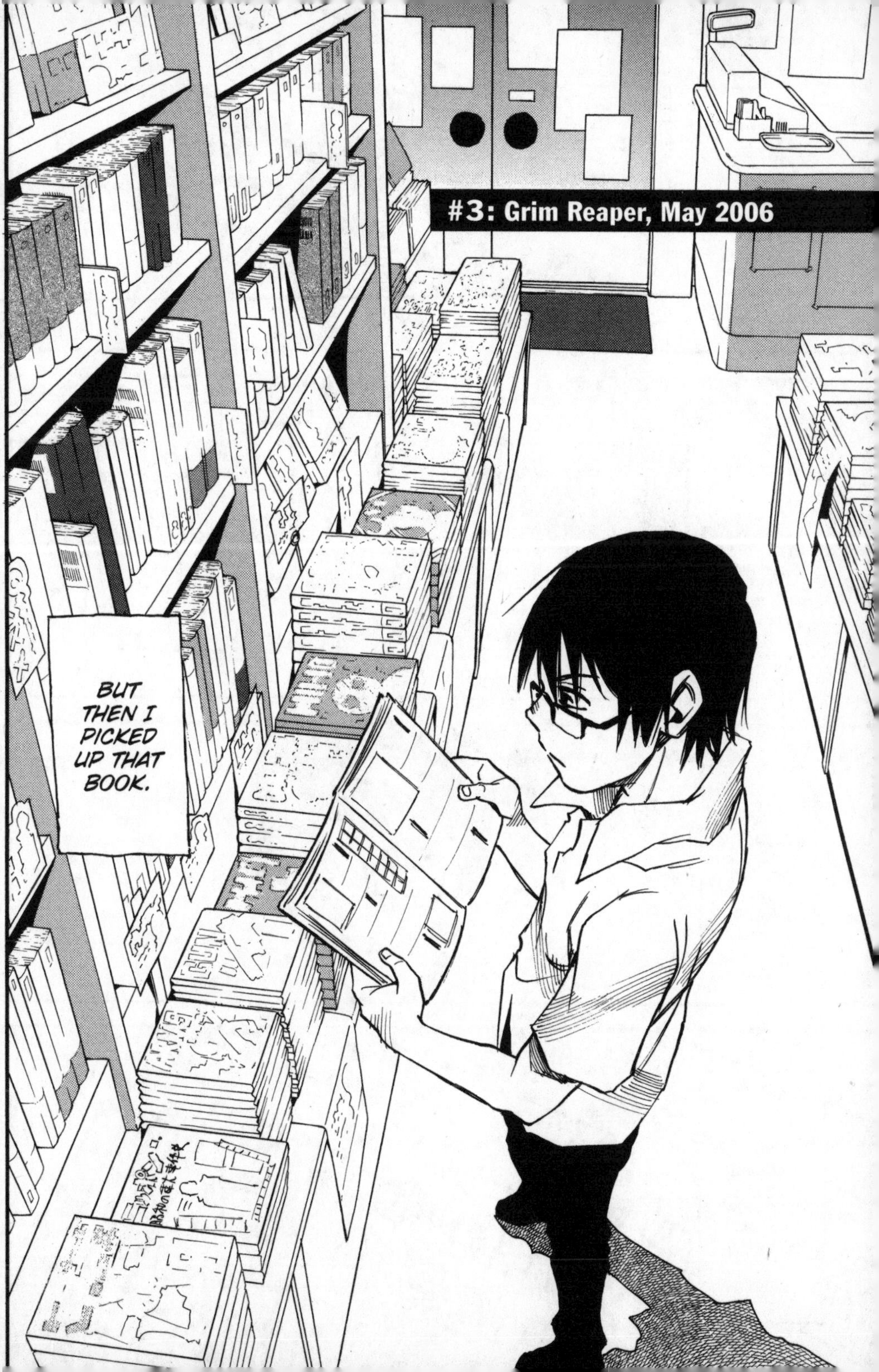
#3: Grim Reaper, May 2006
BUT THEN I PICKED UP THAT BOOK.

HEADING: THE HOKKAIDO ELEMENTARY SCHOOL STUDENT SERIAL KILLER, THE LAST SERIAL KILLER OF THE SHOWA ERA (1926-1989)

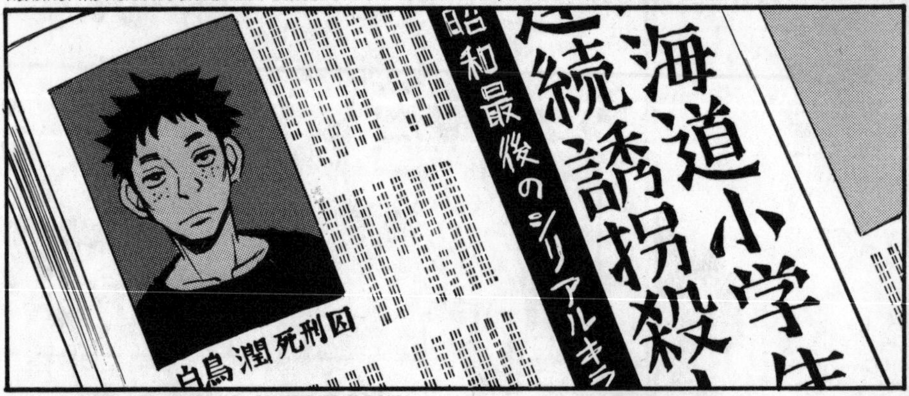
海道小学生
連続誘拐殺
昭和最後のシリアルキラ
白鳥潤死刑囚

CAPTION: JUN SHIRATORI, CONDEMNED TO DEATH

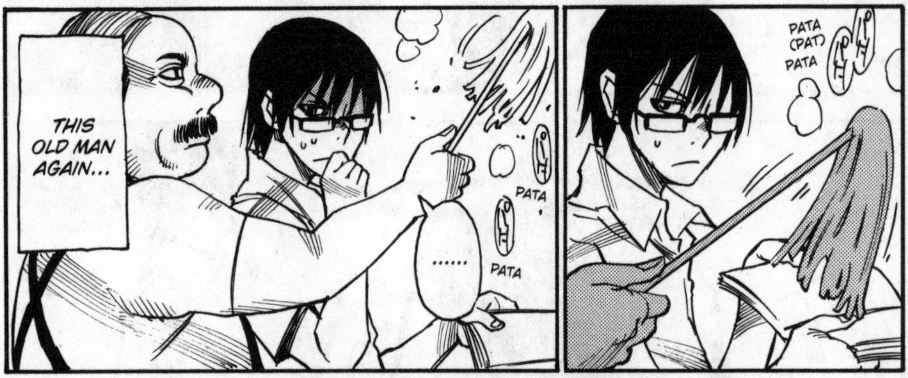
PATA (PAT) PATA
THIS OLD MAN AGAIN...
......
PATA
PATA

SIGN: BOOKSTORE

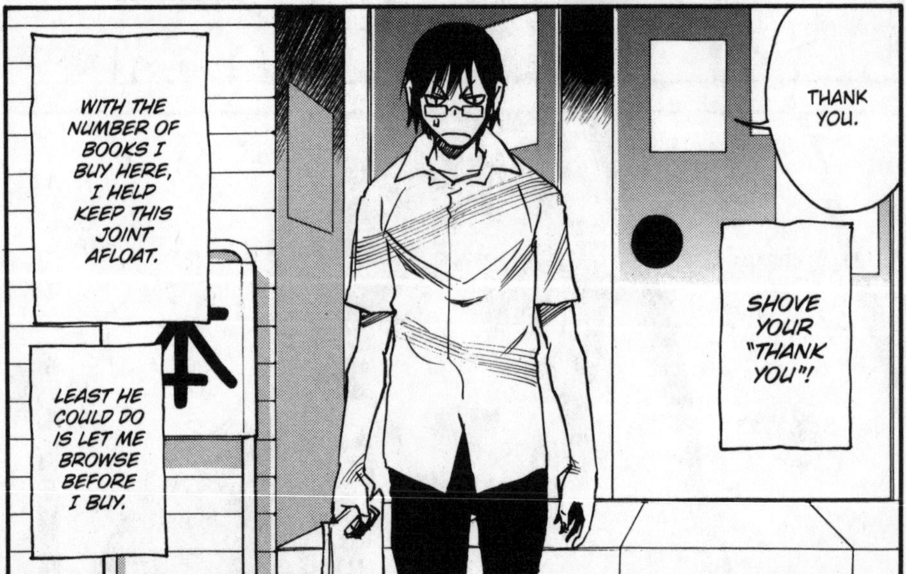
THANK YOU.
SHOVE YOUR "THANK YOU"!
WITH THE NUMBER OF BOOKS I BUY HERE, I HELP KEEP THIS JOINT AFLOAT.
LEAST HE COULD DO IS LET ME BROWSE BEFORE I BUY.

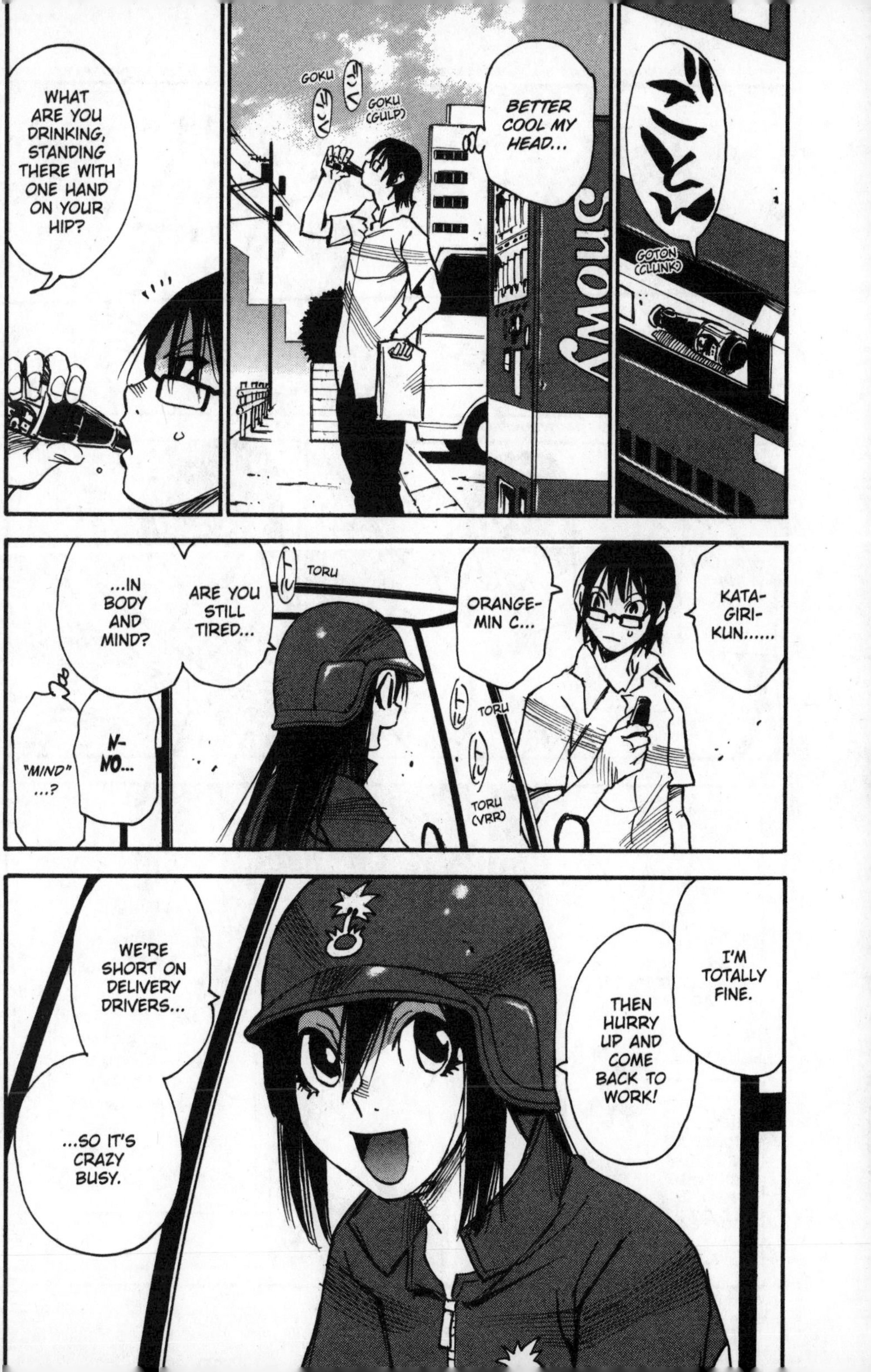
GOTON (CLUNK)
SNOWY
BETTER COOL MY HEAD...
GOKU
GOKU (GULP)
WHAT ARE YOU DRINKING, STANDING THERE WITH ONE HAND ON YOUR HIP?
KATA-GIRI-KUN......
ORANGE-MIN C...
TORU
ARE YOU STILL TIRED...
...IN BODY AND MIND?
TORU
TORU (VRR)
N-NO...
"MIND" ...?
I'M TOTALLY FINE.
THEN HURRY UP AND COME BACK TO WORK!
WE'RE SHORT ON DELIVERY DRIVERS...
...SO IT'S CRAZY BUSY.

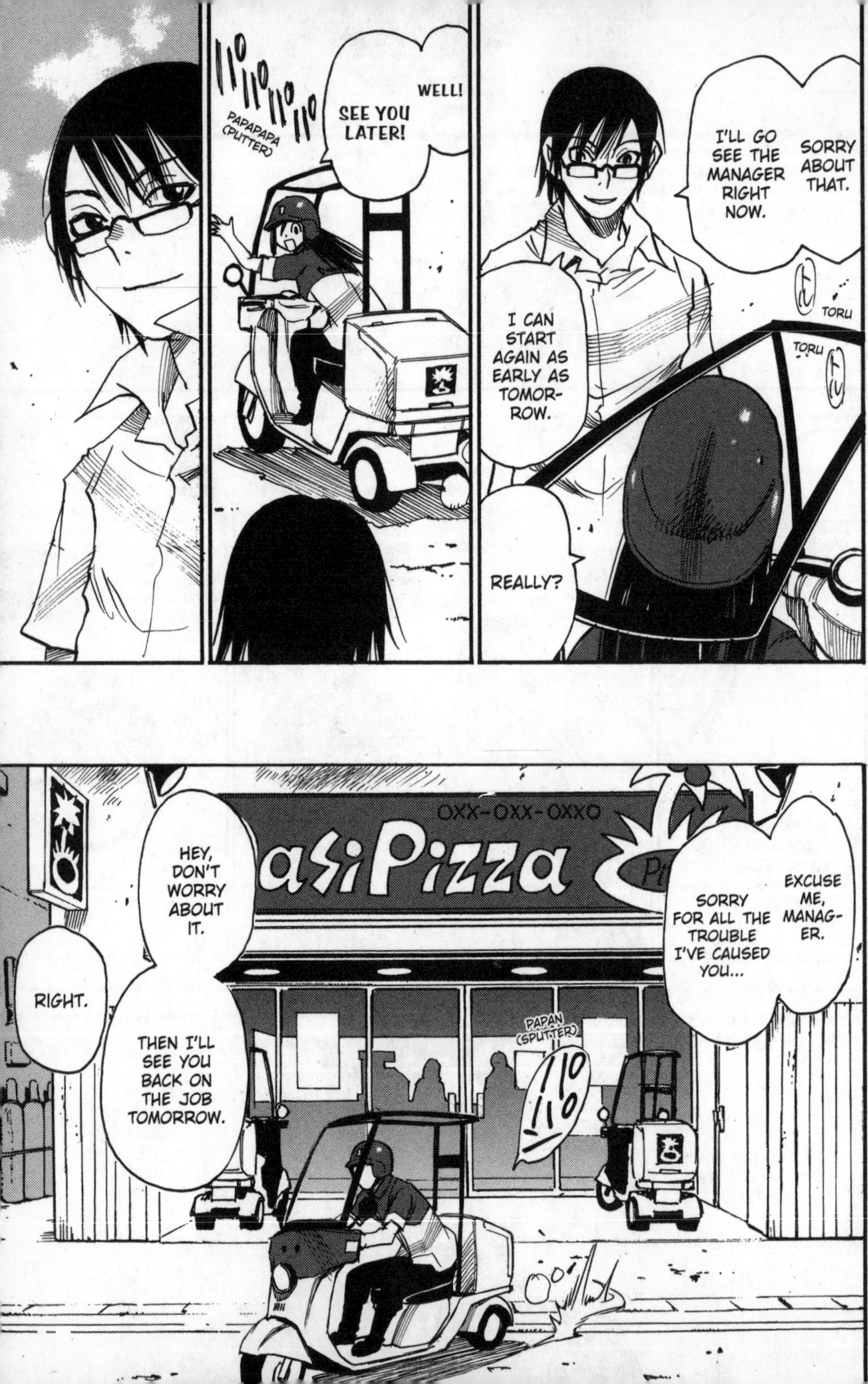
SORRY ABOUT THAT.
I'LL GO SEE THE MANAGER RIGHT NOW.
TORU
TORU
I CAN START AGAIN AS EARLY AS TOMORROW.
REALLY?
WELL!
SEE YOU LATER!
PAPAPAPA (PUTTER)
OXX-OXX-OXXO
asiPizza
EXCUSE ME, MANAGER.
SORRY FOR ALL THE TROUBLE I'VE CAUSED YOU...
HEY, DON'T WORRY ABOUT IT.
RIGHT.
THEN I'LL SEE YOU BACK ON THE JOB TOMORROW.
PAPAN (SPUTTER)

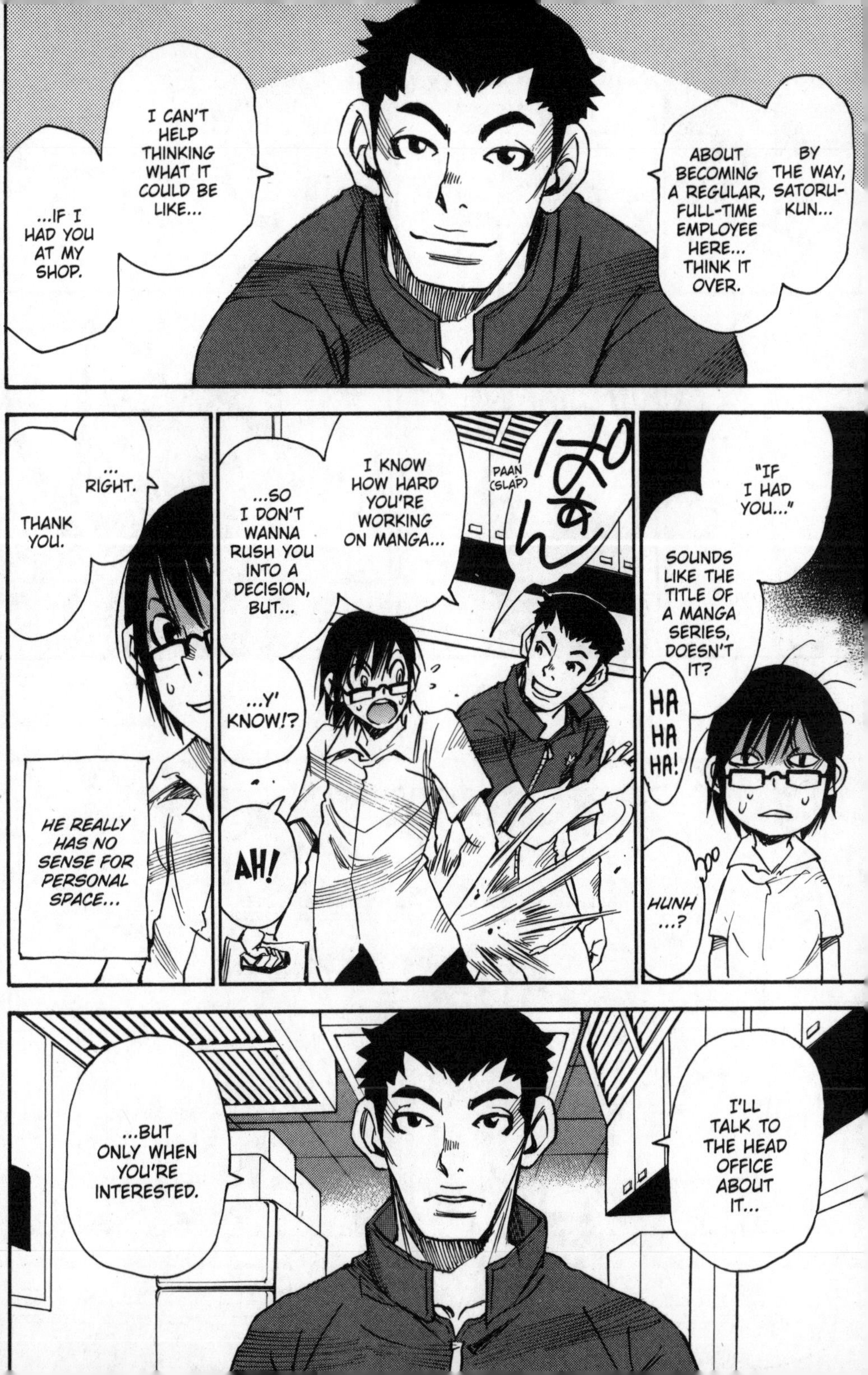
BY THE WAY, SATORU-KUN...
ABOUT BECOMING A REGULAR, FULL-TIME EMPLOYEE HERE... THINK IT OVER.
I CAN'T HELP THINKING WHAT IT COULD BE LIKE...
...IF I HAD YOU AT MY SHOP.
"IF I HAD YOU..."
SOUNDS LIKE THE TITLE OF A MANGA SERIES, DOESN'T IT?
HA HA HA!
HUNH ...?
ぱあん
PAAN (SLAP)
I KNOW HOW HARD YOU'RE WORKING ON MANGA...
...SO I DON'T WANNA RUSH YOU INTO A DECISION, BUT...
...Y' KNOW!?
AH!
...RIGHT.
THANK YOU.
HE REALLY HAS NO SENSE FOR PERSONAL SPACE...
I'LL TALK TO THE HEAD OFFICE ABOUT IT...
...BUT ONLY WHEN YOU'RE INTERESTED.

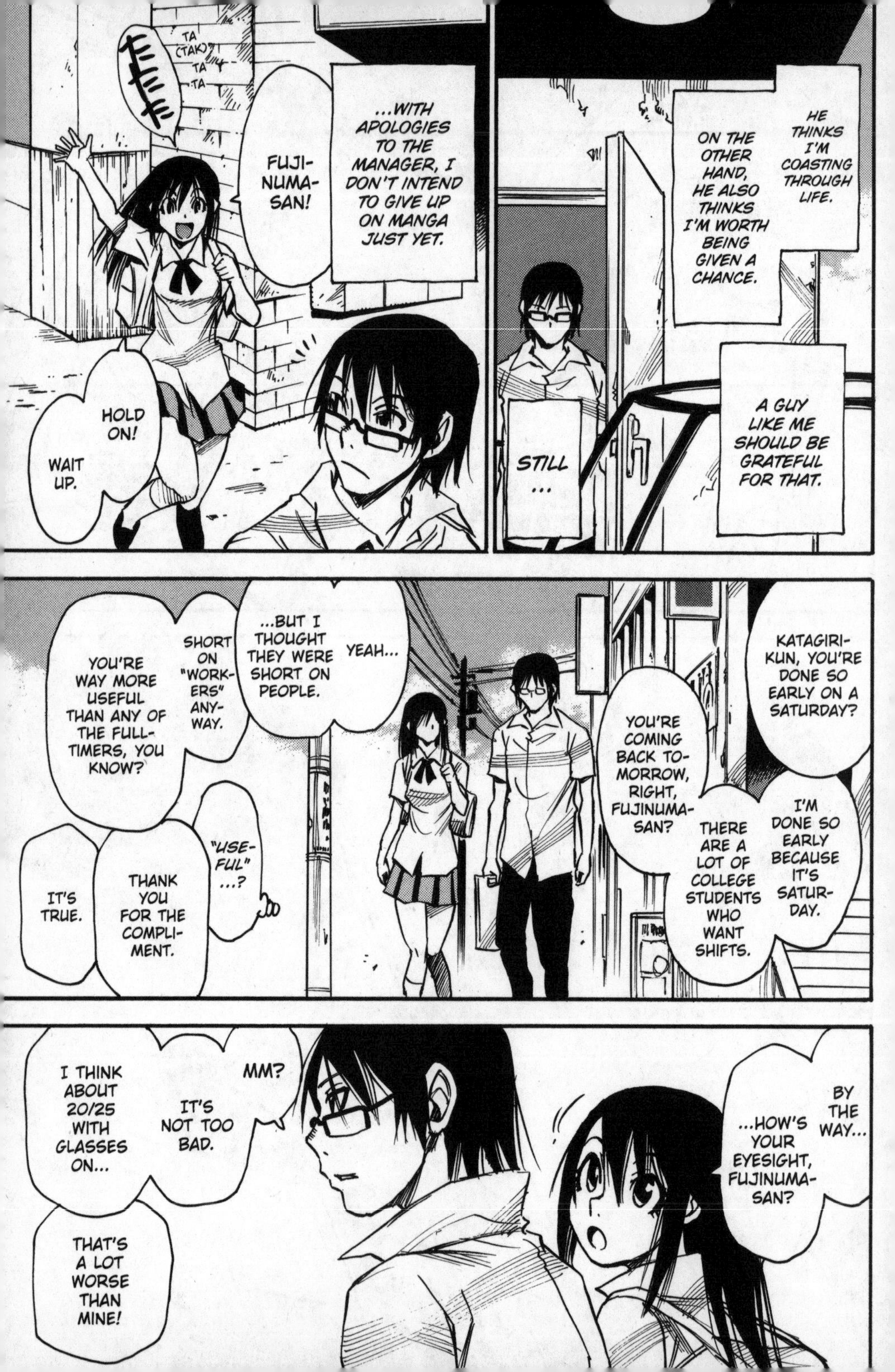
HE THINKS I'M COASTING THROUGH LIFE.
ON THE OTHER HAND, HE ALSO THINKS I'M WORTH BEING GIVEN A CHANCE.
A GUY LIKE ME SHOULD BE GRATEFUL FOR THAT.
STILL ...
...WITH APOLOGIES TO THE MANAGER, I DON'T INTEND TO GIVE UP ON MANGA JUST YET.
FUJI-NUMA-SAN!
TA (TAK) TA TA
HOLD ON!
WAIT UP.
KATAGIRI-KUN, YOU'RE DONE SO EARLY ON A SATURDAY?
I'M DONE SO EARLY BECAUSE IT'S SATUR-DAY.
YOU'RE COMING BACK TO-MORROW, RIGHT, FUJINUMA-SAN?
THERE ARE A LOT OF COLLEGE STUDENTS WHO WANT SHIFTS.
YEAH...
...BUT I THOUGHT THEY WERE SHORT ON PEOPLE.
SHORT ON "WORK-ERS" ANY-WAY.
YOU'RE WAY MORE USEFUL THAN ANY OF THE FULL-TIMERS, YOU KNOW?
"USE-FUL" ...?
THANK YOU FOR THE COMPLI-MENT.
IT'S TRUE.
BY THE WAY...
...HOW'S YOUR EYESIGHT, FUJINUMA-SAN?
MM?
IT'S NOT TOO BAD.
I THINK ABOUT 20/25 WITH GLASSES ON...
THAT'S A LOT WORSE THAN MINE!

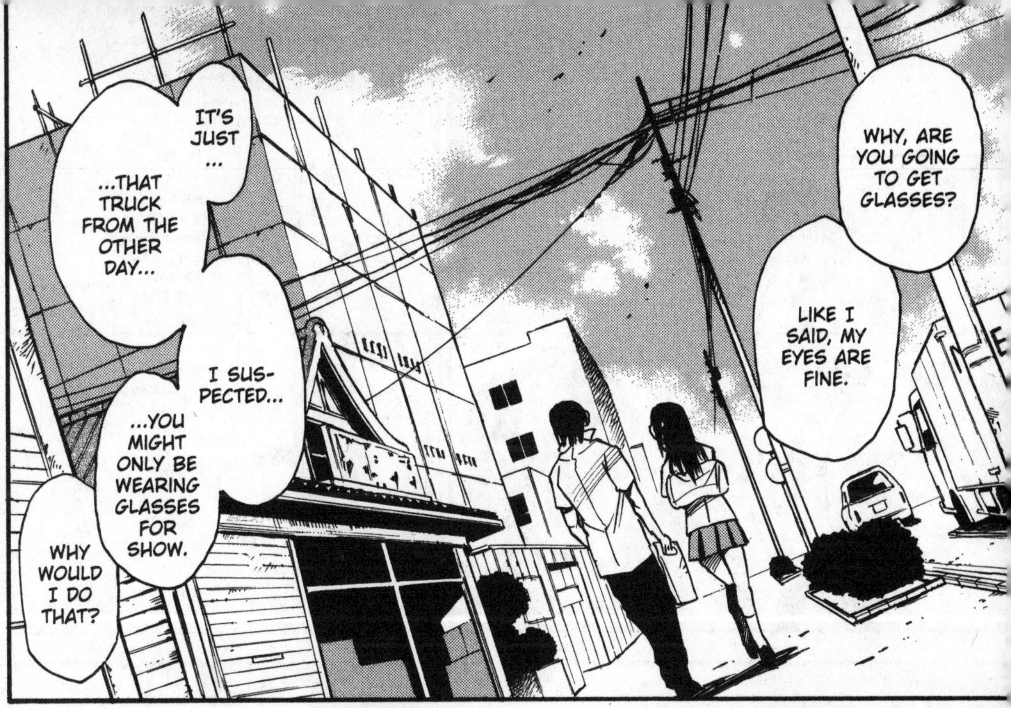
WHY, ARE YOU GOING TO GET GLASSES?
LIKE I SAID, MY EYES ARE FINE.
IT'S JUST ...
...THAT TRUCK FROM THE OTHER DAY...
I SUSPECTED...
...YOU MIGHT ONLY BE WEARING GLASSES FOR SHOW.
WHY WOULD I DO THAT?
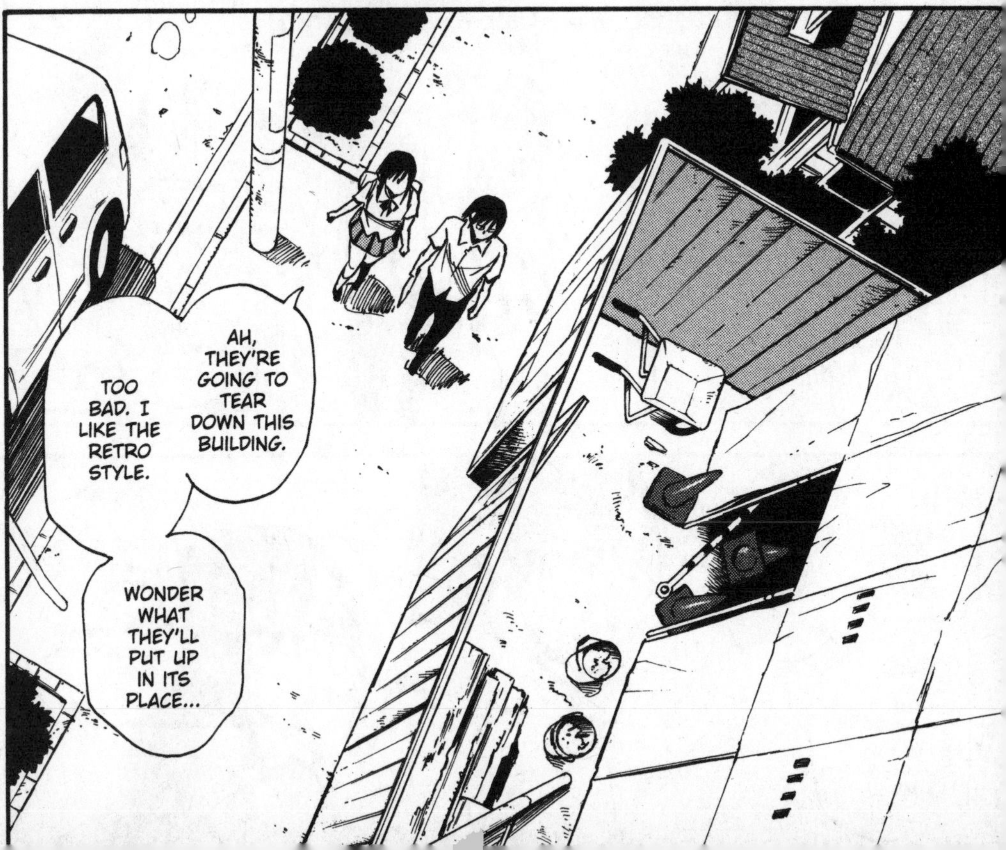
AH, THEY'RE GOING TO TEAR DOWN THIS BUILDING.
TOO BAD. I LIKE THE RETRO STYLE.
WONDER WHAT THEY'LL PUT UP IN ITS PLACE...

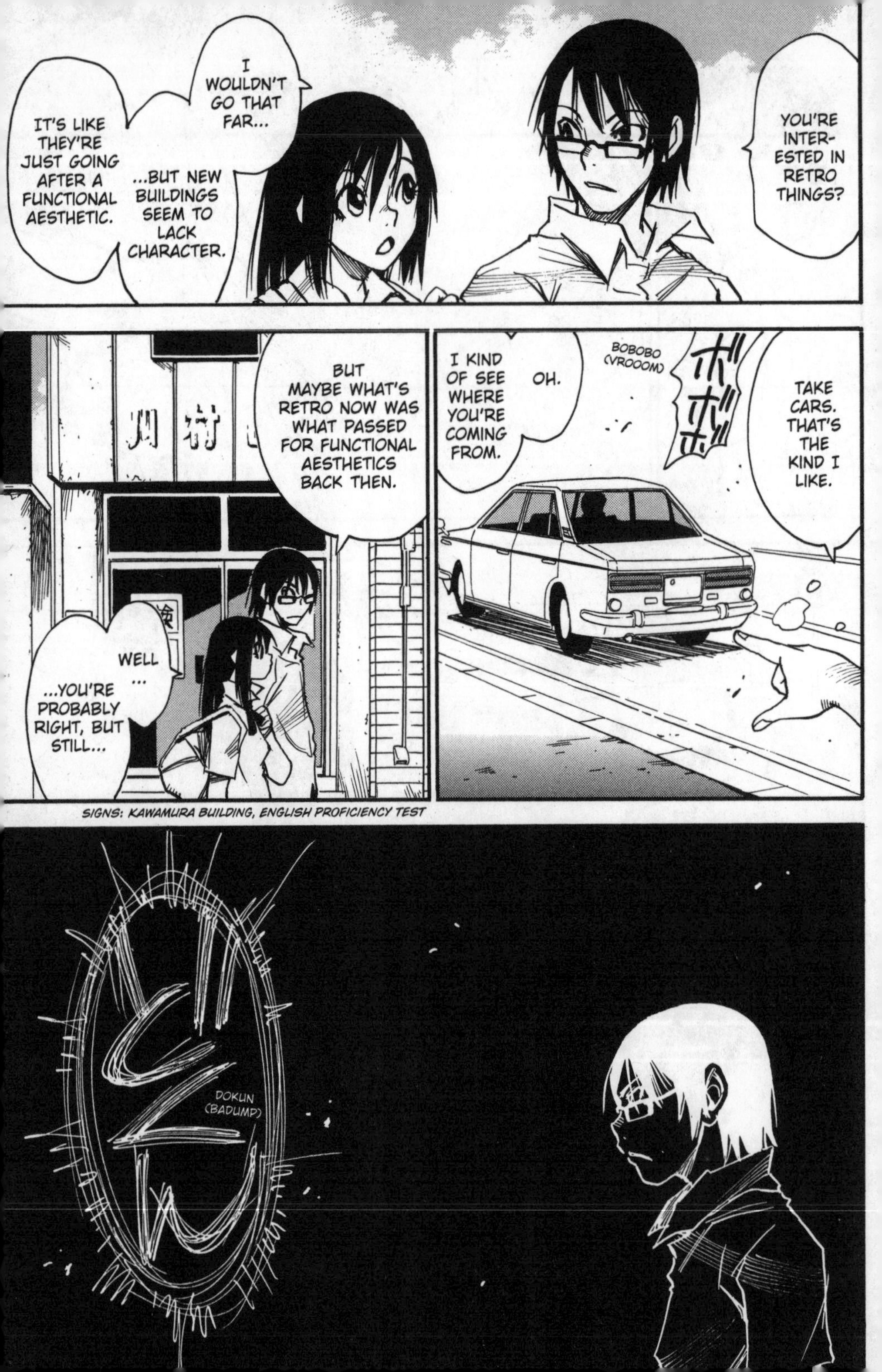
YOU'RE INTERESTED IN RETRO THINGS?
I WOULDN'T GO THAT FAR...
...BUT NEW BUILDINGS SEEM TO LACK CHARACTER.
IT'S LIKE THEY'RE JUST GOING AFTER A FUNCTIONAL AESTHETIC.
TAKE CARS. THAT'S THE KIND I LIKE.
ボボボ
BOBOBO (VROOOM)
OH.
I KIND OF SEE WHERE YOU'RE COMING FROM.
BUT MAYBE WHAT'S RETRO NOW WAS WHAT PASSED FOR FUNCTIONAL AESTHETICS BACK THEN.
WELL...
...YOU'RE PROBABLY RIGHT, BUT STILL...
DOKUN (BADUMP)
SIGNS: KAWAMURA BUILDING, ENGLISH PROFICIENCY TEST

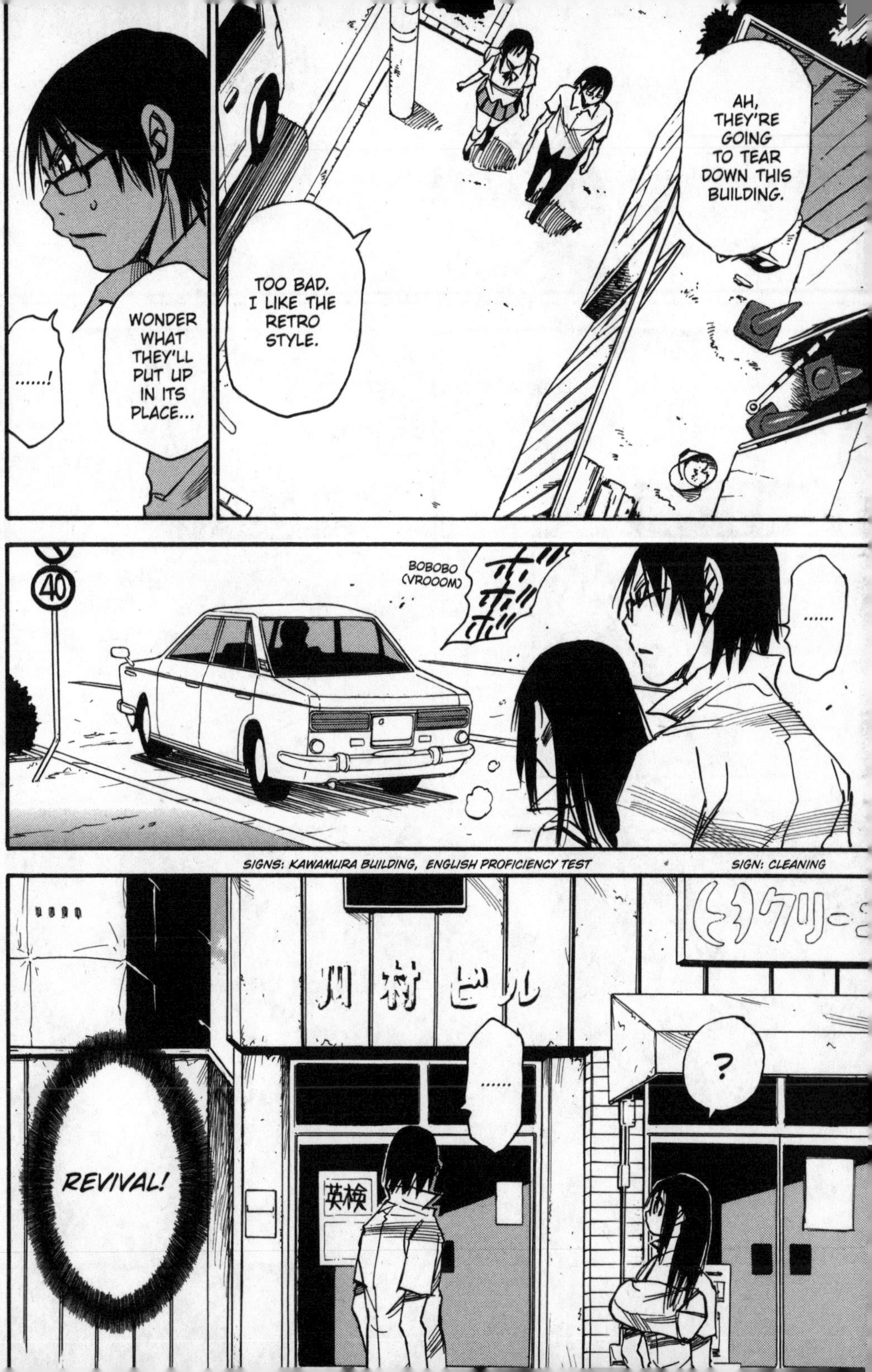
AH, THEY'RE GOING TO TEAR DOWN THIS BUILDING.
TOO BAD. I LIKE THE RETRO STYLE.
WONDER WHAT THEY'LL PUT UP IN ITS PLACE...
......!
40
......
BOBOBO (VROOOM)
SIGN: CLEANING
SIGNS: KAWAMURA BUILDING, ENGLISH PROFICIENCY TEST
川村ビル
?
......
英検
REVIVAL!

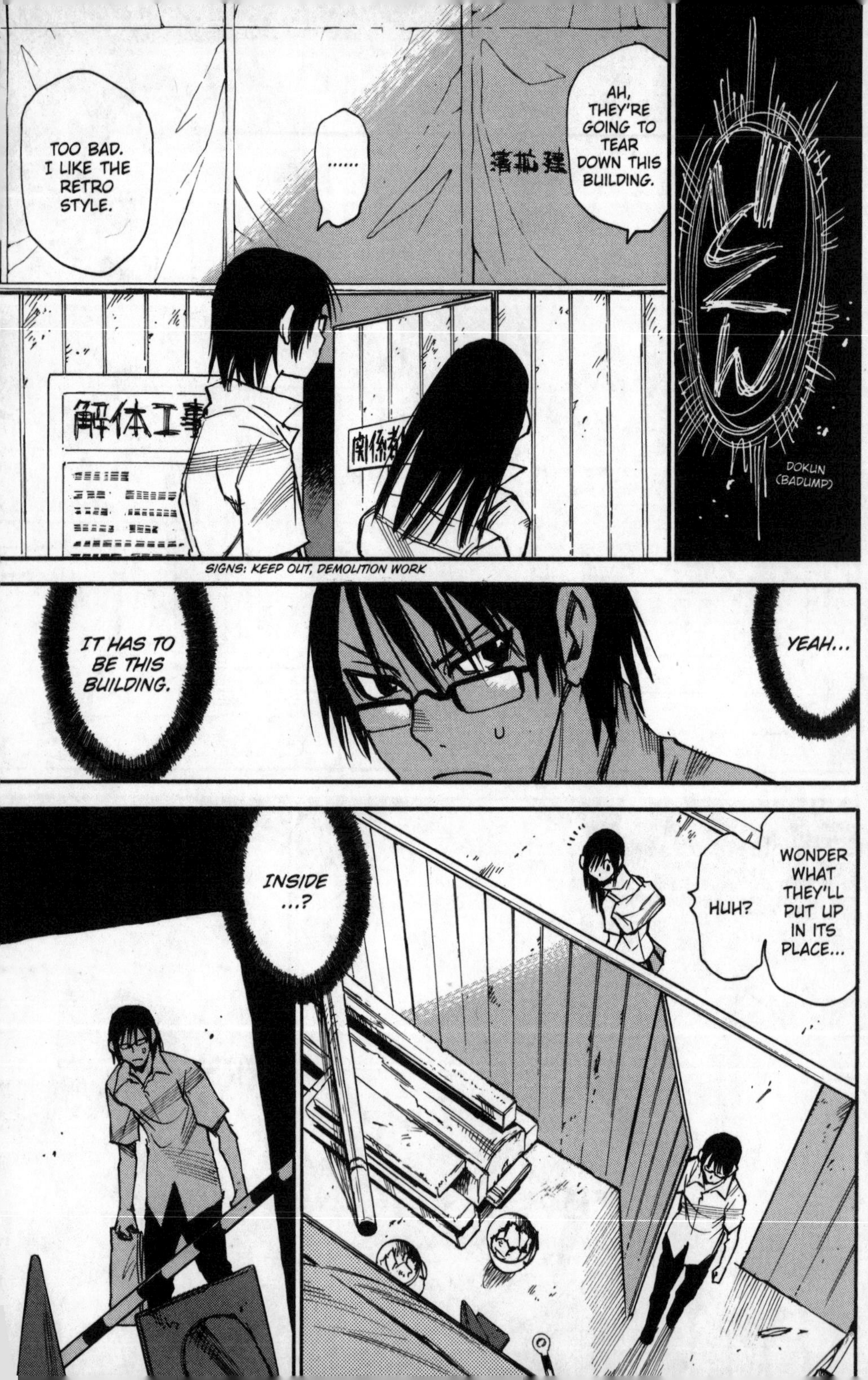
DOKUN (BADUMP)
AH, THEY'RE GOING TO TEAR DOWN THIS BUILDING.
......
TOO BAD. I LIKE THE RETRO STYLE.
解体工事
SIGNS: KEEP OUT, DEMOLITION WORK
YEAH...
IT HAS TO BE THIS BUILDING.
WONDER WHAT THEY'LL PUT UP IN ITS PLACE...
HUH?
INSIDE ...?

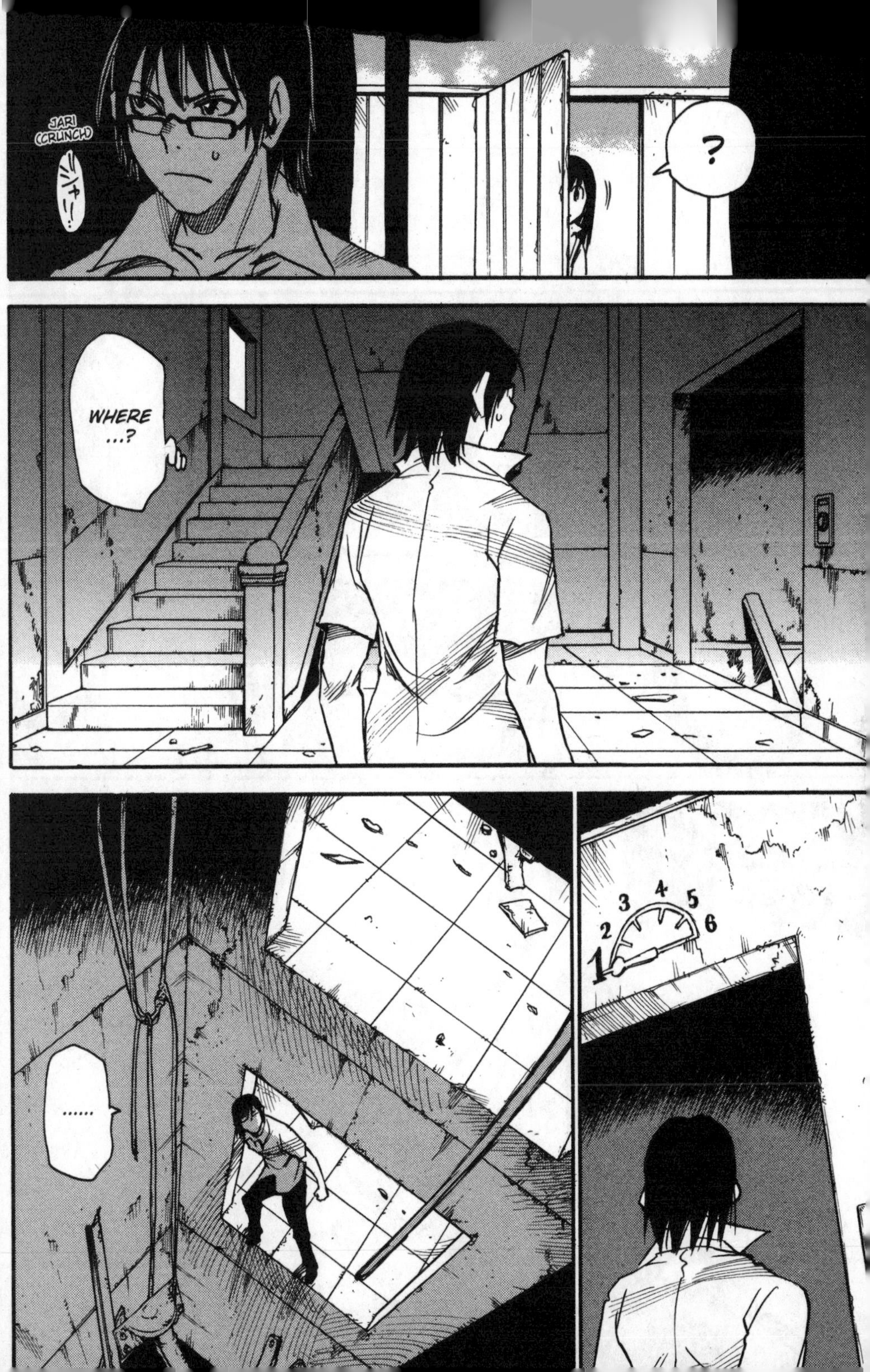
?
JARI (CRUNCH)
WHERE ...?
1 2 3 4 5 6
......

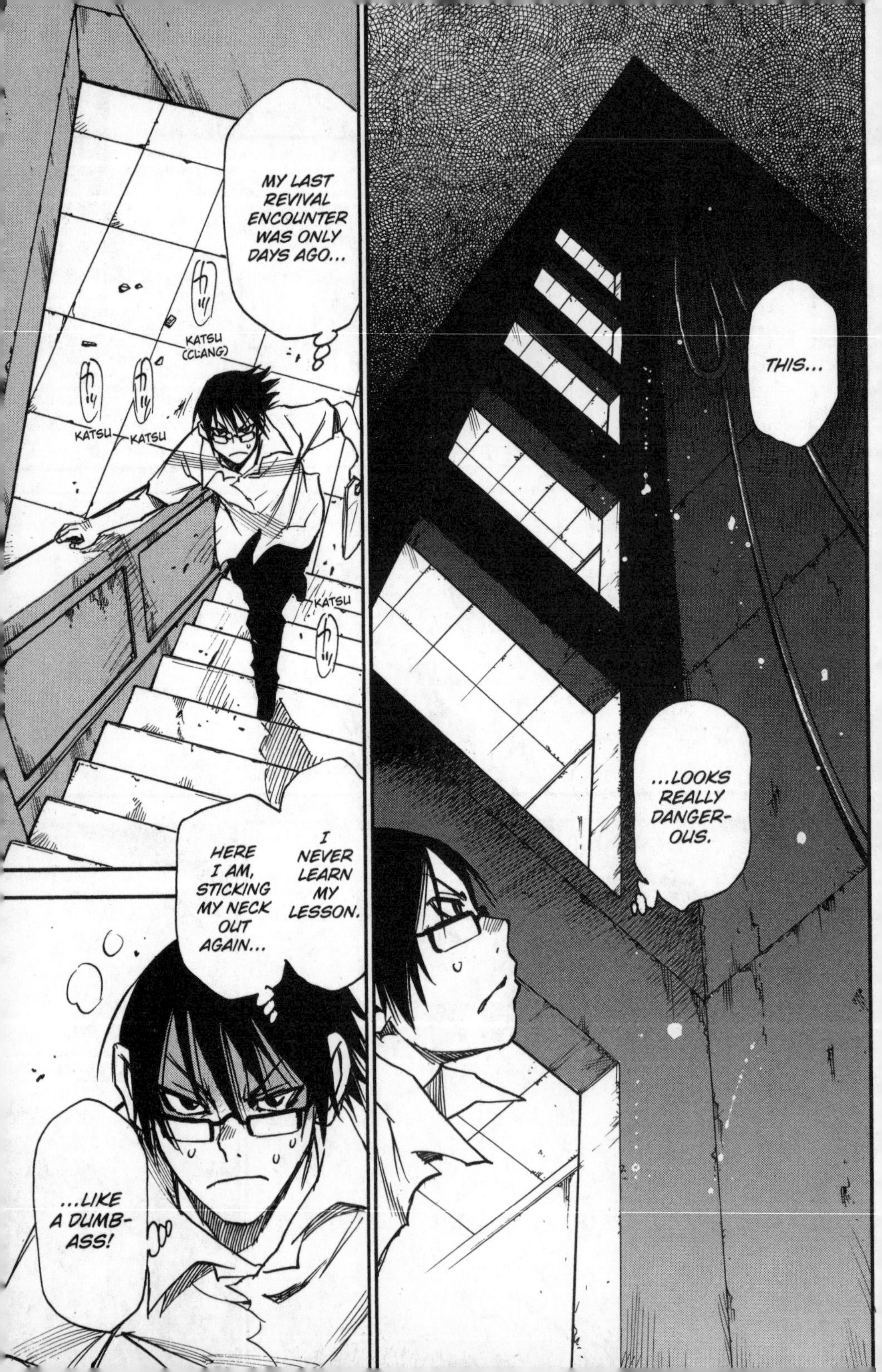
THIS...
...LOOKS REALLY DANGER-OUS.
MY LAST REVIVAL ENCOUNTER WAS ONLY DAYS AGO...
KATSU (CLANG)
KATSU
KATSU
KATSU
I NEVER LEARN MY LESSON.
HERE I AM, STICKING MY NECK OUT AGAIN...
...LIKE A DUMB-ASS!

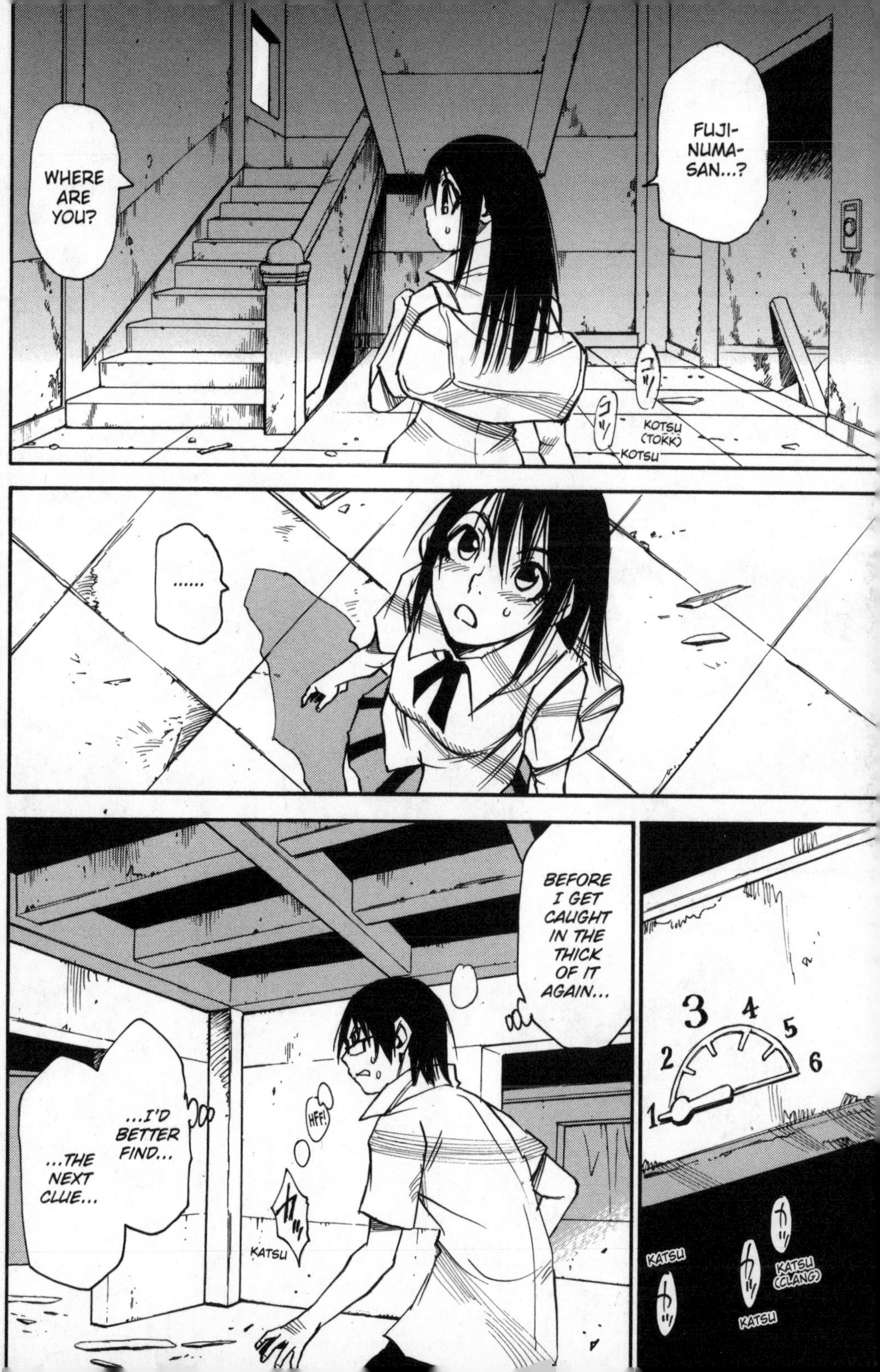
FUJI-NUMA-SAN...?
WHERE ARE YOU?
KOTSU (TOKK)
KOTSU
......
1 2 3 4 5 6
KATSU (CLANG)
KATSU
KATSU
BEFORE I GET CAUGHT IN THE THICK OF IT AGAIN...
HFF!
...I'D BETTER FIND...
...THE NEXT CLUE...
KATSU

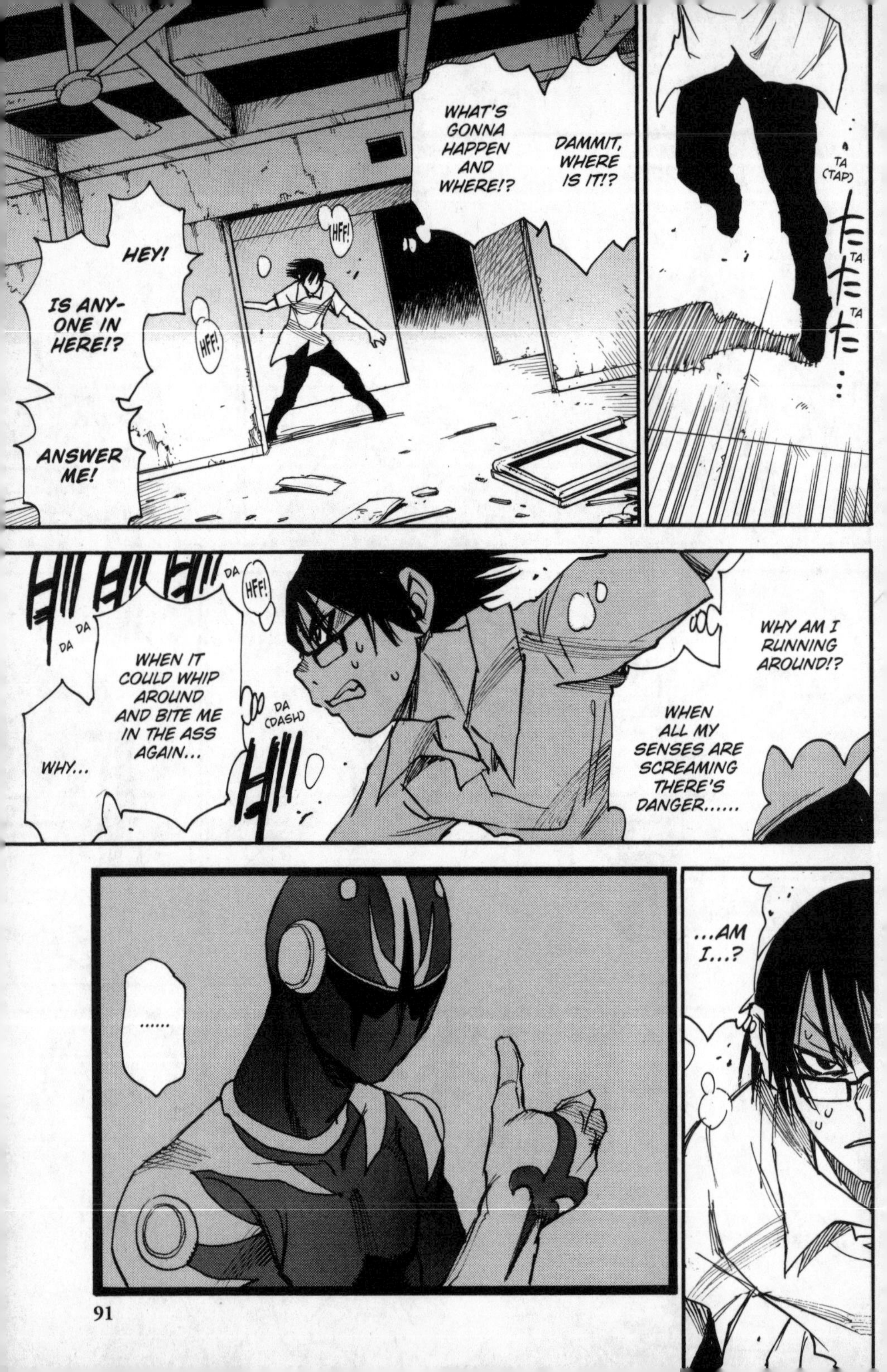
TA (TAP)
TA
TA
DAMMIT, WHERE IS IT!?
WHAT'S GONNA HAPPEN AND WHERE!?
HFF!
HEY!
IS ANY-ONE IN HERE!?
HFF!
ANSWER ME!
WHY AM I RUNNING AROUND!?
WHEN ALL MY SENSES ARE SCREAMING THERE'S DANGER......
HFF!
DA
DA (DASH)
WHEN IT COULD WHIP AROUND AND BITE ME IN THE ASS AGAIN...
WHY...
DA
DA
...AM I...?
......

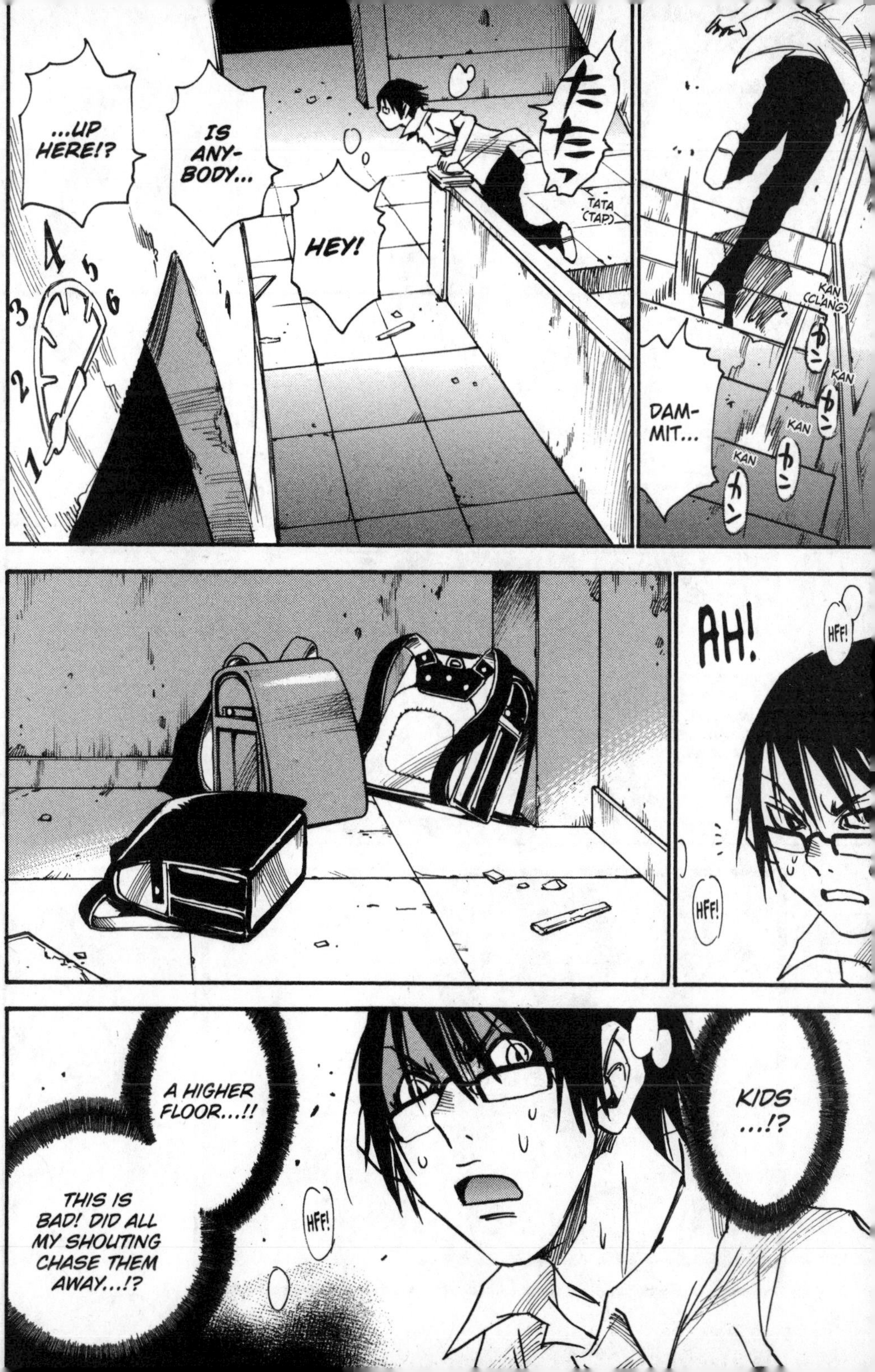
KAN (CLANG)
カン
KAN
カン
KAN
カン
KAN
カン
DAM-MIT...
TATA (TAP)
HEY!
IS ANY-BODY...
...UP HERE!?
AH!
HFF!
HFF!
KIDS ...!?
A HIGHER FLOOR...!!
THIS IS BAD! DID ALL MY SHOUTING CHASE THEM AWAY...!?
HFF!

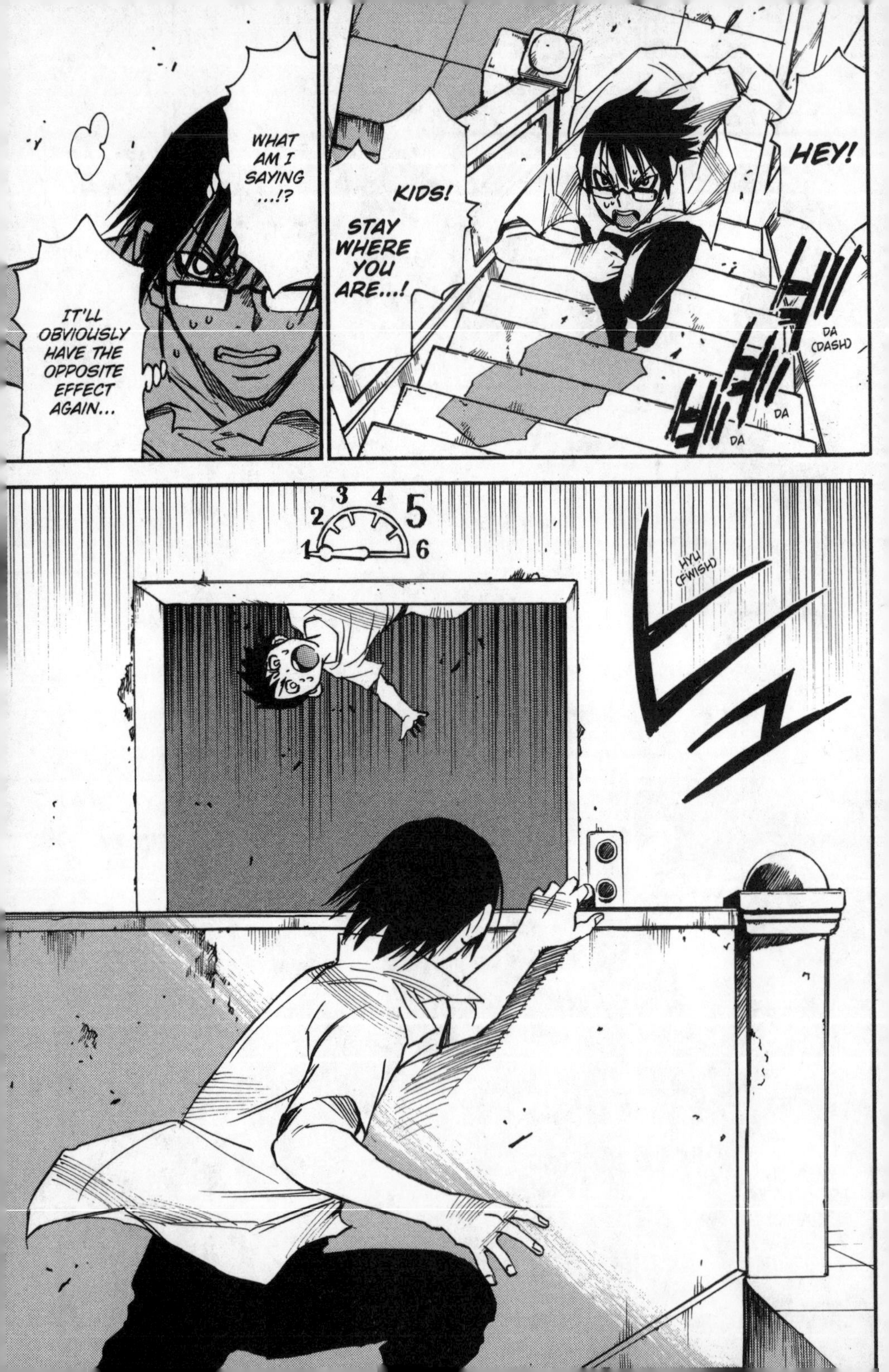
HEY!
KIDS!
STAY WHERE YOU ARE...!
DA (DASH)
DA
DA
WHAT AM I SAYING ...!?
IT'LL OBVIOUSLY HAVE THE OPPOSITE EFFECT AGAIN...
1 2 3 4 5 6
HYU (FWISH)

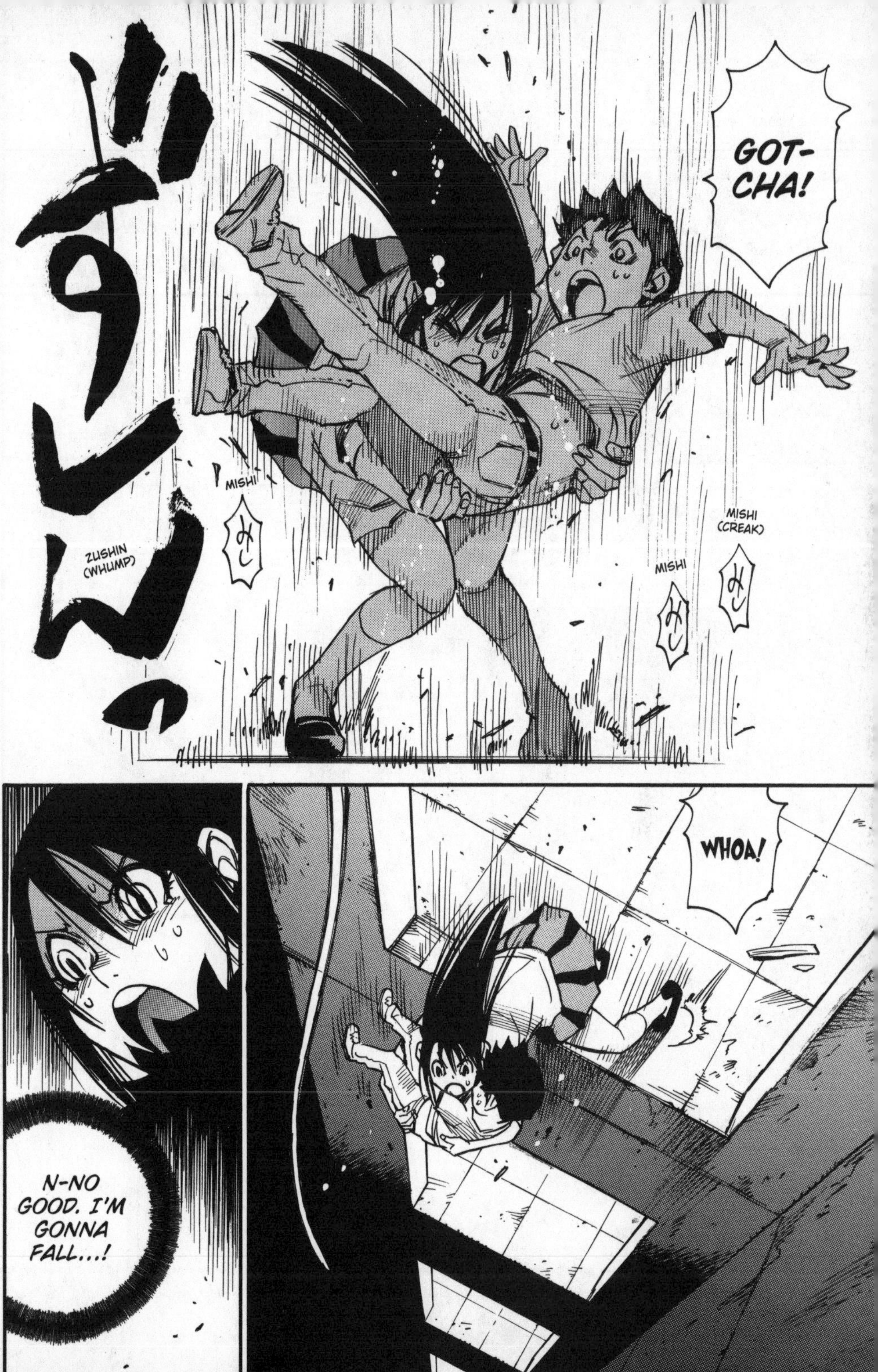
GOT-CHA!
MISHI (CREAK)
MISHI
MISHI
ZUSHIN (WHUMP)
WHOA!
N-NO GOOD. I'M GONNA FALL...!

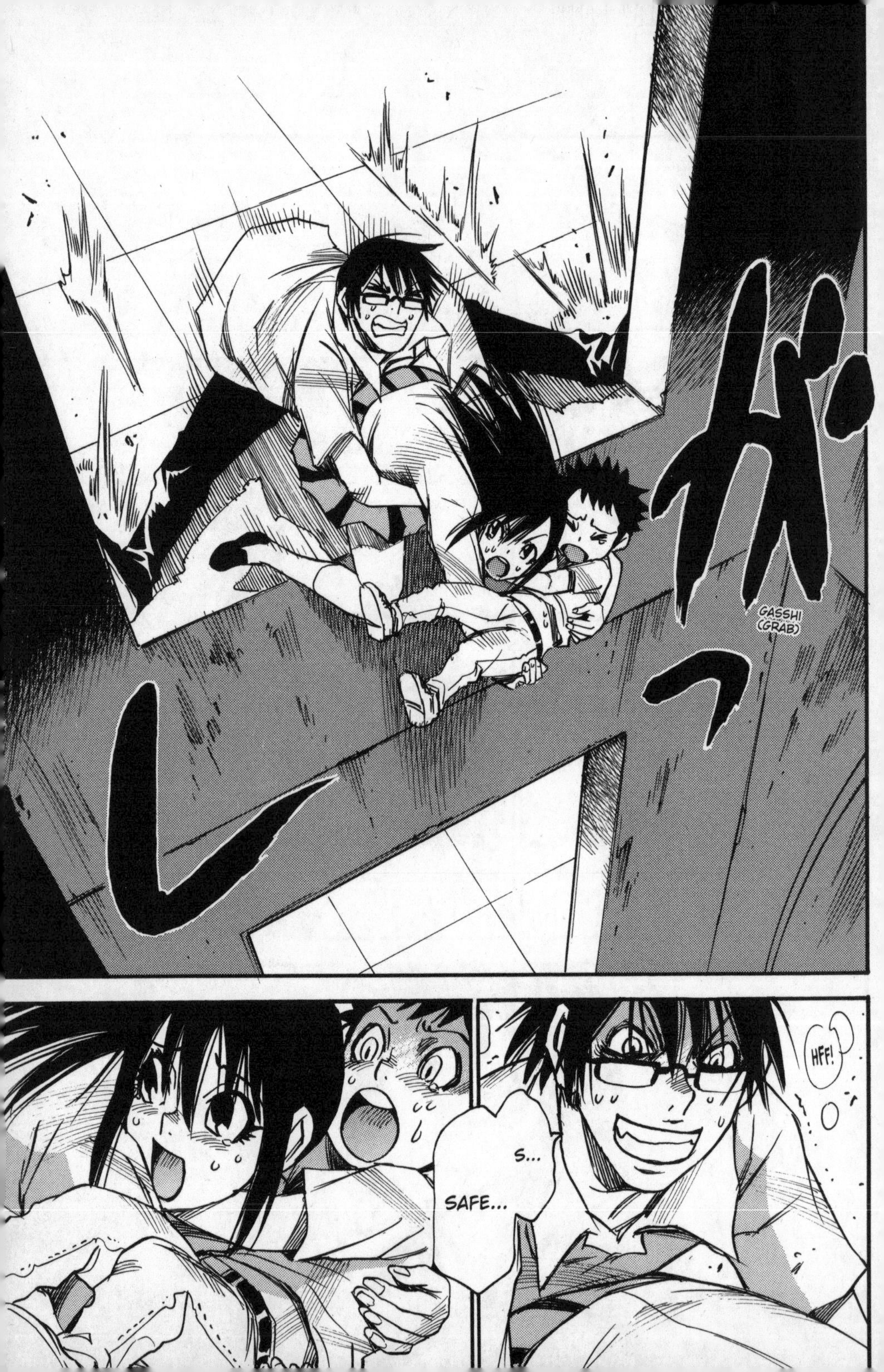
GASSHI
(GRAB)
HFF!
S...
SAFE...

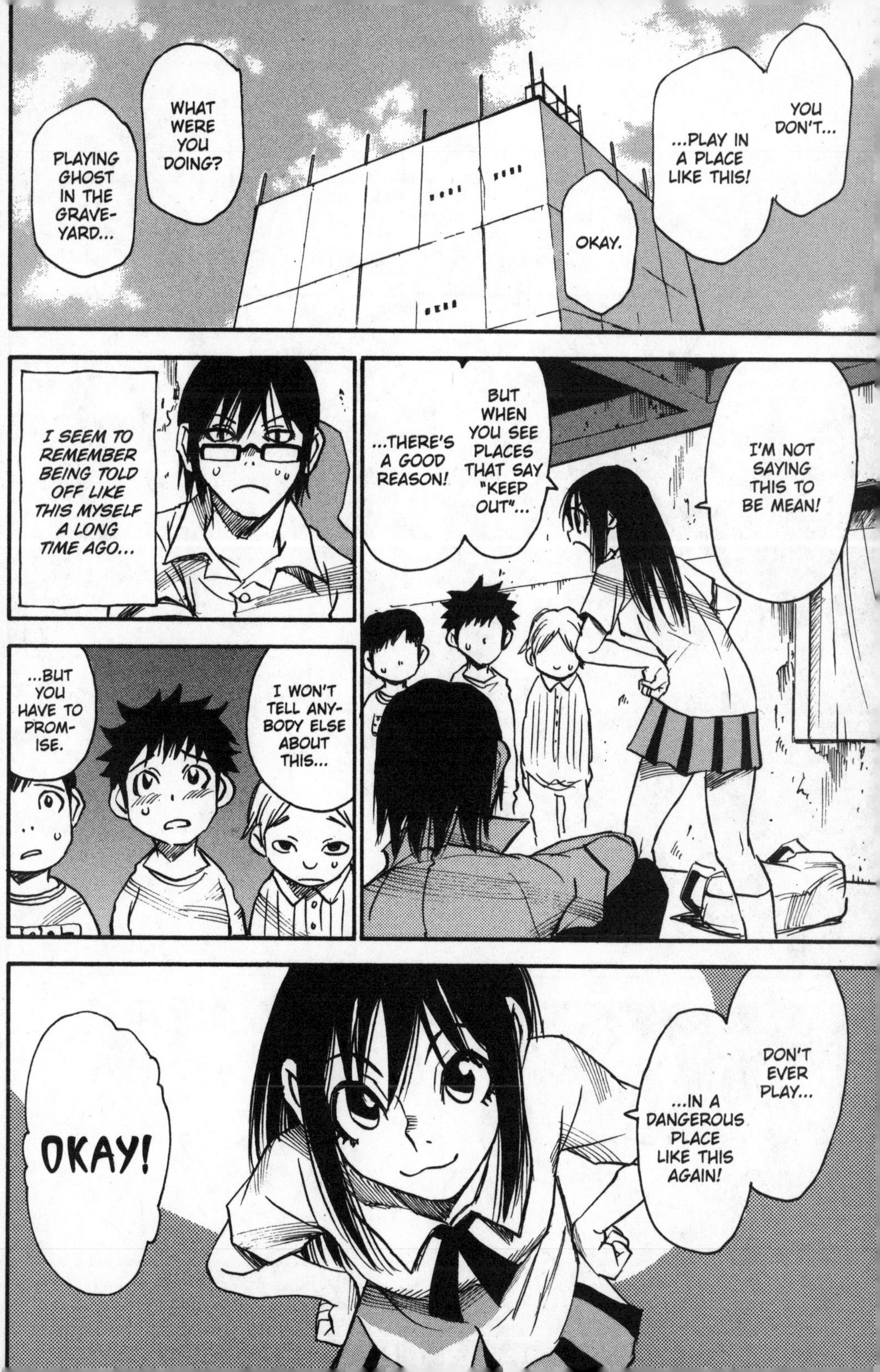
YOU DON'T...
...PLAY IN A PLACE LIKE THIS!
OKAY.
WHAT WERE YOU DOING?
PLAYING GHOST IN THE GRAVE-YARD...
I'M NOT SAYING THIS TO BE MEAN!
BUT WHEN YOU SEE PLACES THAT SAY "KEEP OUT"...
...THERE'S A GOOD REASON!
I SEEM TO REMEMBER BEING TOLD OFF LIKE THIS MYSELF A LONG TIME AGO...
I WON'T TELL ANY-BODY ELSE ABOUT THIS...
...BUT YOU HAVE TO PROM-ISE.
DON'T EVER PLAY...
...IN A DANGEROUS PLACE LIKE THIS AGAIN!
OKAY!

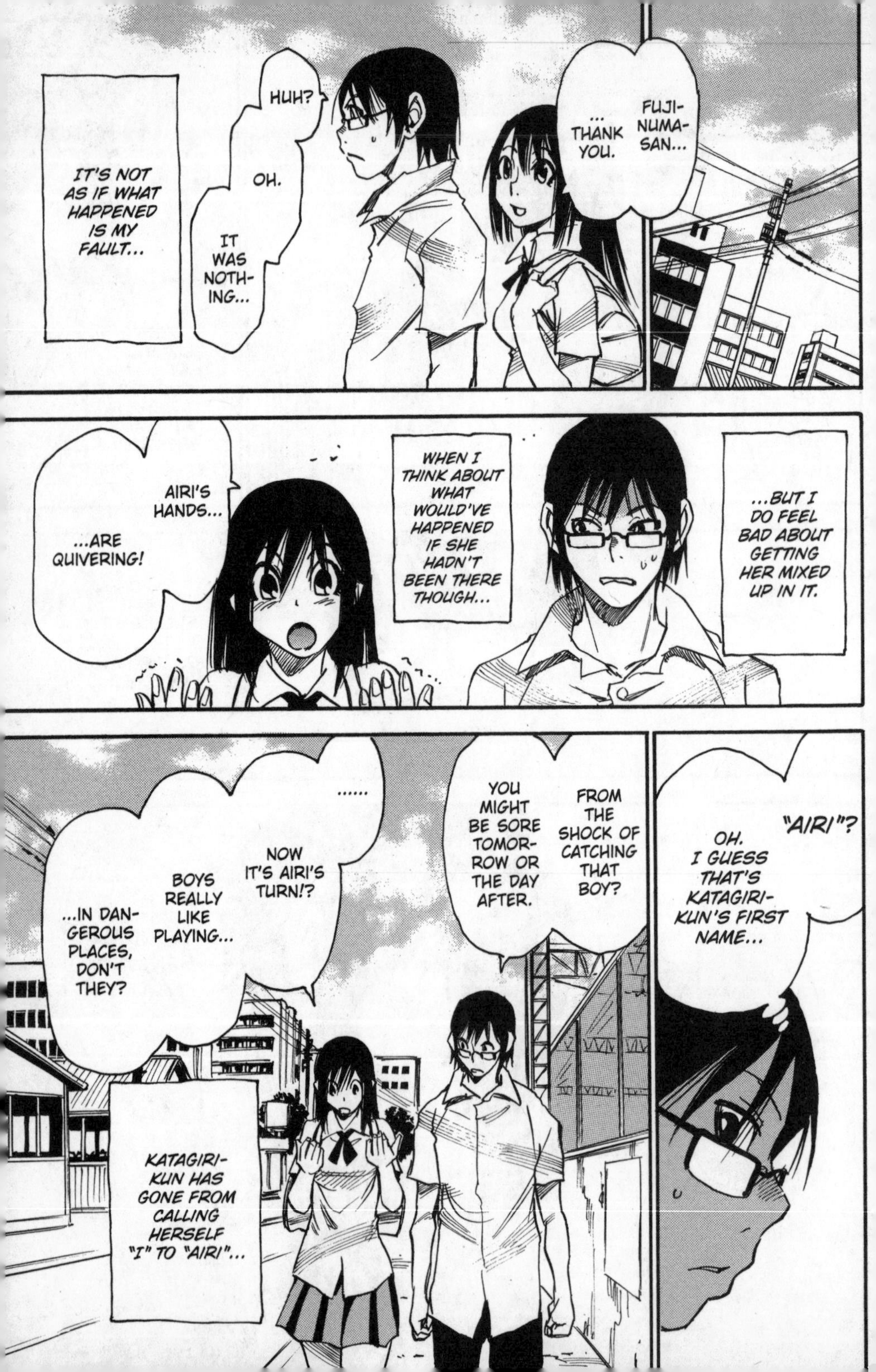
FUJI-NUMA-SAN...
...THANK YOU.
HUH?
OH.
IT WAS NOTHING...
IT'S NOT AS IF WHAT HAPPENED IS MY FAULT...
...BUT I DO FEEL BAD ABOUT GETTING HER MIXED UP IN IT.
WHEN I THINK ABOUT WHAT WOULD'VE HAPPENED IF SHE HADN'T BEEN THERE THOUGH...
AIRI'S HANDS...
...ARE QUIVERING!
"AIRI"?
OH. I GUESS THAT'S KATAGIRI-KUN'S FIRST NAME...
FROM THE SHOCK OF CATCHING THAT BOY?
YOU MIGHT BE SORE TOMORROW OR THE DAY AFTER.
......
NOW IT'S AIRI'S TURN!?
BOYS REALLY LIKE PLAYING...
...IN DANGEROUS PLACES, DON'T THEY?
KATAGIRI-KUN HAS GONE FROM CALLING HERSELF "I" TO "AIRI"...

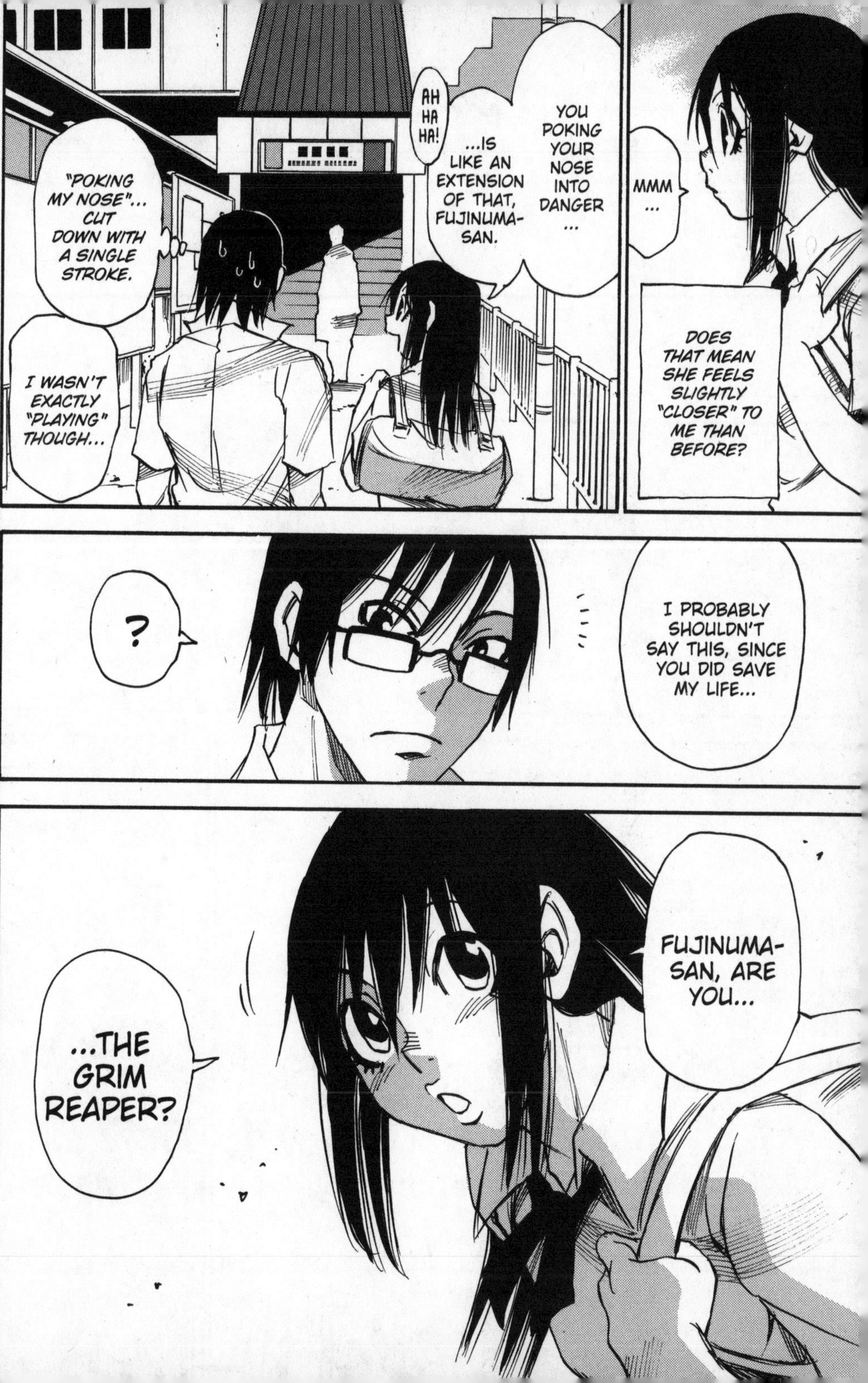
MMM...
DOES THAT MEAN SHE FEELS SLIGHTLY "CLOSER" TO ME THAN BEFORE?
YOU POKING YOUR NOSE INTO DANGER...
...IS LIKE AN EXTENSION OF THAT, FUJINUMA-SAN.
AH HA HA!
"POKING MY NOSE"... CUT DOWN WITH A SINGLE STROKE.
I WASN'T EXACTLY "PLAYING" THOUGH...
I PROBABLY SHOULDN'T SAY THIS, SINCE YOU DID SAVE MY LIFE...
?
FUJINUMA-SAN, ARE YOU...
...THE GRIM REAPER?

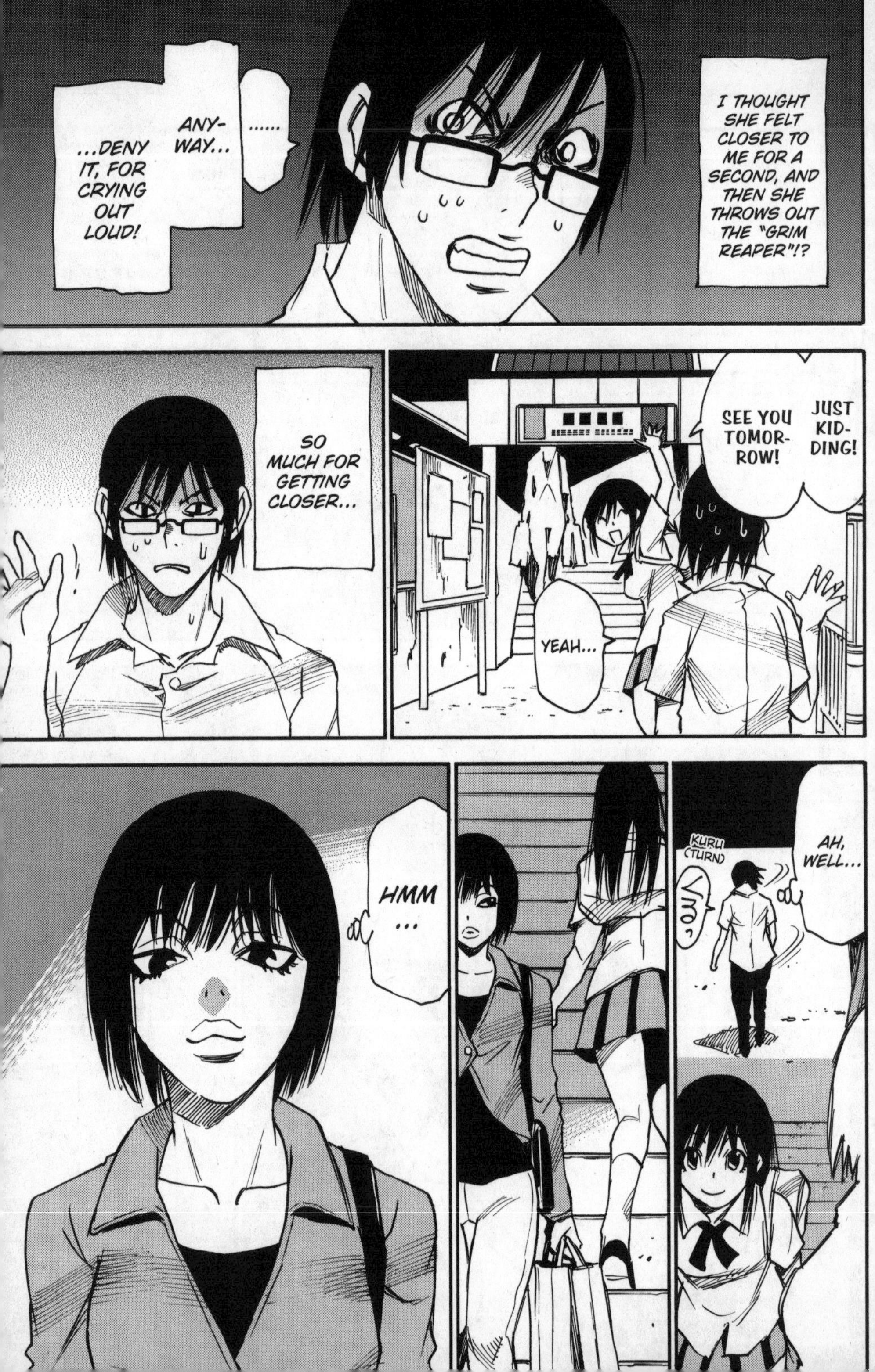
I THOUGHT SHE FELT CLOSER TO ME FOR A SECOND, AND THEN SHE THROWS OUT THE "GRIM REAPER"!?
......
ANY-WAY...
...DENY IT, FOR CRYING OUT LOUD!
JUST KID-DING!
SEE YOU TOMOR-ROW!
YEAH...
SO MUCH FOR GETTING CLOSER...
AH, WELL...
KURU (TURN)
HMM ...

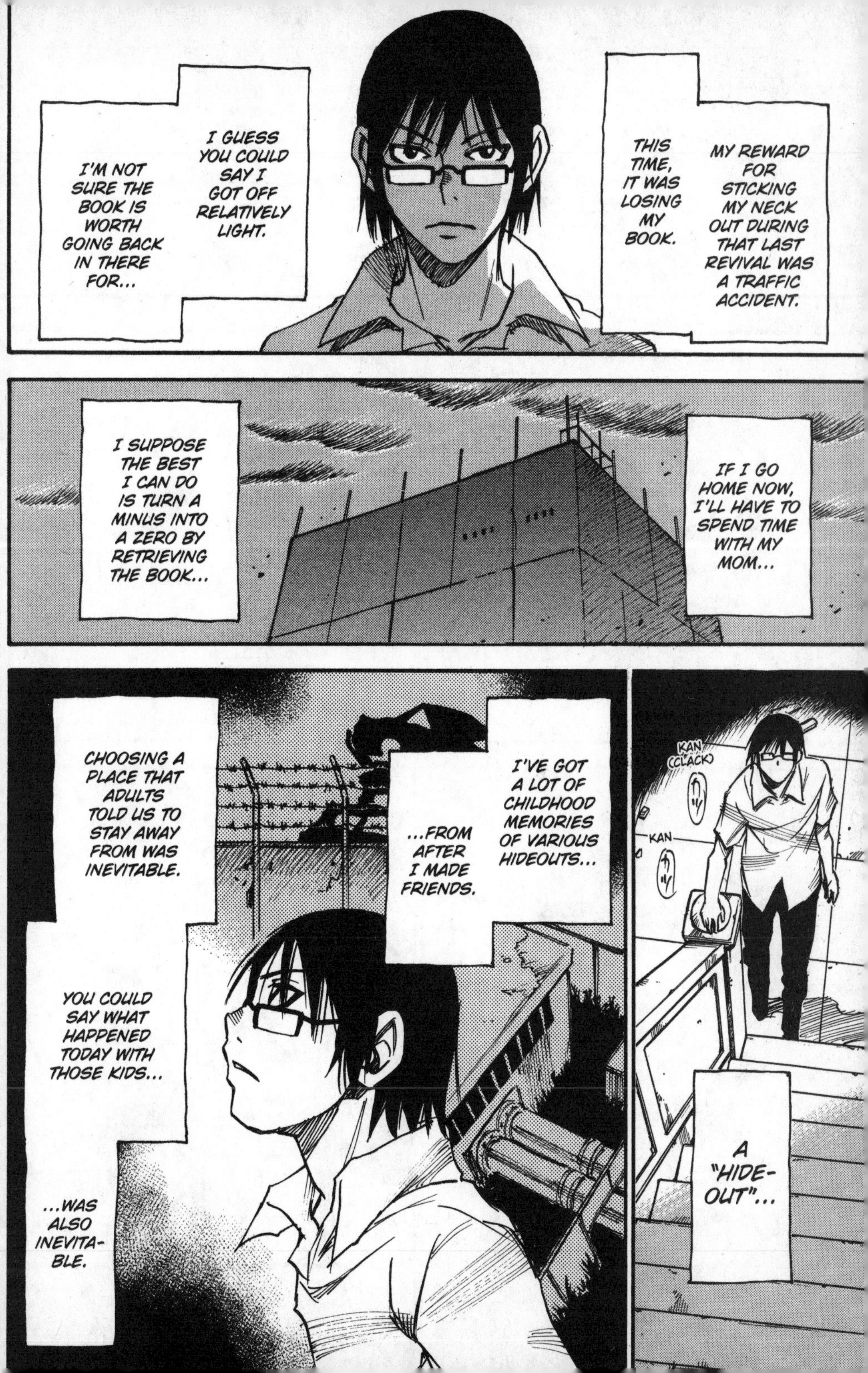
MY REWARD FOR STICKING MY NECK OUT DURING THAT LAST REVIVAL WAS A TRAFFIC ACCIDENT.
THIS TIME, IT WAS LOSING MY BOOK.
I GUESS YOU COULD SAY I GOT OFF RELATIVELY LIGHT.
I'M NOT SURE THE BOOK IS WORTH GOING BACK IN THERE FOR...
IF I GO HOME NOW, I'LL HAVE TO SPEND TIME WITH MY MOM...
I SUPPOSE THE BEST I CAN DO IS TURN A MINUS INTO A ZERO BY RETRIEVING THE BOOK...
KAN (CLACK)
KAN
A "HIDE-OUT"...
I'VE GOT A LOT OF CHILDHOOD MEMORIES OF VARIOUS HIDEOUTS...
...FROM AFTER I MADE FRIENDS.
CHOOSING A PLACE THAT ADULTS TOLD US TO STAY AWAY FROM WAS INEVITABLE.
YOU COULD SAY WHAT HAPPENED TODAY WITH THOSE KIDS...
...WAS ALSO INEVITA-BLE.

"A PLACE THAT'S ONLY SPECIAL TO KIDS."

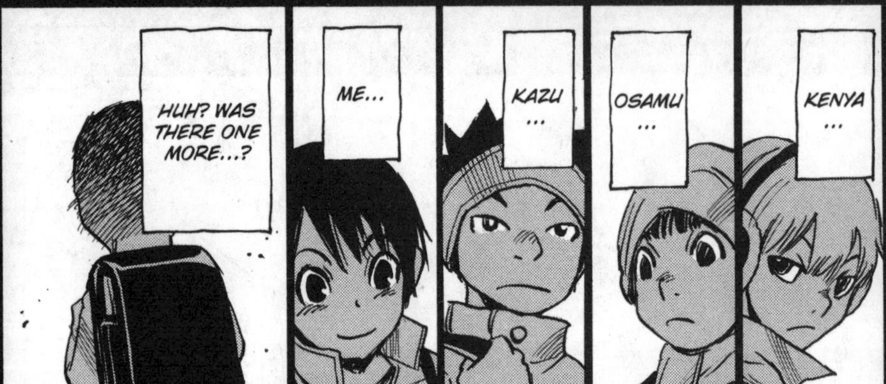
KENYA...
OSAMU...
KAZU...
ME...
HUH? WAS THERE ONE MORE...?
MY MOM WILL GET MAD AT ME.
WE'LL ALL BE GOING, SO IT'S OKAY.
I'M SCARED...
WE HAVEN'T BEEN TO THE HIDEOUT IN A LONG TIME.
......
LET'S MUSTER UP OUR COURAGE AND GO!
......

HE STOPPED COMING TO THE HIDEOUT AFTER THAT FIRST INCIDENT...

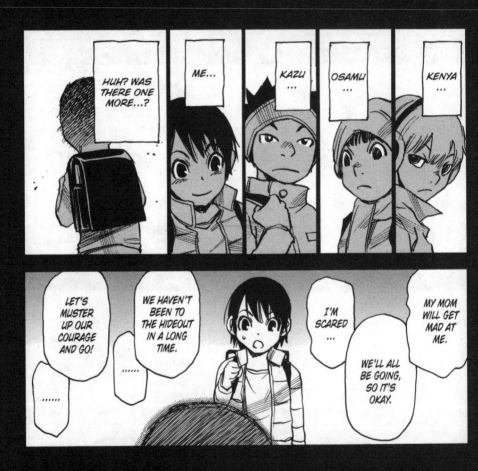

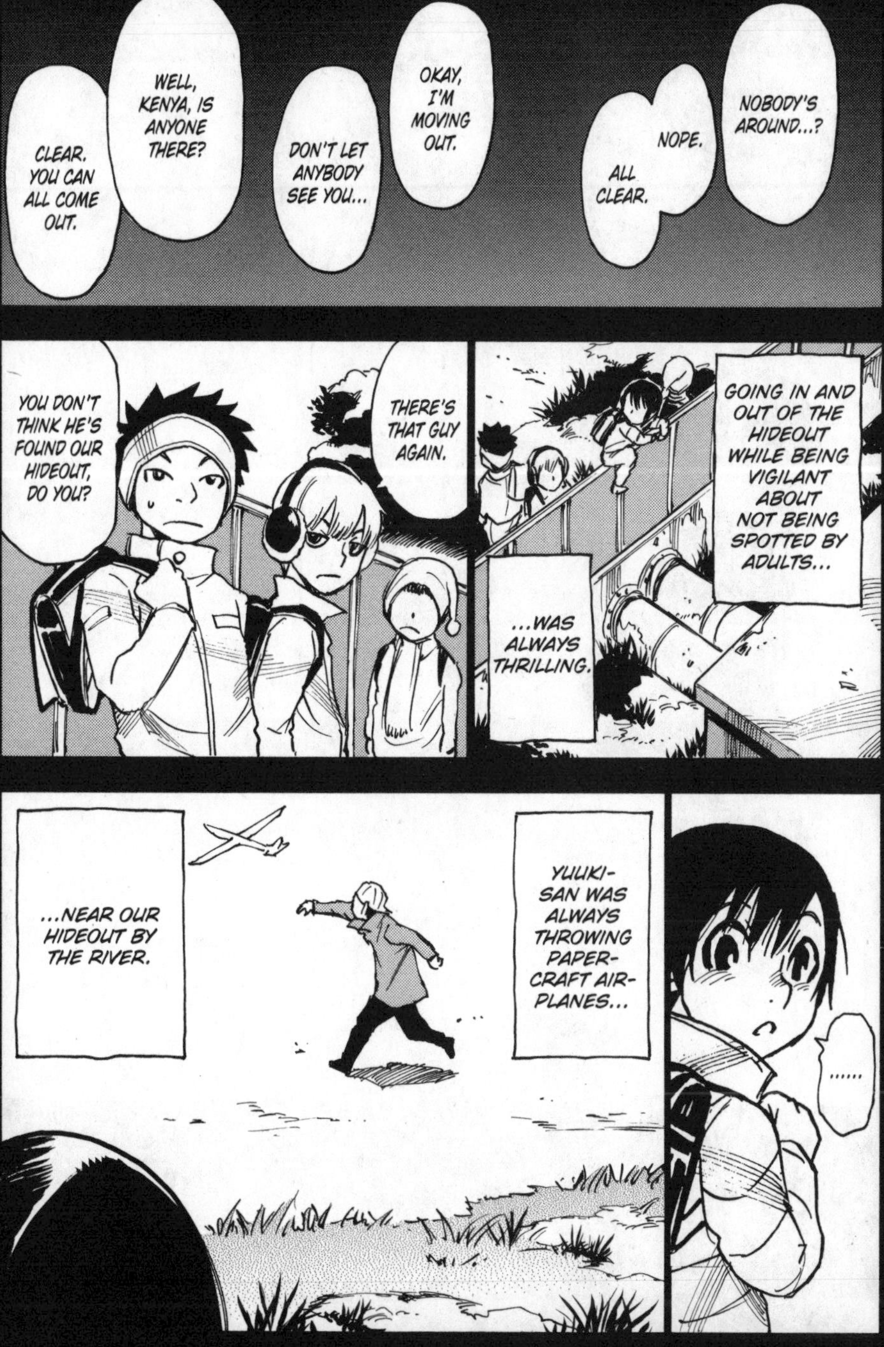
NOBODY'S AROUND...?
NOPE.
ALL CLEAR.
OKAY, I'M MOVING OUT.
DON'T LET ANYBODY SEE YOU...
WELL, KENYA, IS ANYONE THERE?
CLEAR. YOU CAN ALL COME OUT.
GOING IN AND OUT OF THE HIDEOUT WHILE BEING VIGILANT ABOUT NOT BEING SPOTTED BY ADULTS...
...WAS ALWAYS THRILLING.
THERE'S THAT GUY AGAIN.
YOU DON'T THINK HE'S FOUND OUR HIDEOUT, DO YOU?
......
YUUKI-SAN WAS ALWAYS THROWING PAPER-CRAFT AIR-PLANES...
...NEAR OUR HIDEOUT BY THE RIVER.

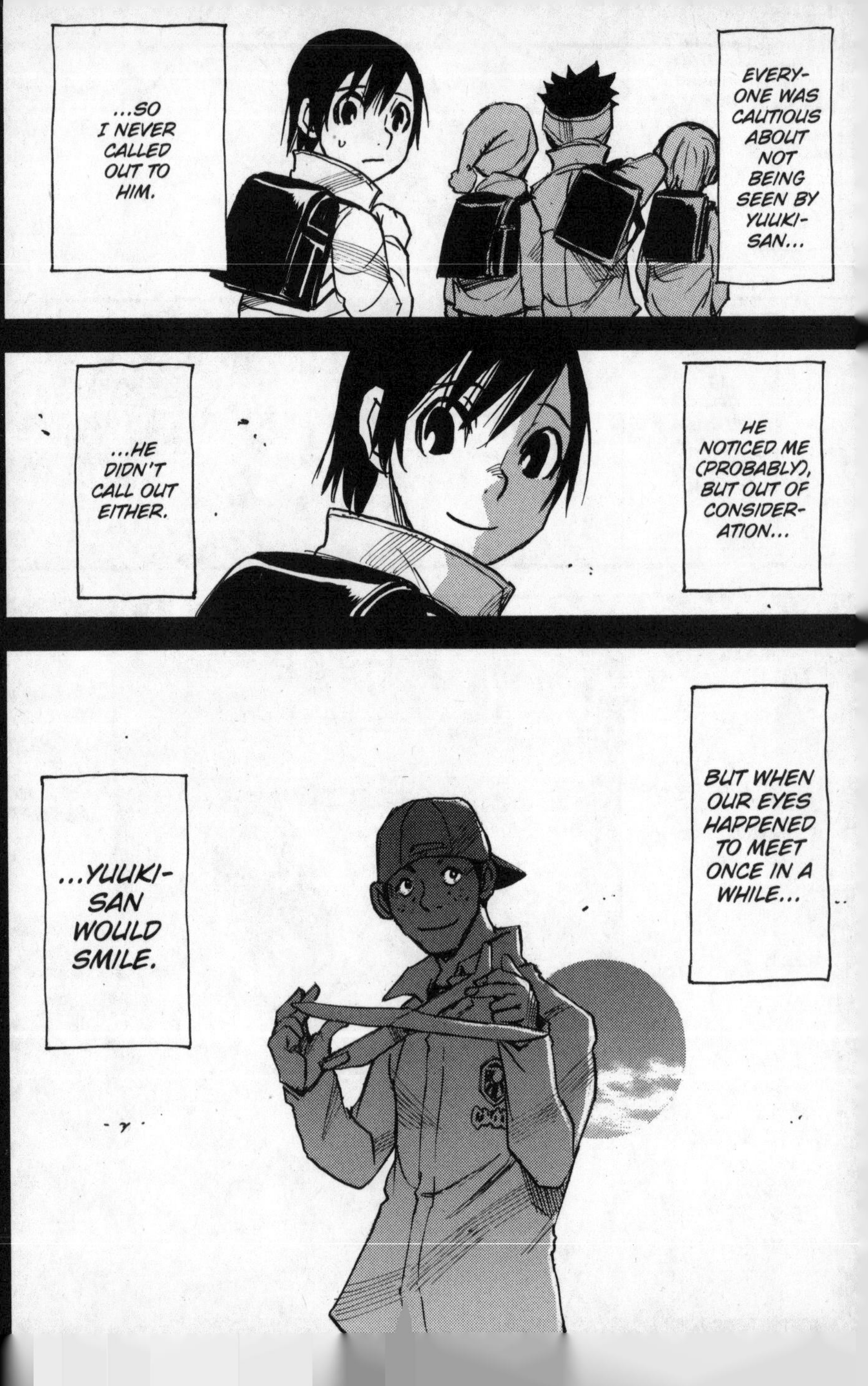
EVERYONE WAS CAUTIOUS ABOUT NOT BEING SEEN BY YUUKI-SAN...
...SO I NEVER CALLED OUT TO HIM.
HE NOTICED ME (PROBABLY), BUT OUT OF CONSIDERATION...
...HE DIDN'T CALL OUT EITHER.
BUT WHEN OUR EYES HAPPENED TO MEET ONCE IN A WHILE...
...YUUKI-SAN WOULD SMILE.

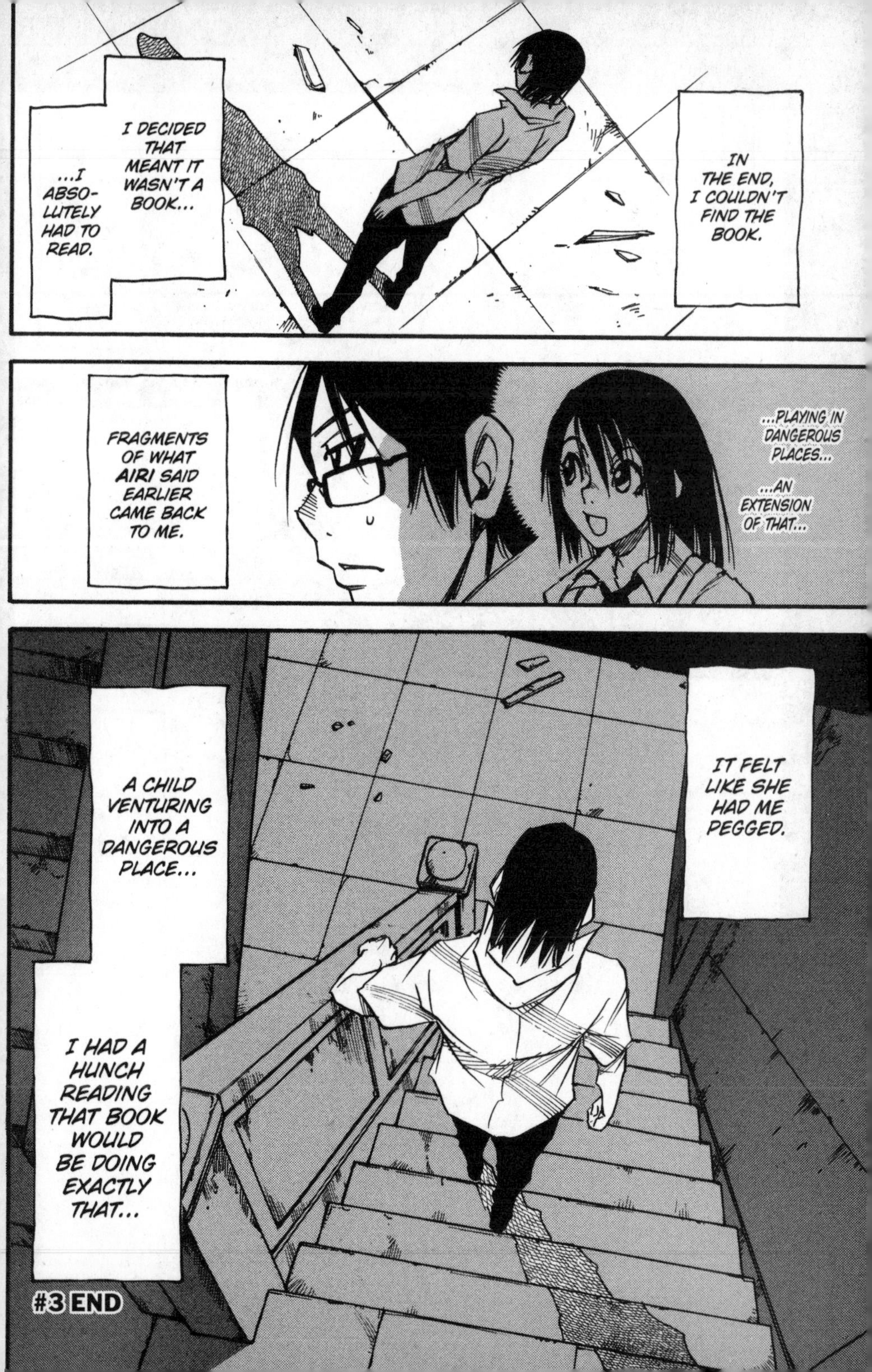
IN THE END, I COULDN'T FIND THE BOOK.
I DECIDED THAT MEANT IT WASN'T A BOOK...
...I ABSOLUTELY HAD TO READ.
...PLAYING IN DANGEROUS PLACES...
...AN EXTENSION OF THAT...
FRAGMENTS OF WHAT AIRI SAID EARLIER CAME BACK TO ME.
IT FELT LIKE SHE HAD ME PEGGED.
A CHILD VENTURING INTO A DANGEROUS PLACE...
I HAD A HUNCH READING THAT BOOK WOULD BE DOING EXACTLY THAT...
#3 END

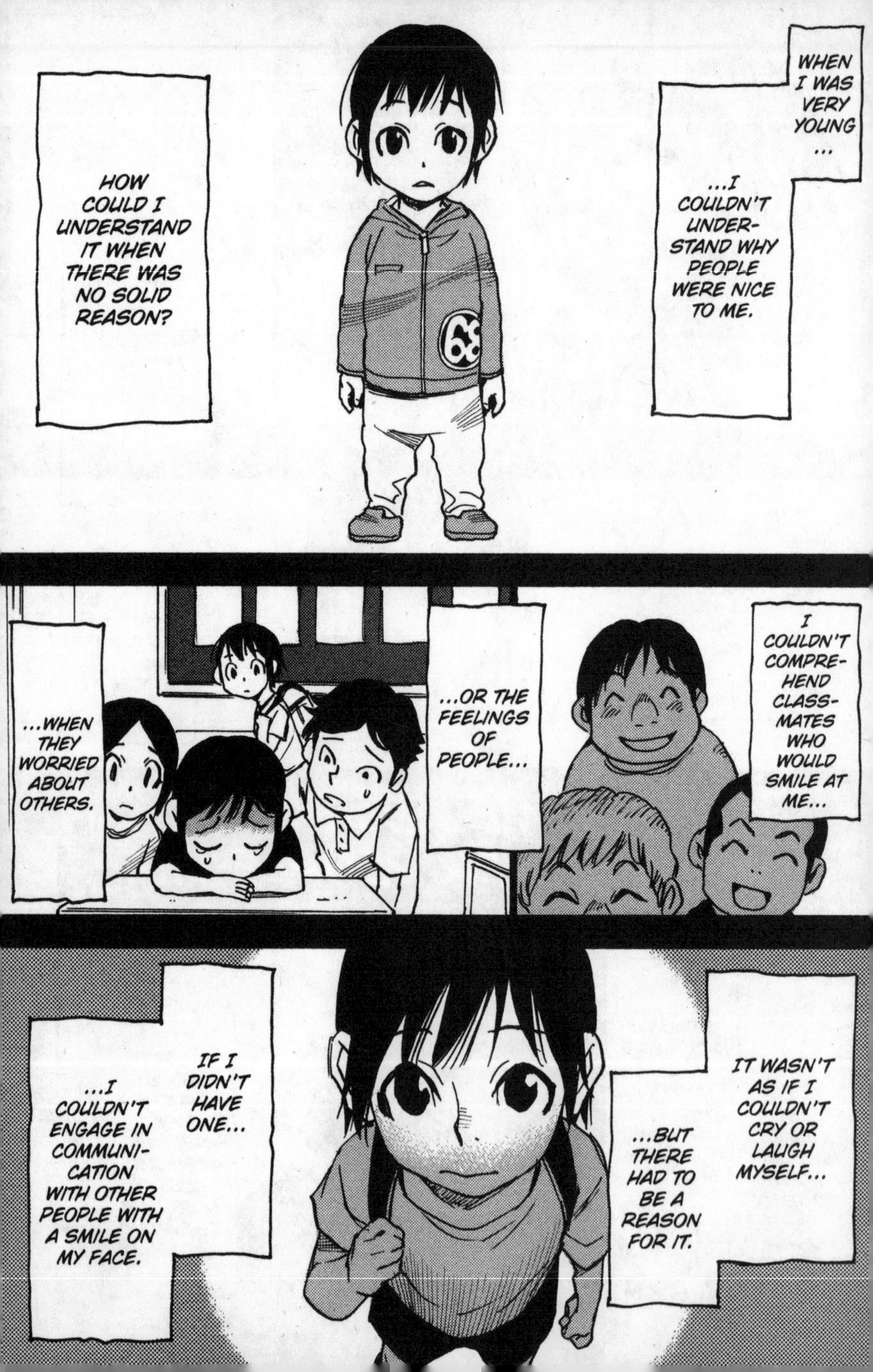
WHEN I WAS VERY YOUNG...
...I COULDN'T UNDER-STAND WHY PEOPLE WERE NICE TO ME.
HOW COULD I UNDERSTAND IT WHEN THERE WAS NO SOLID REASON?
I COULDN'T COMPRE-HEND CLASS-MATES WHO WOULD SMILE AT ME...
...OR THE FEELINGS OF PEOPLE...
...WHEN THEY WORRIED ABOUT OTHERS.
IT WASN'T AS IF I COULDN'T CRY OR LAUGH MYSELF...
...BUT THERE HAD TO BE A REASON FOR IT.
IF I DIDN'T HAVE ONE...
...I COULDN'T ENGAGE IN COMMUNI-CATION WITH OTHER PEOPLE WITH A SMILE ON MY FACE.

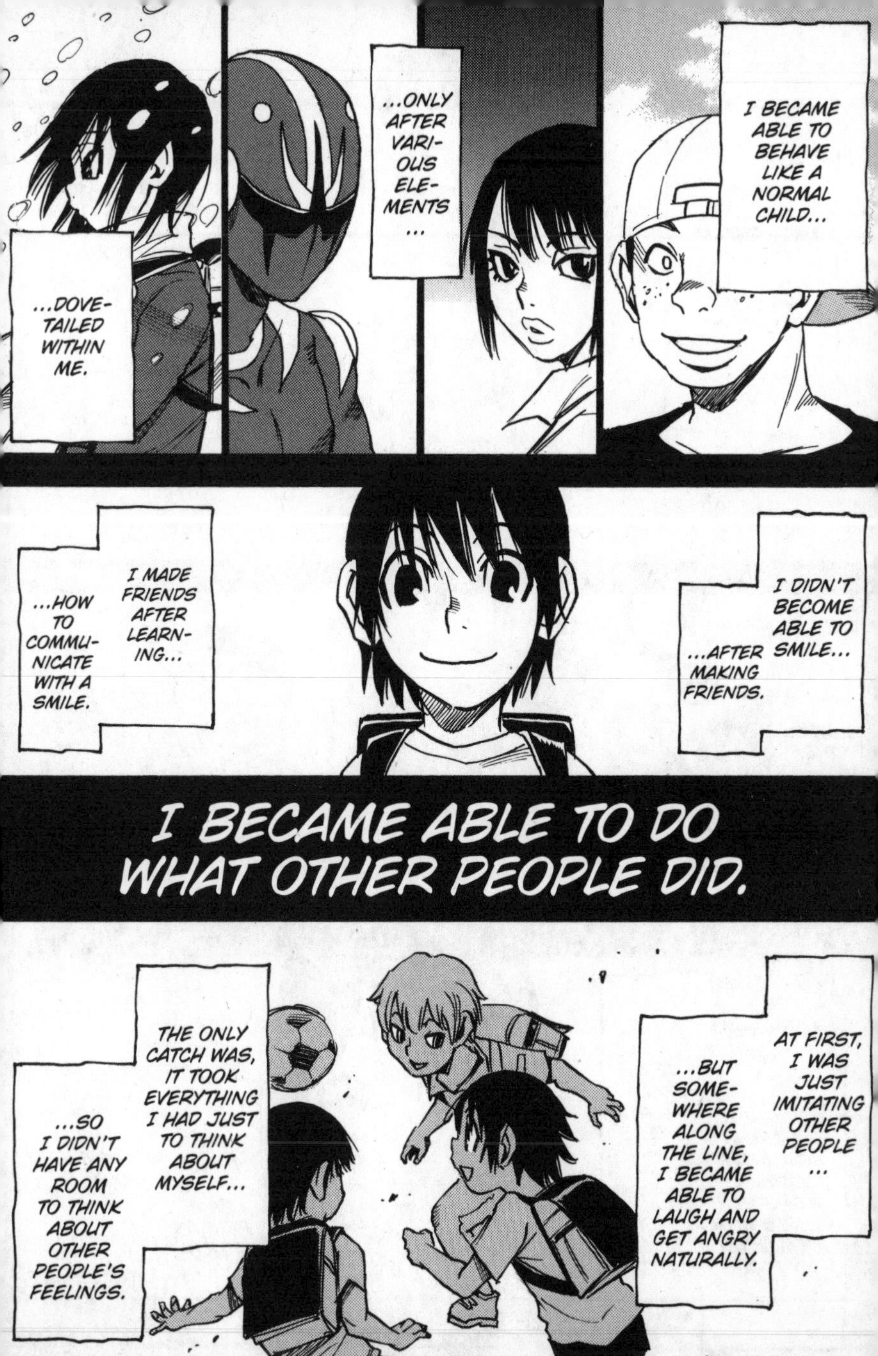

I BECAME ABLE TO BEHAVE LIKE A NORMAL CHILD...
...ONLY AFTER VARI-OUS ELE-MENTS...
...DOVE-TAILED WITHIN ME.
I DIDN'T BECOME ABLE TO SMILE...
...AFTER MAKING FRIENDS.
I MADE FRIENDS AFTER LEARN-ING...
...HOW TO COMMU-NICATE WITH A SMILE.
I BECAME ABLE TO DO WHAT OTHER PEOPLE DID.
AT FIRST, I WAS JUST IMITATING OTHER PEOPLE...
...BUT SOME-WHERE ALONG THE LINE, I BECAME ABLE TO LAUGH AND GET ANGRY NATURALLY.
THE ONLY CATCH WAS, IT TOOK EVERYTHING I HAD JUST TO THINK ABOUT MYSELF...
...SO I DIDN'T HAVE ANY ROOM TO THINK ABOUT OTHER PEOPLE'S FEELINGS.

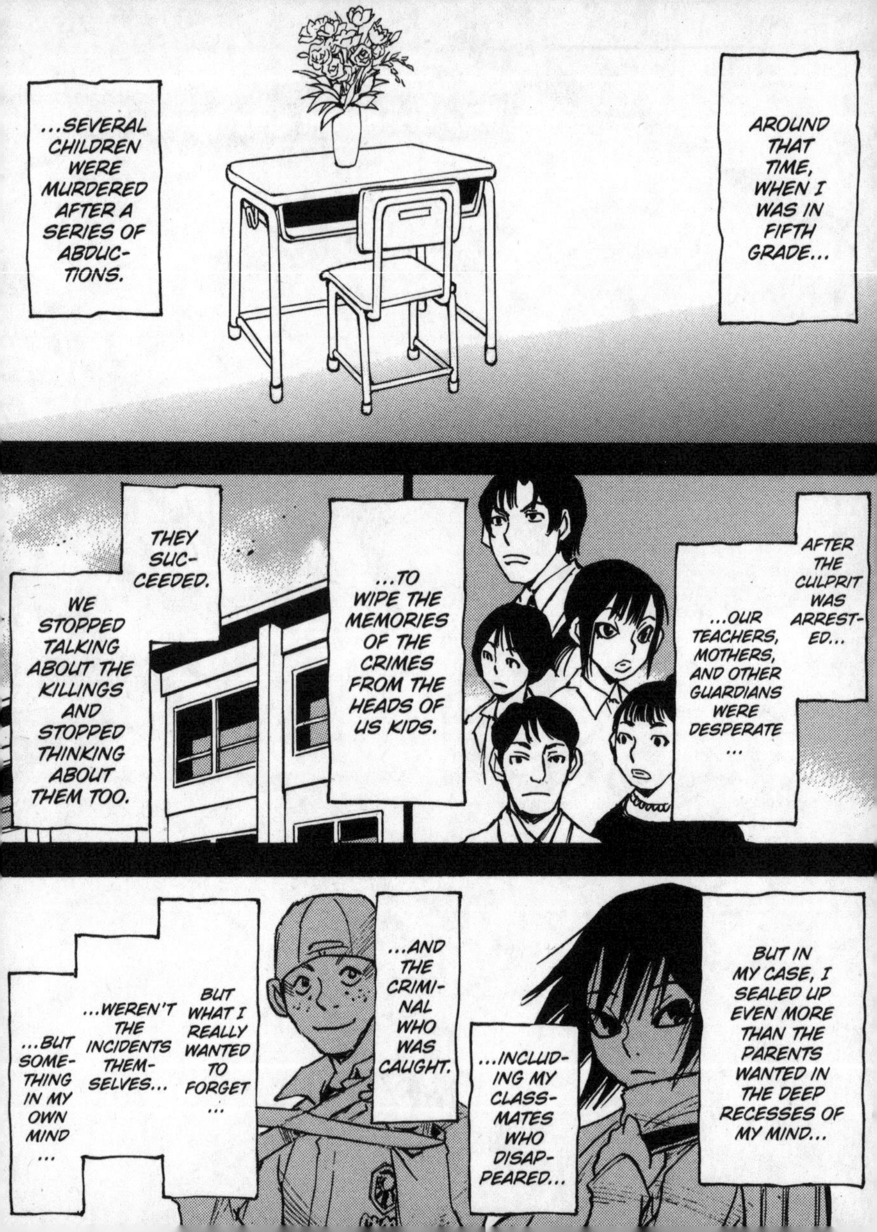
AROUND THAT TIME, WHEN I WAS IN FIFTH GRADE...
...SEVERAL CHILDREN WERE MURDERED AFTER A SERIES OF ABDUCTIONS.
AFTER THE CULPRIT WAS ARRESTED...
...OUR TEACHERS, MOTHERS, AND OTHER GUARDIANS WERE DESPERATE...
...TO WIPE THE MEMORIES OF THE CRIMES FROM THE HEADS OF US KIDS.
THEY SUCCEEDED.
WE STOPPED TALKING ABOUT THE KILLINGS AND STOPPED THINKING ABOUT THEM TOO.
BUT IN MY CASE, I SEALED UP EVEN MORE THAN THE PARENTS WANTED IN THE DEEP RECESSES OF MY MIND...
...INCLUDING MY CLASSMATES WHO DISAPPEARED...
...AND THE CRIMINAL WHO WAS CAUGHT.
BUT WHAT I REALLY WANTED TO FORGET...
...WEREN'T THE INCIDENTS THEMSELVES...
...BUT SOMETHING IN MY OWN MIND...

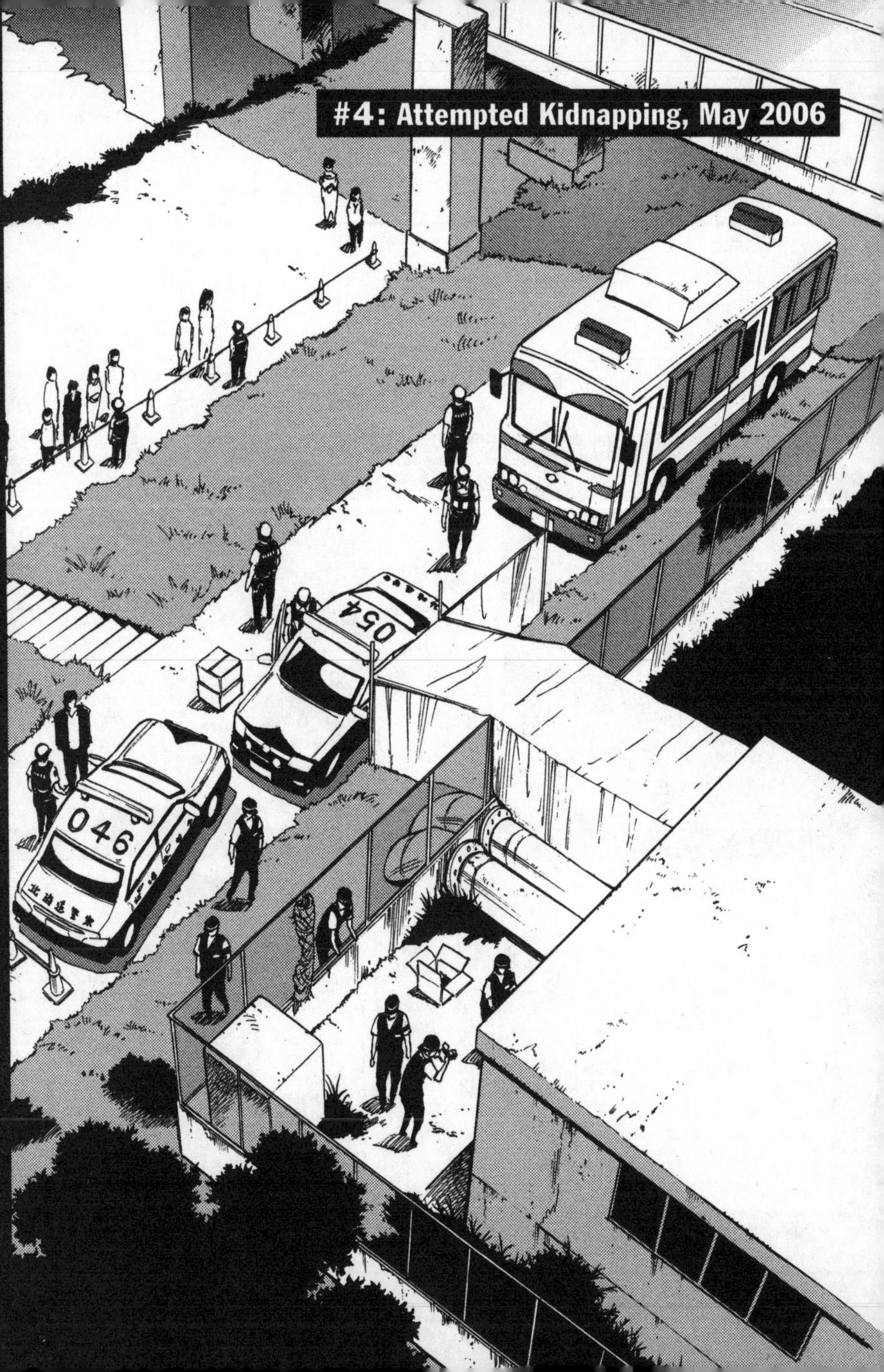
#4: Attempted Kidnapping, May 2006
054
046

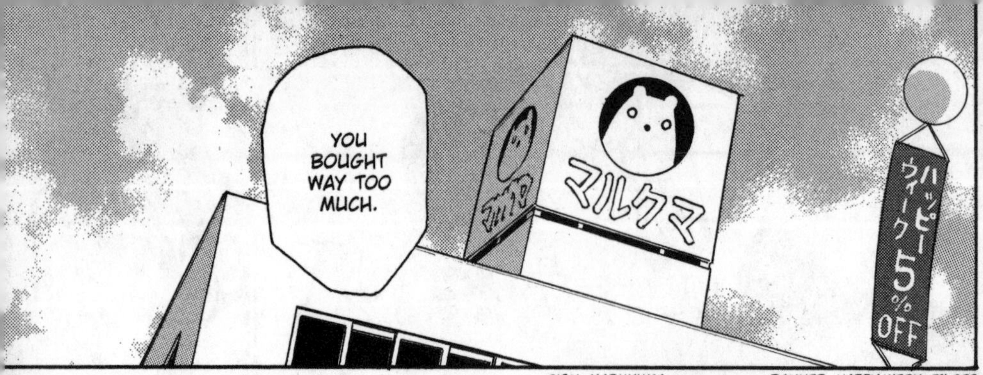
YOU BOUGHT WAY TOO MUCH.
マルクマ
ハッピーウィーク 5% OFF

SIGN: MARUKUMA BANNER: HAPPY WEEK, 5% OFF

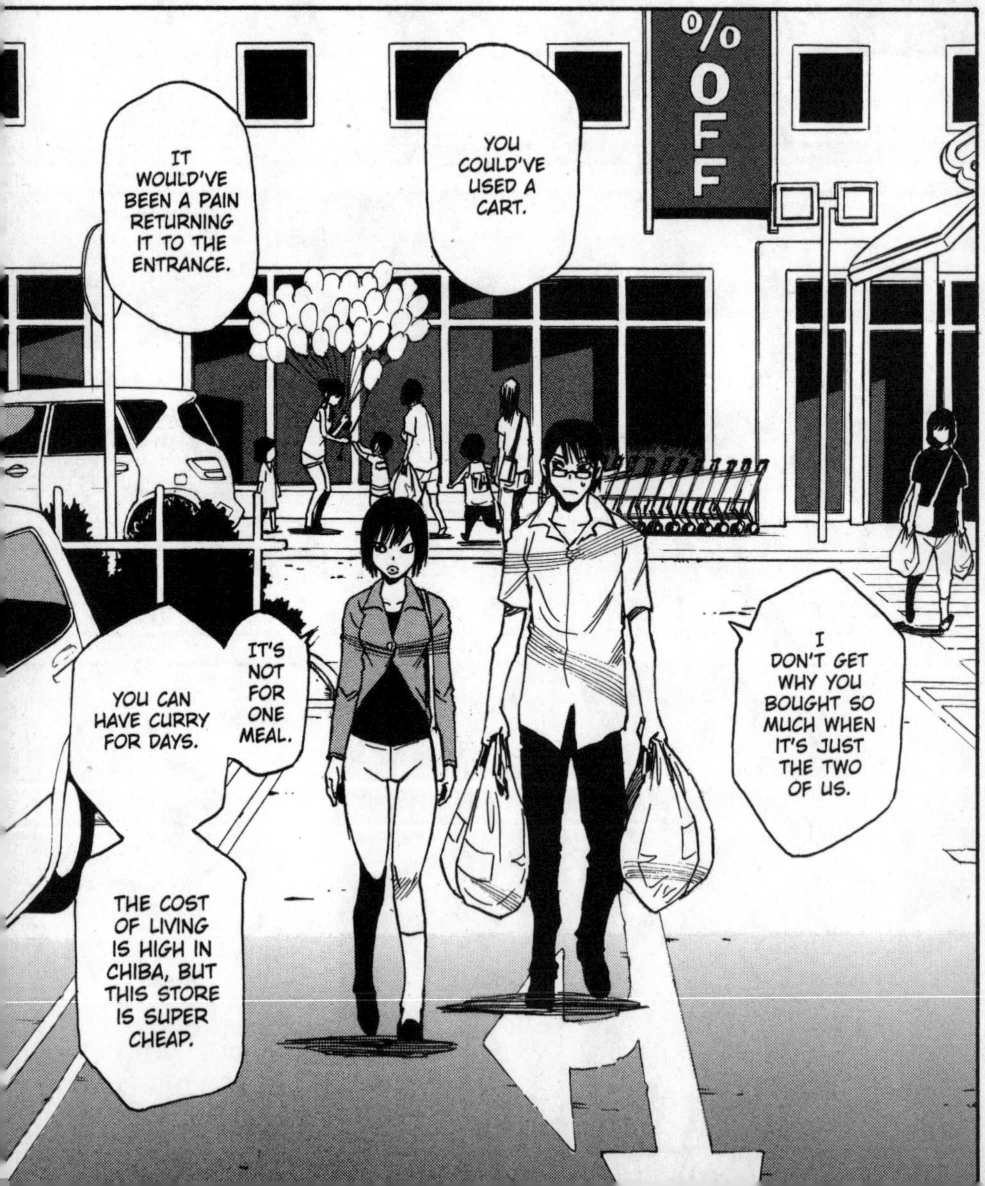
% OFF
YOU COULD'VE USED A CART.
IT WOULD'VE BEEN A PAIN RETURNING IT TO THE ENTRANCE.
I DON'T GET WHY YOU BOUGHT SO MUCH WHEN IT'S JUST THE TWO OF US.
IT'S NOT FOR ONE MEAL.
YOU CAN HAVE CURRY FOR DAYS.
THE COST OF LIVING IS HIGH IN CHIBA, BUT THIS STORE IS SUPER CHEAP.

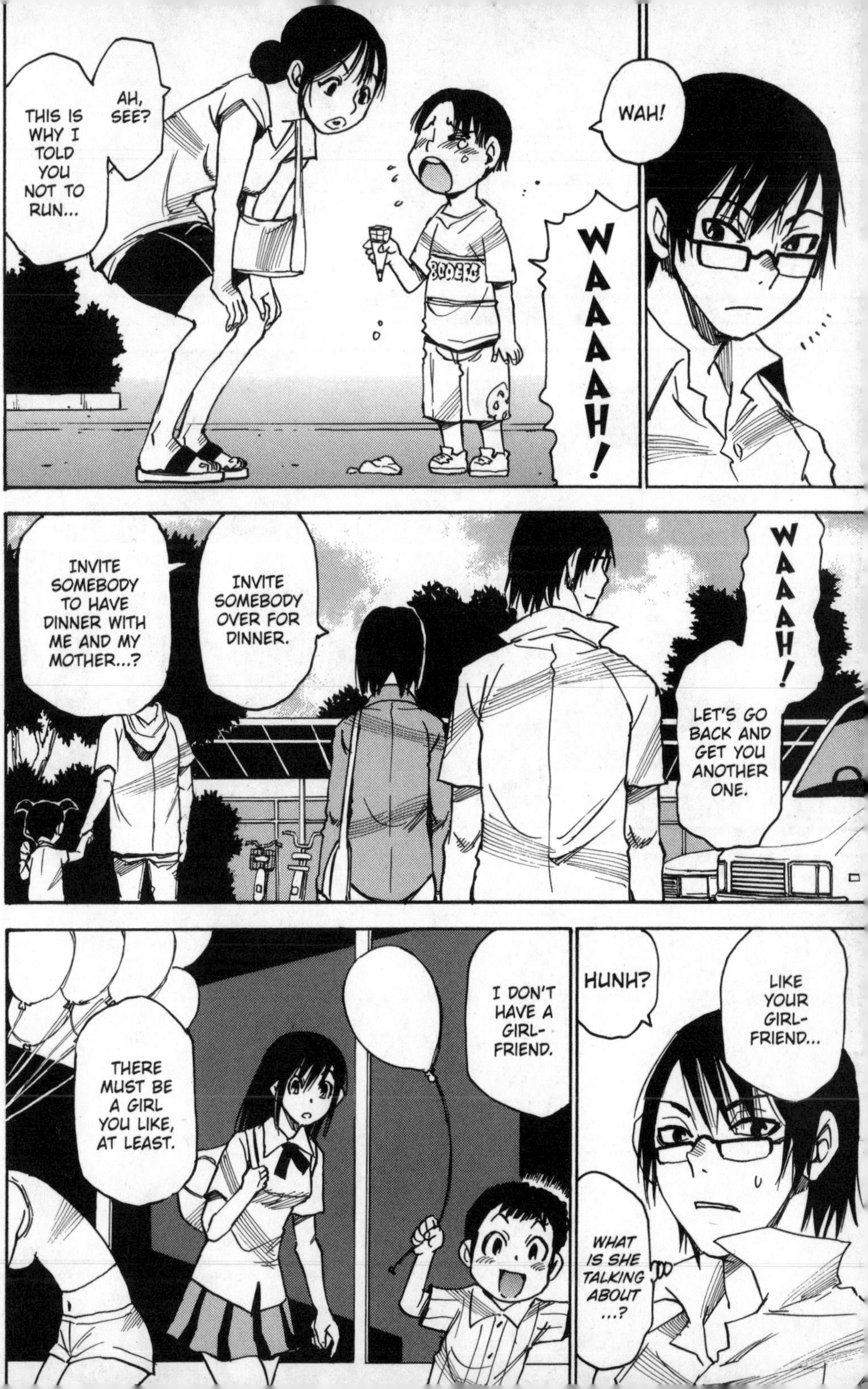
WAH!
WAAAAAH!
AH, SEE?
THIS IS WHY I TOLD YOU NOT TO RUN...
WAAAAH!
LET'S GO BACK AND GET YOU ANOTHER ONE.
INVITE SOMEBODY OVER FOR DINNER.
INVITE SOMEBODY TO HAVE DINNER WITH ME AND MY MOTHER...?
LIKE YOUR GIRL-FRIEND...
HUNH?
WHAT IS SHE TALKING ABOUT ...?
I DON'T HAVE A GIRL-FRIEND.
THERE MUST BE A GIRL YOU LIKE, AT LEAST.

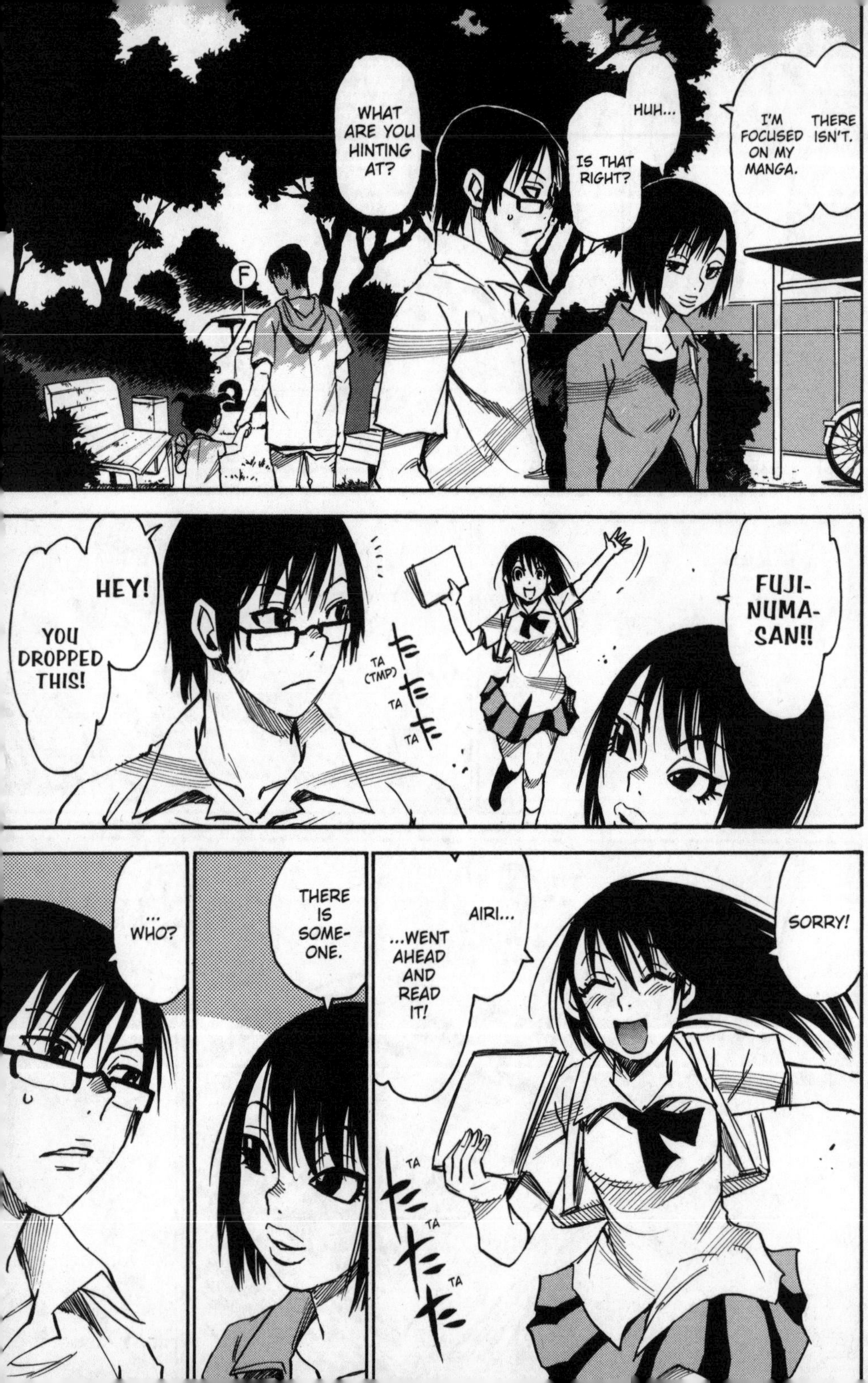
THERE ISN'T. I'M FOCUSED ON MY MANGA.
HUH... IS THAT RIGHT?
WHAT ARE YOU HINTING AT?
FUJI-NUMA-SAN!!
TA (TMP) TA TA
HEY! YOU DROPPED THIS!
SORRY!
AIRI... ...WENT AHEAD AND READ IT!
TA TA TA
THERE IS SOME-ONE.
...WHO?

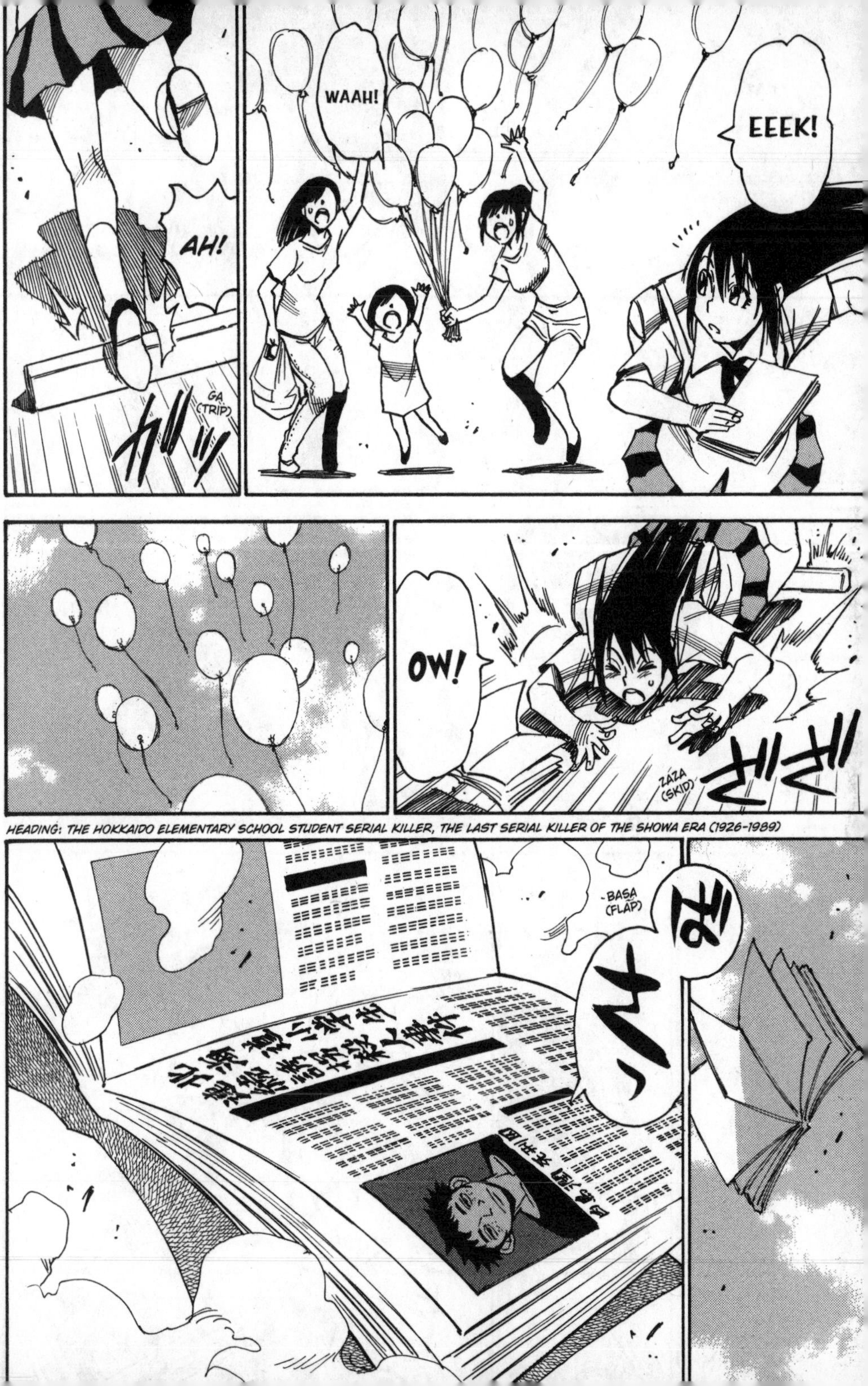
EEEK!
WAAH!
AH!
GA (TRIP)
OW!
ZAZA (SKID)
HEADING: THE HOKKAIDO ELEMENTARY SCHOOL STUDENT SERIAL KILLER, THE LAST SERIAL KILLER OF THE SHOWA ERA (1926-1989)
BASA (FLAP)

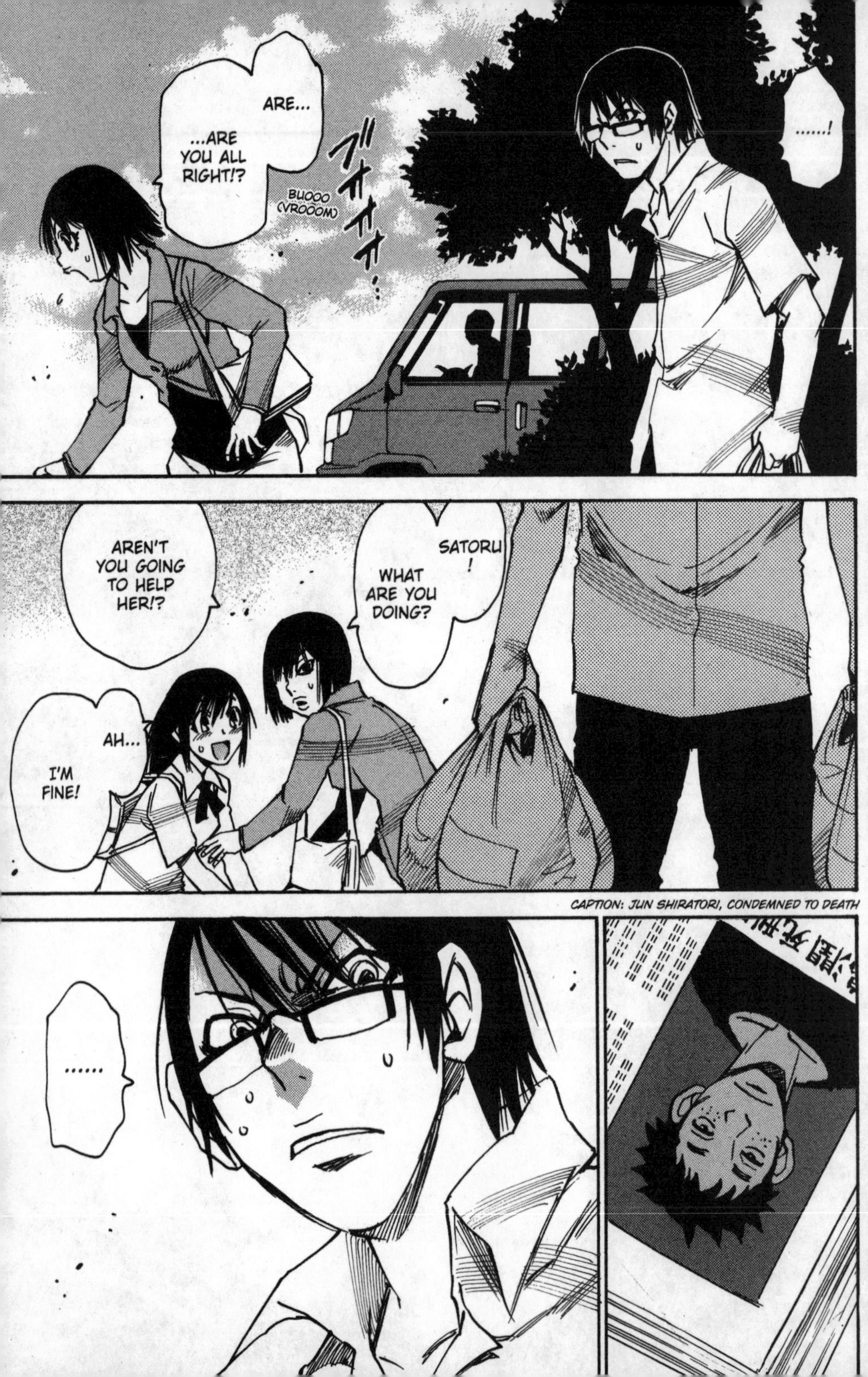
......!
ARE...
...ARE YOU ALL RIGHT!?
BUOOO (VROOOM)
SATORU!
WHAT ARE YOU DOING?
AREN'T YOU GOING TO HELP HER!?
AH...
I'M FINE!
CAPTION: JUN SHIRATORI, CONDEMNED TO DEATH
......

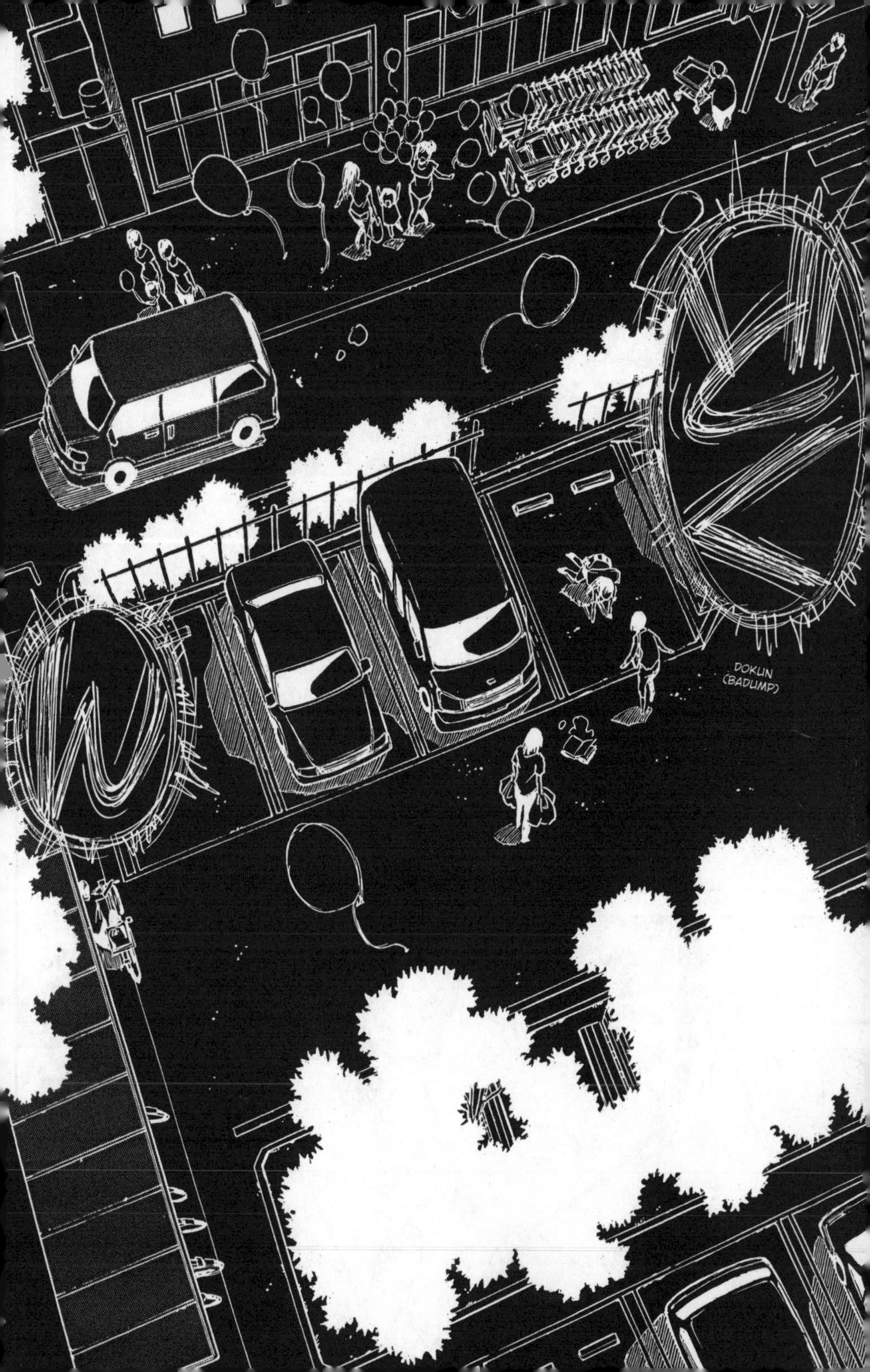
DOKUN
(BADUMP)

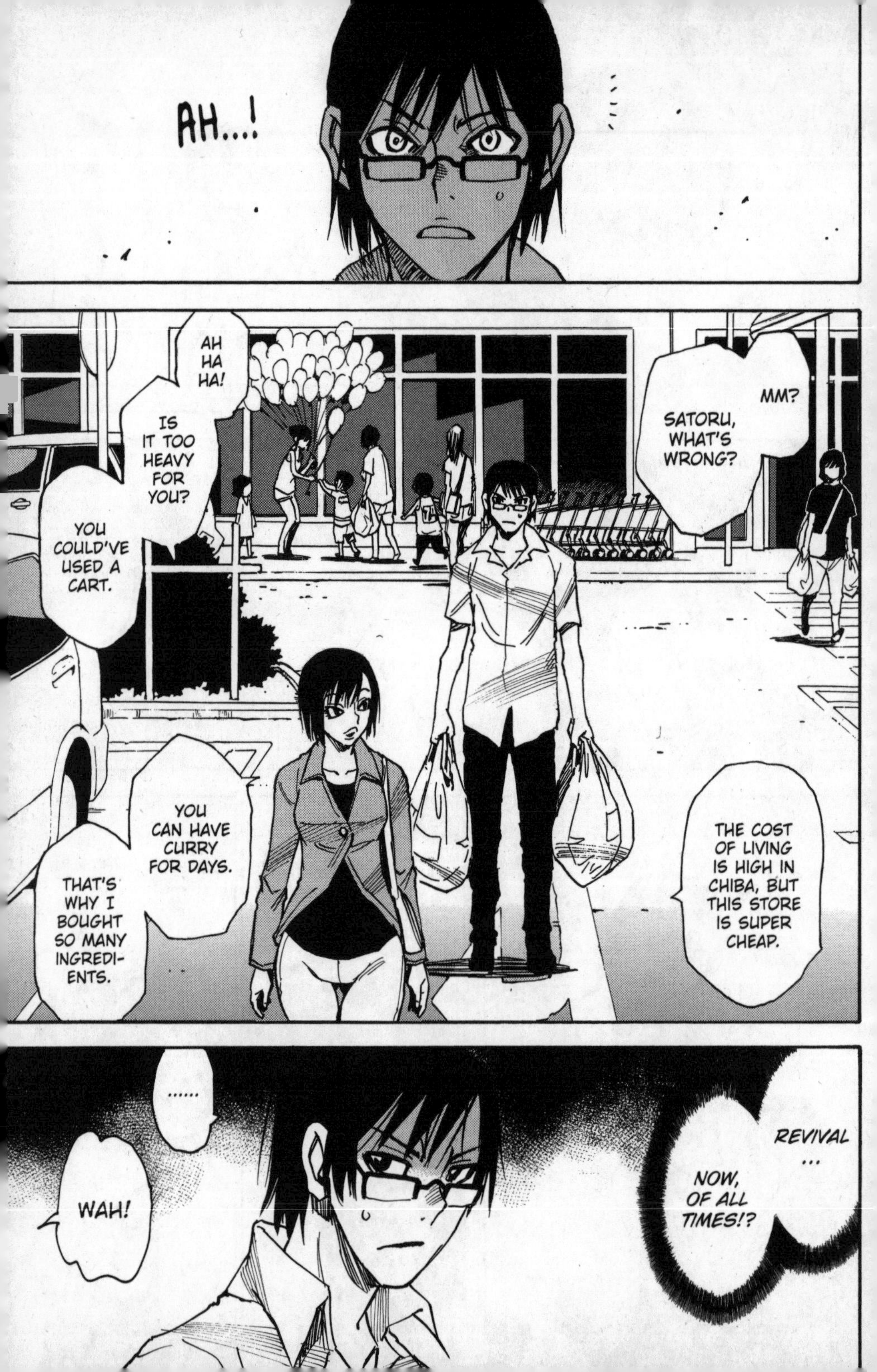
AH...!
MM?
SATORU, WHAT'S WRONG?
AH HA HA!
IS IT TOO HEAVY FOR YOU?
YOU COULD'VE USED A CART.
THE COST OF LIVING IS HIGH IN CHIBA, BUT THIS STORE IS SUPER CHEAP.
YOU CAN HAVE CURRY FOR DAYS.
THAT'S WHY I BOUGHT SO MANY INGREDI-ENTS.
REVIVAL...
NOW, OF ALL TIMES!?
......
WAH!

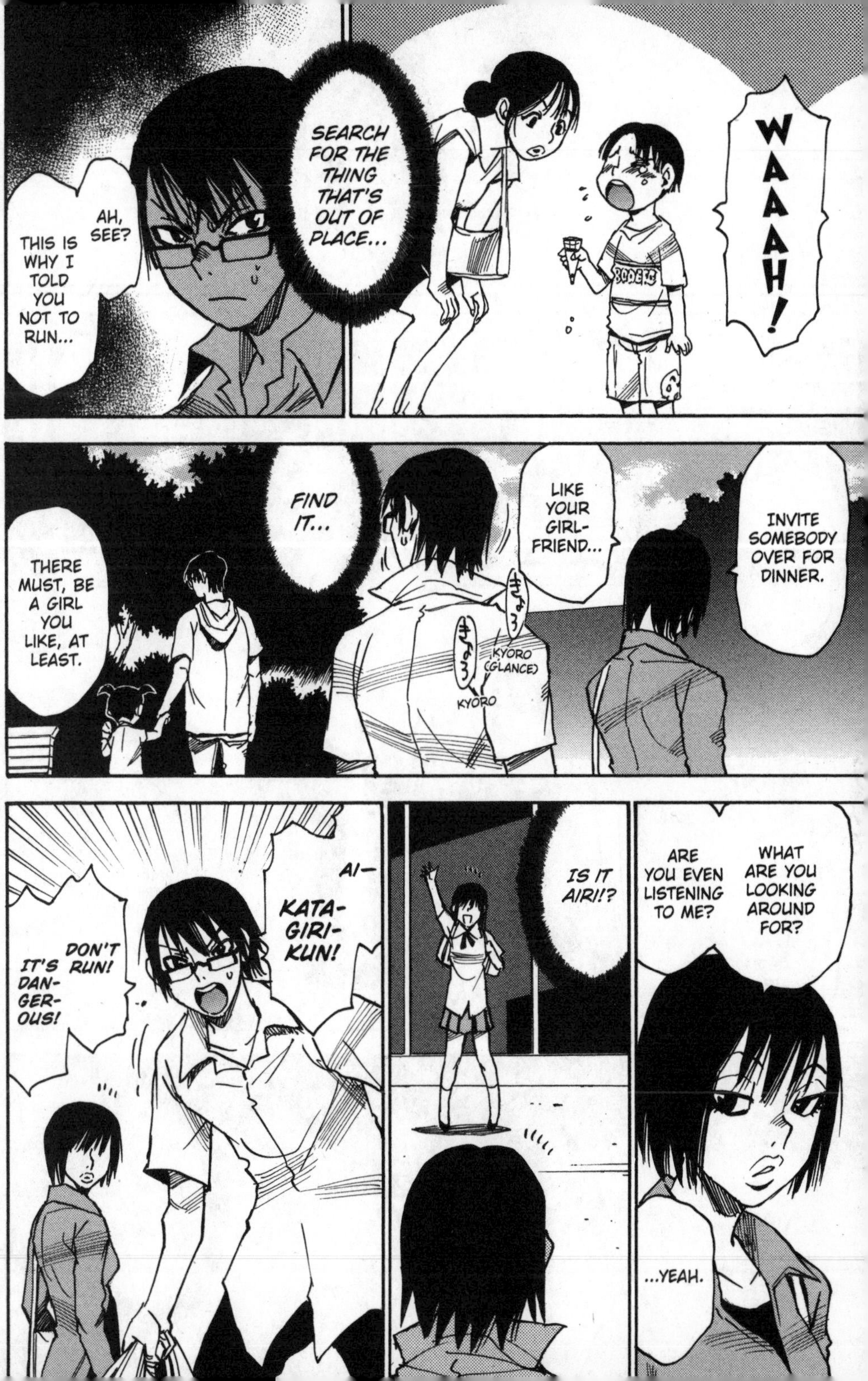
WAAAAH!
SEARCH FOR THE THING THAT'S OUT OF PLACE...
AH, SEE?
THIS IS WHY I TOLD YOU NOT TO RUN...
INVITE SOMEBODY OVER FOR DINNER.
LIKE YOUR GIRL-FRIEND...
きょろ
KYORO (GLANCE)
きょろ
KYORO
FIND IT...
THERE MUST, BE A GIRL YOU LIKE, AT LEAST.
WHAT ARE YOU LOOKING AROUND FOR?
ARE YOU EVEN LISTENING TO ME?
...YEAH.
IS IT AIRI!?
AI—
KATA-GIRI-KUN!
DON'T RUN! IT'S DAN-GER-OUS!

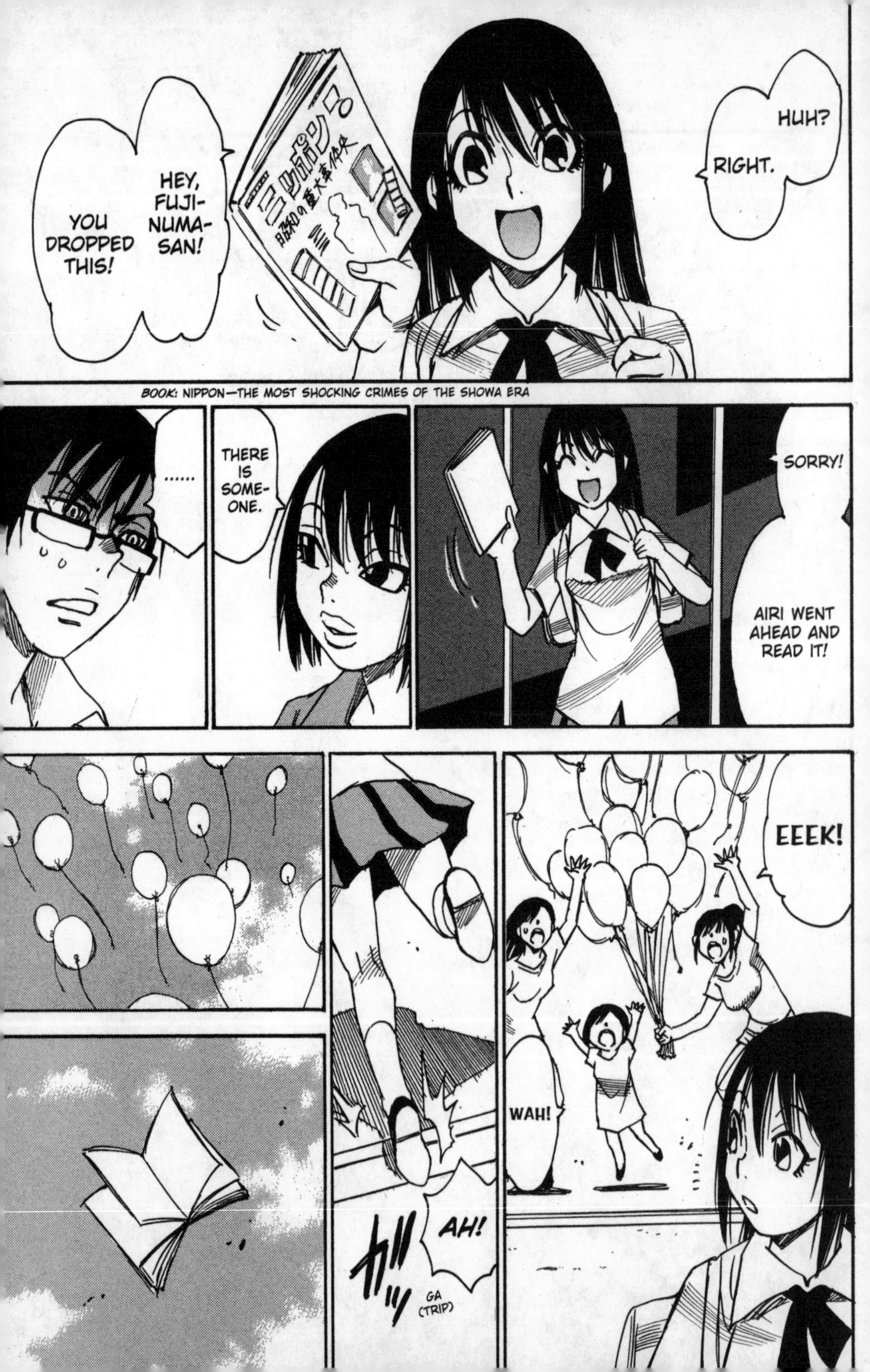
HUH?
RIGHT.
HEY, FUJI-NUMA-SAN!
YOU DROPPED THIS!
BOOK: NIPPON—THE MOST SHOCKING CRIMES OF THE SHOWA ERA
SORRY!
AIRI WENT AHEAD AND READ IT!
THERE IS SOME-ONE.
......
EEEK!
WAH!
AH!
GA (TRIP)

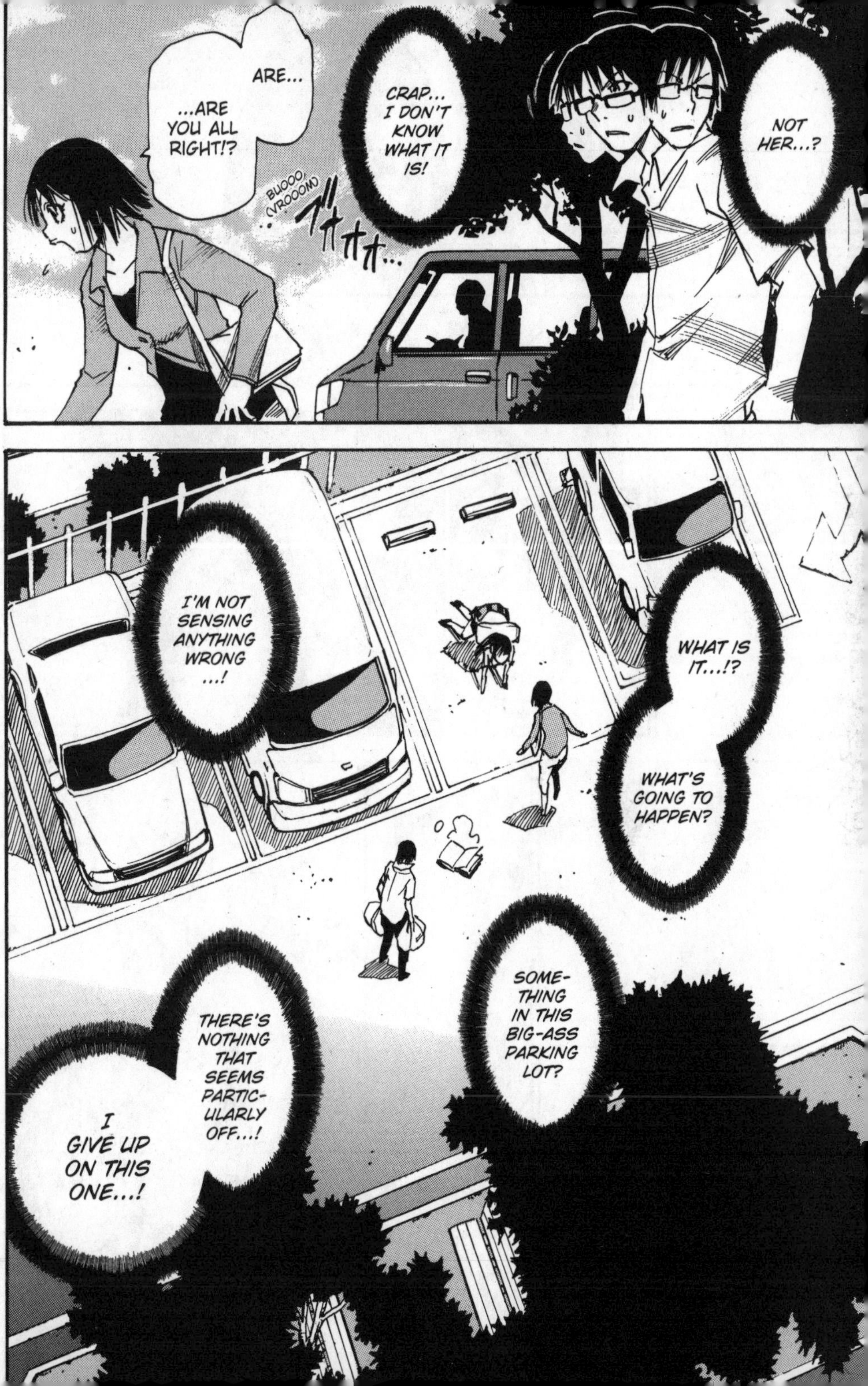
NOT HER...?
CRAP... I DON'T KNOW WHAT IT IS!
BUOOO (VROOOM)
ARE...
...ARE YOU ALL RIGHT!?
WHAT IS IT...!?
WHAT'S GOING TO HAPPEN?
I'M NOT SENSING ANYTHING WRONG ...!
SOME-THING IN THIS BIG-ASS PARKING LOT?
THERE'S NOTHING THAT SEEMS PARTIC-ULARLY OFF...!
I GIVE UP ON THIS ONE...!

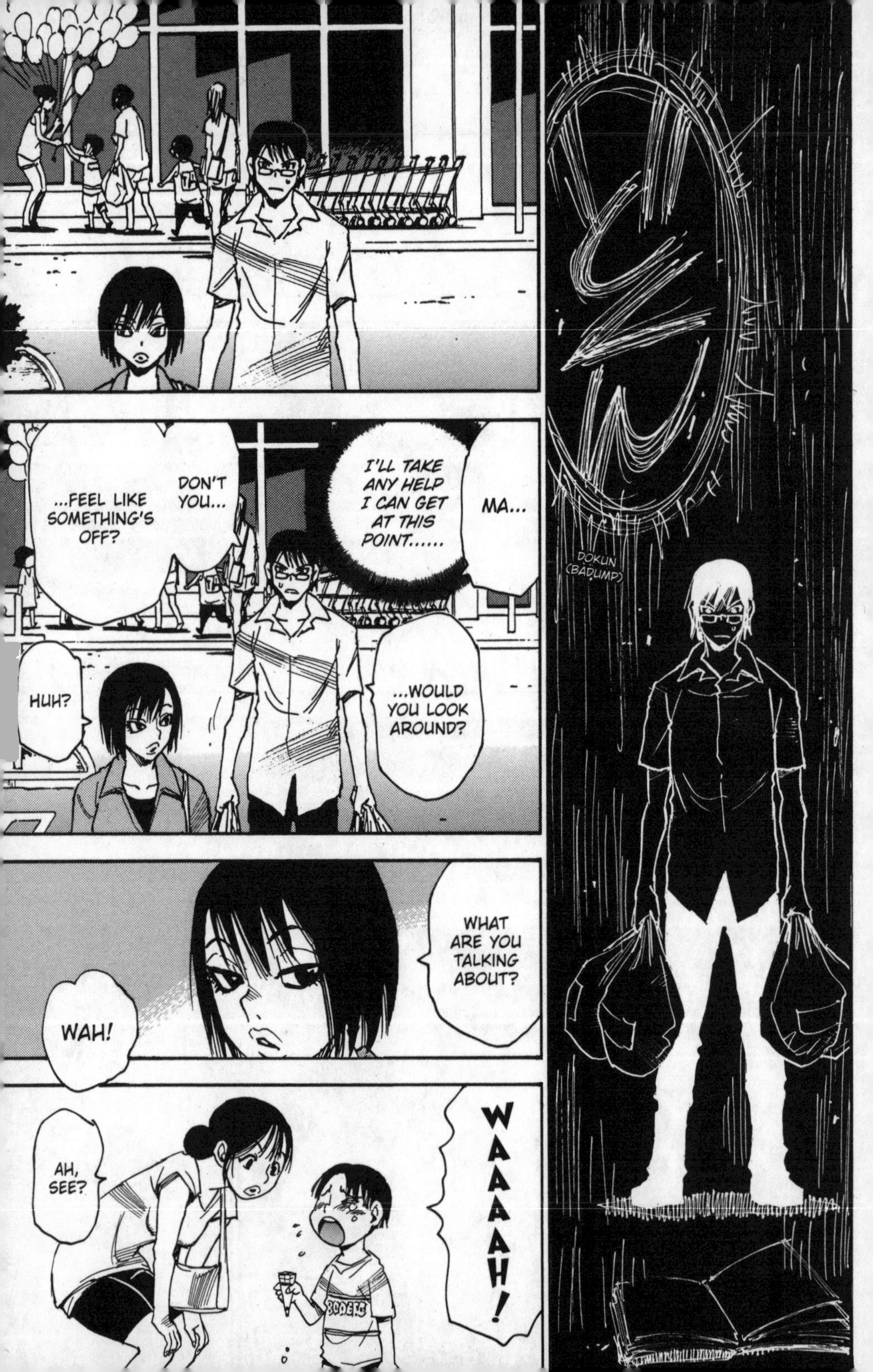
DOKUN
(BADUMP)
MA...
I'LL TAKE ANY HELP I CAN GET AT THIS POINT......
DON'T YOU...
...FEEL LIKE SOMETHING'S OFF?
...WOULD YOU LOOK AROUND?
HUH?
WHAT ARE YOU TALKING ABOUT?
WAH!
WAAAAAH!
AH, SEE?

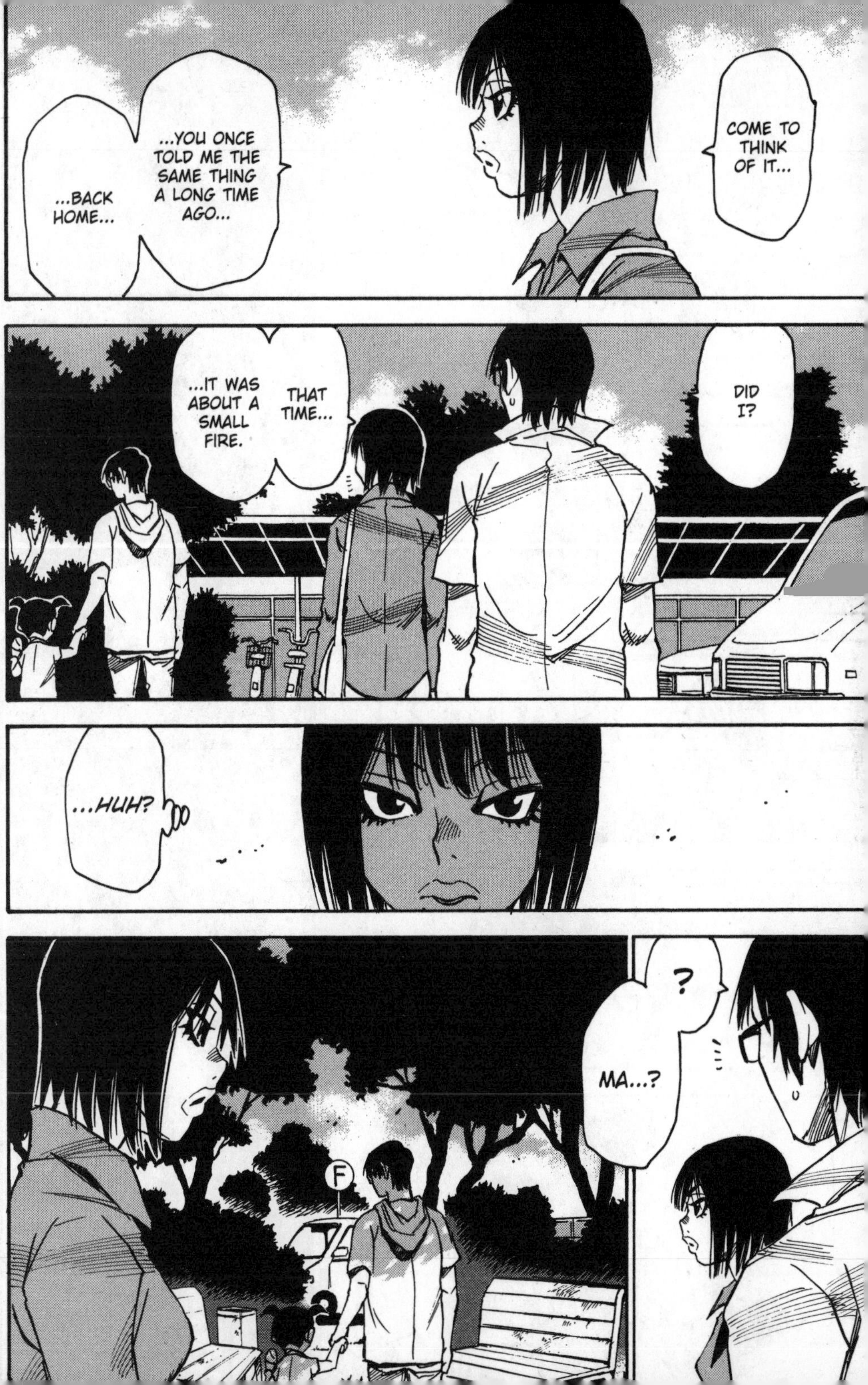
COME TO THINK OF IT...
...YOU ONCE TOLD ME THE SAME THING A LONG TIME AGO...
...BACK HOME...
DID I?
THAT TIME...
...IT WAS ABOUT A SMALL FIRE.
...HUH?
?
MA...?

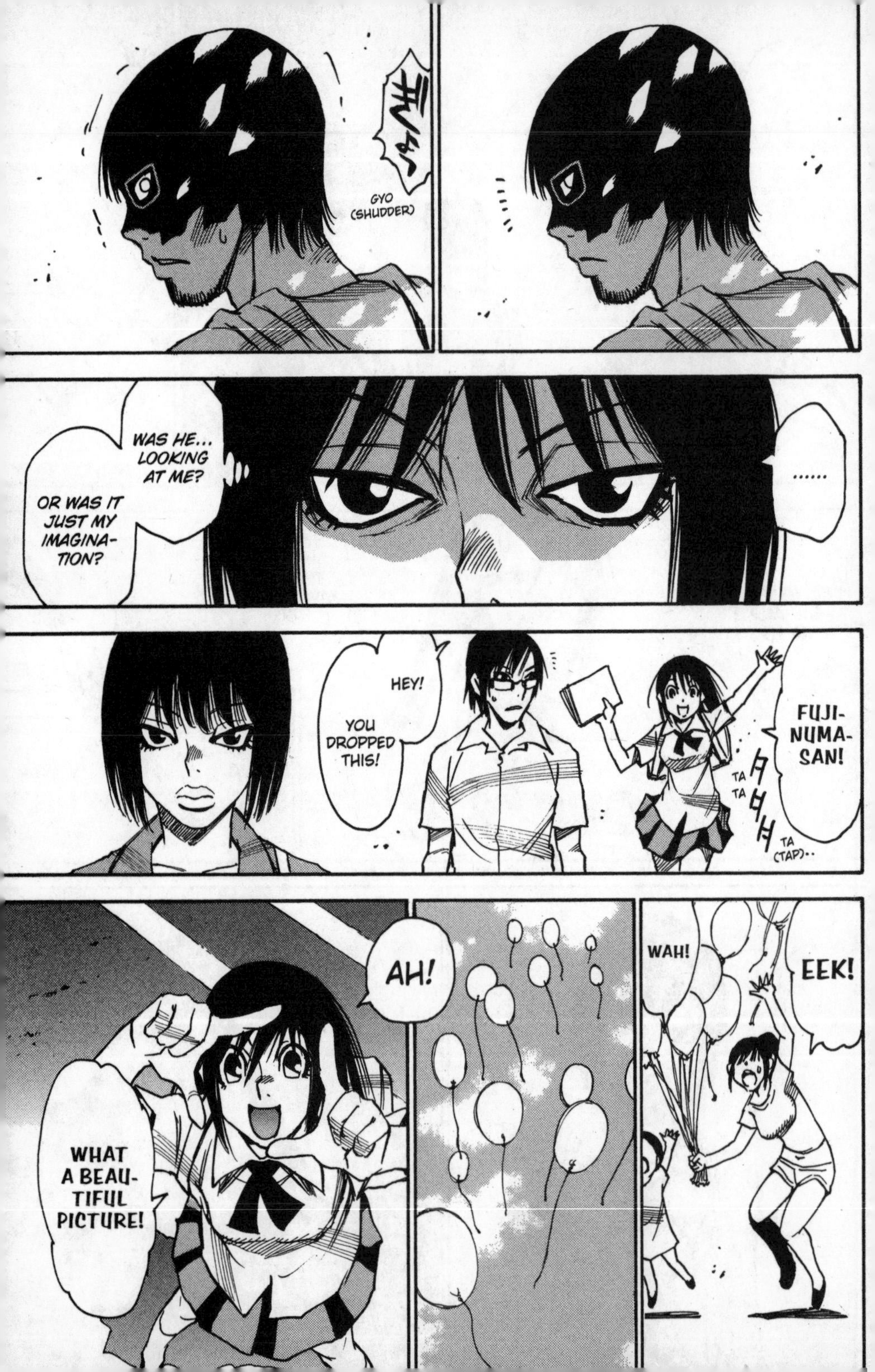

GYO (SHUDDER)
......
WAS HE... LOOKING AT ME?
OR WAS IT JUST MY IMAGINATION?
FUJI-NUMA-SAN!
TA TA TA (TAP)..
HEY!
YOU DROPPED THIS!
EEK!
WAH!
AH!
WHAT A BEAUTIFUL PICTURE!

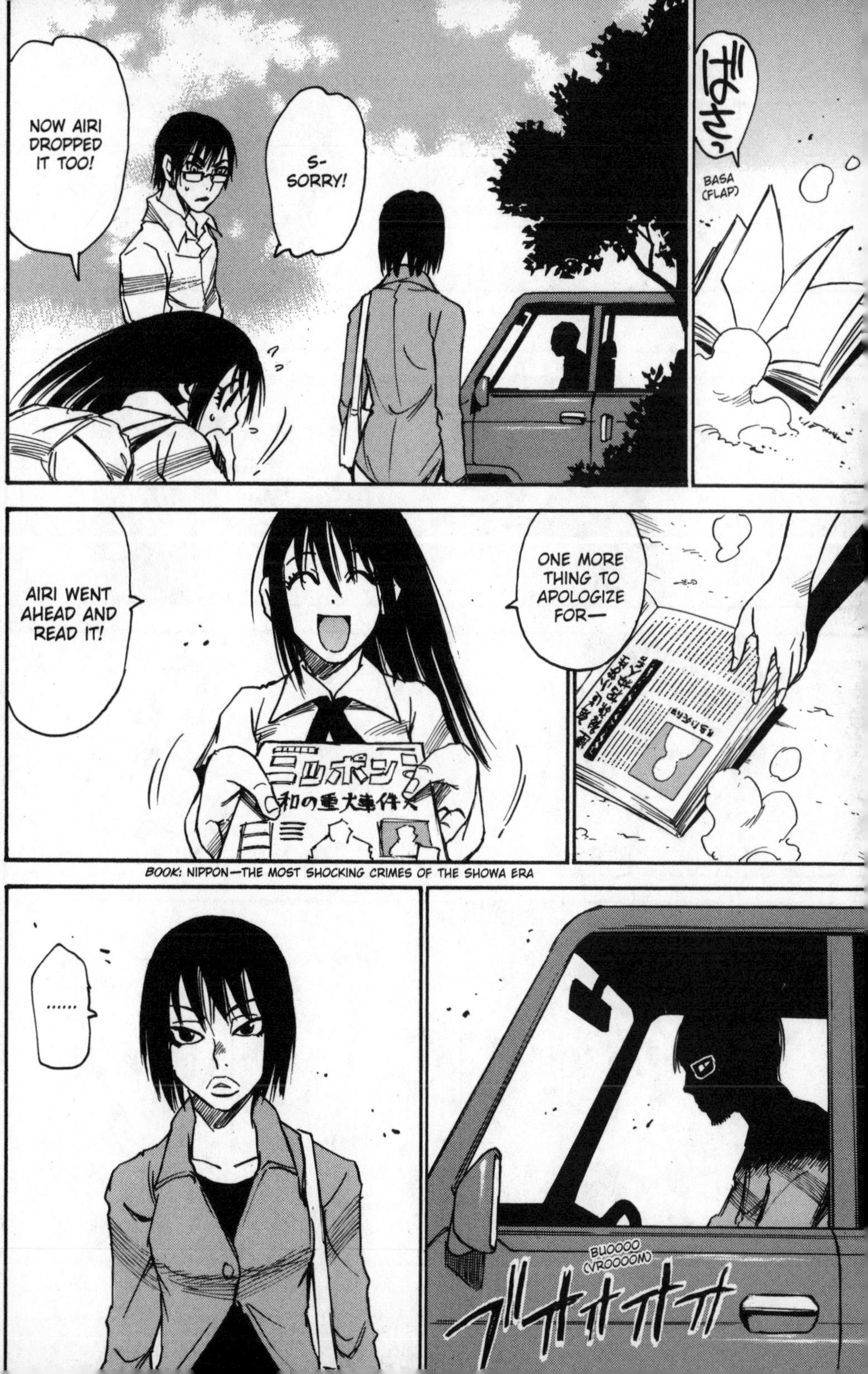
ばさっ
BASA (FLAP)
NOW AIRI DROPPED IT TOO!
S-SORRY!
ONE MORE THING TO APOLOGIZE FOR—
AIRI WENT AHEAD AND READ IT!
ニッポン
和の重大事件
BOOK: NIPPON—THE MOST SHOCKING CRIMES OF THE SHOWA ERA
BUOOOO (VROOOOM)
ブオオオオオ
......

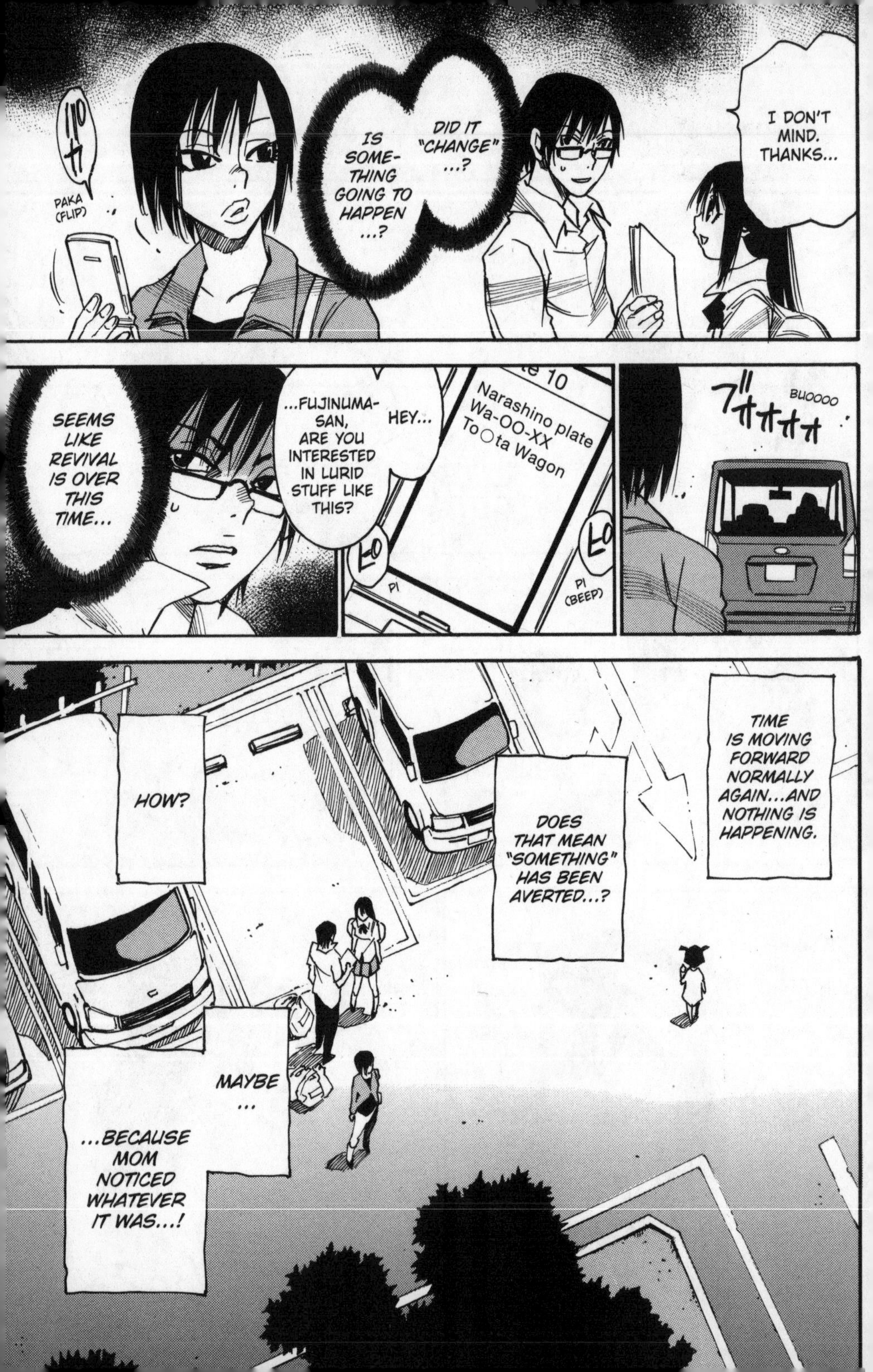
I DON'T MIND. THANKS...
DID IT "CHANGE" ...?
IS SOMETHING GOING TO HAPPEN ...?
PAKA (FLIP)
BUOOOO
Narashino plate Wa-OO-XX To○ta Wagon
PI (BEEP)
PI
HEY...
...FUJINUMA-SAN, ARE YOU INTERESTED IN LURID STUFF LIKE THIS?
SEEMS LIKE REVIVAL IS OVER THIS TIME...
TIME IS MOVING FORWARD NORMALLY AGAIN...AND NOTHING IS HAPPENING.
DOES THAT MEAN "SOMETHING" HAS BEEN AVERTED...?
HOW?
MAYBE ...
...BECAUSE MOM NOTICED WHATEVER IT WAS...!

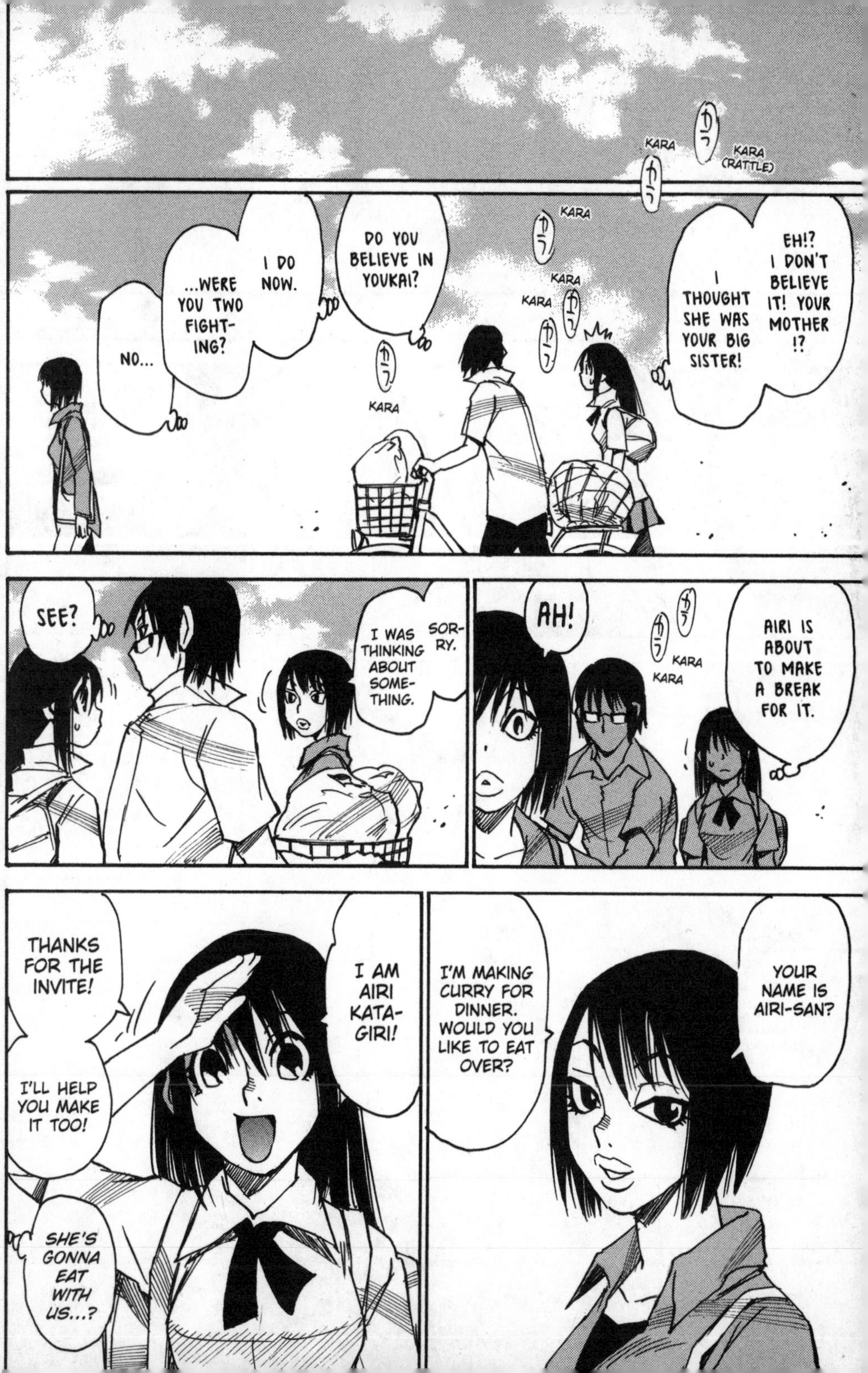
カラ
KARA
KARA (RATTLE)
カラ
KARA
EH!? I DON'T BELIEVE IT! YOUR MOTHER !?
I THOUGHT SHE WAS YOUR BIG SISTER!
カラ
KARA
カラ
KARA
カラ
KARA
カラ
KARA
DO YOU BELIEVE IN YOUKAI?
I DO NOW.
...WERE YOU TWO FIGHTING?
NO...
AIRI IS ABOUT TO MAKE A BREAK FOR IT.
カラ
KARA
カラ
KARA
AH!
SORRY.
I WAS THINKING ABOUT SOMETHING.
SEE?
YOUR NAME IS AIRI-SAN?
I'M MAKING CURRY FOR DINNER. WOULD YOU LIKE TO EAT OVER?
I AM AIRI KATA-GIRI!
THANKS FOR THE INVITE!
I'LL HELP YOU MAKE IT TOO!
SHE'S GONNA EAT WITH US...?

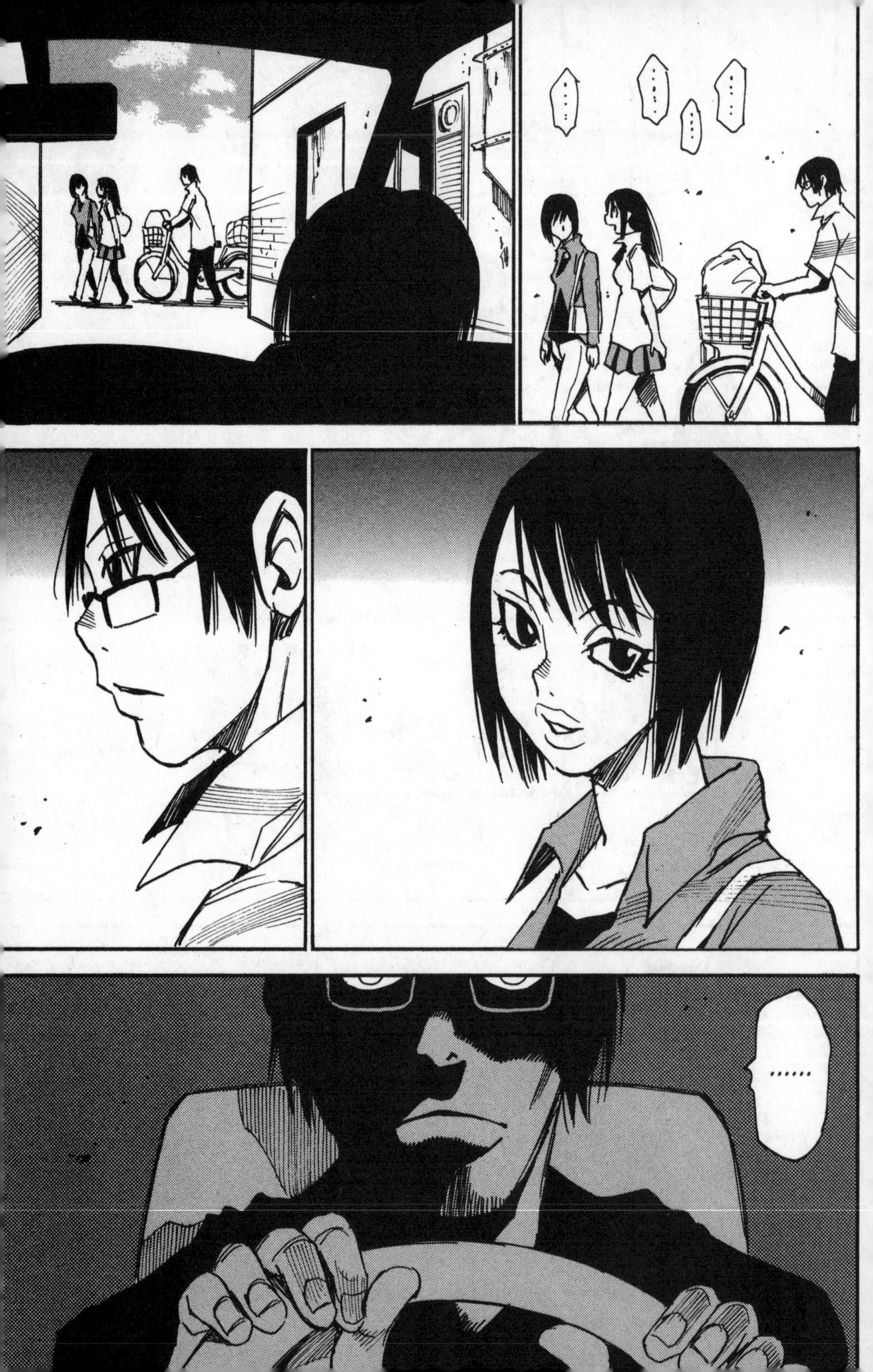
......
......
......
......
......

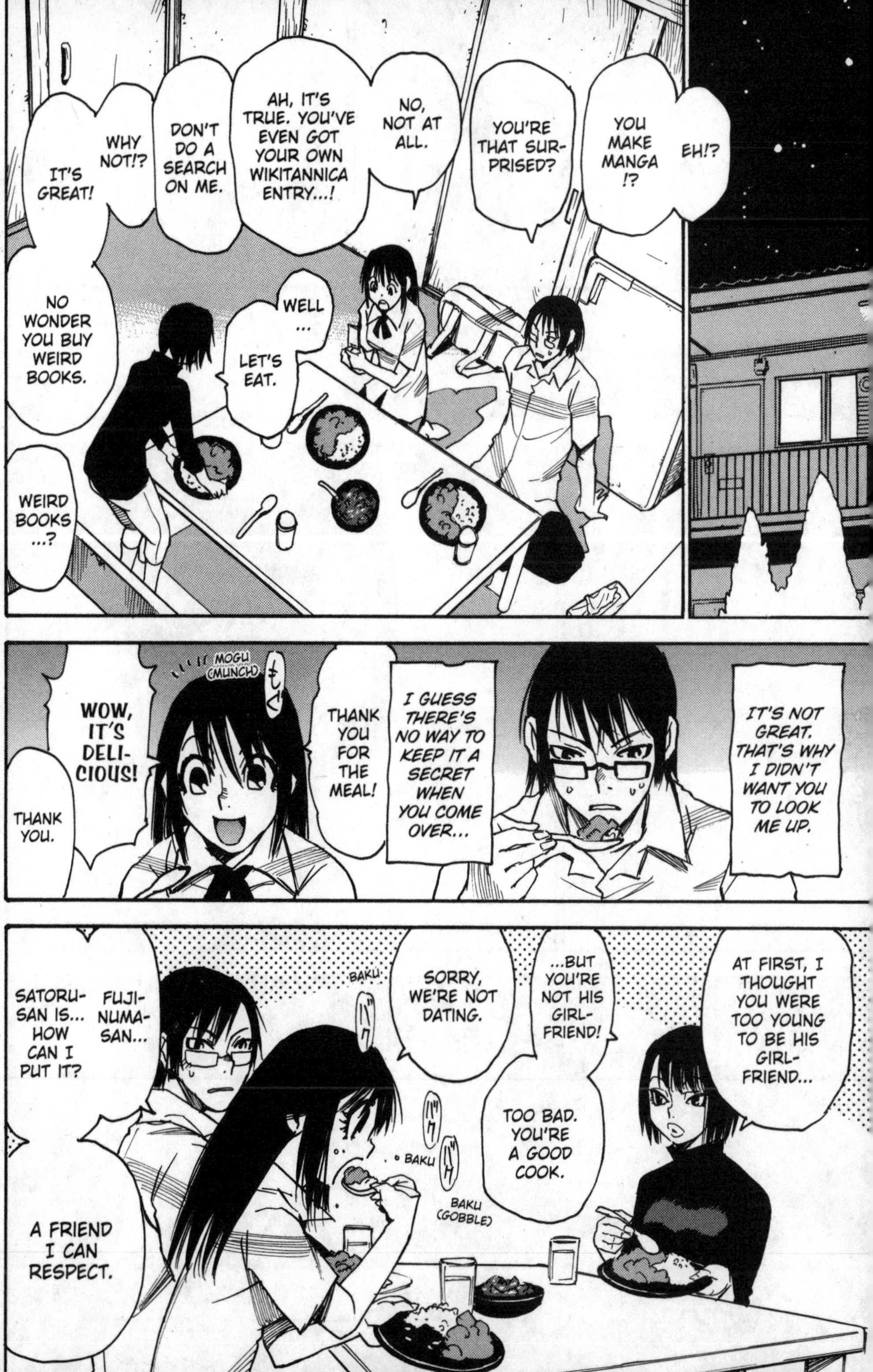
EH!?
YOU MAKE MANGA !?
YOU'RE THAT SUR-PRISED?
NO, NOT AT ALL.
AH, IT'S TRUE. YOU'VE EVEN GOT YOUR OWN WIKITANNICA ENTRY...!
DON'T DO A SEARCH ON ME.
WHY NOT!?
IT'S GREAT!
WELL ...
LET'S EAT.
NO WONDER YOU BUY WEIRD BOOKS.
WEIRD BOOKS ...?
IT'S NOT GREAT. THAT'S WHY I DIDN'T WANT YOU TO LOOK ME UP.
I GUESS THERE'S NO WAY TO KEEP IT A SECRET WHEN YOU COME OVER...
THANK YOU FOR THE MEAL!
MOGU (MUNCH)
WOW, IT'S DELICIOUS!
THANK YOU.
AT FIRST, I THOUGHT YOU WERE TOO YOUNG TO BE HIS GIRL-FRIEND...
...BUT YOU'RE NOT HIS GIRL-FRIEND!
SORRY, WE'RE NOT DATING.
BAKU
TOO BAD. YOU'RE A GOOD COOK.
BAKU
BAKU (GOBBLE)
FUJI-NUMA-SAN...
SATORU-SAN IS... HOW CAN I PUT IT?
A FRIEND I CAN RESPECT.

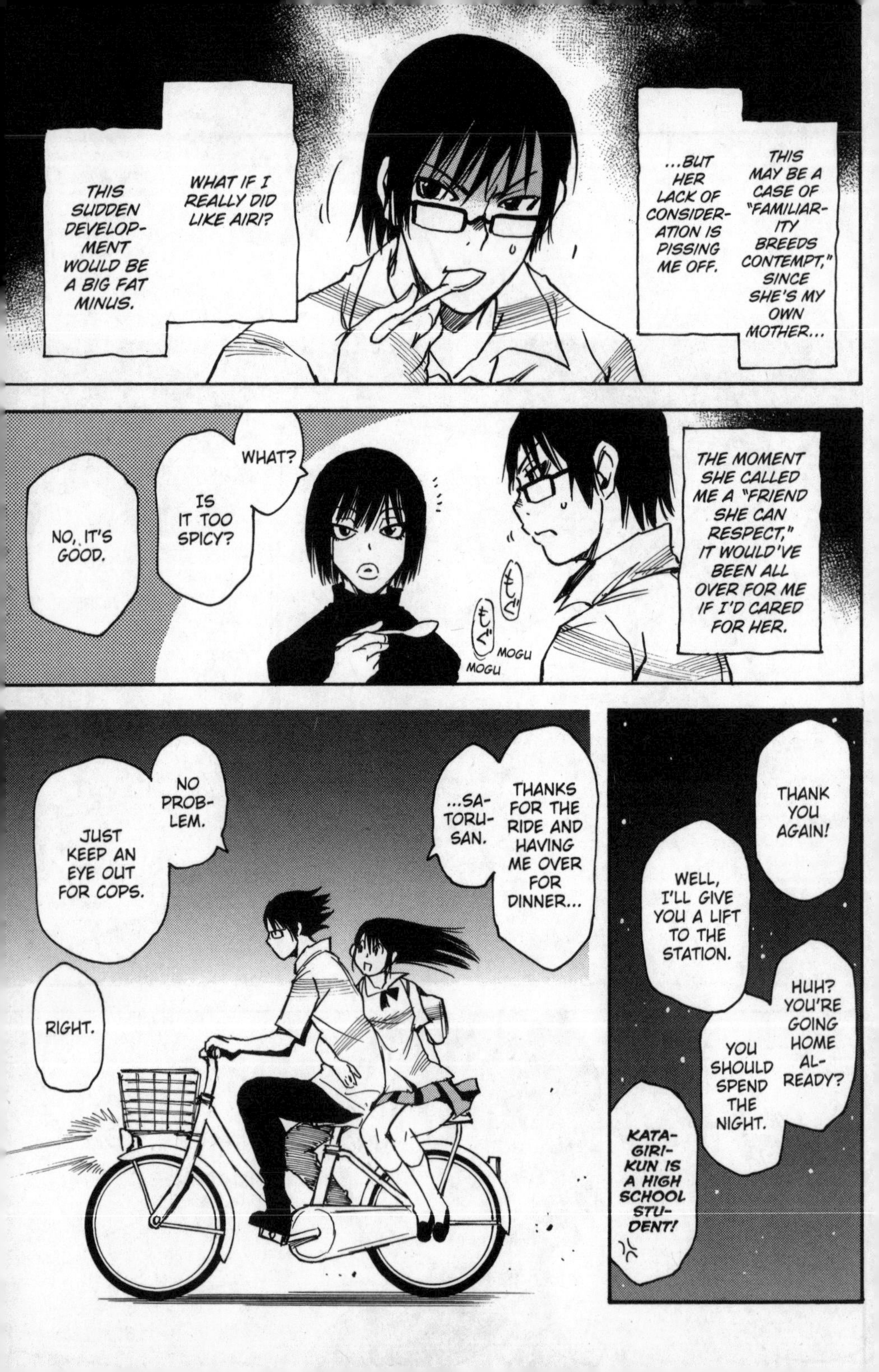
THIS MAY BE A CASE OF "FAMILIARITY BREEDS CONTEMPT," SINCE SHE'S MY OWN MOTHER...
...BUT HER LACK OF CONSIDERATION IS PISSING ME OFF.
WHAT IF I REALLY DID LIKE AIRI?
THIS SUDDEN DEVELOPMENT WOULD BE A BIG FAT MINUS.
THE MOMENT SHE CALLED ME A "FRIEND SHE CAN RESPECT," IT WOULD'VE BEEN ALL OVER FOR ME IF I'D CARED FOR HER.
もぐ
もぐ
MOGU
MOGU
WHAT?
IS IT TOO SPICY?
NO, IT'S GOOD.
THANK YOU AGAIN!
WELL, I'LL GIVE YOU A LIFT TO THE STATION.
HUH? YOU'RE GOING HOME ALREADY?
YOU SHOULD SPEND THE NIGHT.
KATAGIRI-KUN IS A HIGH SCHOOL STUDENT!
THANKS FOR THE RIDE AND HAVING ME OVER FOR DINNER...
...SATORU-SAN.
NO PROBLEM.
JUST KEEP AN EYE OUT FOR COPS.
RIGHT.

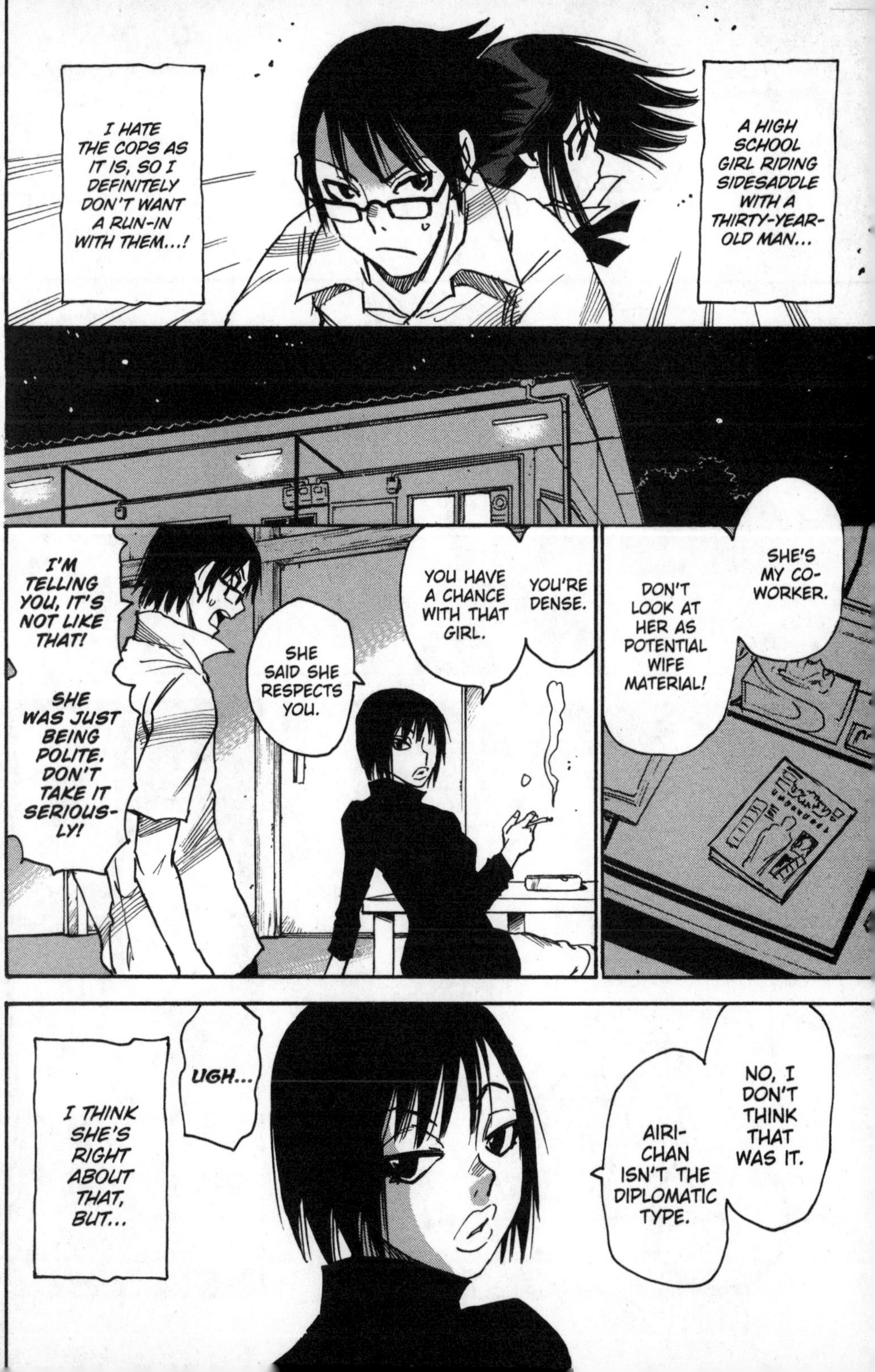
A HIGH SCHOOL GIRL RIDING SIDESADDLE WITH A THIRTY-YEAR-OLD MAN...
I HATE THE COPS AS IT IS, SO I DEFINITELY DON'T WANT A RUN-IN WITH THEM...!
SHE'S MY CO-WORKER.
DON'T LOOK AT HER AS POTENTIAL WIFE MATERIAL!
YOU'RE DENSE.
YOU HAVE A CHANCE WITH THAT GIRL.
SHE SAID SHE RESPECTS YOU.
I'M TELLING YOU, IT'S NOT LIKE THAT!
SHE WAS JUST BEING POLITE. DON'T TAKE IT SERIOUSLY!
NO, I DON'T THINK THAT WAS IT.
AIRI-CHAN ISN'T THE DIPLOMATIC TYPE.
UGH...
I THINK SHE'S RIGHT ABOUT THAT, BUT...

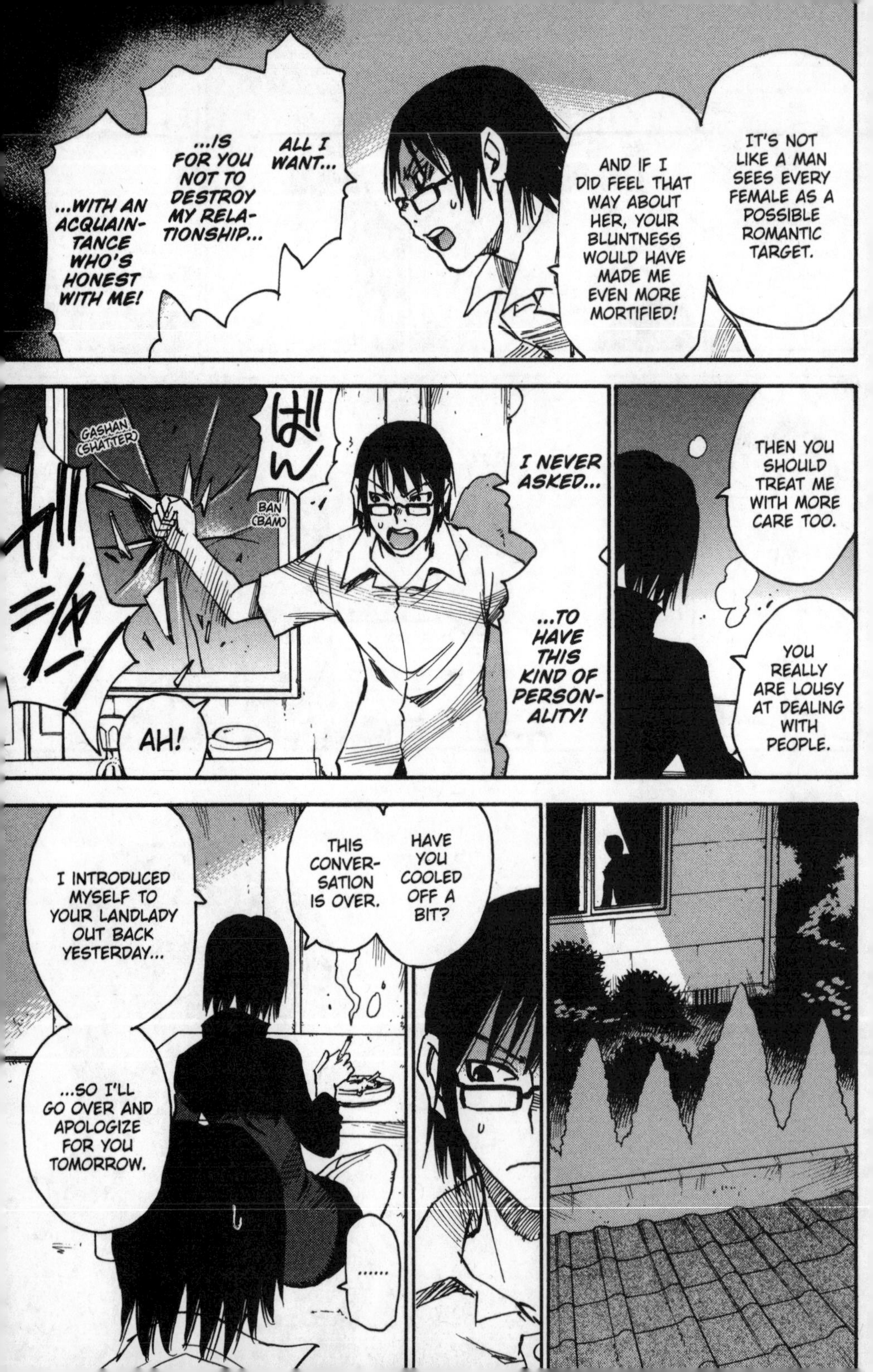
IT'S NOT LIKE A MAN SEES EVERY FEMALE AS A POSSIBLE ROMANTIC TARGET.
AND IF I DID FEEL THAT WAY ABOUT HER, YOUR BLUNTNESS WOULD HAVE MADE ME EVEN MORE MORTIFIED!
ALL I WANT...
...IS FOR YOU NOT TO DESTROY MY RELATIONSHIP...
...WITH AN ACQUAINTANCE WHO'S HONEST WITH ME!
THEN YOU SHOULD TREAT ME WITH MORE CARE TOO.
YOU REALLY ARE LOUSY AT DEALING WITH PEOPLE.
I NEVER ASKED...
...TO HAVE THIS KIND OF PERSONALITY!
ばん
BAN (BAM)
ガシャーン
GASHAN (SHATTER)
AH!
HAVE YOU COOLED OFF A BIT?
THIS CONVERSATION IS OVER.
I INTRODUCED MYSELF TO YOUR LANDLADY OUT BACK YESTERDAY...
...SO I'LL GO OVER AND APOLOGIZE FOR YOU TOMORROW.
......

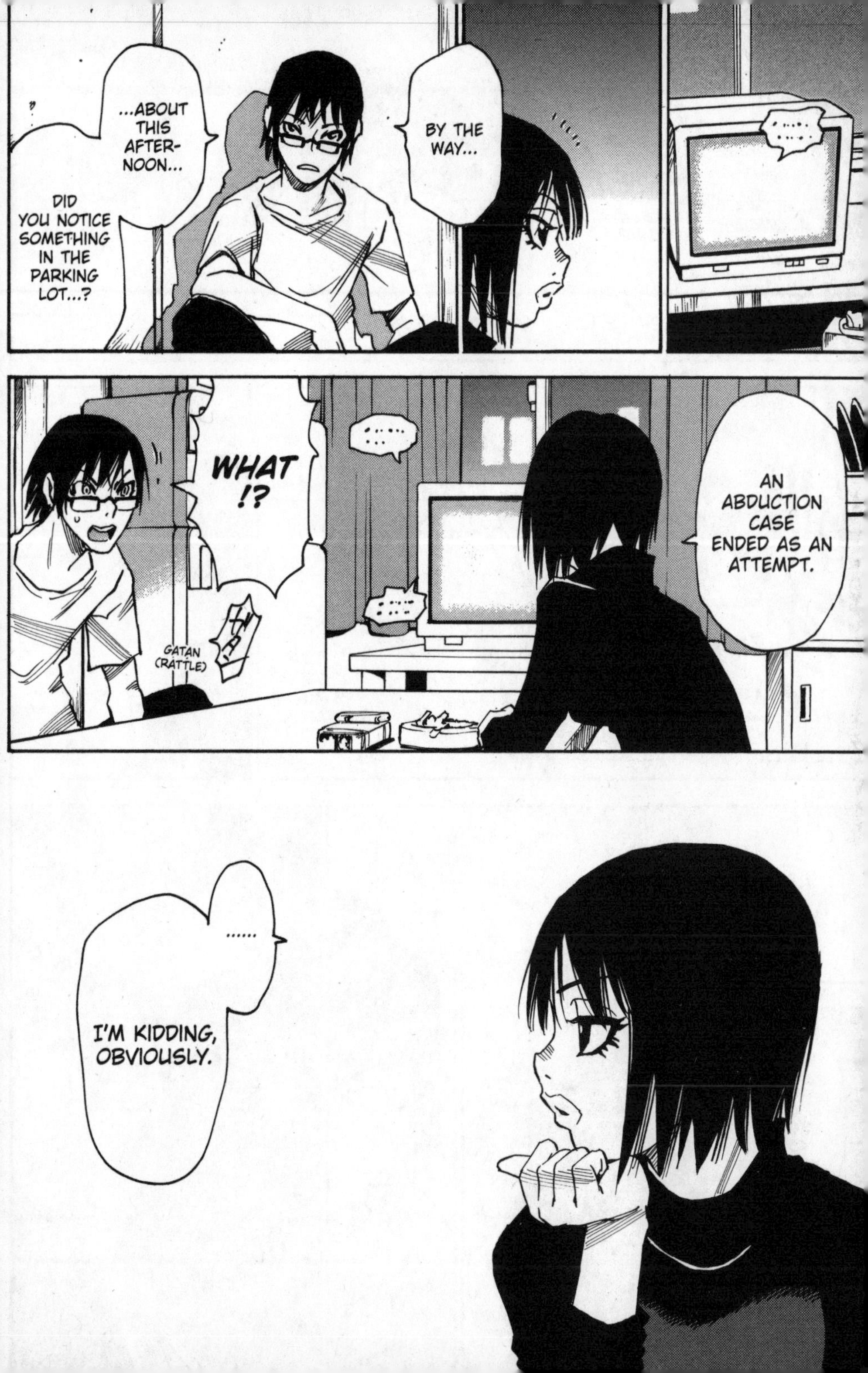

BY THE WAY...
...ABOUT THIS AFTERNOON...
DID YOU NOTICE SOMETHING IN THE PARKING LOT...?
AN ABDUCTION CASE ENDED AS AN ATTEMPT.
WHAT!?
GATAN (RATTLE)
......
I'M KIDDING, OBVIOUSLY.

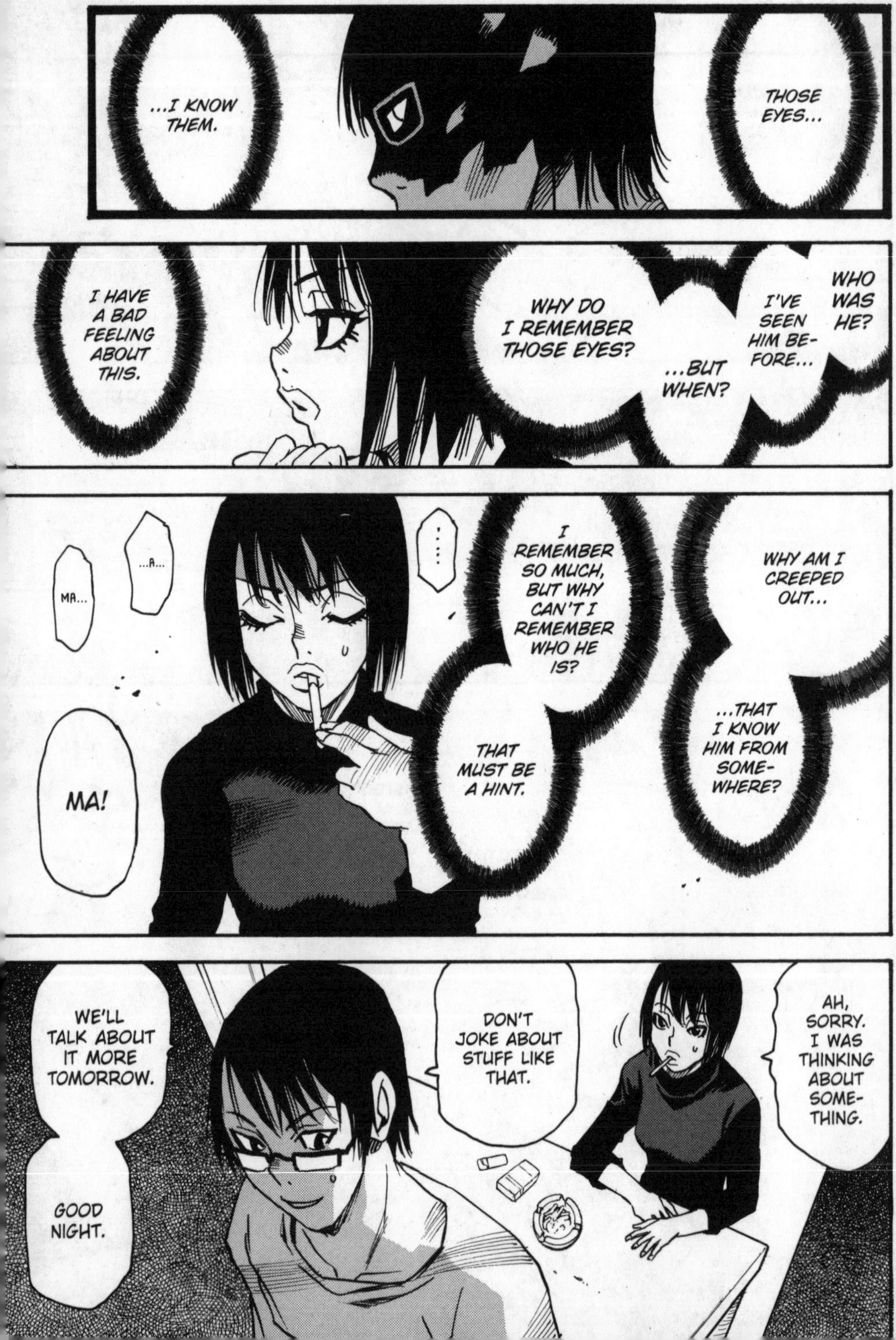
THOSE EYES...
...I KNOW THEM.
WHO WAS HE?
I'VE SEEN HIM BE-FORE...
...BUT WHEN?
WHY DO I REMEMBER THOSE EYES?
I HAVE A BAD FEELING ABOUT THIS.
WHY AM I CREEPED OUT...
...THAT I KNOW HIM FROM SOME-WHERE?
I REMEMBER SO MUCH, BUT WHY CAN'T I REMEMBER WHO HE IS?
THAT MUST BE A HINT.
......
...A...
MA...
MA!
AH, SORRY. I WAS THINKING ABOUT SOME-THING.
DON'T JOKE ABOUT STUFF LIKE THAT.
WE'LL TALK ABOUT IT MORE TOMORROW.
GOOD NIGHT.

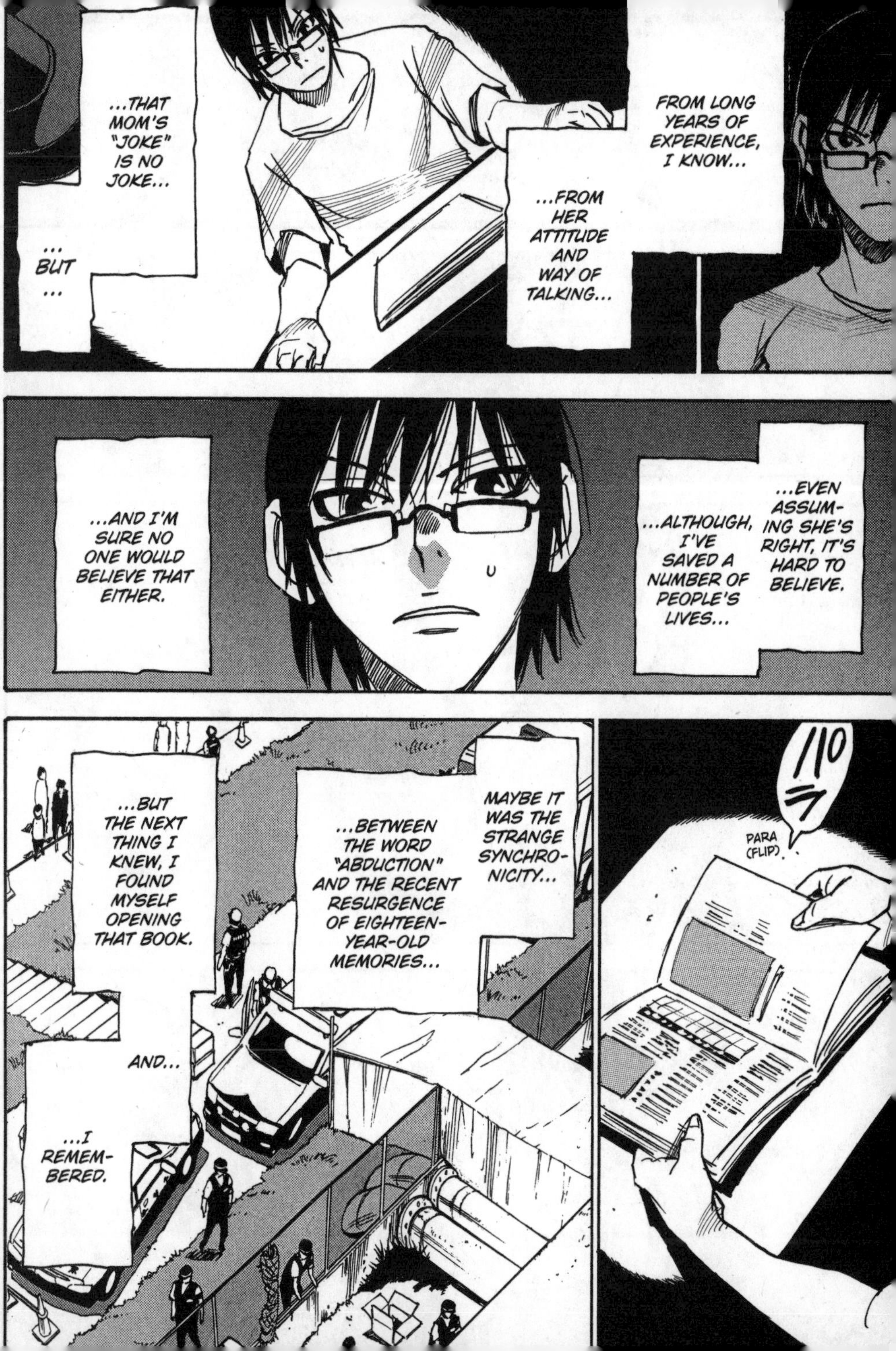
FROM LONG YEARS OF EXPERIENCE, I KNOW...
...FROM HER ATTITUDE AND WAY OF TALKING...
...THAT MOM'S "JOKE" IS NO JOKE...
...BUT...
...EVEN ASSUMING SHE'S RIGHT, IT'S HARD TO BELIEVE.
...ALTHOUGH, I'VE SAVED A NUMBER OF PEOPLE'S LIVES...
...AND I'M SURE NO ONE WOULD BELIEVE THAT EITHER.
パラ
PARA (FLIP)
MAYBE IT WAS THE STRANGE SYNCHRONICITY...
...BETWEEN THE WORD "ABDUCTION" AND THE RECENT RESURGENCE OF EIGHTEEN-YEAR-OLD MEMORIES...
...BUT THE NEXT THING I KNEW, I FOUND MYSELF OPENING THAT BOOK.
AND...
...I REMEMBERED.

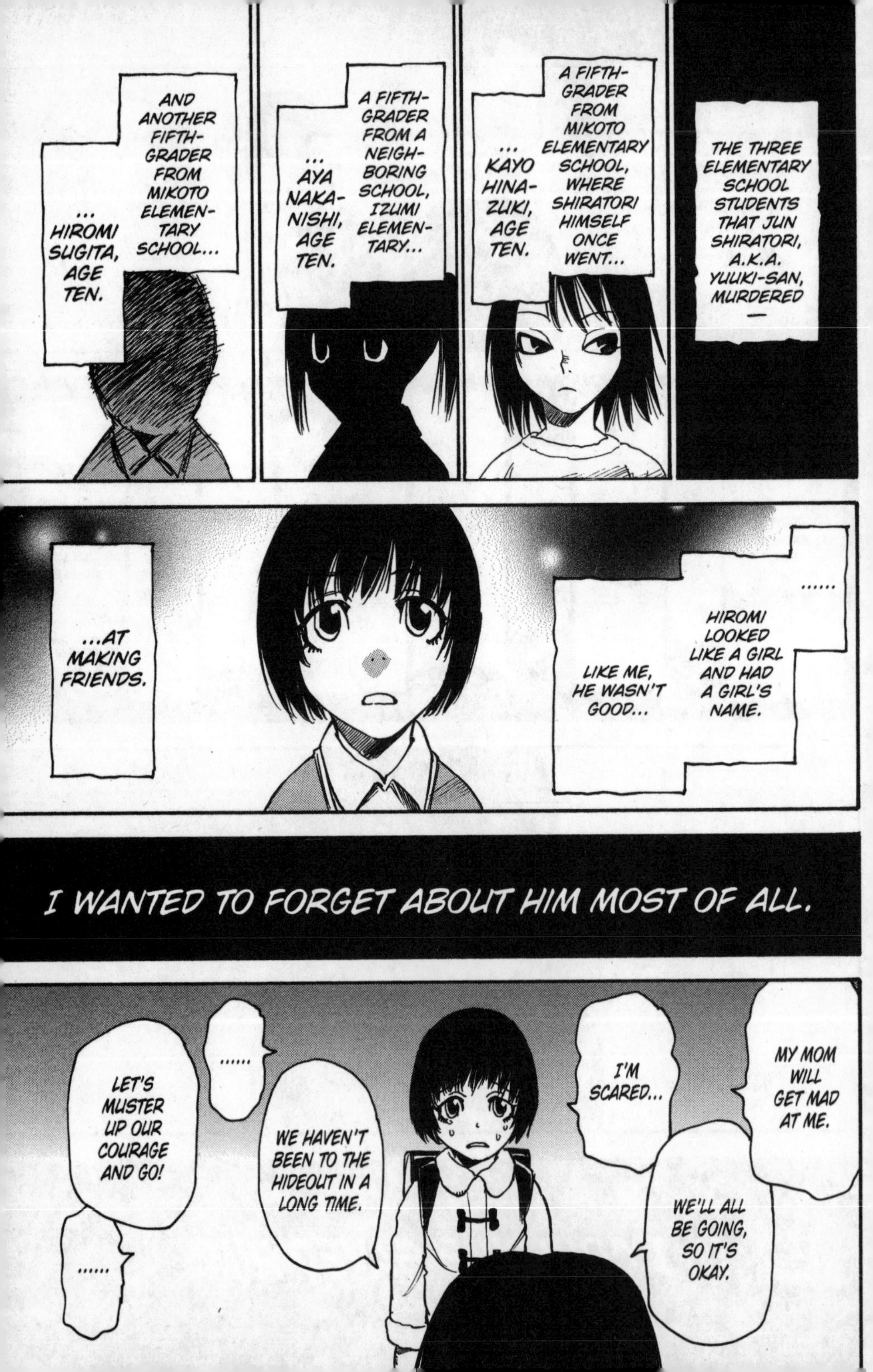
THE THREE ELEMENTARY SCHOOL STUDENTS THAT JUN SHIRATORI, A.K.A. YUUKI-SAN, MURDERED —
A FIFTH-GRADER FROM MIKOTO ELEMENTARY SCHOOL, WHERE SHIRATORI HIMSELF ONCE WENT...
...KAYO HINAZUKI, AGE TEN.
A FIFTH-GRADER FROM A NEIGHBORING SCHOOL, IZUMI ELEMENTARY...
...AYA NAKANISHI, AGE TEN.
AND ANOTHER FIFTH-GRADER FROM MIKOTO ELEMENTARY SCHOOL...
...HIROMI SUGITA, AGE TEN.
......
HIROMI LOOKED LIKE A GIRL AND HAD A GIRL'S NAME.
LIKE ME, HE WASN'T GOOD...
...AT MAKING FRIENDS.
I WANTED TO FORGET ABOUT HIM MOST OF ALL.
MY MOM WILL GET MAD AT ME.
I'M SCARED...
WE'LL ALL BE GOING, SO IT'S OKAY.
WE HAVEN'T BEEN TO THE HIDEOUT IN A LONG TIME.
......
LET'S MUSTER UP OUR COURAGE AND GO!
......

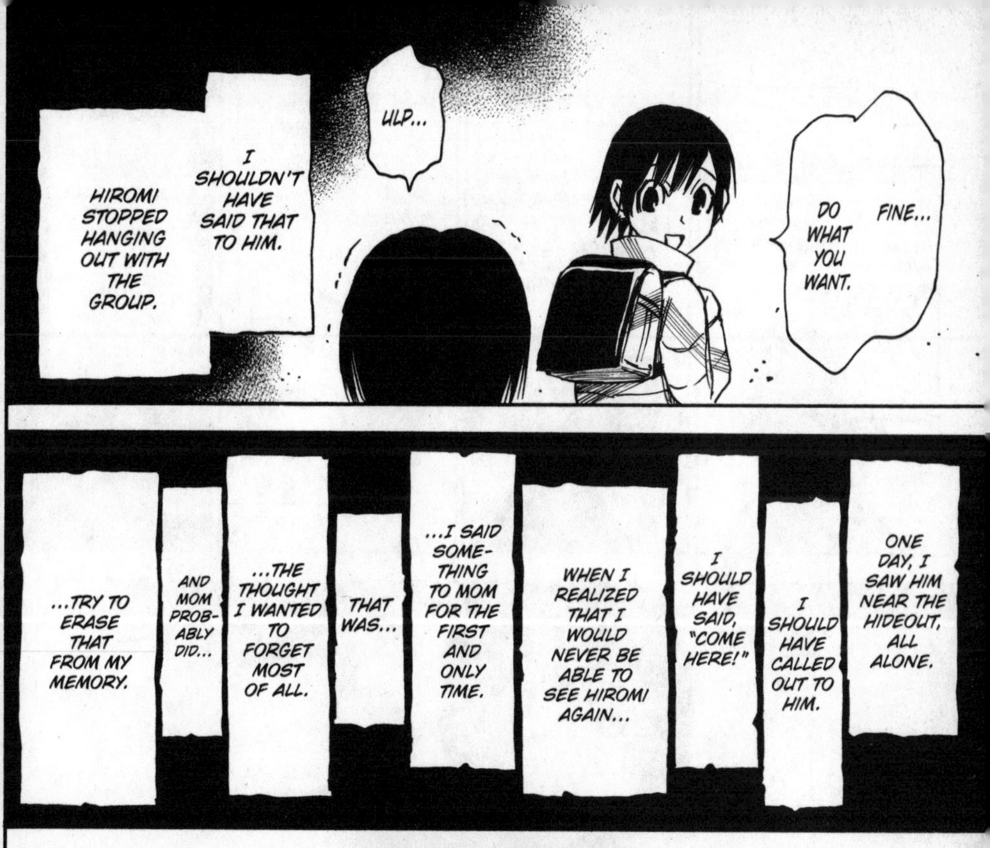
FINE... DO WHAT YOU WANT.
ULP...
I SHOULDN'T HAVE SAID THAT TO HIM.
HIROMI STOPPED HANGING OUT WITH THE GROUP.
ONE DAY, I SAW HIM NEAR THE HIDEOUT, ALL ALONE.
I SHOULD HAVE CALLED OUT TO HIM.
I SHOULD HAVE SAID, "COME HERE!"
WHEN I REALIZED THAT I WOULD NEVER BE ABLE TO SEE HIROMI AGAIN...
...I SAID SOMETHING TO MOM FOR THE FIRST AND ONLY TIME.
THAT WAS...
...THE THOUGHT I WANTED TO FORGET MOST OF ALL.
AND MOM PROBABLY DID...
...TRY TO ERASE THAT FROM MY MEMORY.

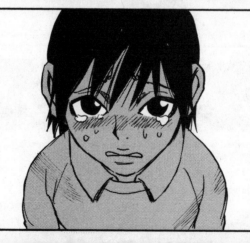

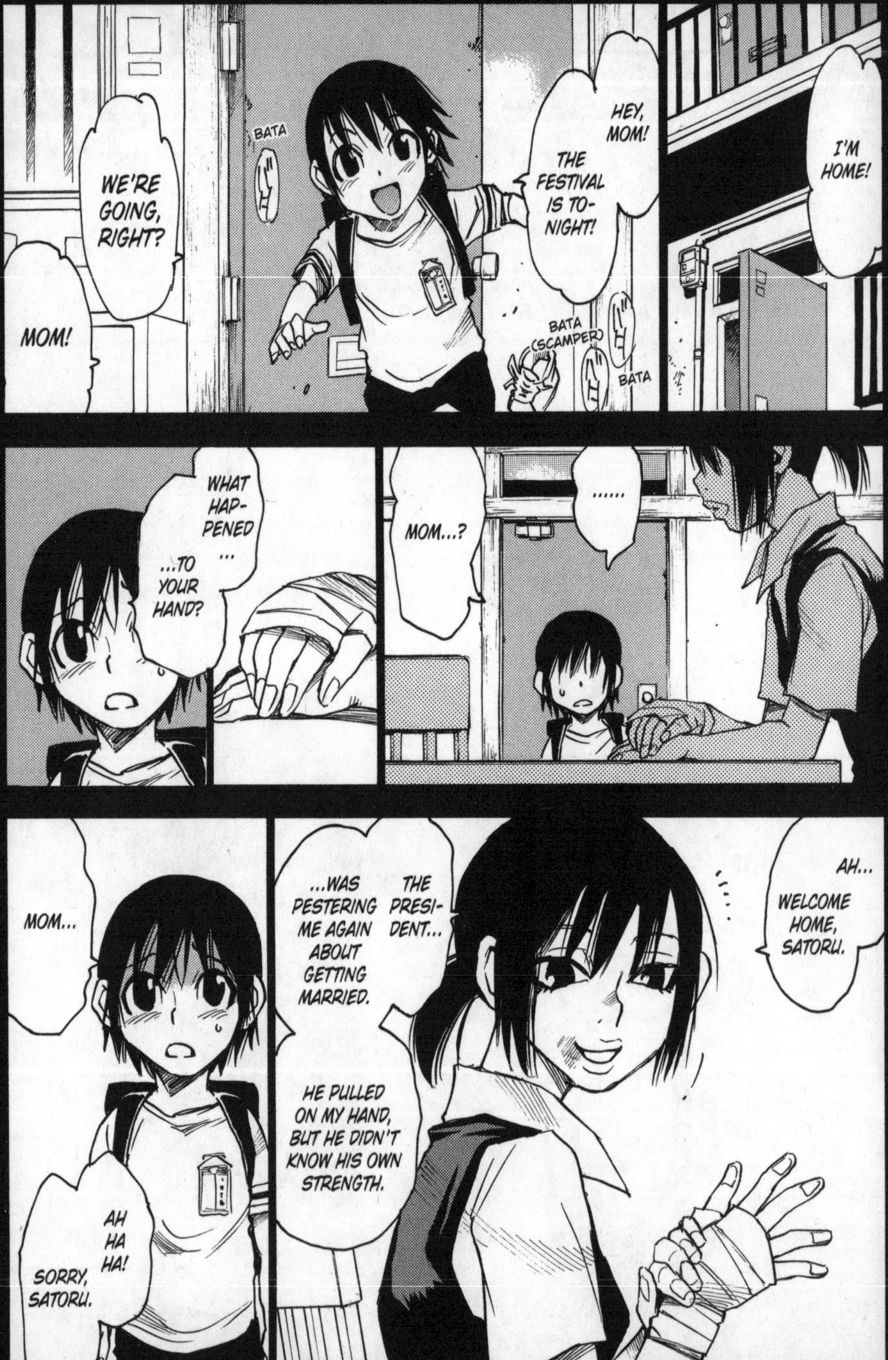
I'M HOME!
HEY, MOM!
THE FESTIVAL IS TO-NIGHT!
BATA
BATA (SCAMPER)
BATA
BATA
WE'RE GOING, RIGHT?
MOM!
......
MOM...?
WHAT HAP-PENED ...
...TO YOUR HAND?
AH... WELCOME HOME, SATORU.
THE PRESI-DENT...
...WAS PESTERING ME AGAIN ABOUT GETTING MARRIED.
HE PULLED ON MY HAND, BUT HE DIDN'T KNOW HIS OWN STRENGTH.
AH HA HA!
SORRY, SATORU.
MOM...

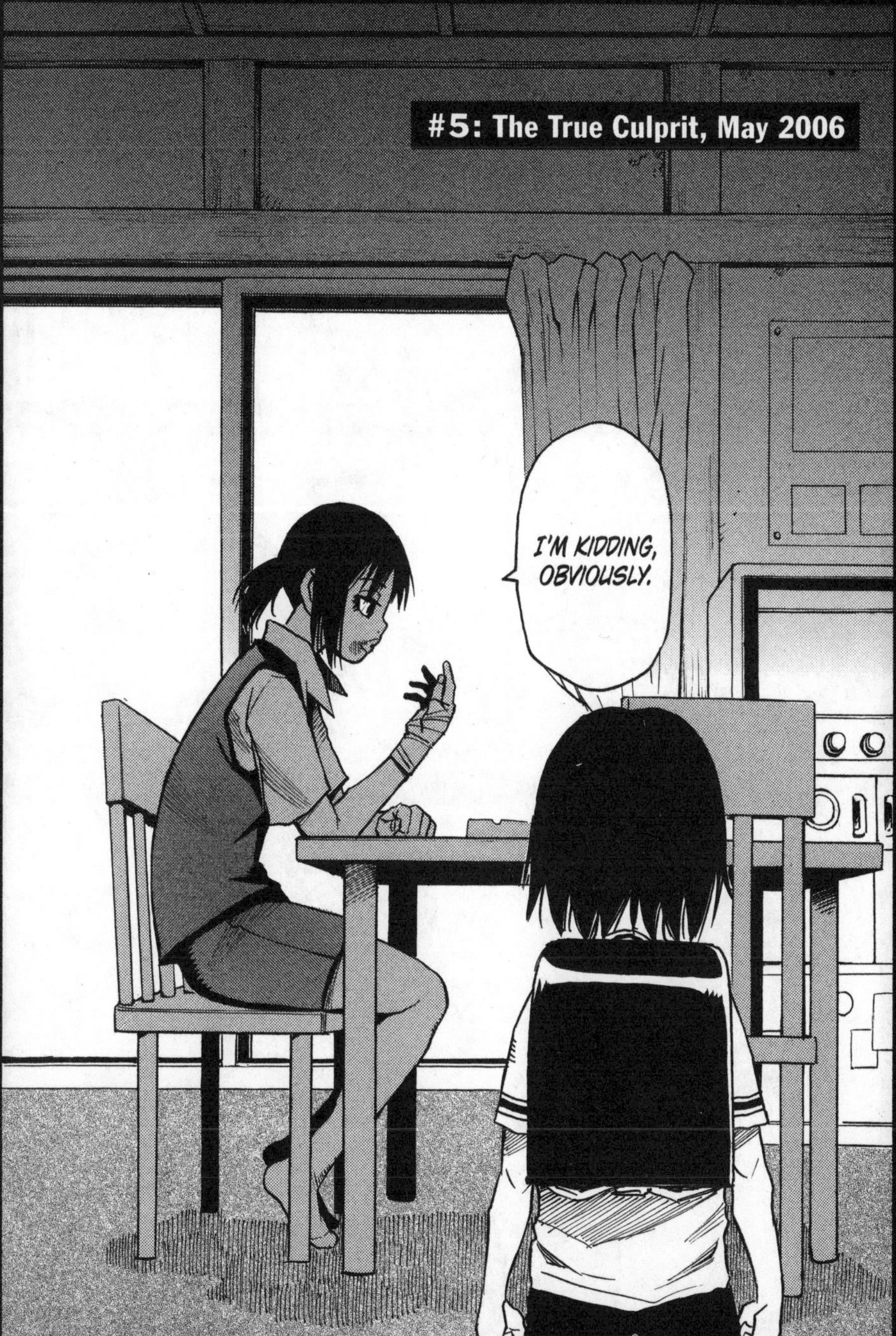
#5: The True Culprit, May 2006
I'M KIDDING, OBVIOUSLY.

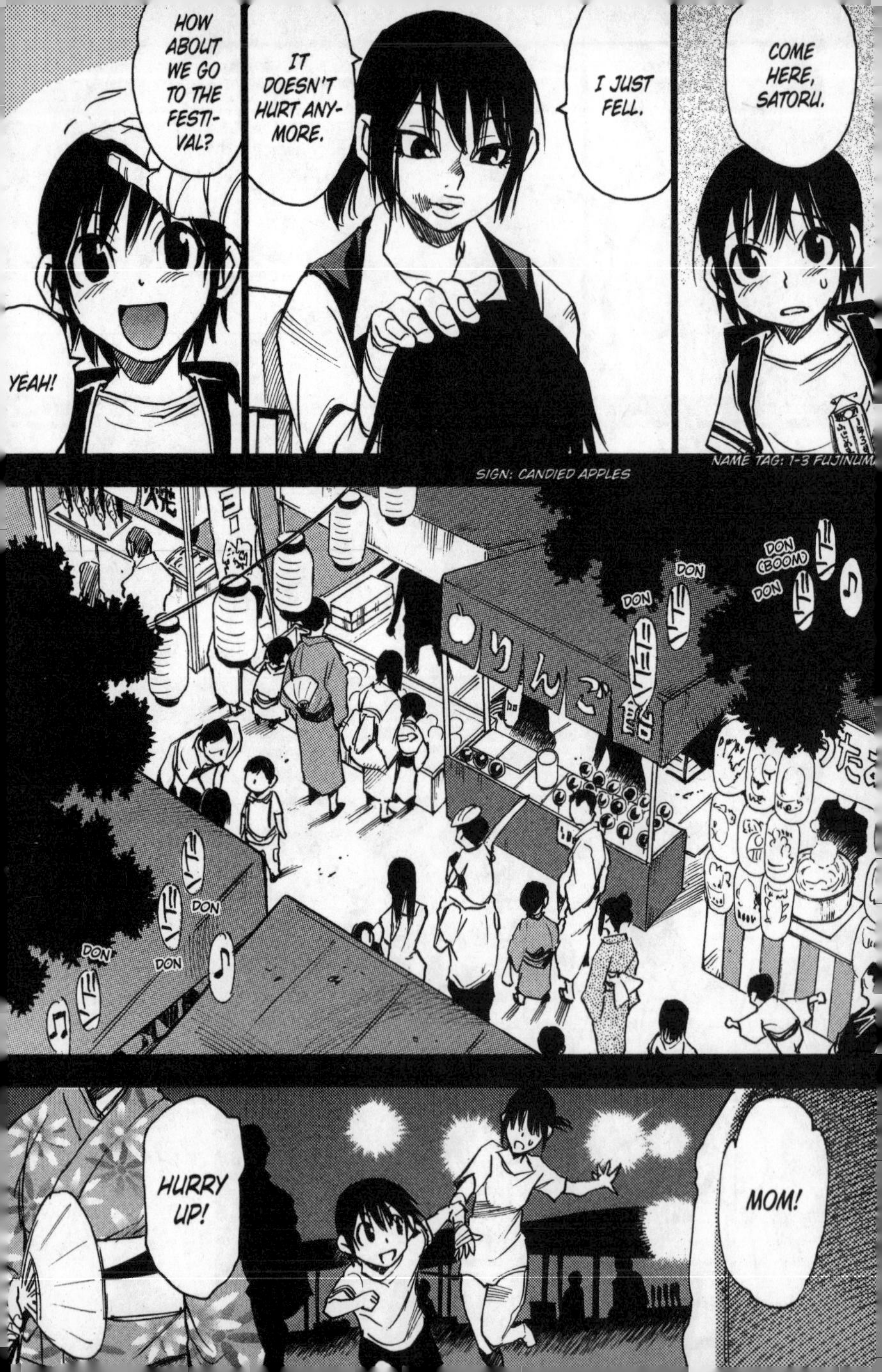
COME HERE, SATORU.
NAME TAG: 1-3 FUJINUM
I JUST FELL.
IT DOESN'T HURT ANYMORE.
HOW ABOUT WE GO TO THE FESTIVAL?
YEAH!
SIGN: CANDIED APPLES
DON (BOOM)
DON
DON
DON
DON
DON
DON
MOM!
HURRY UP!

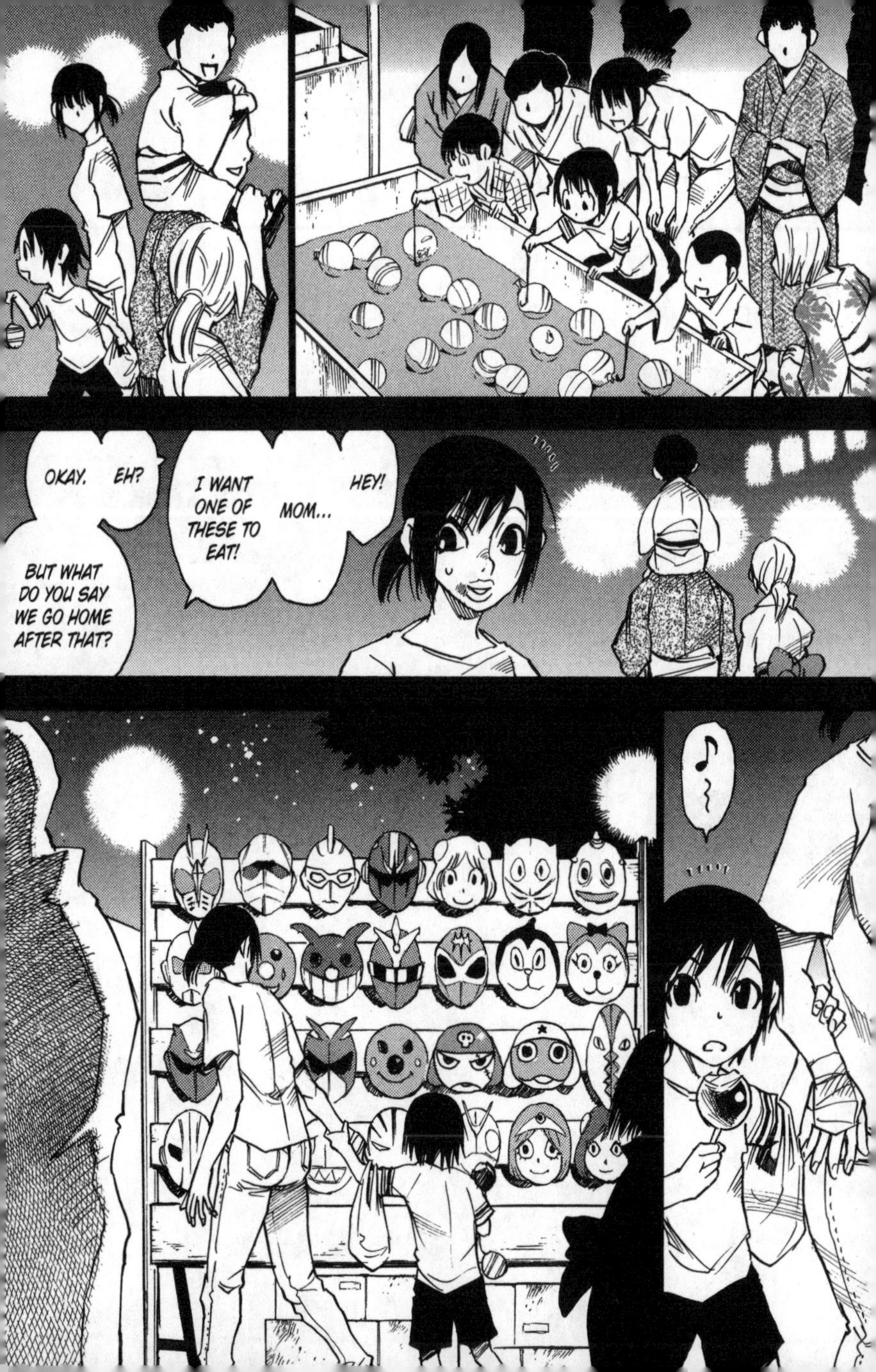
HEY!
MOM...
I WANT ONE OF THESE TO EAT!
OKAY.
EH?
BUT WHAT DO YOU SAY WE GO HOME AFTER THAT?
♪

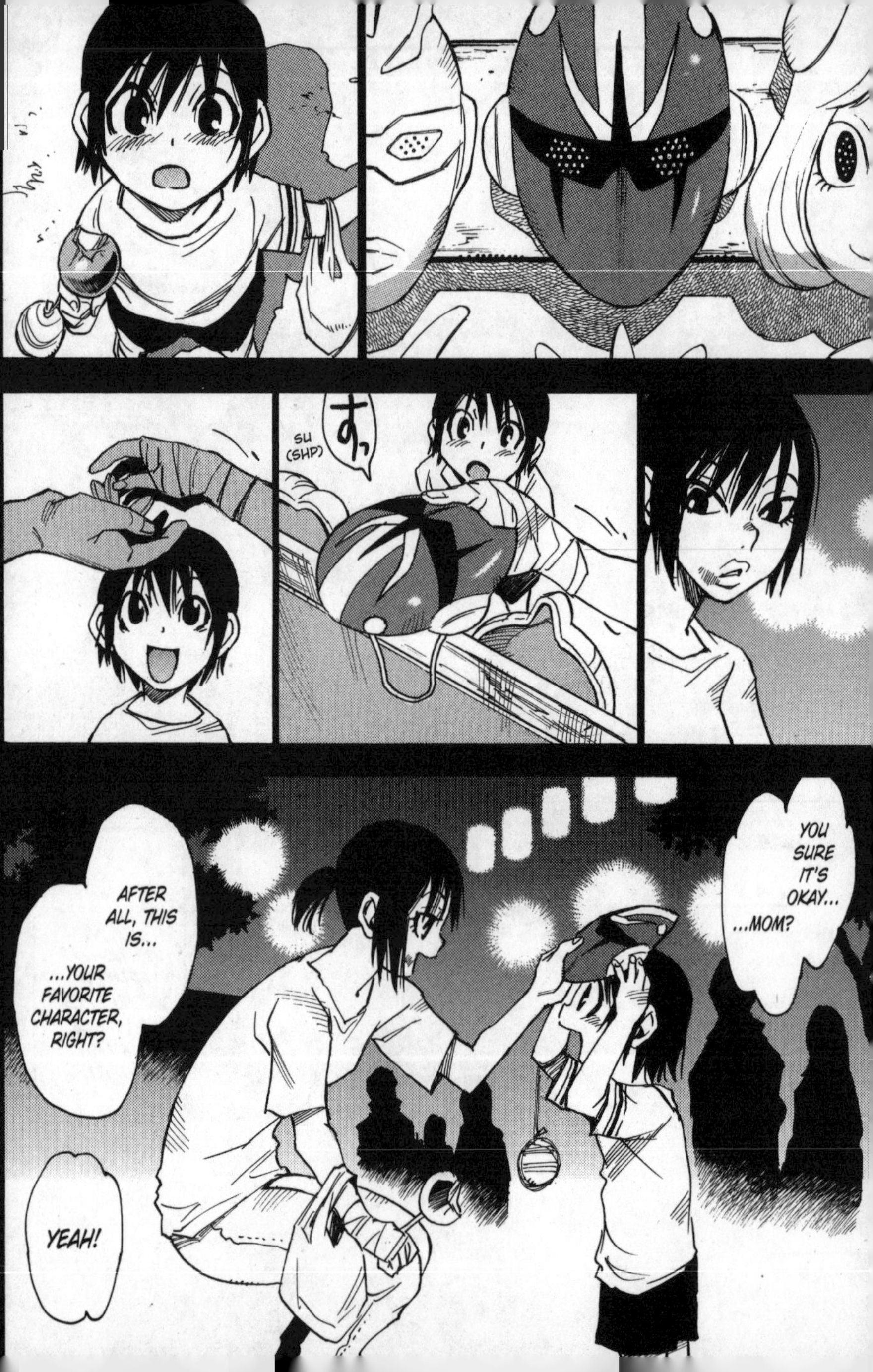
すっ
SU (SHP)
YOU SURE IT'S OKAY... ...MOM?
AFTER ALL, THIS IS... ...YOUR FAVORITE CHARACTER, RIGHT?
YEAH!

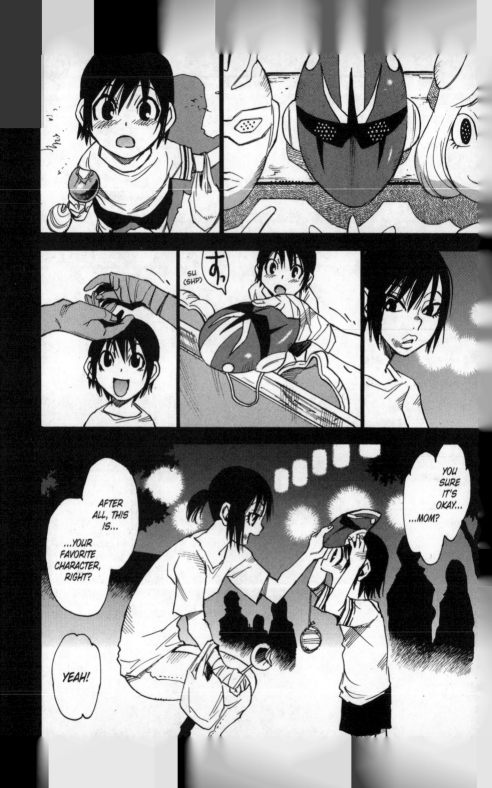

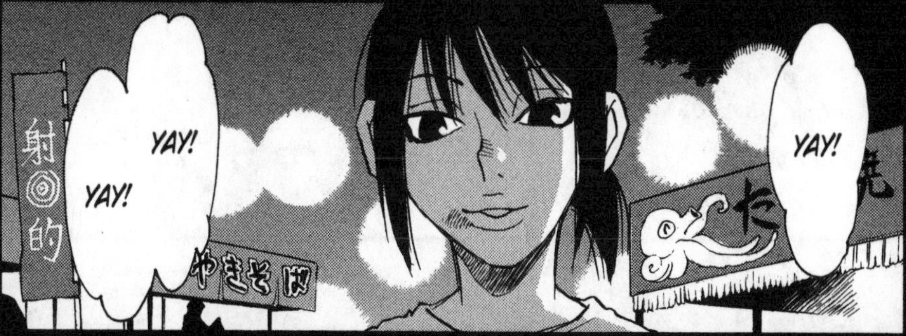
YAY!
YAY!
YAY!
射的
やきそば
SIGNS: TARGET PRACTICE, YAKISOBA
SIGN: TAKOYAKI

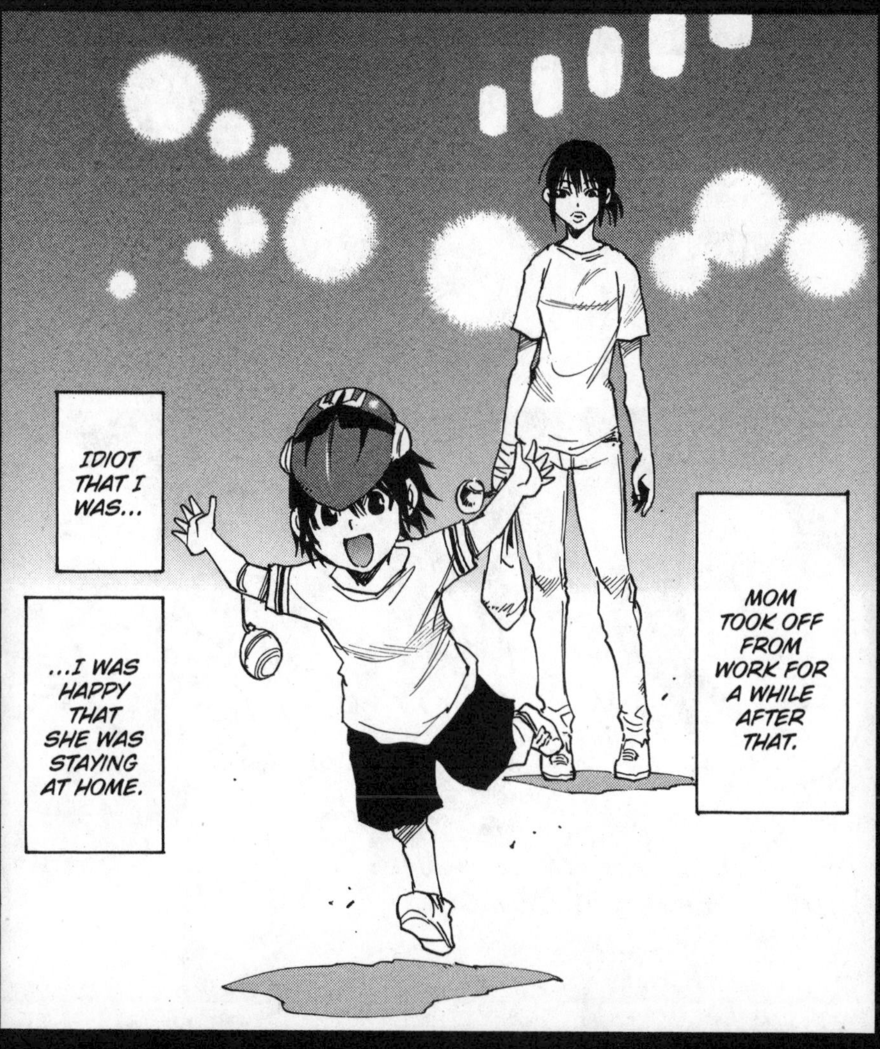
MOM TOOK OFF FROM WORK FOR A WHILE AFTER THAT.
IDIOT THAT I WAS...
...I WAS HAPPY THAT SHE WAS STAYING AT HOME.

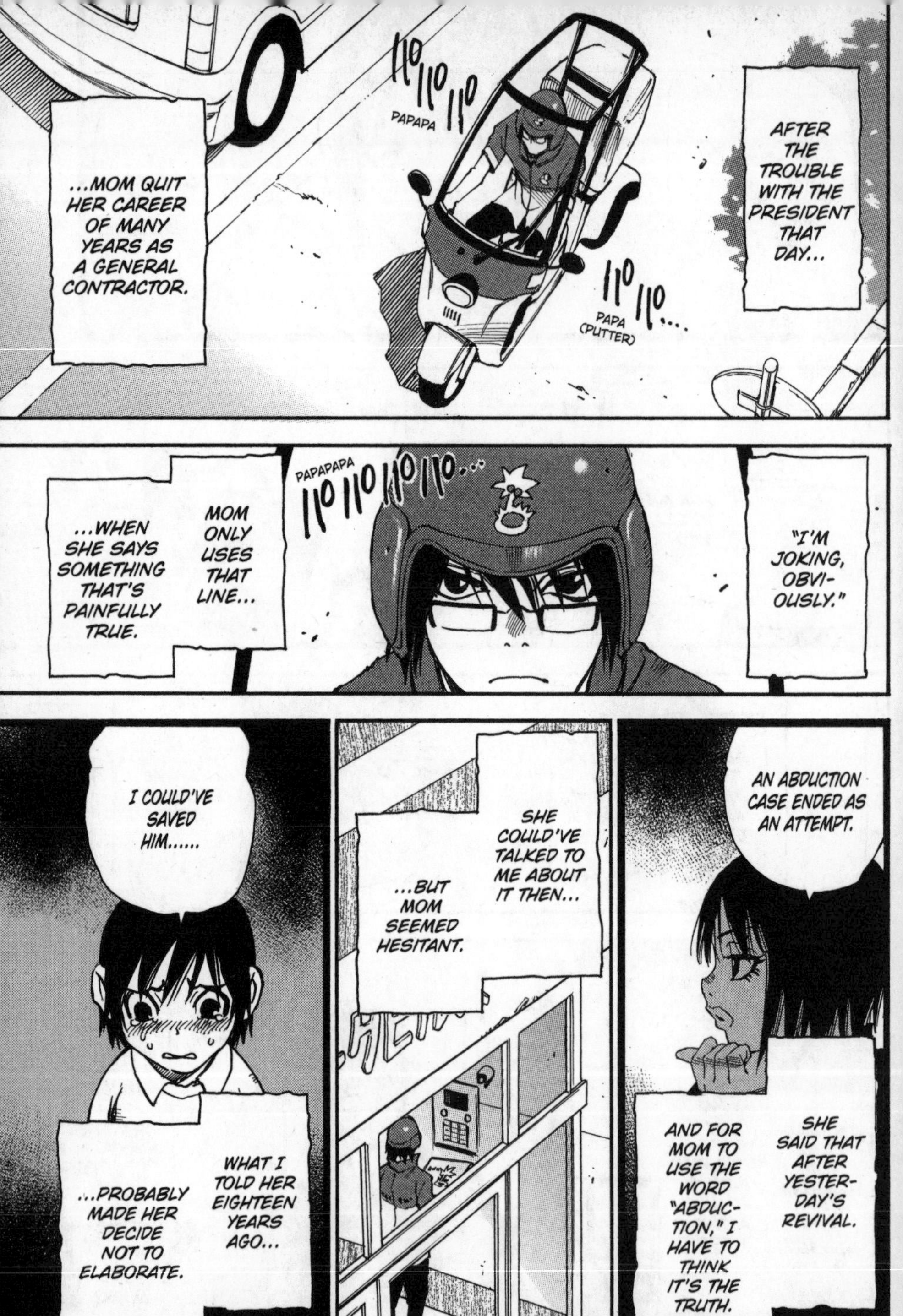
AFTER THE TROUBLE WITH THE PRESIDENT THAT DAY...
PAPAPA
...MOM QUIT HER CAREER OF MANY YEARS AS A GENERAL CONTRACTOR.
PAPA (PUTTER)
"I'M JOKING, OBVIOUSLY."
PAPAPAPA
MOM ONLY USES THAT LINE...
...WHEN SHE SAYS SOMETHING THAT'S PAINFULLY TRUE.
AN ABDUCTION CASE ENDED AS AN ATTEMPT.
SHE SAID THAT AFTER YESTERDAY'S REVIVAL.
AND FOR MOM TO USE THE WORD "ABDUCTION," I HAVE TO THINK IT'S THE TRUTH.
SHE COULD'VE TALKED TO ME ABOUT IT THEN...
...BUT MOM SEEMED HESITANT.
I COULD'VE SAVED HIM......
WHAT I TOLD HER EIGHTEEN YEARS AGO...
...PROBABLY MADE HER DECIDE NOT TO ELABORATE.

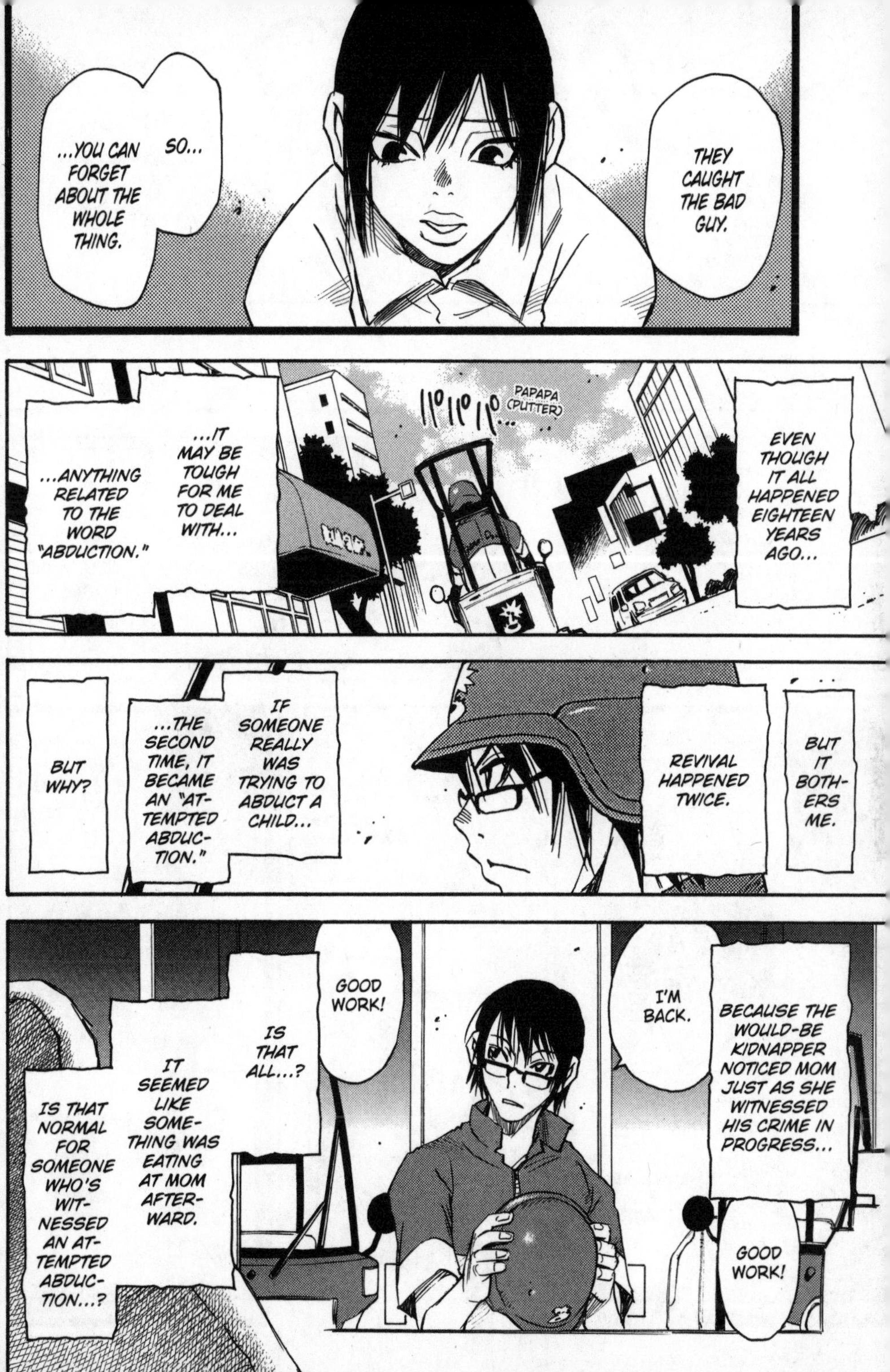
THEY CAUGHT THE BAD GUY.
SO...
...YOU CAN FORGET ABOUT THE WHOLE THING.
EVEN THOUGH IT ALL HAPPENED EIGHTEEN YEARS AGO...
PAPAPA (PUTTER)
...IT MAY BE TOUGH FOR ME TO DEAL WITH...
...ANYTHING RELATED TO THE WORD "ABDUCTION."
BUT IT BOTHERS ME.
REVIVAL HAPPENED TWICE.
IF SOMEONE REALLY WAS TRYING TO ABDUCT A CHILD...
...THE SECOND TIME, IT BECAME AN "ATTEMPTED ABDUCTION."
BUT WHY?
BECAUSE THE WOULD-BE KIDNAPPER NOTICED MOM JUST AS SHE WITNESSED HIS CRIME IN PROGRESS...
I'M BACK.
GOOD WORK!
GOOD WORK!
IS THAT ALL...?
IT SEEMED LIKE SOMETHING WAS EATING AT MOM AFTERWARD.
IS THAT NORMAL FOR SOMEONE WHO'S WITNESSED AN ATTEMPTED ABDUCTION...?

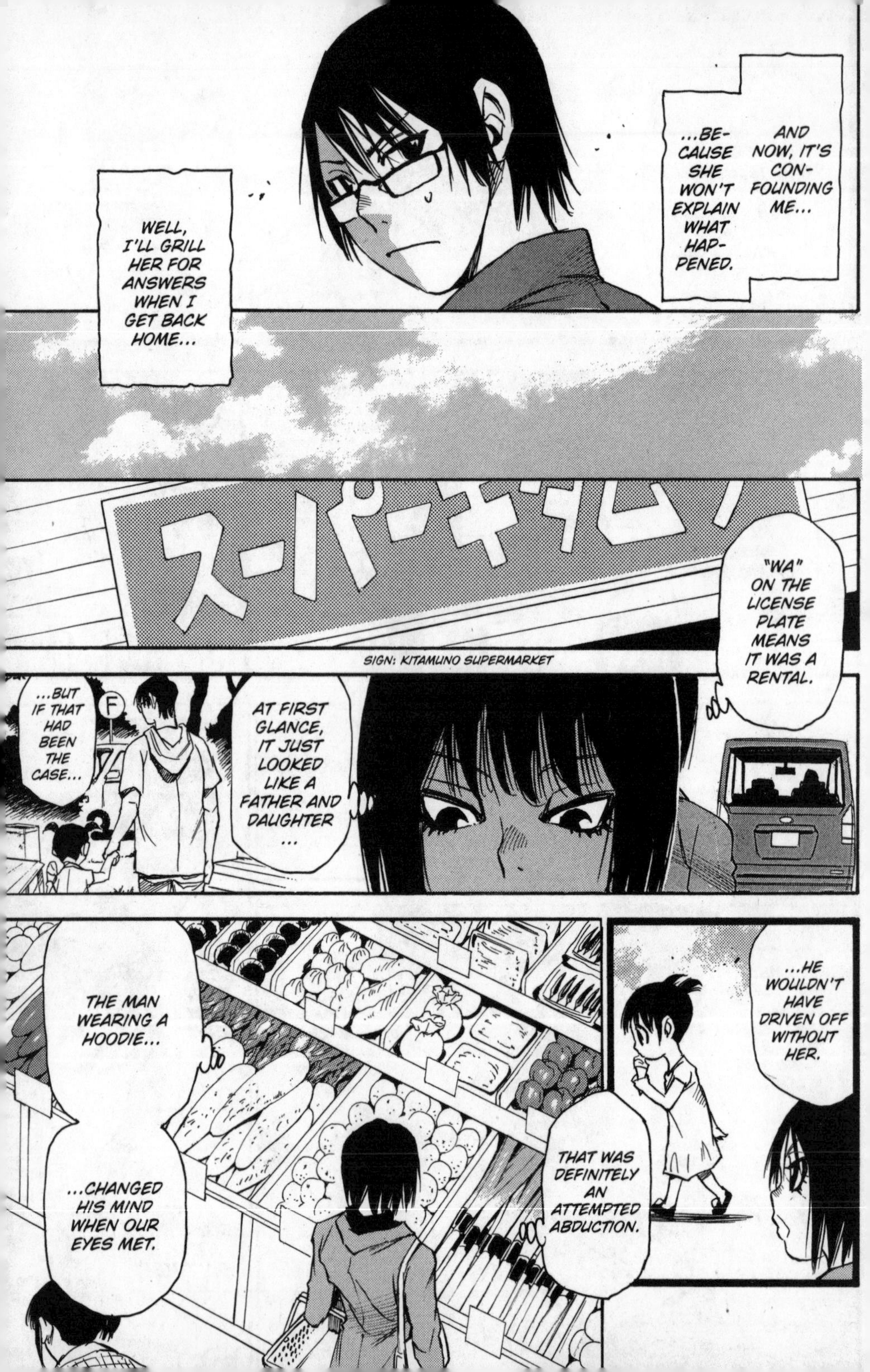
AND NOW, IT'S CONFOUNDING ME...
...BECAUSE SHE WON'T EXPLAIN WHAT HAPPENED.
WELL, I'LL GRILL HER FOR ANSWERS WHEN I GET BACK HOME...
SIGN: KITAMUNO SUPERMARKET
"WA" ON THE LICENSE PLATE MEANS IT WAS A RENTAL.
AT FIRST GLANCE, IT JUST LOOKED LIKE A FATHER AND DAUGHTER...
...BUT IF THAT HAD BEEN THE CASE...
...HE WOULDN'T HAVE DRIVEN OFF WITHOUT HER.
THAT WAS DEFINITELY AN ATTEMPTED ABDUCTION.
THE MAN WEARING A HOODIE...
...CHANGED HIS MIND WHEN OUR EYES MET.

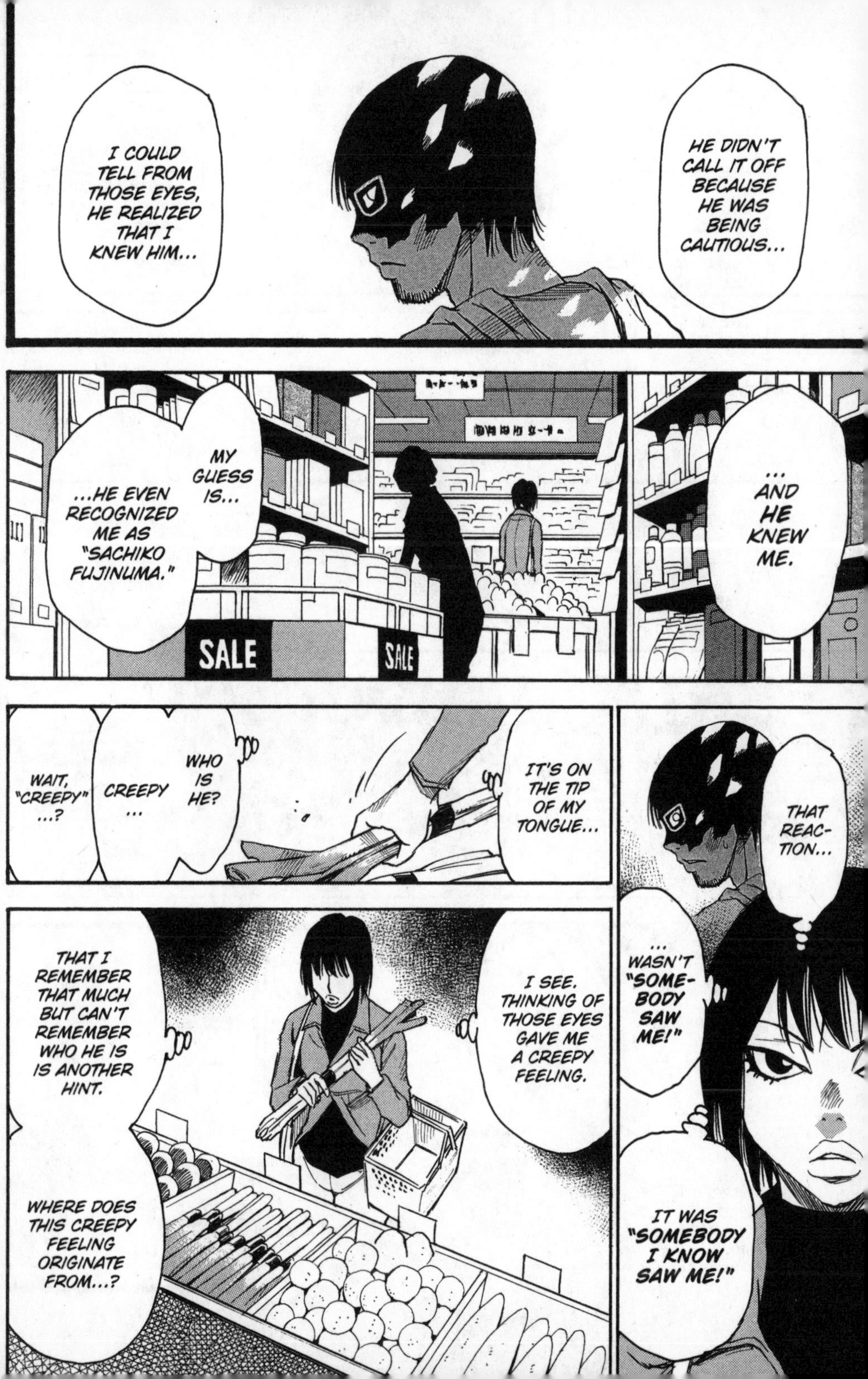
HE DIDN'T CALL IT OFF BECAUSE HE WAS BEING CAUTIOUS...
I COULD TELL FROM THOSE EYES, HE REALIZED THAT I KNEW HIM...
... AND HE KNEW ME.
MY GUESS IS...
...HE EVEN RECOGNIZED ME AS "SACHIKO FUJINUMA."
SALE
SALE
THAT REACTION...
... WASN'T "SOMEBODY SAW ME!"
IT WAS "SOMEBODY I KNOW SAW ME!"
IT'S ON THE TIP OF MY TONGUE...
WHO IS HE?
CREEPY ...
WAIT, "CREEPY" ...?
I SEE. THINKING OF THOSE EYES GAVE ME A CREEPY FEELING.
THAT I REMEMBER THAT MUCH BUT CAN'T REMEMBER WHO HE IS IS ANOTHER HINT.
WHERE DOES THIS CREEPY FEELING ORIGINATE FROM...?

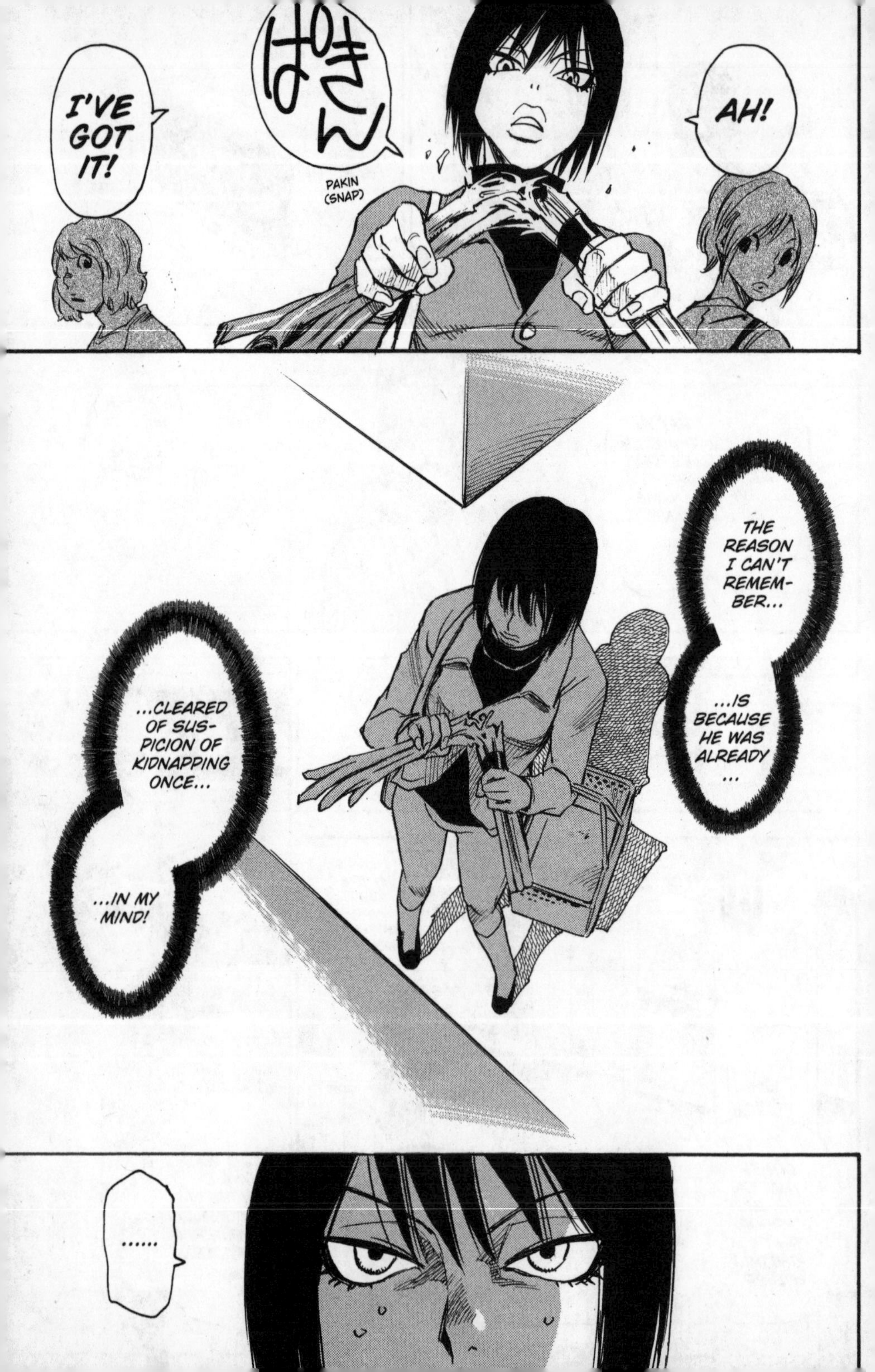
AH!
ぱきん
PAKIN (SNAP)
I'VE GOT IT!
THE REASON I CAN'T REMEMBER...
...IS BECAUSE HE WAS ALREADY...
...CLEARED OF SUSPICION OF KIDNAPPING ONCE...
...IN MY MIND!
......

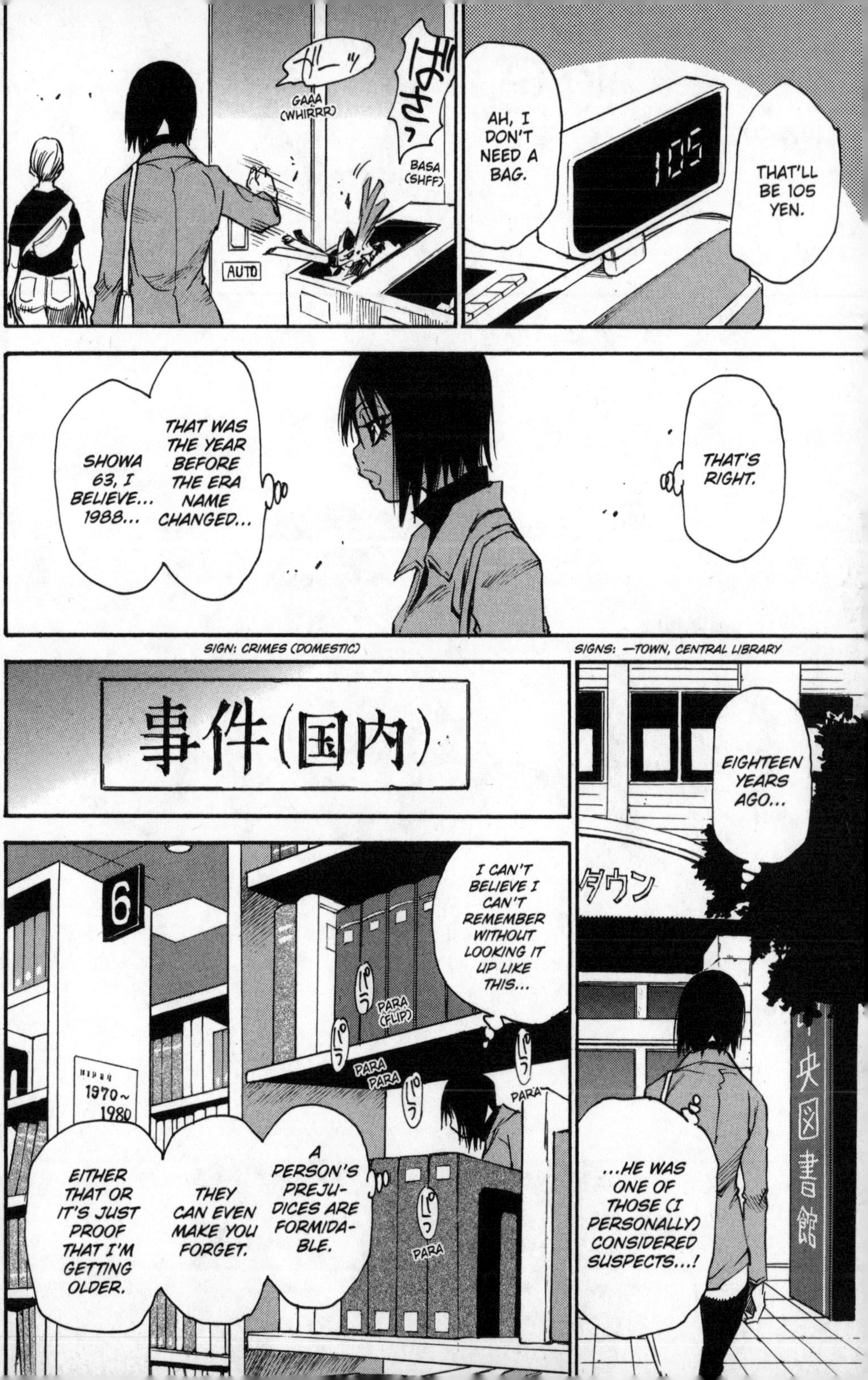
THAT'LL BE 105 YEN.
105
AH, I DON'T NEED A BAG.
ぱさっ
BASA (SHFF)
ガーッ
GAAA (WHIRRR)
AUTO
THAT'S RIGHT.
SHOWA 63, I BELIEVE... 1988...
THAT WAS THE YEAR BEFORE THE ERA NAME CHANGED...
SIGNS: —TOWN, CENTRAL LIBRARY
タウン
央図書館
EIGHTEEN YEARS AGO...
...HE WAS ONE OF THOSE (I PERSONALLY) CONSIDERED SUSPECTS...!
SIGN: CRIMES (DOMESTIC)
事件(国内)
6
1970~1980
I CAN'T BELIEVE I CAN'T REMEMBER WITHOUT LOOKING IT UP LIKE THIS...
パラ
PARA (FLIP)
PARA PARA
PARA
A PERSON'S PREJUDICES ARE FORMIDABLE.
THEY CAN EVEN MAKE YOU FORGET.
EITHER THAT OR IT'S JUST PROOF THAT I'M GETTING OLDER.
PARA

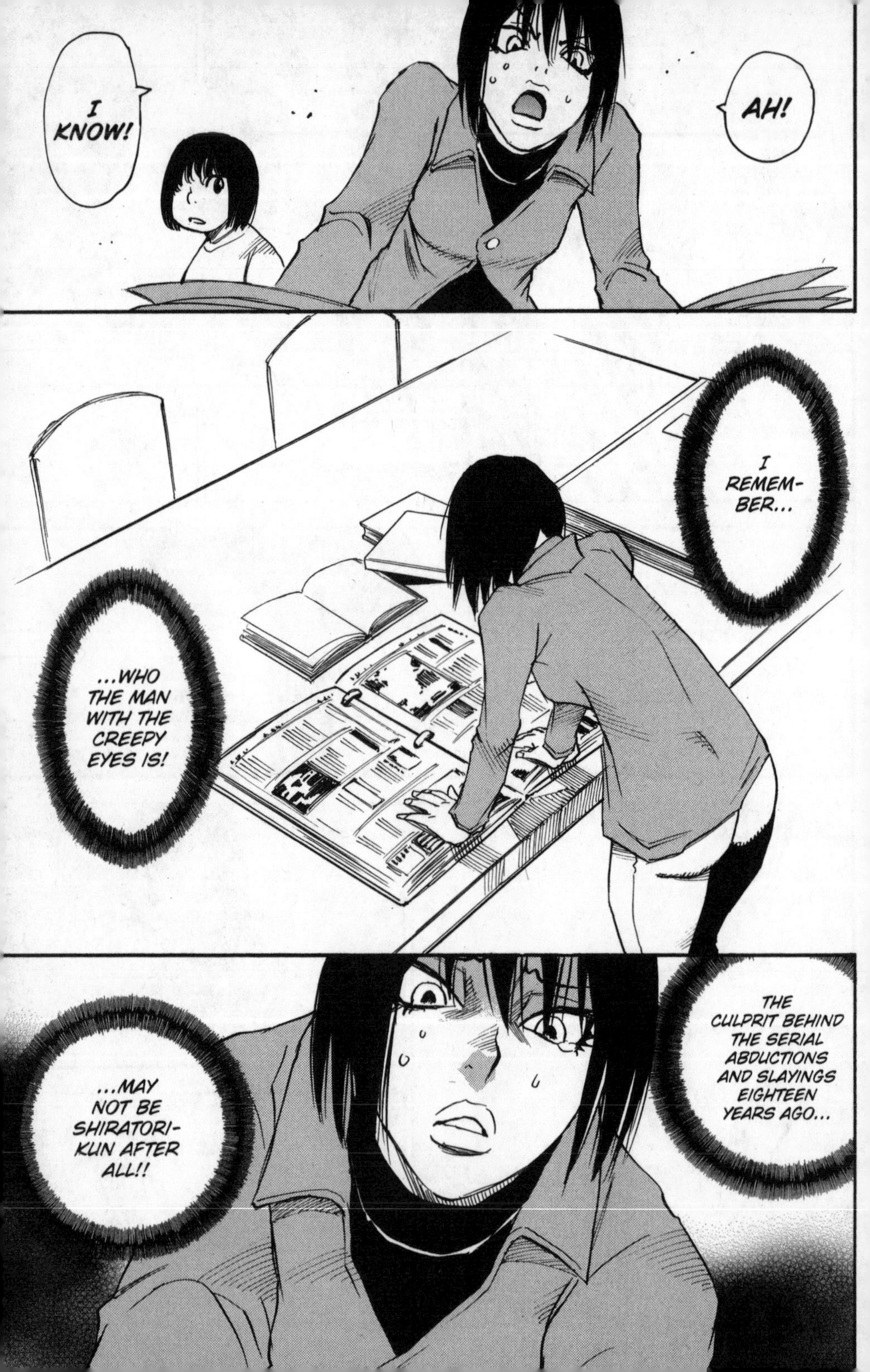
AH!
I KNOW!
I REMEMBER...
...WHO THE MAN WITH THE CREEPY EYES IS!
THE CULPRIT BEHIND THE SERIAL ABDUCTIONS AND SLAYINGS EIGHTEEN YEARS AGO...
...MAY NOT BE SHIRATORI-KUN AFTER ALL!!

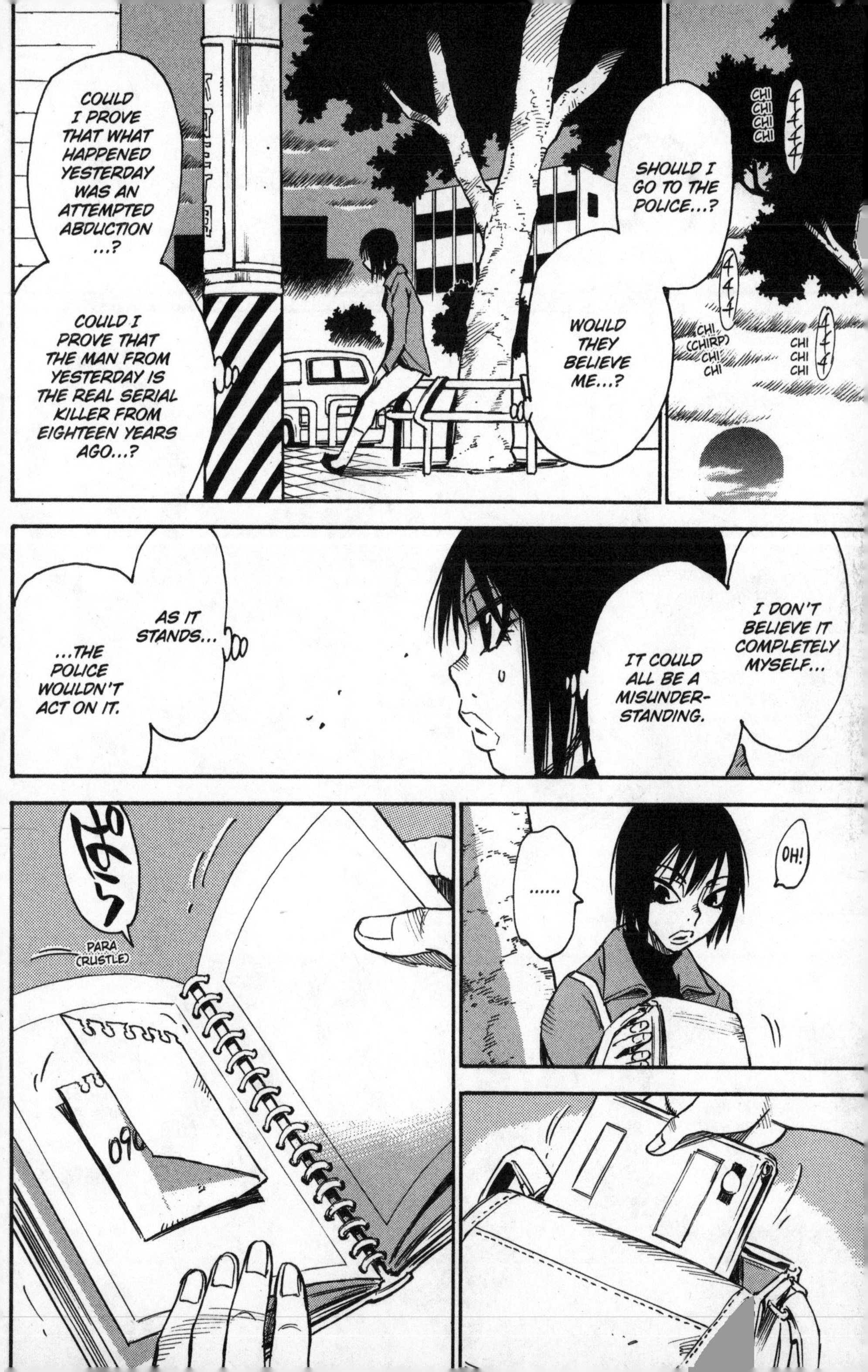
CHI CHI CHI CHI
SHOULD I GO TO THE POLICE...?
WOULD THEY BELIEVE ME...?
CHI (CHIRP) CHI CHI
CHI CHI CHI
COULD I PROVE THAT WHAT HAPPENED YESTERDAY WAS AN ATTEMPTED ABDUCTION ...?
COULD I PROVE THAT THE MAN FROM YESTERDAY IS THE REAL SERIAL KILLER FROM EIGHTEEN YEARS AGO...?
I DON'T BELIEVE IT COMPLETELY MYSELF...
IT COULD ALL BE A MISUNDERSTANDING.
AS IT STANDS...
...THE POLICE WOULDN'T ACT ON IT.
OH!
......
PARA (RUSTLE)
090

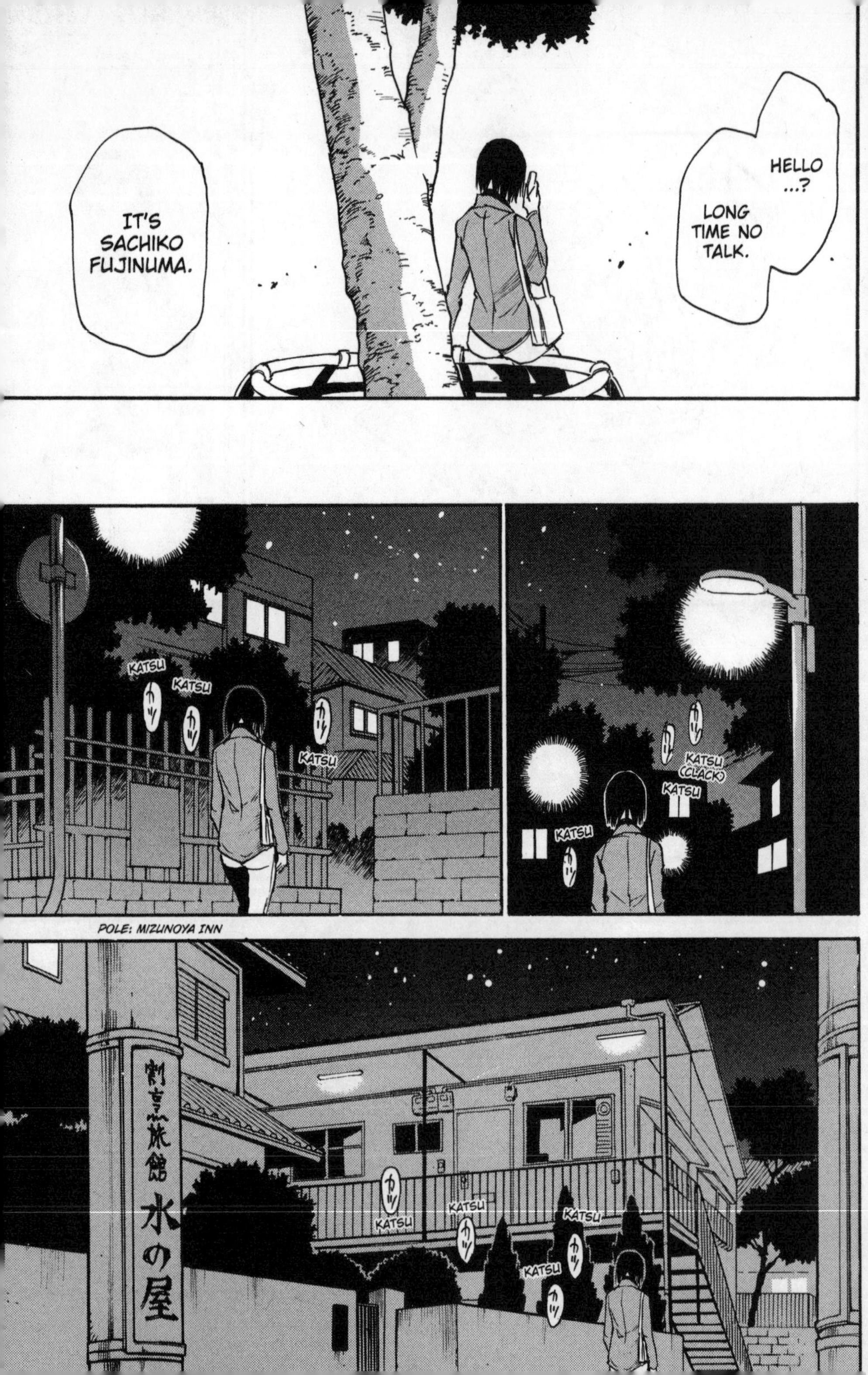
HELLO ...?
LONG TIME NO TALK.
IT'S SACHIKO FUJINUMA.
カッ
カッ
KATSU (CLACK)
KATSU
KATSU
カッ
KATSU
カッ
KATSU
カッ
カッ
KATSU
POLE: MIZUNOYA INN
割烹旅館 水の屋
カッ
KATSU
KATSU
カッ
KATSU
カッ
KATSU
カッ

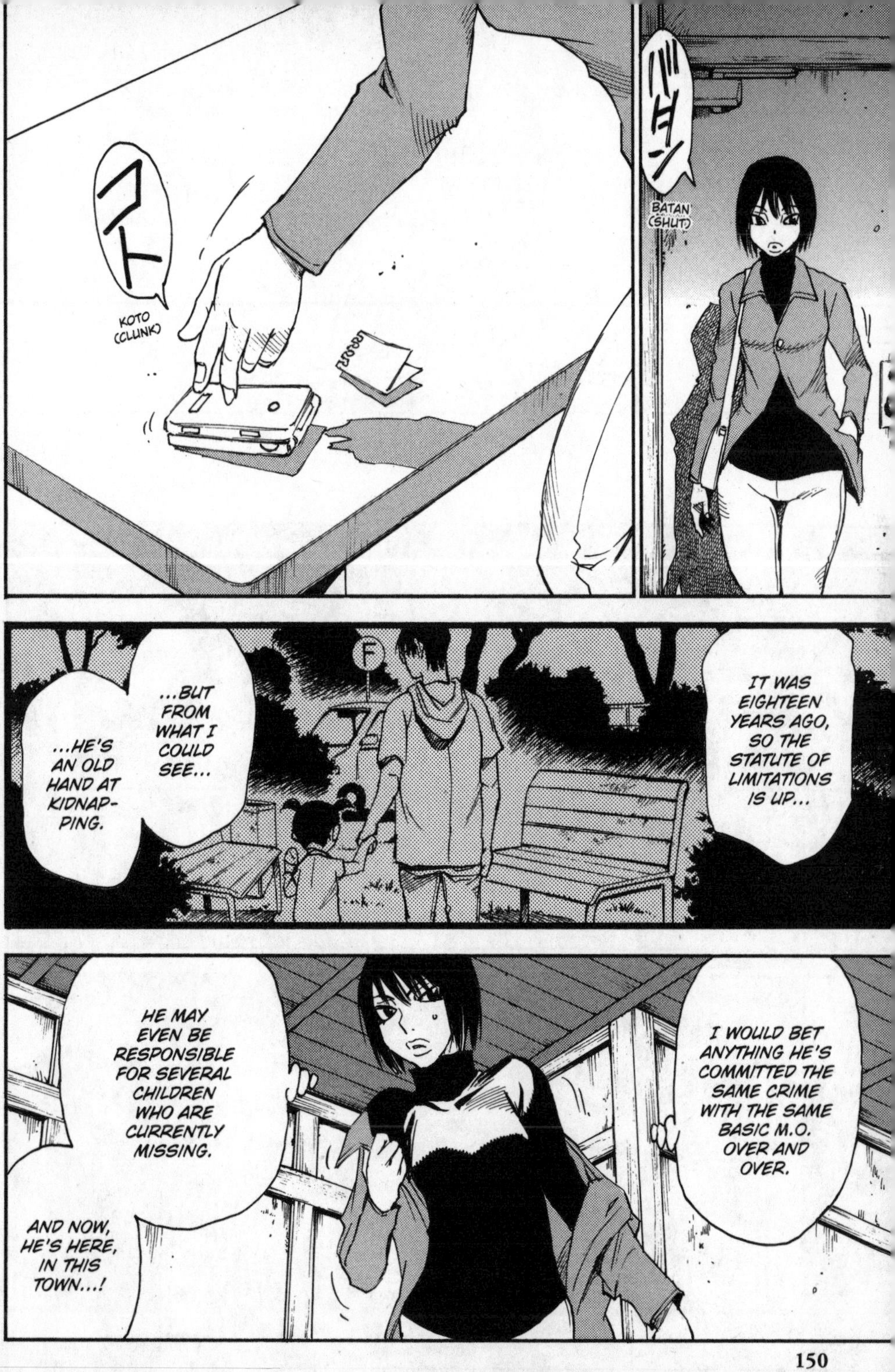
バタン
BATAN (SHUT)
コト
KOTO (CLUNK)
IT WAS EIGHTEEN YEARS AGO, SO THE STATUTE OF LIMITATIONS IS UP...
...BUT FROM WHAT I COULD SEE...
...HE'S AN OLD HAND AT KIDNAP-PING.
I WOULD BET ANYTHING HE'S COMMITTED THE SAME CRIME WITH THE SAME BASIC M.O. OVER AND OVER.
HE MAY EVEN BE RESPONSIBLE FOR SEVERAL CHILDREN WHO ARE CURRENTLY MISSING.
AND NOW, HE'S HERE, IN THIS TOWN...!

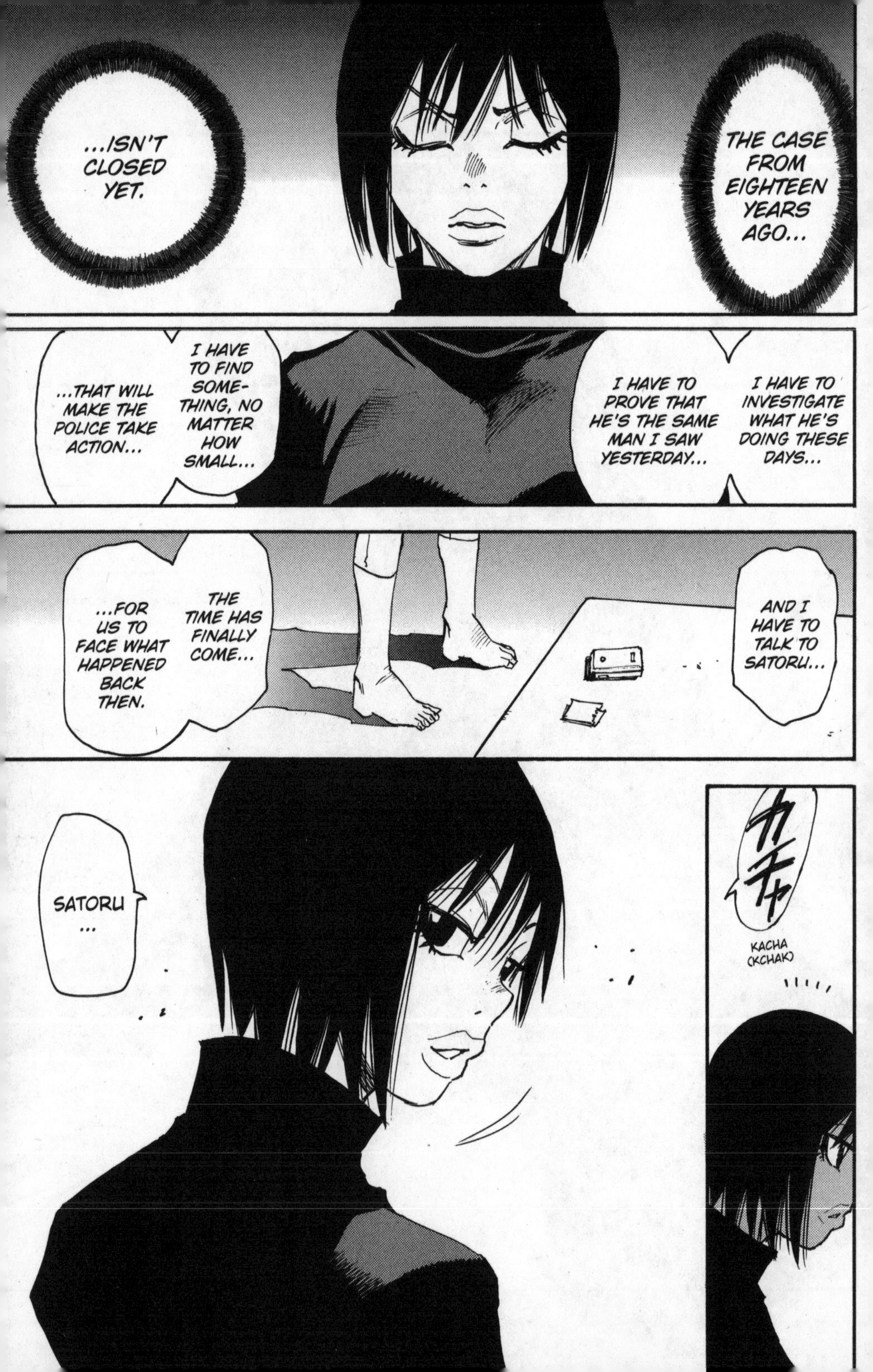
THE CASE FROM EIGHTEEN YEARS AGO...
...ISN'T CLOSED YET.
I HAVE TO INVESTIGATE WHAT HE'S DOING THESE DAYS...
I HAVE TO PROVE THAT HE'S THE SAME MAN I SAW YESTERDAY...
I HAVE TO FIND SOME-THING, NO MATTER HOW SMALL...
...THAT WILL MAKE THE POLICE TAKE ACTION...
AND I HAVE TO TALK TO SATORU...
THE TIME HAS FINALLY COME...
...FOR US TO FACE WHAT HAPPENED BACK THEN.
カチャ
KACHA (KCHAK)
SATORU ...

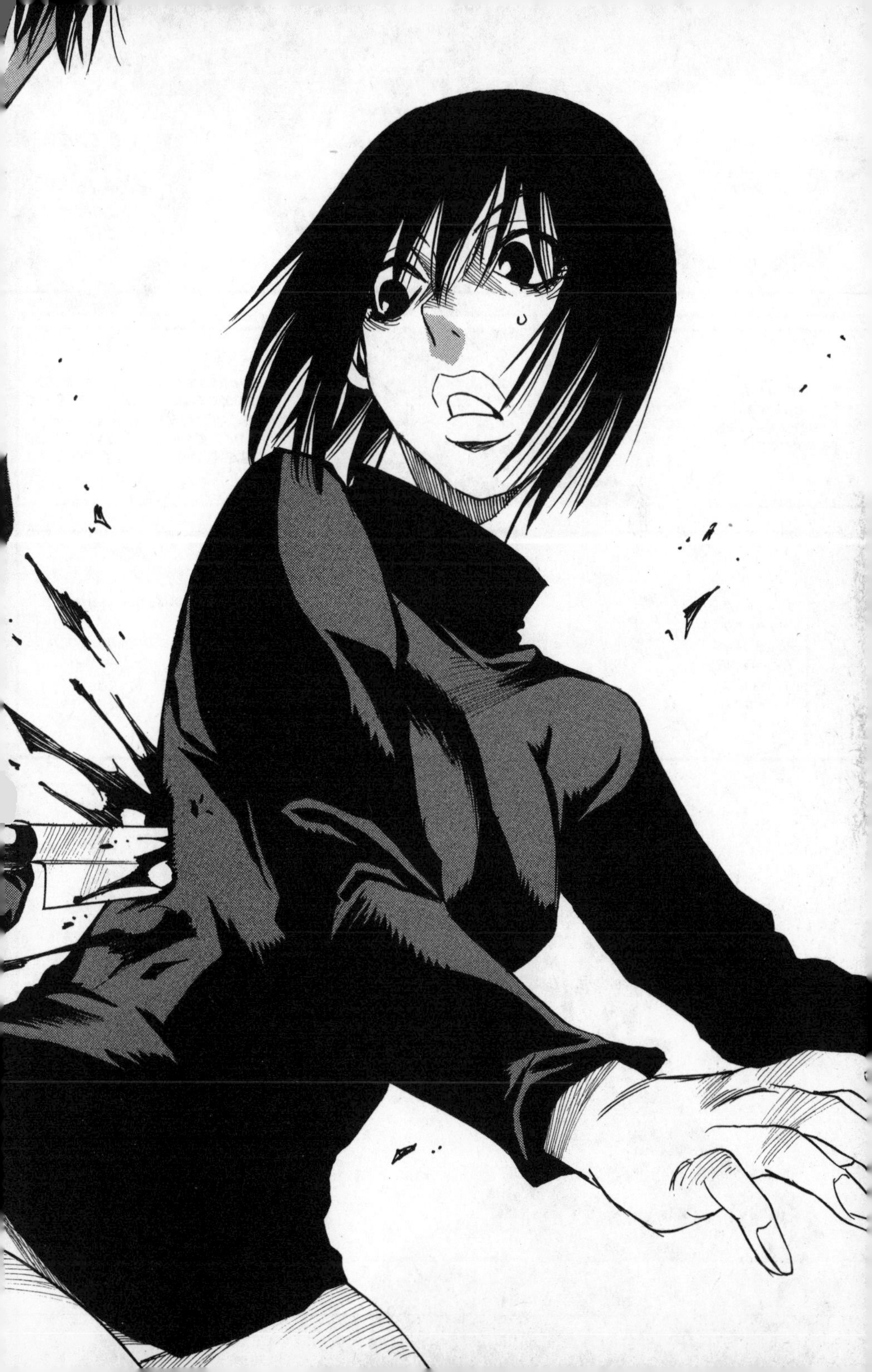

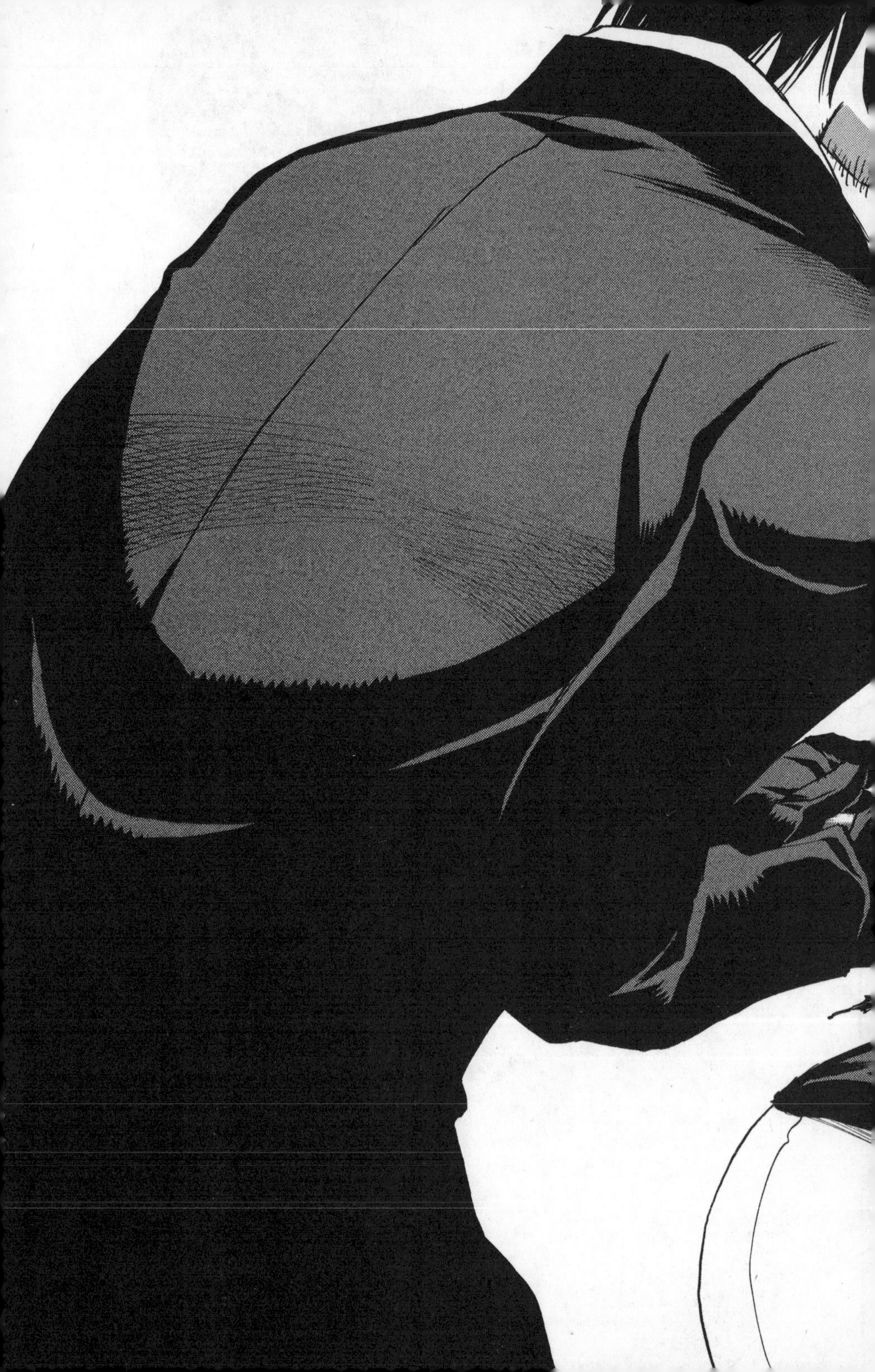

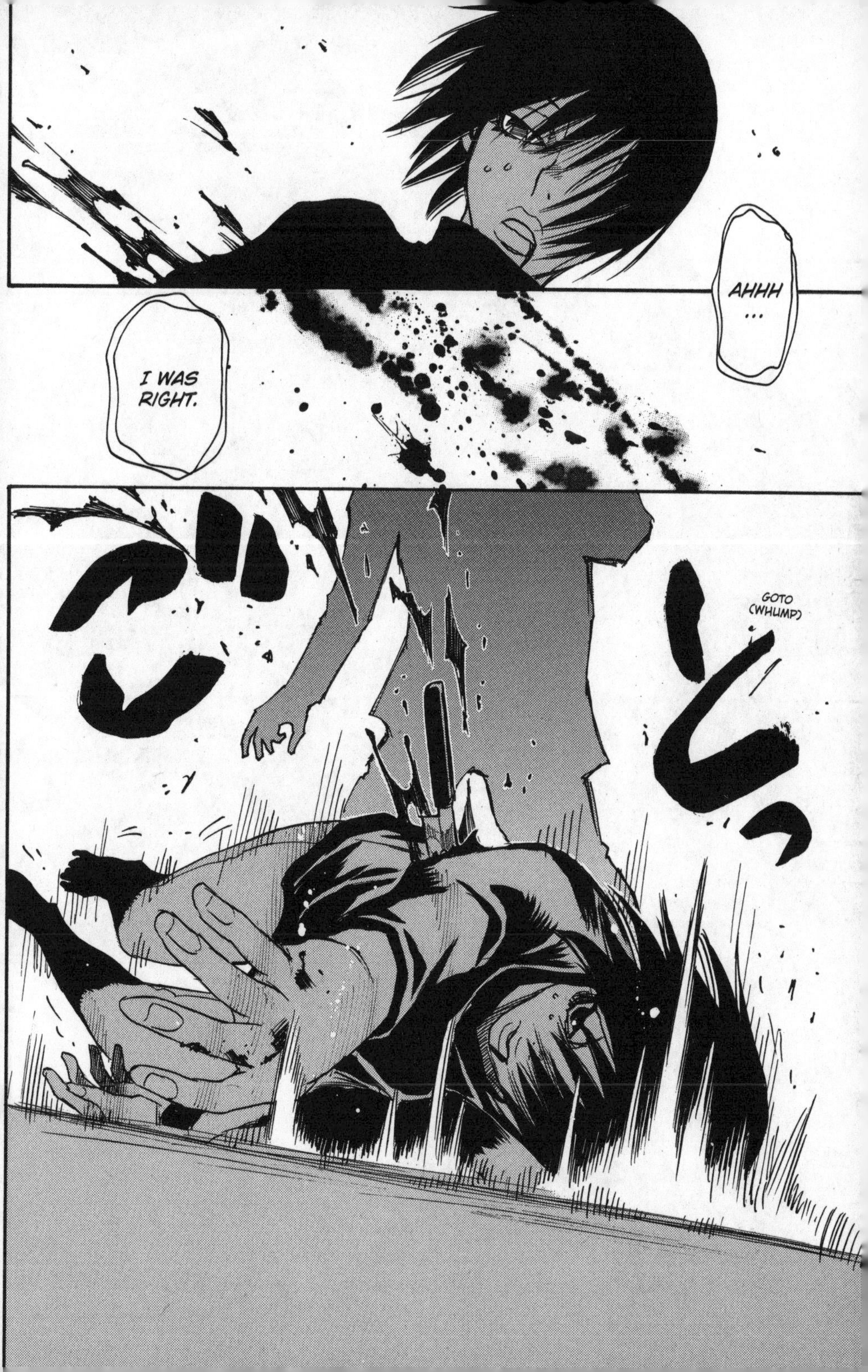
AHHH
...
I WAS RIGHT.
GOTO (WHUMP)

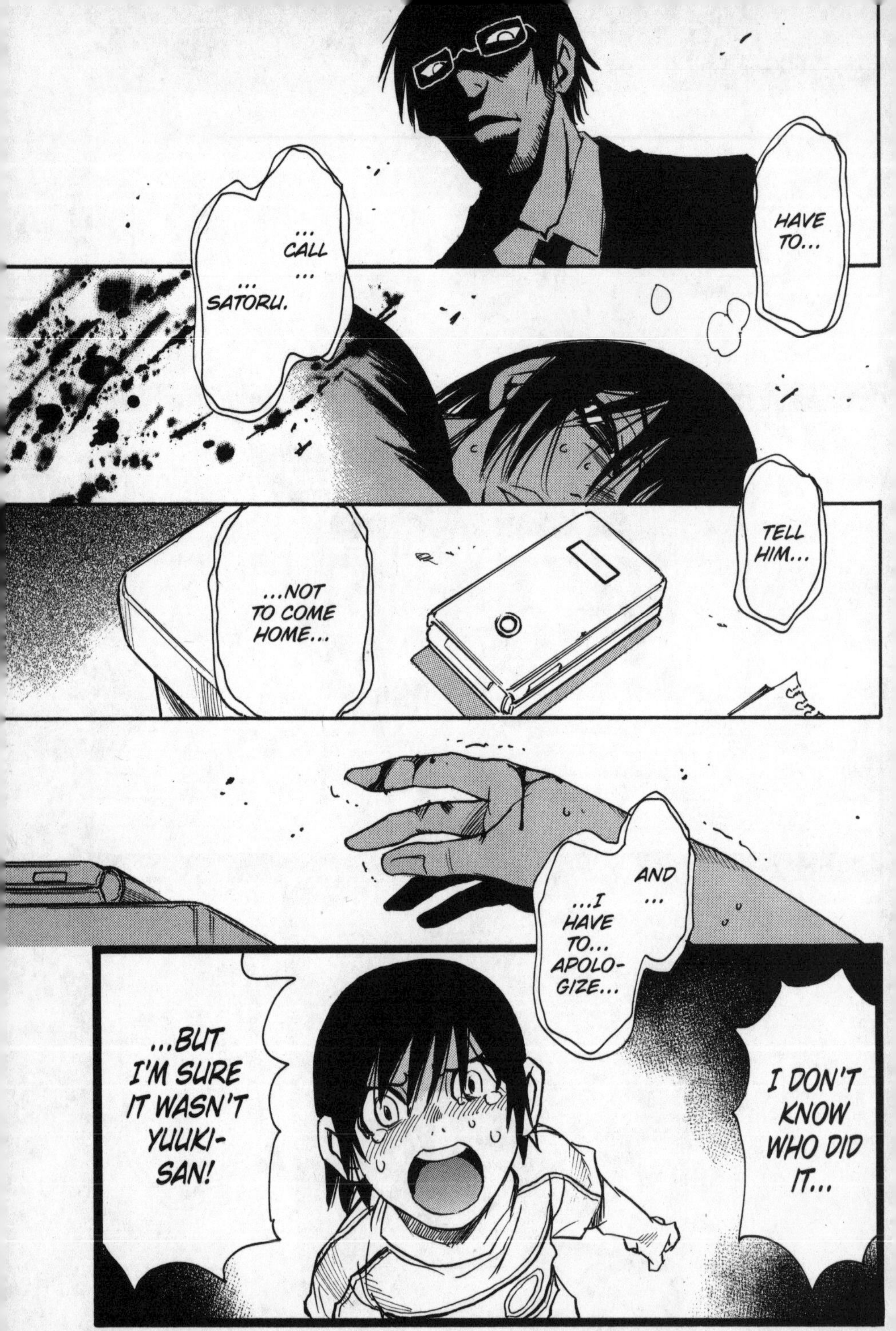
HAVE TO...
... CALL ... ... SATORU.
TELL HIM...
...NOT TO COME HOME...
AND ... ...I HAVE TO... APOLOGIZE...
I DON'T KNOW WHO DID IT...
...BUT I'M SURE IT WASN'T YUUKI-SAN!

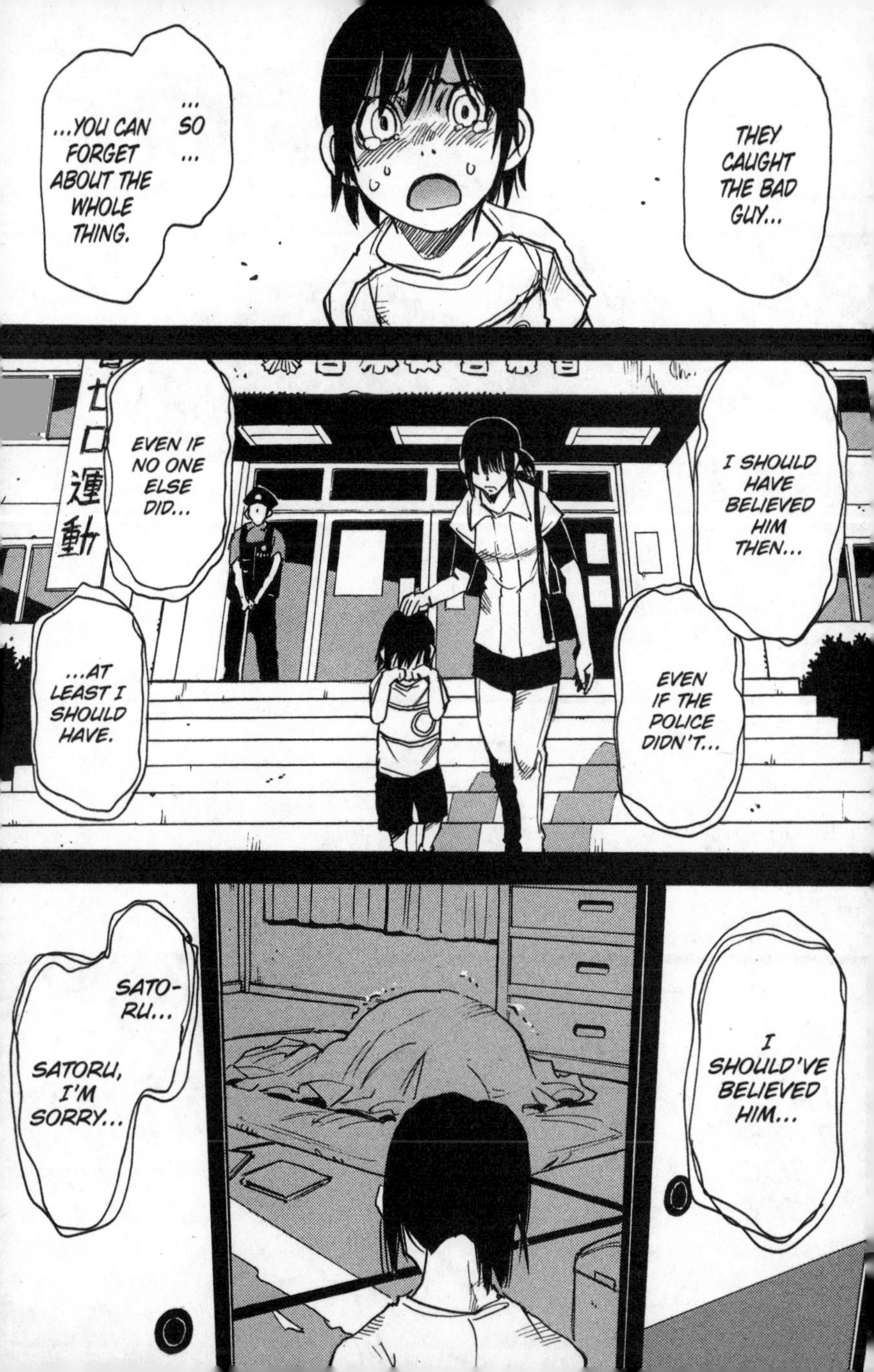
THEY CAUGHT THE BAD GUY...
...SO...
...YOU CAN FORGET ABOUT THE WHOLE THING.
I SHOULD HAVE BELIEVED HIM THEN...
EVEN IF THE POLICE DIDN'T...
EVEN IF NO ONE ELSE DID...
...AT LEAST I SHOULD HAVE.
I SHOULD'VE BELIEVED HIM...
SATO-RU...
SATORU, I'M SORRY...

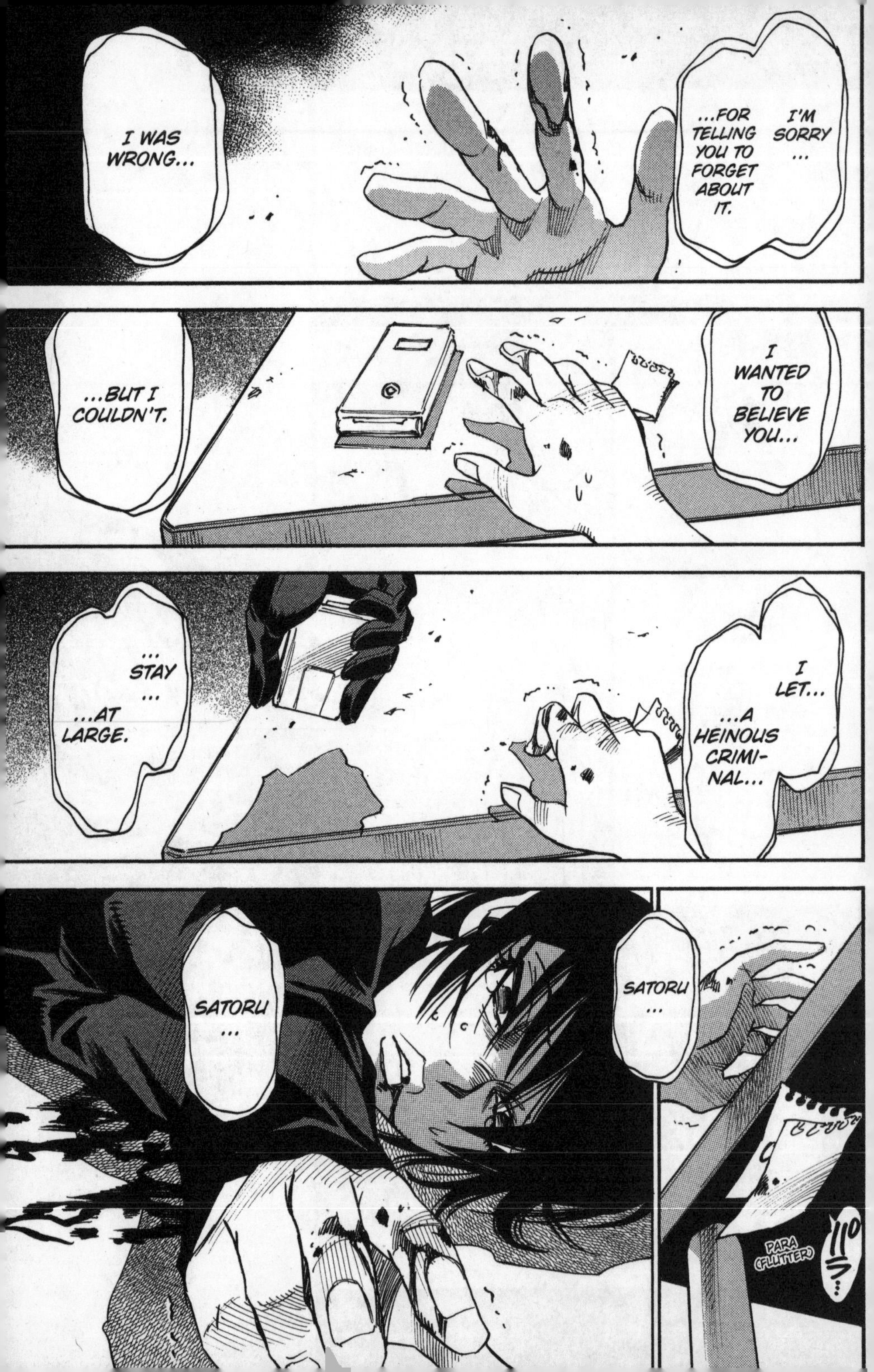
I'M SORRY ...
...FOR TELLING YOU TO FORGET ABOUT IT.
I WAS WRONG...
I WANTED TO BELIEVE YOU...
...BUT I COULDN'T.
I LET... ...A HEINOUS CRIMINAL...
... STAY ... ...AT LARGE.
SATORU ...
PARA (FLUTTER)
SATORU ...

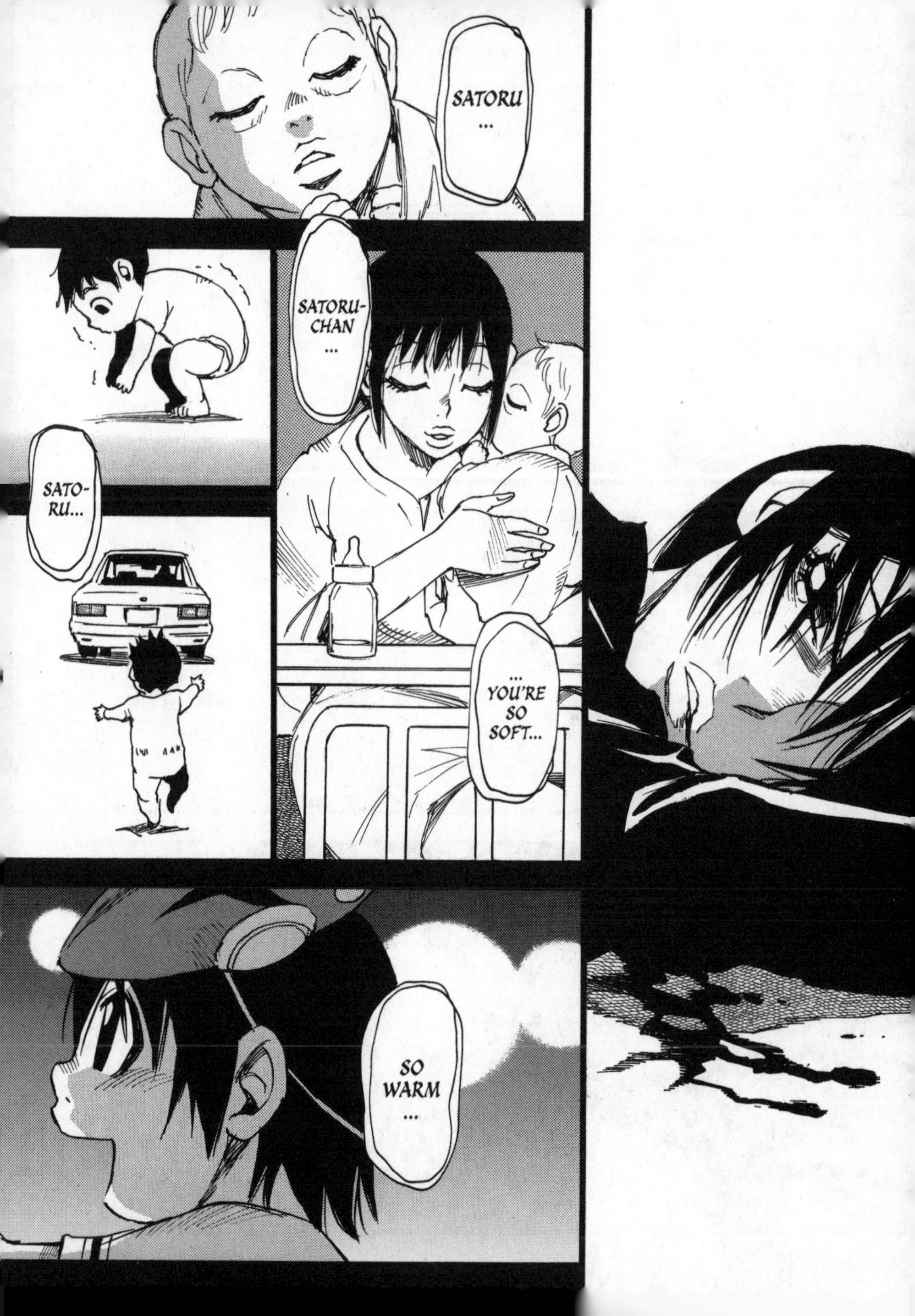
SATORU ...
SATORU-CHAN ...
... YOU'RE SO SOFT...
SATO-RU...
SO WARM ...

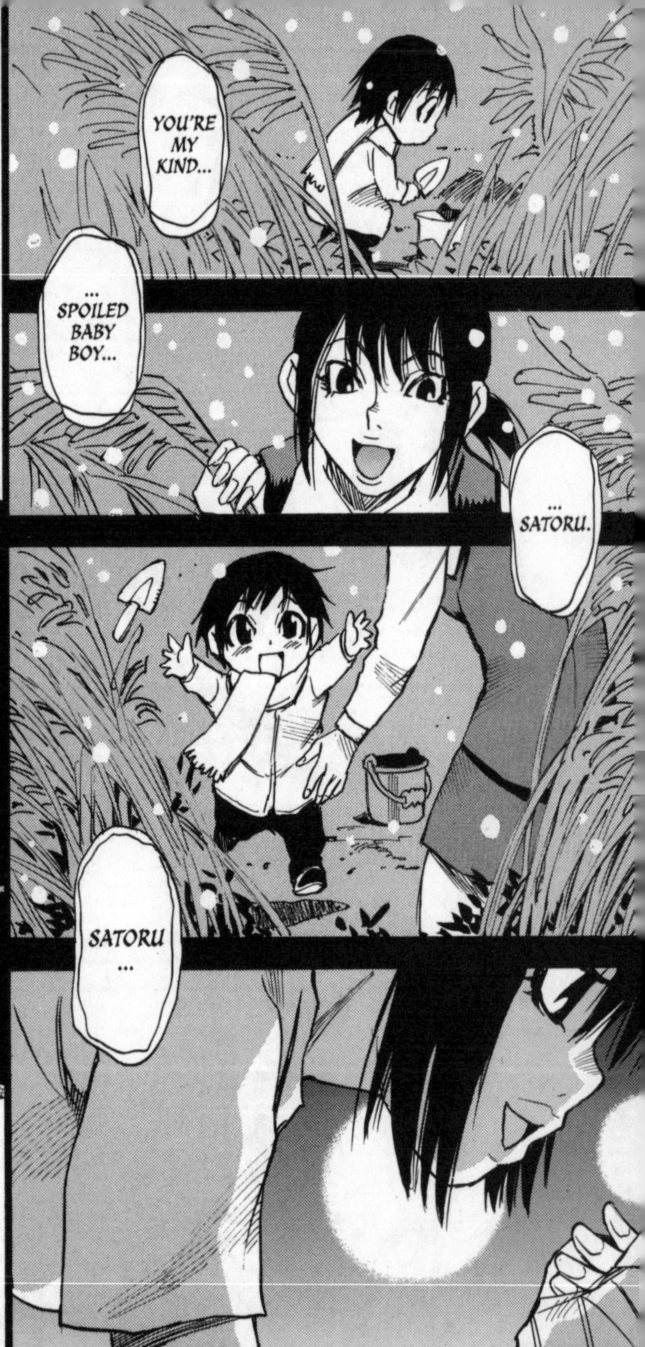
YOU'RE MY KIND...
... SPOILED BABY BOY...
... SATORU.
SATORU ...
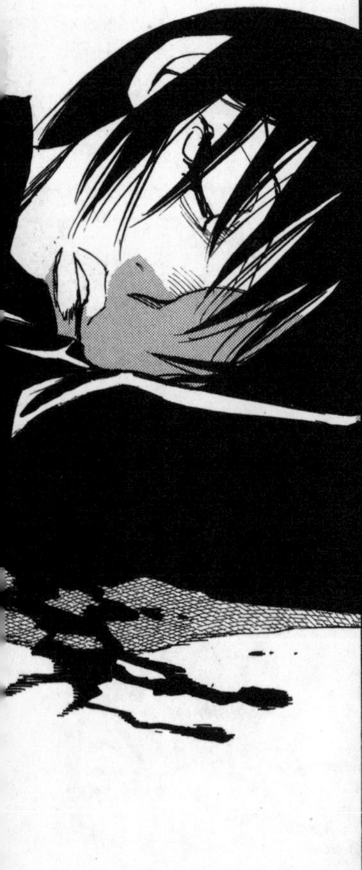

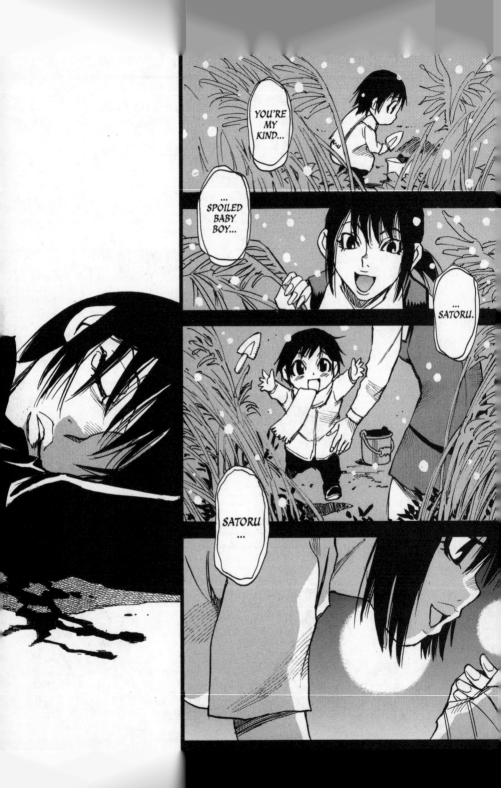

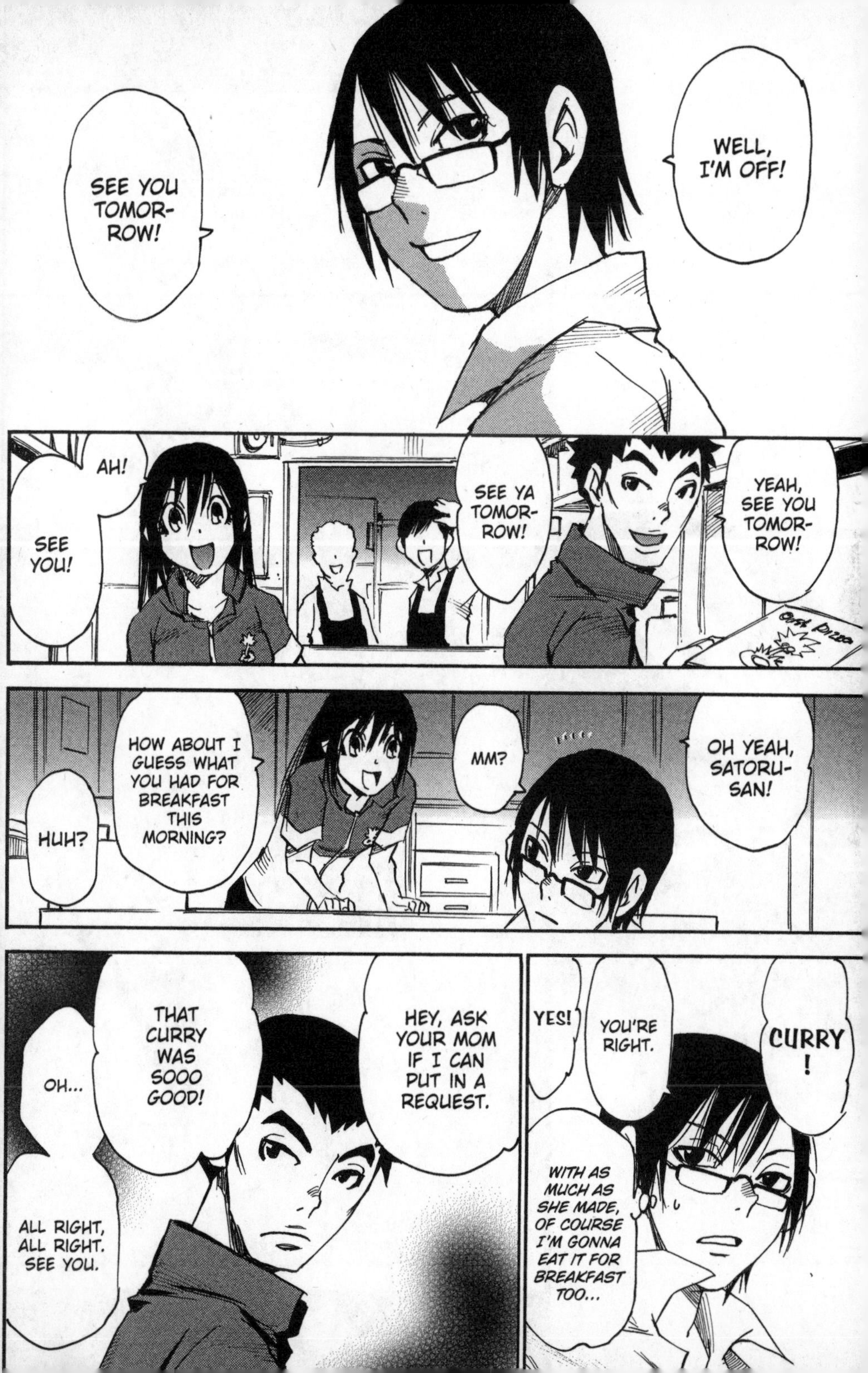
WELL, I'M OFF!
SEE YOU TOMORROW!
YEAH, SEE YOU TOMORROW!
SEE YA TOMORROW!
AH!
SEE YOU!
OH YEAH, SATORU-SAN!
....
MM?
HOW ABOUT I GUESS WHAT YOU HAD FOR BREAKFAST THIS MORNING?
HUH?
CURRY!
YOU'RE RIGHT.
YES!
WITH AS MUCH AS SHE MADE, OF COURSE I'M GONNA EAT IT FOR BREAKFAST TOO...
HEY, ASK YOUR MOM IF I CAN PUT IN A REQUEST.
THAT CURRY WAS SOOO GOOD!
OH...
ALL RIGHT, ALL RIGHT. SEE YOU.

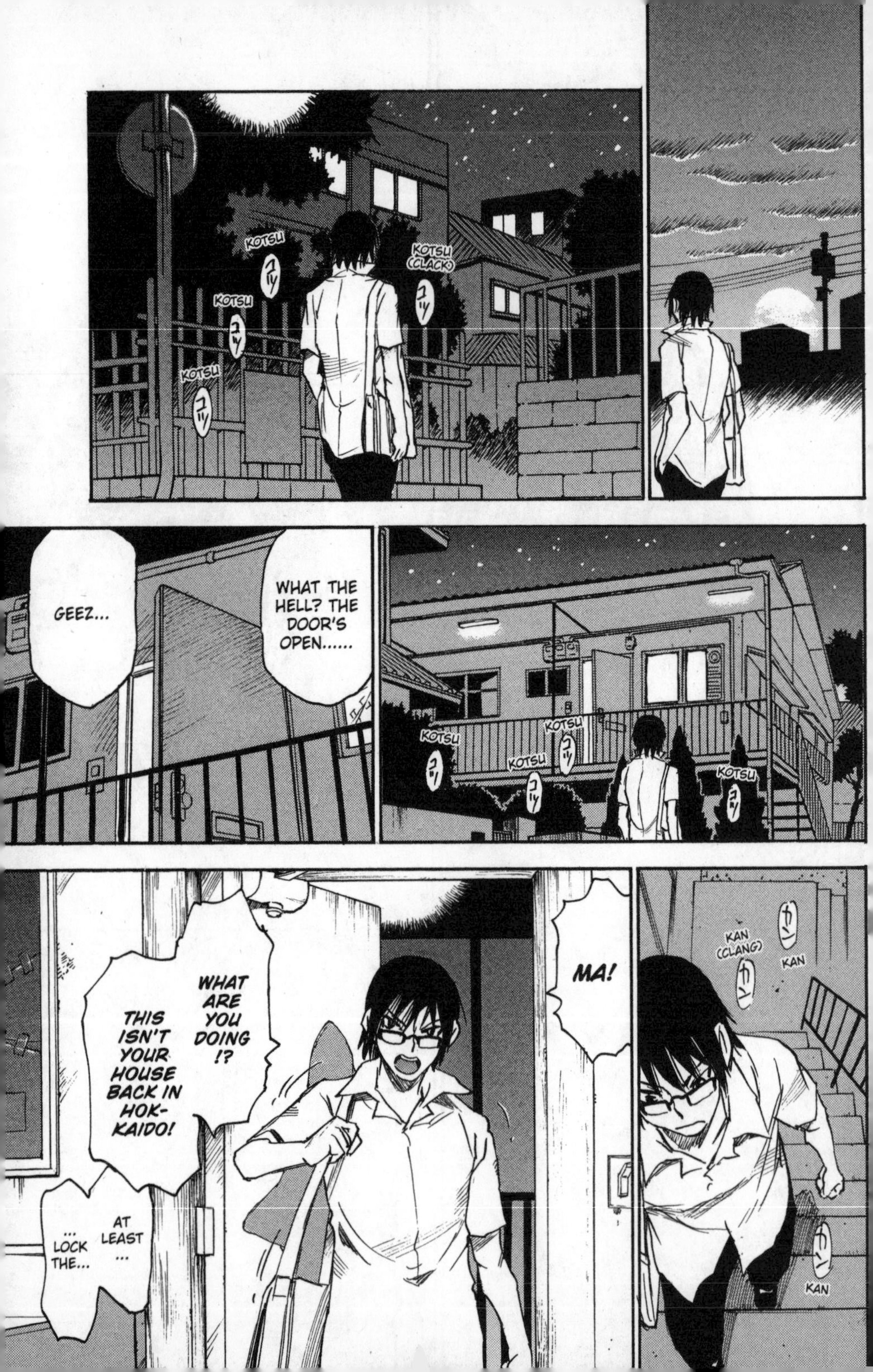
KOTSU (CLACK)
コツ
KOTSU
コツ
KOTSU
コツ
KOTSU
コツ
KOTSU
コツ
KOTSU
コツ
KOTSU
コツ
KOTSU
コツ
WHAT THE HELL? THE DOOR'S OPEN......
GEEZ...
KAN (CLANG)
カン
KAN
カン
カン
KAN
MA!
WHAT ARE YOU DOING!?
THIS ISN'T YOUR HOUSE BACK IN HOK-KAIDO!
AT LEAST...
...LOCK THE...

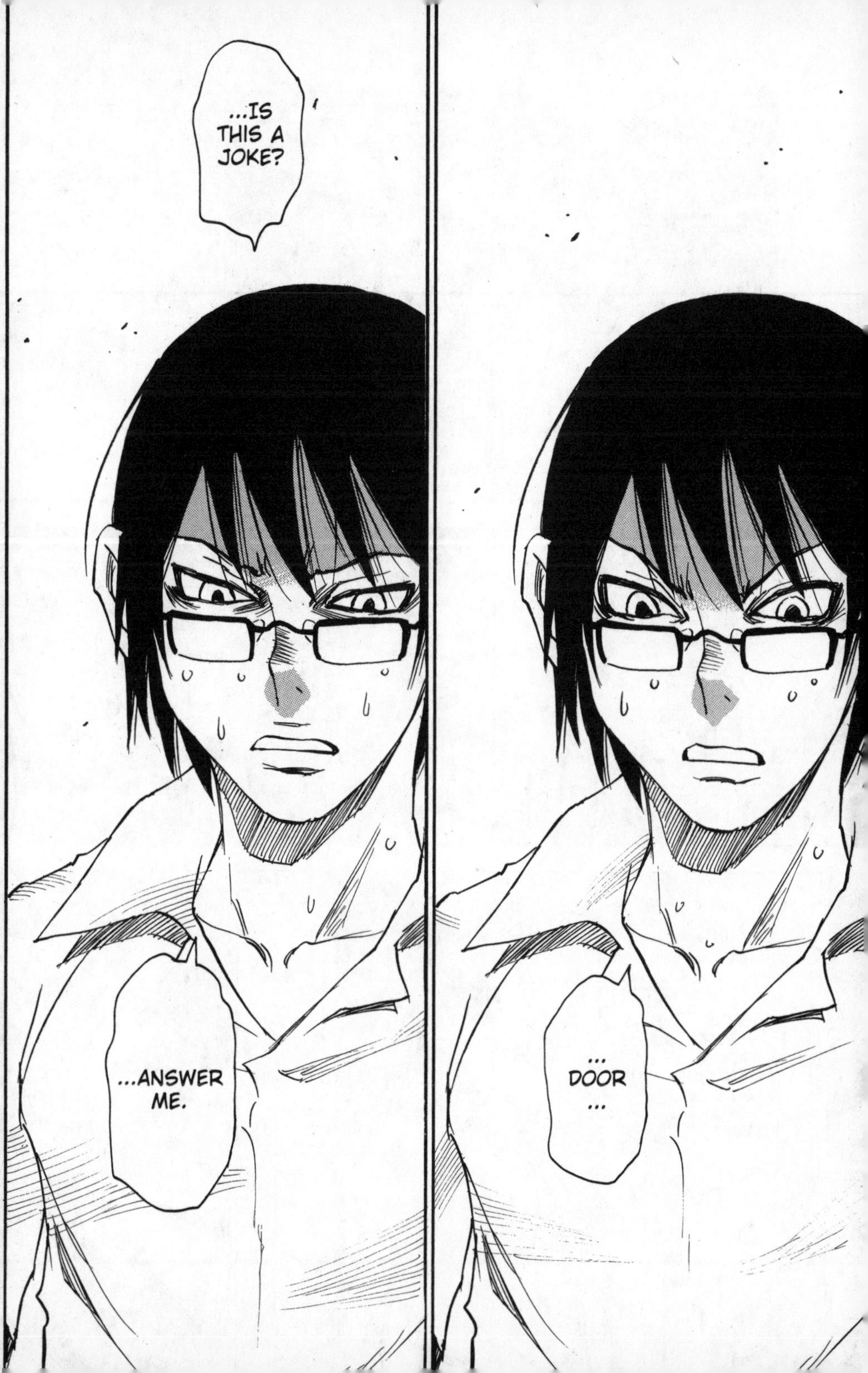
... DOOR ...
...IS THIS A JOKE?
...ANSWER ME.

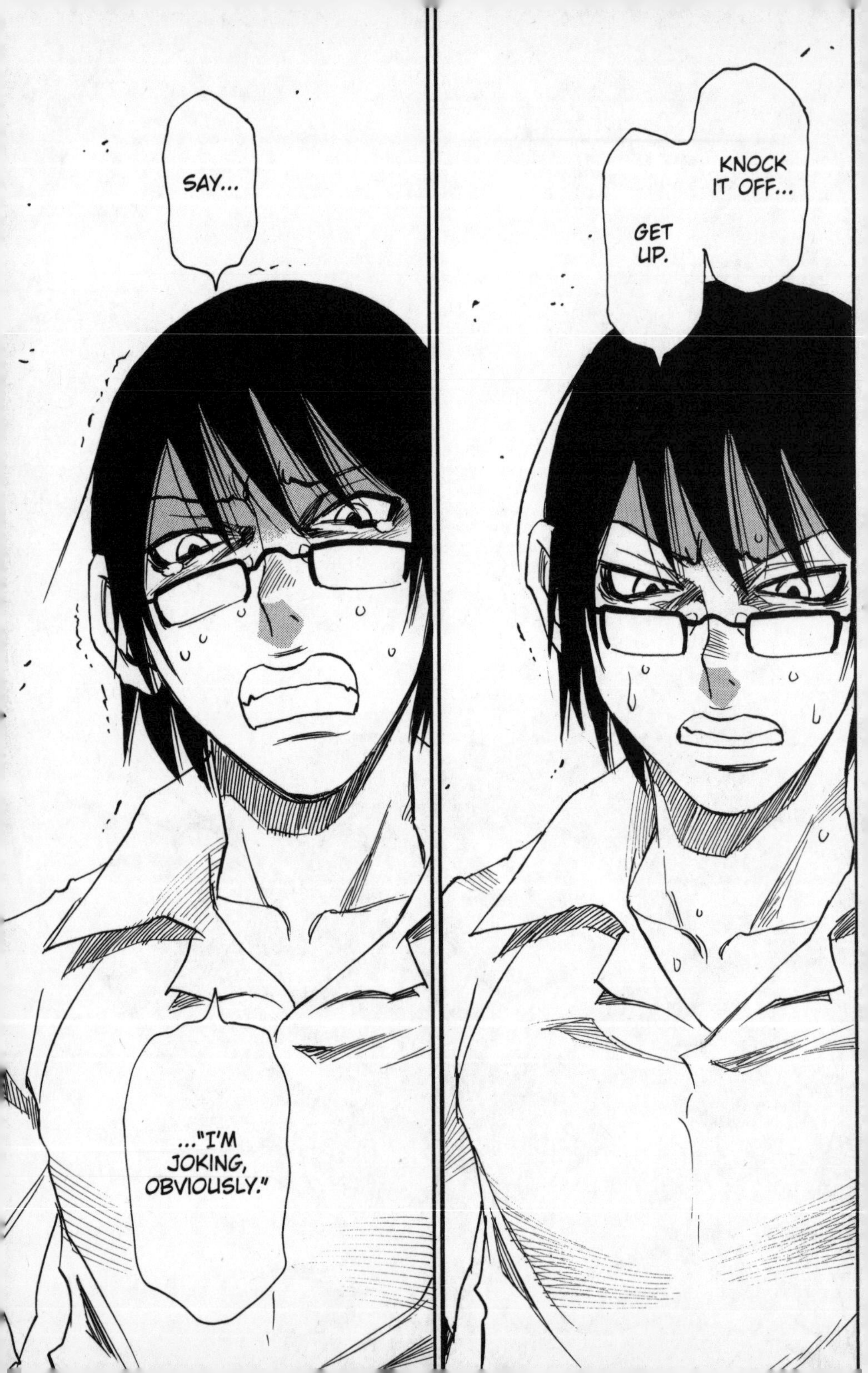
KNOCK IT OFF...
GET UP.
SAY...
..."I'M JOKING, OBVIOUSLY."

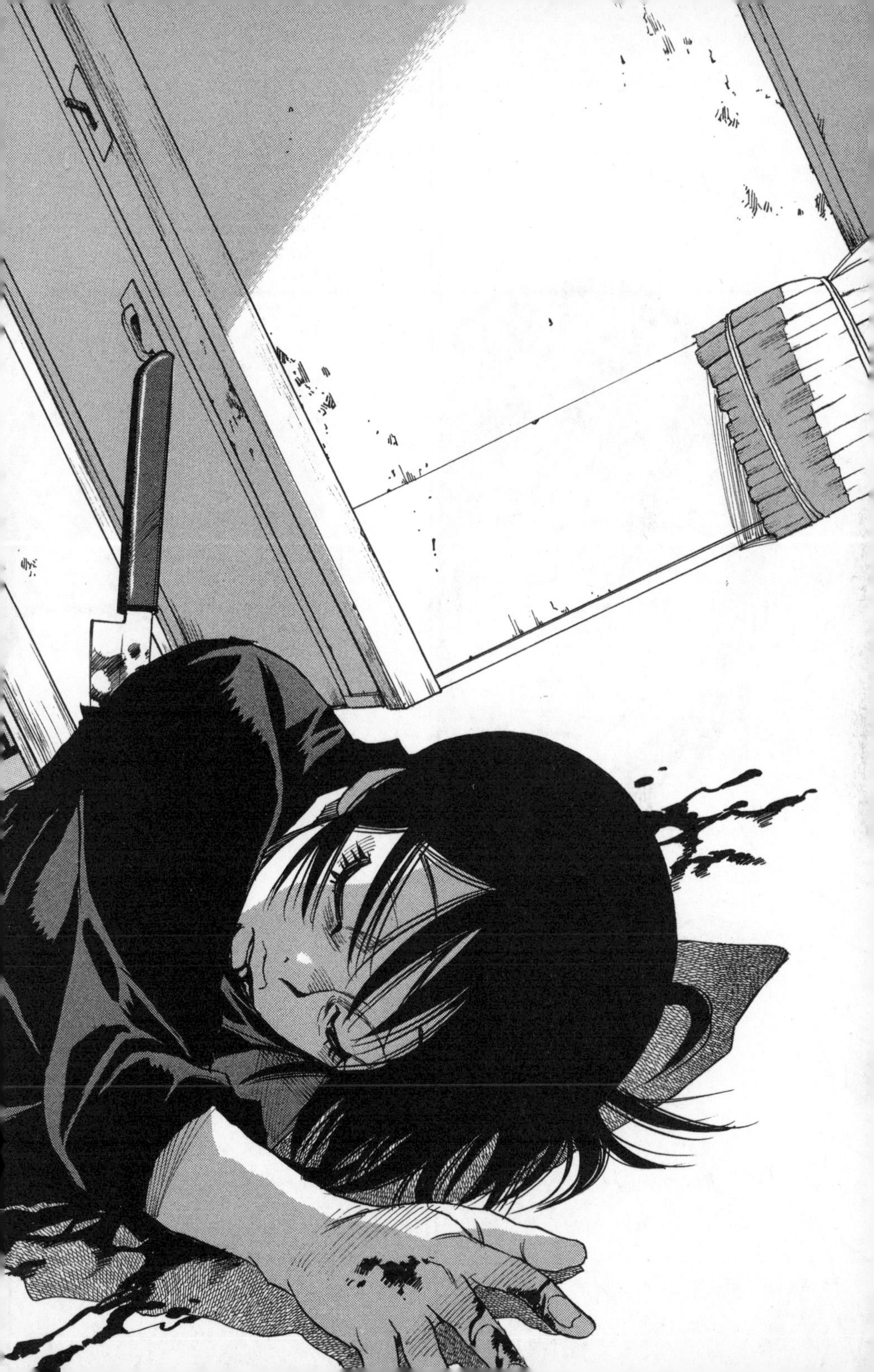

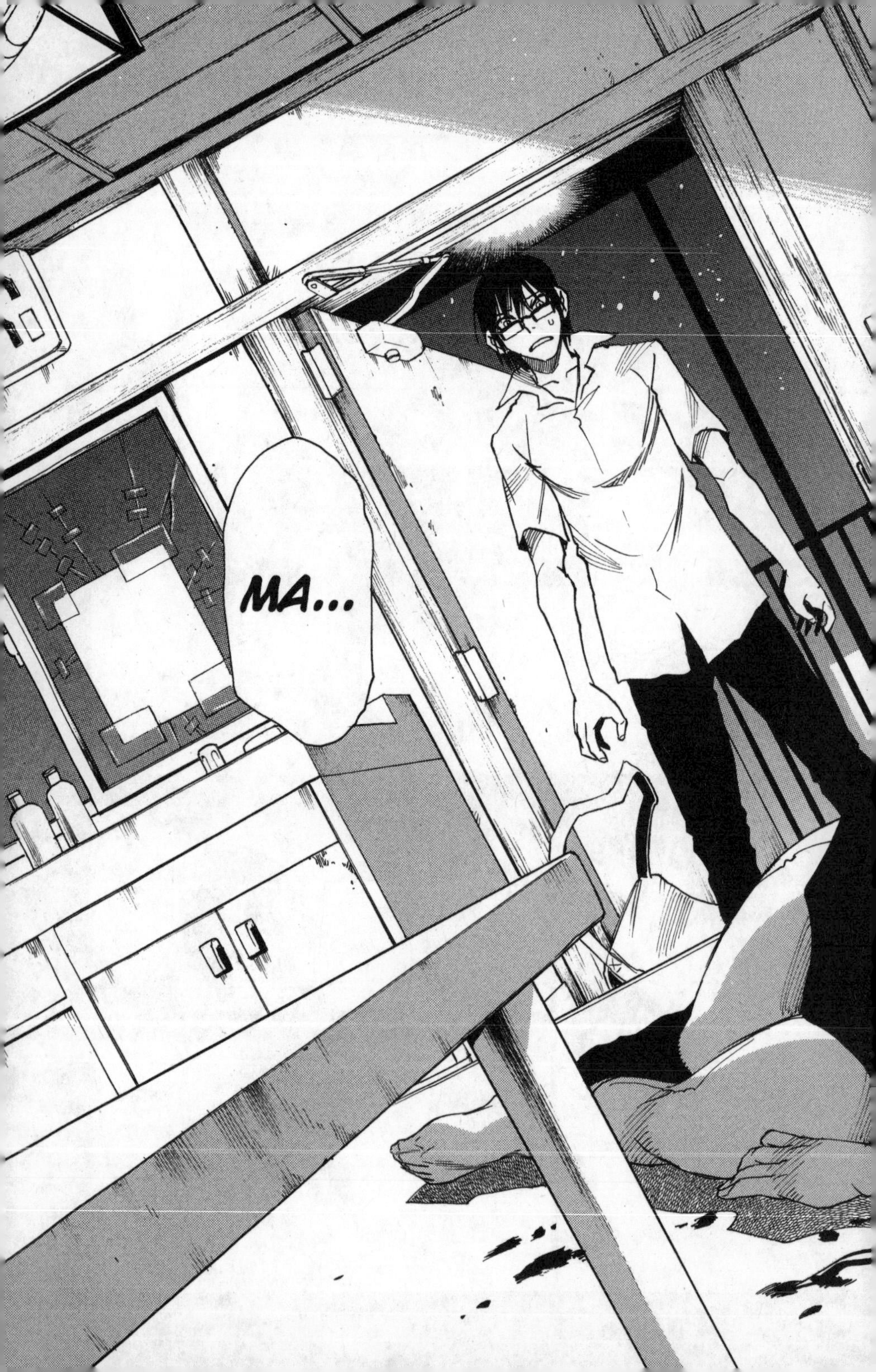
MA...

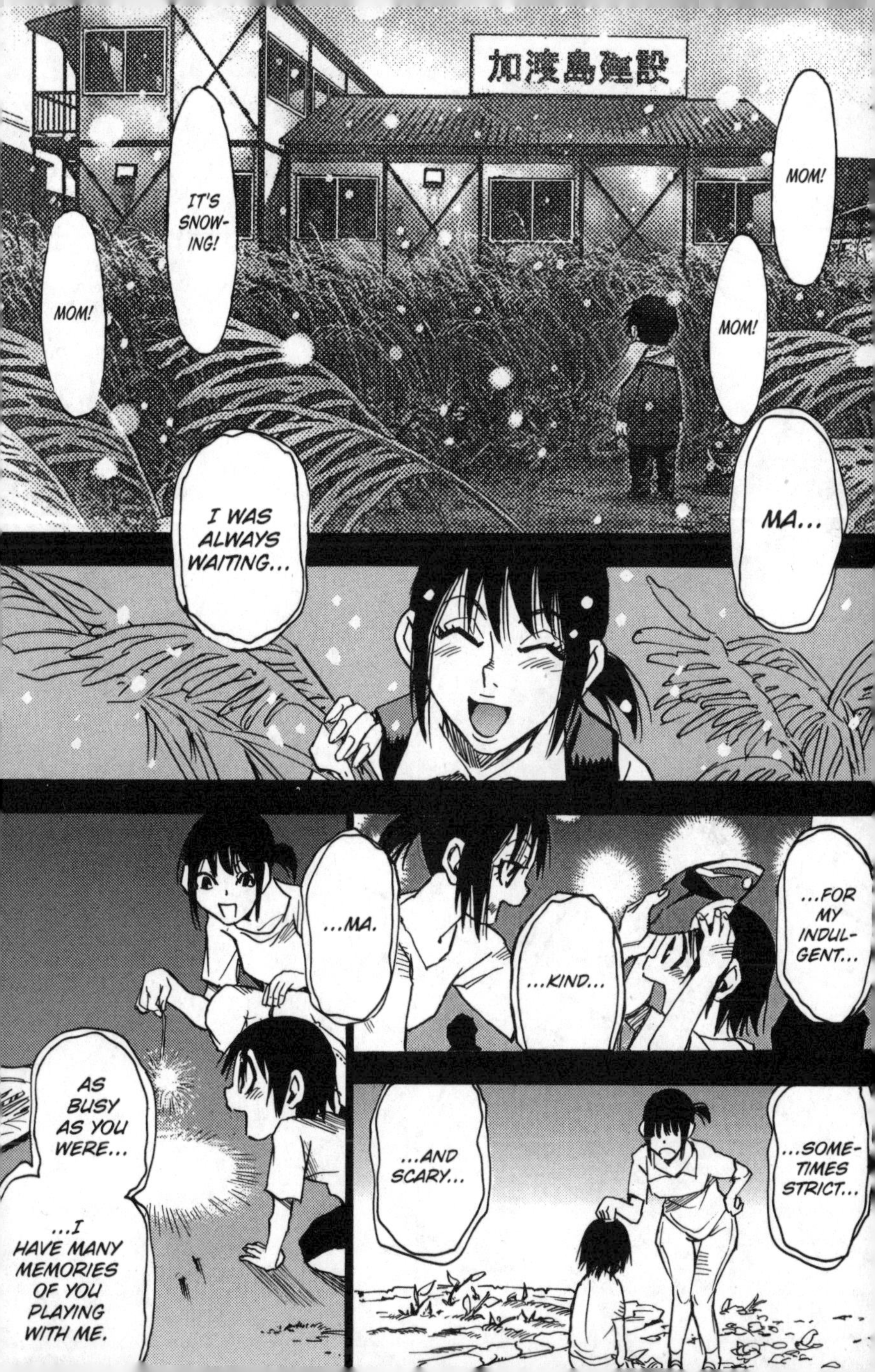
MOM!
MOM!
IT'S SNOWING!
MOM!
MA...
I WAS ALWAYS WAITING...
...FOR MY INDULGENT...
...KIND...
...MA.
...SOMETIMES STRICT...
...AND SCARY...
AS BUSY AS YOU WERE...
...I HAVE MANY MEMORIES OF YOU PLAYING WITH ME.

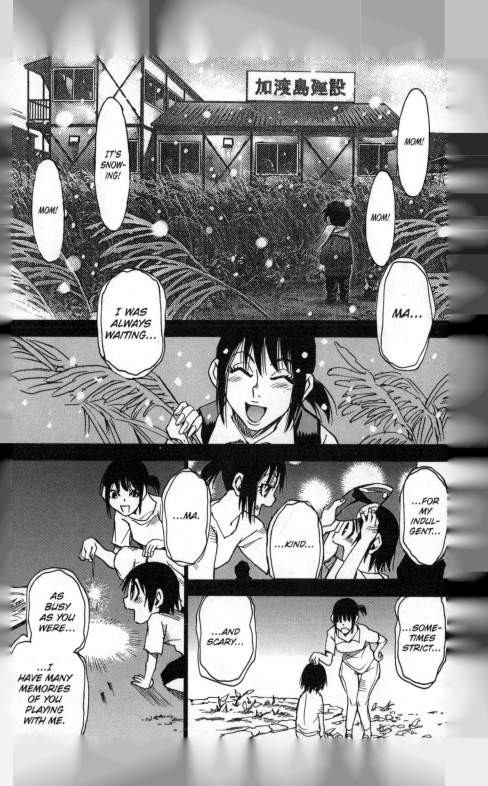

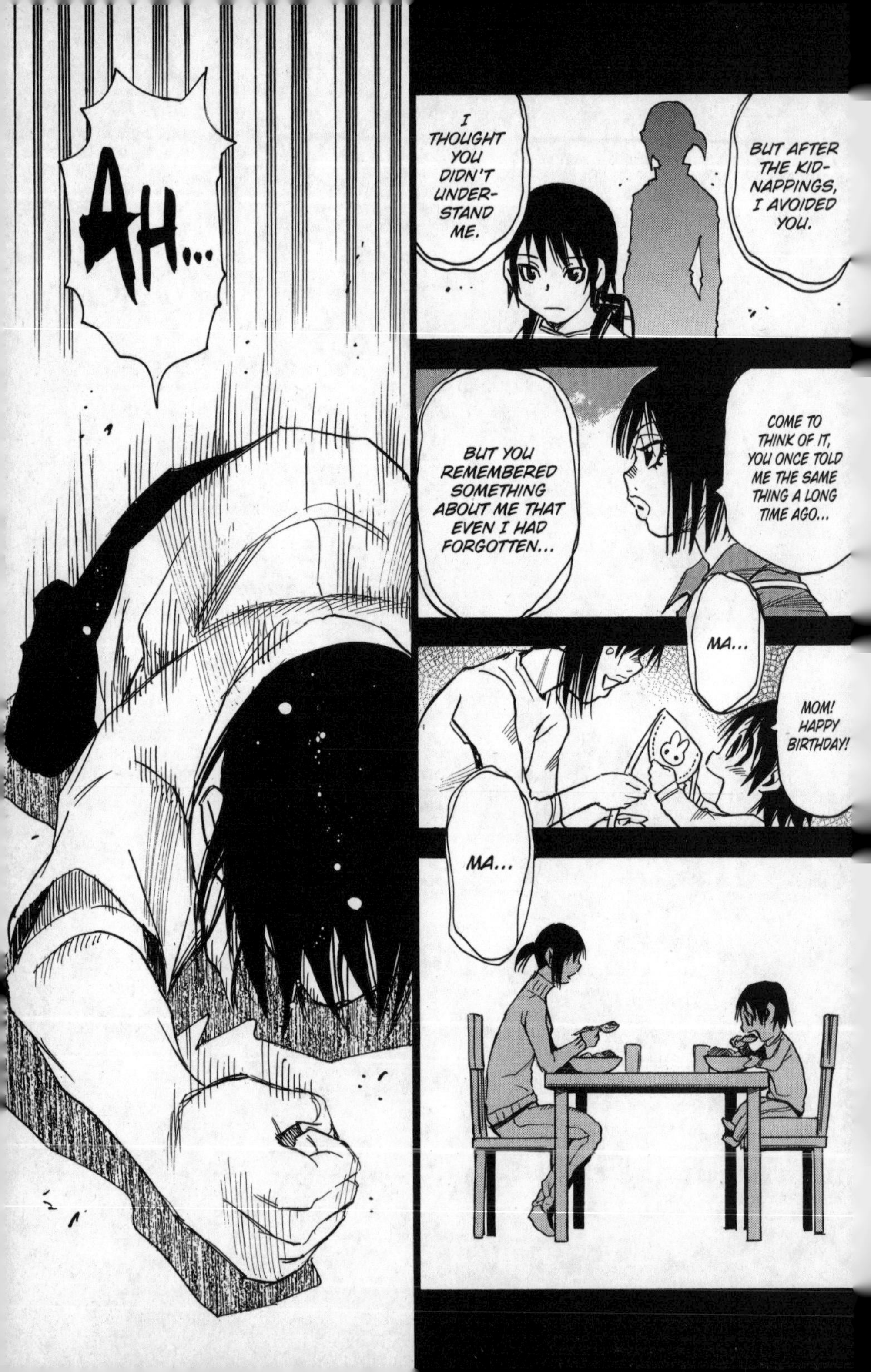
BUT AFTER THE KID-NAPPINGS, I AVOIDED YOU.
I THOUGHT YOU DIDN'T UNDER-STAND ME.
COME TO THINK OF IT, YOU ONCE TOLD ME THE SAME THING A LONG TIME AGO...
BUT YOU REMEMBERED SOMETHING ABOUT ME THAT EVEN I HAD FORGOTTEN...
MA...
MOM! HAPPY BIRTHDAY!
MA...
AH...

MA...!!!

#5 END

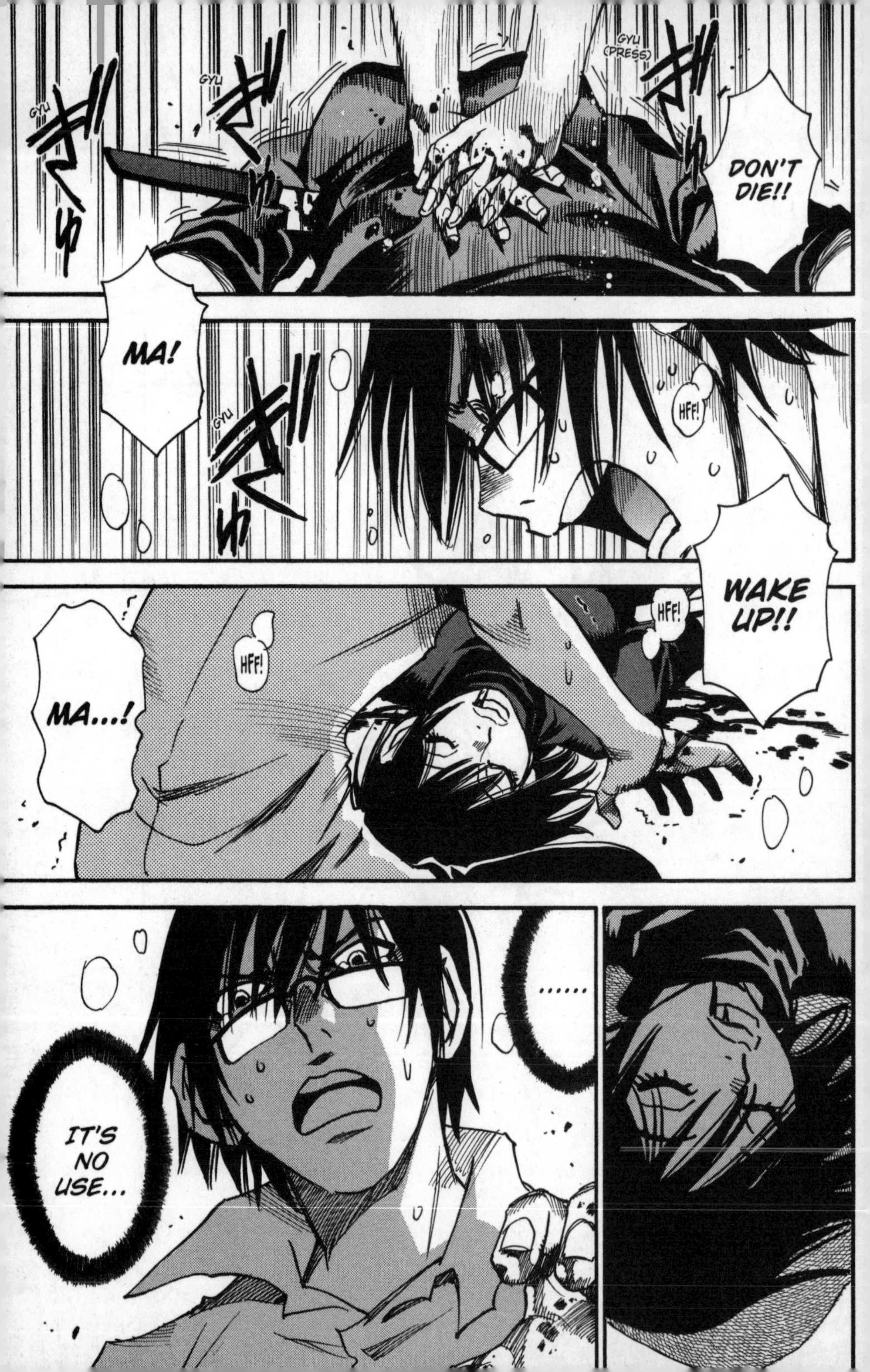
GYU (PRESS)
DON'T DIE!!
GYU
GYU
HFF!
WAKE UP!!
GYU
MA!
HFF!
HFF!
MA...!
......
IT'S NO USE...

#6: Fugitive, February 1988

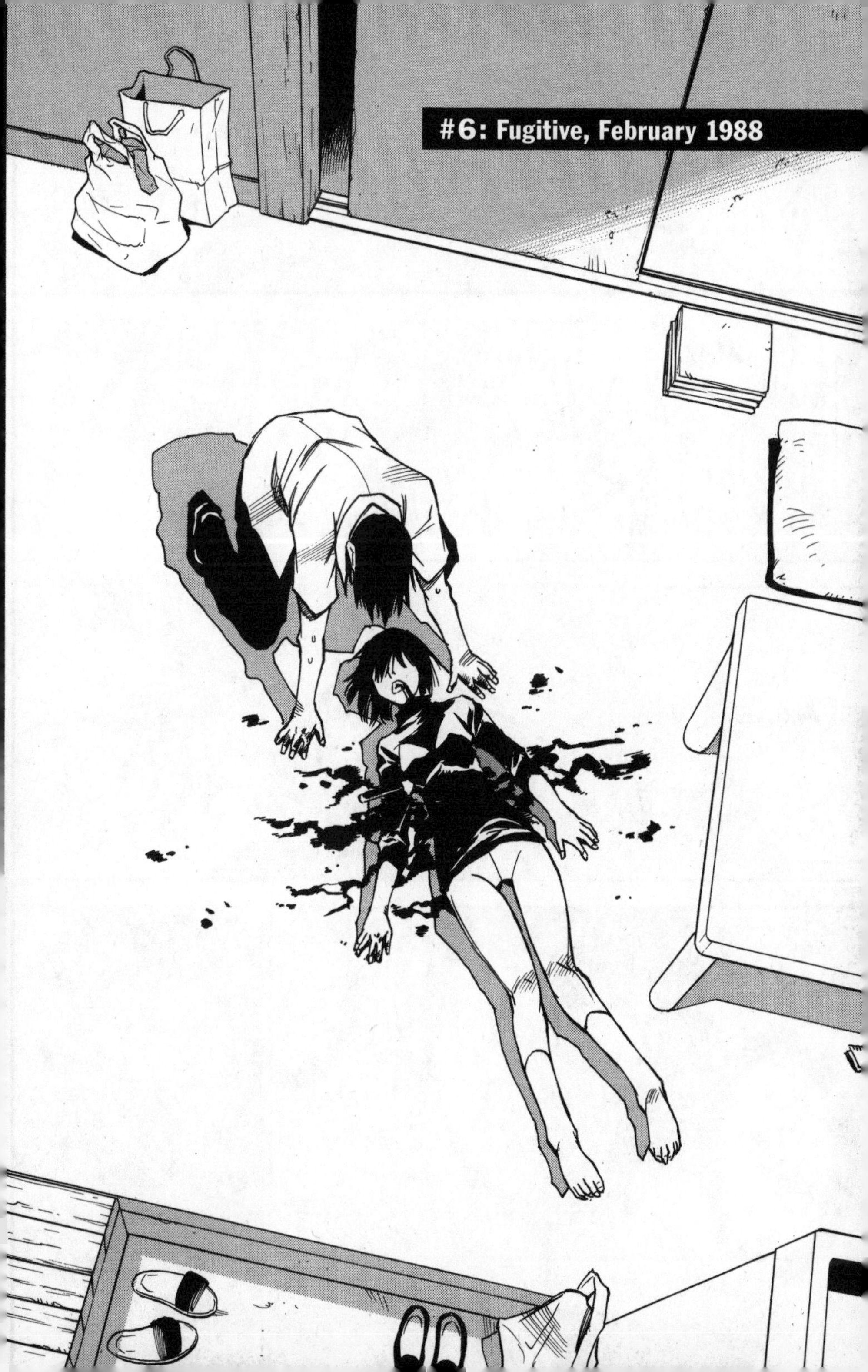

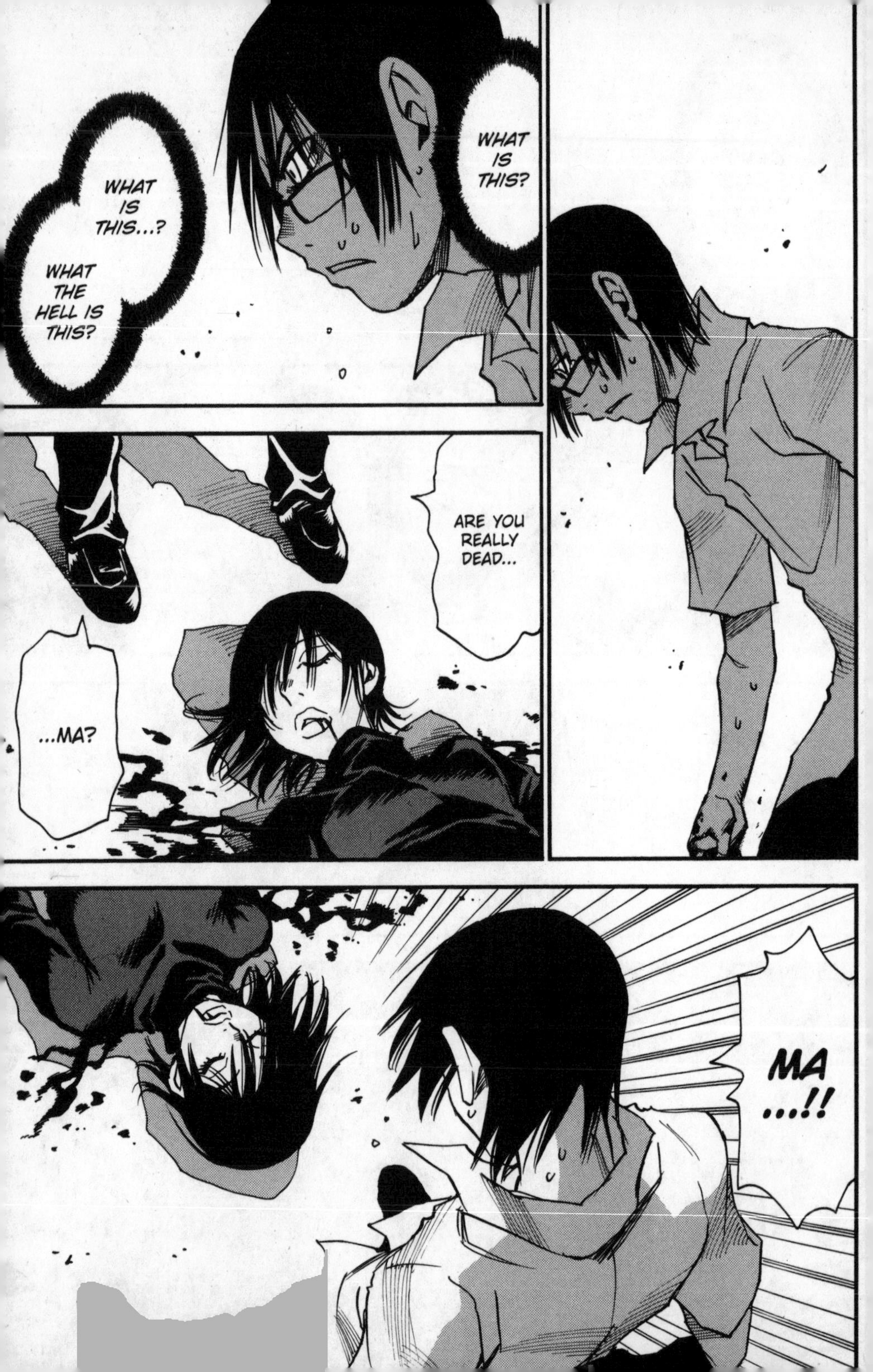
WHAT IS THIS?
WHAT IS THIS...?
WHAT THE HELL IS THIS?
ARE YOU REALLY DEAD...
...MA?
MA ...!!

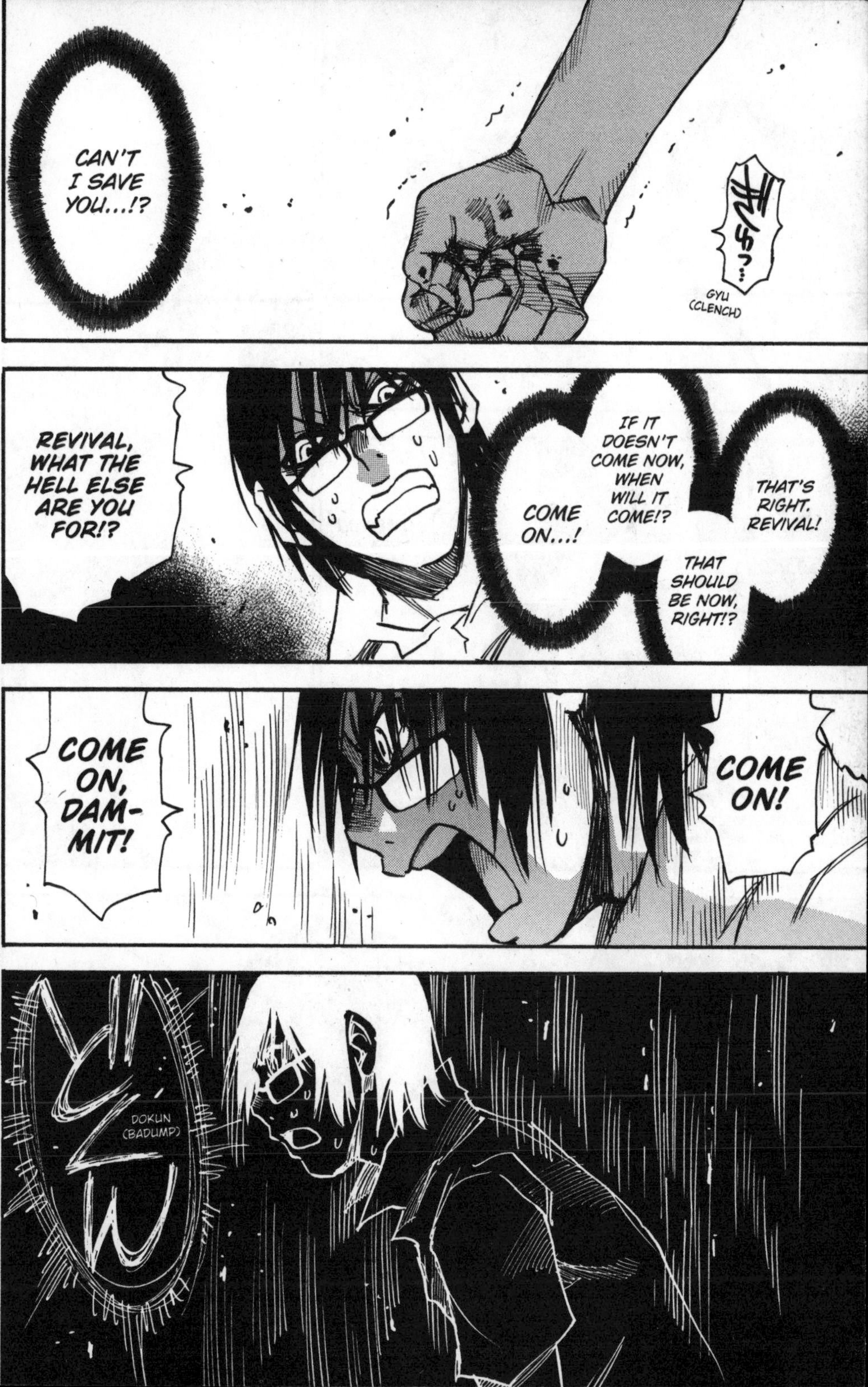
GYU (CLENCH)
CAN'T I SAVE YOU...!?
THAT'S RIGHT. REVIVAL!
THAT SHOULD BE NOW, RIGHT!?
IF IT DOESN'T COME NOW, WHEN WILL IT COME!?
COME ON...!
REVIVAL, WHAT THE HELL ELSE ARE YOU FOR!?
COME ON!
COME ON, DAM-MIT!
DOKUN (BADUMP)

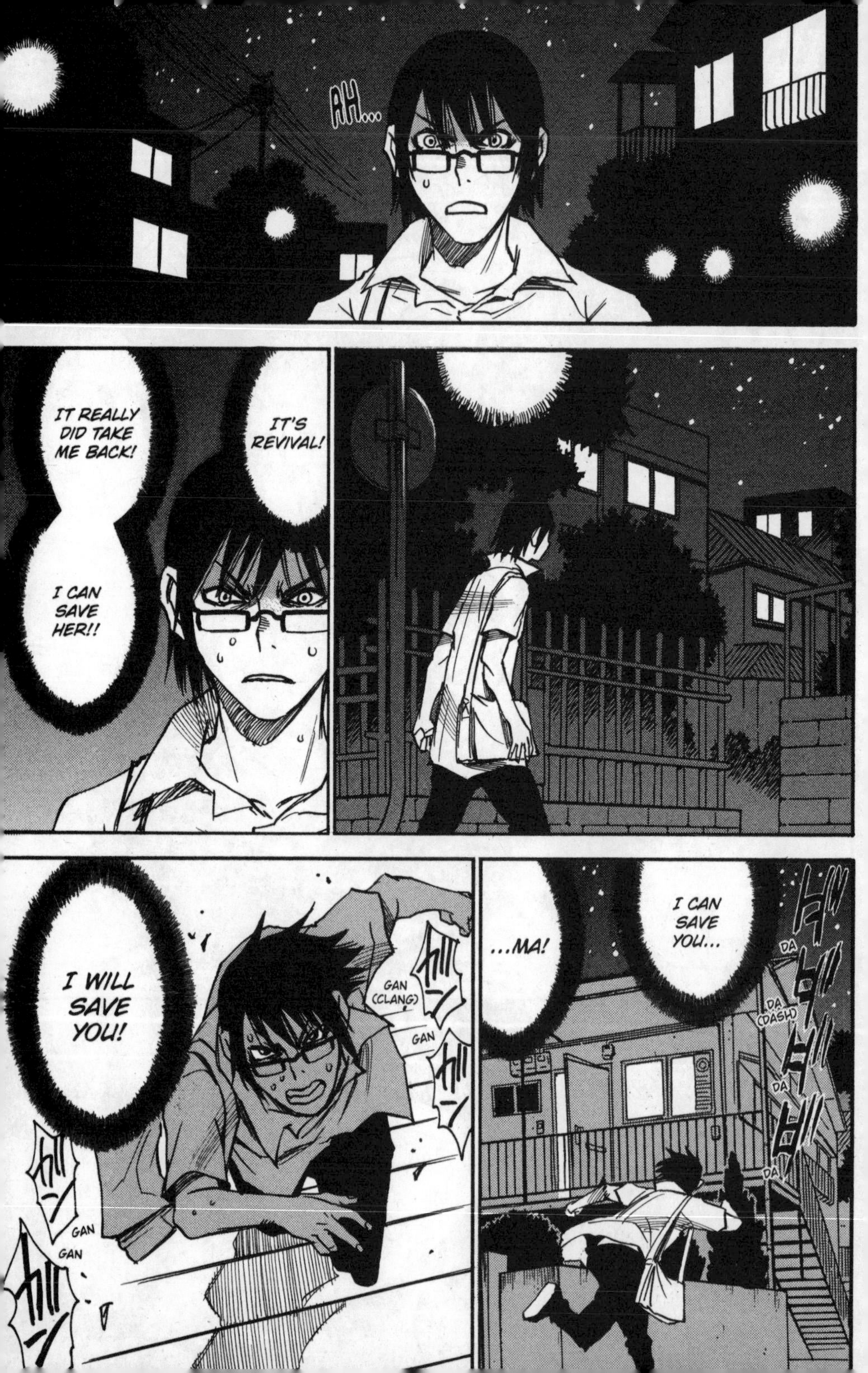
AH...
IT'S REVIVAL!
IT REALLY DID TAKE ME BACK!
I CAN SAVE HER!!
I CAN SAVE YOU...
...MA!
DA
DA (DASH)
DA
DA
GAN (CLANG)
GAN
I WILL SAVE YOU!
GAN
GAN

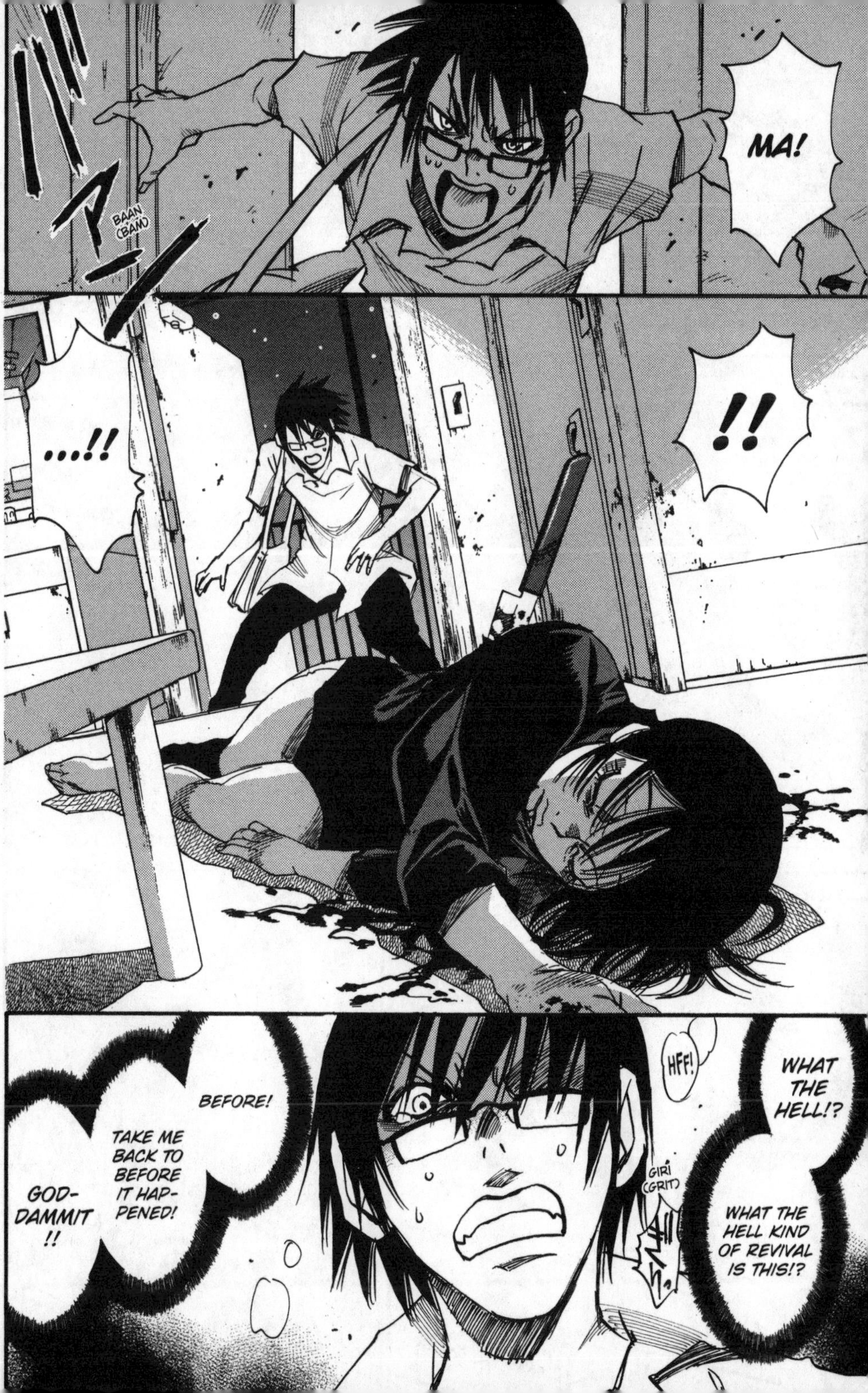
MA!
BAAN (BAM)
!!
...!!
WHAT THE HELL!?
HFF!
GIRI (GRIT)
WHAT THE HELL KIND OF REVIVAL IS THIS!?
BEFORE!
TAKE ME BACK TO BEFORE IT HAPPENED!
GOD-DAMMIT !!

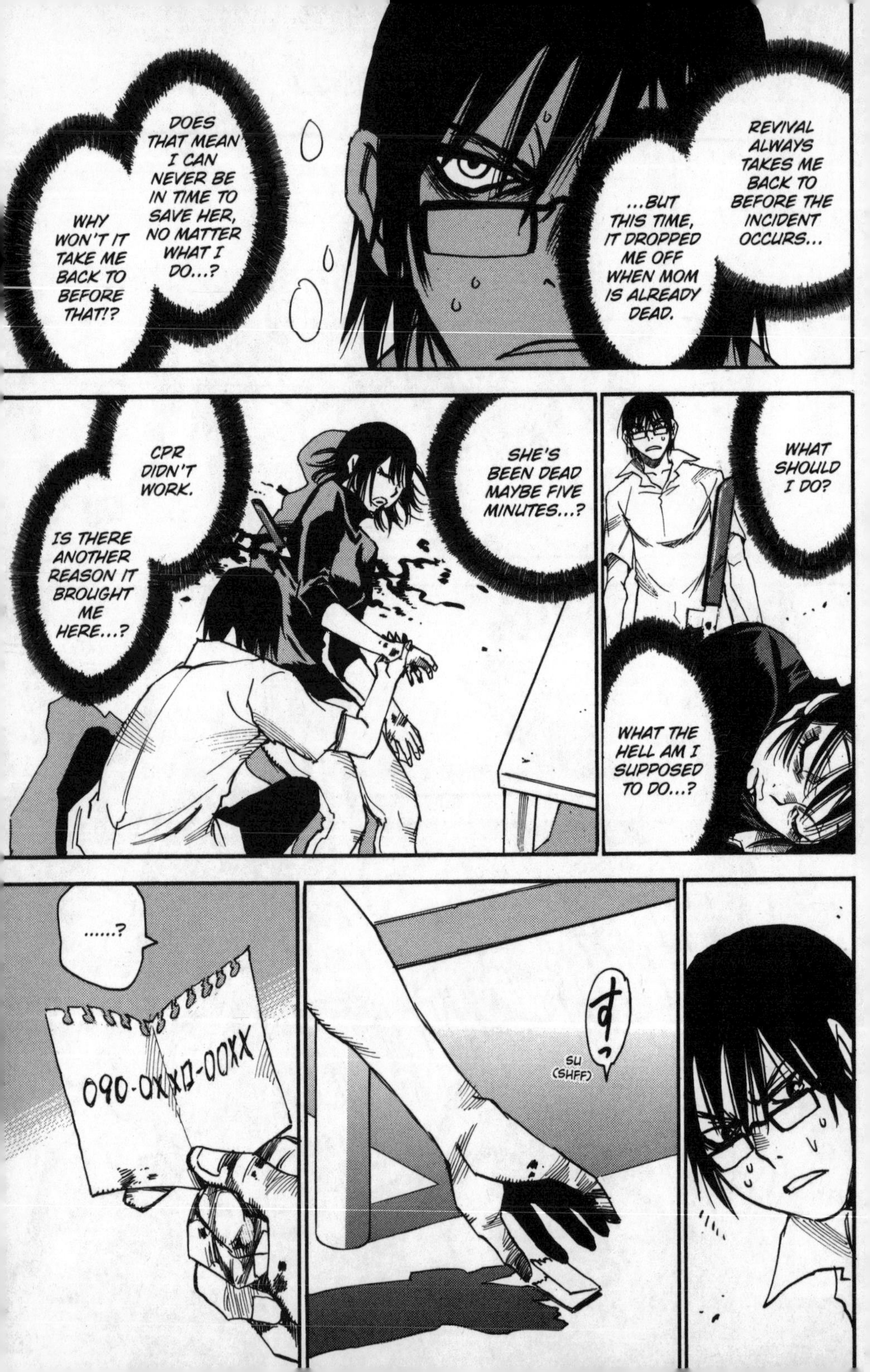
REVIVAL ALWAYS TAKES ME BACK TO BEFORE THE INCIDENT OCCURS...
...BUT THIS TIME, IT DROPPED ME OFF WHEN MOM IS ALREADY DEAD.
DOES THAT MEAN I CAN NEVER BE IN TIME TO SAVE HER, NO MATTER WHAT I DO...?
WHY WON'T IT TAKE ME BACK TO BEFORE THAT!?
WHAT SHOULD I DO?
WHAT THE HELL AM I SUPPOSED TO DO...?
SHE'S BEEN DEAD MAYBE FIVE MINUTES...?
CPR DIDN'T WORK.
IS THERE ANOTHER REASON IT BROUGHT ME HERE...?
すっ
SU (SHFF)
......?
090-○XX□-○○XX

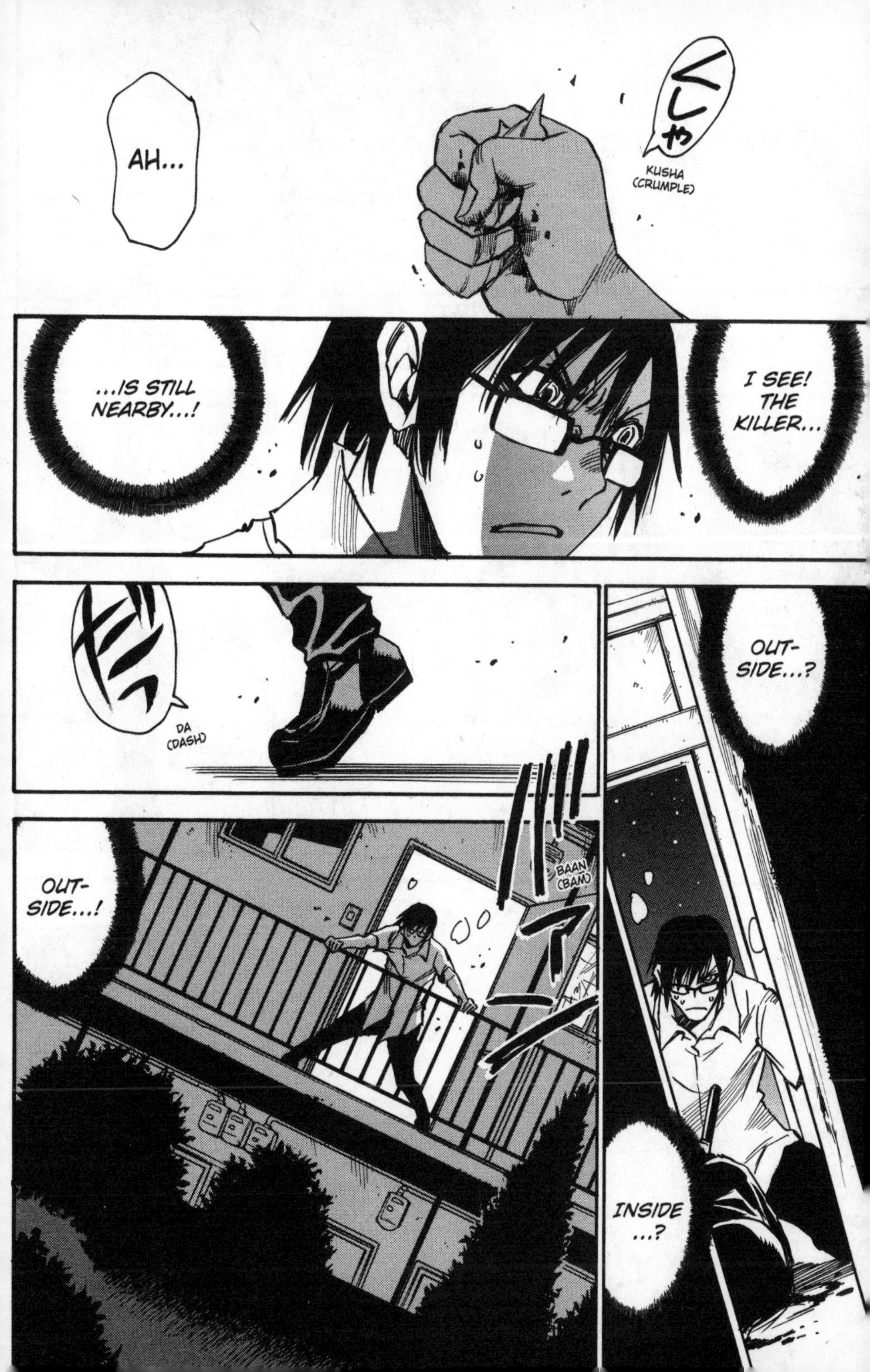
くしゃ
KUSHA (CRUMPLE)
AH...
I SEE! THE KILLER...
...IS STILL NEARBY...!
OUT-SIDE...?
INSIDE ...?
ダッ
DA (DASH)
BAAN (BAM)
OUT-SIDE...!

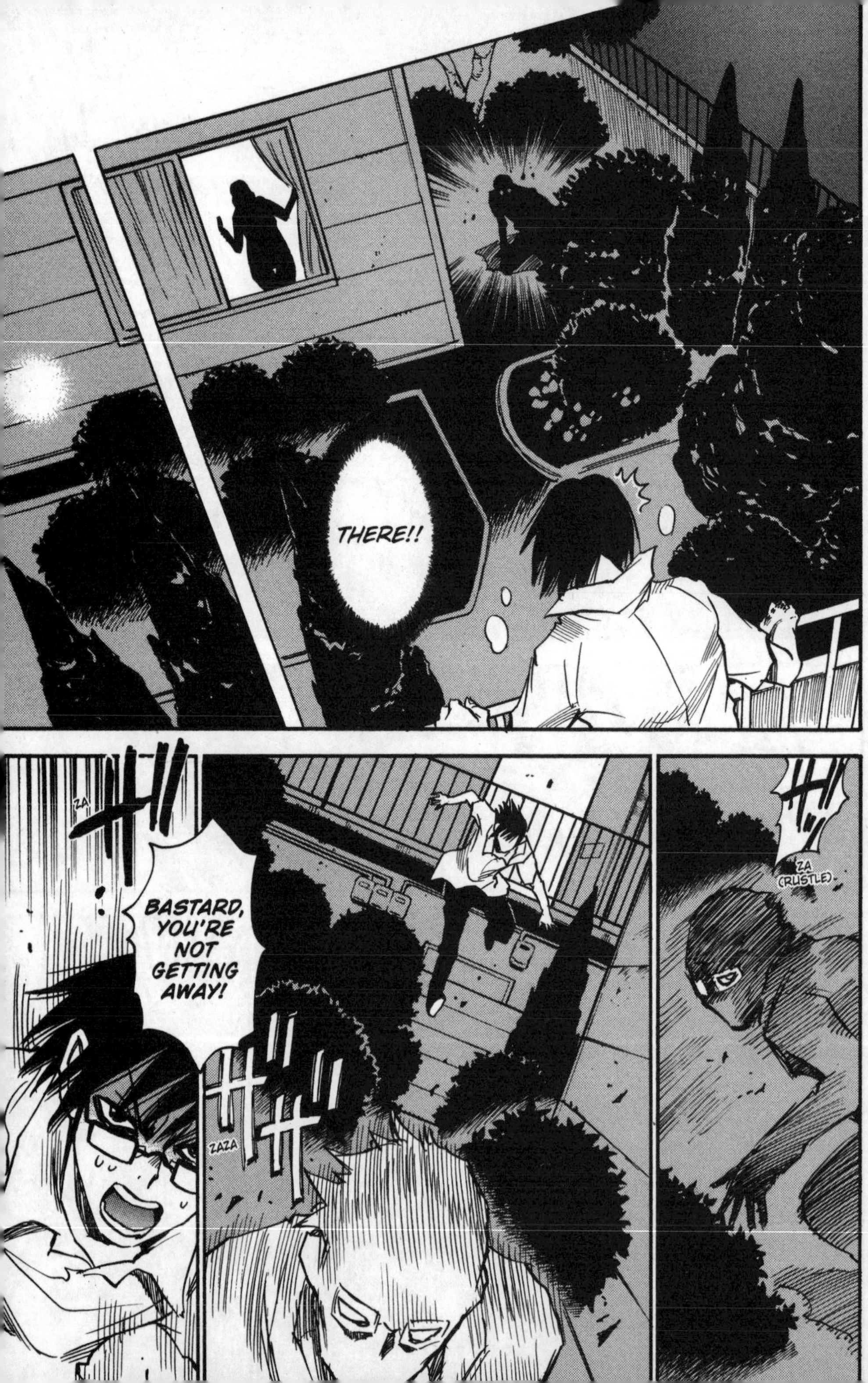
THERE!!
ZA
(RUSTLE)
ZA
BASTARD, YOU'RE NOT GETTING AWAY!
ZAZA

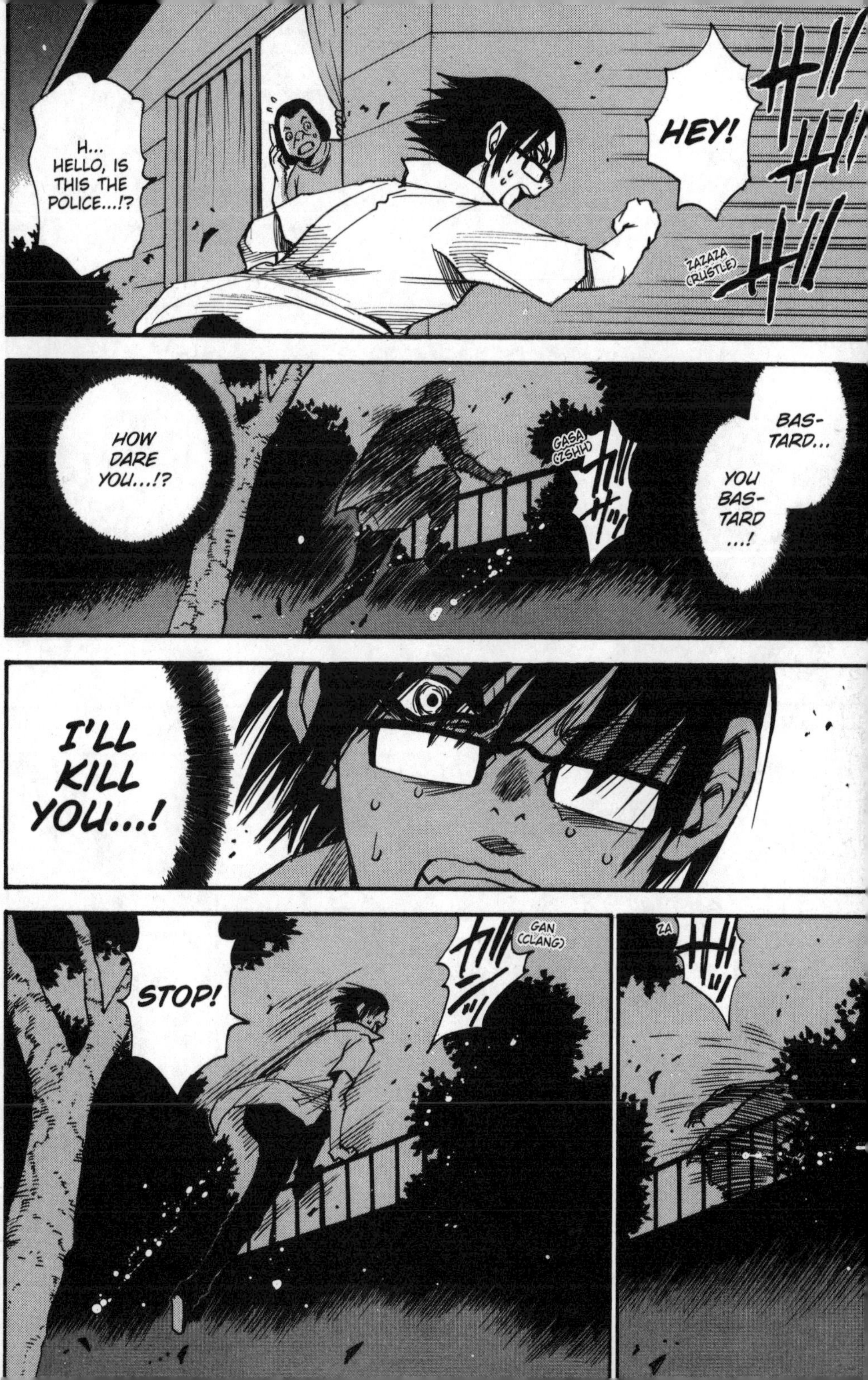
HEY!
ZAZAZA (RUSTLE)
H... HELLO, IS THIS THE POLICE...!?
BASTARD...
YOU BASTARD...!
GASA (ZSHH)
HOW DARE YOU...!?
I'LL KILL YOU...!
ZA
GAN (CLANG)
STOP!

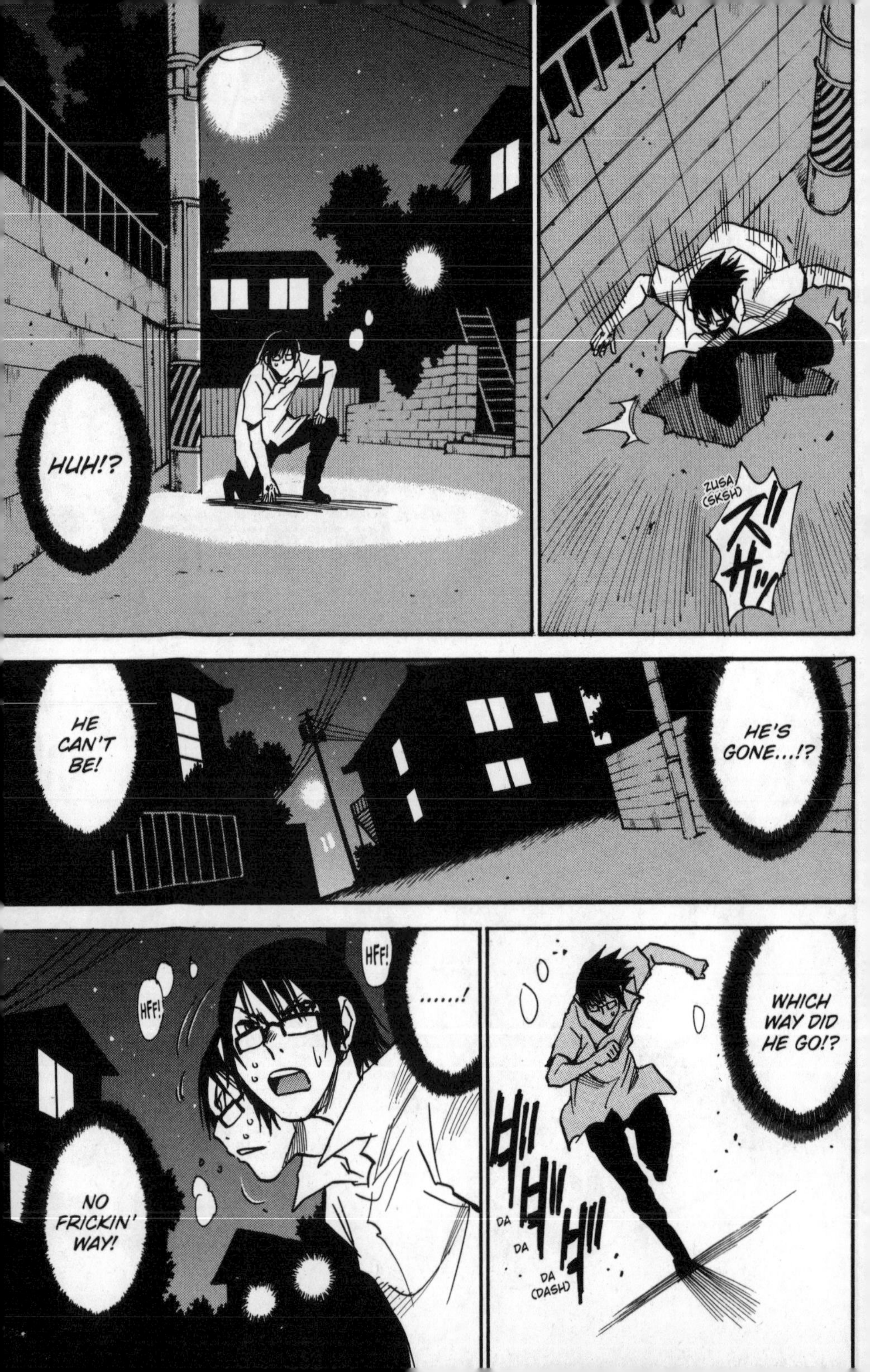
ZUSA (SKSH)
HUH!?
HE'S GONE...!?
HE CAN'T BE!
WHICH WAY DID HE GO!?
DA DA DA (DASH)
HFF!
......!
HFF!
NO FRICKIN' WAY!

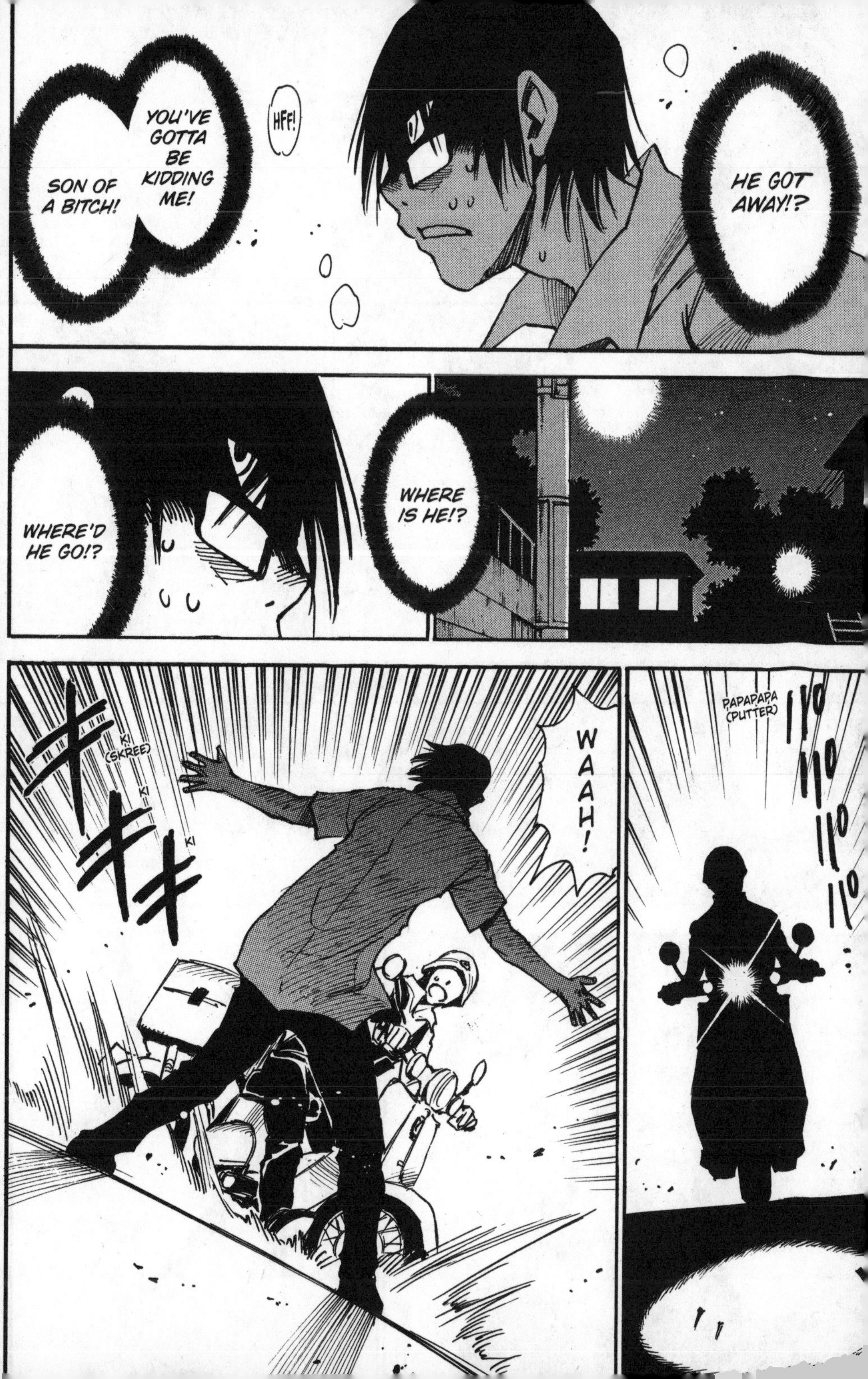
HE GOT AWAY!?
HFF!
YOU'VE GOTTA BE KIDDING ME!
SON OF A BITCH!
WHERE IS HE!?
WHERE'D HE GO!?
PAPAPAPA (PUTTER)
WAAAH!
KI (SKREE)
KI
KI

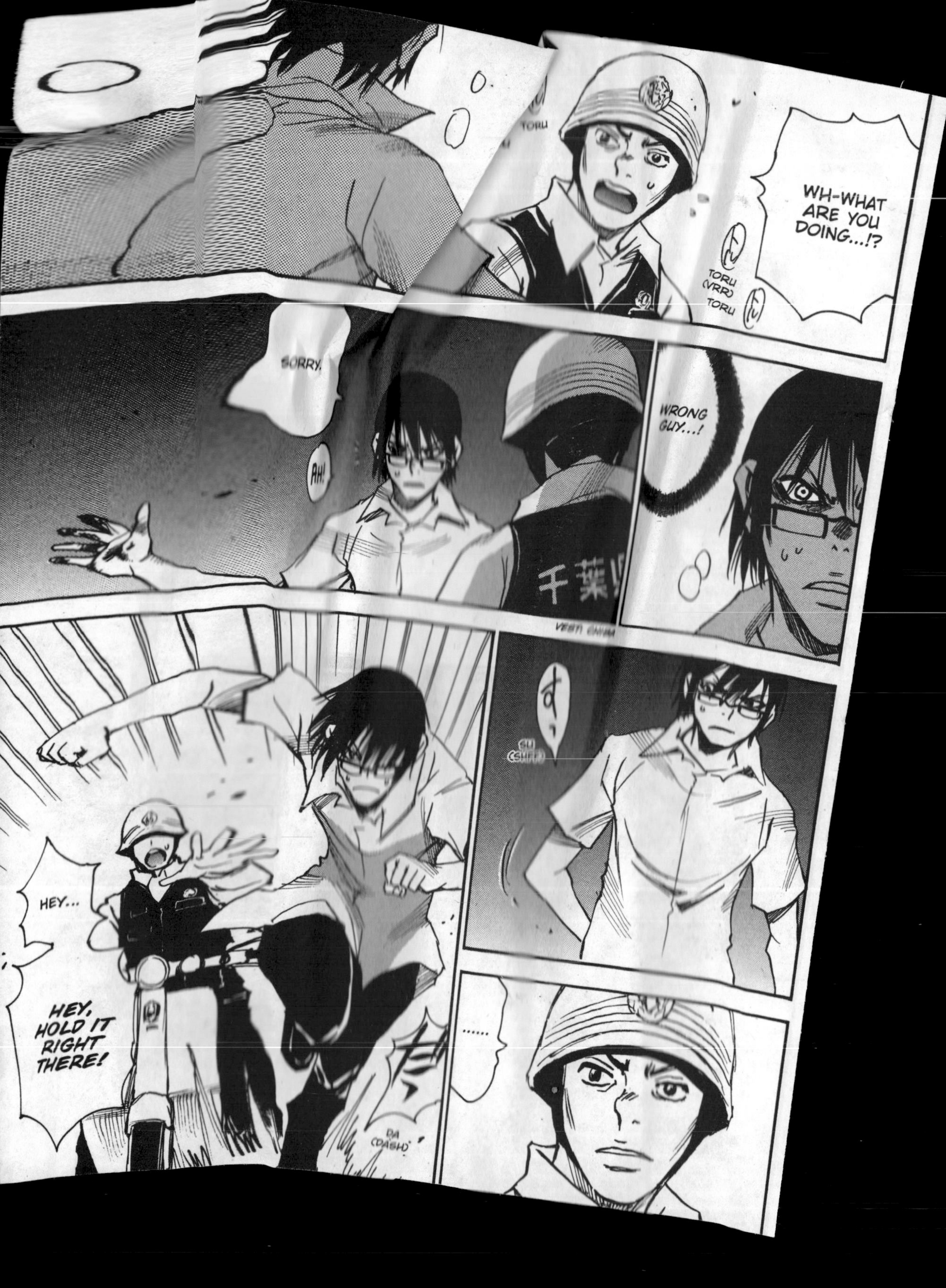
TORU
WH-WHAT ARE YOU DOING...!?
TORU (VRR) TORU
WRONG GUY...!
SORRY.
AH!
千葉県
VEST: CHIBA
す
SU (SHFF)
......
HEY...
HEY, HOLD IT RIGHT THERE!
DA (DASH)

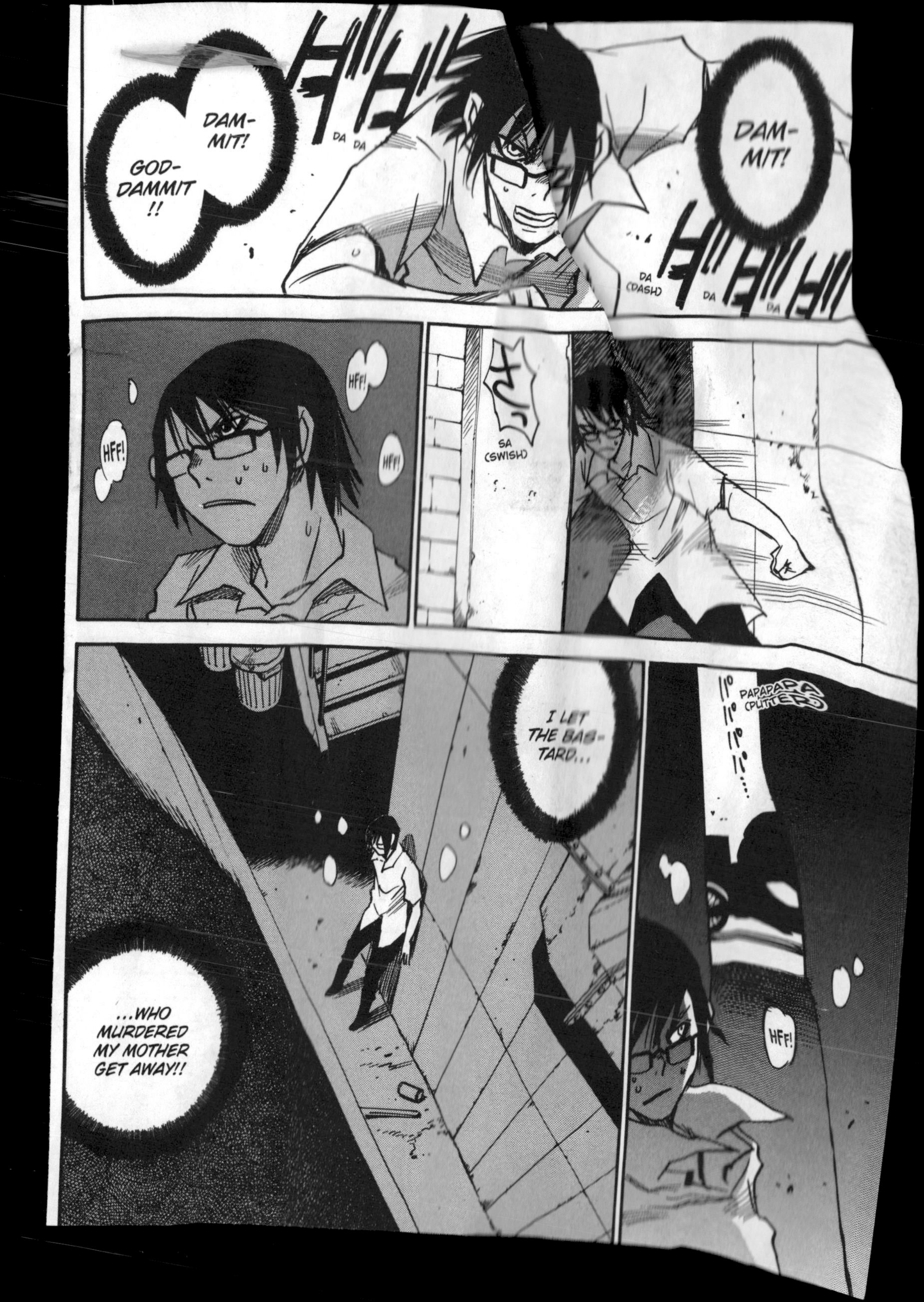
DAM-MIT!
DA (DASH) DA DA
DA DA
DAM-MIT!
GOD-DAMMIT !!
さっ
SA (SWISH)
HFF!
HFF!
HFF!
PAPAPAPA (PUTTER)
I LET THE BAS-TARD...
HFF!
...WHO MURDERED MY MOTHER GET AWAY!!

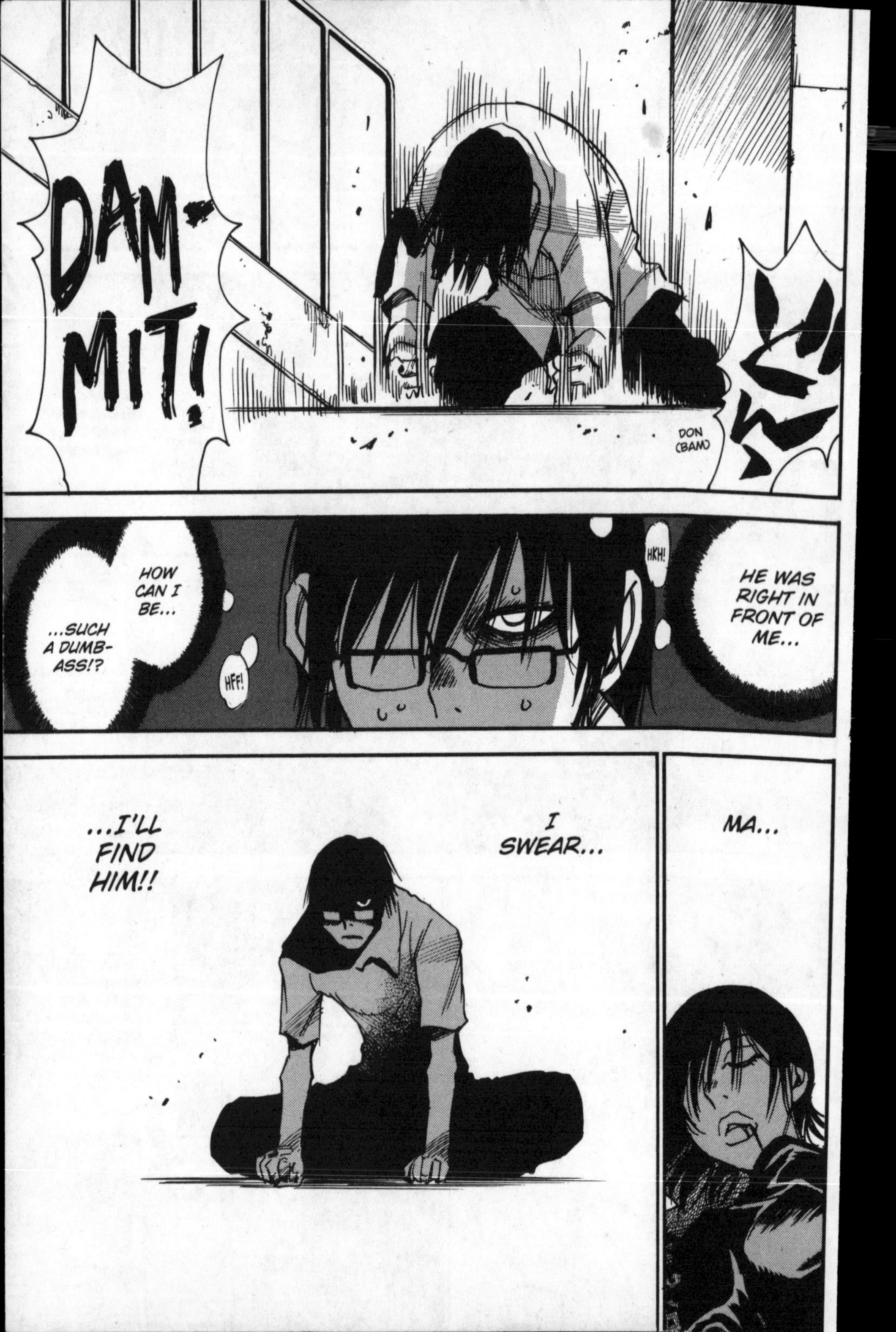
DON (BAM)
DAM-MIT!
HE WAS RIGHT IN FRONT OF ME...
HKH!
HFF!
HOW CAN I BE...
...SUCH A DUMB-ASS!?
MA...
I SWEAR...
...I'LL FIND HIM!!

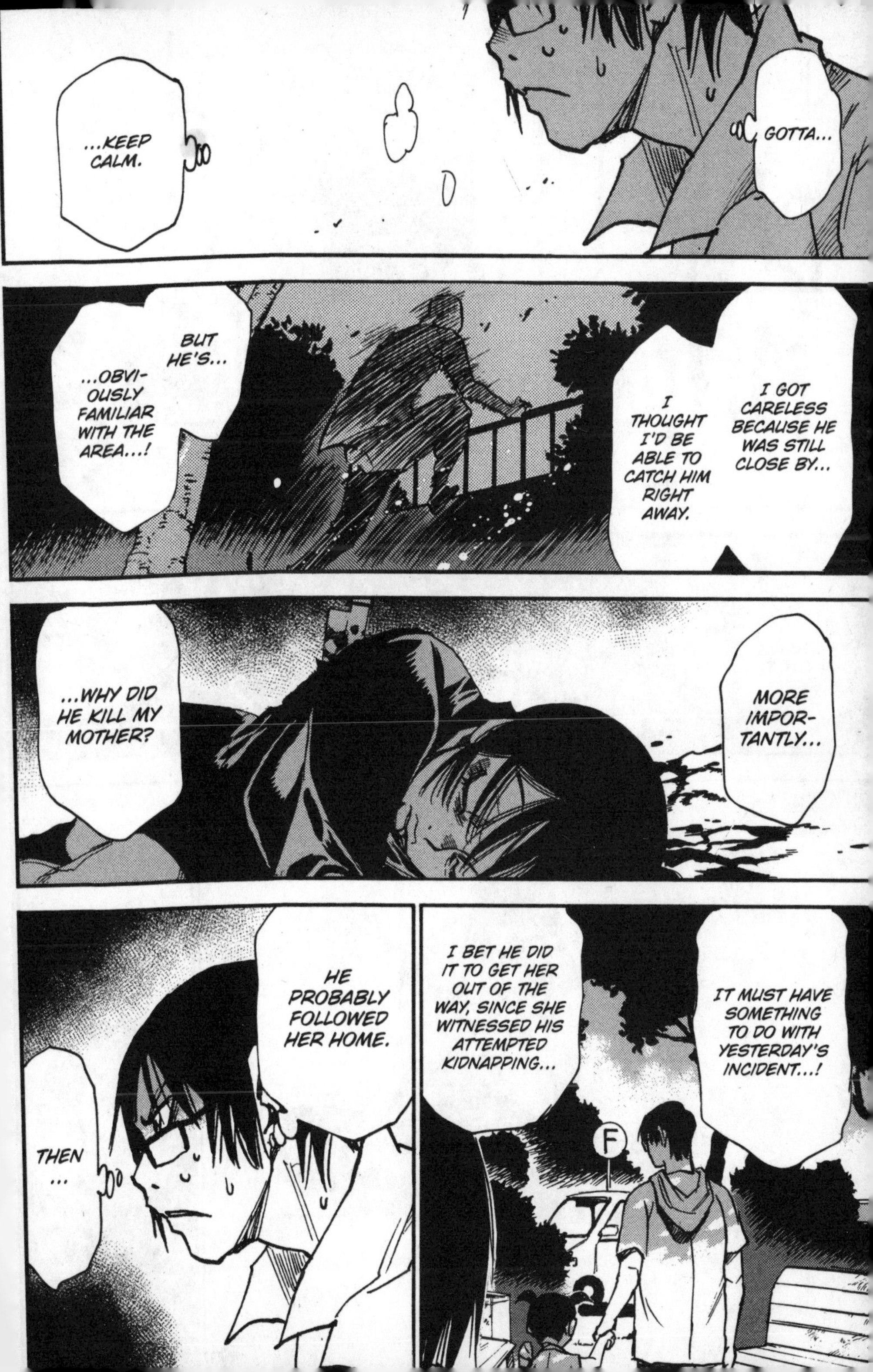
GOTTA...
...KEEP CALM.
I GOT CARELESS BECAUSE HE WAS STILL CLOSE BY...
I THOUGHT I'D BE ABLE TO CATCH HIM RIGHT AWAY.
BUT HE'S...
...OBVIOUSLY FAMILIAR WITH THE AREA...!
MORE IMPORTANTLY...
...WHY DID HE KILL MY MOTHER?
IT MUST HAVE SOMETHING TO DO WITH YESTERDAY'S INCIDENT...!
I BET HE DID IT TO GET HER OUT OF THE WAY, SINCE SHE WITNESSED HIS ATTEMPTED KIDNAPPING...
F
HE PROBABLY FOLLOWED HER HOME.
THEN...

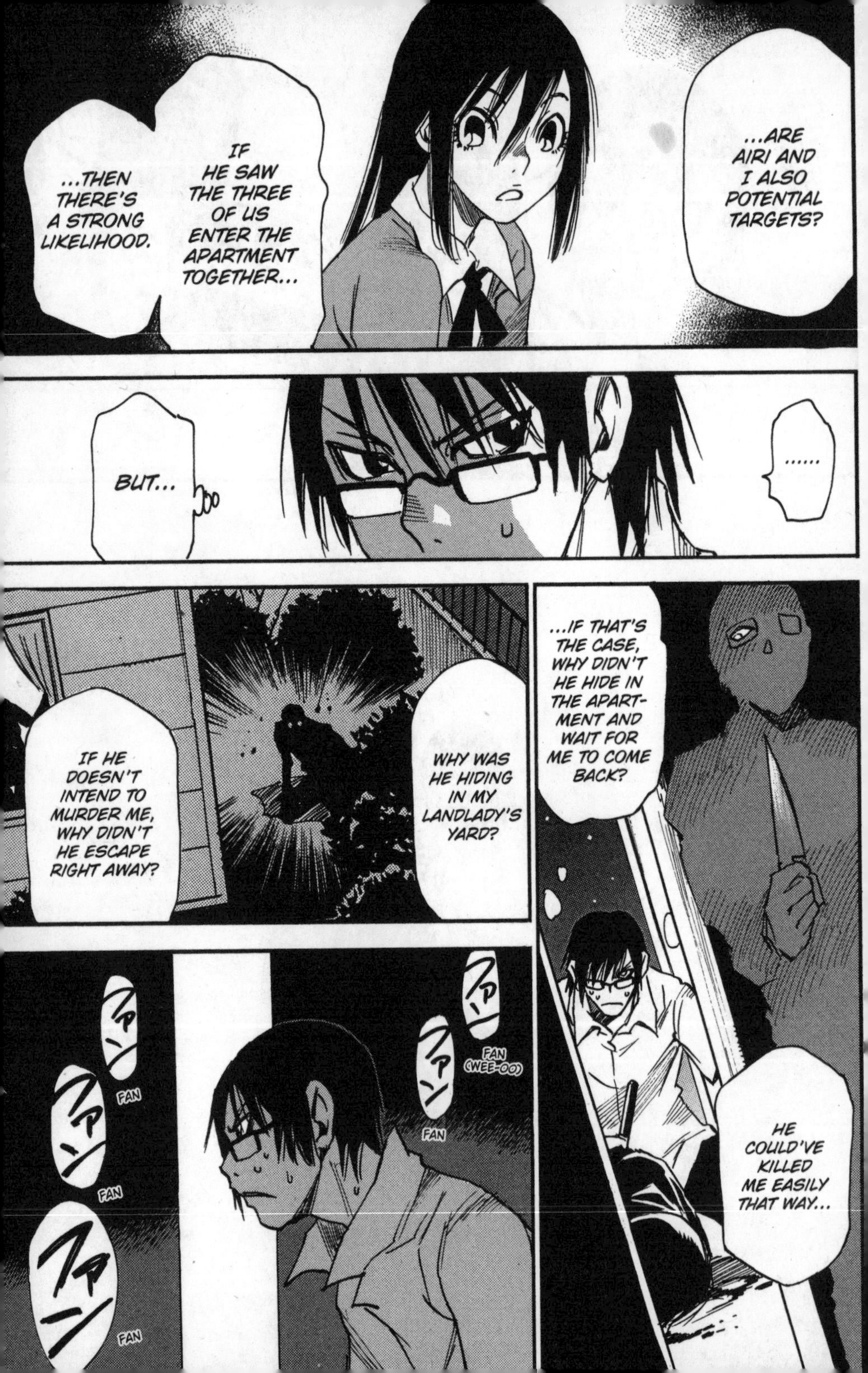
...ARE AIRI AND I ALSO POTENTIAL TARGETS?
IF HE SAW THE THREE OF US ENTER THE APARTMENT TOGETHER...
...THEN THERE'S A STRONG LIKELIHOOD.
......
BUT...
...IF THAT'S THE CASE, WHY DIDN'T HE HIDE IN THE APART-MENT AND WAIT FOR ME TO COME BACK?
HE COULD'VE KILLED ME EASILY THAT WAY...
WHY WAS HE HIDING IN MY LANDLADY'S YARD?
IF HE DOESN'T INTEND TO MURDER ME, WHY DIDN'T HE ESCAPE RIGHT AWAY?
FAN (WEE-OO)
FAN
FAN
FAN
FAN

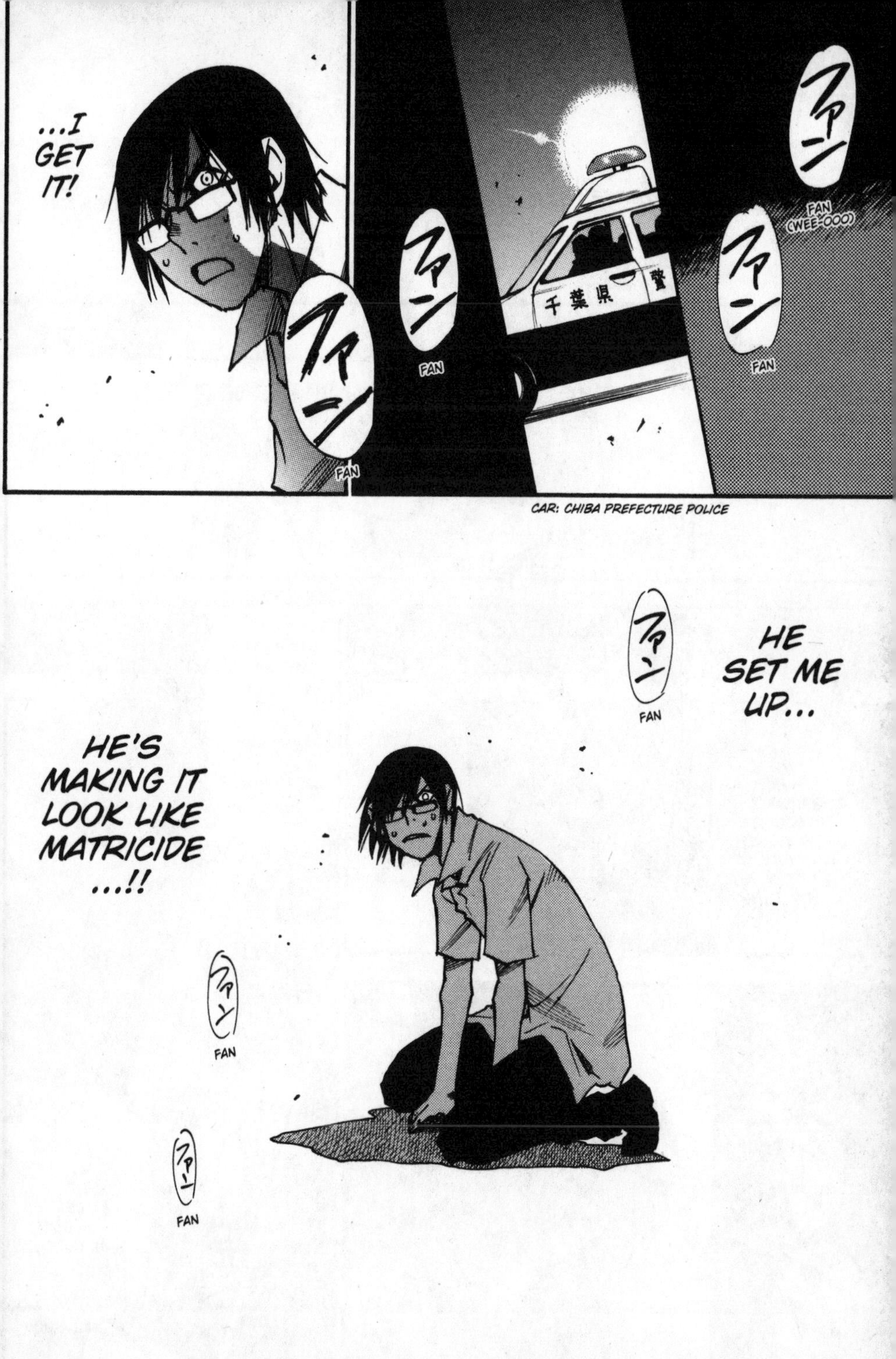
ファン
FAN (WEE-OOO)
ファン
FAN
千葉県警
ファン
FAN
...I GET IT!
ファン
FAN
CAR: CHIBA PREFECTURE POLICE
ファン
FAN
HE SET ME UP...
HE'S MAKING IT LOOK LIKE MATRICIDE ...!!
ファン
FAN
ファン
FAN

A COP ...!?

CRAP ...!

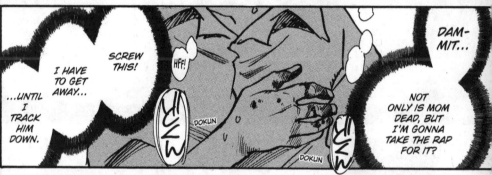

...UNTIL I TRACK HIM DOWN.

I HAVE TO GET AWAY...

SCREW THIS!

HFF!

DAMMIT...

NOT ONLY IS MOM DEAD, BUT I'M GONNA TAKE THE RAP FOR IT?

SEND ME BACK!

SEND ME BACK BEFORE THAT!

AND DON'T MAKE IT HALF-ASSED LIKE THIS LAST TIME, AFTER THE DEED WAS DONE...!!

HEY...

REVIVAL... SEND ME BACK!!

HOW CAN I GET OUT OF THIS...!?

GIVE ME EVERYTHING YOU'VE GOT...!!

SEND ME BACK!!

SEND ME BACK!!

HFF!

SEND ME BACK!!

HFF!

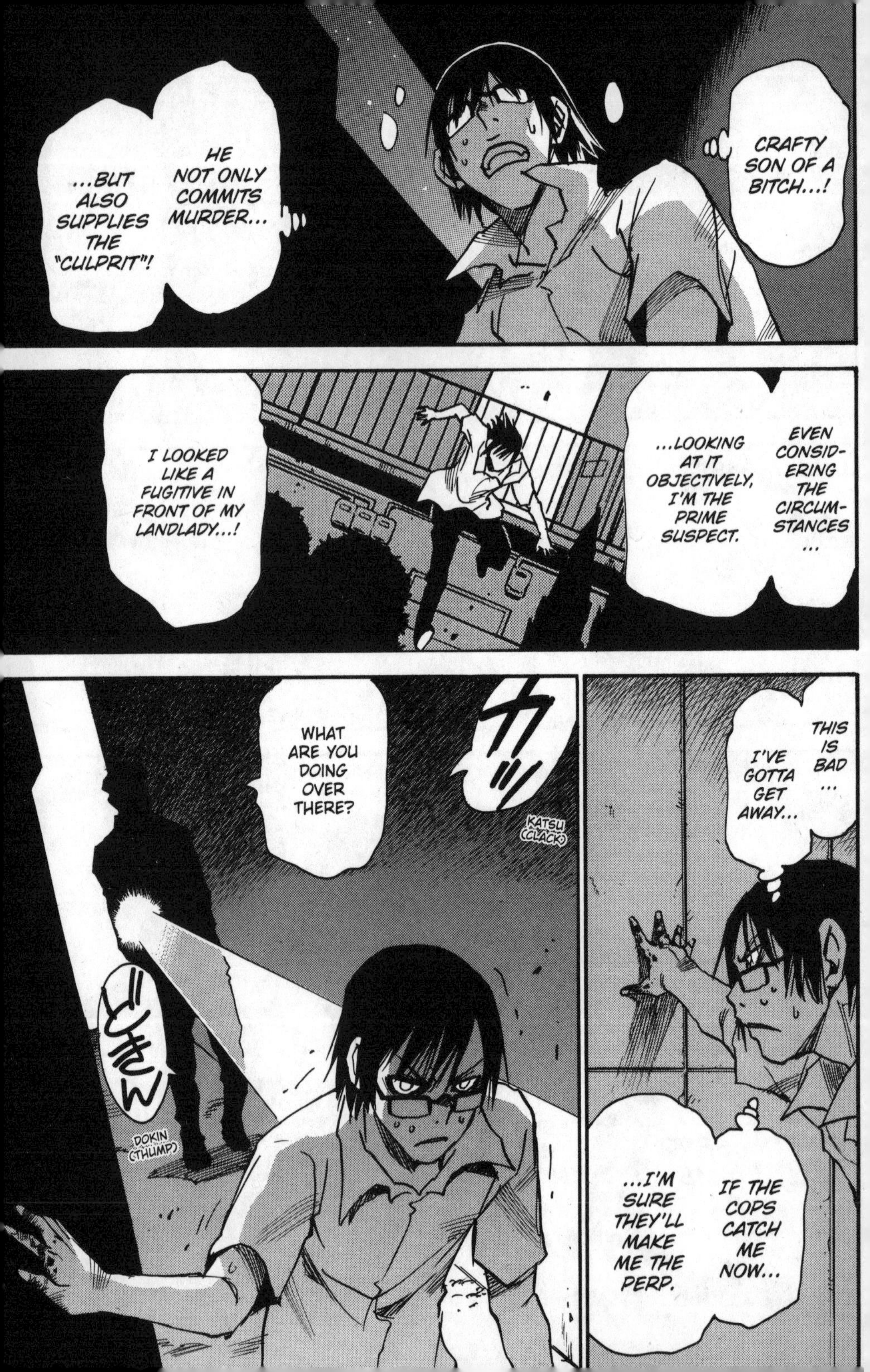
CRAFTY SON OF A BITCH...!
HE NOT ONLY COMMITS MURDER...
...BUT ALSO SUPPLIES THE "CULPRIT"!
EVEN CONSIDERING THE CIRCUMSTANCES...
...LOOKING AT IT OBJECTIVELY, I'M THE PRIME SUSPECT.
I LOOKED LIKE A FUGITIVE IN FRONT OF MY LANDLADY...!
THIS IS BAD...
I'VE GOTTA GET AWAY...
IF THE COPS CATCH ME NOW...
...I'M SURE THEY'LL MAKE ME THE PERP.
カッ
KATSU (CLACK)
WHAT ARE YOU DOING OVER THERE?
どきん
DOKIN (THUMP)

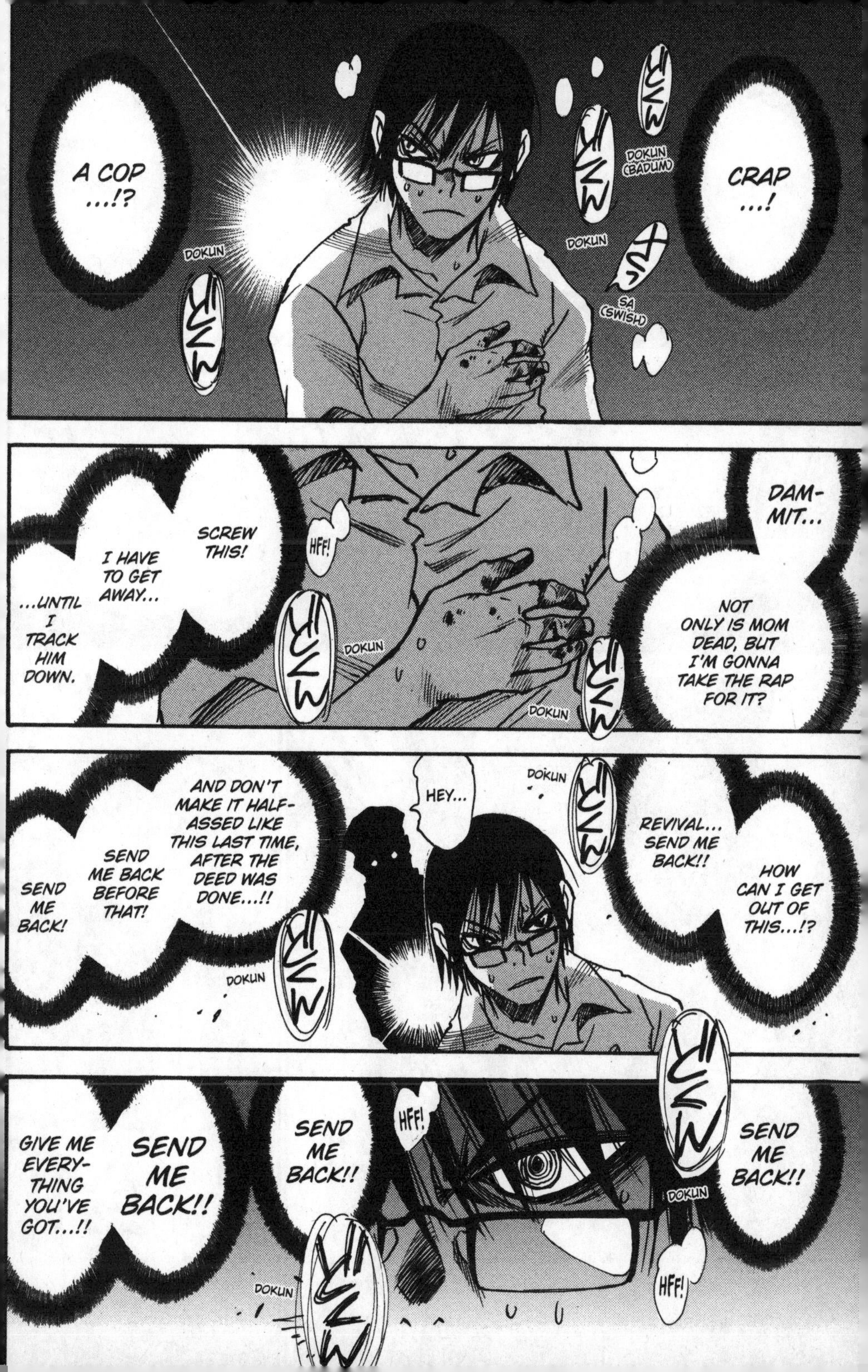
CRAP ...!
DOKUN (BADUM)
DOKUN
SA (SWISH)
A COP ...!?
DOKUN
DAM-MIT...
NOT ONLY IS MOM DEAD, BUT I'M GONNA TAKE THE RAP FOR IT?
DOKUN
HFF!
DOKUN
SCREW THIS!
I HAVE TO GET AWAY...
...UNTIL I TRACK HIM DOWN.
HOW CAN I GET OUT OF THIS...!?
REVIVAL... SEND ME BACK!!
DOKUN
HEY...
AND DON'T MAKE IT HALF-ASSED LIKE THIS LAST TIME, AFTER THE DEED WAS DONE...!!
SEND ME BACK BEFORE THAT!
DOKUN
SEND ME BACK!
SEND ME BACK!!
DOKUN
HFF!
HFF!
SEND ME BACK!!
SEND ME BACK!!
DOKUN
GIVE ME EVERY-THING YOU'VE GOT...!!

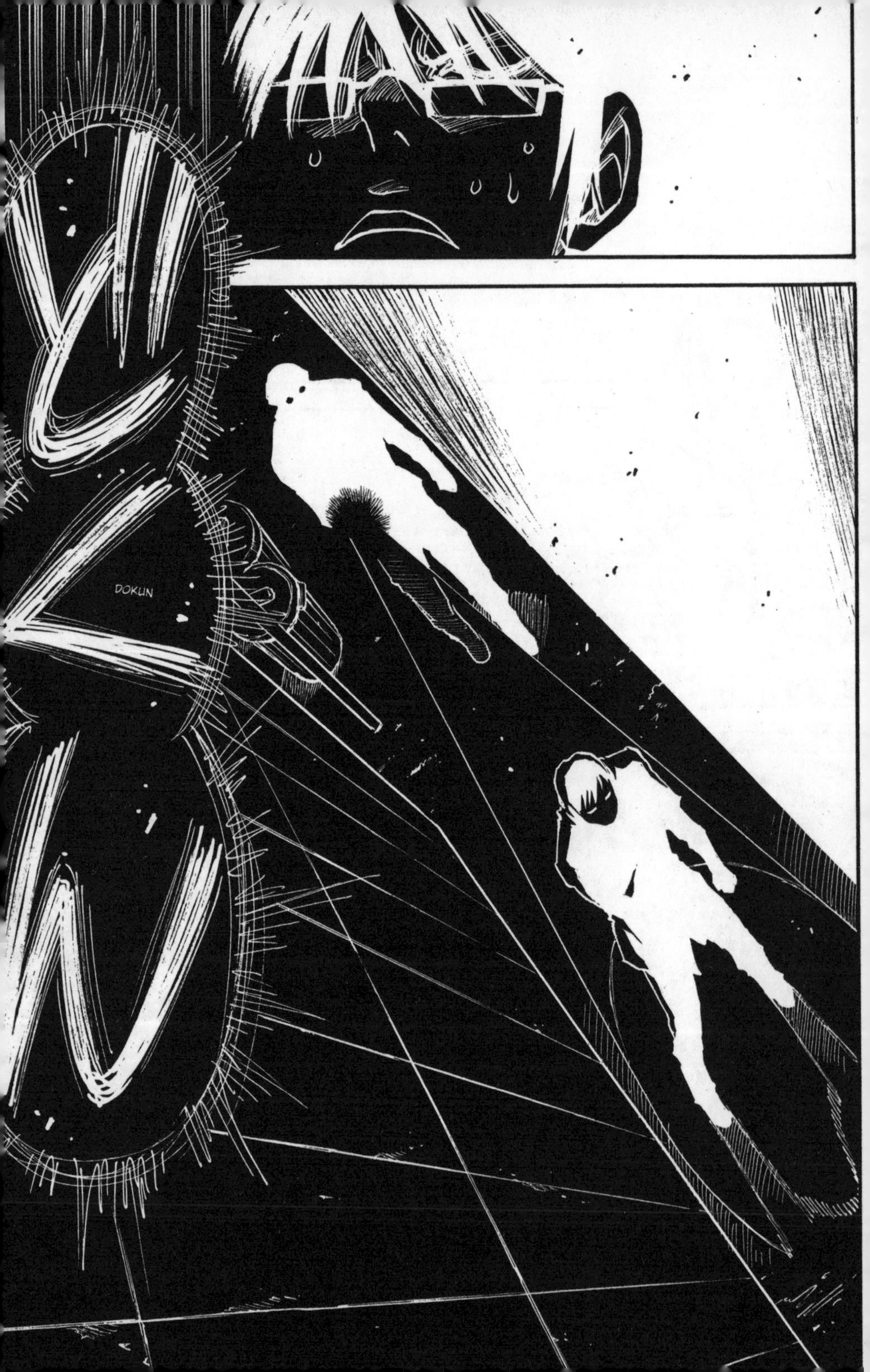
DOKUN

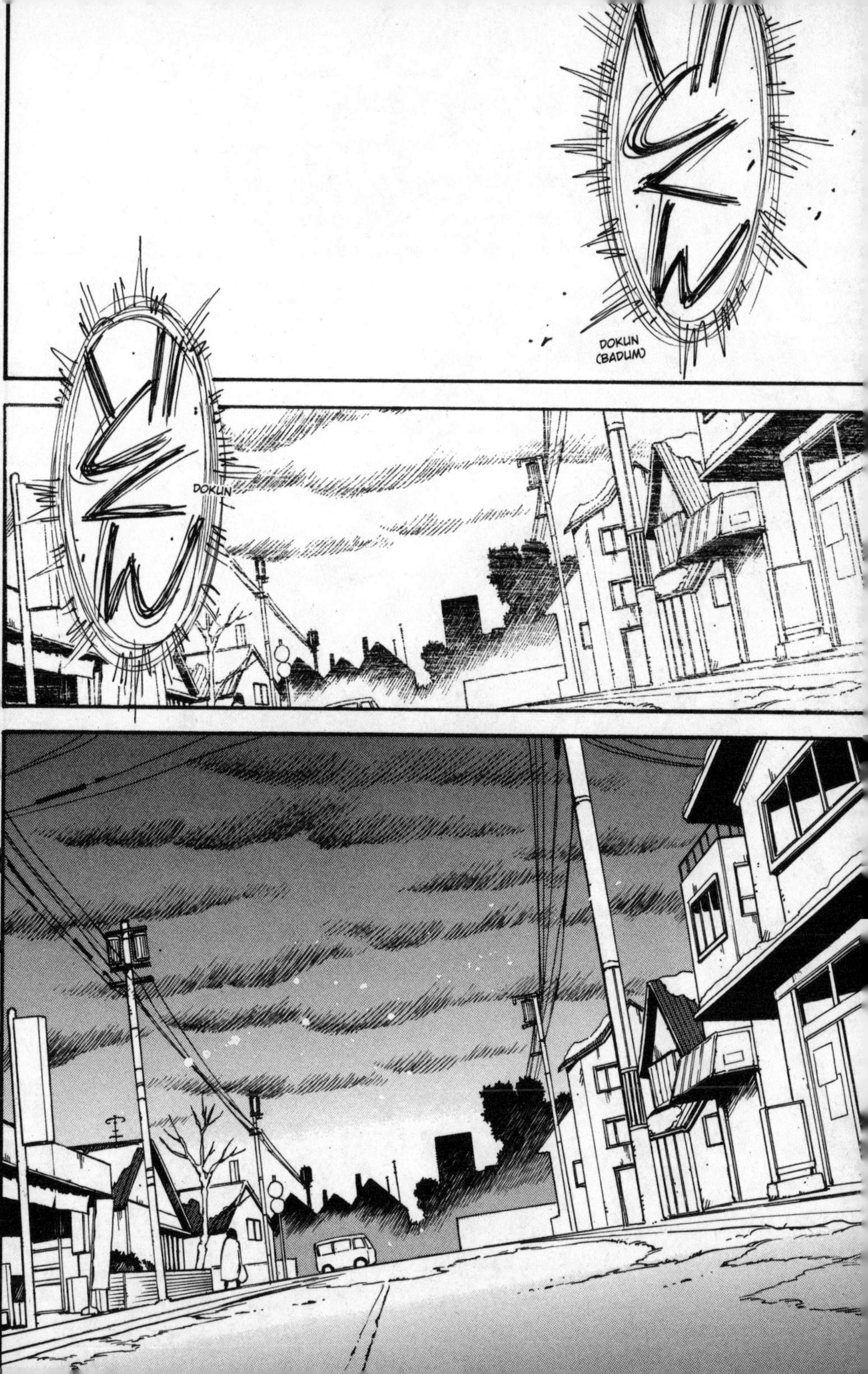
DOKUN
(BADUM)
DOKUN

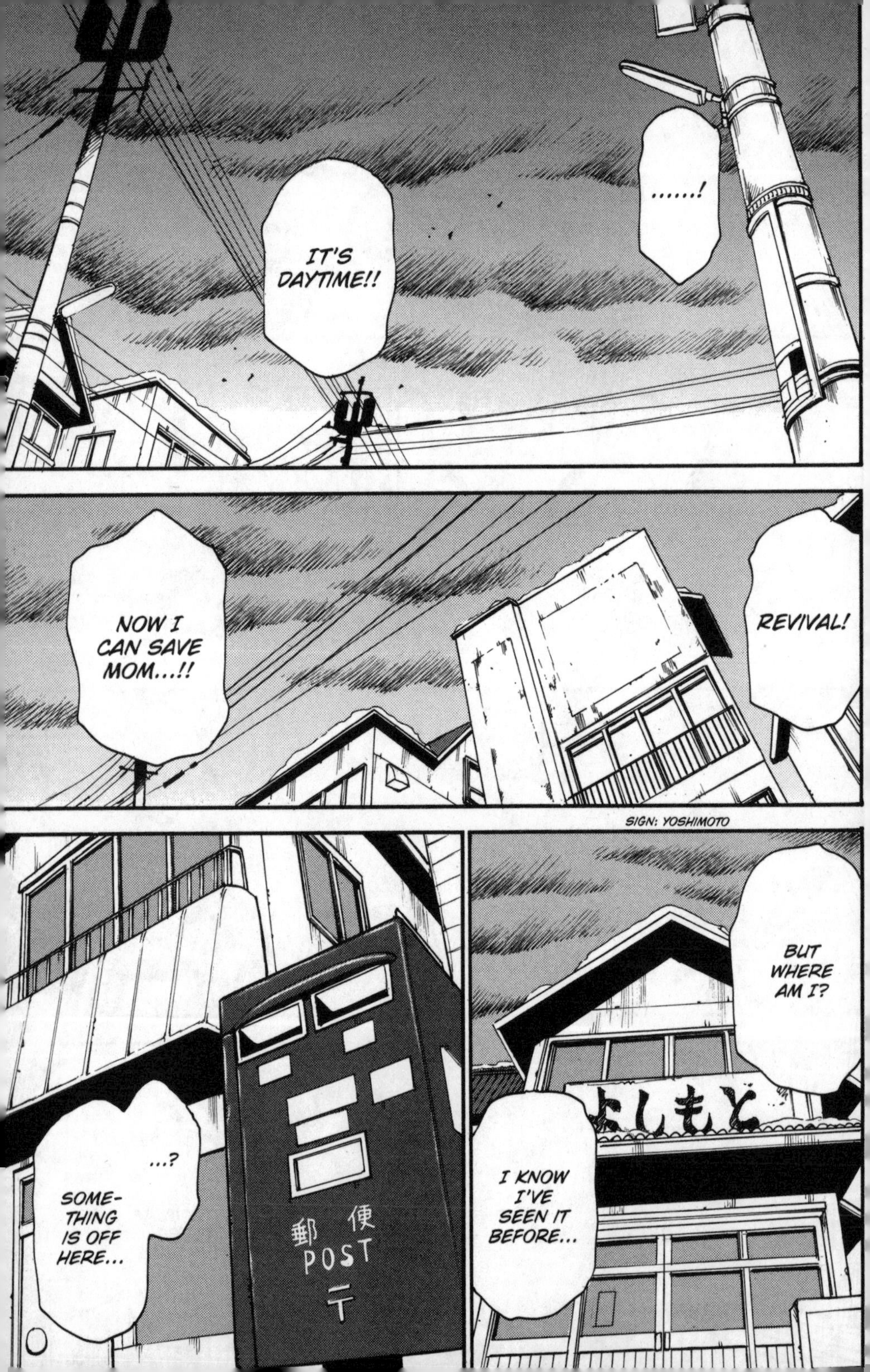
......!
IT'S DAYTIME!!
REVIVAL!
NOW I CAN SAVE MOM...!!
SIGN: YOSHIMOTO
BUT WHERE AM I?
よしもと
I KNOW I'VE SEEN IT BEFORE...
...?
SOME-THING IS OFF HERE...
郵便
POST
〒

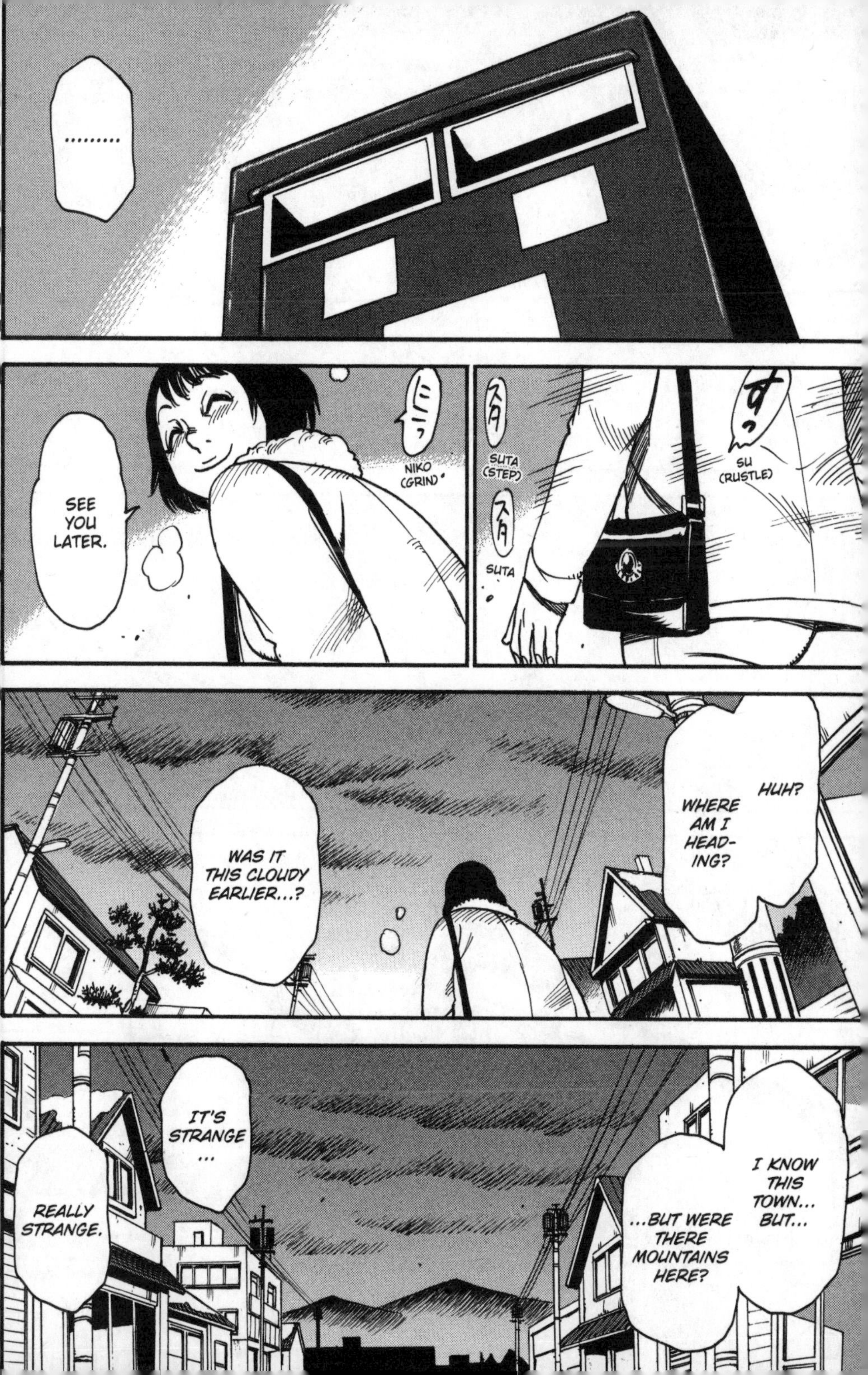
....
すっ
SU (RUSTLE)
スタ
SUTA (STEP)
スタ
SUTA
ニコっ
NIKO (GRIN)
SEE YOU LATER.
HUH?
WHERE AM I HEAD-ING?
WAS IT THIS CLOUDY EARLIER...?
I KNOW THIS TOWN... BUT...
...BUT WERE THERE MOUNTAINS HERE?
IT'S STRANGE...
REALLY STRANGE.

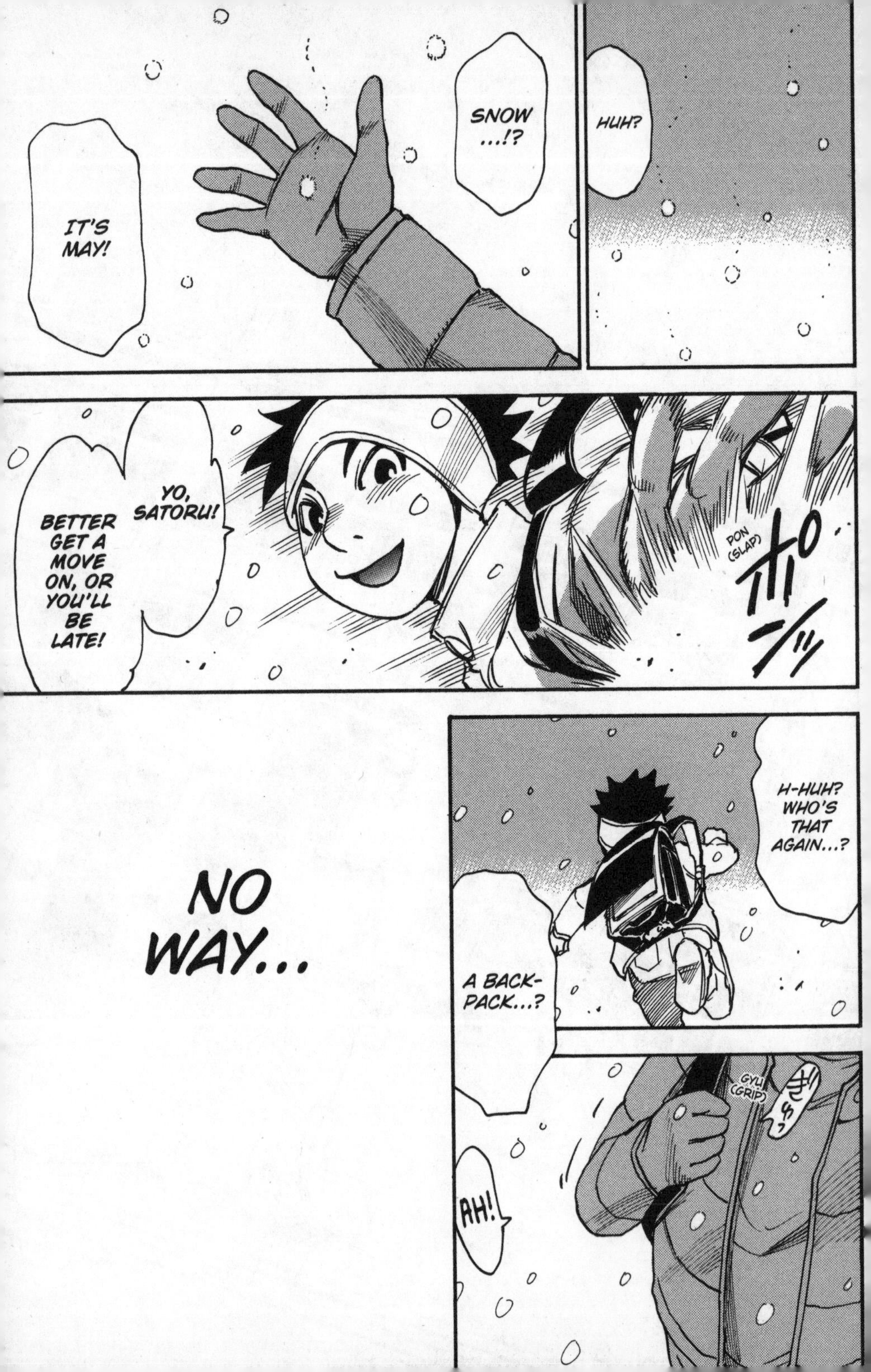
HUH?
SNOW ...!?
IT'S MAY!
PON (SLAP)
YO, SATORU!
BETTER GET A MOVE ON, OR YOU'LL BE LATE!
H-HUH? WHO'S THAT AGAIN...?
A BACK-PACK...?
GYU (GRIP)
AH!
NO WAY...

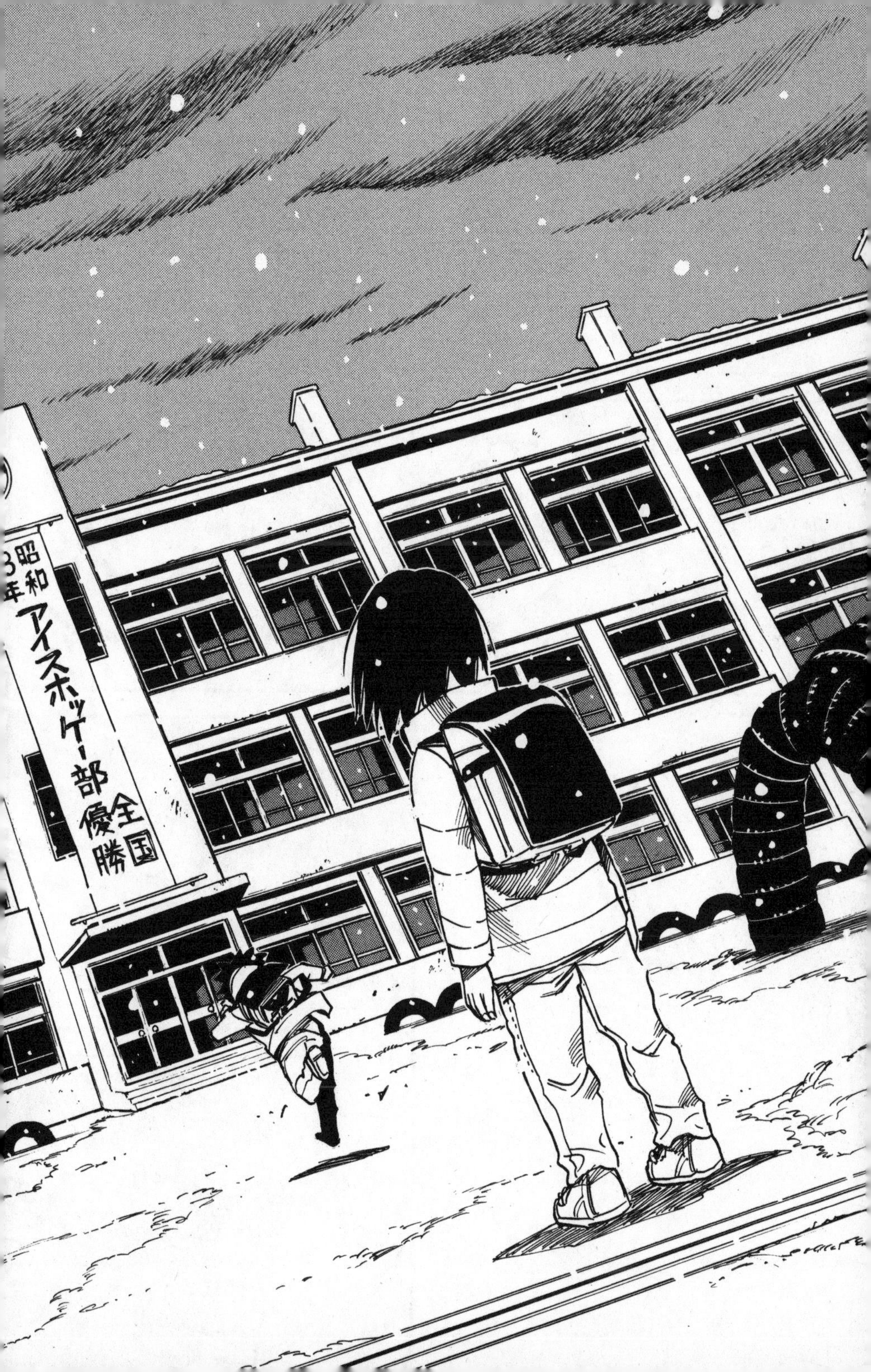
昭和
3年
アイスホッケー部
全国
優勝

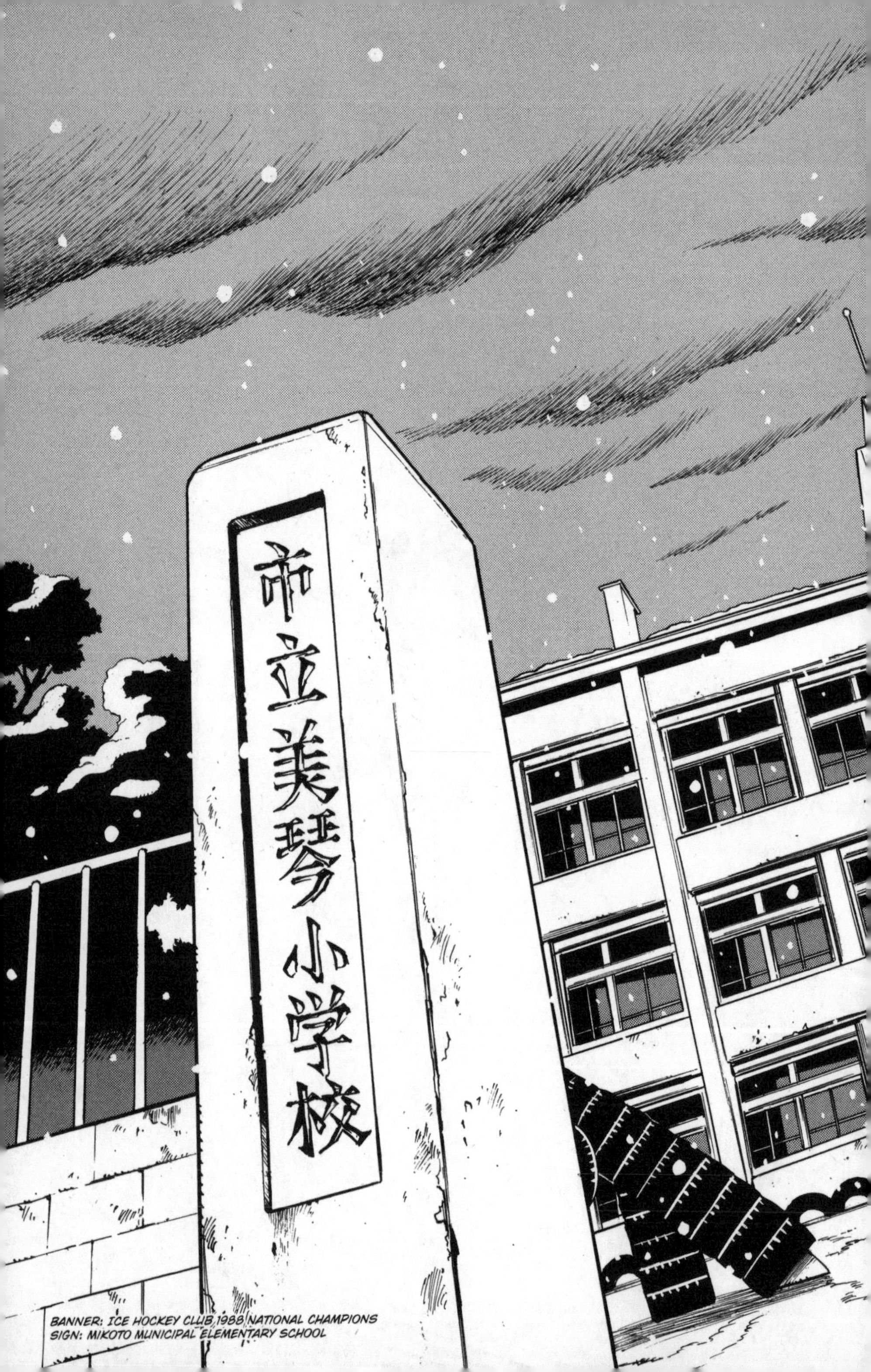
市立美琴小学校
BANNER: ICE HOCKEY CLUB 1988 NATIONAL CHAMPIONS
SIGN: MIKOTO MUNICIPAL ELEMENTARY SCHOOL

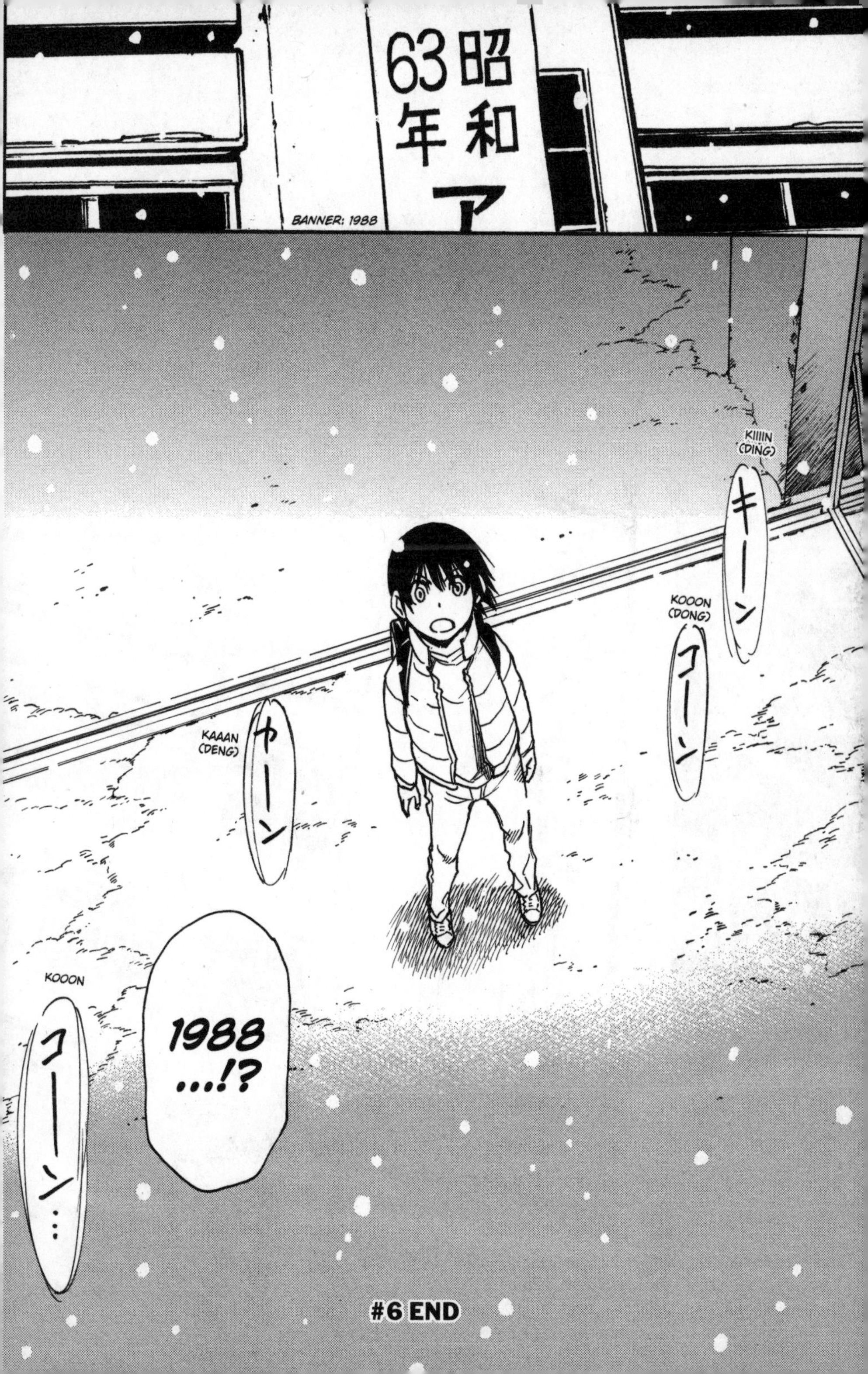
昭和63年
ア
BANNER: 1988
キーン
KIIIN (DING)
コーン
KOOON (DONG)
ヤーン
KAAAN (DENG)
1988...!?
コーン…
KOOON
#6 END

STAFF

Kei Sanbe

Yoichiro Tomita
Manami 18-years-old
Shuuei Takagi
Zukku Ozaki
Kouji Kikuta

Keishi Kanesada

BOOK DESIGN
Yukio Hoshino
VOLARE inc.

EDITOR
Tsunenori Matsumiya

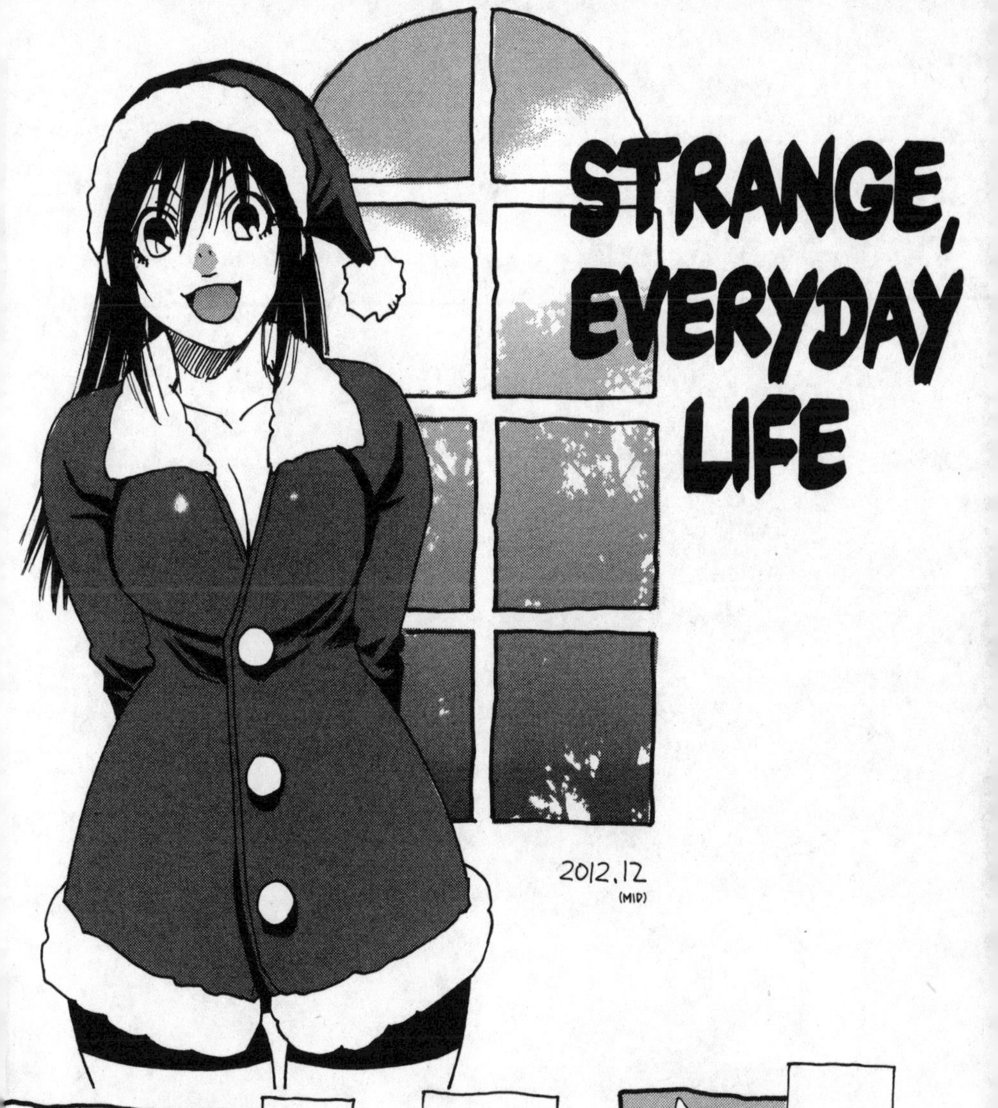
STRANGE, EVERYDAY LIFE
2012.12 (MID)

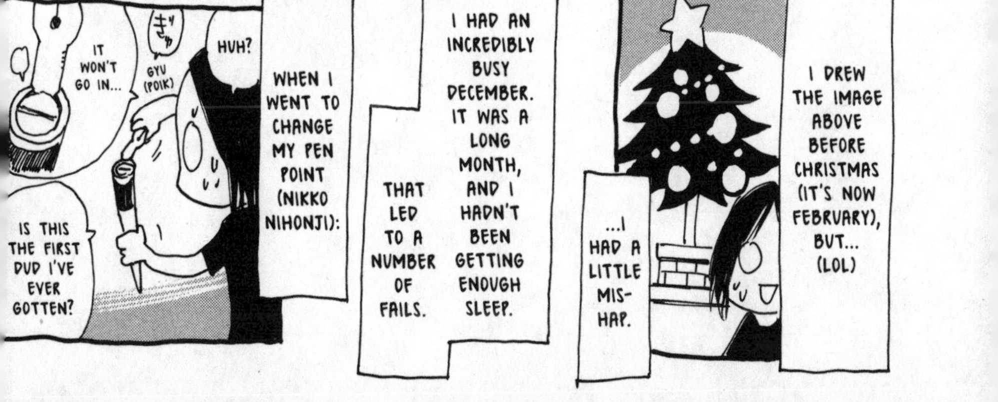
I DREW THE IMAGE ABOVE BEFORE CHRISTMAS (IT'S NOW FEBRUARY), BUT... (LOL)
...I HAD A LITTLE MIS-HAP.
I HAD AN INCREDIBLY BUSY DECEMBER. IT WAS A LONG MONTH, AND I HADN'T BEEN GETTING ENOUGH SLEEP.
THAT LED TO A NUMBER OF FAILS.
WHEN I WENT TO CHANGE MY PEN POINT (NIKKO NIHONJI):
HUH?
GYU (POIK)
IT WON'T GO IN...
IS THIS THE FIRST DUD I'VE EVER GOTTEN?

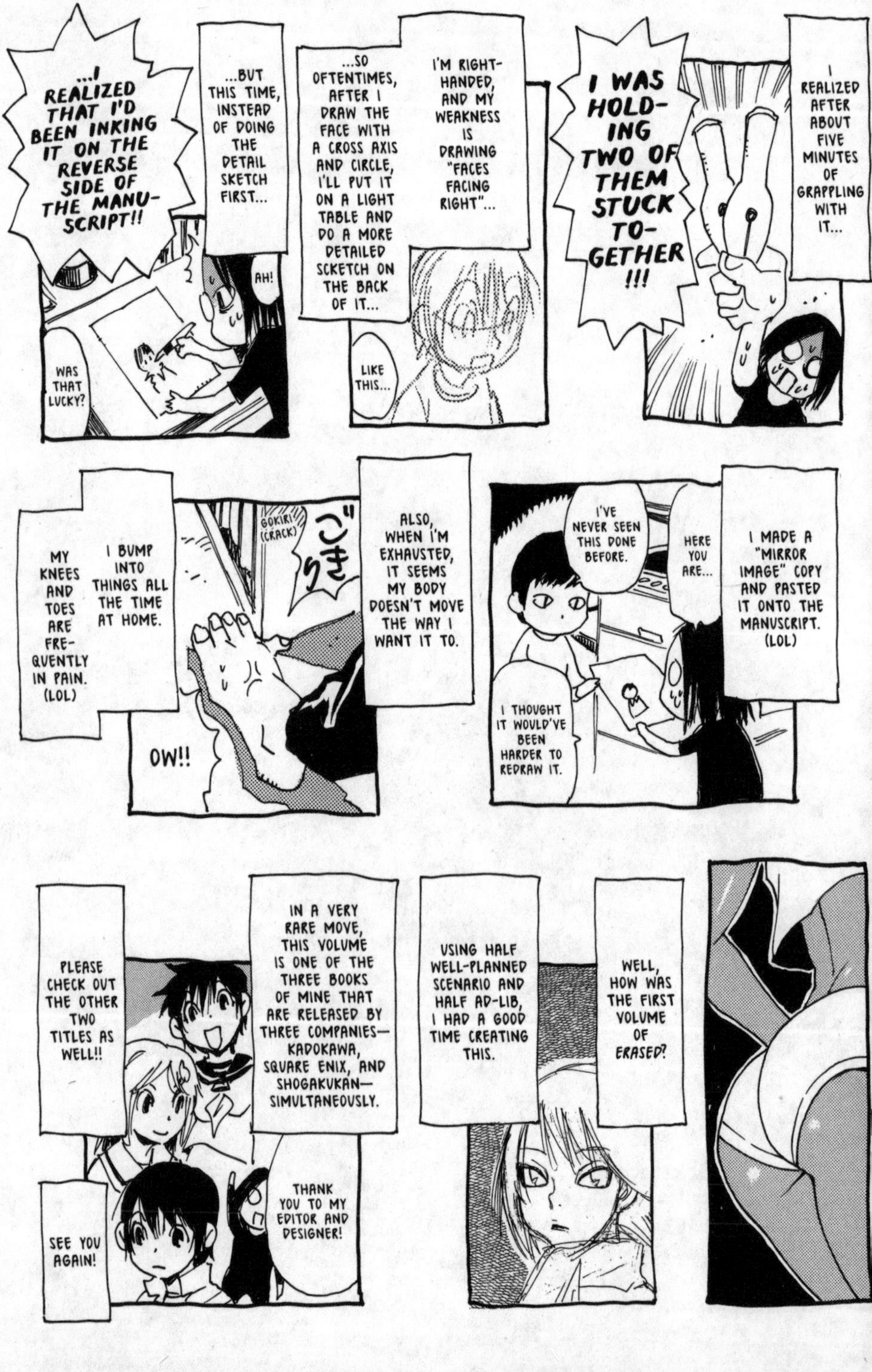
I REALIZED AFTER ABOUT FIVE MINUTES OF GRAPPLING WITH IT...
I WAS HOLDING TWO OF THEM STUCK TOGETHER!!!
I'M RIGHT-HANDED, AND MY WEAKNESS IS DRAWING "FACES FACING RIGHT"...
...SO OFTENTIMES, AFTER I DRAW THE FACE WITH A CROSS AXIS AND CIRCLE, I'LL PUT IT ON A LIGHT TABLE AND DO A MORE DETAILED SCKETCH ON THE BACK OF IT...
LIKE THIS...
...BUT THIS TIME, INSTEAD OF DOING THE DETAIL SKETCH FIRST...
...I REALIZED THAT I'D BEEN INKING IT ON THE REVERSE SIDE OF THE MANU-SCRIPT!!
AH!
WAS THAT LUCKY?
I MADE A "MIRROR IMAGE" COPY AND PASTED IT ONTO THE MANUSCRIPT. (LOL)
HERE YOU ARE...
I'VE NEVER SEEN THIS DONE BEFORE.
I THOUGHT IT WOULD'VE BEEN HARDER TO REDRAW IT.
ALSO, WHEN I'M EXHAUSTED, IT SEEMS MY BODY DOESN'T MOVE THE WAY I WANT IT TO.
ごきり
GOKIRI (CRACK)
OW!!
I BUMP INTO THINGS ALL THE TIME AT HOME.
MY KNEES AND TOES ARE FRE-QUENTLY IN PAIN. (LOL)
WELL, HOW WAS THE FIRST VOLUME OF ERASED?
USING HALF WELL-PLANNED SCENARIO AND HALF AD-LIB, I HAD A GOOD TIME CREATING THIS.
IN A VERY RARE MOVE, THIS VOLUME IS ONE OF THE THREE BOOKS OF MINE THAT ARE RELEASED BY THREE COMPANIES—KADOKAWA, SQUARE ENIX, AND SHOGAKUKAN—SIMULTANEOUSLY.
PLEASE CHECK OUT THE OTHER TWO TITLES AS WELL!!
THANK YOU TO MY EDITOR AND DESIGNER!
SEE YOU AGAIN!

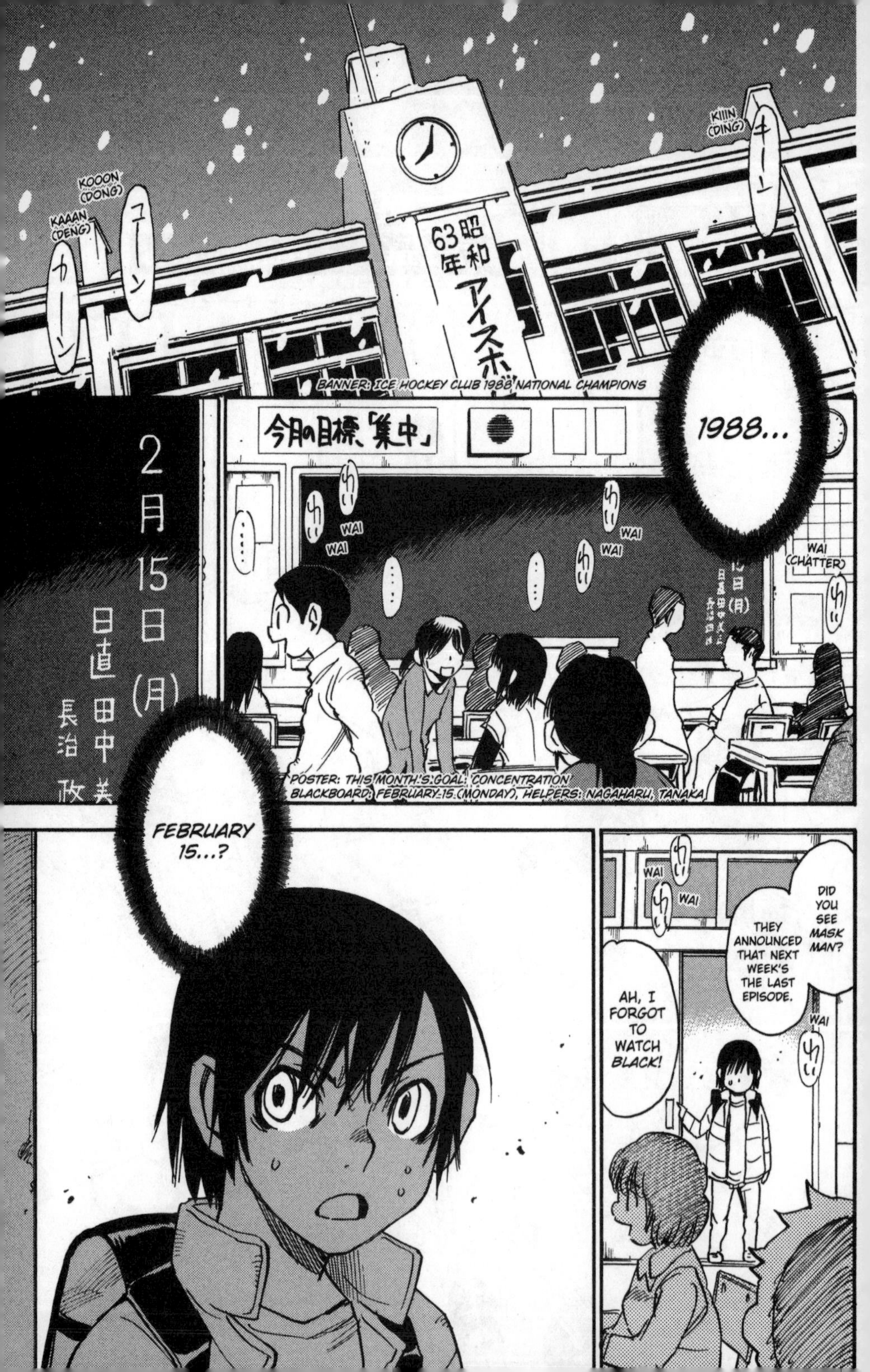
KIIN (DING)
キーン
昭和63年 アイスホ
KOOON (DONG)
コーン
KAAAN (DENG)
カーン
BANNER: ICE HOCKEY CLUB 1988 NATIONAL CHAMPIONS
1988...
今月の目標「集中」
WAI (CHATTER)
WAI
WAI
WAI
WAI
2月15日(月)
POSTER: THIS MONTH'S GOAL: CONCENTRATION
BLACKBOARD: FEBRUARY 15 (MONDAY), HELPERS: NAGAHARU, TANAKA
DID YOU SEE MASK MAN?
THEY ANNOUNCED THAT NEXT WEEK'S THE LAST EPISODE.
AH, I FORGOT TO WATCH BLACK!
WAI
WAI
WAI
FEBRUARY 15...?

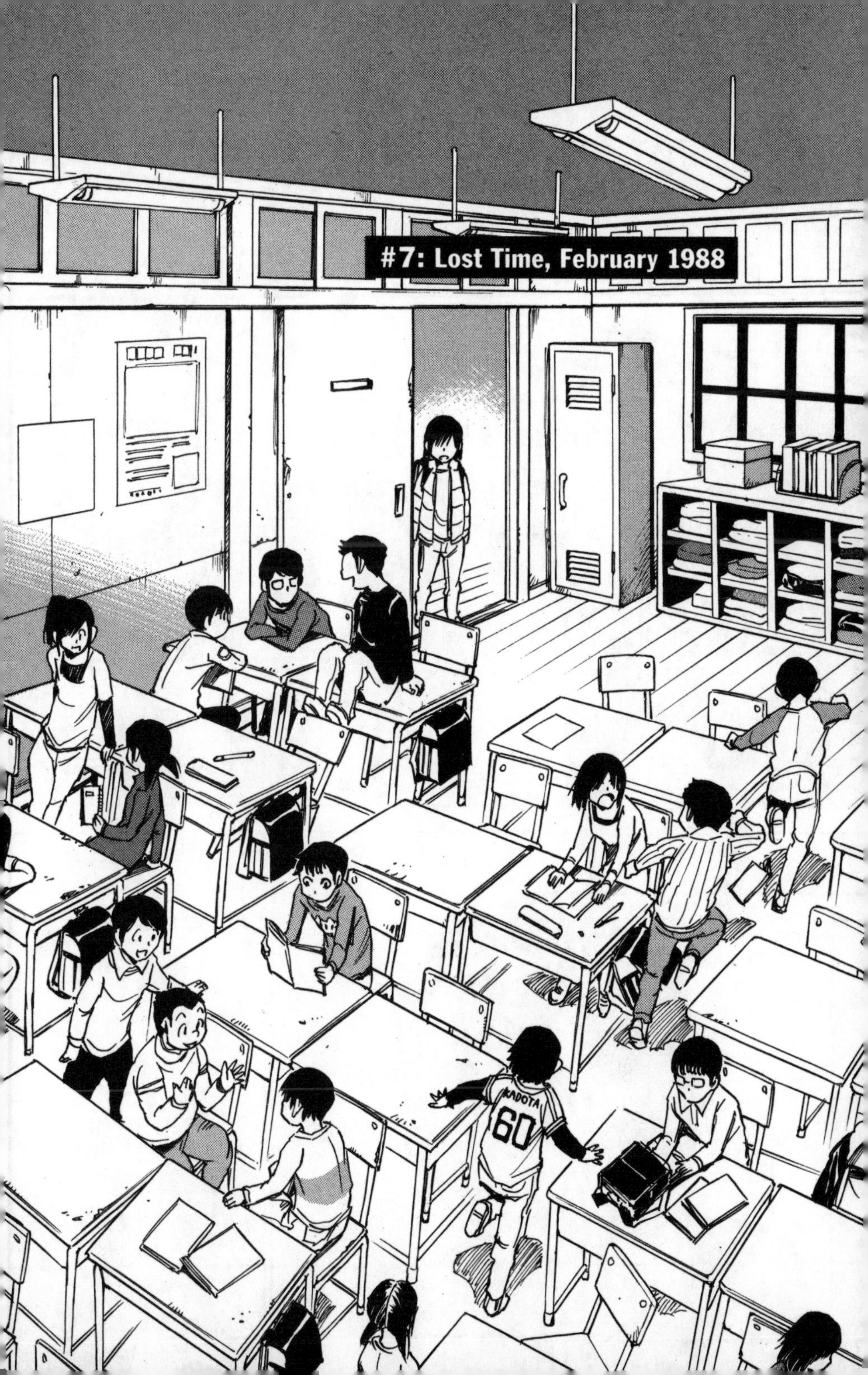
#7: Lost Time, February 1988
KADOTA
60

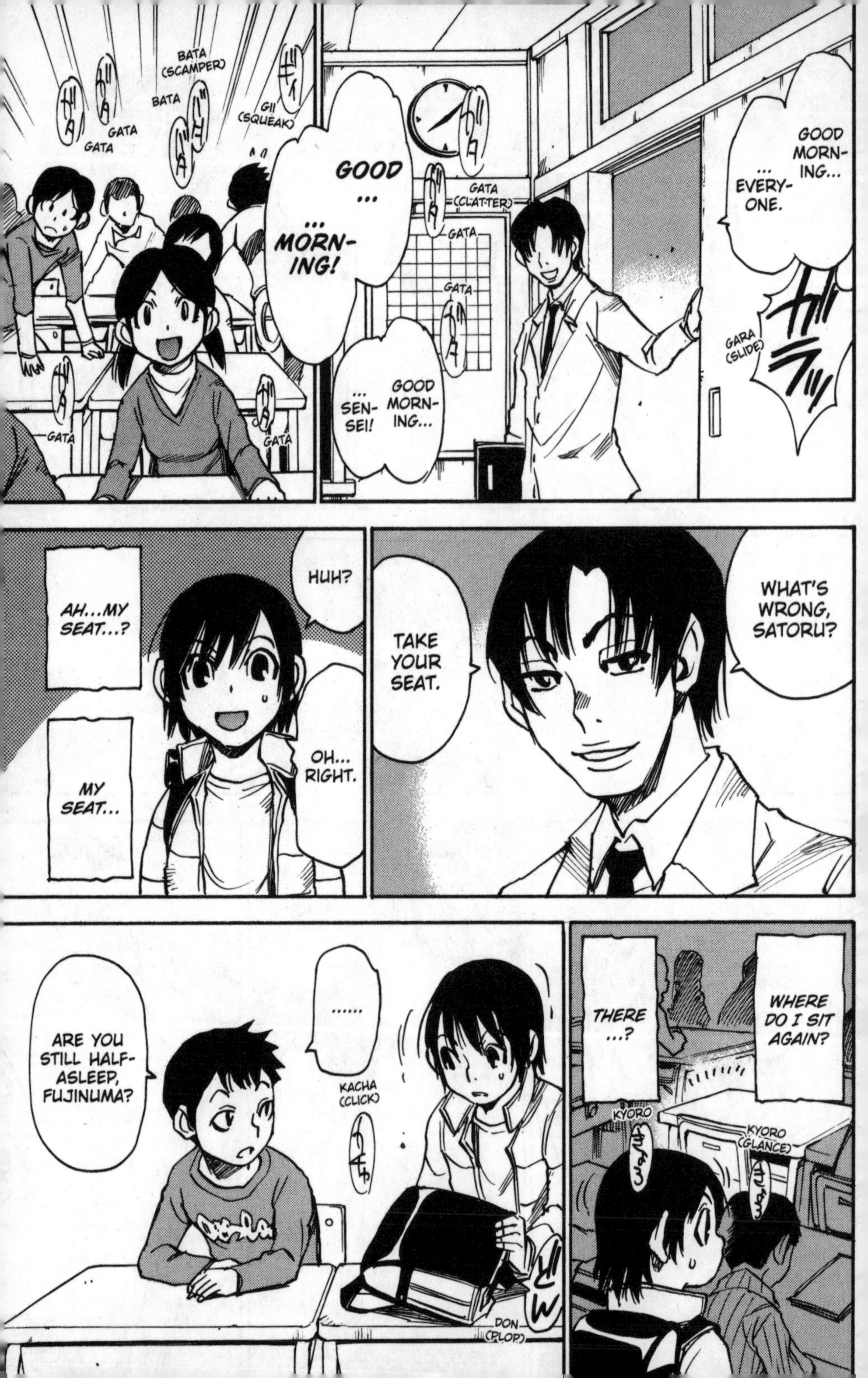
GARA (SLIDE)
GOOD MORNING... ...EVERYONE.
GATA (CLATTER)
GATA
GATA
GOOD MORNING... ...SENSEI!
GOOD ... ...MORNING!
GII (SQUEAK)
BATA (SCAMPER)
BATA
GATA
GATA
GATA
GATA
WHAT'S WRONG, SATORU?
TAKE YOUR SEAT.
HUH?
AH...MY SEAT...?
OH... RIGHT.
MY SEAT...
WHERE DO I SIT AGAIN?
THERE ...?
KYORO (GLANCE)
KYORO
......
KACHA (CLICK)
DON (PLOP)
ARE YOU STILL HALF-ASLEEP, FUJINUMA?

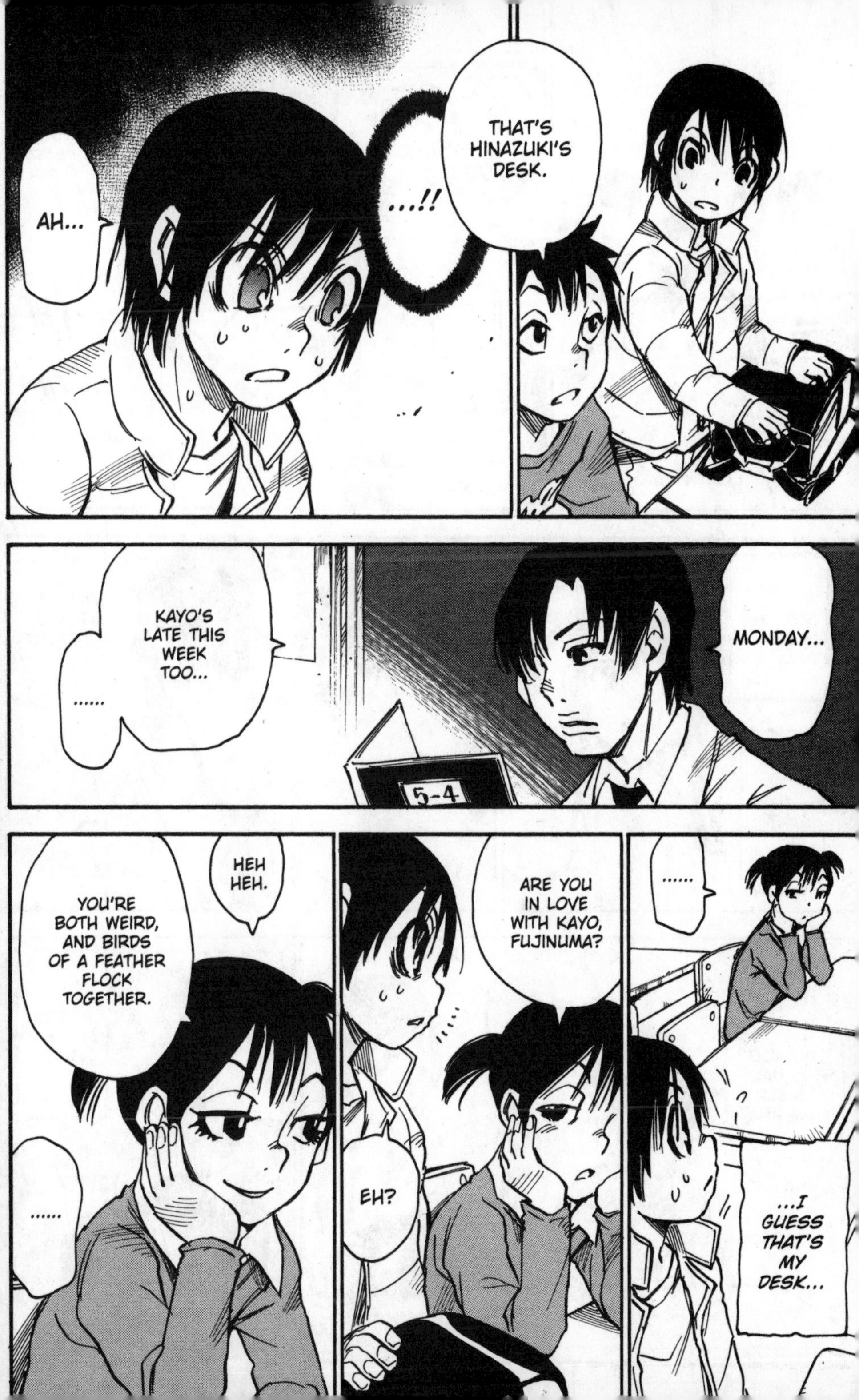
THAT'S HINAZUKI'S DESK.
...!!
AH...
MONDAY...
KAYO'S LATE THIS WEEK TOO...
......
......
...I GUESS THAT'S MY DESK...
ARE YOU IN LOVE WITH KAYO, FUJINUMA?
EH?
HEH HEH.
YOU'RE BOTH WEIRD, AND BIRDS OF A FEATHER FLOCK TOGETHER.
......

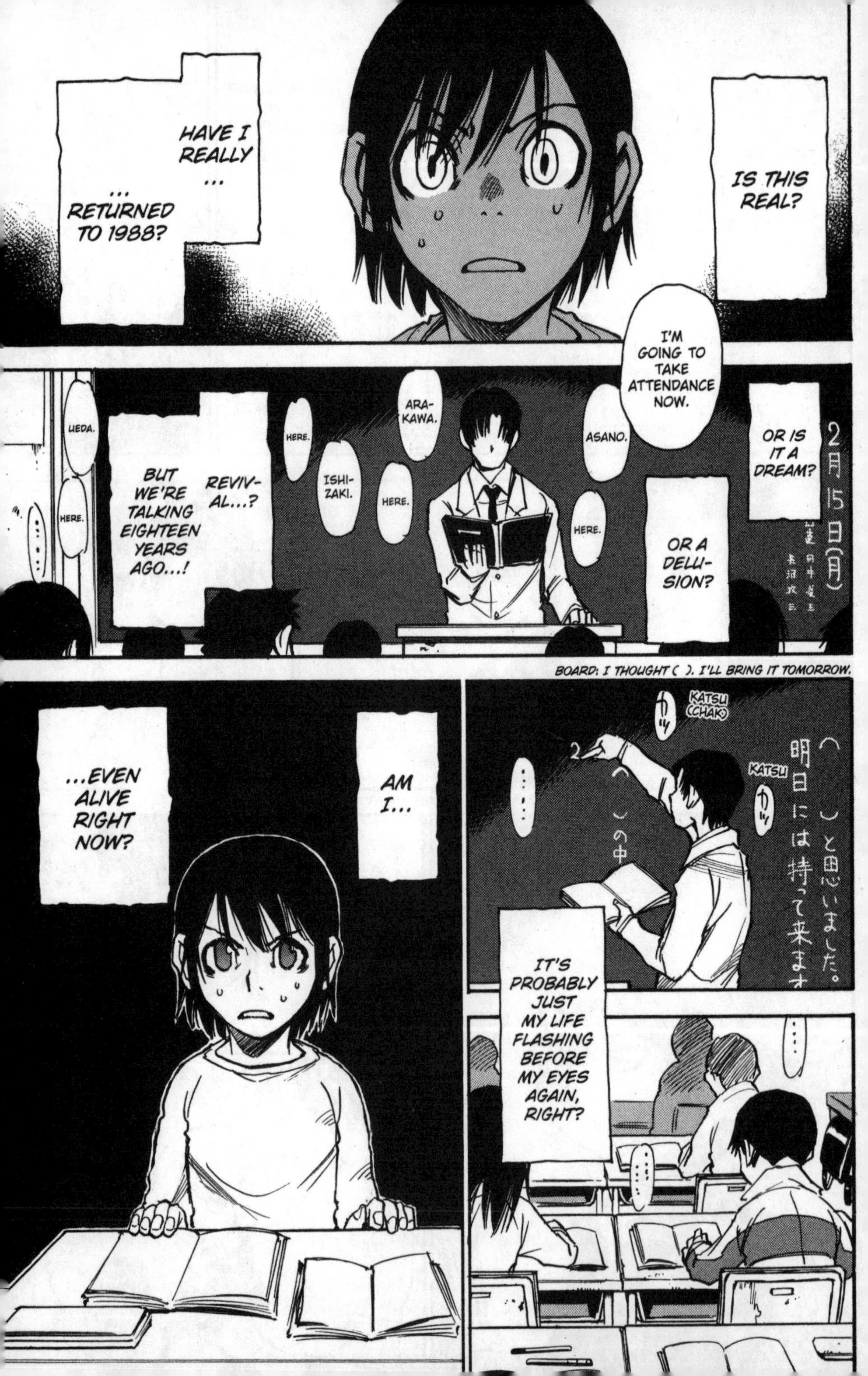
IS THIS REAL?
HAVE I REALLY ... ... RETURNED TO 1988?
I'M GOING TO TAKE ATTENDANCE NOW.
OR IS IT A DREAM?
2月15日(月)
ASANO.
HERE.
OR A DELUSION?
ARA-KAWA.
HERE.
ISHI-ZAKI.
HERE.
REVIV-AL...?
BUT WE'RE TALKING EIGHTEEN YEARS AGO...!
UEDA.
HERE.
...
BOARD: I THOUGHT ( ). I'LL BRING IT TOMORROW.
カッ
KATSU (CHAK)
カッ
KATSU
（　）と思いました。明日には持って来ま
（　）の中
...
IT'S PROBABLY JUST MY LIFE FLASHING BEFORE MY EYES AGAIN, RIGHT?
...
...
AM I...
...EVEN ALIVE RIGHT NOW?

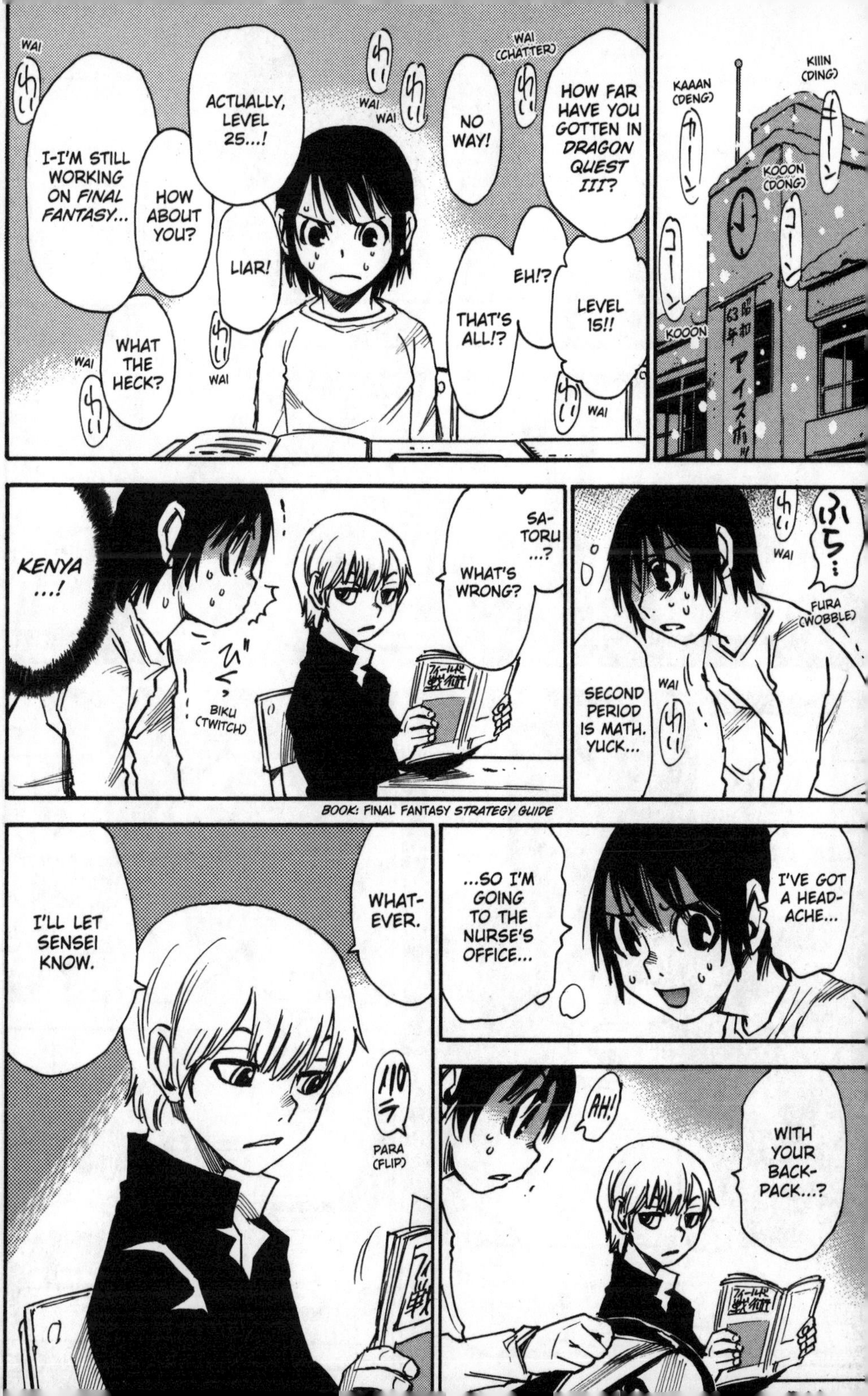
KIIIN (DING)
KAAAN (DENG)
KOOON (DONG)
KOOON
WAI (CHATTER)
HOW FAR HAVE YOU GOTTEN IN *DRAGON QUEST III*?
NO WAY!
WAI
WAI
LEVEL 15!!
EH!?
THAT'S ALL!?
WAI
ACTUALLY, LEVEL 25...!
HOW ABOUT YOU?
LIAR!
WAI
I-I'M STILL WORKING ON *FINAL FANTASY*...
WAI
WHAT THE HECK?
WAI
WAI
ふら…
FURA (WOBBLE)
WAI
SECOND PERIOD IS MATH. YUCK...
SA-TORU ...?
WHAT'S WRONG?
KENYA ...!
BIKU (TWITCH)
BOOK: *FINAL FANTASY STRATEGY GUIDE*
I'VE GOT A HEAD-ACHE...
...SO I'M GOING TO THE NURSE'S OFFICE...
WITH YOUR BACK-PACK...?
AH!
WHAT-EVER.
I'LL LET SENSEI KNOW.
PARA (FLIP)

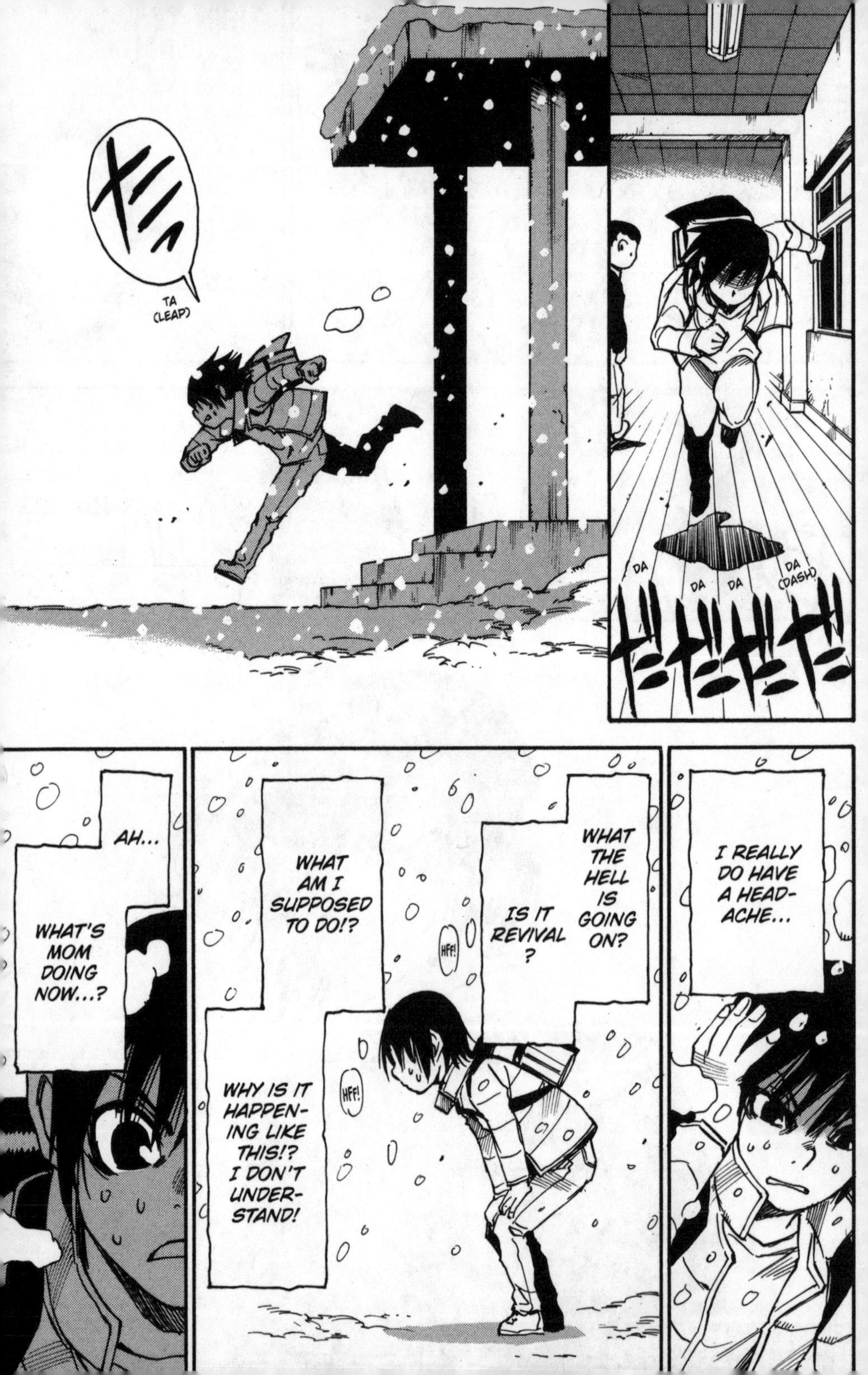
DA DA DA DA (DASH)
TA (LEAP)
I REALLY DO HAVE A HEAD-ACHE...
WHAT THE HELL IS GOING ON?
IS IT REVIVAL?
HFF!
WHAT AM I SUPPOSED TO DO!?
HFF!
WHY IS IT HAPPEN-ING LIKE THIS!? I DON'T UNDER-STAND!
AH...
WHAT'S MOM DOING NOW...?

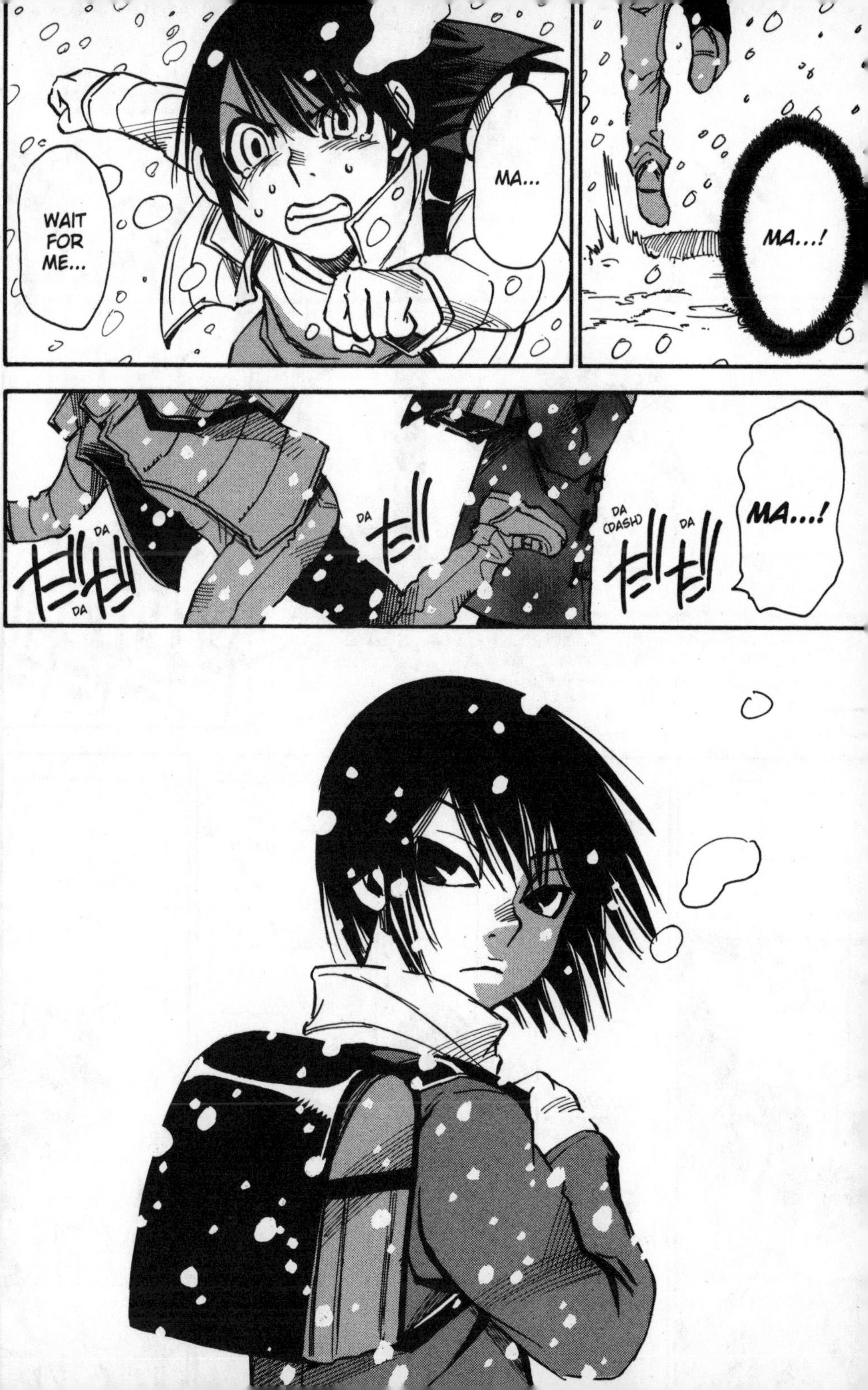
MA...!
MA...
WAIT FOR ME...
MA...!
DA
DA (DASH)
DA
DA
DA

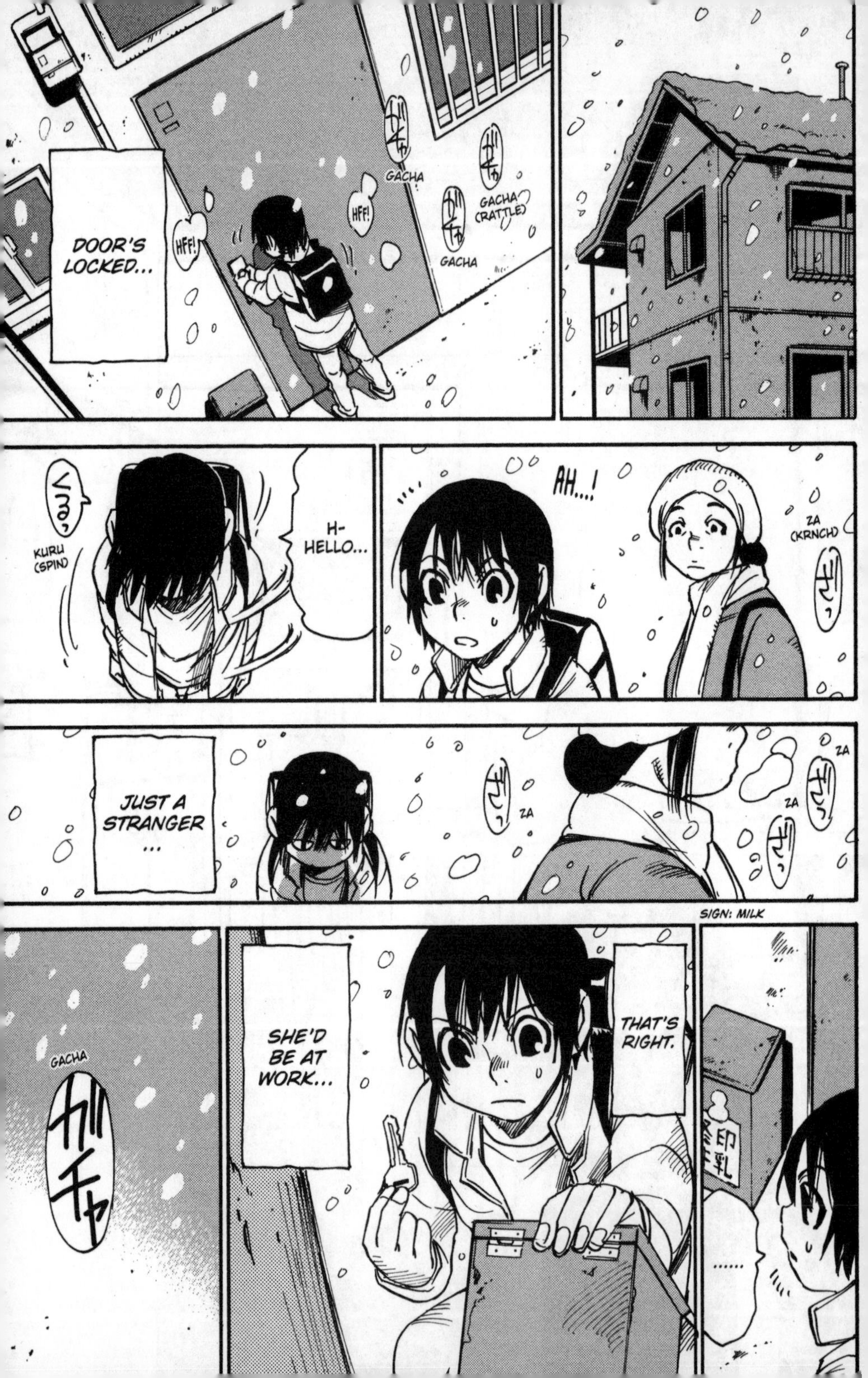
GACHA
GACHA (RATTLE)
HFF!
GACHA
HFF!
DOOR'S LOCKED...
AH...!
ZA (KRNCH)
...
H-HELLO...
KURU (SPIN)
ZA
ZA
ZA
JUST A STRANGER...
SIGN: MILK
......
THAT'S RIGHT.
SHE'D BE AT WORK...
GACHA
ガチャ

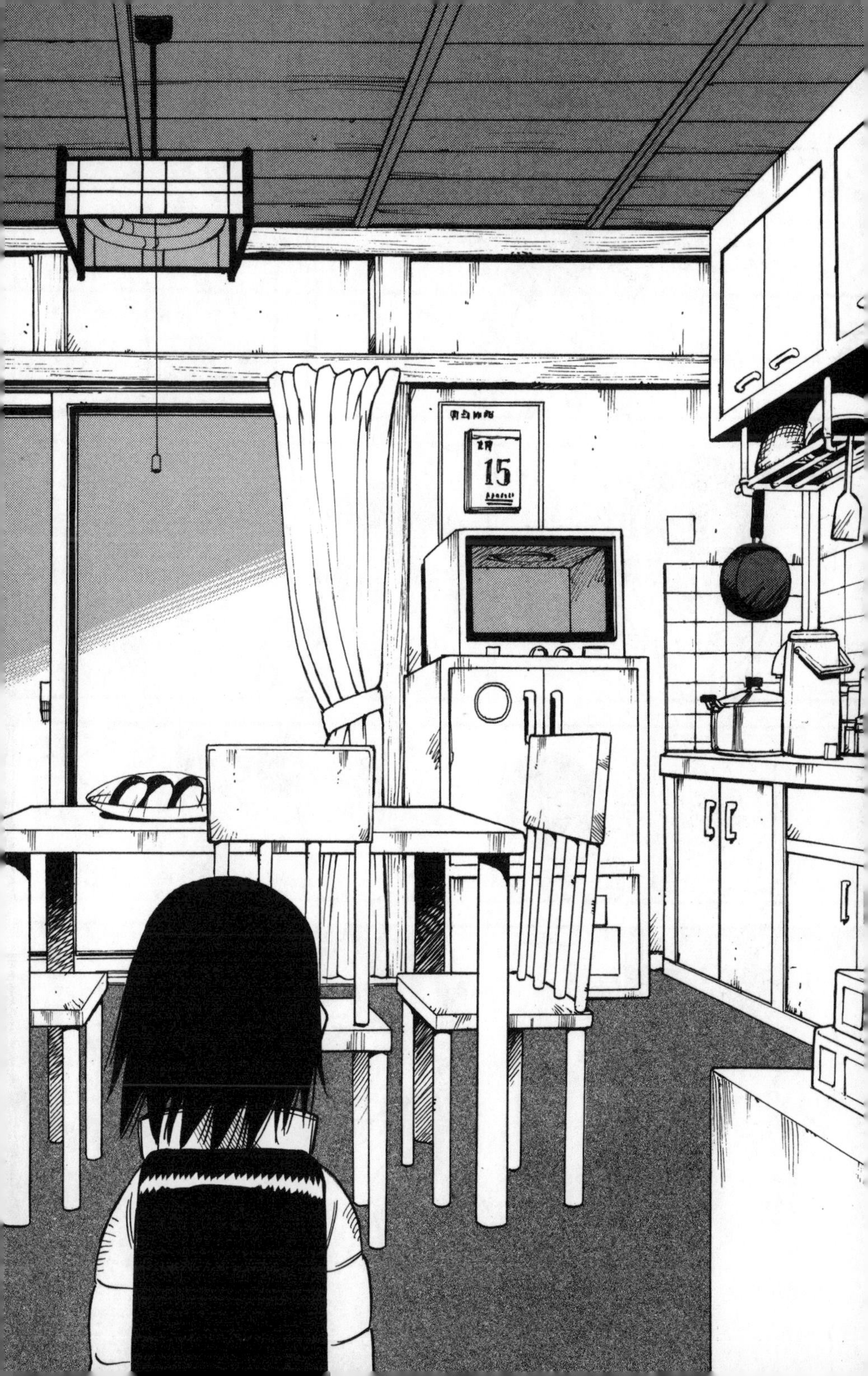
15

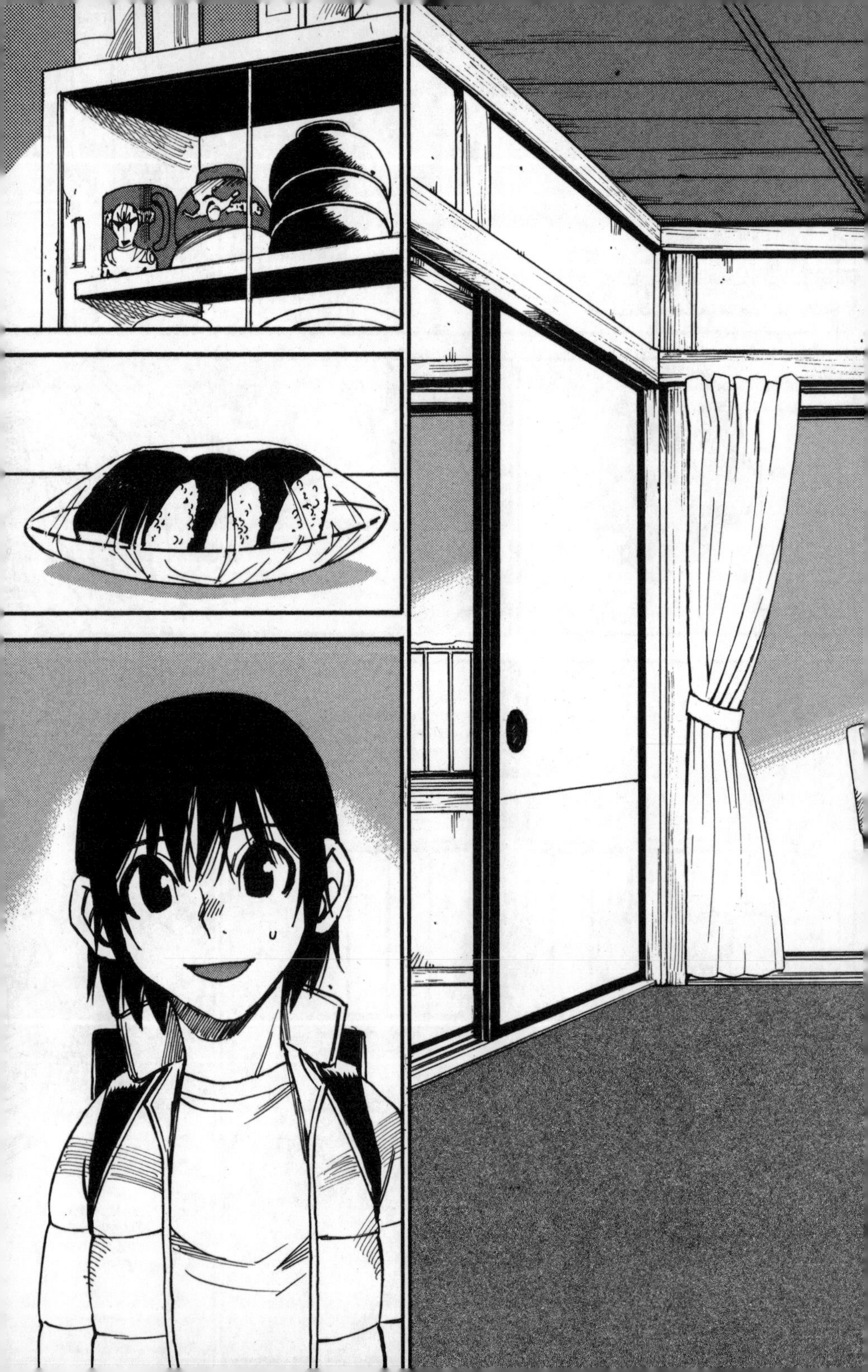

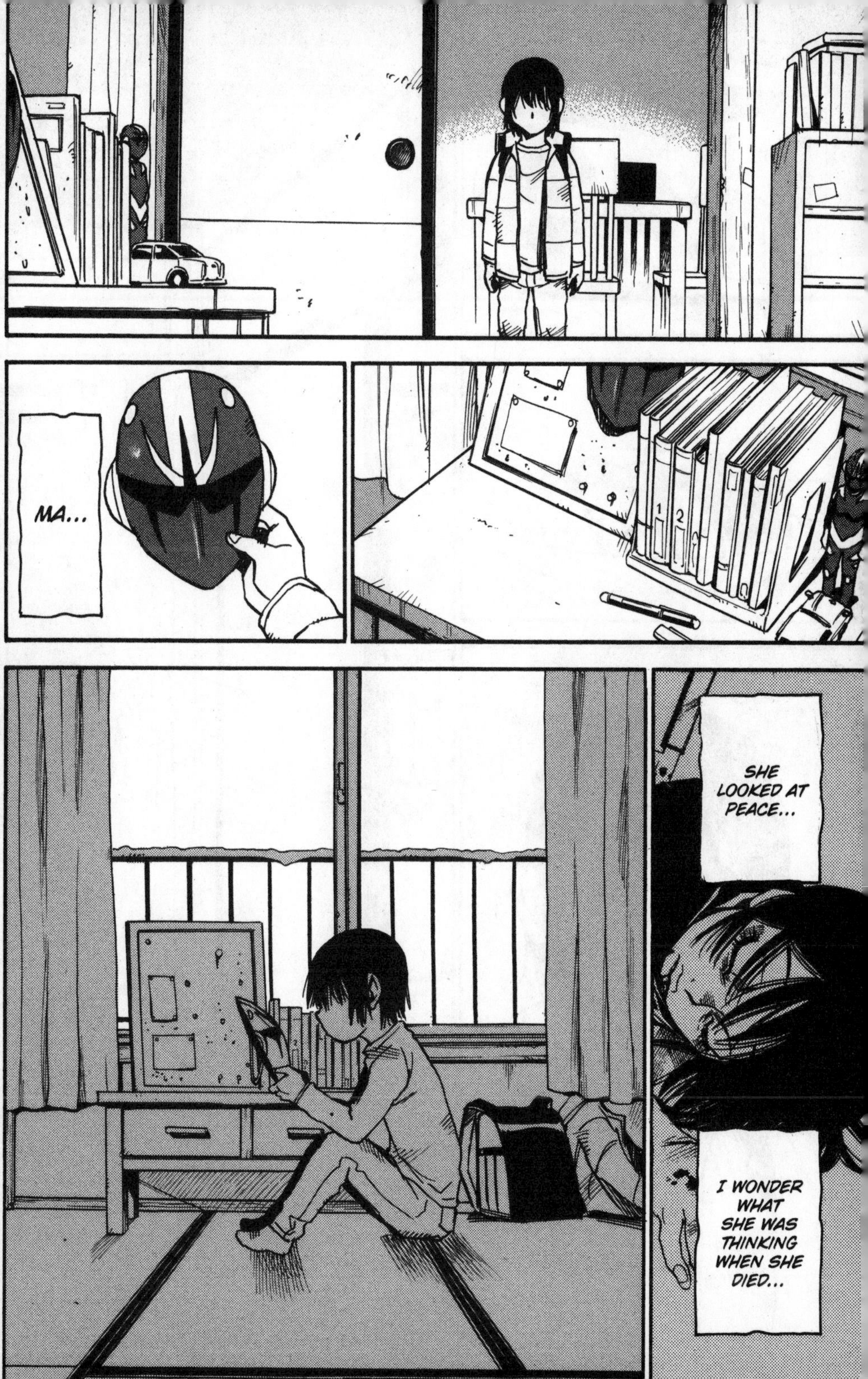
MA...
SHE LOOKED AT PEACE...
I WONDER WHAT SHE WAS THINKING WHEN SHE DIED...

カチャ
KACHA (CHAK)
KACHA
カチャ
I'M HOME!
みし
MISHI (CREAK)
みし
MISHI
みし…
MISHI
カチッ
KACHI (CLICK)
SATORU ...
AH...

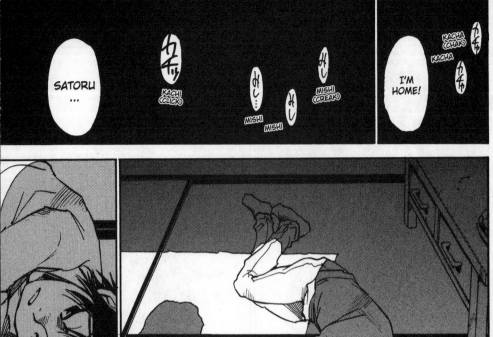

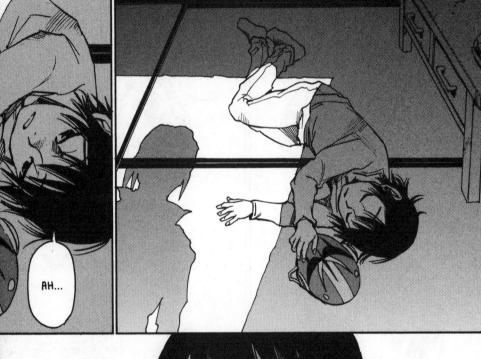

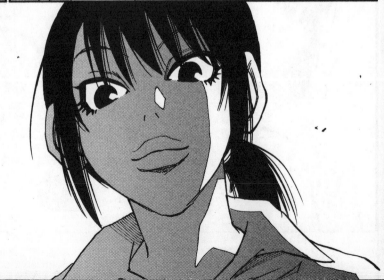

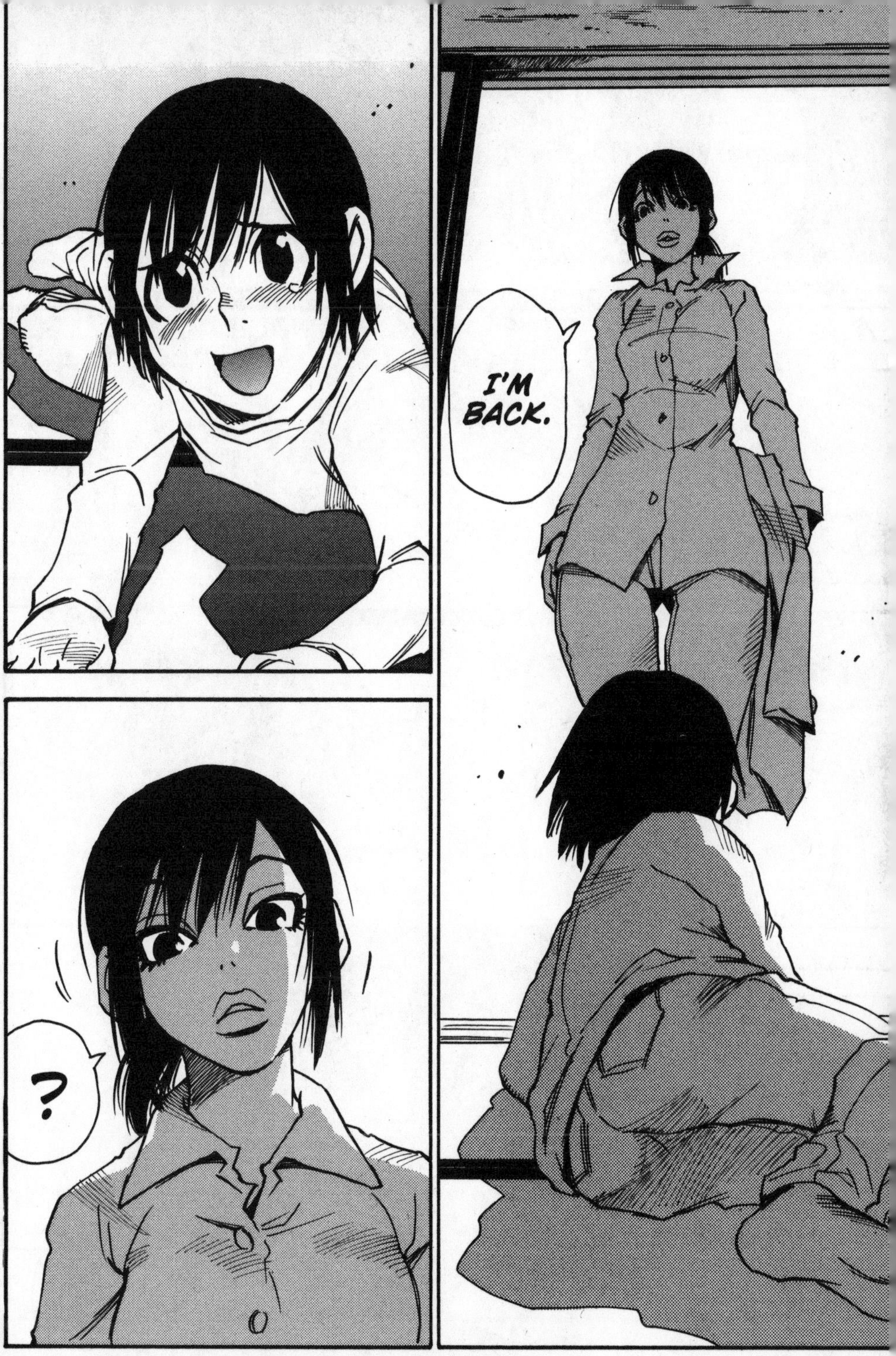
I'M BACK.
?

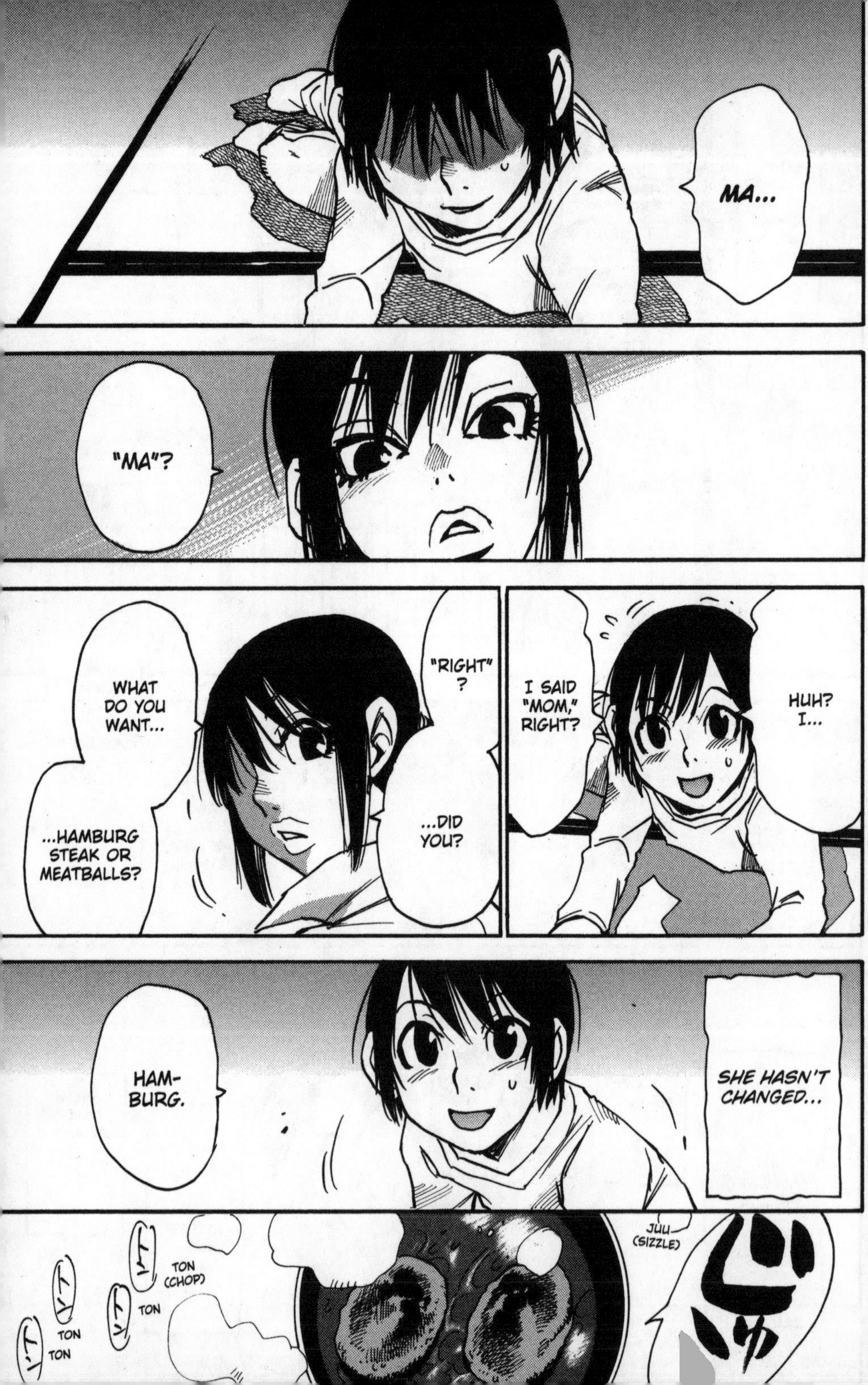
MA...
"MA"?
HUH? I...
I SAID "MOM," RIGHT?
"RIGHT"?
...DID YOU?
WHAT DO YOU WANT...
...HAMBURG STEAK OR MEATBALLS?
SHE HASN'T CHANGED...
HAM-BURG.
JUU (SIZZLE)
TON (CHOP)
TON
TON
TON

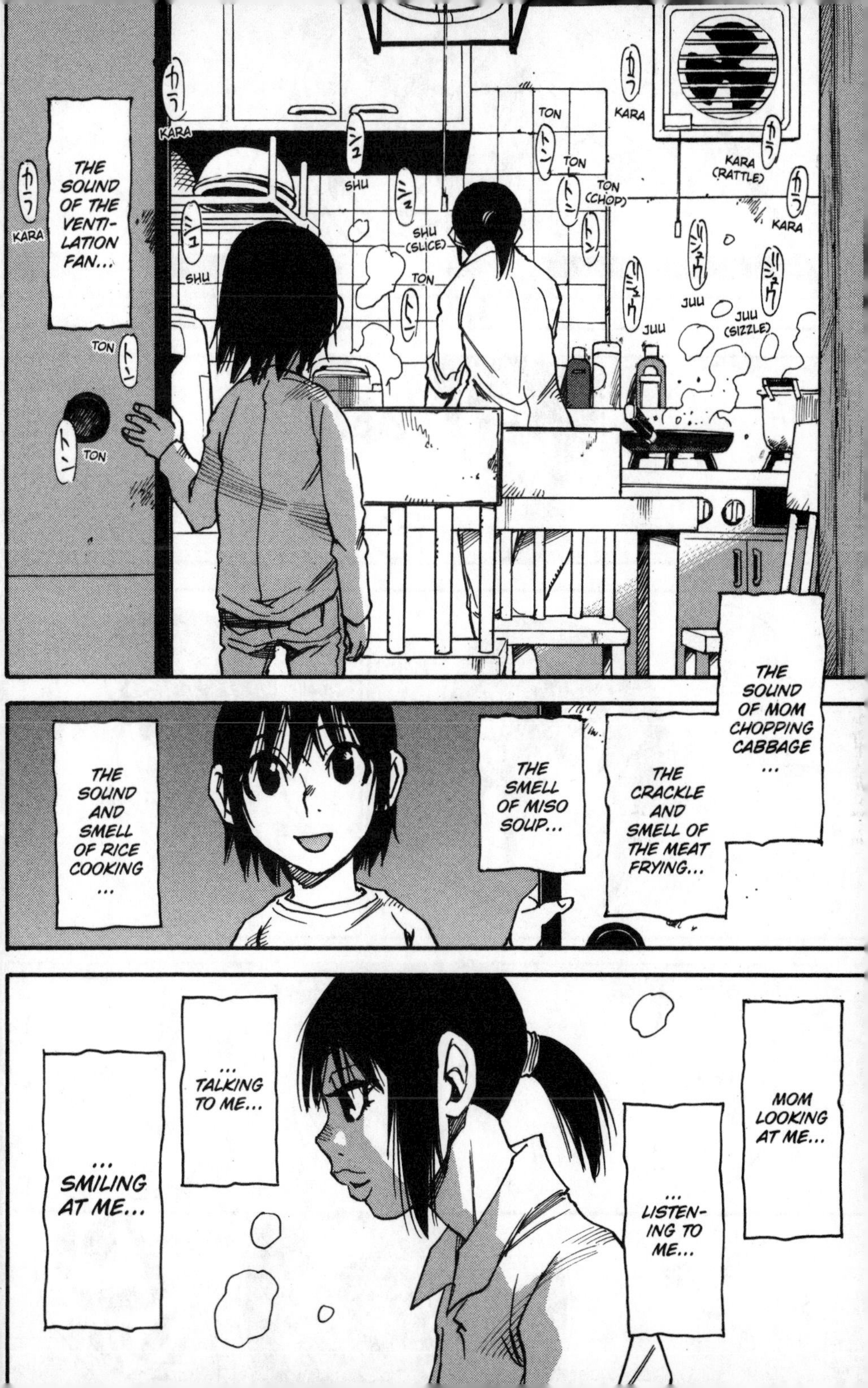
カラ
KARA
カラ
KARA (RATTLE)
カラ
KARA
トン
TON
トン
TON
トン
TON (CHOP)
ジュウ
JUU
ジュウ
JUU (SIZZLE)
ジュウ
JUU
シュ
SHU
シュ
SHU (SLICE)
シュ
SHU
トン
TON
カラ
KARA
THE SOUND OF THE VENTILATION FAN...
カラ
KARA
トン
TON
トン
TON
THE SOUND OF MOM CHOPPING CABBAGE...
THE CRACKLE AND SMELL OF THE MEAT FRYING...
THE SMELL OF MISO SOUP...
THE SOUND AND SMELL OF RICE COOKING...
MOM LOOKING AT ME...
... LISTENING TO ME...
... TALKING TO ME...
... SMILING AT ME...

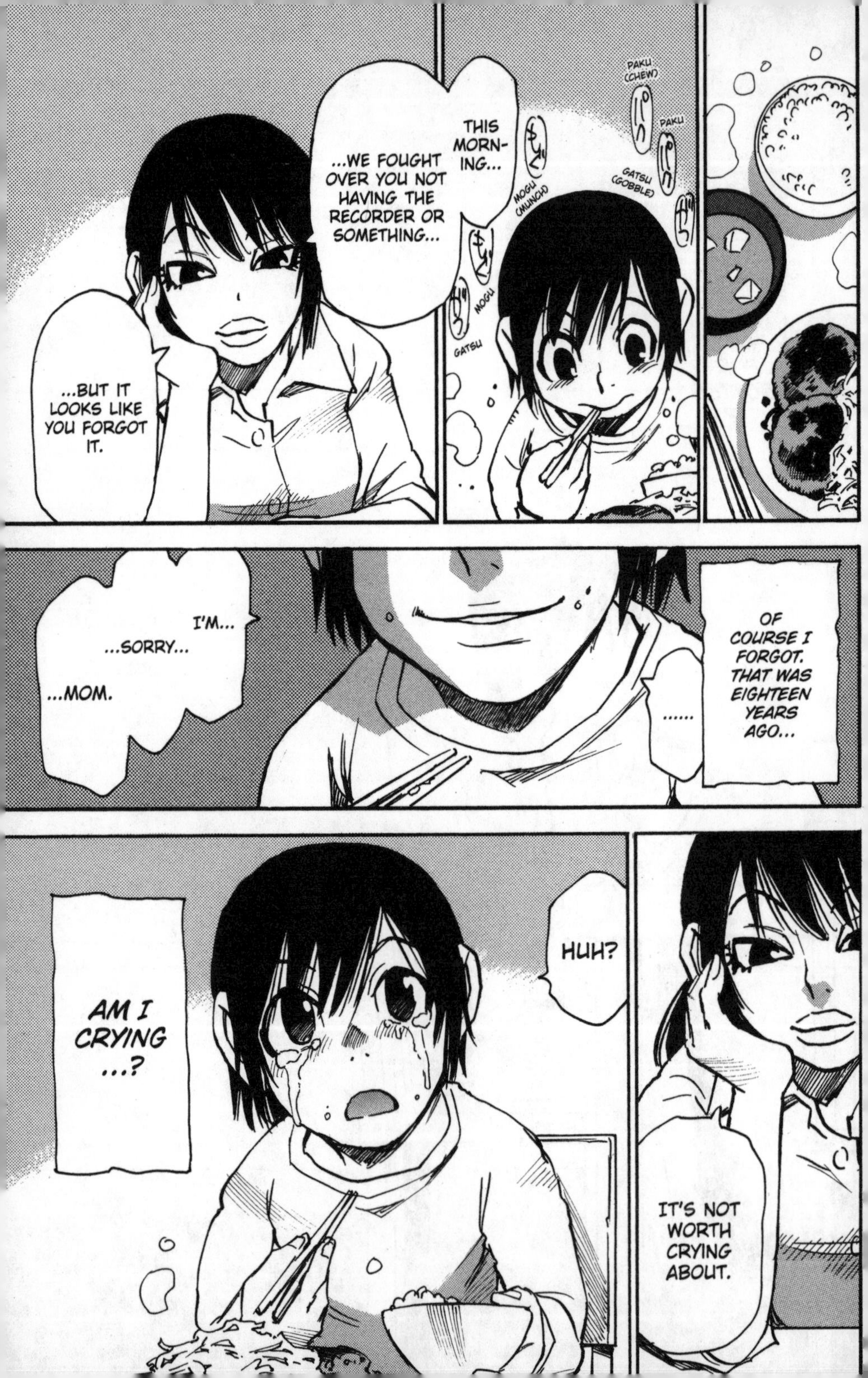
PAKU (CHEW)
PAKU
GATSU (GOBBLE)
THIS MORNING...
...WE FOUGHT OVER YOU NOT HAVING THE RECORDER OR SOMETHING...
MOGU (MUNCH)
MOGU
GATSU
...BUT IT LOOKS LIKE YOU FORGOT IT.
OF COURSE I FORGOT. THAT WAS EIGHTEEN YEARS AGO...
......
I'M...
...SORRY...
...MOM.
IT'S NOT WORTH CRYING ABOUT.
HUH?
AM I CRYING ...?

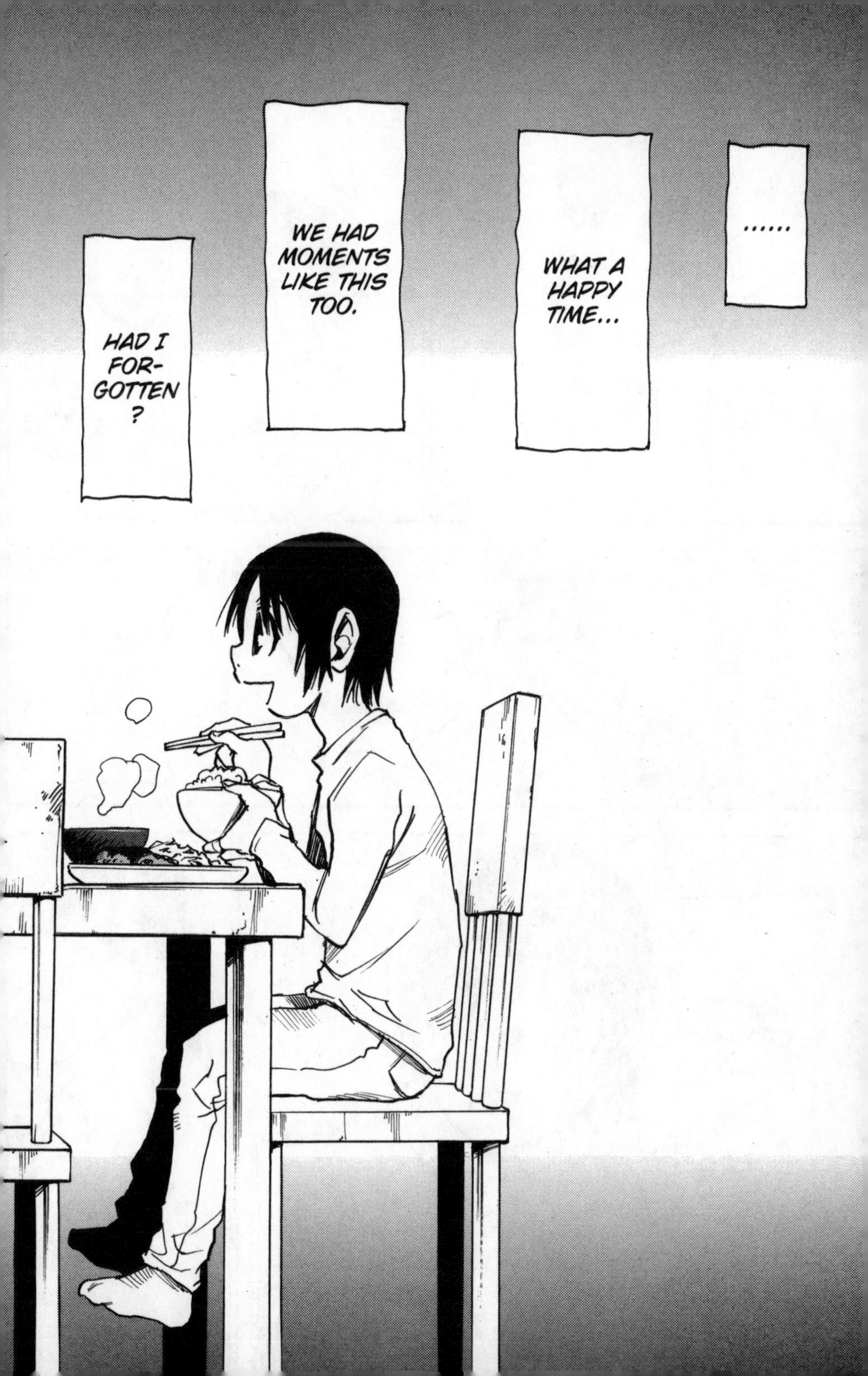
......
WHAT A HAPPY TIME...
WE HAD MOMENTS LIKE THIS TOO.
HAD I FORGOTTEN?

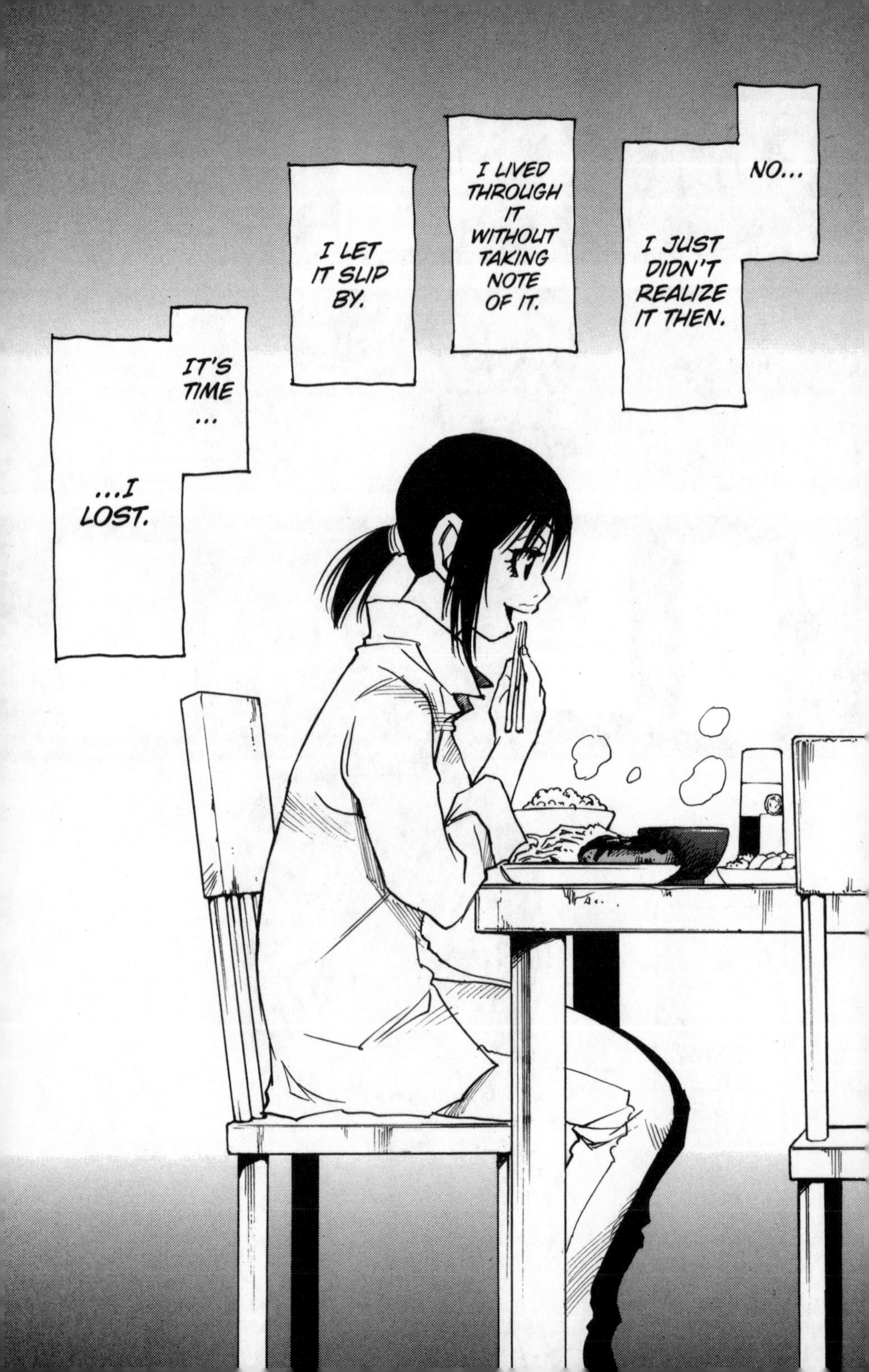
NO...
I JUST DIDN'T REALIZE IT THEN.
I LIVED THROUGH IT WITHOUT TAKING NOTE OF IT.
I LET IT SLIP BY.
IT'S TIME...
...I LOST.

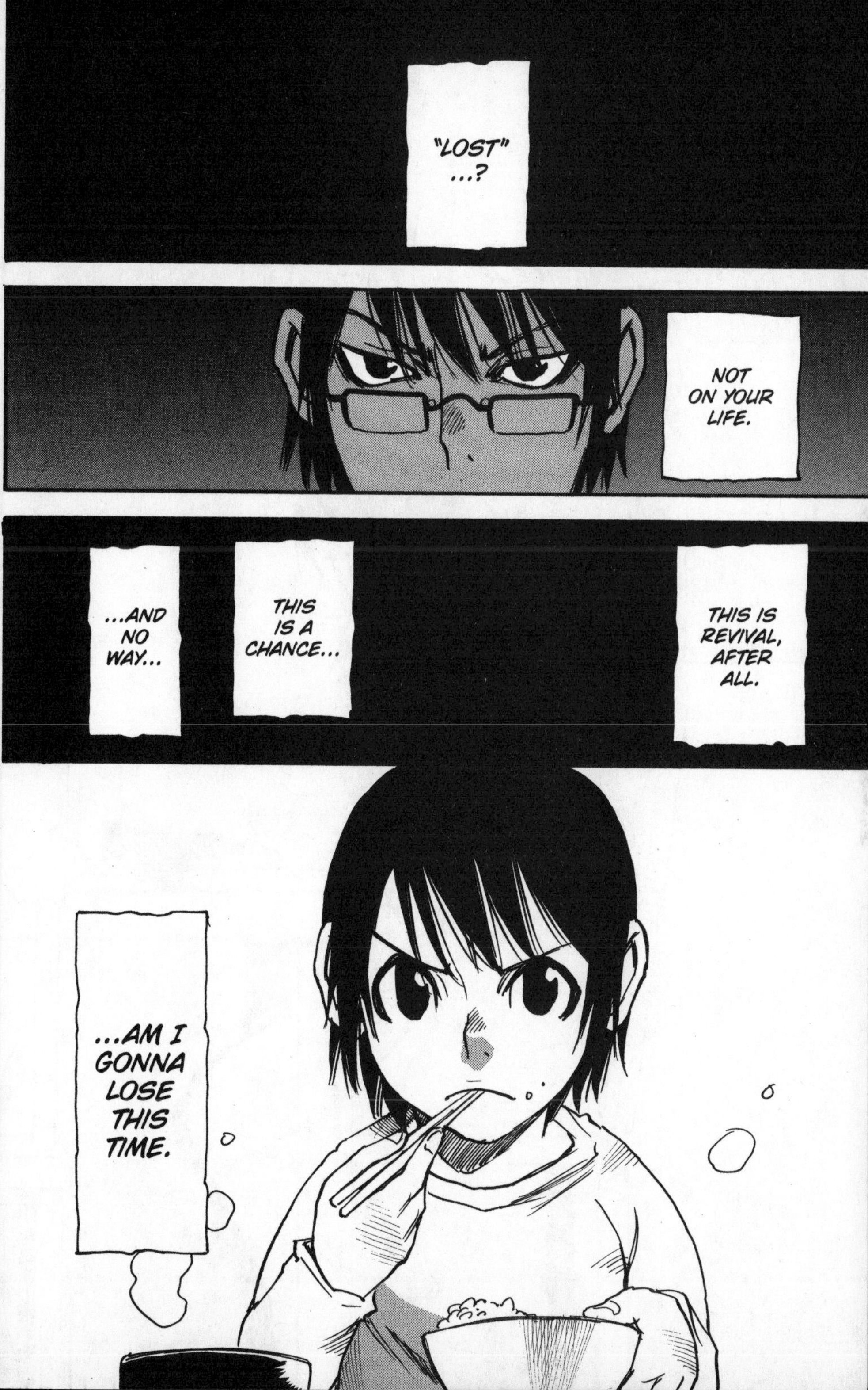
"LOST" ...?
NOT ON YOUR LIFE.
THIS IS REVIVAL, AFTER ALL.
THIS IS A CHANCE...
...AND NO WAY...
...AM I GONNA LOSE THIS TIME.

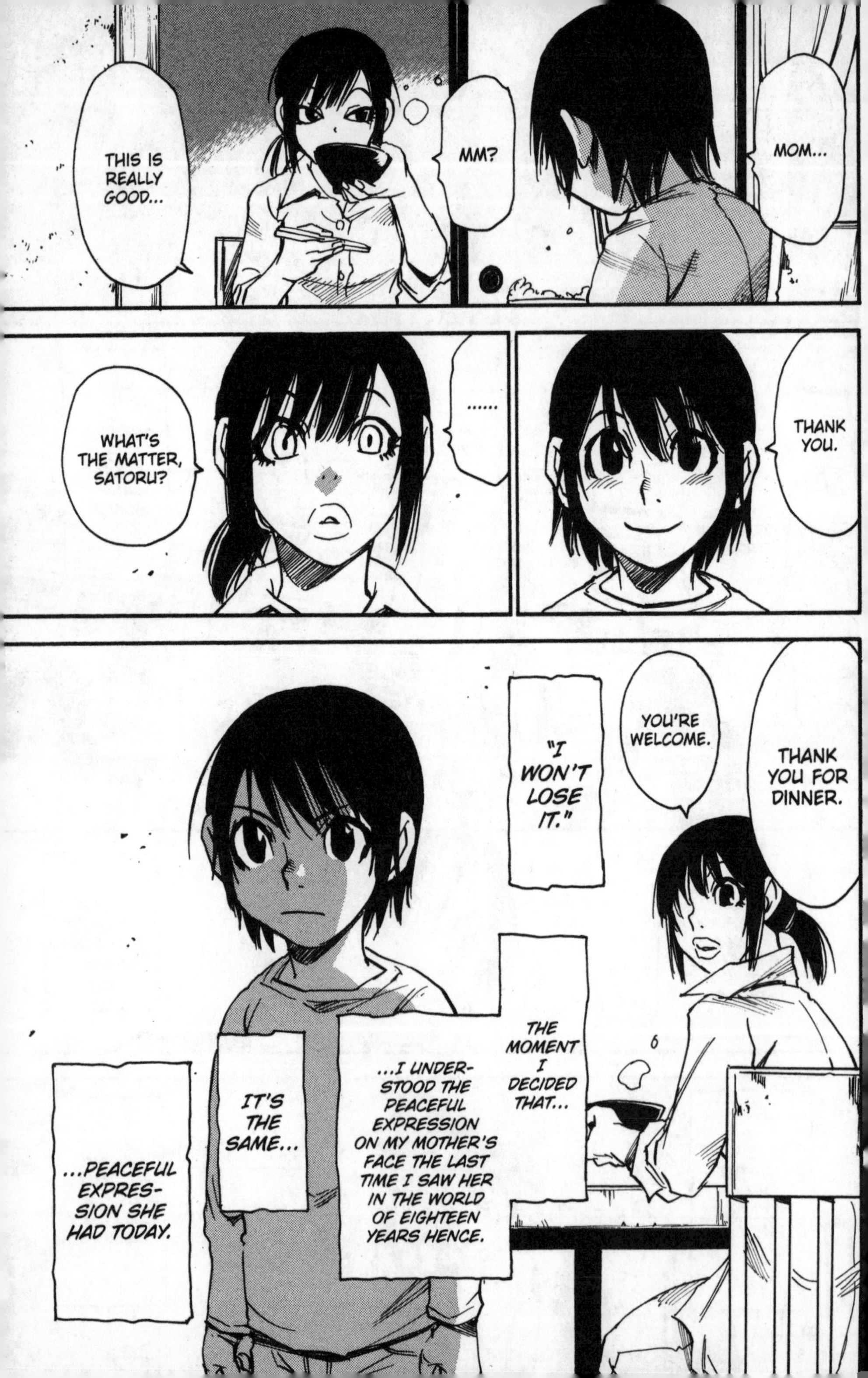
MOM...
MM?
THIS IS REALLY GOOD...
THANK YOU.
......
WHAT'S THE MATTER, SATORU?
THANK YOU FOR DINNER.
YOU'RE WELCOME.
"I WON'T LOSE IT."
THE MOMENT I DECIDED THAT...
...I UNDERSTOOD THE PEACEFUL EXPRESSION ON MY MOTHER'S FACE THE LAST TIME I SAW HER IN THE WORLD OF EIGHTEEN YEARS HENCE.
IT'S THE SAME...
...PEACEFUL EXPRESSION SHE HAD TODAY.

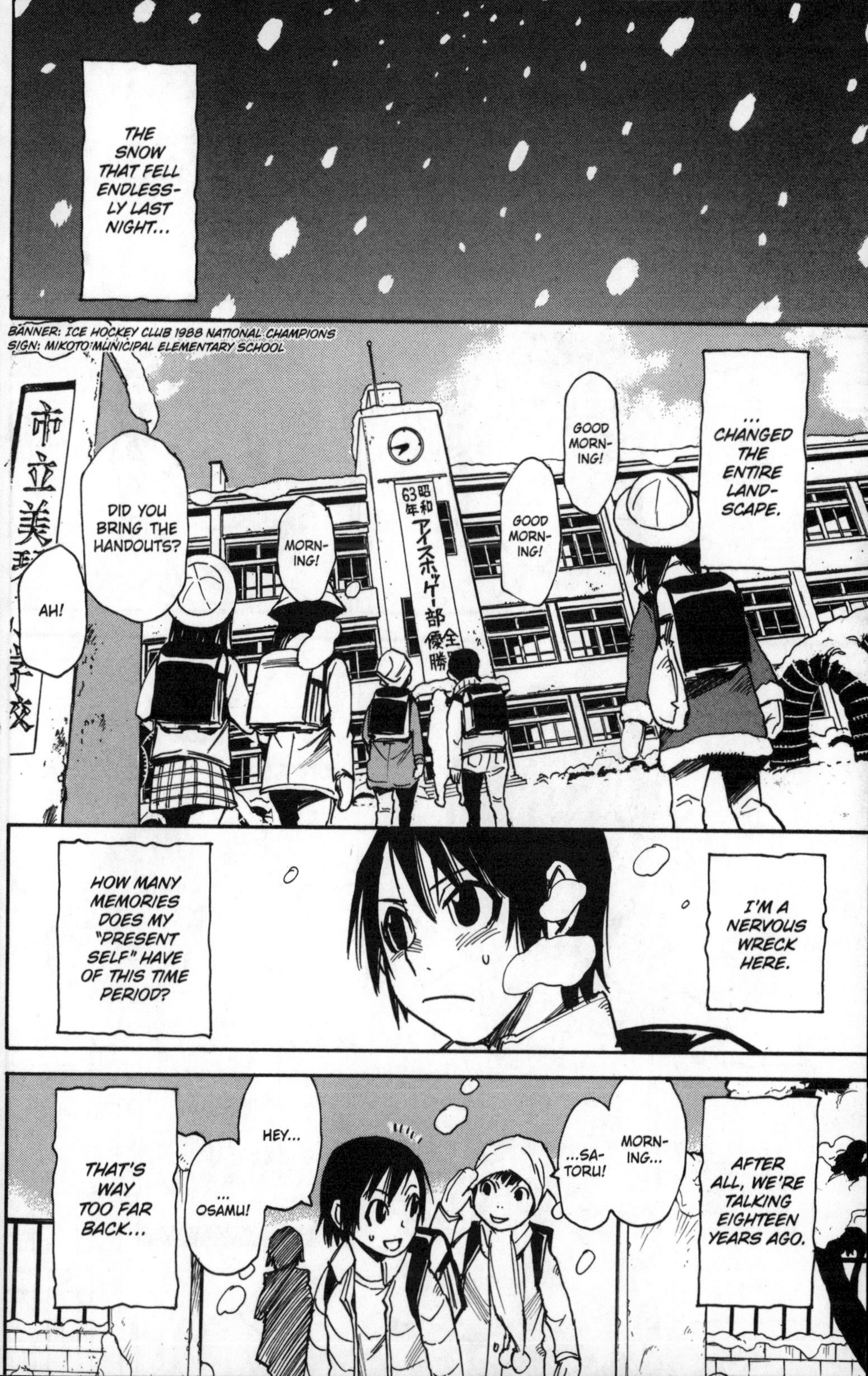
THE SNOW THAT FELL ENDLESSLY LAST NIGHT...
BANNER: ICE HOCKEY CLUB 1988 NATIONAL CHAMPIONS
SIGN: MIKOTO MUNICIPAL ELEMENTARY SCHOOL
...CHANGED THE ENTIRE LANDSCAPE.
GOOD MORNING!
GOOD MORNING!
MORNING!
DID YOU BRING THE HANDOUTS?
AH!
I'M A NERVOUS WRECK HERE.
HOW MANY MEMORIES DOES MY "PRESENT SELF" HAVE OF THIS TIME PERIOD?
AFTER ALL, WE'RE TALKING EIGHTEEN YEARS AGO.
MORNING...
...SATORU!
HEY...
...OSAMU!
THAT'S WAY TOO FAR BACK...

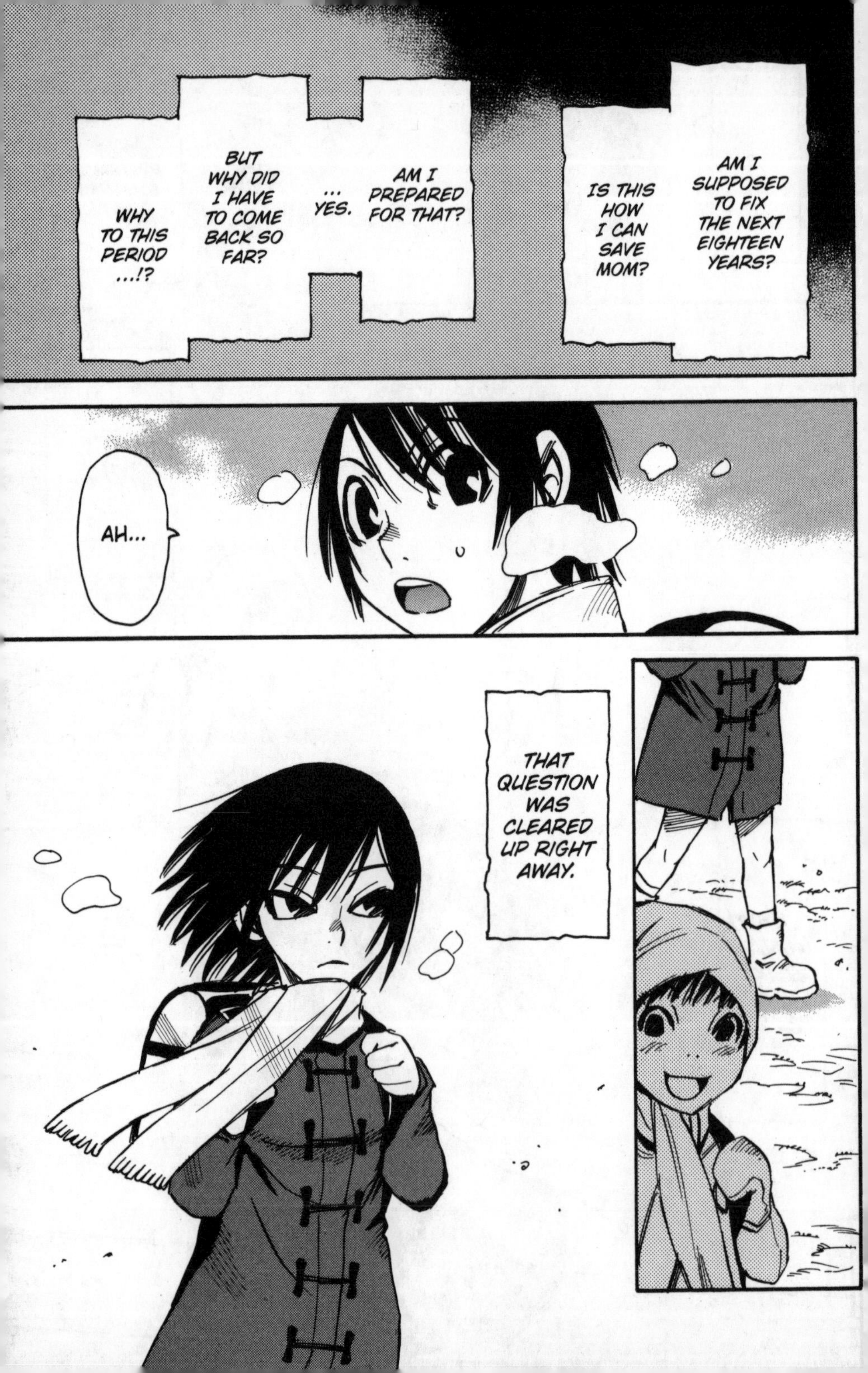
AM I SUPPOSED TO FIX THE NEXT EIGHTEEN YEARS?
IS THIS HOW I CAN SAVE MOM?
AM I PREPARED FOR THAT?
... YES.
BUT WHY DID I HAVE TO COME BACK SO FAR?
WHY TO THIS PERIOD ...!?
AH...
THAT QUESTION WAS CLEARED UP RIGHT AWAY.

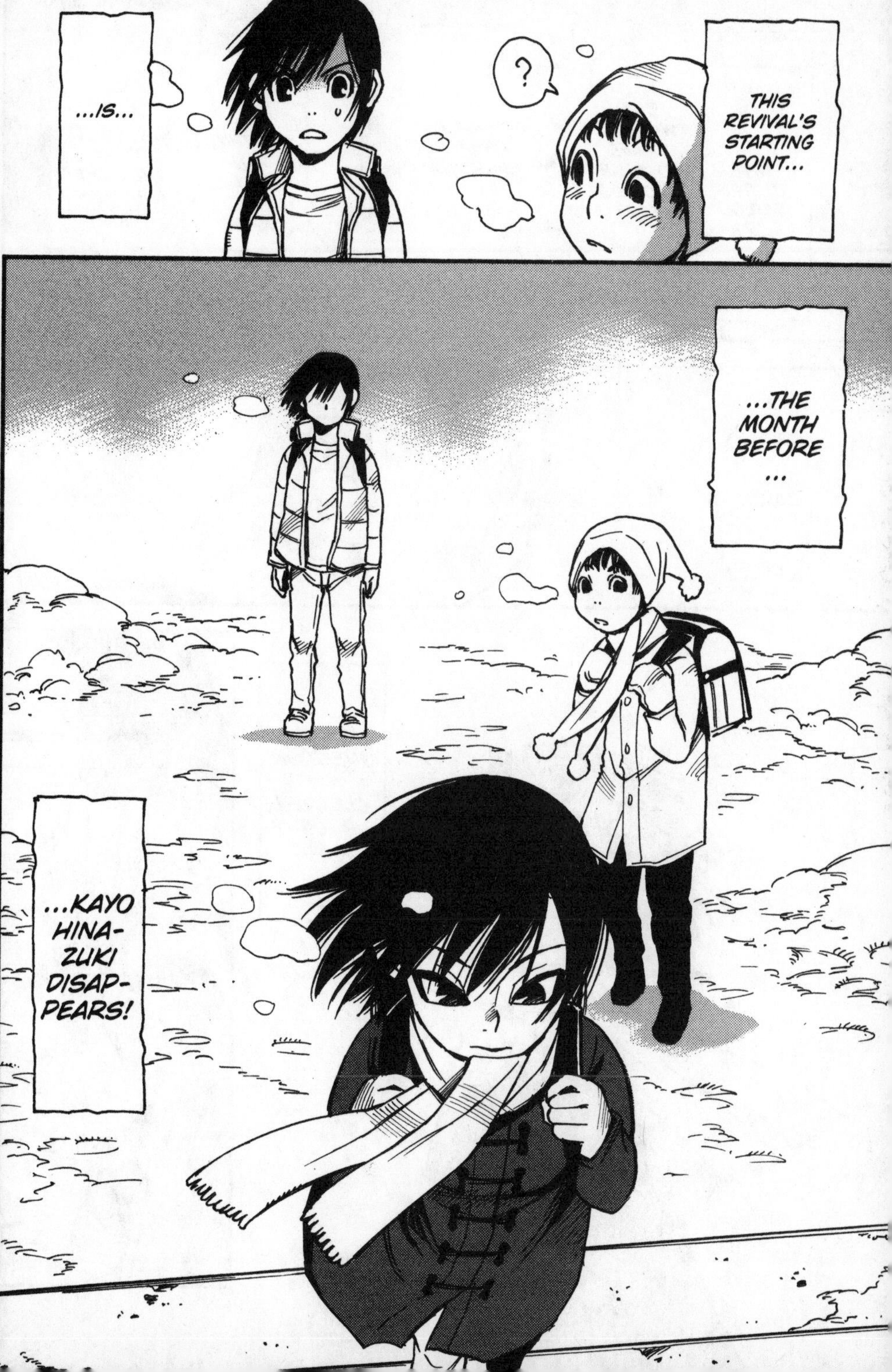
THIS REVIVAL'S STARTING POINT...
?
...IS...
...THE MONTH BEFORE ...
...KAYO HINA-ZUKI DISAP-PEARS!

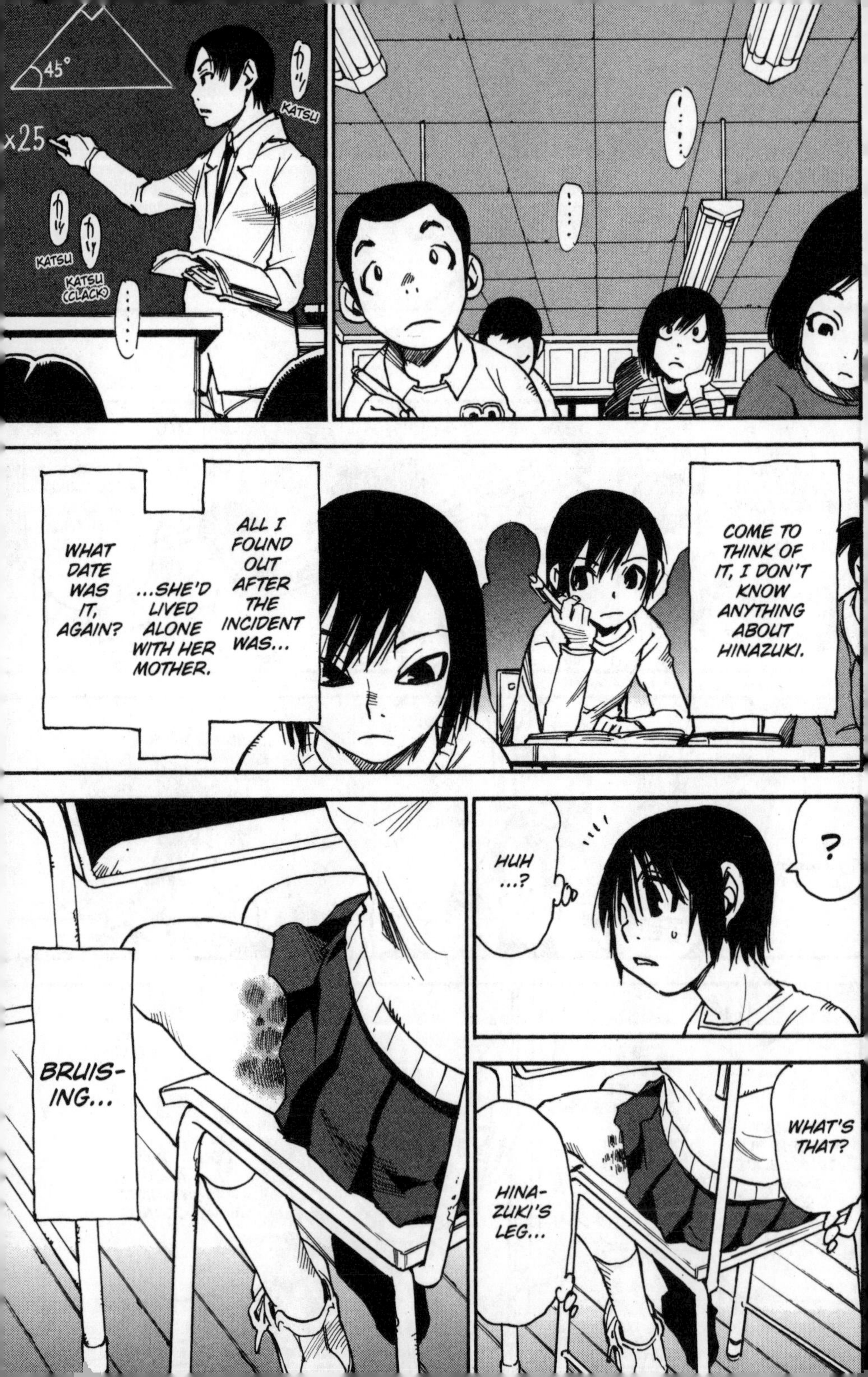
......
45°
x25
KATSU
KATSU
KATSU (CLACK)
......
COME TO THINK OF IT, I DON'T KNOW ANYTHING ABOUT HINAZUKI.
ALL I FOUND OUT AFTER THE INCIDENT WAS...
...SHE'D LIVED ALONE WITH HER MOTHER.
WHAT DATE WAS IT, AGAIN?
?
HUH ...?
WHAT'S THAT?
HINA-ZUKI'S LEG...
BRUIS-ING...

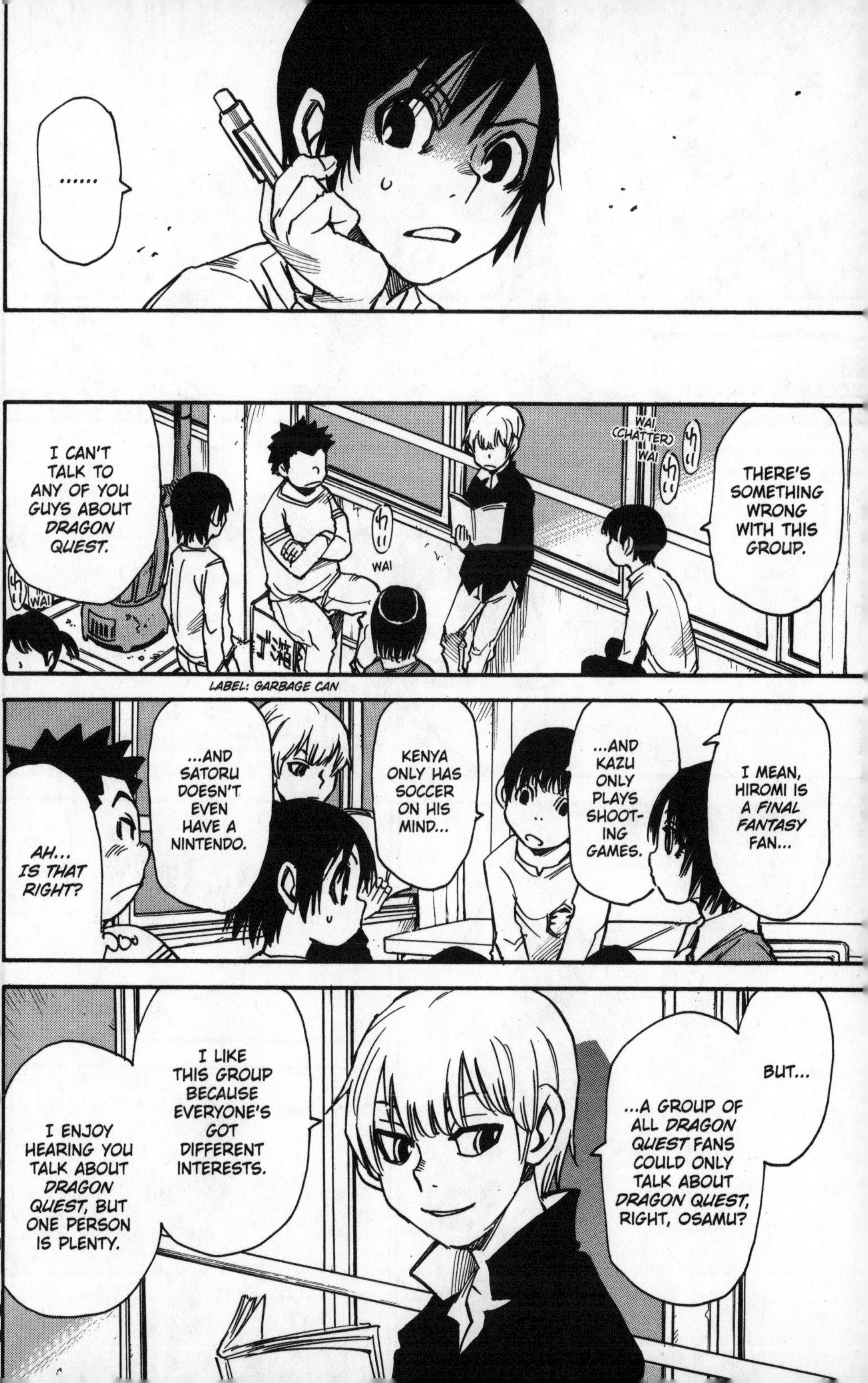
......
WAI (CHATTER) WAI
THERE'S SOMETHING WRONG WITH THIS GROUP.
WAI
I CAN'T TALK TO ANY OF YOU GUYS ABOUT *DRAGON QUEST*.
WAI
LABEL: GARBAGE CAN
I MEAN, HIROMI IS A *FINAL FANTASY* FAN...
...AND KAZU ONLY PLAYS SHOOTING GAMES.
KENYA ONLY HAS SOCCER ON HIS MIND...
...AND SATORU DOESN'T EVEN HAVE A NINTENDO.
AH... IS THAT RIGHT?
BUT...
...A GROUP OF ALL *DRAGON QUEST* FANS COULD ONLY TALK ABOUT *DRAGON QUEST*, RIGHT, OSAMU?
I LIKE THIS GROUP BECAUSE EVERYONE'S GOT DIFFERENT INTERESTS.
I ENJOY HEARING YOU TALK ABOUT *DRAGON QUEST*, BUT ONE PERSON IS PLENTY.

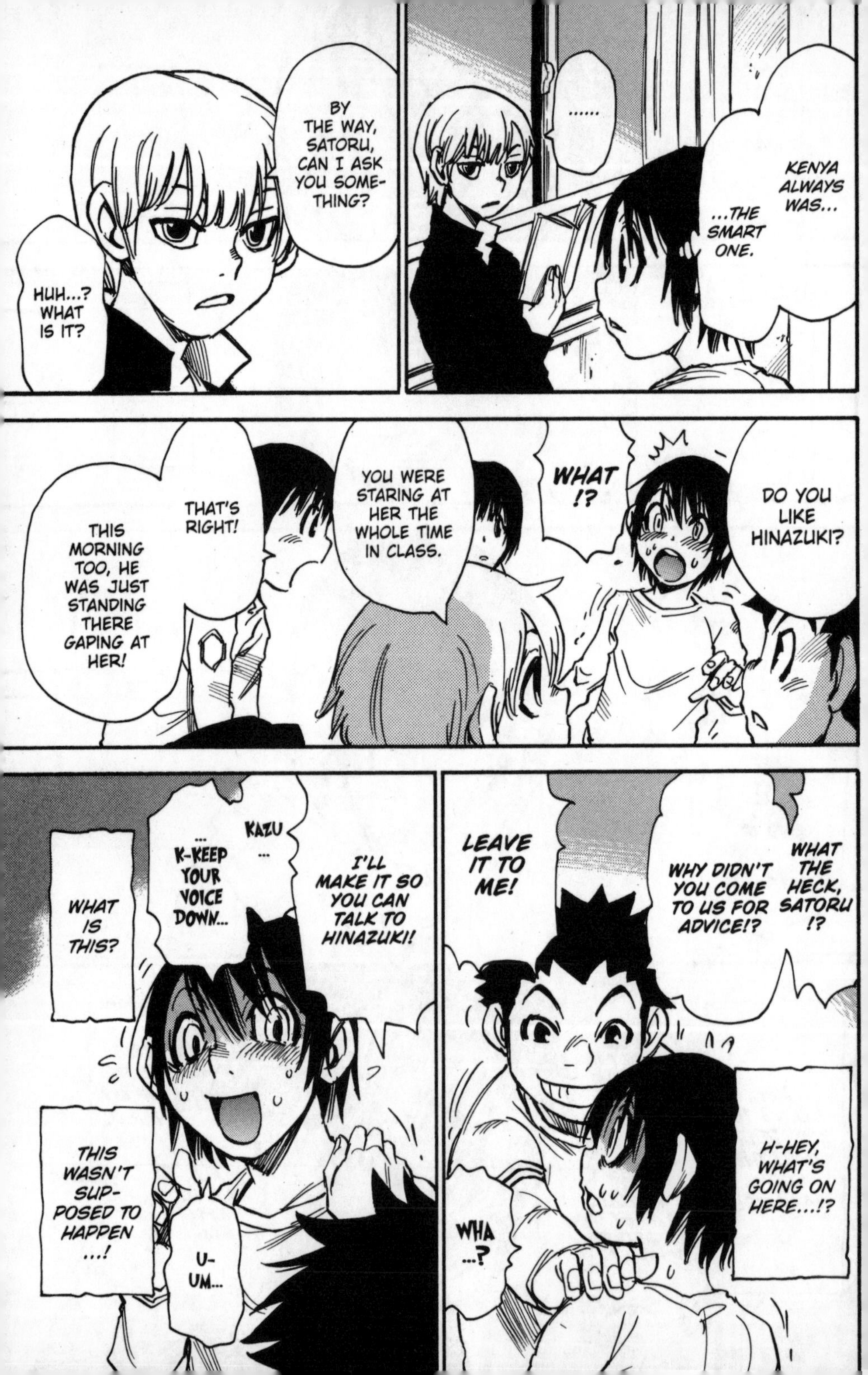
KENYA ALWAYS WAS...
...THE SMART ONE.
......
BY THE WAY, SATORU, CAN I ASK YOU SOMETHING?
HUH...? WHAT IS IT?
DO YOU LIKE HINAZUKI?
WHAT!?
YOU WERE STARING AT HER THE WHOLE TIME IN CLASS.
THAT'S RIGHT!
THIS MORNING TOO, HE WAS JUST STANDING THERE GAPING AT HER!
WHAT THE HECK, SATORU!?
WHY DIDN'T YOU COME TO US FOR ADVICE!?
LEAVE IT TO ME!
H-HEY, WHAT'S GOING ON HERE...!?
WHA...?
I'LL MAKE IT SO YOU CAN TALK TO HINAZUKI!
KAZU...
...K-KEEP YOUR VOICE DOWN...
WHAT IS THIS?
THIS WASN'T SUPPOSED TO HAPPEN...!
U-UM...

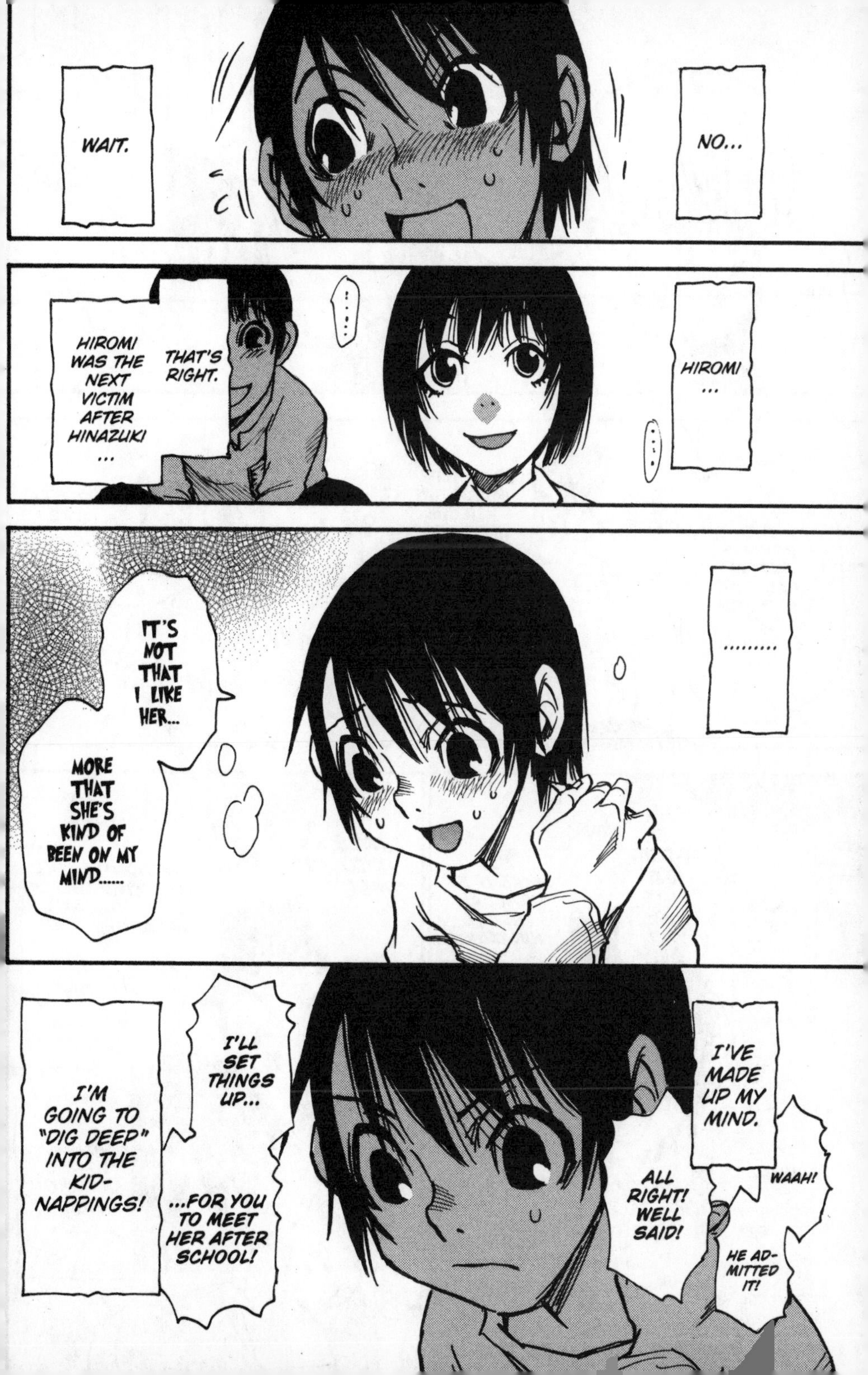
NO...
WAIT.
HIROMI ...
THAT'S RIGHT.
HIROMI WAS THE NEXT VICTIM AFTER HINAZUKI ...
....
IT'S NOT THAT I LIKE HER...
MORE THAT SHE'S KIND OF BEEN ON MY MIND......
I'VE MADE UP MY MIND.
WAAH!
ALL RIGHT! WELL SAID!
HE AD-MITTED IT!
I'LL SET THINGS UP...
...FOR YOU TO MEET HER AFTER SCHOOL!
I'M GOING TO "DIG DEEP" INTO THE KID-NAPPINGS!

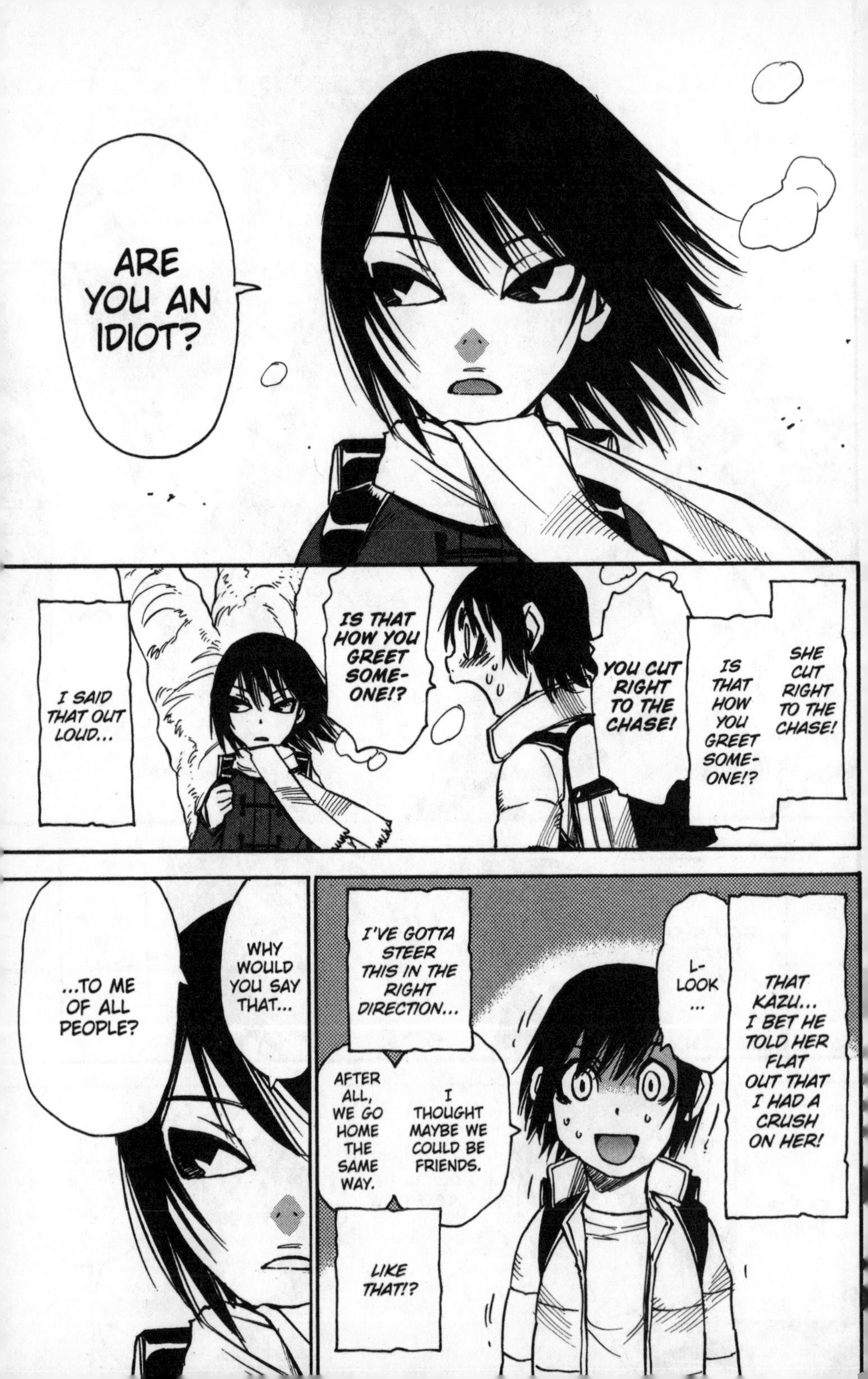
ARE YOU AN IDIOT?
SHE CUT RIGHT TO THE CHASE!
IS THAT HOW YOU GREET SOMEONE!?
YOU CUT RIGHT TO THE CHASE!
IS THAT HOW YOU GREET SOMEONE!?
I SAID THAT OUT LOUD...
THAT KAZU... I BET HE TOLD HER FLAT OUT THAT I HAD A CRUSH ON HER!
L-LOOK...
I'VE GOTTA STEER THIS IN THE RIGHT DIRECTION...
I THOUGHT MAYBE WE COULD BE FRIENDS.
AFTER ALL, WE GO HOME THE SAME WAY.
LIKE THAT!?
WHY WOULD YOU SAY THAT...
...TO ME OF ALL PEOPLE?

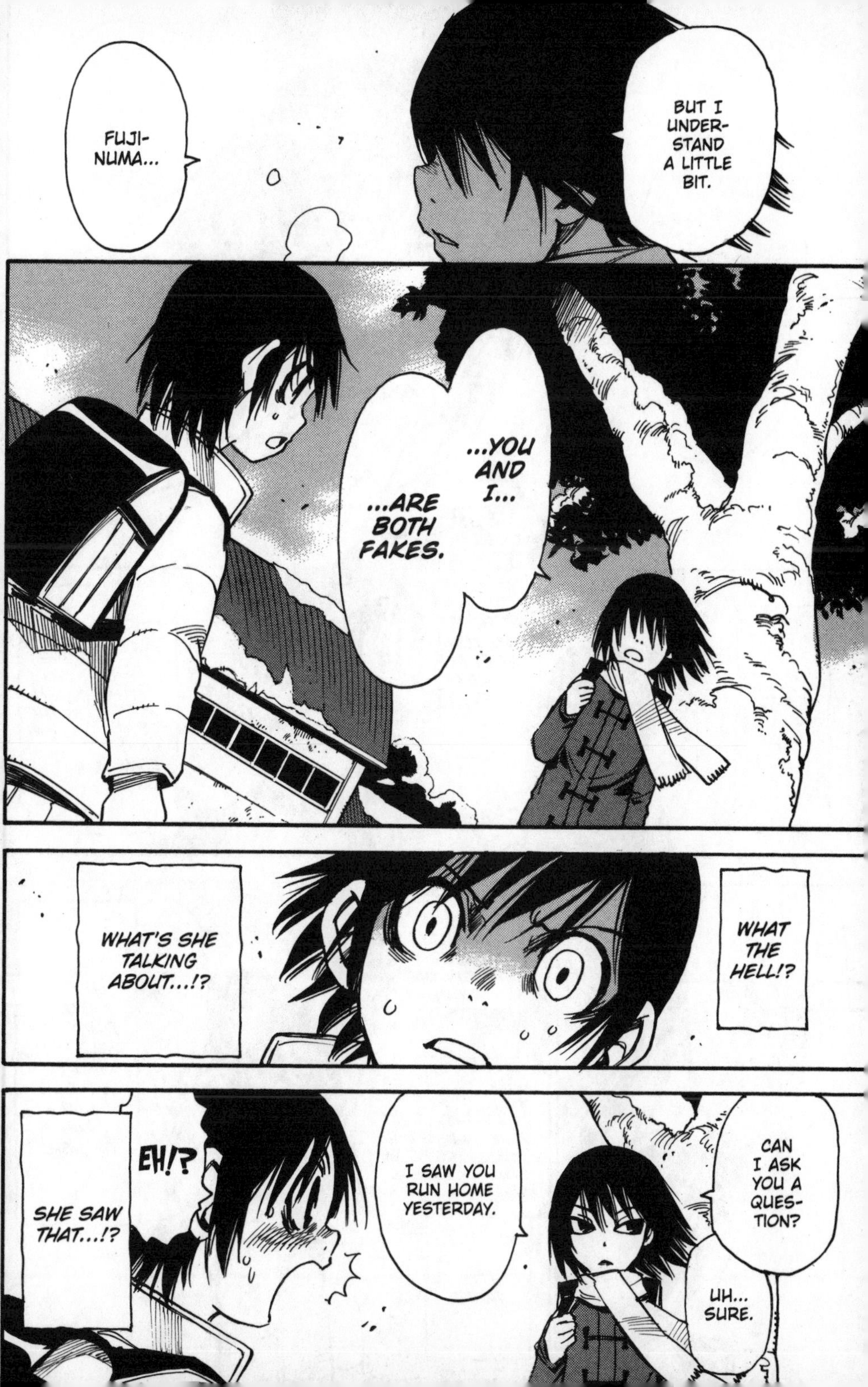
BUT I UNDER-STAND A LITTLE BIT.
FUJI-NUMA...
...YOU AND I...
...ARE BOTH FAKES.
WHAT THE HELL!?
WHAT'S SHE TALKING ABOUT...!?
CAN I ASK YOU A QUES-TION?
UH... SURE.
I SAW YOU RUN HOME YESTERDAY.
EH!?
SHE SAW THAT...!?

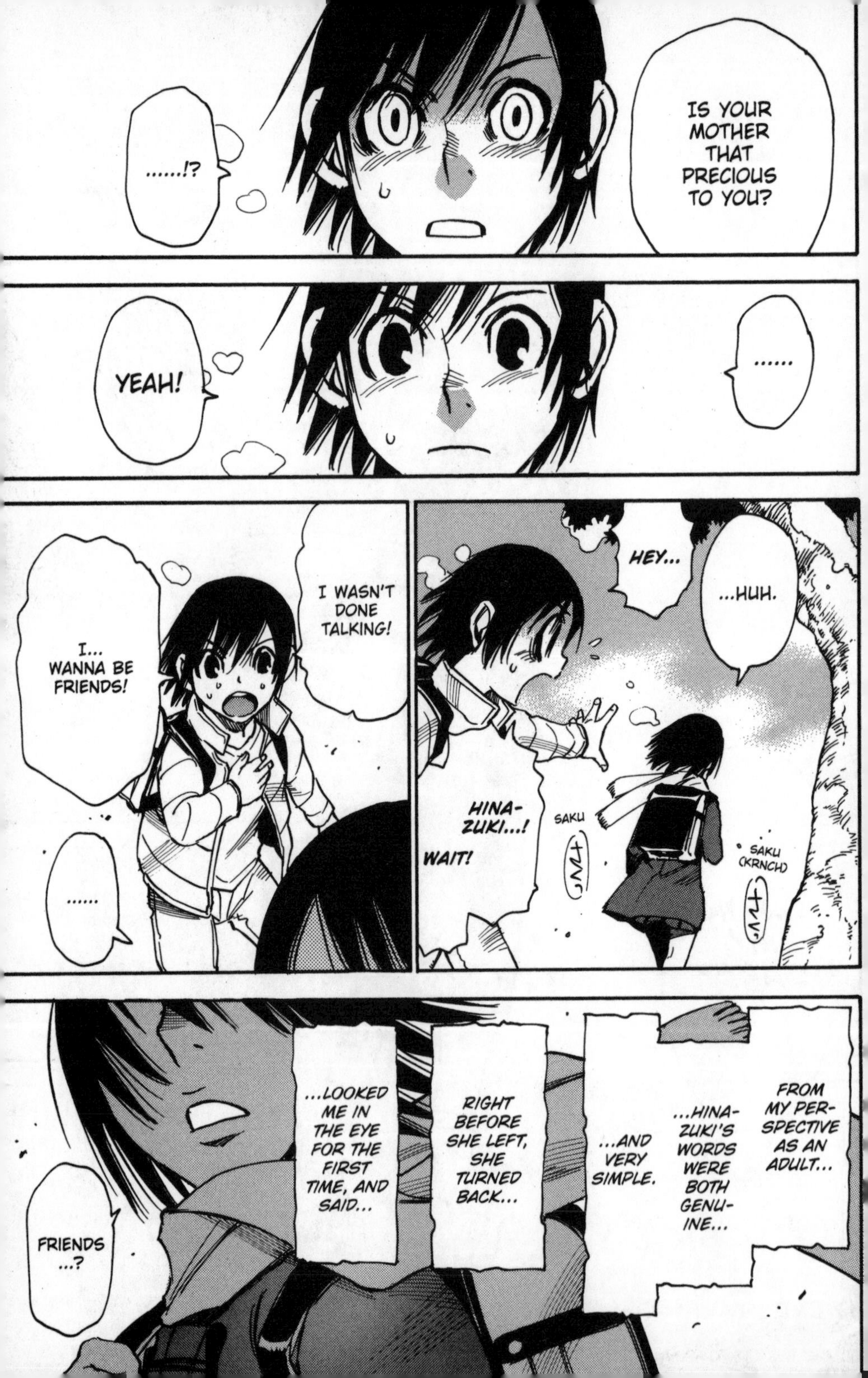

IS YOUR MOTHER THAT PRECIOUS TO YOU?
......!?
......
YEAH!
...HUH.
HEY...
HINA-ZUKI...!
WAIT!
SAKU
SAKU (KRNCH)
I WASN'T DONE TALKING!
I... WANNA BE FRIENDS!
......
FROM MY PER-SPECTIVE AS AN ADULT...
...HINA-ZUKI'S WORDS WERE BOTH GENU-INE...
...AND VERY SIMPLE.
RIGHT BEFORE SHE LEFT, SHE TURNED BACK...
...LOOKED ME IN THE EYE FOR THE FIRST TIME, AND SAID...
FRIENDS...?

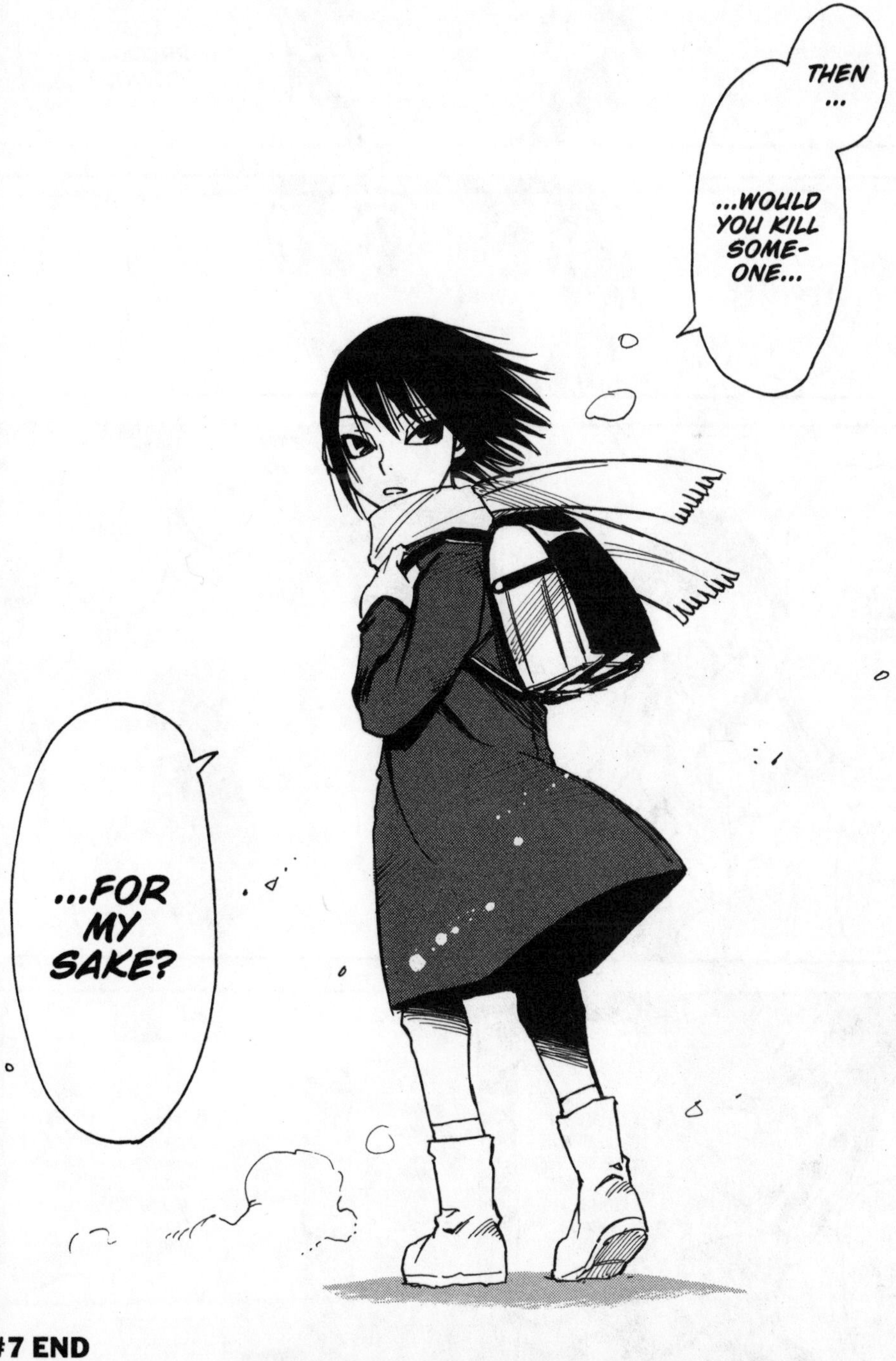
THEN ...
...WOULD YOU KILL SOME-ONE...
...FOR MY SAKE?

#7 END

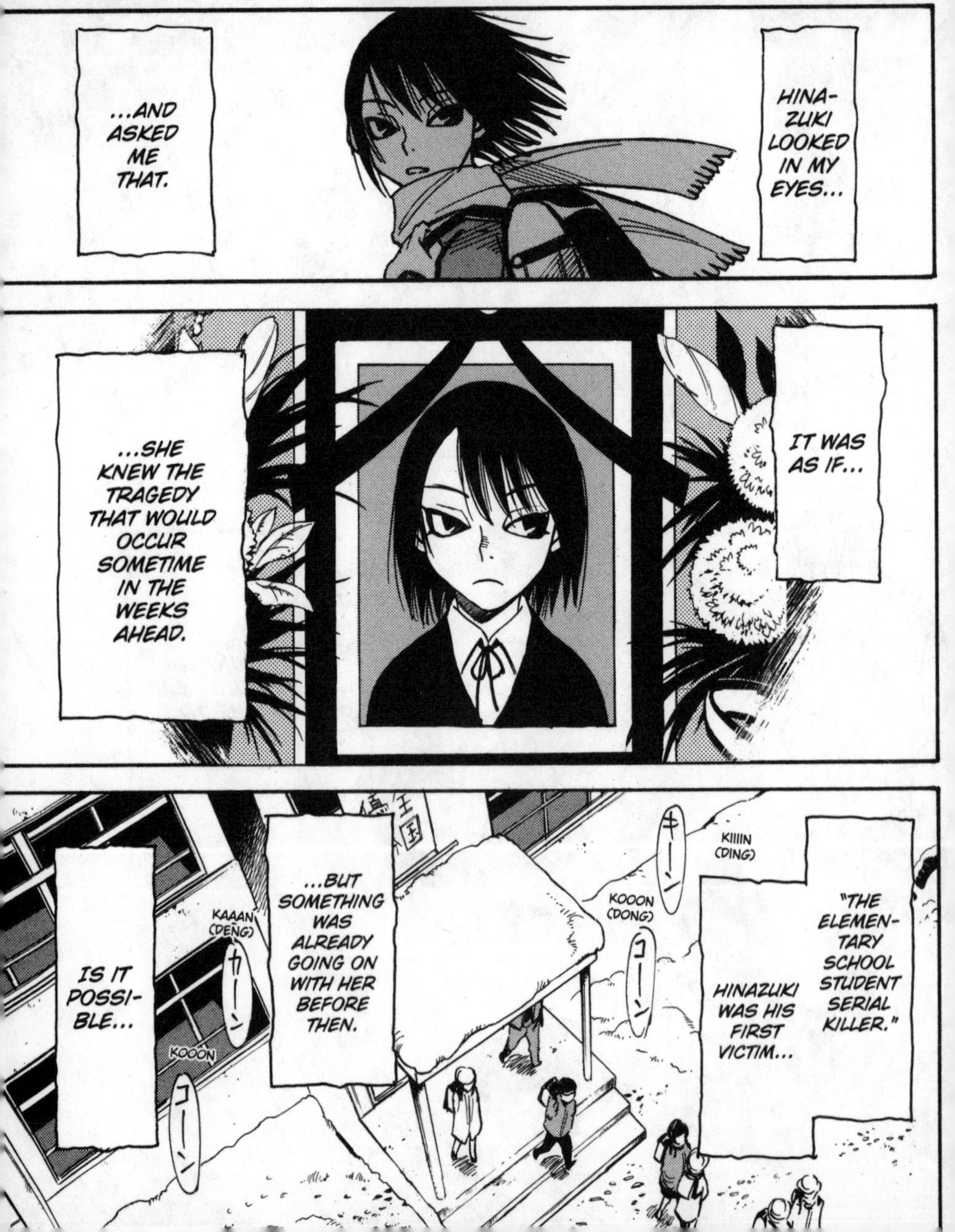
HINA-ZUKI LOOKED IN MY EYES...
...AND ASKED ME THAT.
IT WAS AS IF...
...SHE KNEW THE TRAGEDY THAT WOULD OCCUR SOMETIME IN THE WEEKS AHEAD.
"THE ELEMENTARY SCHOOL STUDENT SERIAL KILLER."
HINAZUKI WAS HIS FIRST VICTIM...
KIIIN (DING)
KOOON (DONG)
...BUT SOMETHING WAS ALREADY GOING ON WITH HER BEFORE THEN.
KAAAN (DENG)
IS IT POSSI-BLE...
KOOON

#8: The Town Without Me, February 1988

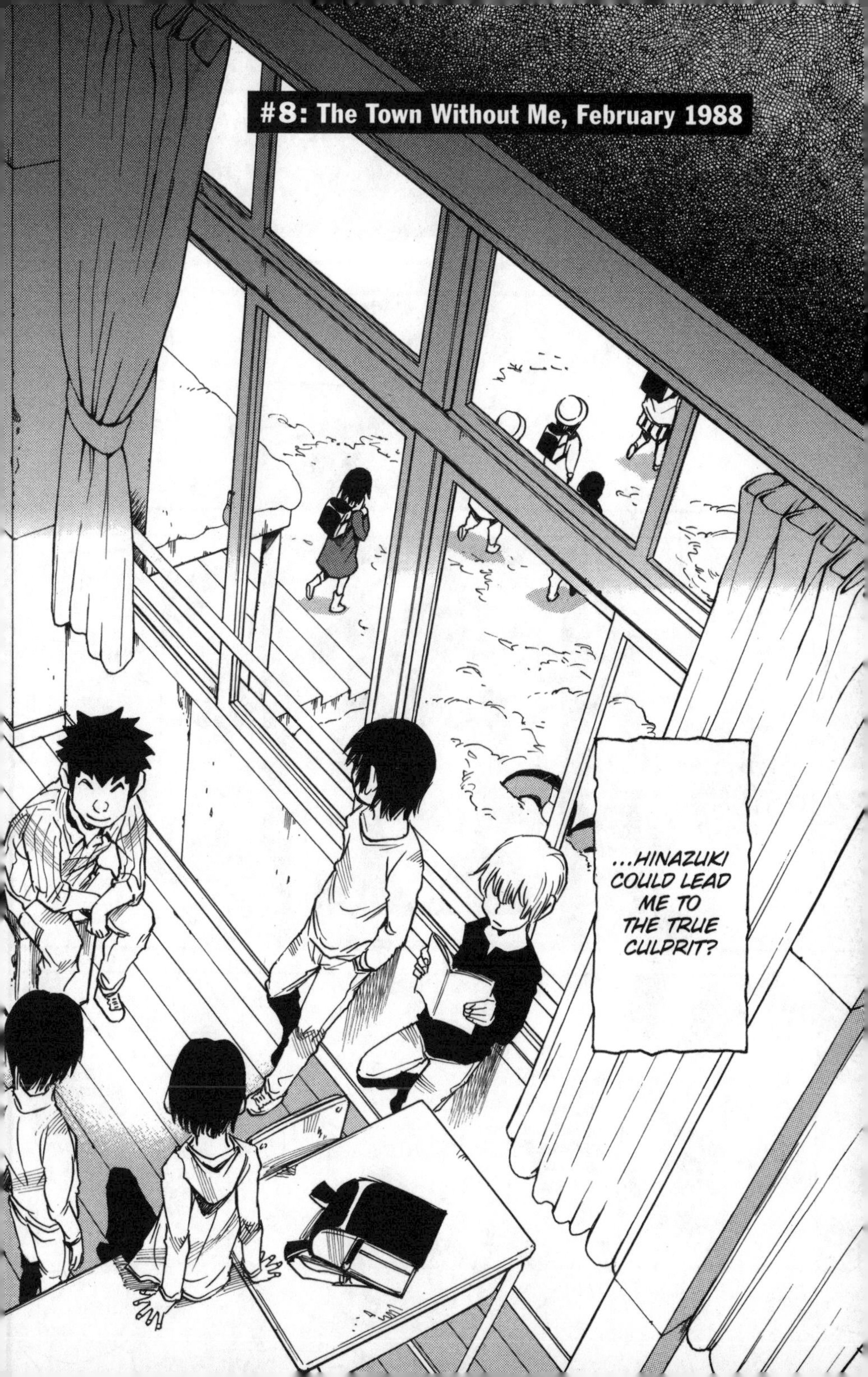
...HINAZUKI COULD LEAD ME TO THE TRUE CULPRIT?

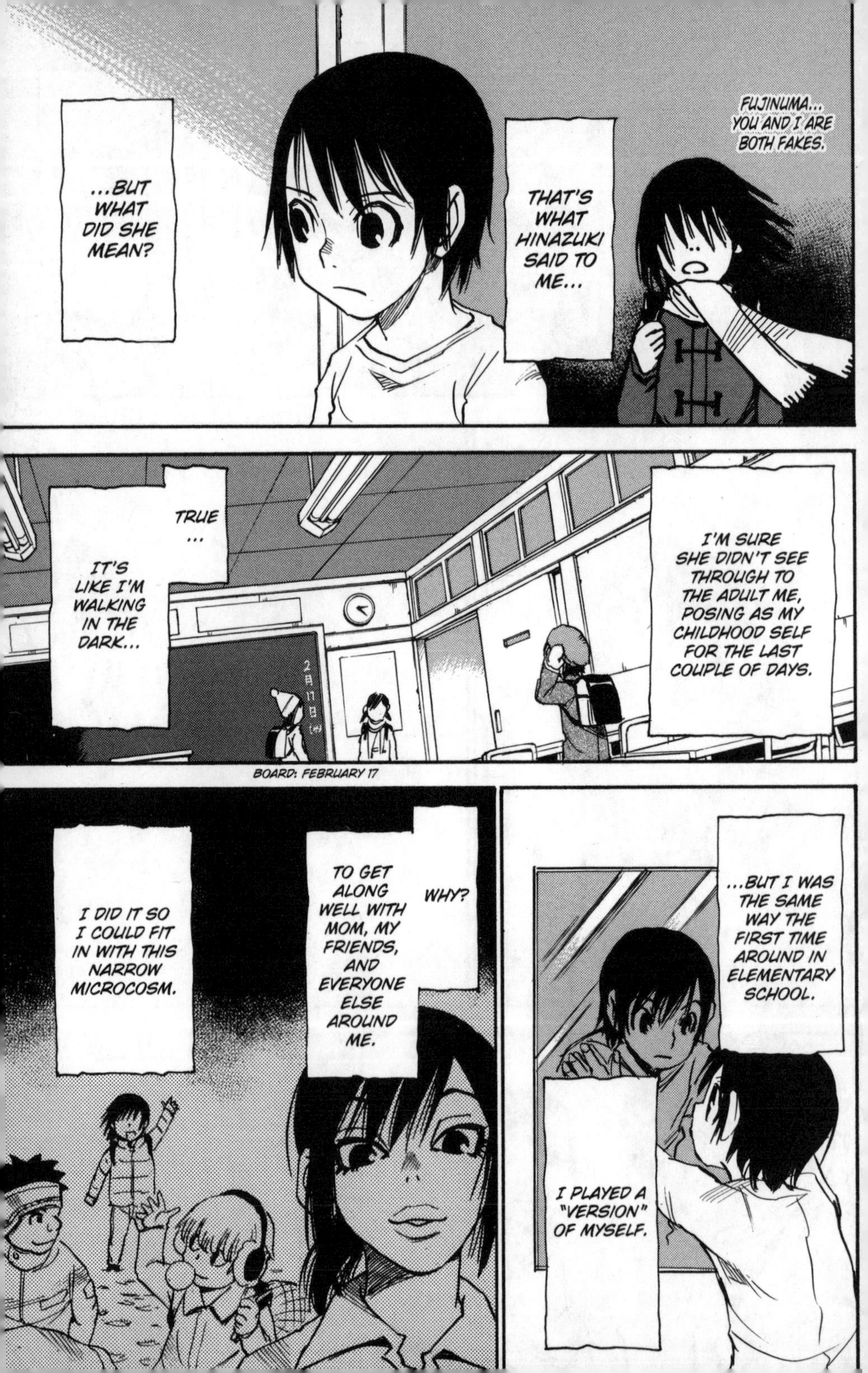
FUJINUMA... YOU AND I ARE BOTH FAKES.
THAT'S WHAT HINAZUKI SAID TO ME...
...BUT WHAT DID SHE MEAN?
I'M SURE SHE DIDN'T SEE THROUGH TO THE ADULT ME, POSING AS MY CHILDHOOD SELF FOR THE LAST COUPLE OF DAYS.
TRUE ...
IT'S LIKE I'M WALKING IN THE DARK...
BOARD: FEBRUARY 17
...BUT I WAS THE SAME WAY THE FIRST TIME AROUND IN ELEMENTARY SCHOOL.
I PLAYED A "VERSION" OF MYSELF.
WHY?
TO GET ALONG WELL WITH MOM, MY FRIENDS, AND EVERYONE ELSE AROUND ME.
I DID IT SO I COULD FIT IN WITH THIS NARROW MICROCOSM.

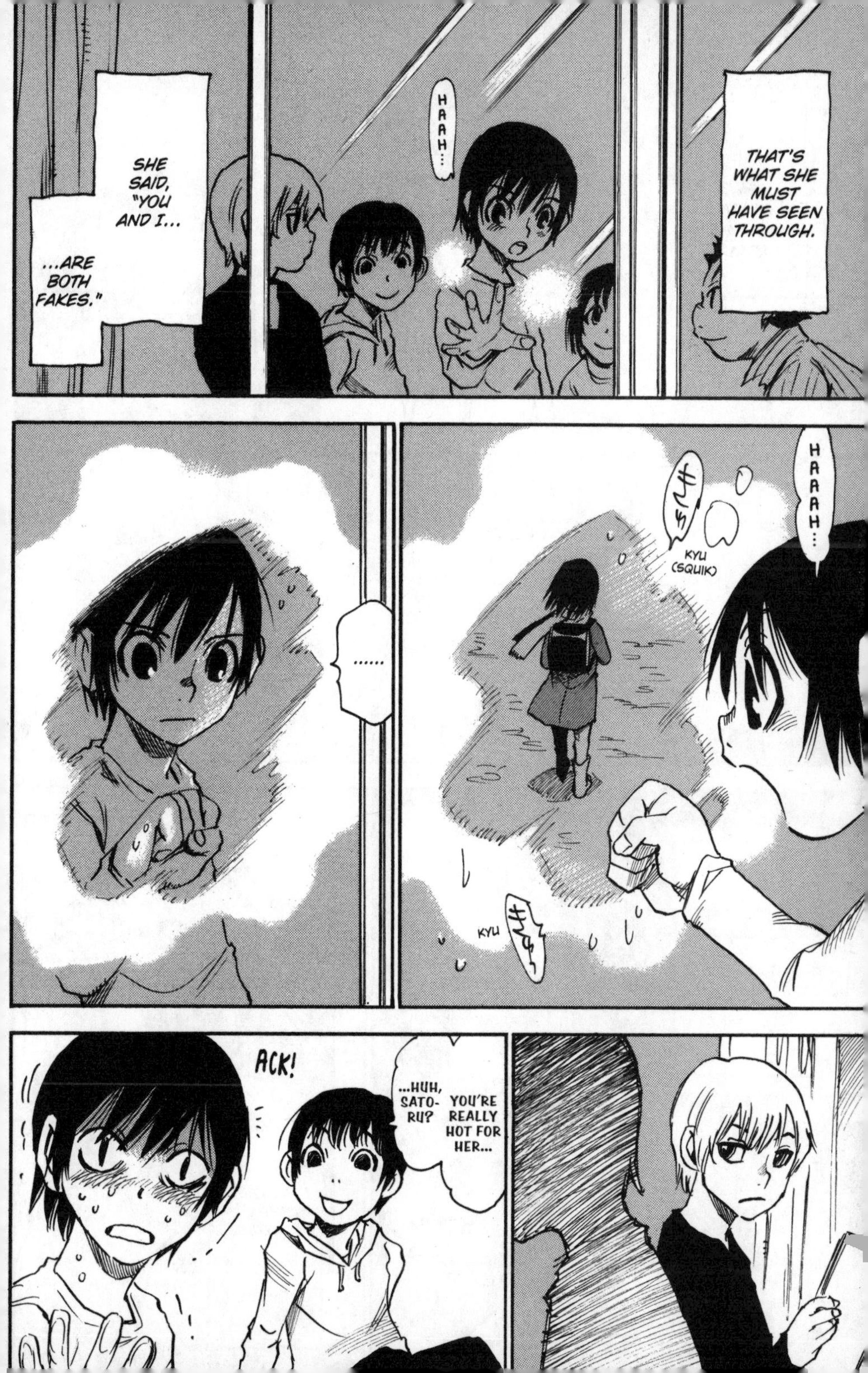
THAT'S WHAT SHE MUST HAVE SEEN THROUGH.
H A A H...
SHE SAID, "YOU AND I...
...ARE BOTH FAKES."
H A A A A H...
KYU (SQUIK)
KYU
......
...HUH, SATO-RU?
YOU'RE REALLY HOT FOR HER...
ACK!

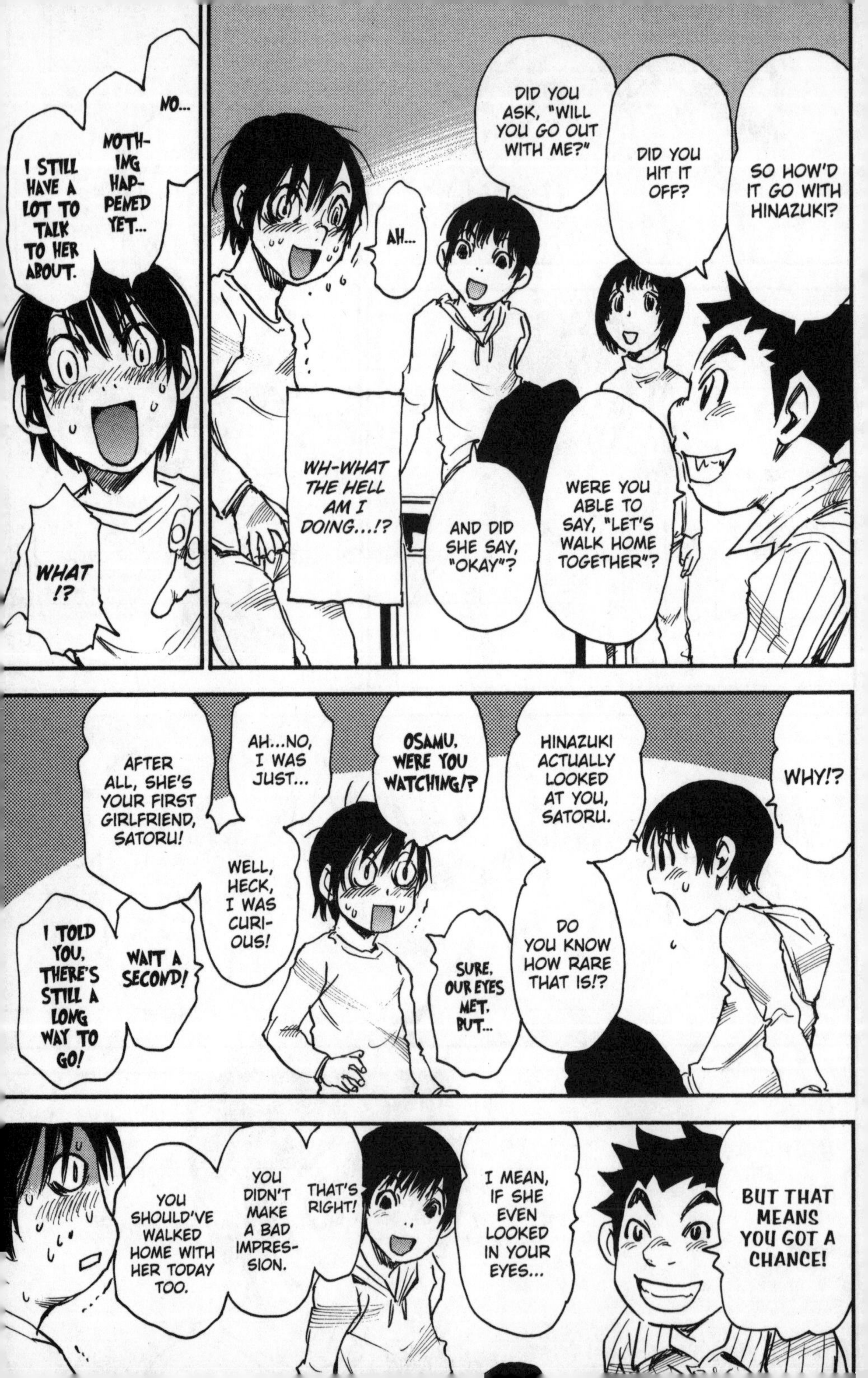
SO HOW'D IT GO WITH HINAZUKI?
DID YOU HIT IT OFF?
DID YOU ASK, "WILL YOU GO OUT WITH ME?"
AH...
WERE YOU ABLE TO SAY, "LET'S WALK HOME TOGETHER"?
AND DID SHE SAY, "OKAY"?
WH-WHAT THE HELL AM I DOING...!?
NO...
NOTHING HAPPENED YET...
I STILL HAVE A LOT TO TALK TO HER ABOUT.
WHAT!?
WHY!?
HINAZUKI ACTUALLY LOOKED AT YOU, SATORU.
DO YOU KNOW HOW RARE THAT IS!?
OSAMU, WERE YOU WATCHING!?
SURE, OUR EYES MET. BUT...
AH...NO, I WAS JUST...
WELL, HECK, I WAS CURIOUS!
AFTER ALL, SHE'S YOUR FIRST GIRLFRIEND, SATORU!
WAIT A SECOND!
I TOLD YOU, THERE'S STILL A LONG WAY TO GO!
BUT THAT MEANS YOU GOT A CHANCE!
I MEAN, IF SHE EVEN LOOKED IN YOUR EYES...
THAT'S RIGHT!
YOU DIDN'T MAKE A BAD IMPRESSION.
YOU SHOULD'VE WALKED HOME WITH HER TODAY TOO.

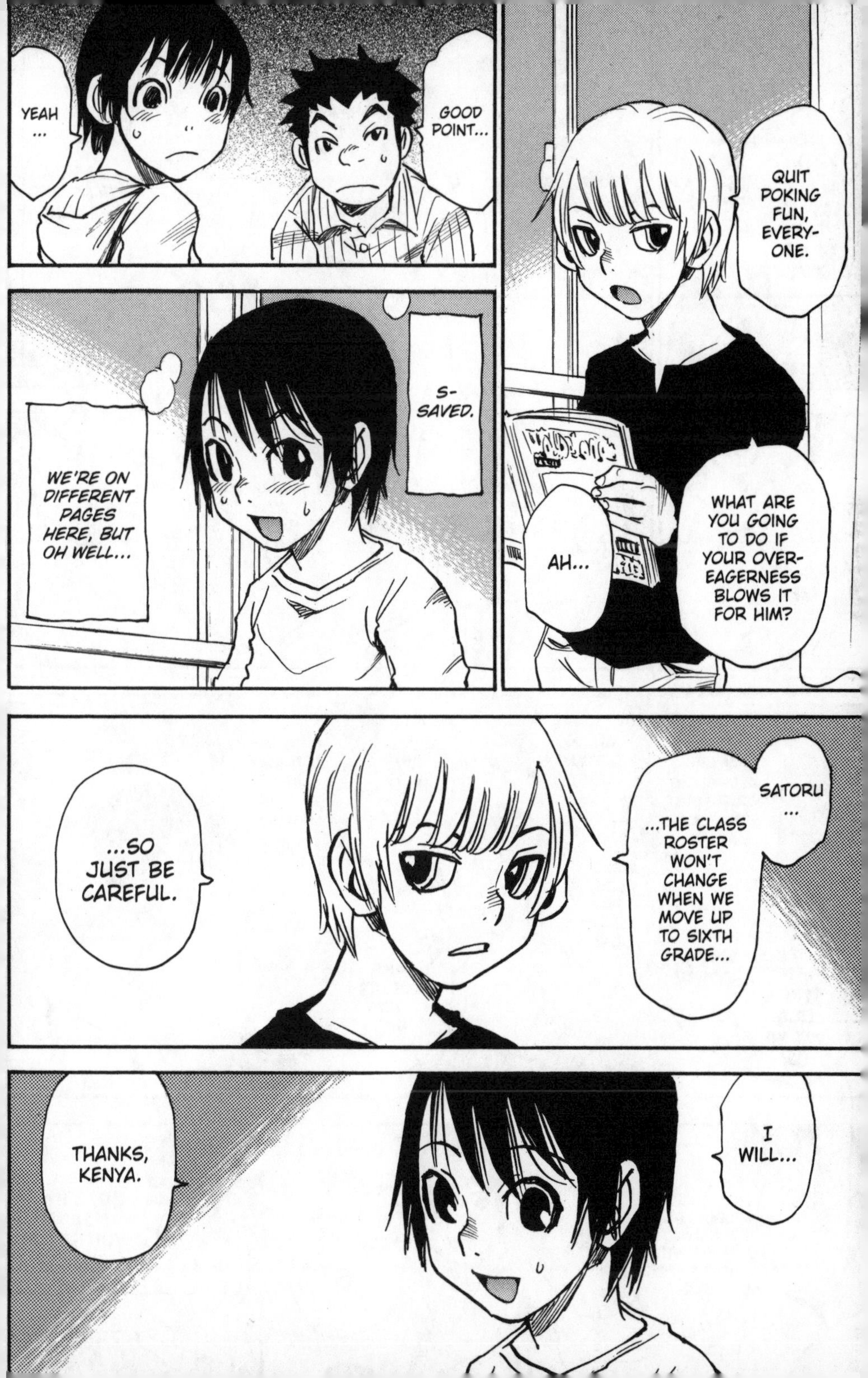
QUIT POKING FUN, EVERY-ONE.
WHAT ARE YOU GOING TO DO IF YOUR OVER-EAGERNESS BLOWS IT FOR HIM?
AH...
GOOD POINT...
YEAH ...
S-SAVED.
WE'RE ON DIFFERENT PAGES HERE, BUT OH WELL...
SATORU ...
...THE CLASS ROSTER WON'T CHANGE WHEN WE MOVE UP TO SIXTH GRADE...
...SO JUST BE CAREFUL.
I WILL...
THANKS, KENYA.

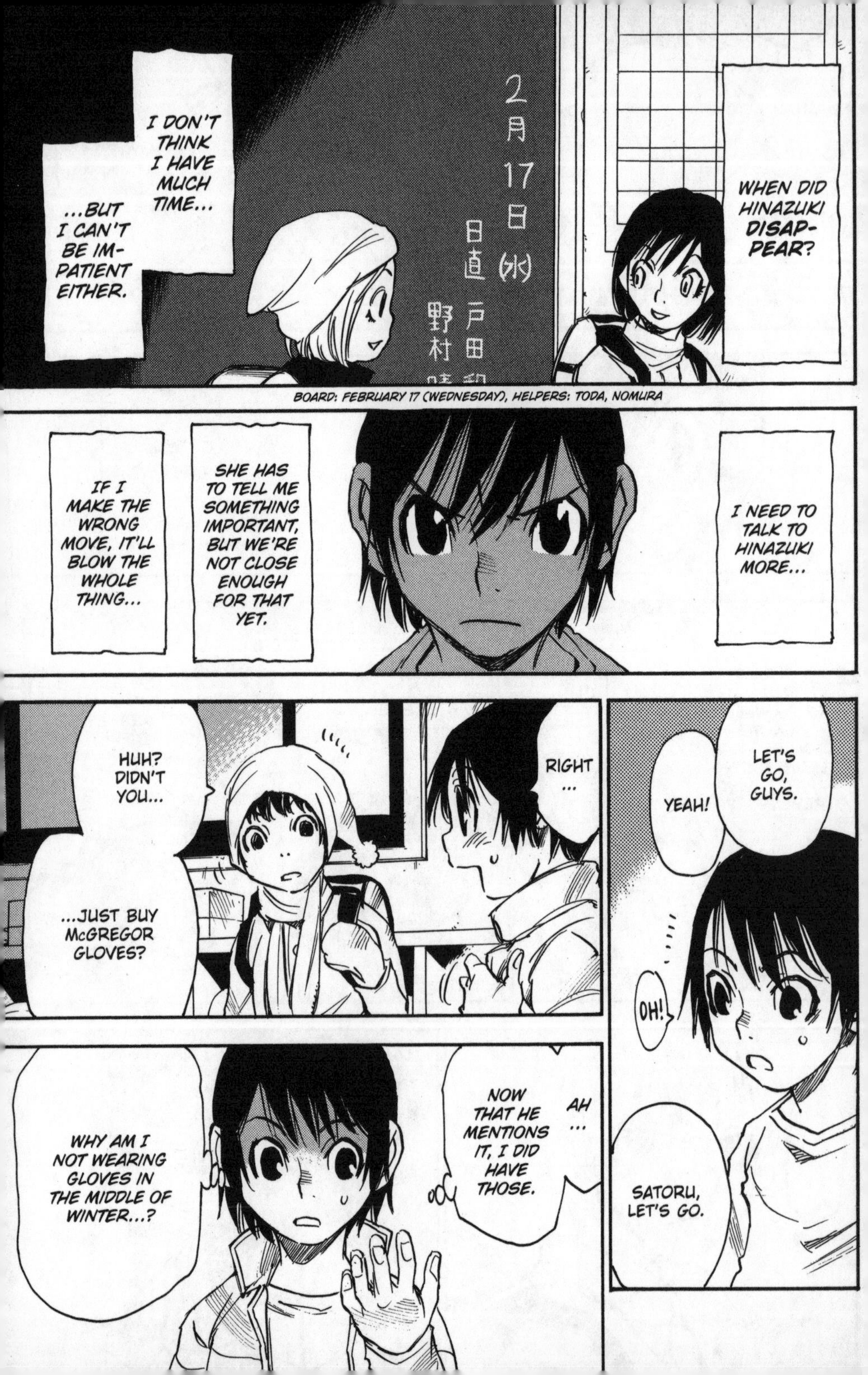
WHEN DID HINAZUKI DISAPPEAR?
I DON'T THINK I HAVE MUCH TIME...
...BUT I CAN'T BE IMPATIENT EITHER.
2月17日(水)
日直 戸田
野村
BOARD: FEBRUARY 17 (WEDNESDAY), HELPERS: TODA, NOMURA
I NEED TO TALK TO HINAZUKI MORE...
SHE HAS TO TELL ME SOMETHING IMPORTANT, BUT WE'RE NOT CLOSE ENOUGH FOR THAT YET.
IF I MAKE THE WRONG MOVE, IT'LL BLOW THE WHOLE THING...
LET'S GO, GUYS.
YEAH!
OH!
SATORU, LET'S GO.
HUH? DIDN'T YOU... ...JUST BUY McGREGOR GLOVES?
RIGHT...
AH...
NOW THAT HE MENTIONS IT, I DID HAVE THOSE.
WHY AM I NOT WEARING GLOVES IN THE MIDDLE OF WINTER...?

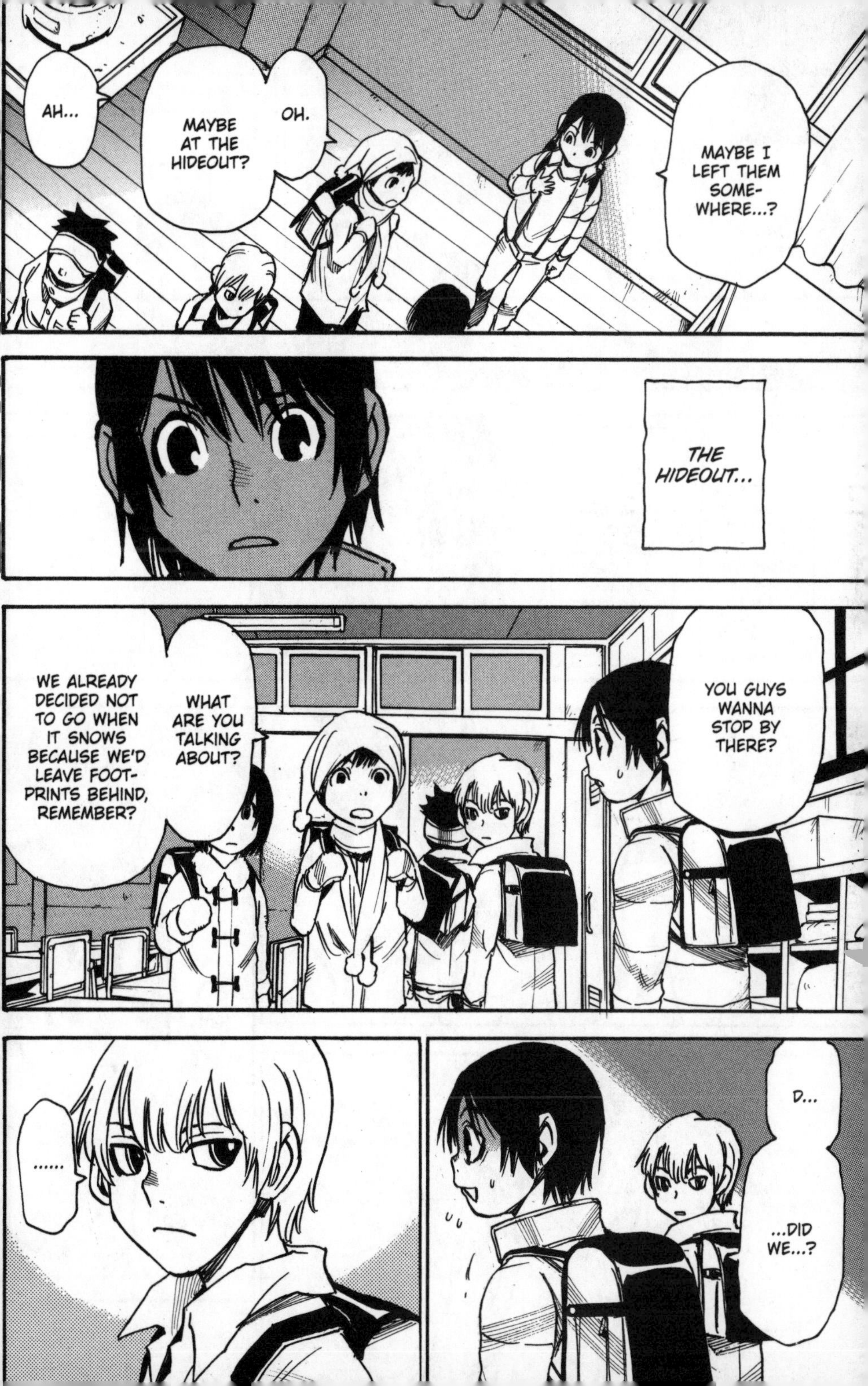
MAYBE I LEFT THEM SOME-WHERE...?
OH.
MAYBE AT THE HIDEOUT?
AH...
THE HIDEOUT...
YOU GUYS WANNA STOP BY THERE?
WHAT ARE YOU TALKING ABOUT?
WE ALREADY DECIDED NOT TO GO WHEN IT SNOWS BECAUSE WE'D LEAVE FOOT-PRINTS BEHIND, REMEMBER?
D...
...DID WE...?
......

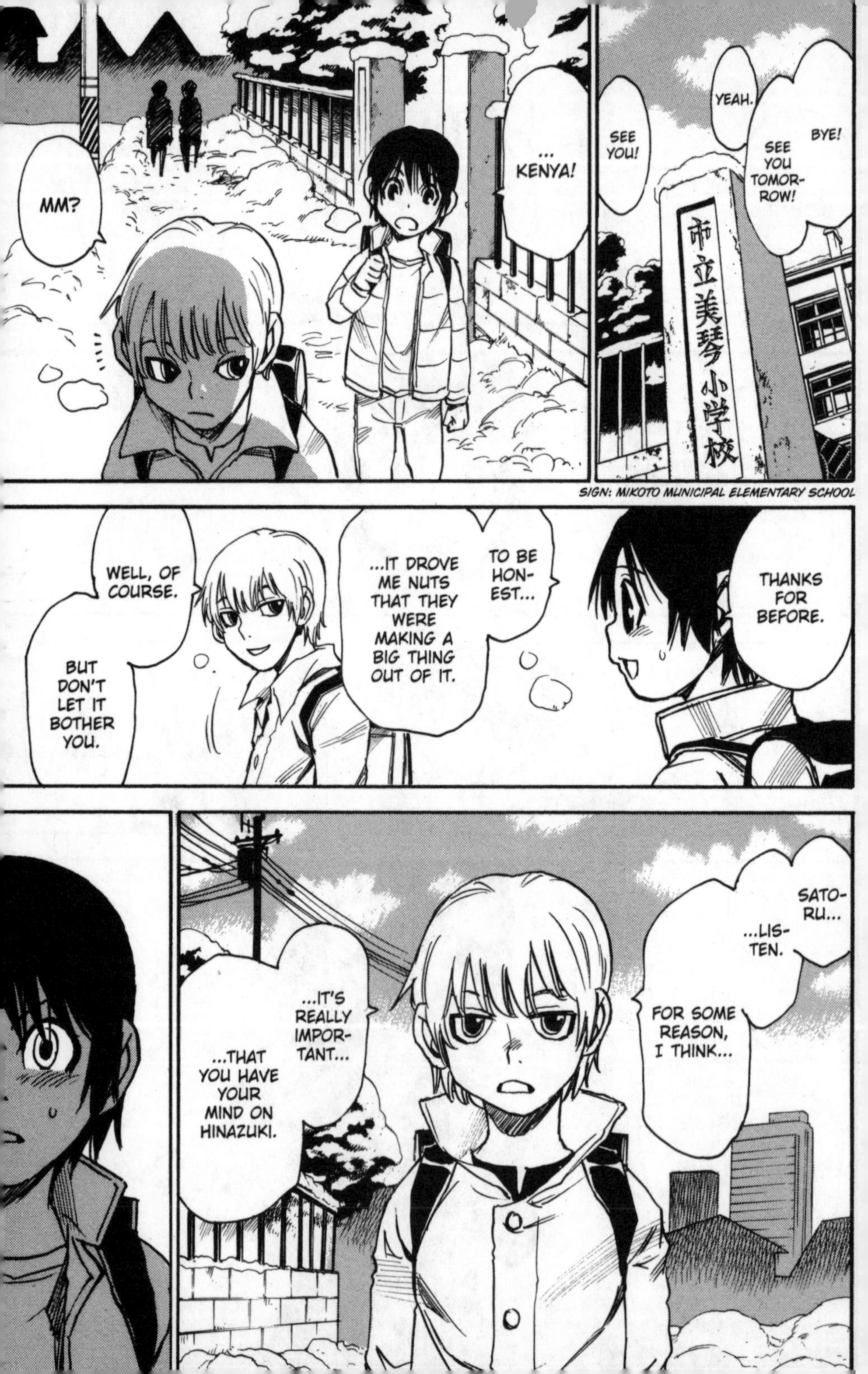
BYE! SEE YOU TOMORROW!
YEAH.
SEE YOU!
市立美琴小学校
...KENYA!
MM?
SIGN: MIKOTO MUNICIPAL ELEMENTARY SCHOOL
THANKS FOR BEFORE.
TO BE HONEST...
...IT DROVE ME NUTS THAT THEY WERE MAKING A BIG THING OUT OF IT.
WELL, OF COURSE.
BUT DON'T LET IT BOTHER YOU.
SATORU...
...LISTEN.
FOR SOME REASON, I THINK...
...IT'S REALLY IMPORTANT...
...THAT YOU HAVE YOUR MIND ON HINAZUKI.

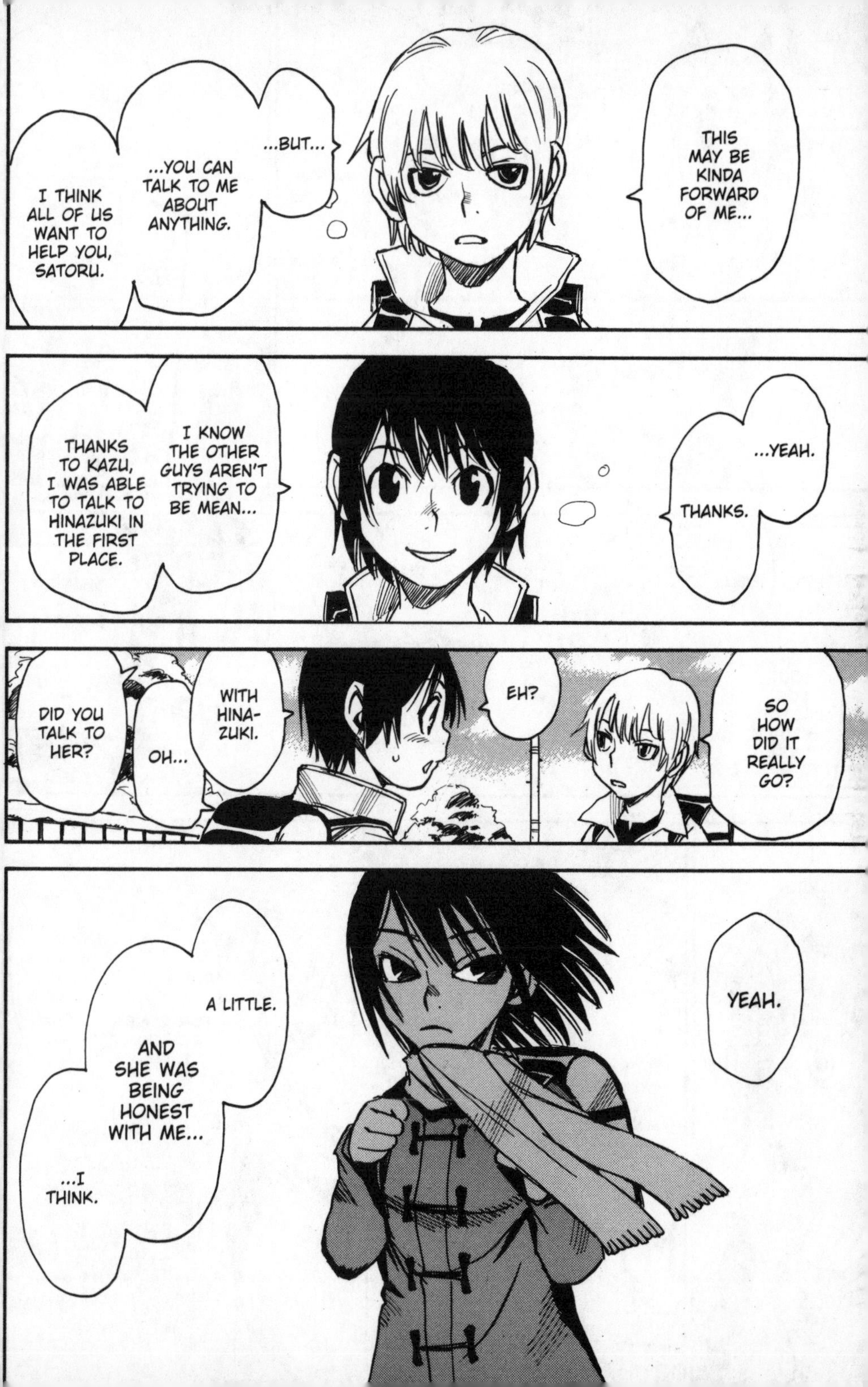
THIS MAY BE KINDA FORWARD OF ME...
...BUT...
...YOU CAN TALK TO ME ABOUT ANYTHING.
I THINK ALL OF US WANT TO HELP YOU, SATORU.
...YEAH.
THANKS.
I KNOW THE OTHER GUYS AREN'T TRYING TO BE MEAN...
THANKS TO KAZU, I WAS ABLE TO TALK TO HINAZUKI IN THE FIRST PLACE.
SO HOW DID IT REALLY GO?
EH?
WITH HINA-ZUKI.
OH...
DID YOU TALK TO HER?
YEAH.
A LITTLE.
AND SHE WAS BEING HONEST WITH ME...
...I THINK.

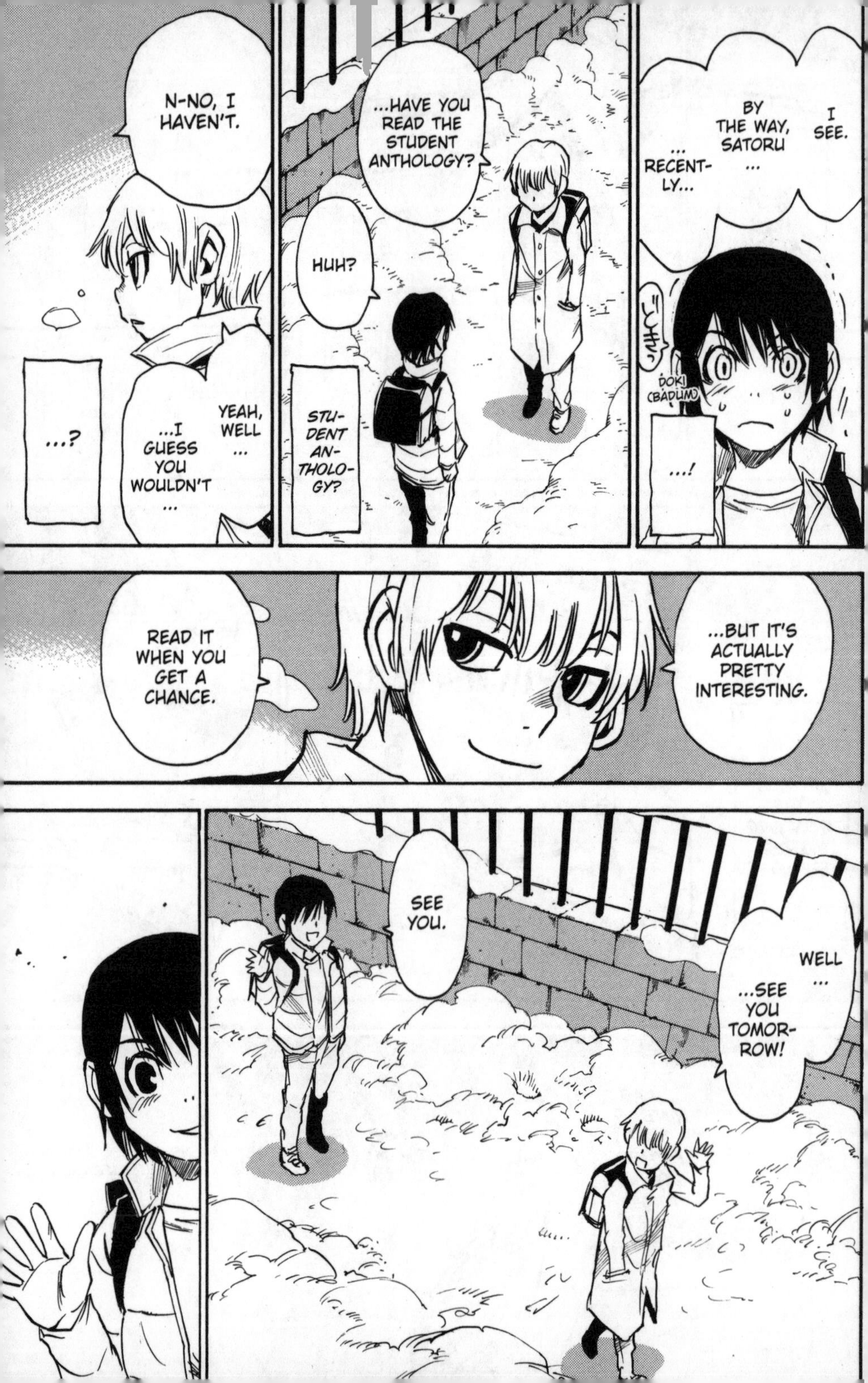
I SEE.
BY THE WAY, SATORU ...
... RECENT-LY...
DOKI (BADUM)
...!
...HAVE YOU READ THE STUDENT ANTHOLOGY?
HUH?
STU-DENT AN-THOLO-GY?
N-NO, I HAVEN'T.
YEAH, WELL ...
...I GUESS YOU WOULDN'T ...
...?
...BUT IT'S ACTUALLY PRETTY INTERESTING.
READ IT WHEN YOU GET A CHANCE.
WELL ...
...SEE YOU TOMOR-ROW!
SEE YOU.

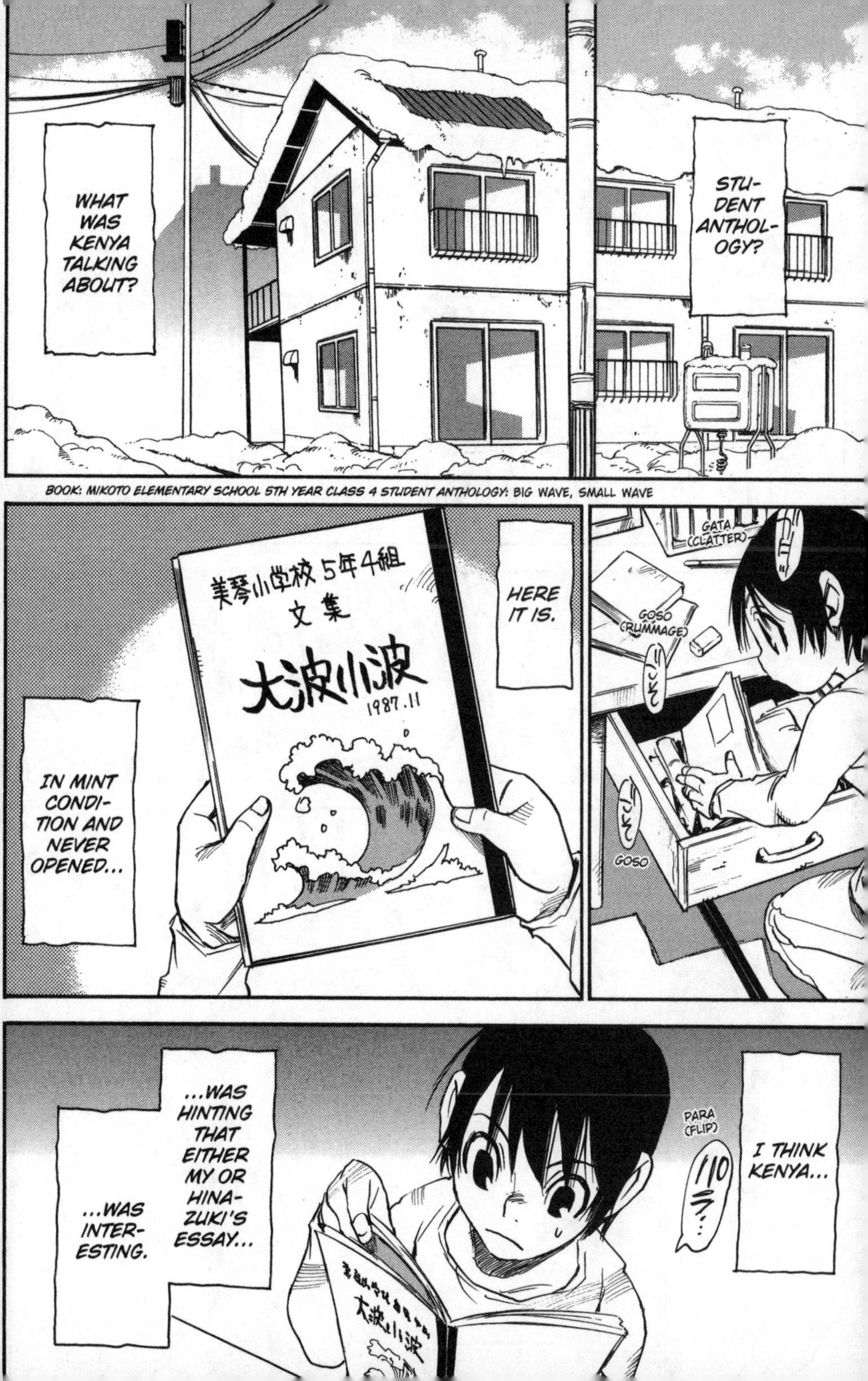
STUDENT ANTHOLOGY?
WHAT WAS KENYA TALKING ABOUT?
BOOK: MIKOTO ELEMENTARY SCHOOL 5TH YEAR CLASS 4 STUDENT ANTHOLOGY: BIG WAVE, SMALL WAVE
GATA (CLATTER)
GOSO (RUMMAGE)
GOSO
HERE IT IS.
美琴小学校 5年4組
文集
大波小波
1987.11
IN MINT CONDITION AND NEVER OPENED...
I THINK KENYA...
PARA (FLIP)
...WAS HINTING THAT EITHER MY OR HINAZUKI'S ESSAY...
...WAS INTERESTING.
大波小波

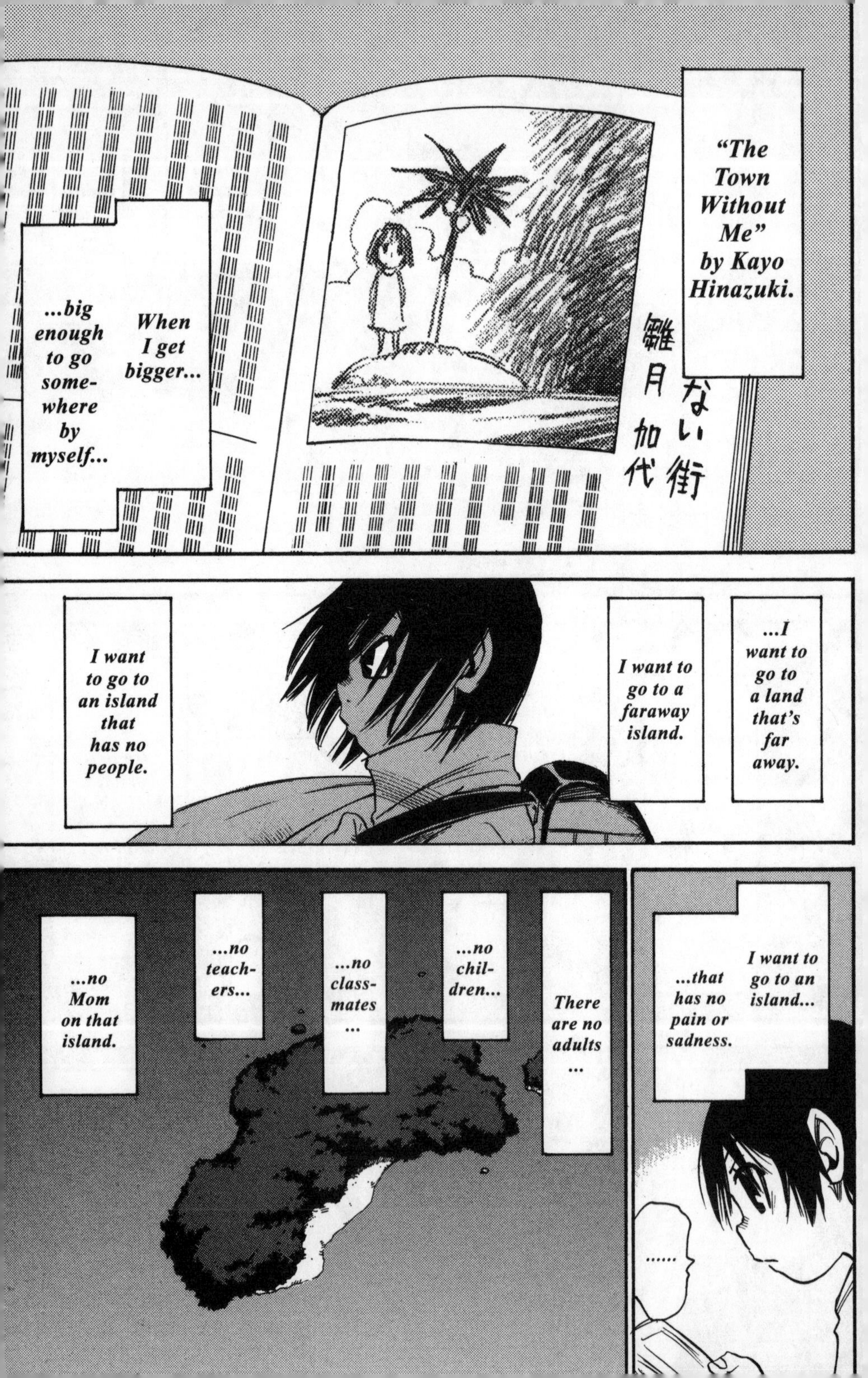
"The Town Without Me" by Kayo Hinazuki.
ない街
雛月加代
When I get bigger...
...big enough to go somewhere by myself...
...I want to go to a land that's far away.
I want to go to a faraway island.
I want to go to an island that has no people.
I want to go to an island...
...that has no pain or sadness.
......
There are no adults...
...no children...
...no classmates...
...no teachers...
...no Mom on that island.

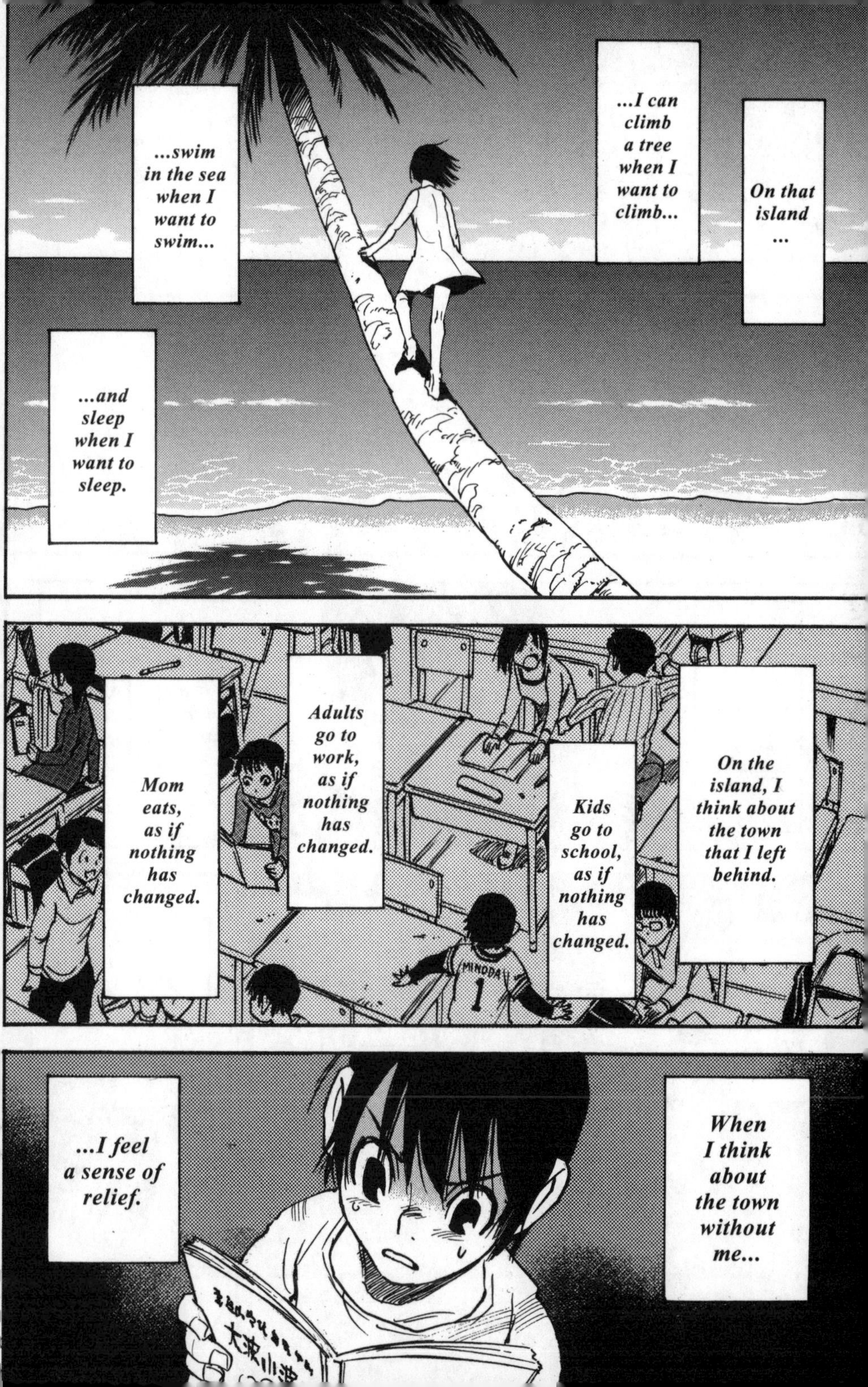
On that island...
...I can climb a tree when I want to climb...
...swim in the sea when I want to swim...
...and sleep when I want to sleep.
On the island, I think about the town that I left behind.
Kids go to school, as if nothing has changed.
Adults go to work, as if nothing has changed.
Mom eats, as if nothing has changed.
MINODA
1
When I think about the town without me...
...I feel a sense of relief.

I want to go far, far away.

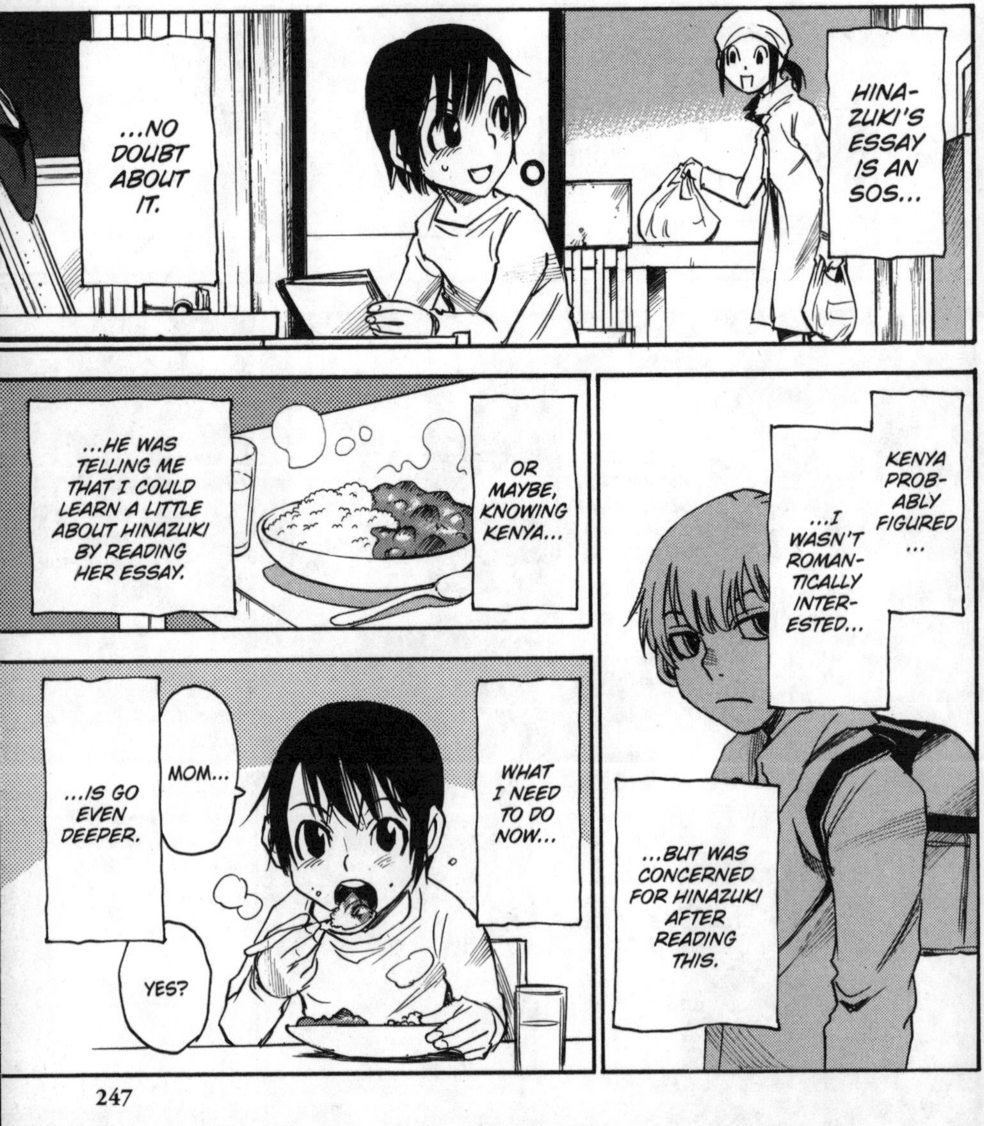
HINAZUKI'S ESSAY IS AN SOS...
...NO DOUBT ABOUT IT.
KENYA PROBABLY FIGURED...
...I WASN'T ROMANTICALLY INTERESTED...
...BUT WAS CONCERNED FOR HINAZUKI AFTER READING THIS.
OR MAYBE, KNOWING KENYA...
...HE WAS TELLING ME THAT I COULD LEARN A LITTLE ABOUT HINAZUKI BY READING HER ESSAY.
WHAT I NEED TO DO NOW...
MOM...
...IS GO EVEN DEEPER.
YES?

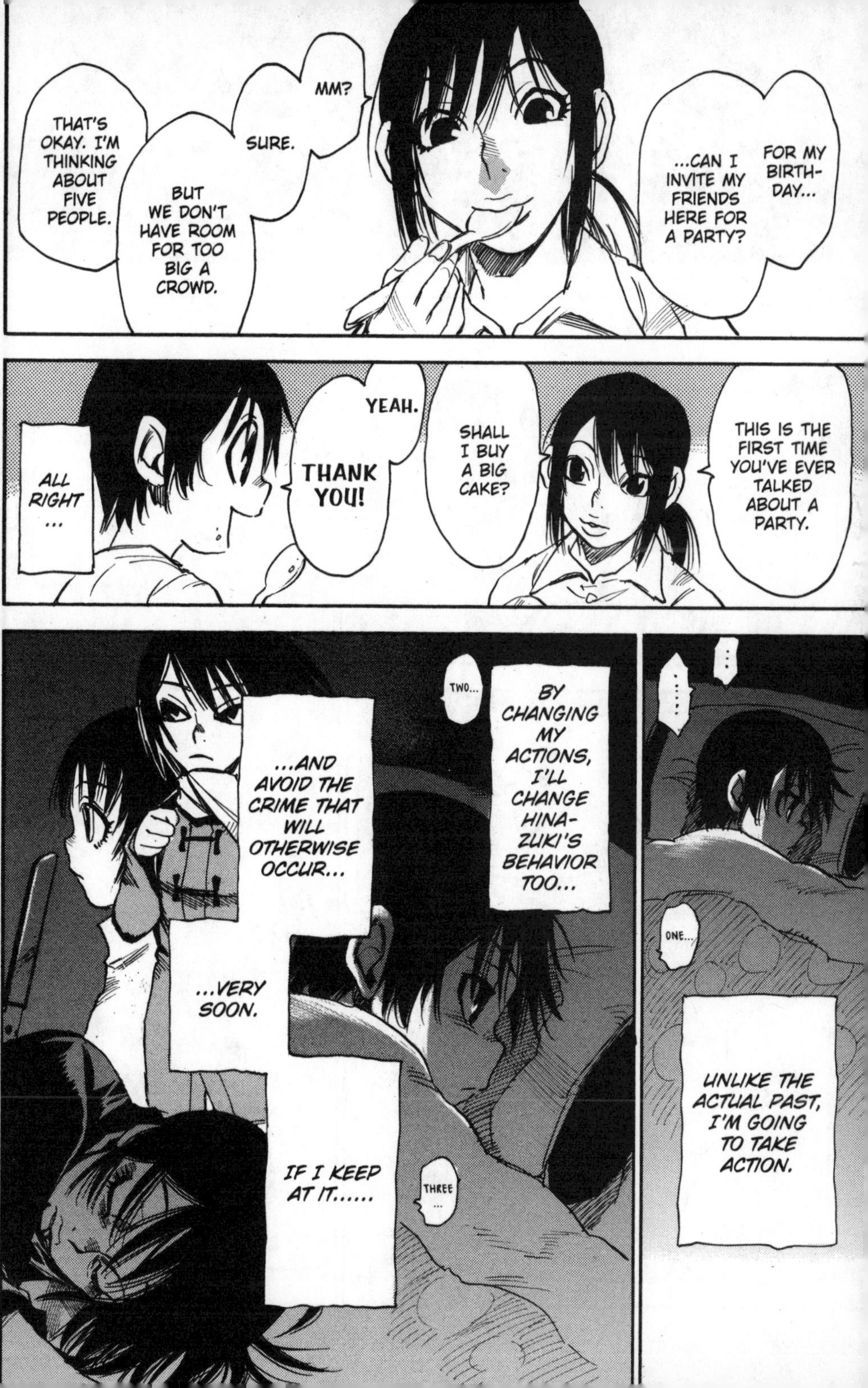
FOR MY BIRTHDAY...
...CAN I INVITE MY FRIENDS HERE FOR A PARTY?
MM?
SURE.
BUT WE DON'T HAVE ROOM FOR TOO BIG A CROWD.
THAT'S OKAY. I'M THINKING ABOUT FIVE PEOPLE.
THIS IS THE FIRST TIME YOU'VE EVER TALKED ABOUT A PARTY.
SHALL I BUY A BIG CAKE?
YEAH.
THANK YOU!
ALL RIGHT ...
......
...
ONE...
UNLIKE THE ACTUAL PAST, I'M GOING TO TAKE ACTION.
TWO...
BY CHANGING MY ACTIONS, I'LL CHANGE HINA-ZUKI'S BEHAVIOR TOO...
...AND AVOID THE CRIME THAT WILL OTHERWISE OCCUR...
...VERY SOON.
IF I KEEP AT IT......
THREE ...

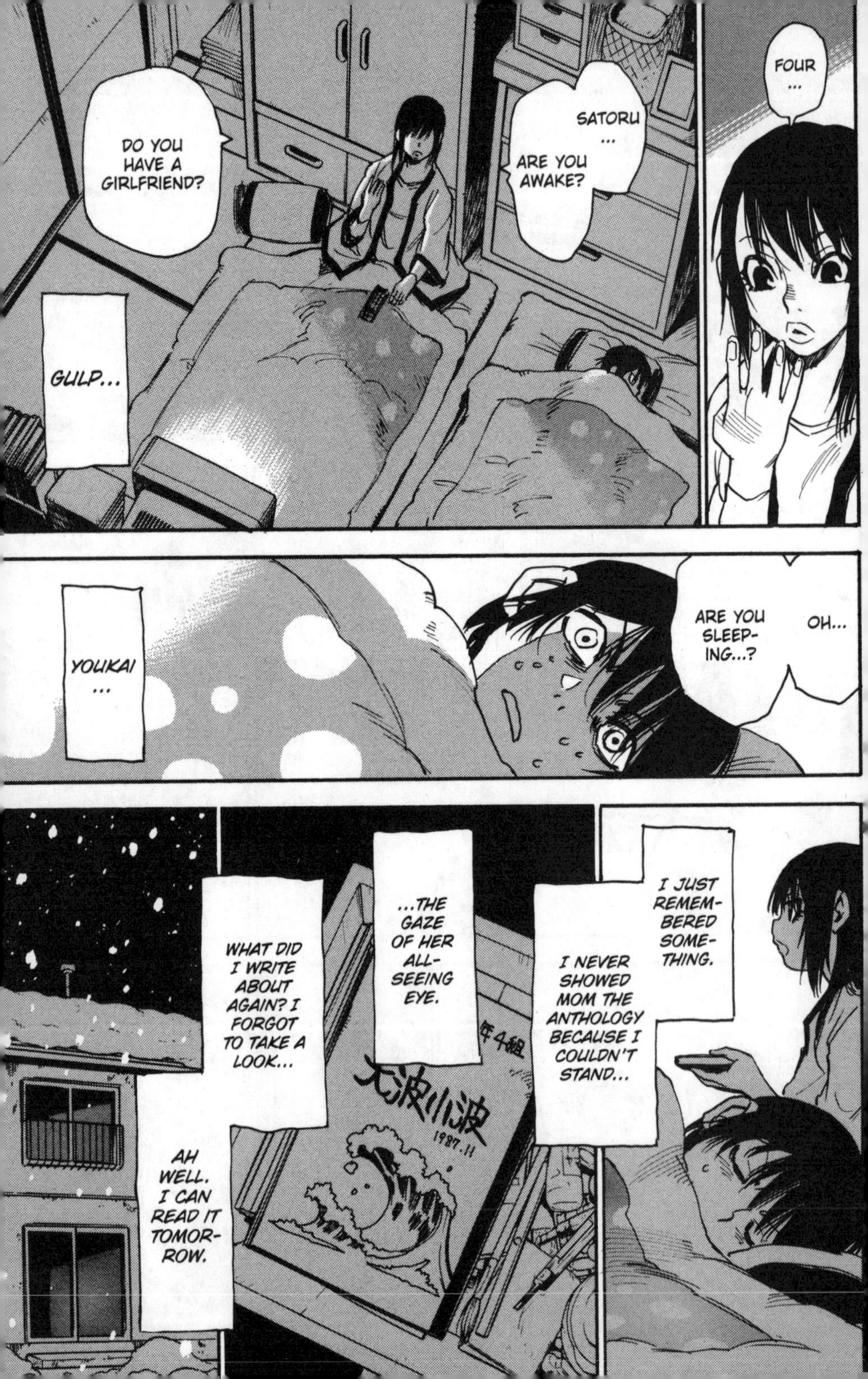
FOUR ...
SATORU ...
ARE YOU AWAKE?
DO YOU HAVE A GIRLFRIEND?
GULP...
OH...
ARE YOU SLEEPING...?
YOUKAI ...
I JUST REMEMBERED SOMETHING.
I NEVER SHOWED MOM THE ANTHOLOGY BECAUSE I COULDN'T STAND...
...THE GAZE OF HER ALL-SEEING EYE.
年4組
大波小波
1987.11
WHAT DID I WRITE ABOUT AGAIN? I FORGOT TO TAKE A LOOK...
AH WELL. I CAN READ IT TOMORROW.

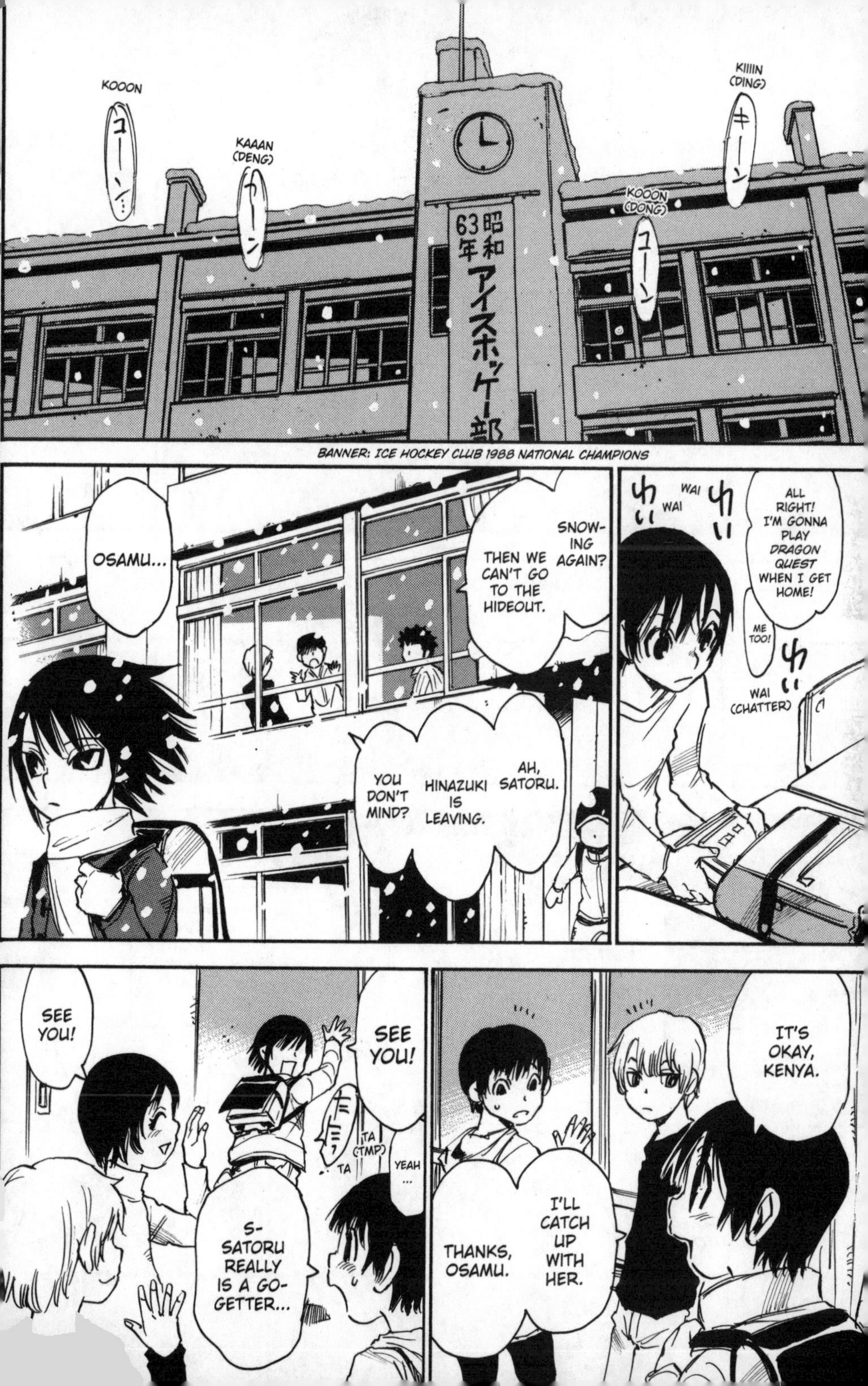
KIIIN (DING)
キーン
KOOON (DONG)
コーン
KAAAN (DENG)
カーン
KOOON
コーン…
昭和63年アイスホッケー部
BANNER: ICE HOCKEY CLUB 1988 NATIONAL CHAMPIONS
WAI WAI
ALL RIGHT! I'M GONNA PLAY *DRAGON QUEST* WHEN I GET HOME!
ME TOO!
WAI (CHATTER)
SNOWING AGAIN?
THEN WE CAN'T GO TO THE HIDEOUT.
AH, SATORU.
HINAZUKI IS LEAVING.
YOU DON'T MIND?
OSAMU...
IT'S OKAY, KENYA.
I'LL CATCH UP WITH HER.
THANKS, OSAMU.
YEAH...
SEE YOU!
TA TA (TMP)
SEE YOU!
S-SATORU REALLY IS A GO-GETTER...

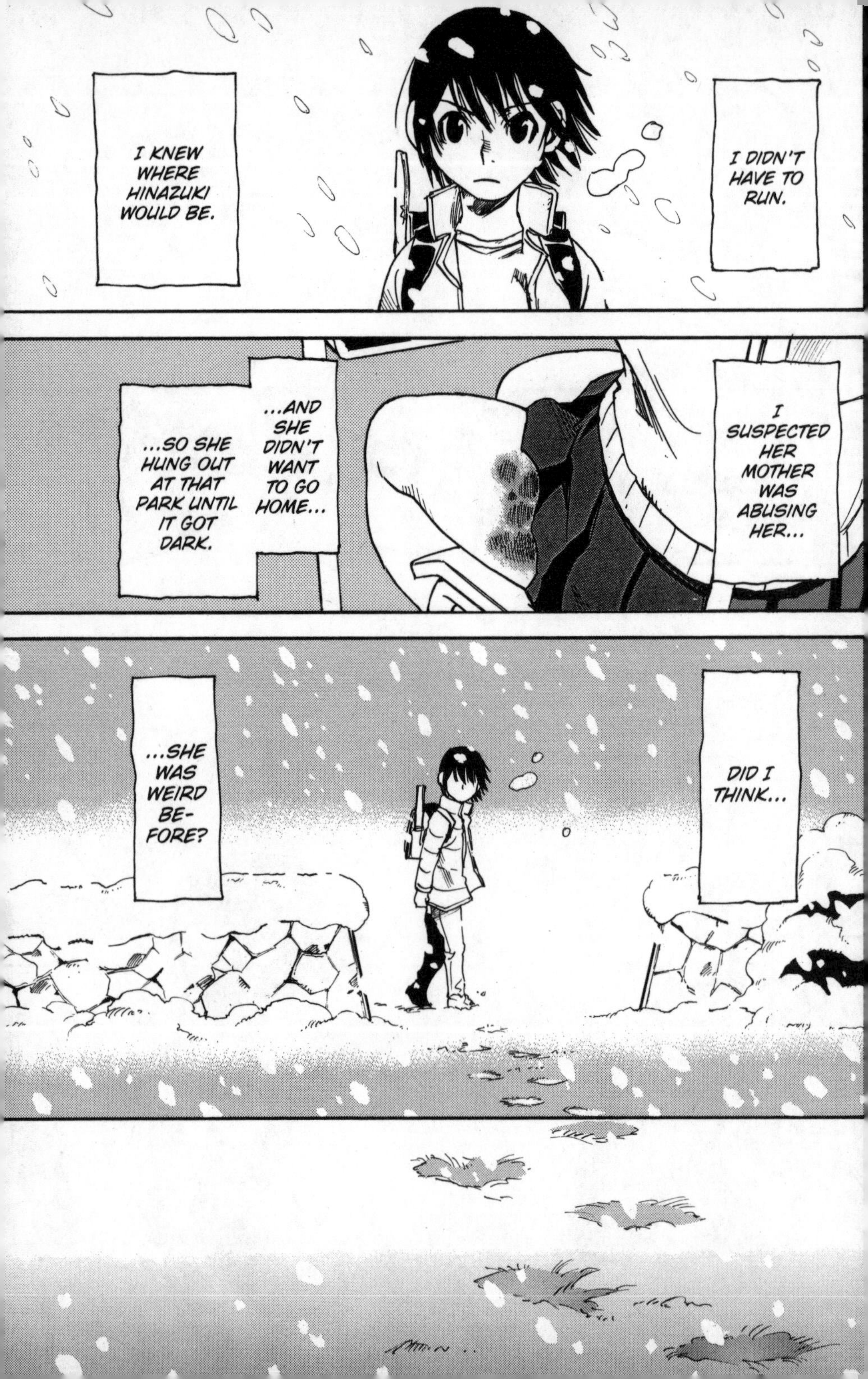
I DIDN'T HAVE TO RUN.
I KNEW WHERE HINAZUKI WOULD BE.
I SUSPECTED HER MOTHER WAS ABUSING HER...
...AND SHE DIDN'T WANT TO GO HOME...
...SO SHE HUNG OUT AT THAT PARK UNTIL IT GOT DARK.
DID I THINK...
...SHE WAS WEIRD BE-FORE?

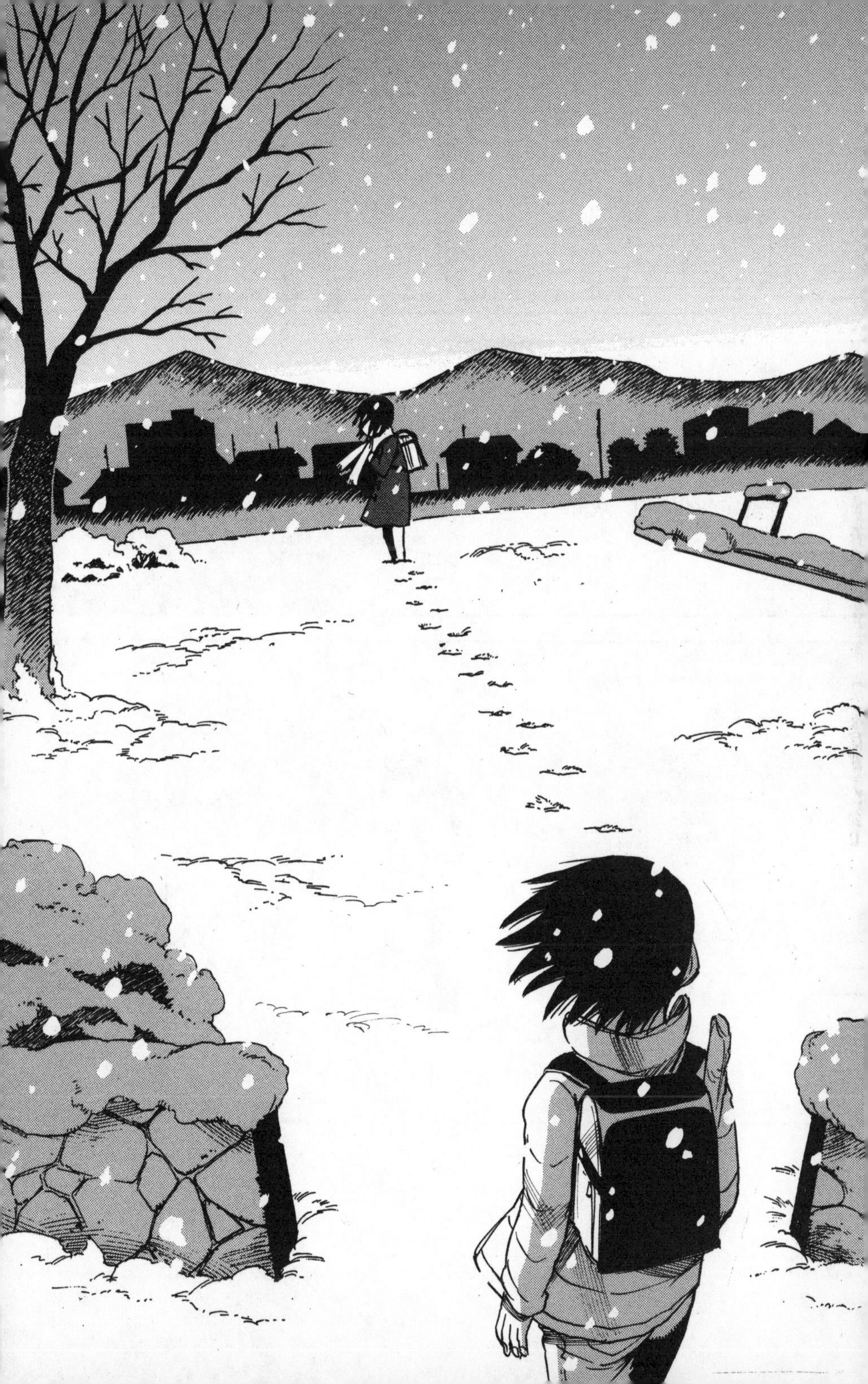

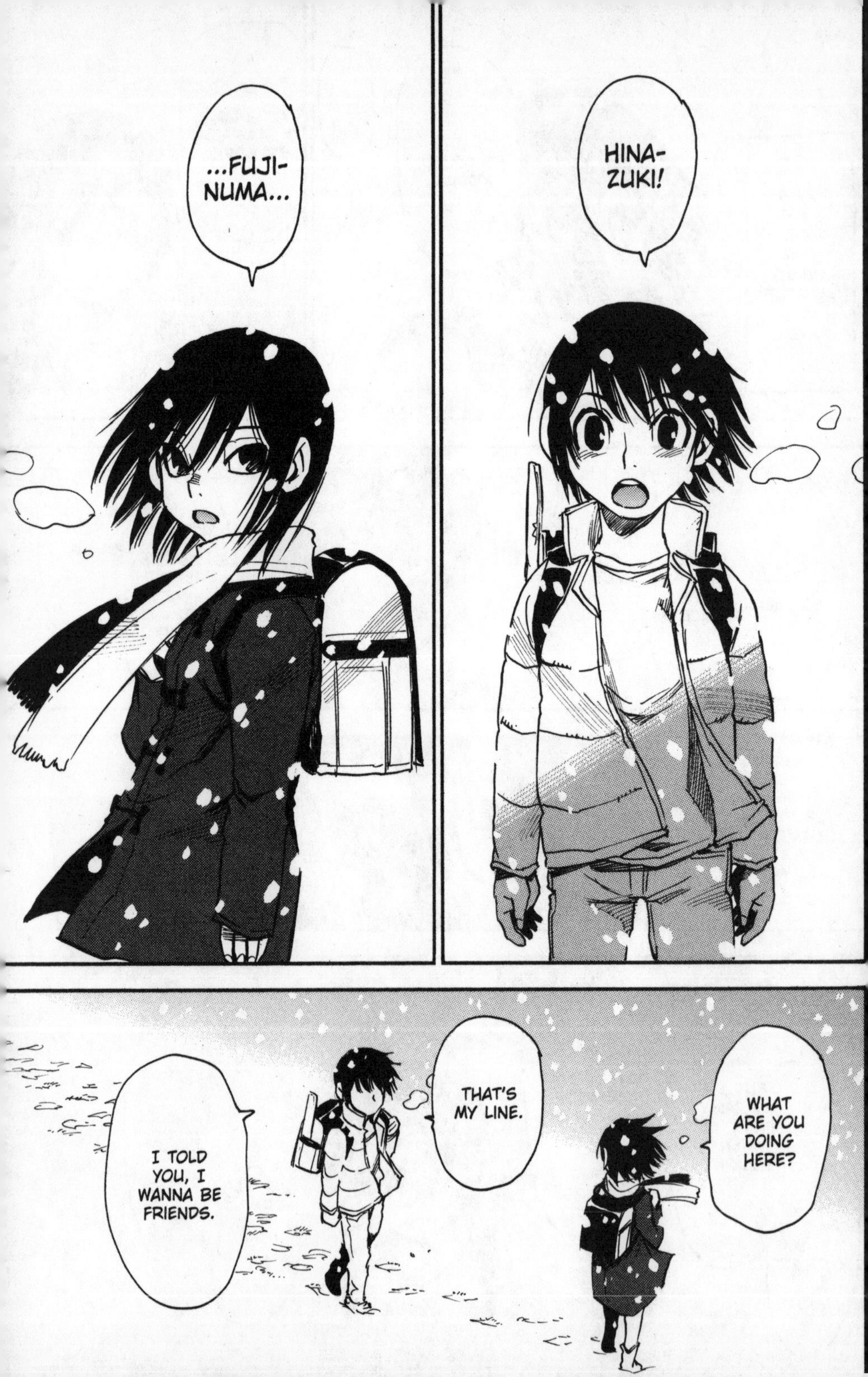
HINA-ZUKI!
...FUJI-NUMA...
WHAT ARE YOU DOING HERE?
THAT'S MY LINE.
I TOLD YOU, I WANNA BE FRIENDS.

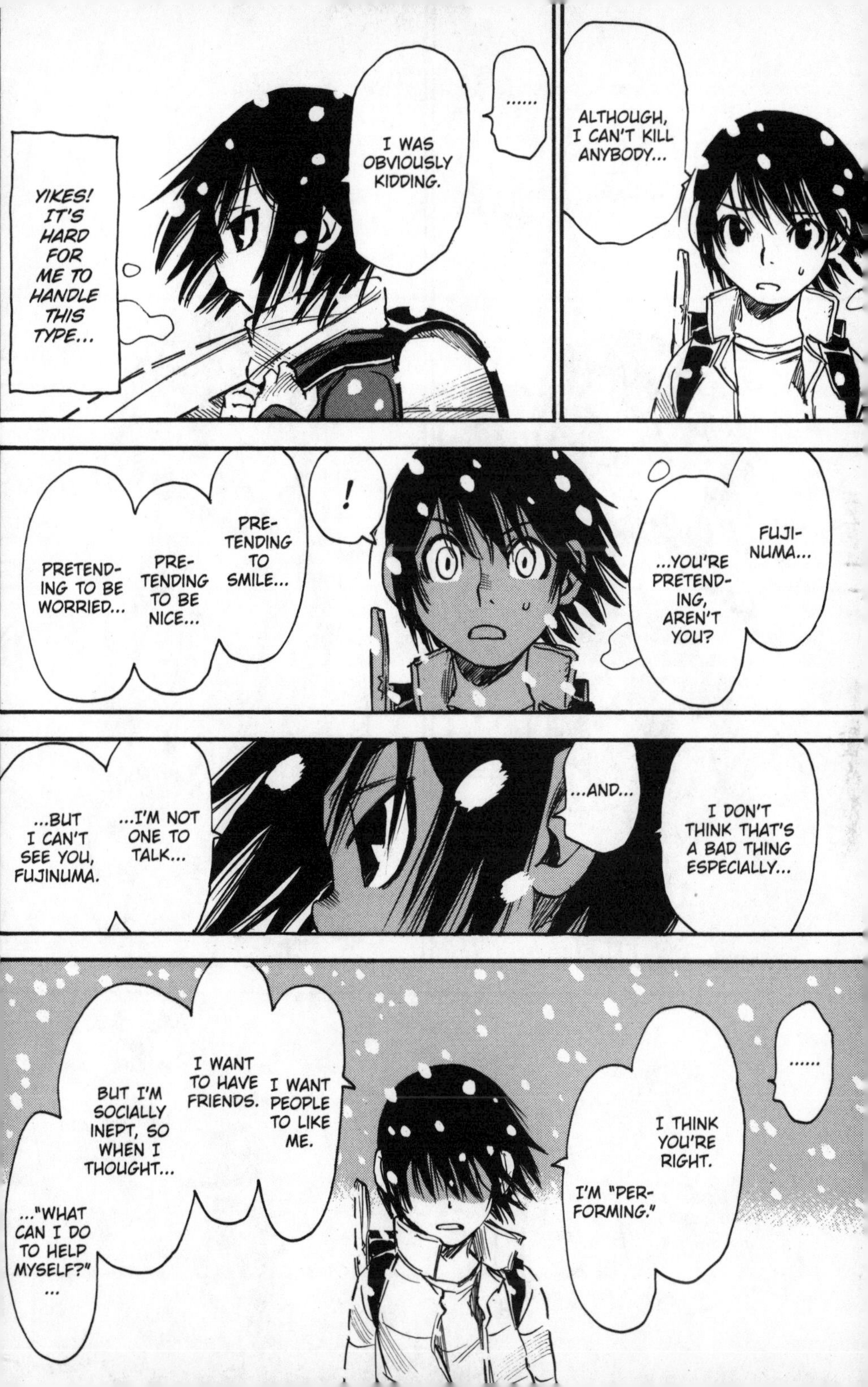
ALTHOUGH, I CAN'T KILL ANYBODY...
......
I WAS OBVIOUSLY KIDDING.
YIKES! IT'S HARD FOR ME TO HANDLE THIS TYPE...
FUJI-NUMA...
...YOU'RE PRETEND-ING, AREN'T YOU?
!
PRE-TENDING TO SMILE...
PRE-TENDING TO BE NICE...
PRETEND-ING TO BE WORRIED...
I DON'T THINK THAT'S A BAD THING ESPECIALLY...
...AND...
...I'M NOT ONE TO TALK...
...BUT I CAN'T SEE YOU, FUJINUMA.
......
I THINK YOU'RE RIGHT.
I'M "PER-FORMING."
I WANT PEOPLE TO LIKE ME.
I WANT TO HAVE FRIENDS.
BUT I'M SOCIALLY INEPT, SO WHEN I THOUGHT...
..."WHAT CAN I DO TO HELP MYSELF?" ...

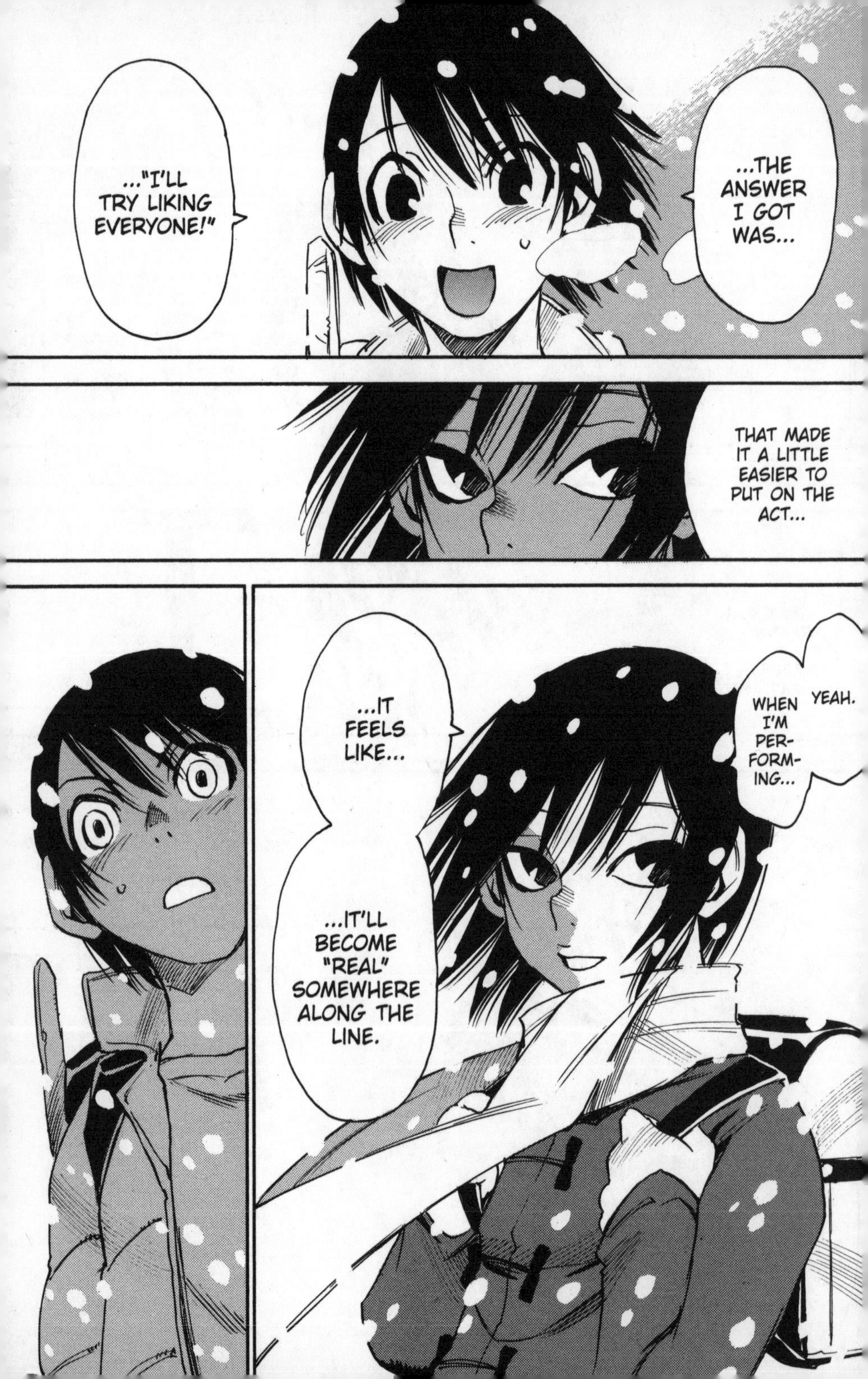
...THE ANSWER I GOT WAS...
..."I'LL TRY LIKING EVERYONE!"
THAT MADE IT A LITTLE EASIER TO PUT ON THE ACT...
YEAH.
WHEN I'M PER-FORM-ING...
...IT FEELS LIKE...
...IT'LL BECOME "REAL" SOMEWHERE ALONG THE LINE.

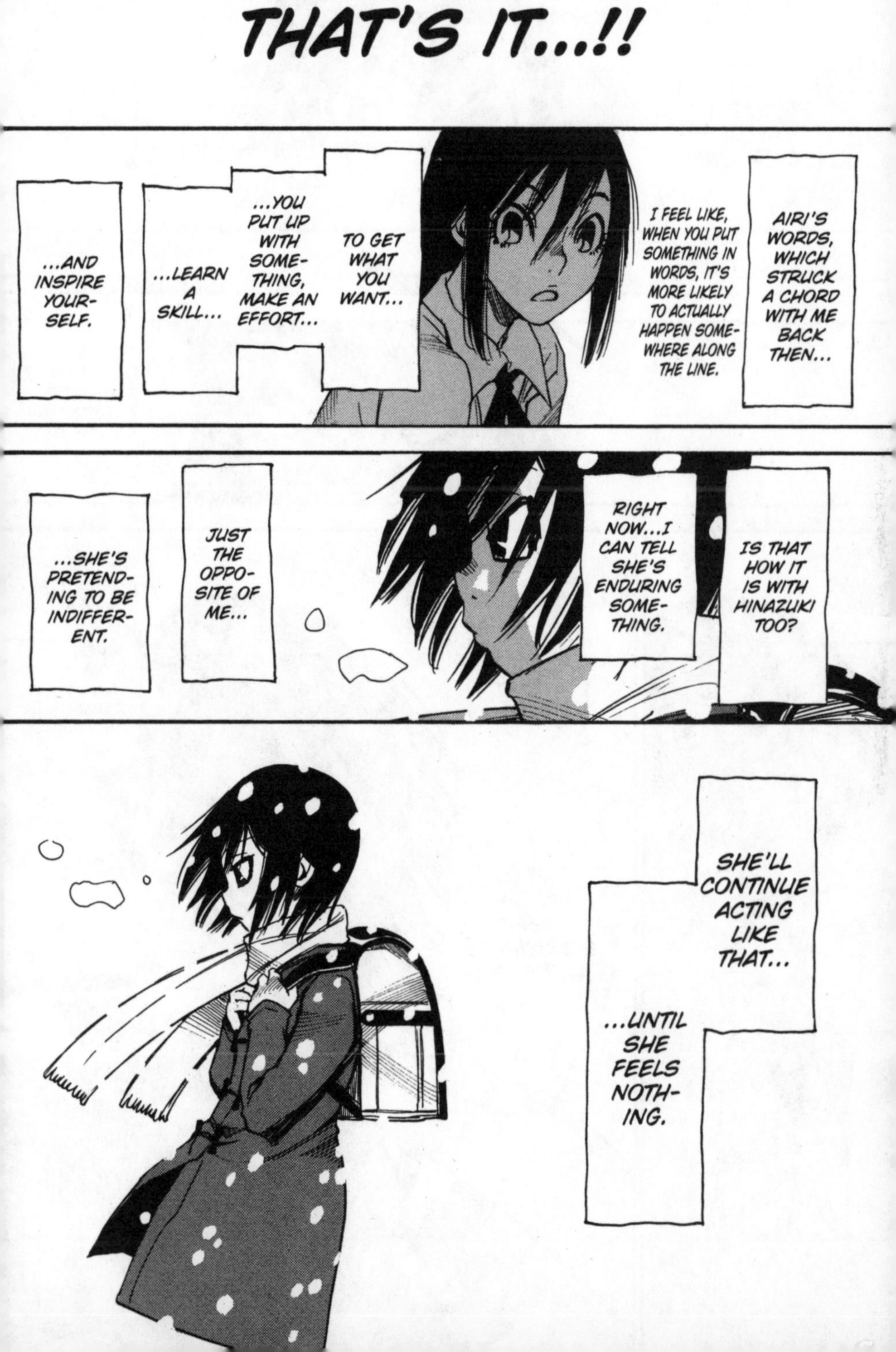
THAT'S IT...!!
AIRI'S WORDS, WHICH STRUCK A CHORD WITH ME BACK THEN...
I FEEL LIKE, WHEN YOU PUT SOMETHING IN WORDS, IT'S MORE LIKELY TO ACTUALLY HAPPEN SOMEWHERE ALONG THE LINE.
TO GET WHAT YOU WANT...
...YOU PUT UP WITH SOMETHING, MAKE AN EFFORT...
...LEARN A SKILL...
...AND INSPIRE YOURSELF.
IS THAT HOW IT IS WITH HINAZUKI TOO?
RIGHT NOW...I CAN TELL SHE'S ENDURING SOMETHING.
JUST THE OPPOSITE OF ME...
...SHE'S PRETENDING TO BE INDIFFERENT.
SHE'LL CONTINUE ACTING LIKE THAT...
...UNTIL SHE FEELS NOTHING.

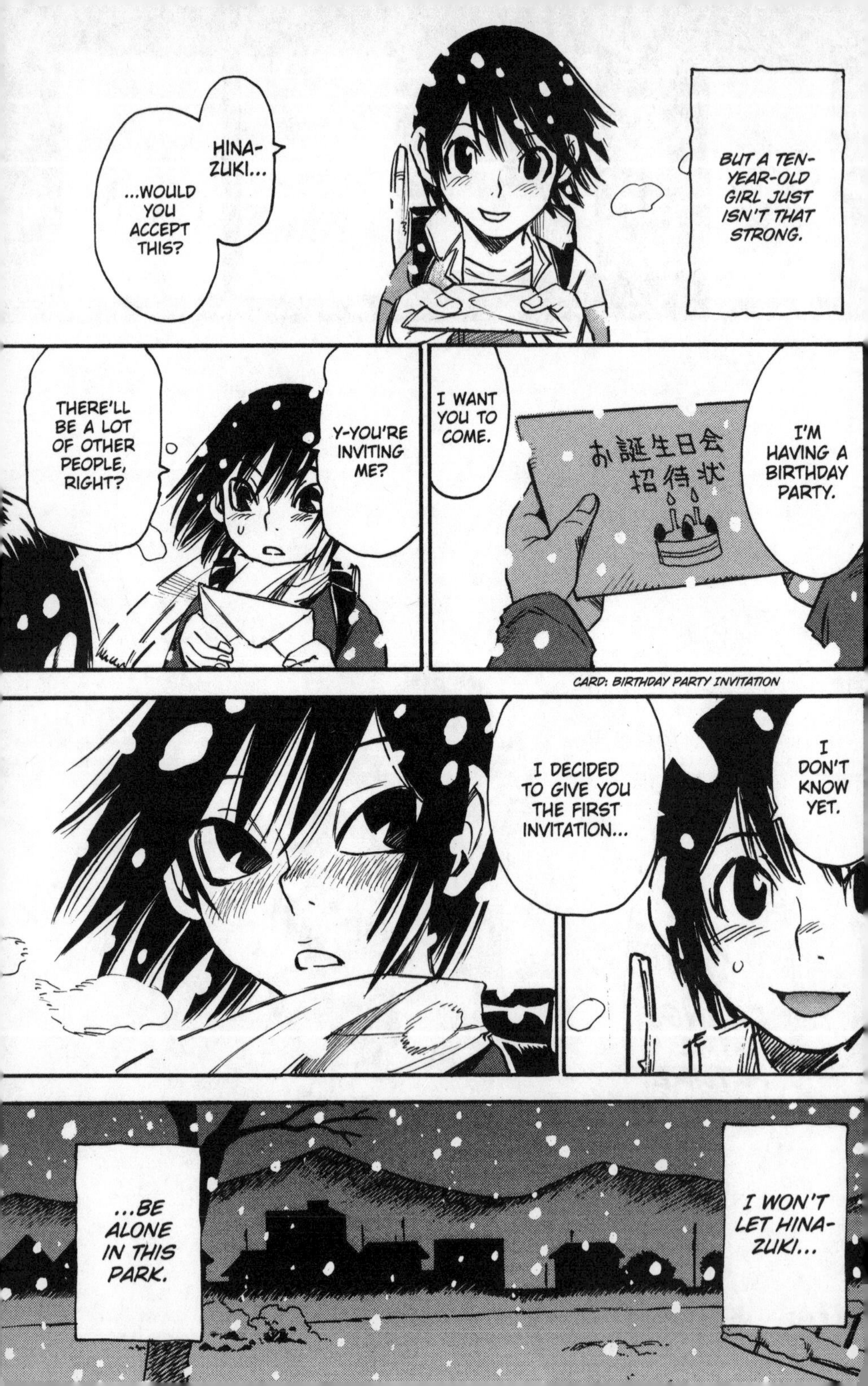
BUT A TEN-YEAR-OLD GIRL JUST ISN'T THAT STRONG.
HINA-ZUKI...
...WOULD YOU ACCEPT THIS?
I'M HAVING A BIRTHDAY PARTY.
I WANT YOU TO COME.
お誕生日会
招待状
Y-YOU'RE INVITING ME?
THERE'LL BE A LOT OF OTHER PEOPLE, RIGHT?
CARD: BIRTHDAY PARTY INVITATION
I DON'T KNOW YET.
I DECIDED TO GIVE YOU THE FIRST INVITATION...
I WON'T LET HINA-ZUKI...
...BE ALONE IN THIS PARK.

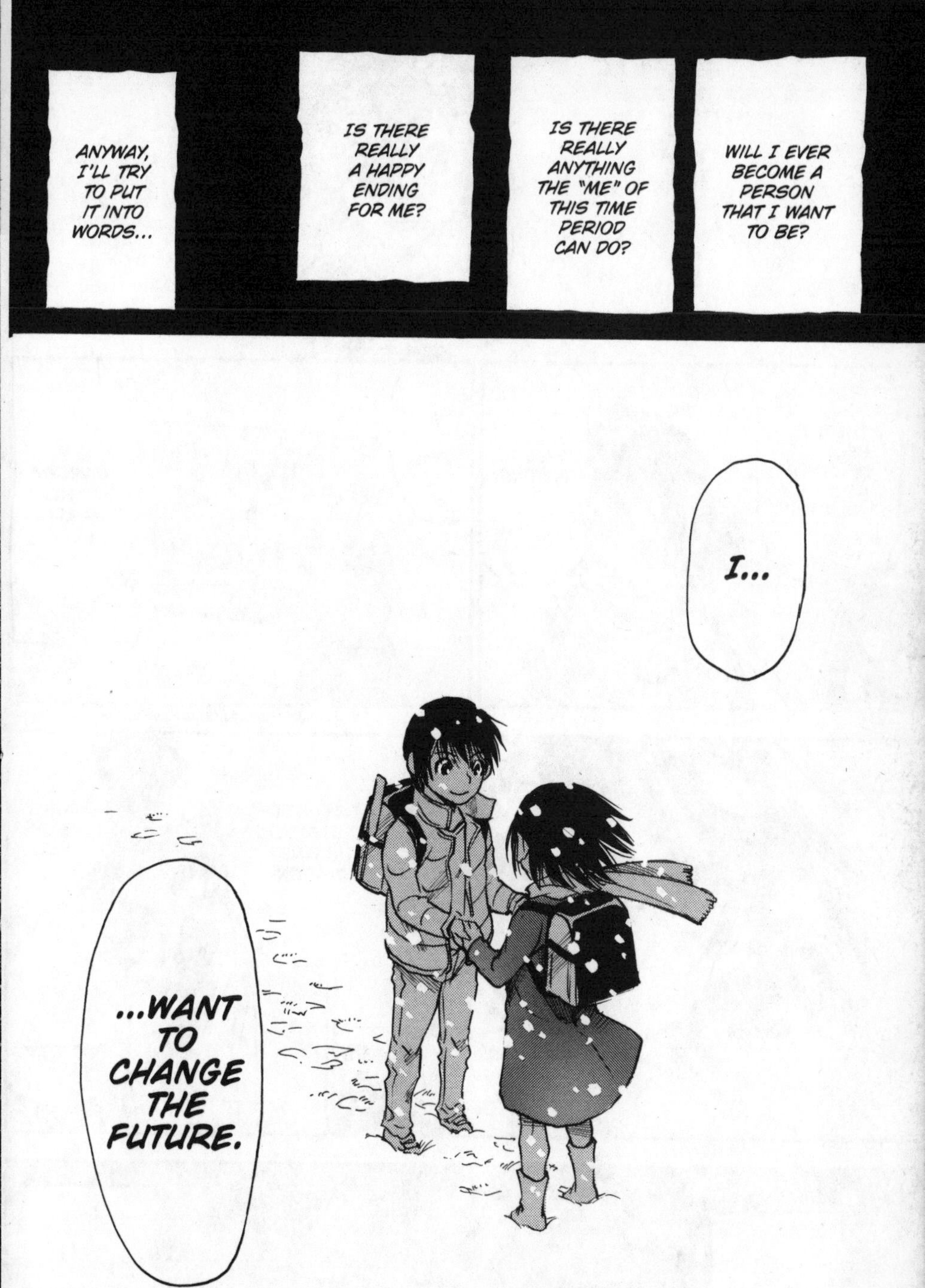
WILL I EVER BECOME A PERSON THAT I WANT TO BE?
IS THERE REALLY ANYTHING THE "ME" OF THIS TIME PERIOD CAN DO?
IS THERE REALLY A HAPPY ENDING FOR ME?
ANYWAY, I'LL TRY TO PUT IT INTO WORDS...
I...
...WANT TO CHANGE THE FUTURE.

#8 END

WHEN I'M PERFORMING, IT FEELS LIKE IT'LL BECOME "REAL" SOMEWHERE ALONG THE LINE.

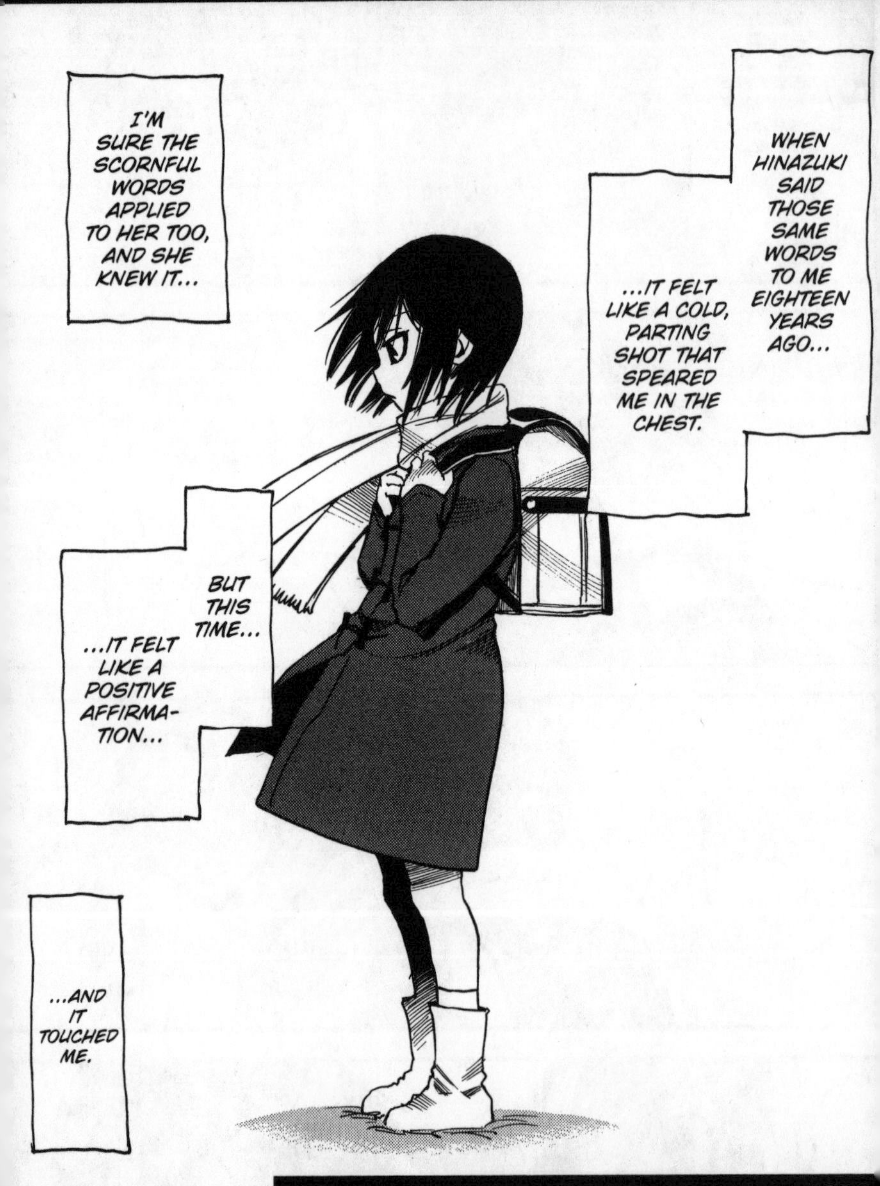
WHEN HINAZUKI SAID THOSE SAME WORDS TO ME EIGHTEEN YEARS AGO...
...IT FELT LIKE A COLD, PARTING SHOT THAT SPEARED ME IN THE CHEST.
I'M SURE THE SCORNFUL WORDS APPLIED TO HER TOO, AND SHE KNEW IT...
BUT THIS TIME...
...IT FELT LIKE A POSITIVE AFFIRMATION...
...AND IT TOUCHED ME.

#9: The Beginning of Failure, February 1988

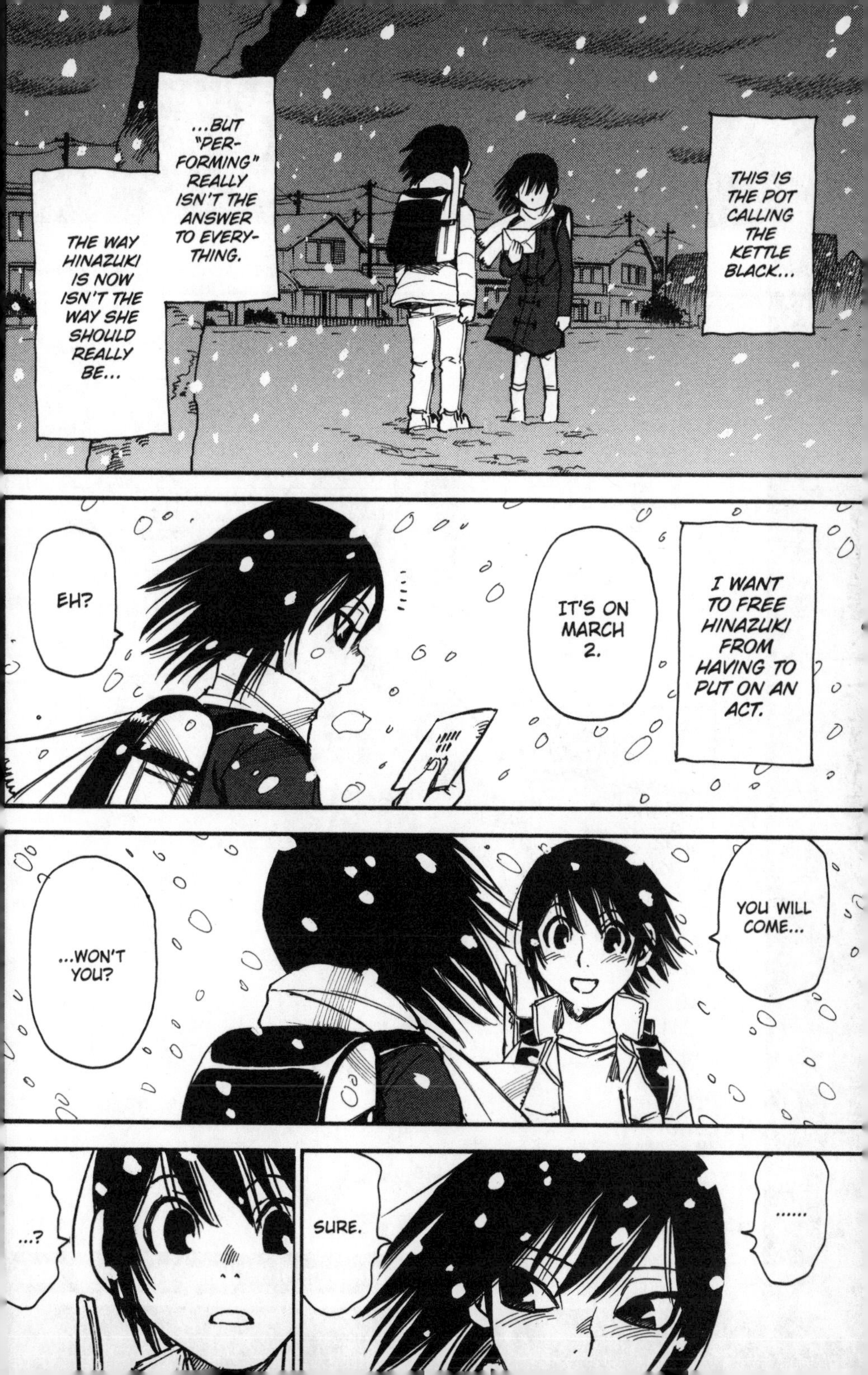
THIS IS THE POT CALLING THE KETTLE BLACK...
...BUT "PERFORMING" REALLY ISN'T THE ANSWER TO EVERYTHING.
THE WAY HINAZUKI IS NOW ISN'T THE WAY SHE SHOULD REALLY BE...
I WANT TO FREE HINAZUKI FROM HAVING TO PUT ON AN ACT.
IT'S ON MARCH 2.
EH?
YOU WILL COME...
...WON'T YOU?
......
SURE.
...?

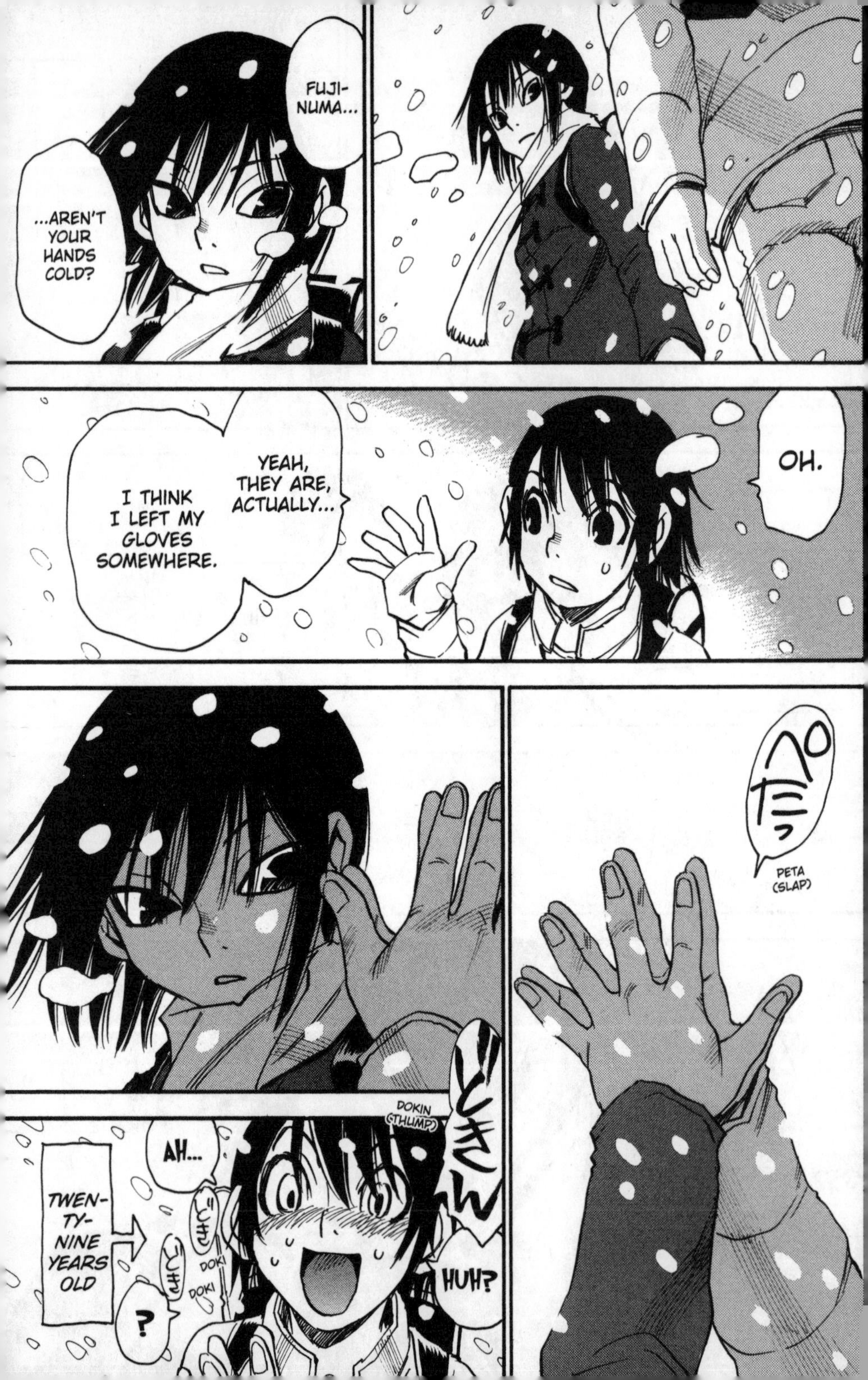
FUJI-NUMA...
...AREN'T YOUR HANDS COLD?
OH.
YEAH, THEY ARE, ACTUALLY...
I THINK I LEFT MY GLOVES SOMEWHERE.
ペタッ
PETA (SLAP)
DOKIN (THUMP)
AH...
HUH?
DOKI
DOKI
TWENTY-NINE YEARS OLD
?

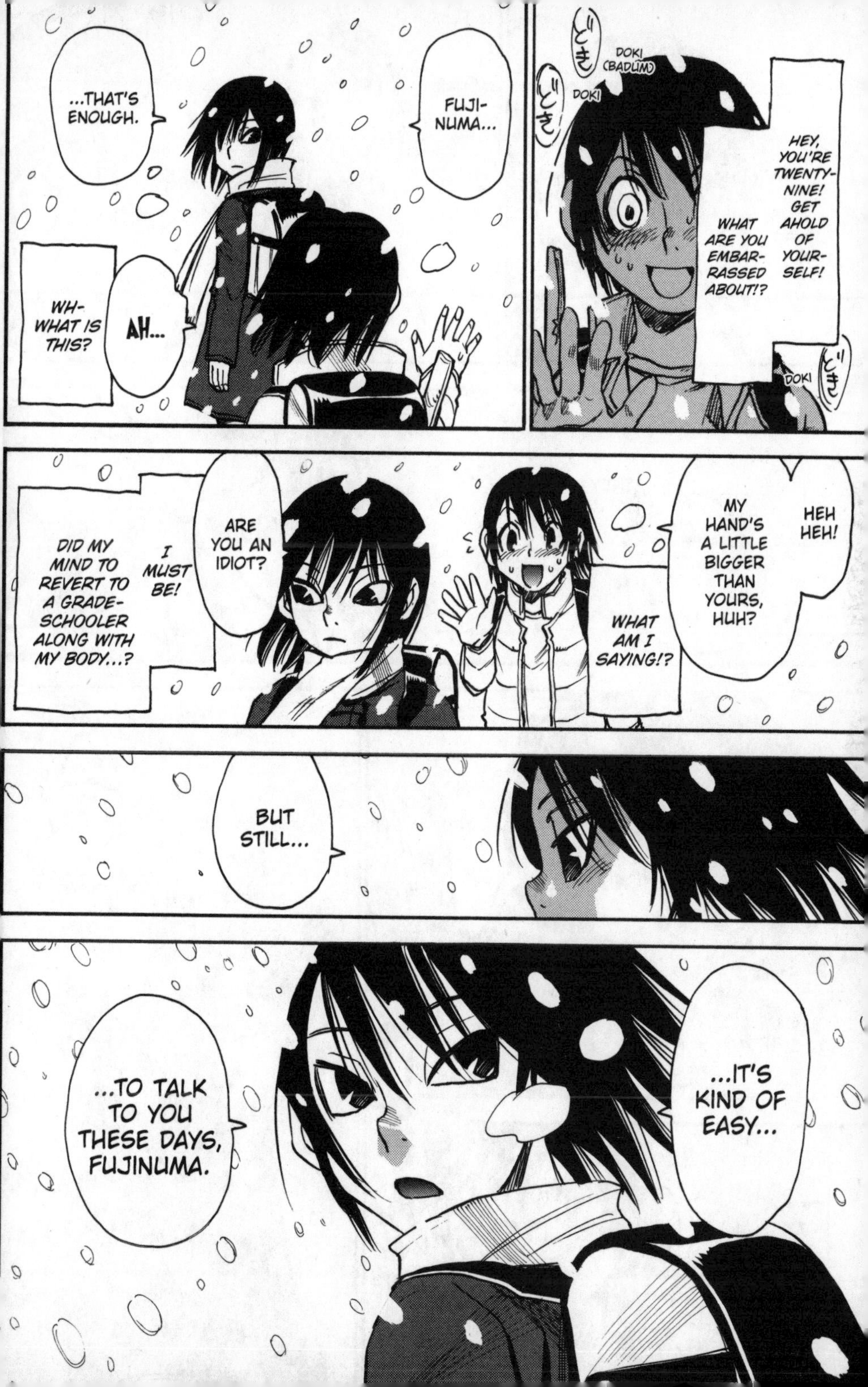
どき
DOKI (BADUM)
どき
DOKI
HEY, YOU'RE TWENTY-NINE! GET AHOLD OF YOURSELF!
WHAT ARE YOU EMBARRASSED ABOUT!?
どき
DOKI
FUJI-NUMA...
...THAT'S ENOUGH.
AH...
WH-WHAT IS THIS?
HEH HEH!
MY HAND'S A LITTLE BIGGER THAN YOURS, HUH?
WHAT AM I SAYING!?
ARE YOU AN IDIOT?
I MUST BE!
DID MY MIND TO REVERT TO A GRADE-SCHOOLER ALONG WITH MY BODY...?
BUT STILL...
...IT'S KIND OF EASY...
...TO TALK TO YOU THESE DAYS, FUJINUMA.

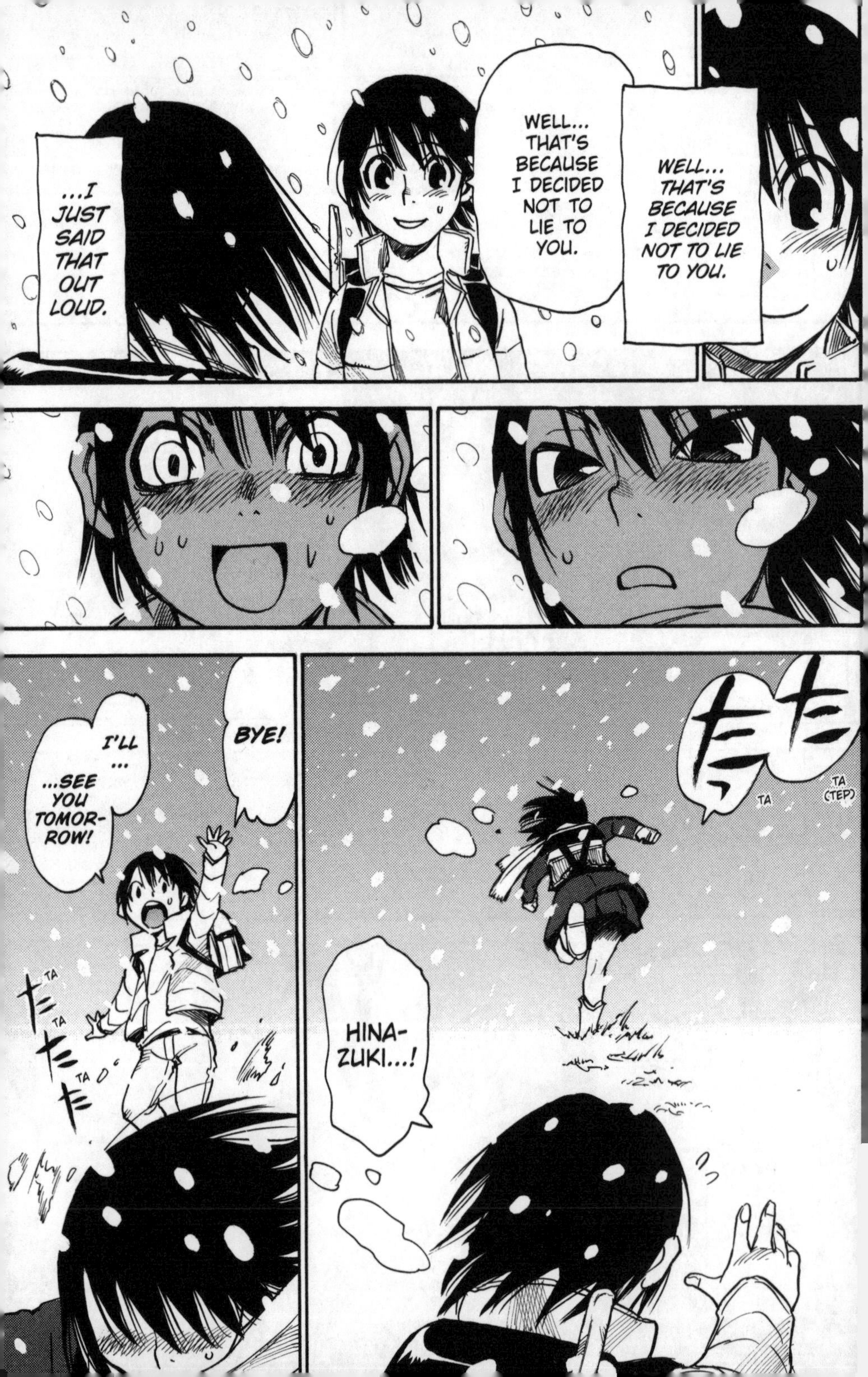
WELL... THAT'S BECAUSE I DECIDED NOT TO LIE TO YOU.
WELL... THAT'S BECAUSE I DECIDED NOT TO LIE TO YOU.
...I JUST SAID THAT OUT LOUD.
TA TA (TEP)
HINA-ZUKI...!
BYE!
I'LL...
...SEE YOU TOMOR-ROW!
TA TA TA

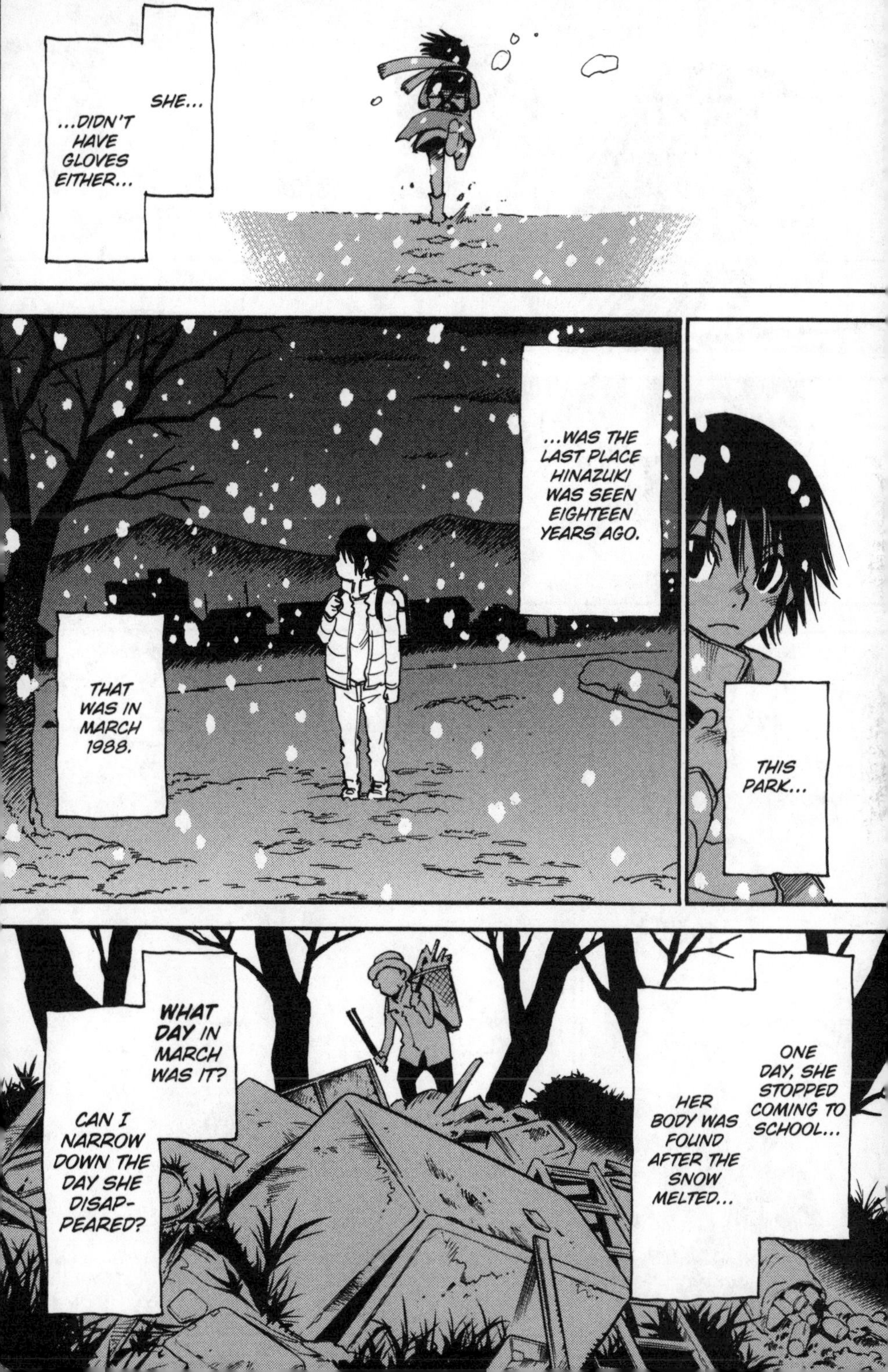
SHE...
...DIDN'T HAVE GLOVES EITHER...
THIS PARK...
...WAS THE LAST PLACE HINAZUKI WAS SEEN EIGHTEEN YEARS AGO.
THAT WAS IN MARCH 1988.
ONE DAY, SHE STOPPED COMING TO SCHOOL...
HER BODY WAS FOUND AFTER THE SNOW MELTED...
WHAT DAY IN MARCH WAS IT?
CAN I NARROW DOWN THE DAY SHE DISAP-PEARED?

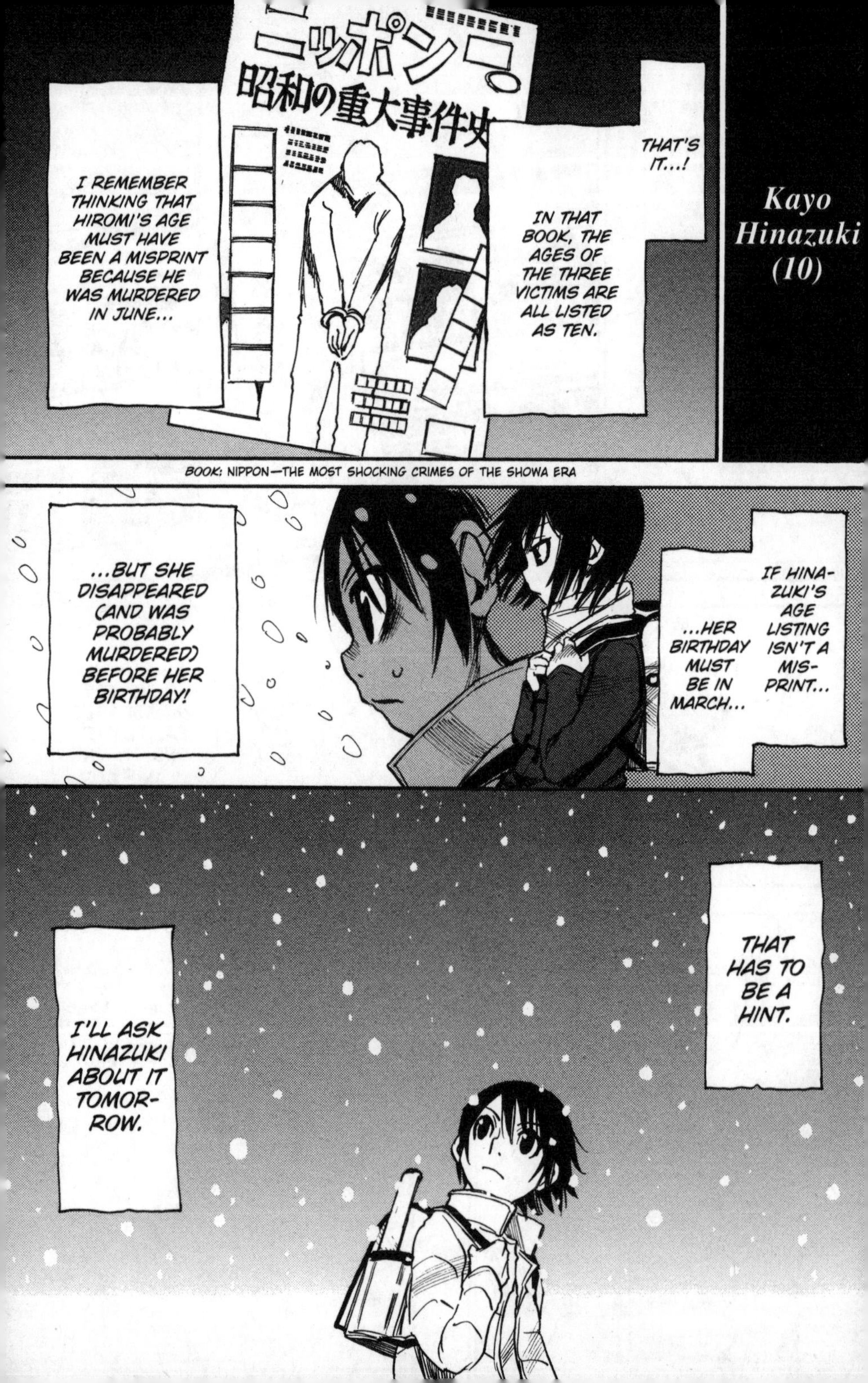
Kayo Hinazuki (10)
THAT'S IT...!
IN THAT BOOK, THE AGES OF THE THREE VICTIMS ARE ALL LISTED AS TEN.
I REMEMBER THINKING THAT HIROMI'S AGE MUST HAVE BEEN A MISPRINT BECAUSE HE WAS MURDERED IN JUNE...
BOOK: NIPPON—THE MOST SHOCKING CRIMES OF THE SHOWA ERA
IF HINA-ZUKI'S AGE LISTING ISN'T A MIS-PRINT...
...HER BIRTHDAY MUST BE IN MARCH...
...BUT SHE DISAPPEARED (AND WAS PROBABLY MURDERED) BEFORE HER BIRTHDAY!
THAT HAS TO BE A HINT.
I'LL ASK HINAZUKI ABOUT IT TOMOR-ROW.

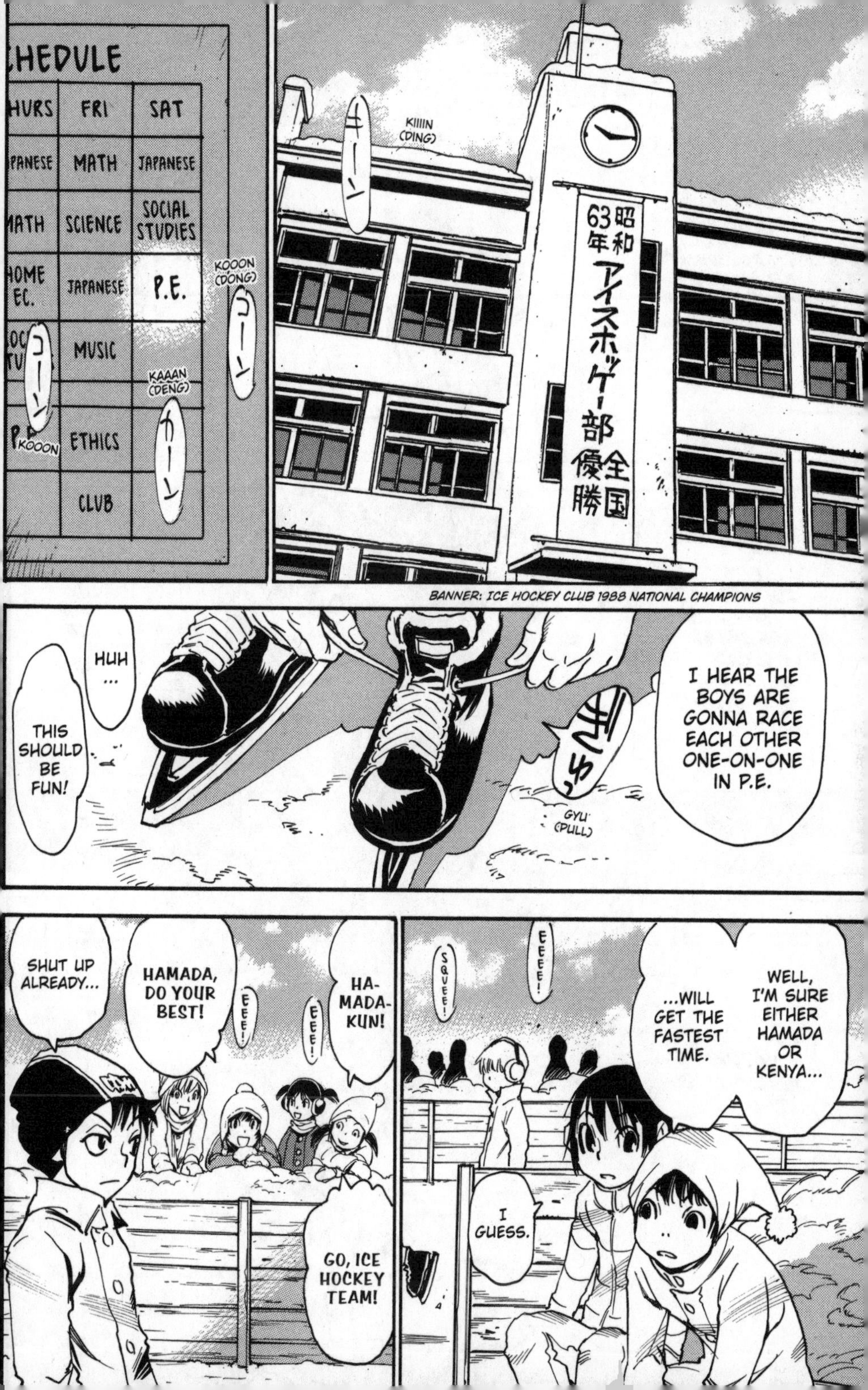
KIIIN (DING)
キーン
昭和63年
アイスホッケー部
全国優勝
KOOON (DONG)
コーン
KAAAN (DENG)
カーン
KOOON
コーン
CHEDULE
HURS FRI SAT
PANESE MATH JAPANESE
MATH SCIENCE SOCIAL STUDIES
HOME EC. JAPANESE P.E.
MUSIC
ETHICS
CLUB
BANNER: ICE HOCKEY CLUB 1988 NATIONAL CHAMPIONS
I HEAR THE BOYS ARE GONNA RACE EACH OTHER ONE-ON-ONE IN P.E.
きゅっ
GYU (PULL)
HUH...
THIS SHOULD BE FUN!
WELL, I'M SURE EITHER HAMADA OR KENYA...
...WILL GET THE FASTEST TIME.
EEEE!
SQUEE!
I GUESS.
HA-MADA-KUN!
EEE!
EEE!
HAMADA, DO YOUR BEST!
SHUT UP ALREADY...
GO, ICE HOCKEY TEAM!

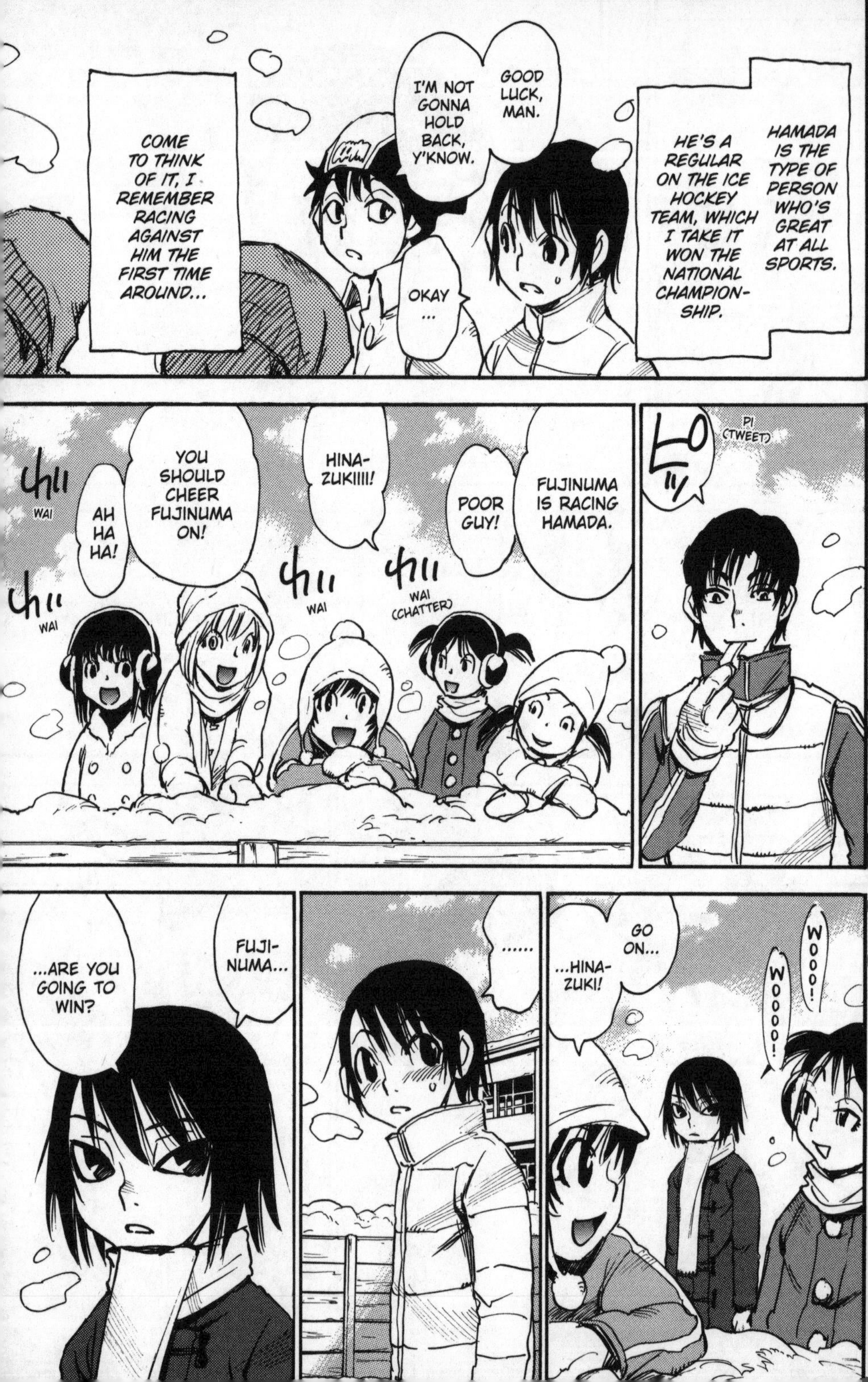
HAMADA IS THE TYPE OF PERSON WHO'S GREAT AT ALL SPORTS.
HE'S A REGULAR ON THE ICE HOCKEY TEAM, WHICH I TAKE IT WON THE NATIONAL CHAMPION-SHIP.
GOOD LUCK, MAN.
I'M NOT GONNA HOLD BACK, Y'KNOW.
OKAY...
COME TO THINK OF IT, I REMEMBER RACING AGAINST HIM THE FIRST TIME AROUND...
ピッ
PI (TWEET)
FUJINUMA IS RACING HAMADA.
POOR GUY!
HINA-ZUKIIII!
YOU SHOULD CHEER FUJINUMA ON!
AH HA HA!
わい
WAI (CHATTER)
わい
WAI
わい
WAI
わい
WAI
WOOOO!
WOOOO!
GO ON...
...HINA-ZUKI!
......
FUJI-NUMA...
...ARE YOU GOING TO WIN?

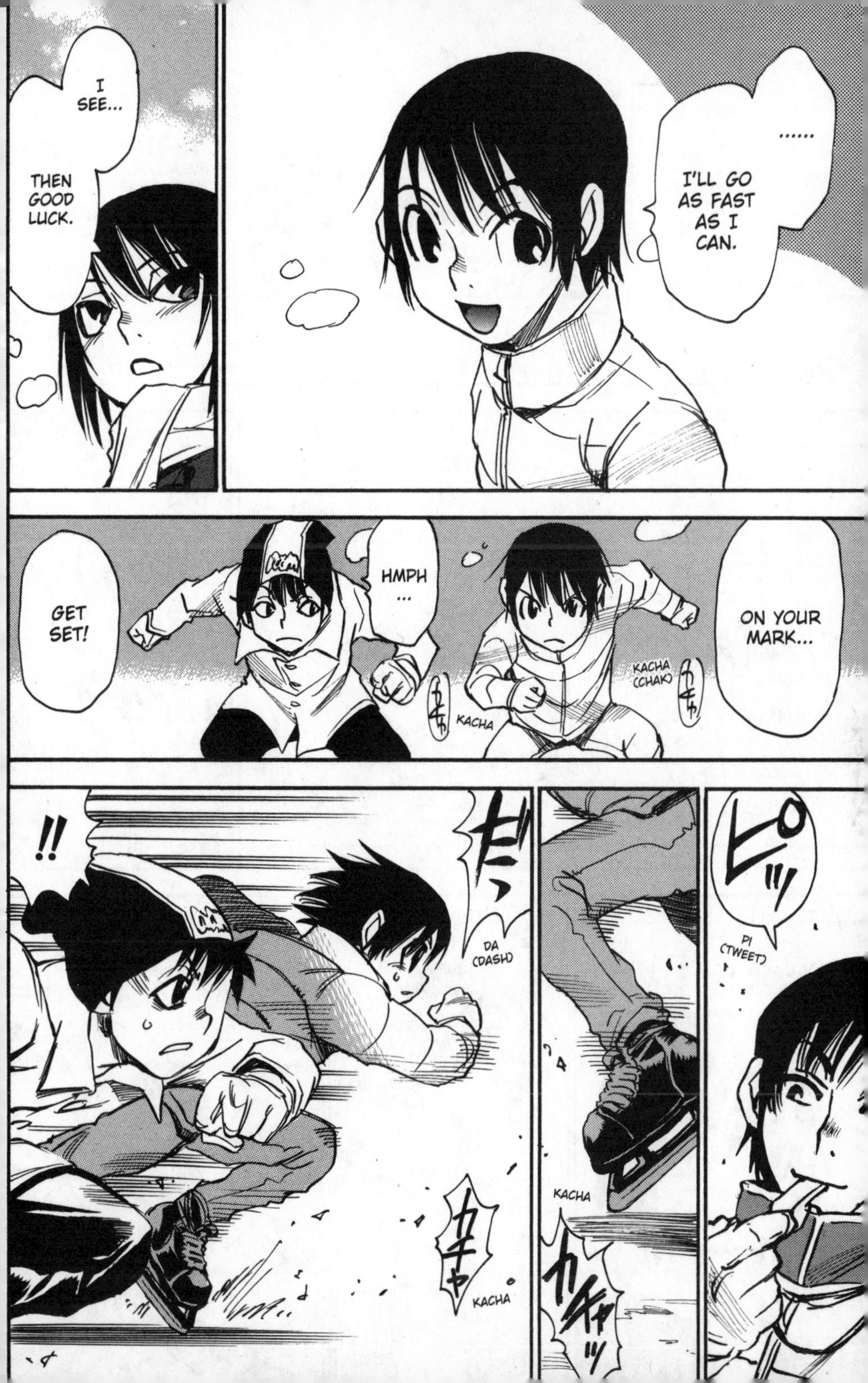
......
I'LL GO AS FAST AS I CAN.
I SEE...
THEN GOOD LUCK.
ON YOUR MARK...
KACHA (CHAK)
KACHA
HMPH ...
GET SET!
PI (TWEET)
KACHA
DA (DASH)
KACHA
!!

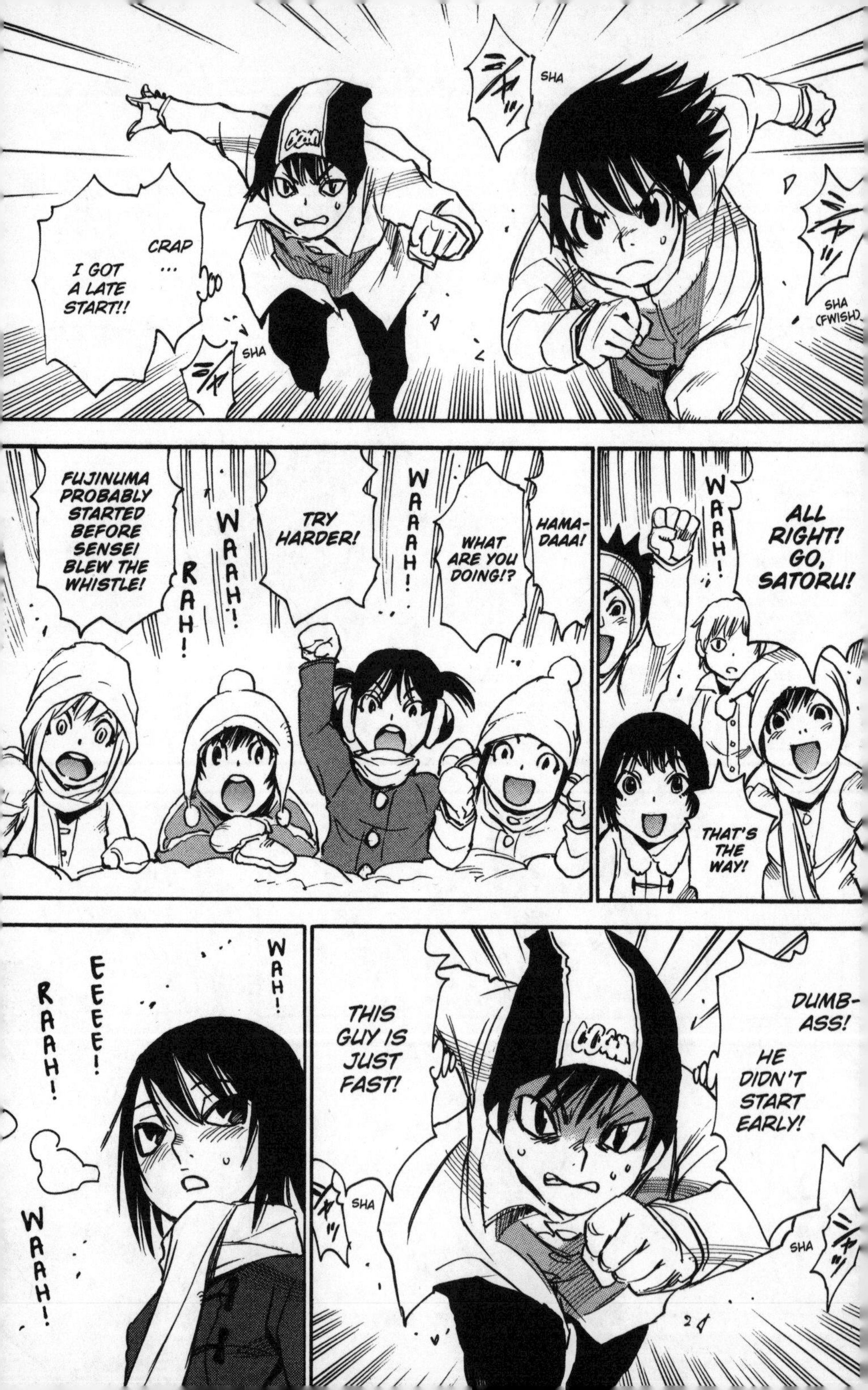
SHA
SHA (FWISH)
CRAP...
I GOT A LATE START!!
SHA
WAAH!
ALL RIGHT! GO, SATORU!
THAT'S THE WAY!
HAMA-DAAA!
WHAT ARE YOU DOING!?
WAAAAH!
TRY HARDER!
WAAH!
RAH!
FUJINUMA PROBABLY STARTED BEFORE SENSEI BLEW THE WHISTLE!
DUMB-ASS!
HE DIDN'T START EARLY!
THIS GUY IS JUST FAST!
SHA
SHA
WAH!
EEEE!
RAAAH!
WAAH!

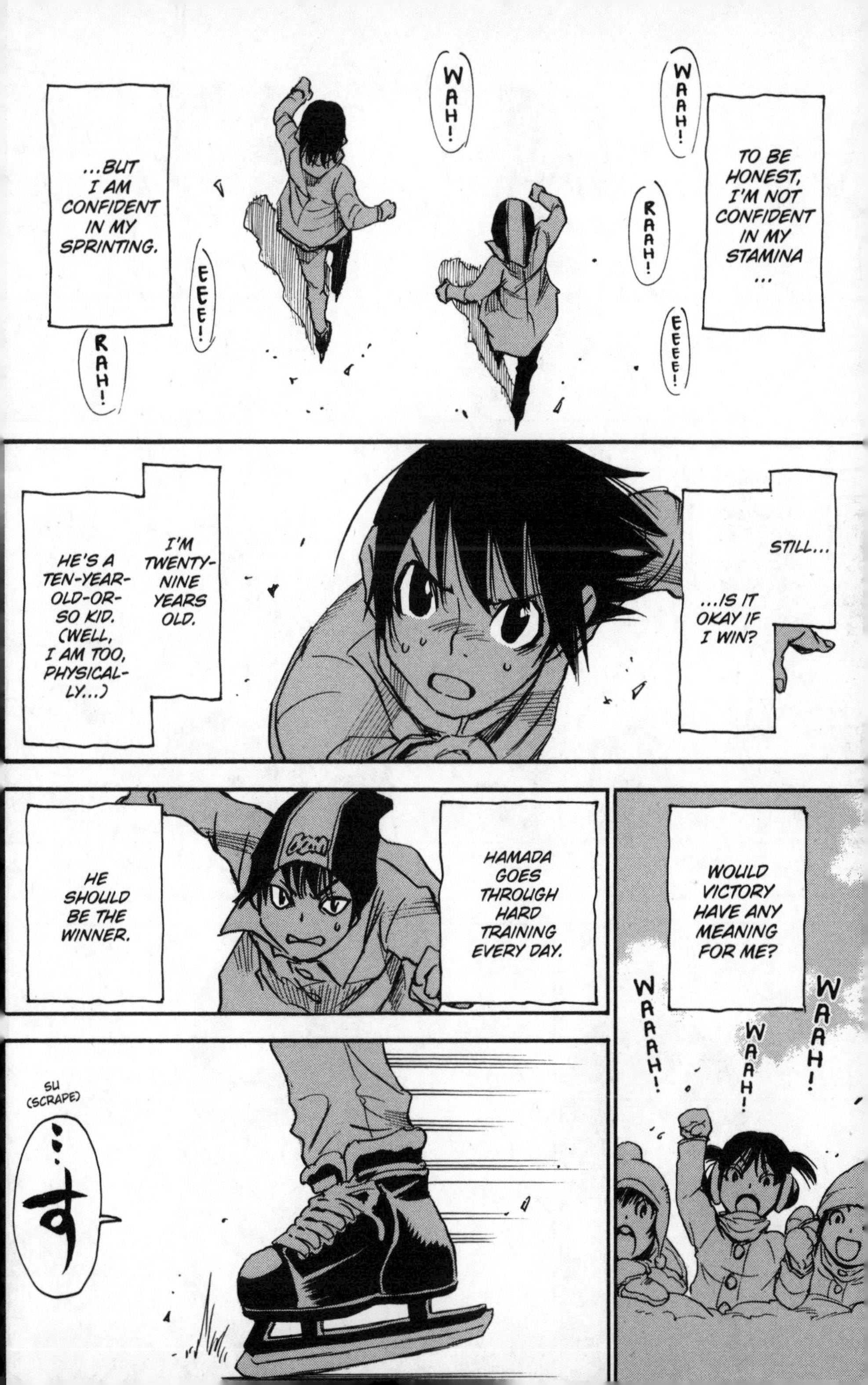
TO BE HONEST, I'M NOT CONFIDENT IN MY STAMINA ...
WAAAH!
RAAH!
EEEE!
WAH!
...BUT I AM CONFIDENT IN MY SPRINTING.
EEE!
RAH!
STILL...
...IS IT OKAY IF I WIN?
I'M TWENTY-NINE YEARS OLD.
HE'S A TEN-YEAR-OLD-OR-SO KID. (WELL, I AM TOO, PHYSICALLY...)
WOULD VICTORY HAVE ANY MEANING FOR ME?
WAAH!
WAAH!
WAAAH!
HAMADA GOES THROUGH HARD TRAINING EVERY DAY.
HE SHOULD BE THE WINNER.
す
SU (SCRAPE)

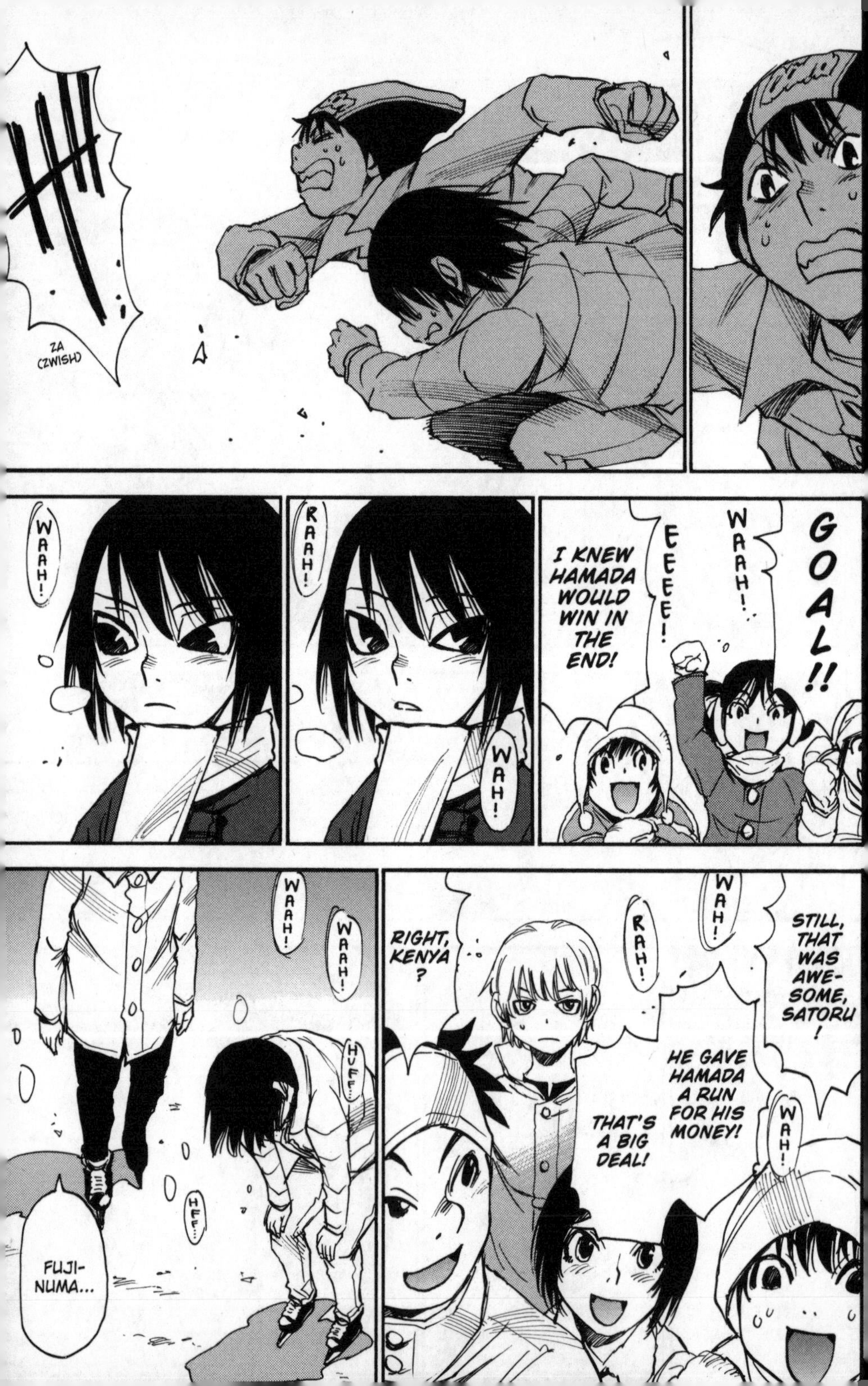
ZA (ZWISH)
GOAL!!
WAAH!
EEEE!
I KNEW HAMADA WOULD WIN IN THE END!
RAAH!
WAH!
WAAH!
STILL, THAT WAS AWESOME, SATORU!
WAH!
RAH!
RIGHT, KENYA?
HE GAVE HAMADA A RUN FOR HIS MONEY!
THAT'S A BIG DEAL!
WAH!
WAAH!
WAAH!
HUFF...
HFF...
FUJINUMA...

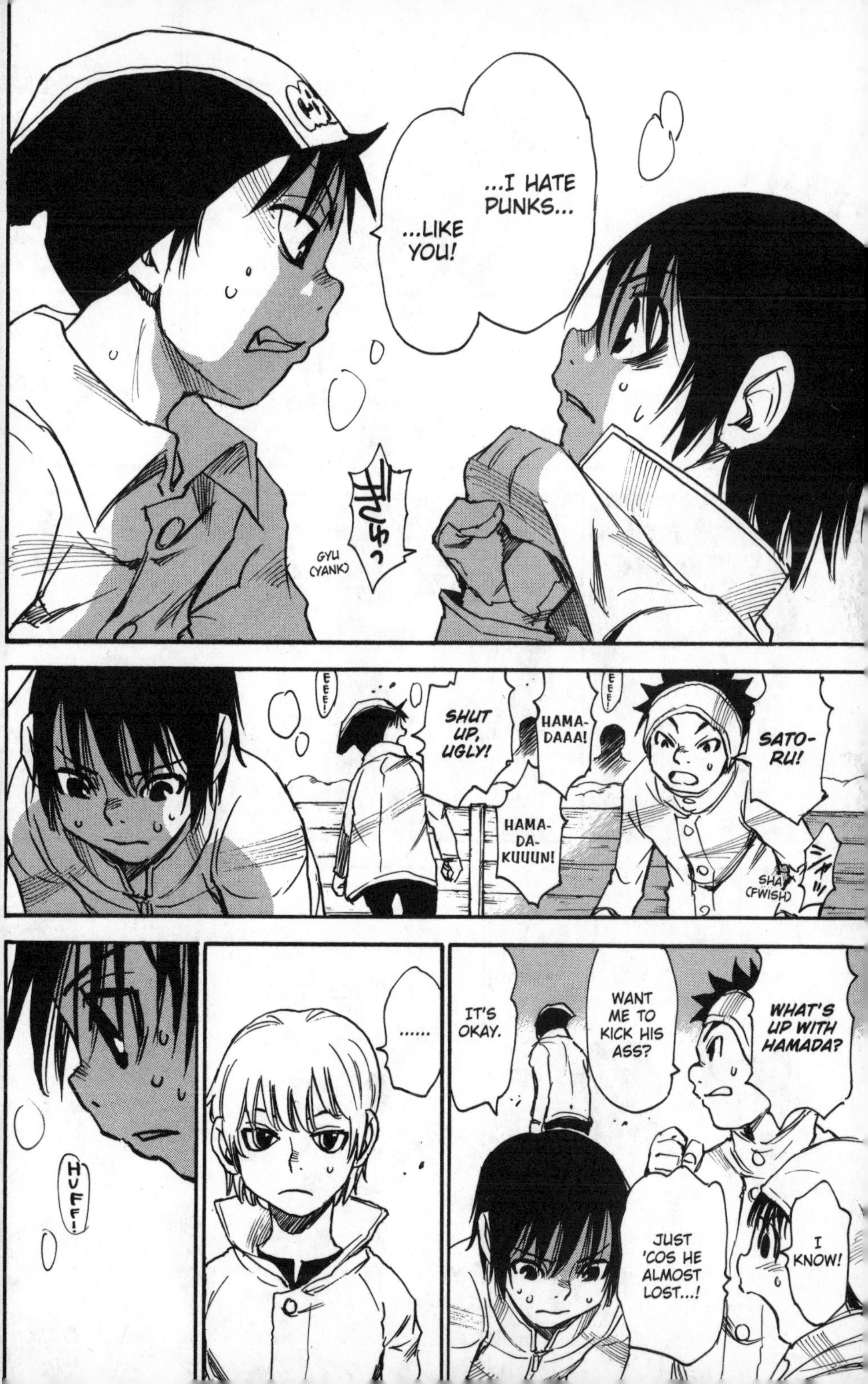
...I HATE PUNKS...
...LIKE YOU!
GYU (YANK)
SATO-RU!
SHA (FWISH)
HAMA-DAAA!
HAMA-DA-KUUUN!
SHUT UP, UGLY!
WHAT'S UP WITH HAMADA?
I KNOW!
WANT ME TO KICK HIS ASS?
JUST 'COS HE ALMOST LOST...!
IT'S OKAY.
......
HUFF!

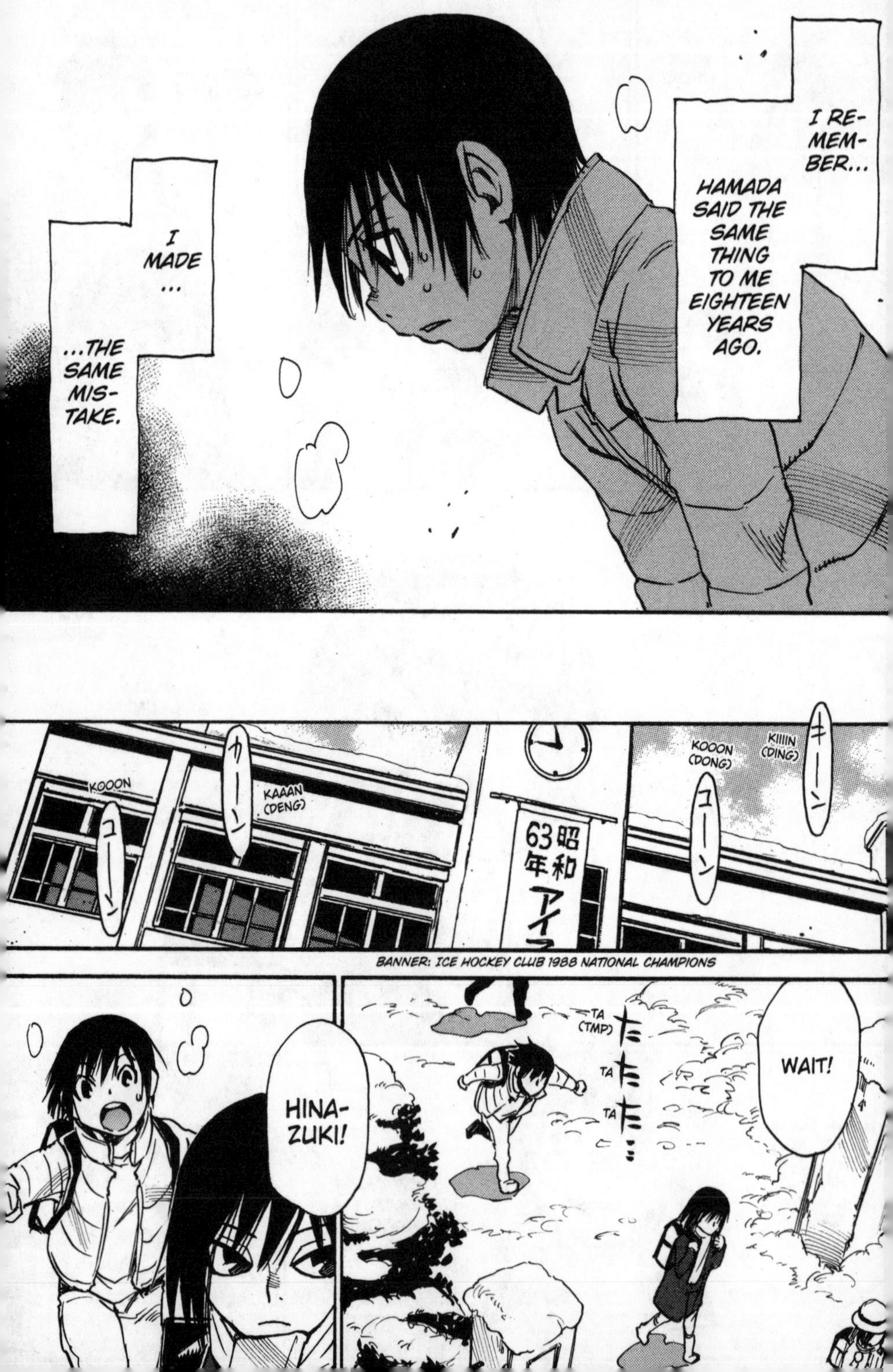
I RE-MEM-BER...
HAMADA SAID THE SAME THING TO ME EIGHTEEN YEARS AGO.
I MADE...
...THE SAME MIS-TAKE.
キーン
KIIIN (DING)
コーン
KOOON (DONG)
カーン
KAAAN (DENG)
コーン
KOOON
BANNER: ICE HOCKEY CLUB 1988 NATIONAL CHAMPIONS
WAIT!
たたた
TA (TMP) TA TA
HINA-ZUKI!

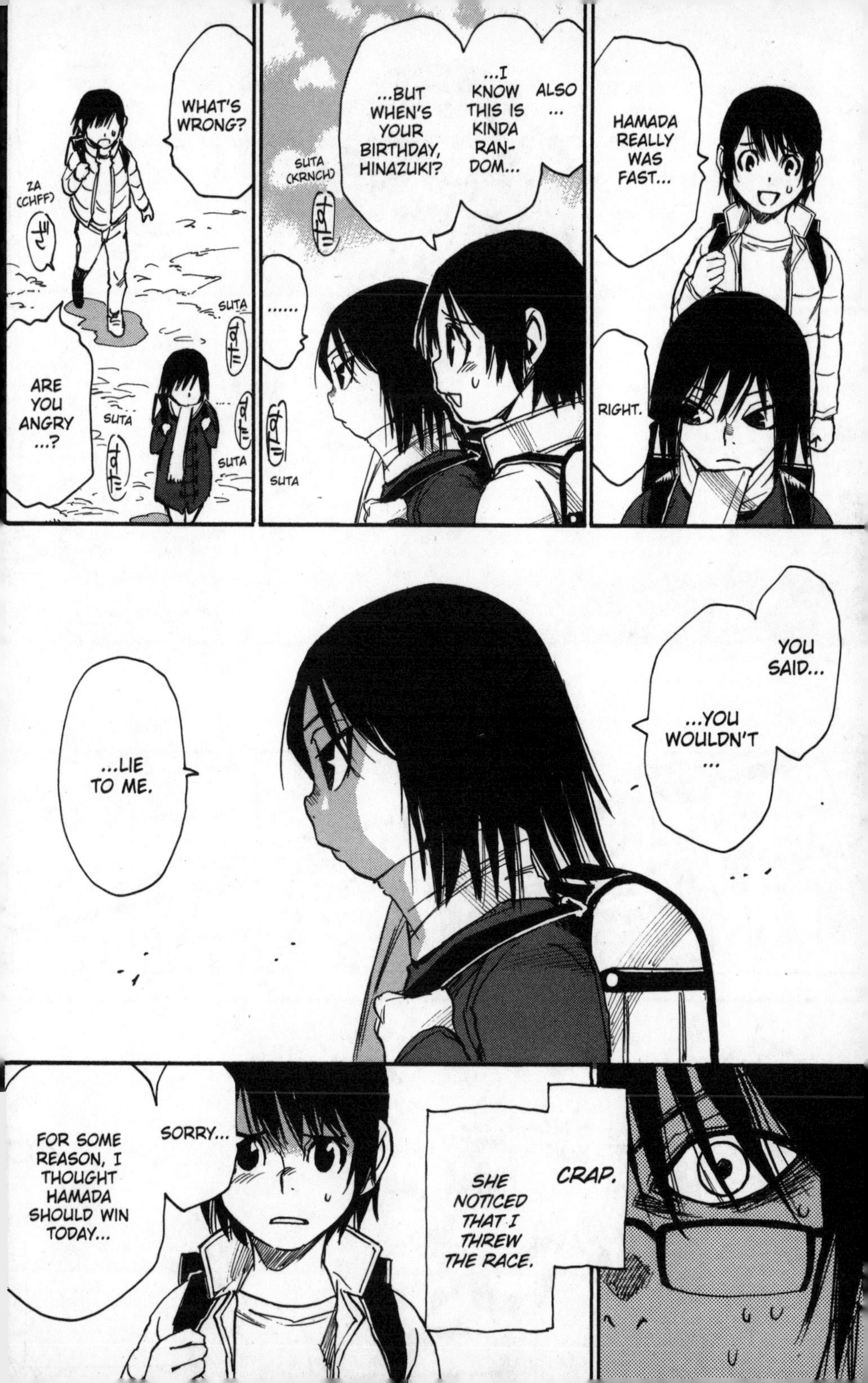
HAMADA REALLY WAS FAST...
RIGHT.
ALSO ...
...I KNOW THIS IS KINDA RAN-DOM...
...BUT WHEN'S YOUR BIRTHDAY, HINAZUKI?
SUTA (KRNCH)
......
SUTA
WHAT'S WRONG?
ZA (CHFF)
SUTA
...
SUTA
SUTA
ARE YOU ANGRY ...?
YOU SAID...
...YOU WOULDN'T ...
...LIE TO ME.
CRAP.
SHE NOTICED THAT I THREW THE RACE.
SORRY...
FOR SOME REASON, I THOUGHT HAMADA SHOULD WIN TODAY...

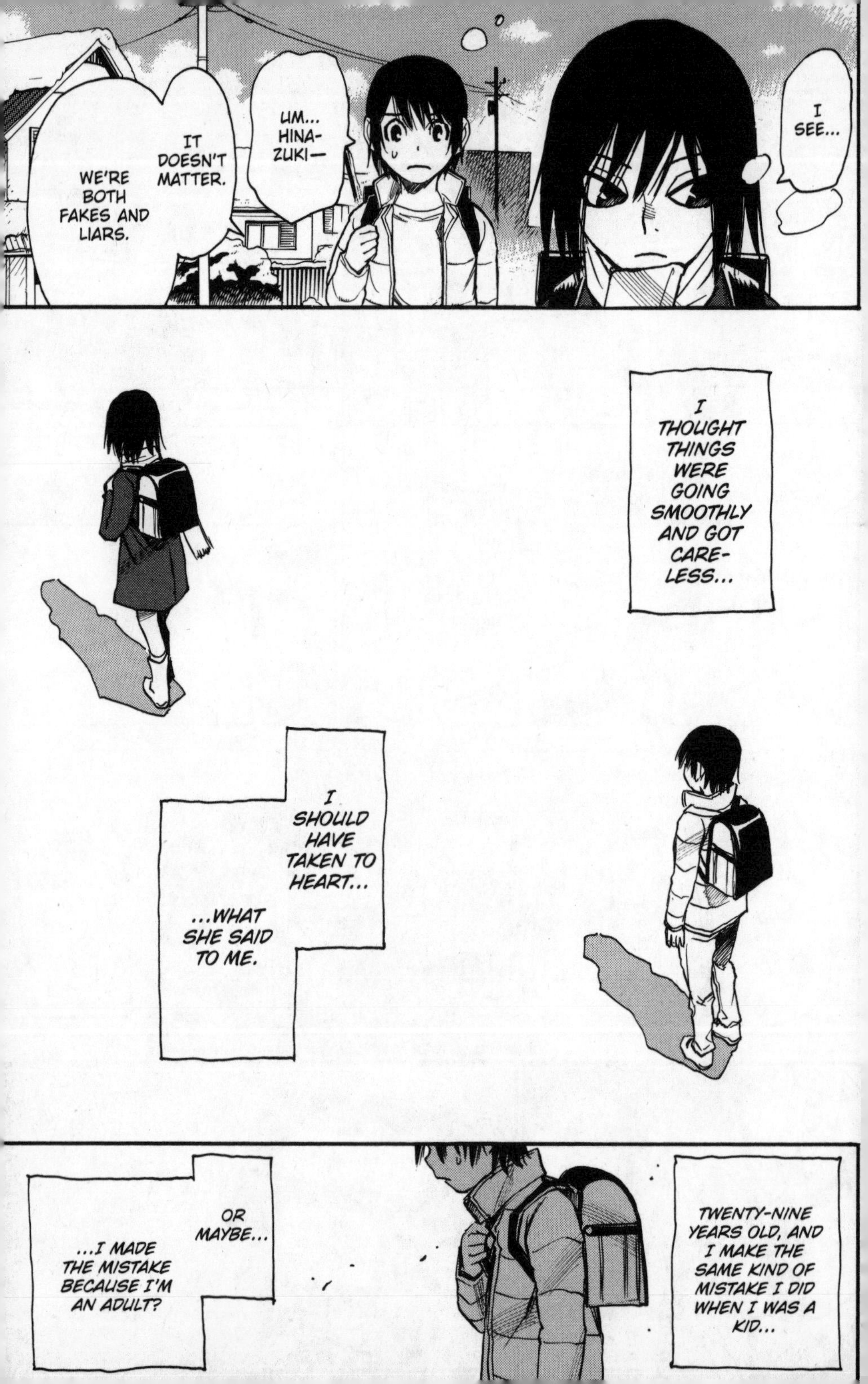
I SEE...
UM... HINA-ZUKI—
IT DOESN'T MATTER.
WE'RE BOTH FAKES AND LIARS.
I THOUGHT THINGS WERE GOING SMOOTHLY AND GOT CARE-LESS...
I SHOULD HAVE TAKEN TO HEART...
...WHAT SHE SAID TO ME.
TWENTY-NINE YEARS OLD, AND I MAKE THE SAME KIND OF MISTAKE I DID WHEN I WAS A KID...
OR MAYBE...
...I MADE THE MISTAKE BECAUSE I'M AN ADULT?

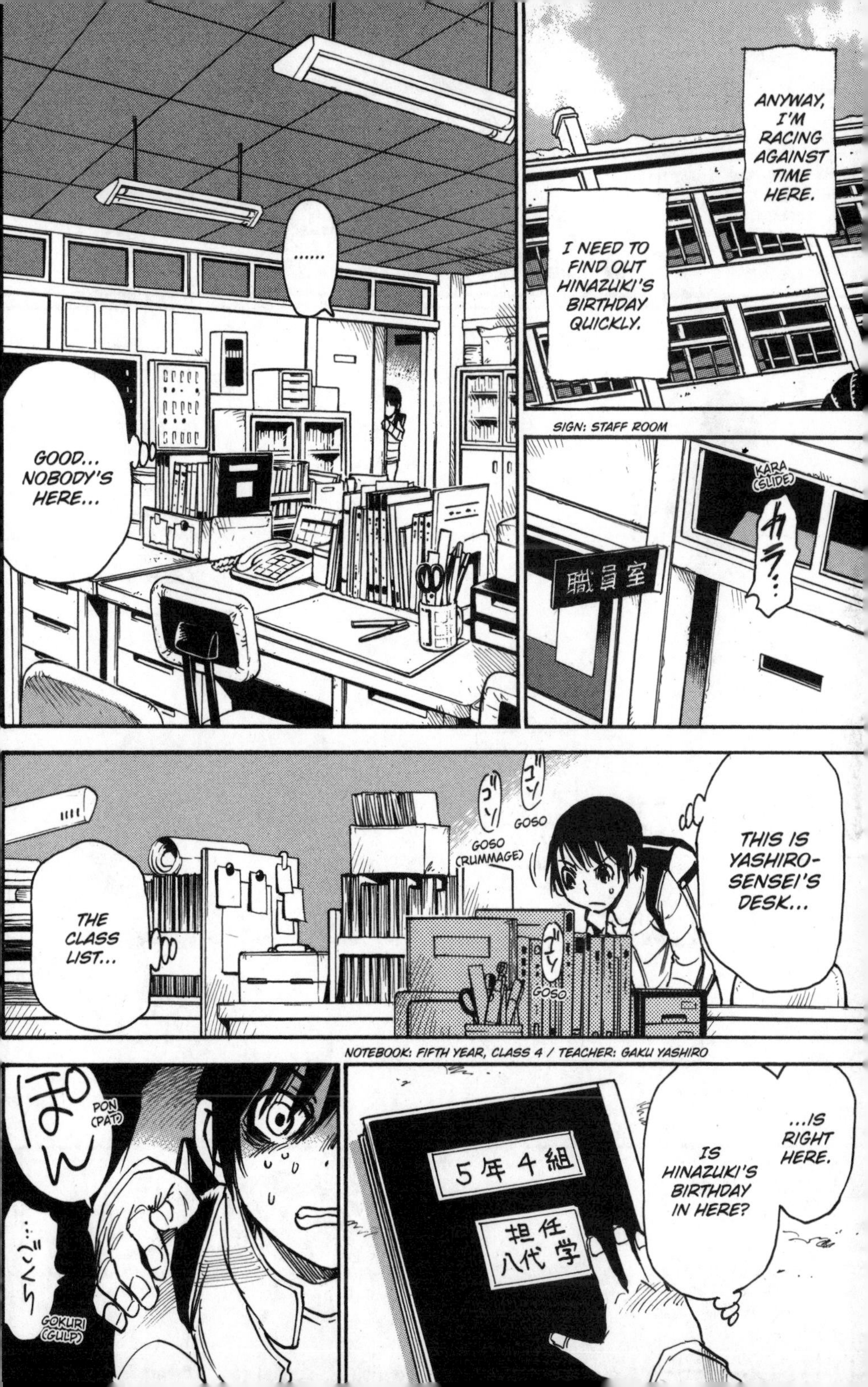
ANYWAY, I'M RACING AGAINST TIME HERE.
I NEED TO FIND OUT HINAZUKI'S BIRTHDAY QUICKLY.
SIGN: STAFF ROOM
職員室
カラ…
KARA (SLIDE)
......
GOOD... NOBODY'S HERE...
THIS IS YASHIRO-SENSEI'S DESK...
ゴソ
GOSO
ゴソ
GOSO (RUMMAGE)
ゴソ
GOSO
THE CLASS LIST...
NOTEBOOK: FIFTH YEAR, CLASS 4 / TEACHER: GAKU YASHIRO
...IS RIGHT HERE.
IS HINAZUKI'S BIRTHDAY IN HERE?
5年4組
担任 八代学
ぽん
PON (PAT)
ごくり…
GOKURI (GULP)

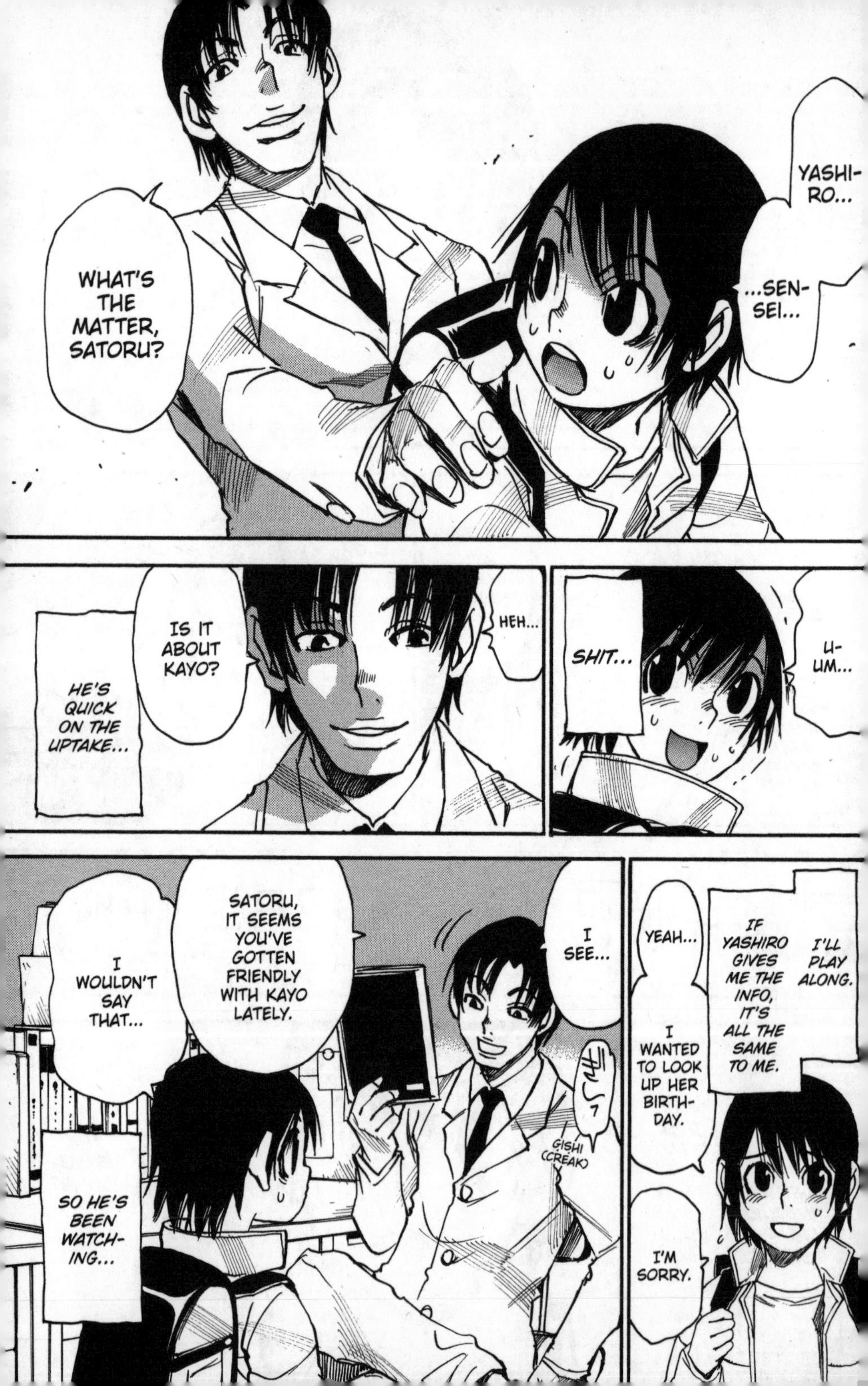
YASHIRO...
...SENSEI...
WHAT'S THE MATTER, SATORU?
U-UM...
SHIT...
HEH...
IS IT ABOUT KAYO?
HE'S QUICK ON THE UPTAKE...
I'LL PLAY ALONG.
IF YASHIRO GIVES ME THE INFO, IT'S ALL THE SAME TO ME.
YEAH...
I WANTED TO LOOK UP HER BIRTHDAY.
I'M SORRY.
I SEE...
GISHI (CREAK)
SATORU, IT SEEMS YOU'VE GOTTEN FRIENDLY WITH KAYO LATELY.
I WOULDN'T SAY THAT...
SO HE'S BEEN WATCHING...

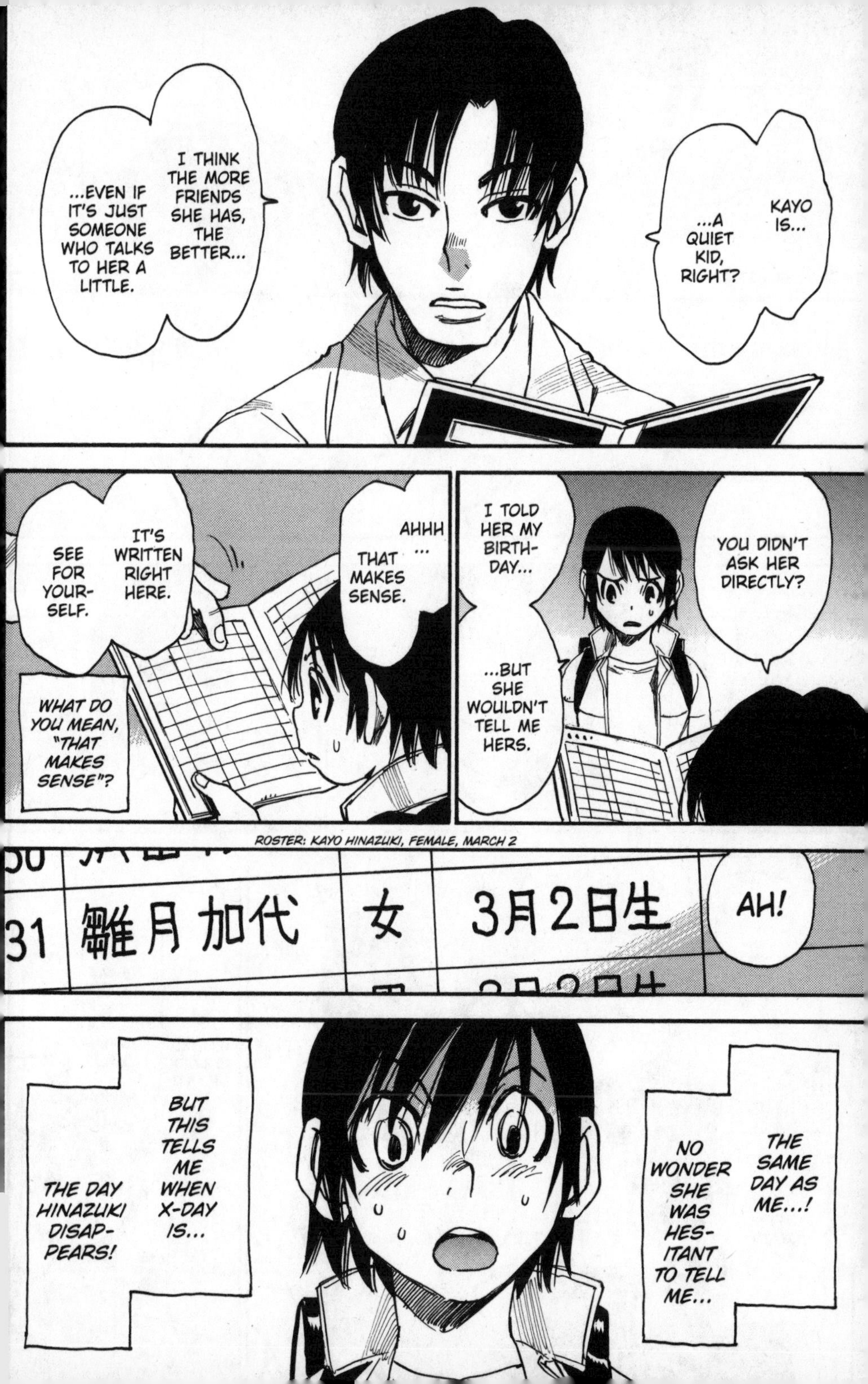
KAYO IS...
...A QUIET KID, RIGHT?
I THINK THE MORE FRIENDS SHE HAS, THE BETTER...
...EVEN IF IT'S JUST SOMEONE WHO TALKS TO HER A LITTLE.
YOU DIDN'T ASK HER DIRECTLY?
I TOLD HER MY BIRTH-DAY...
...BUT SHE WOULDN'T TELL ME HERS.
AHHH... THAT MAKES SENSE.
WHAT DO YOU MEAN, "THAT MAKES SENSE"?
IT'S WRITTEN RIGHT HERE.
SEE FOR YOUR-SELF.
AH!
31 雛月加代 女 3月2日生
ROSTER: KAYO HINAZUKI, FEMALE, MARCH 2
THE SAME DAY AS ME...!
NO WONDER SHE WAS HES-ITANT TO TELL ME...
BUT THIS TELLS ME WHEN X-DAY IS...
THE DAY HINAZUKI DISAP-PEARS!

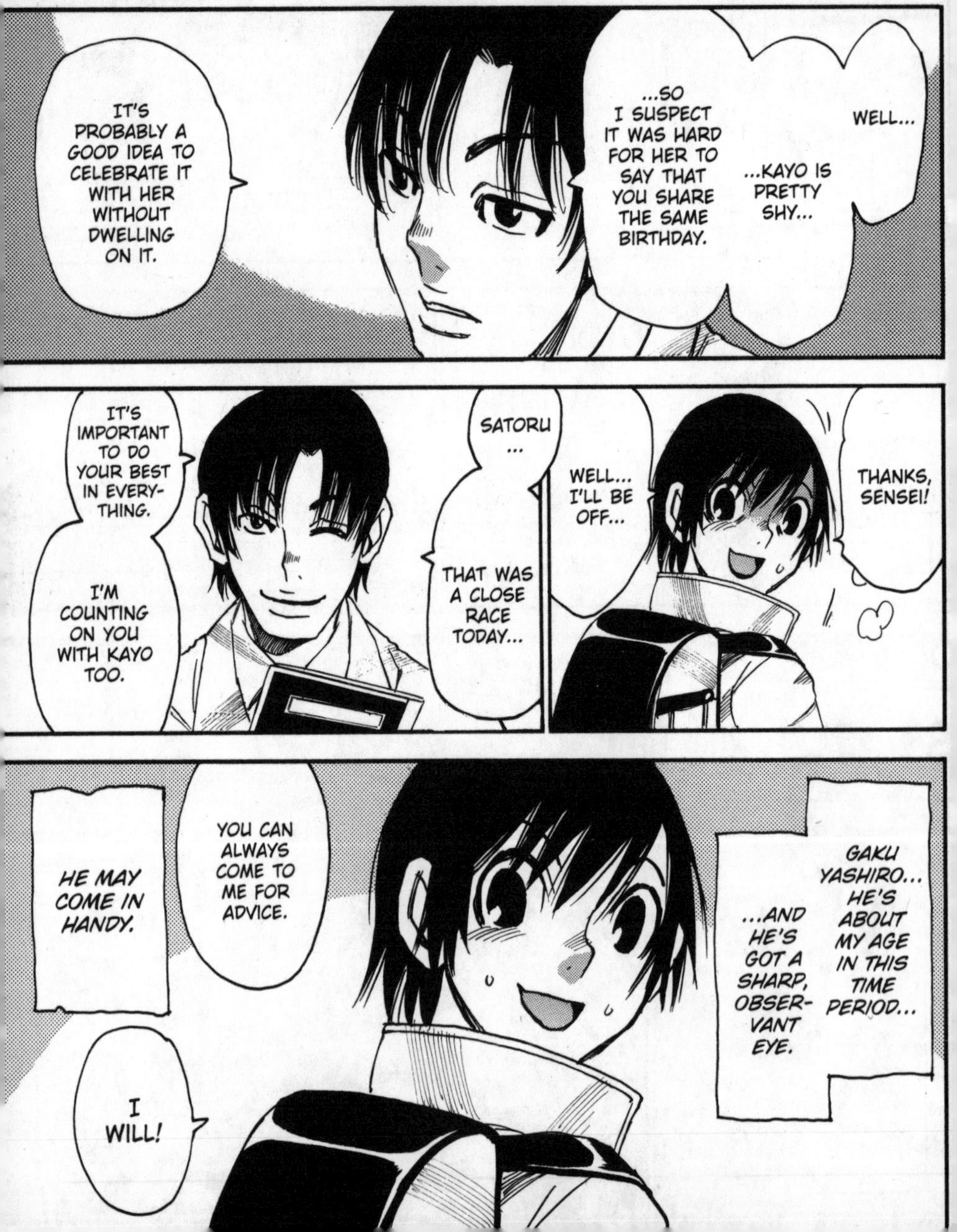
WELL...
...KAYO IS PRETTY SHY...
...SO I SUSPECT IT WAS HARD FOR HER TO SAY THAT YOU SHARE THE SAME BIRTHDAY.
IT'S PROBABLY A GOOD IDEA TO CELEBRATE IT WITH HER WITHOUT DWELLING ON IT.
THANKS, SENSEI!
WELL... I'LL BE OFF...
SATORU...
THAT WAS A CLOSE RACE TODAY...
IT'S IMPORTANT TO DO YOUR BEST IN EVERY-THING.
I'M COUNTING ON YOU WITH KAYO TOO.
GAKU YASHIRO... HE'S ABOUT MY AGE IN THIS TIME PERIOD...
...AND HE'S GOT A SHARP, OBSERVANT EYE.
YOU CAN ALWAYS COME TO ME FOR ADVICE.
HE MAY COME IN HANDY.
I WILL!

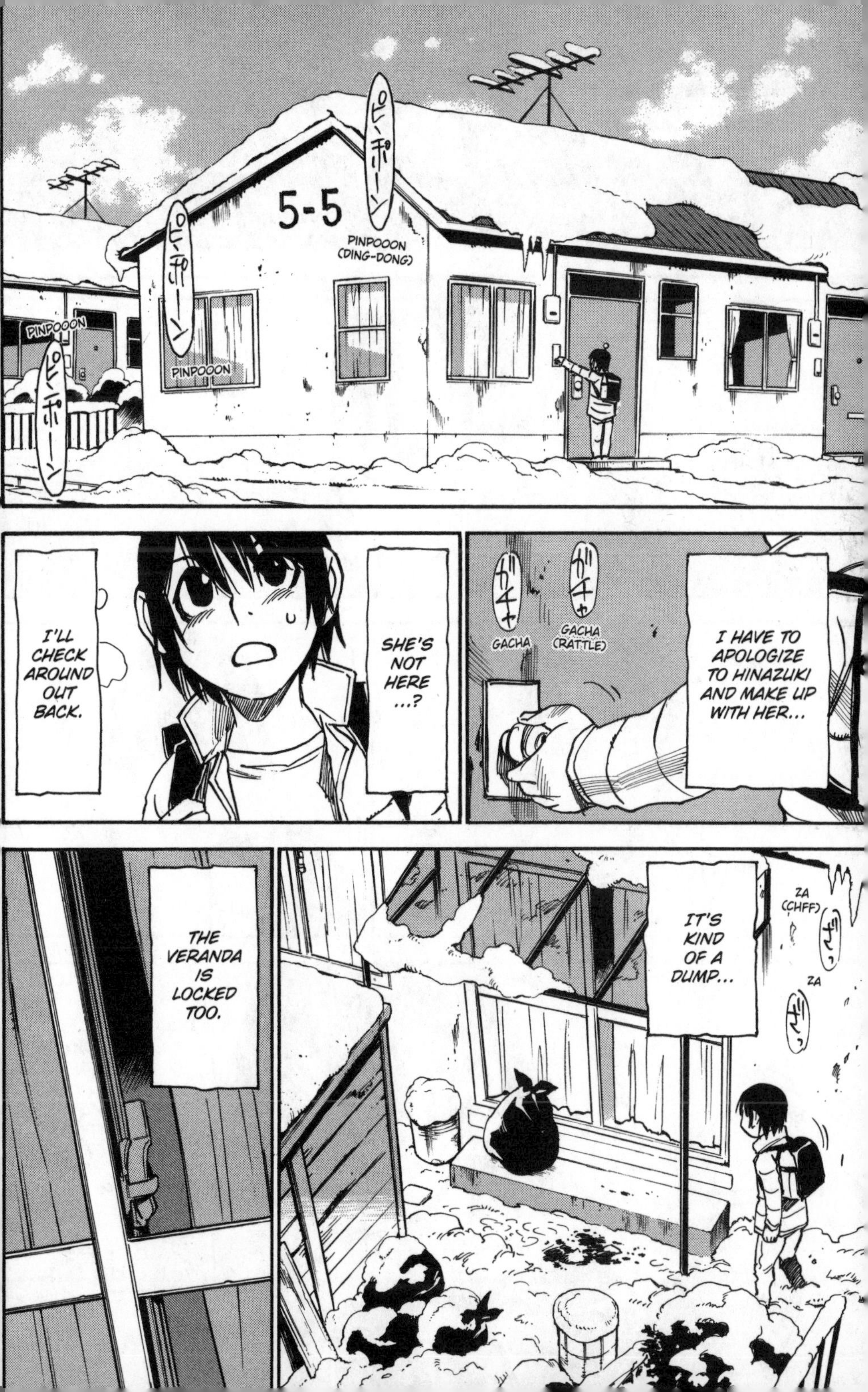

5-5
ピンポーン
PINPOOON (DING-DONG)
ピンポーン
PINPOOON
PINPOOON
ピンポーン
I HAVE TO APOLOGIZE TO HINAZUKI AND MAKE UP WITH HER...
ガチャ
GACHA (RATTLE)
ガチャ
GACHA
SHE'S NOT HERE ...?
I'LL CHECK AROUND OUT BACK.
ざっ
ZA (CHFF)
ざっ
ZA
IT'S KIND OF A DUMP...
THE VERANDA IS LOCKED TOO.

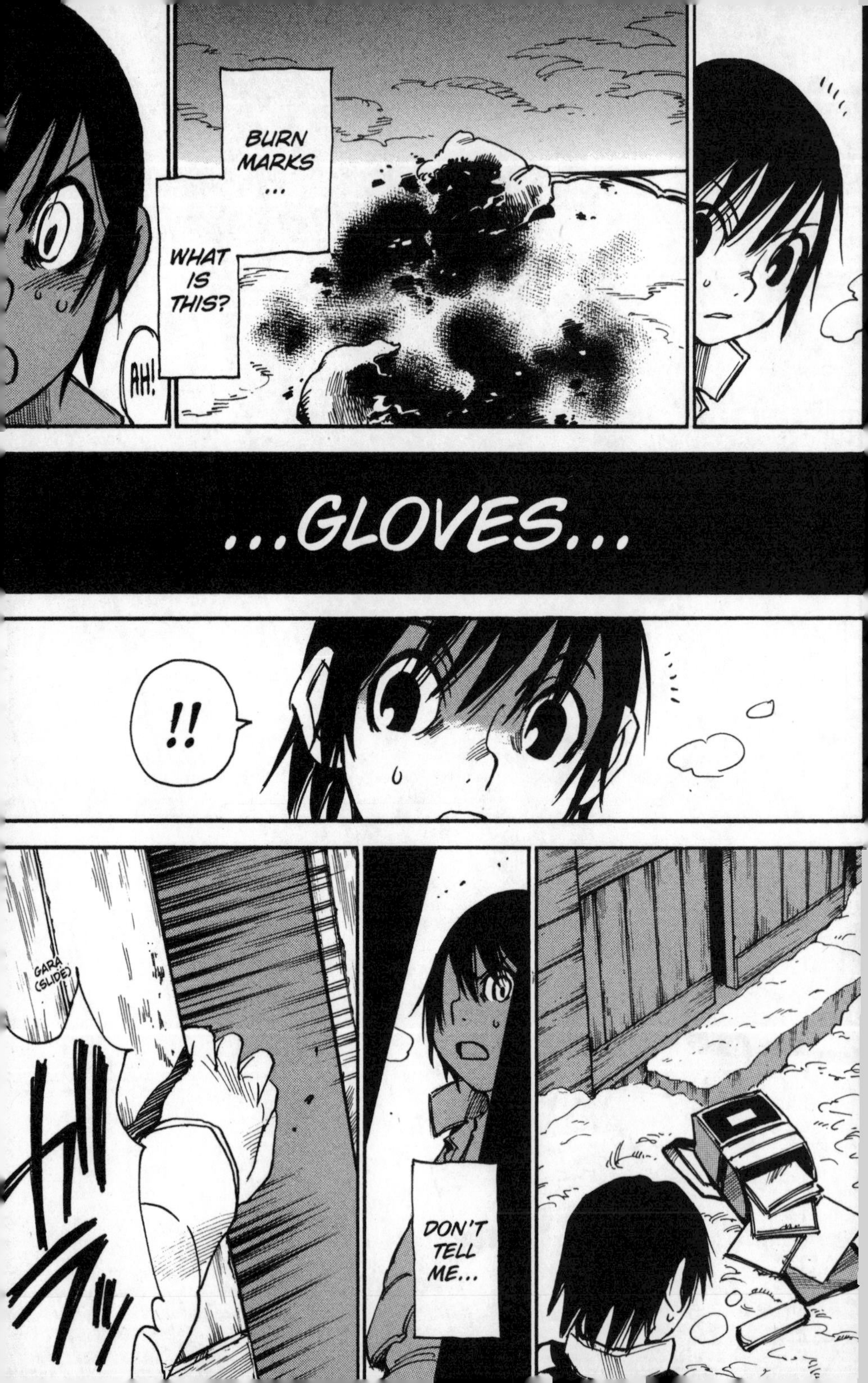
BURN MARKS ...
WHAT IS THIS?
AH!
...GLOVES...
!!
DON'T TELL ME...
GARA (SLIDE)

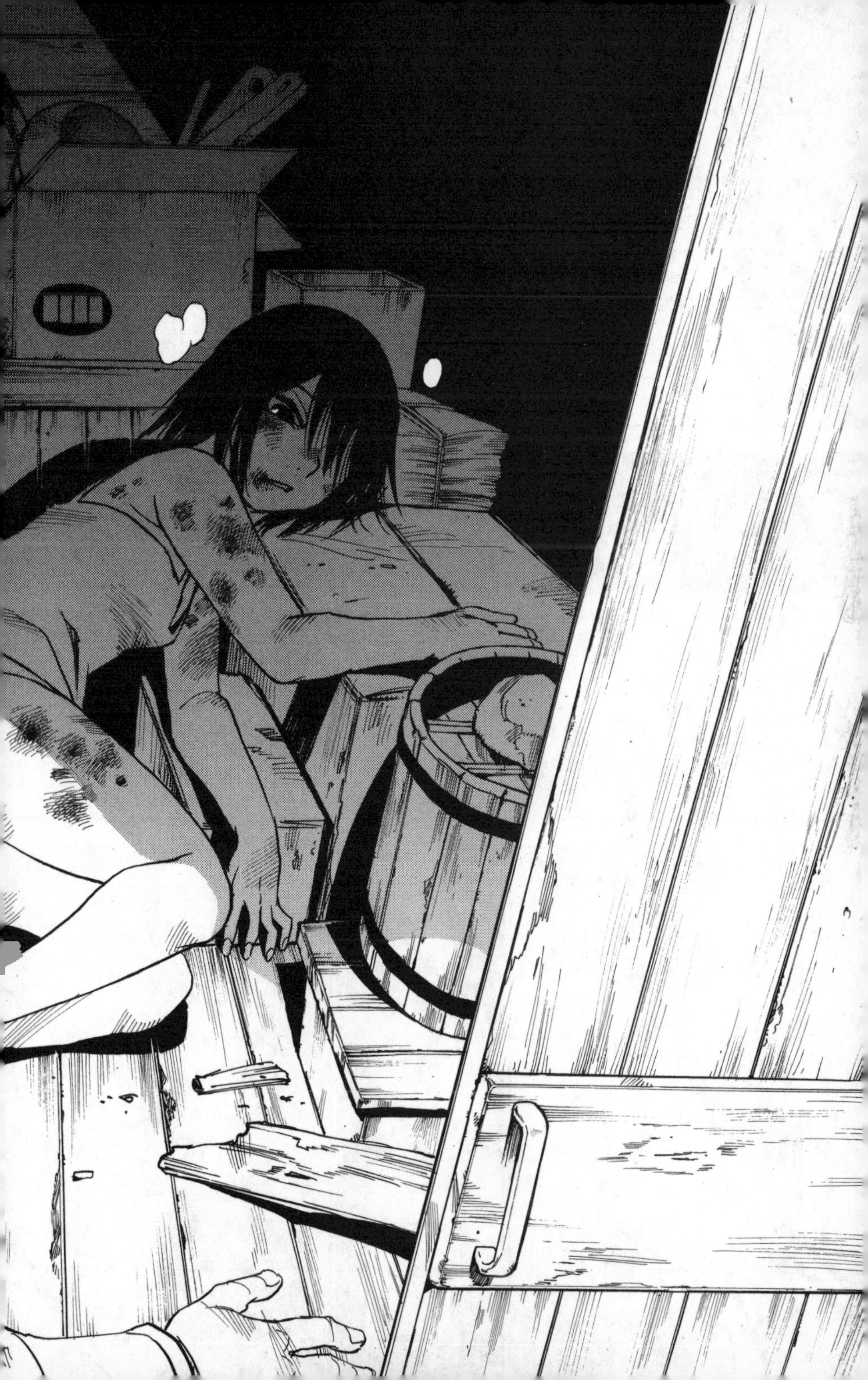

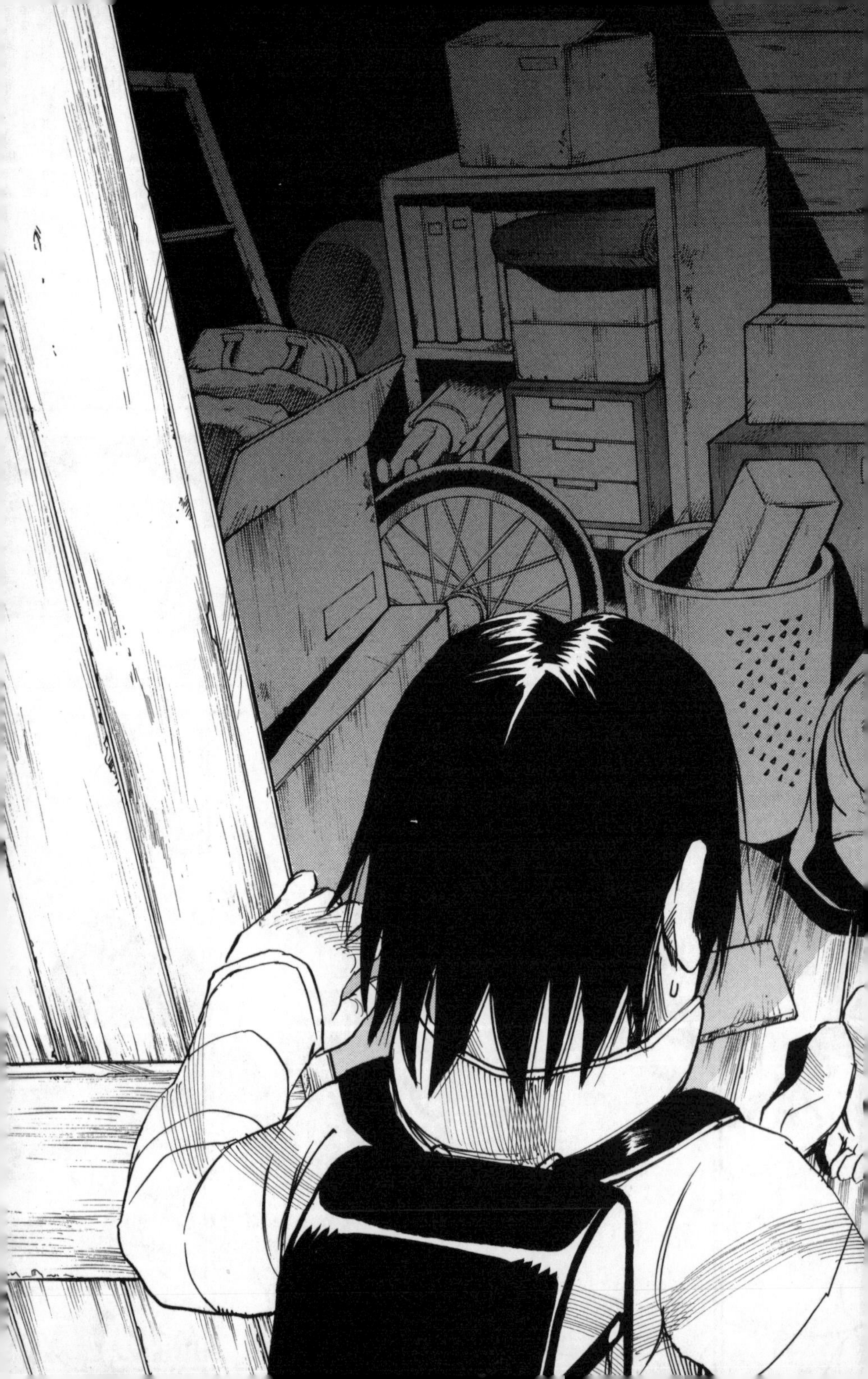

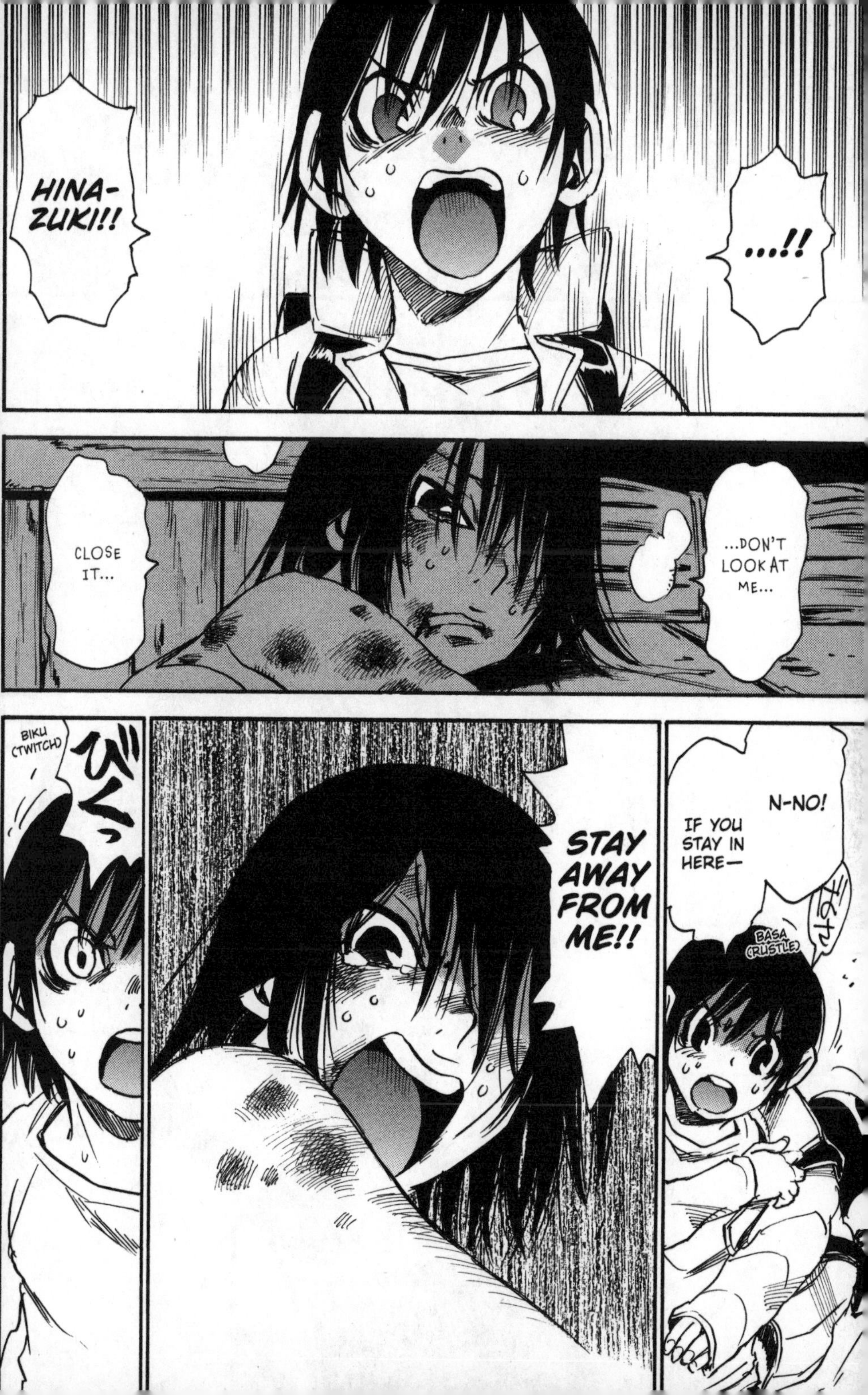
...!!
HINA-ZUKI!!
...DON'T LOOK AT ME...
CLOSE IT...
N-NO!
IF YOU STAY IN HERE—
BASA (RUSTLE)
STAY AWAY FROM ME!!
BIKU (TWITCH)

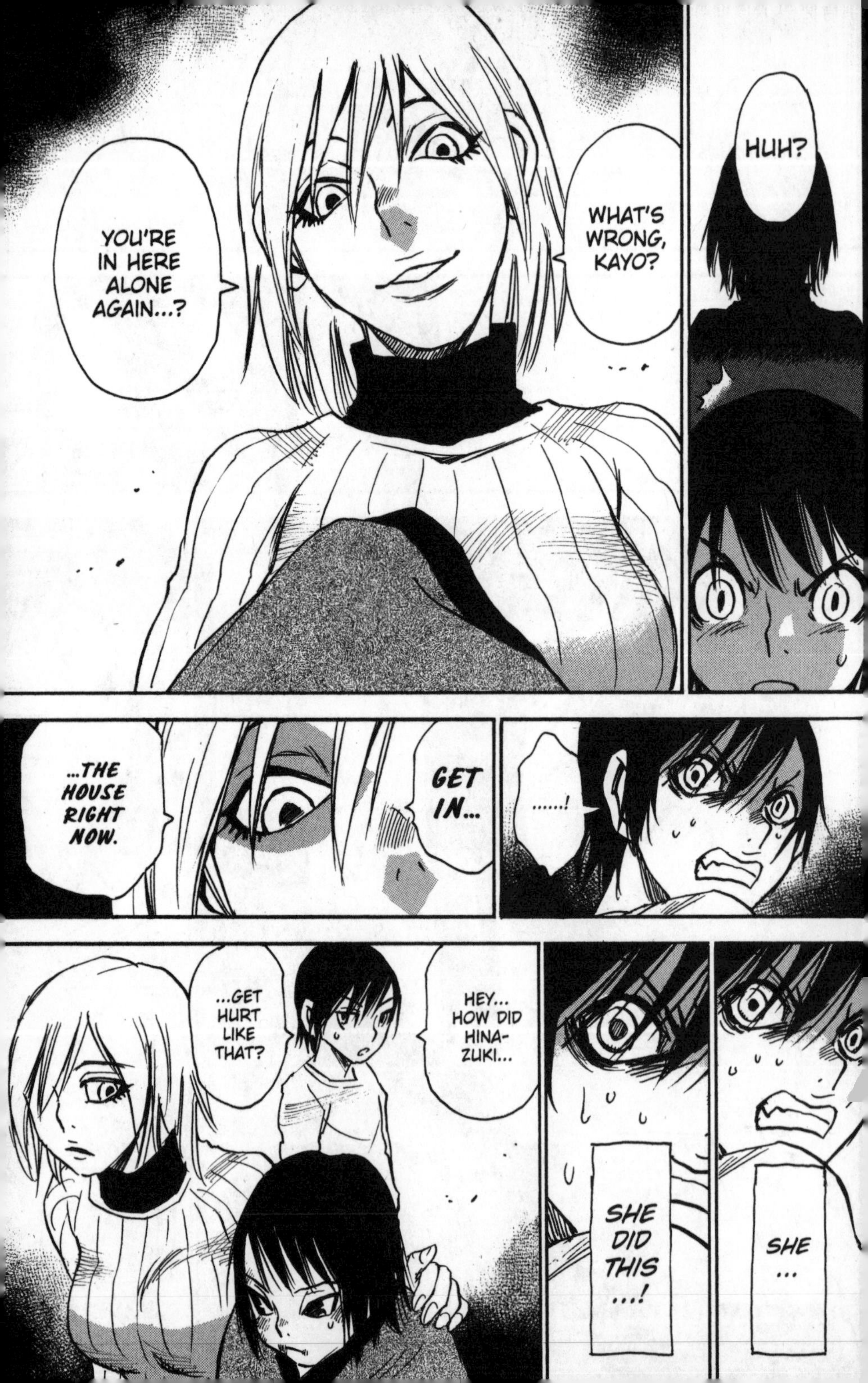
HUH?
WHAT'S WRONG, KAYO?
YOU'RE IN HERE ALONE AGAIN...?
......!
GET IN...
...THE HOUSE RIGHT NOW.
SHE ...
SHE DID THIS ...!
HEY... HOW DID HINA-ZUKI...
...GET HURT LIKE THAT?

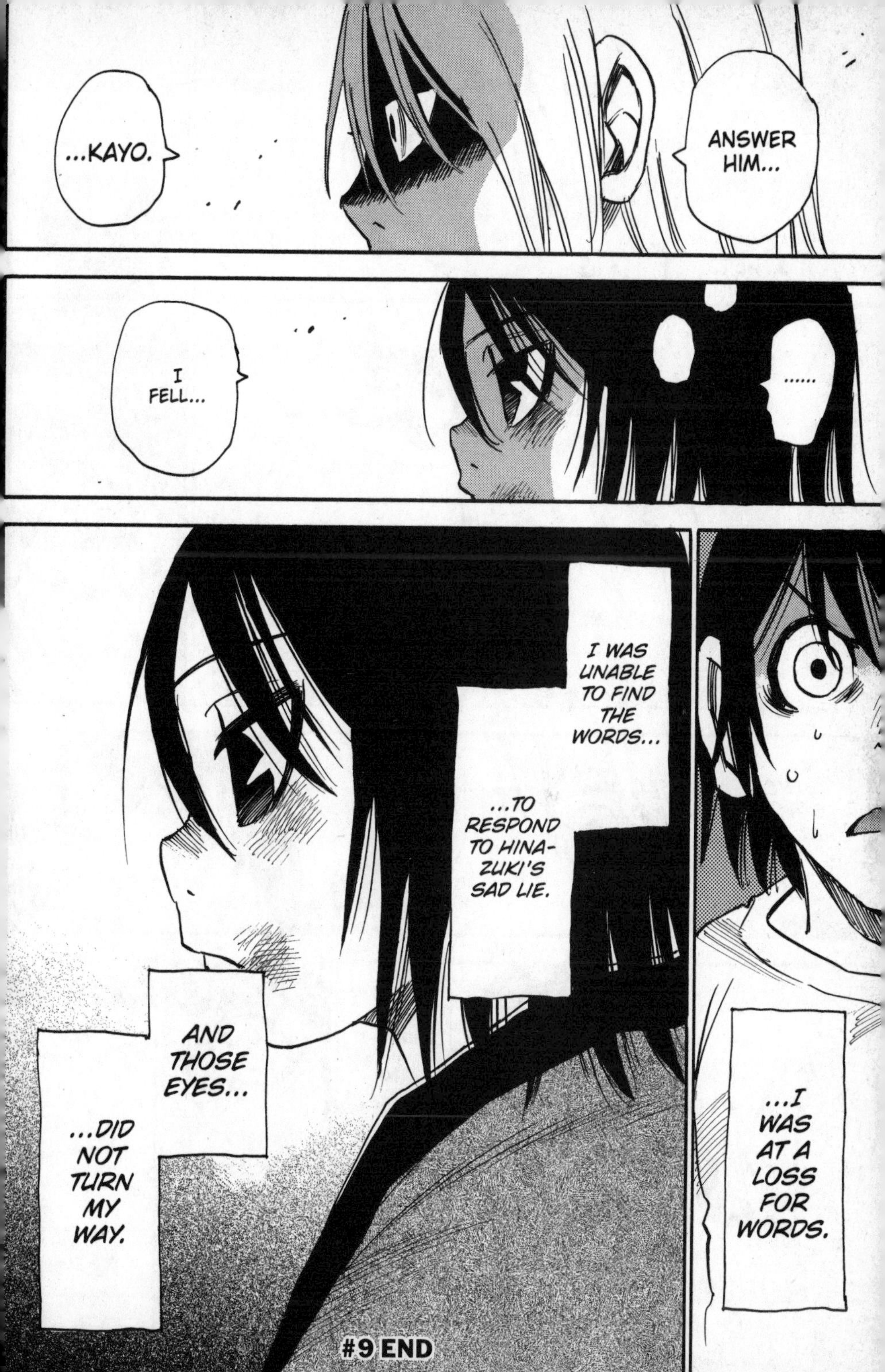
ANSWER HIM...
...KAYO.
......
I FELL...
...I WAS AT A LOSS FOR WORDS.
I WAS UNABLE TO FIND THE WORDS...
...TO RESPOND TO HINA-ZUKI'S SAD LIE.
AND THOSE EYES...
...DID NOT TURN MY WAY.

#9 END

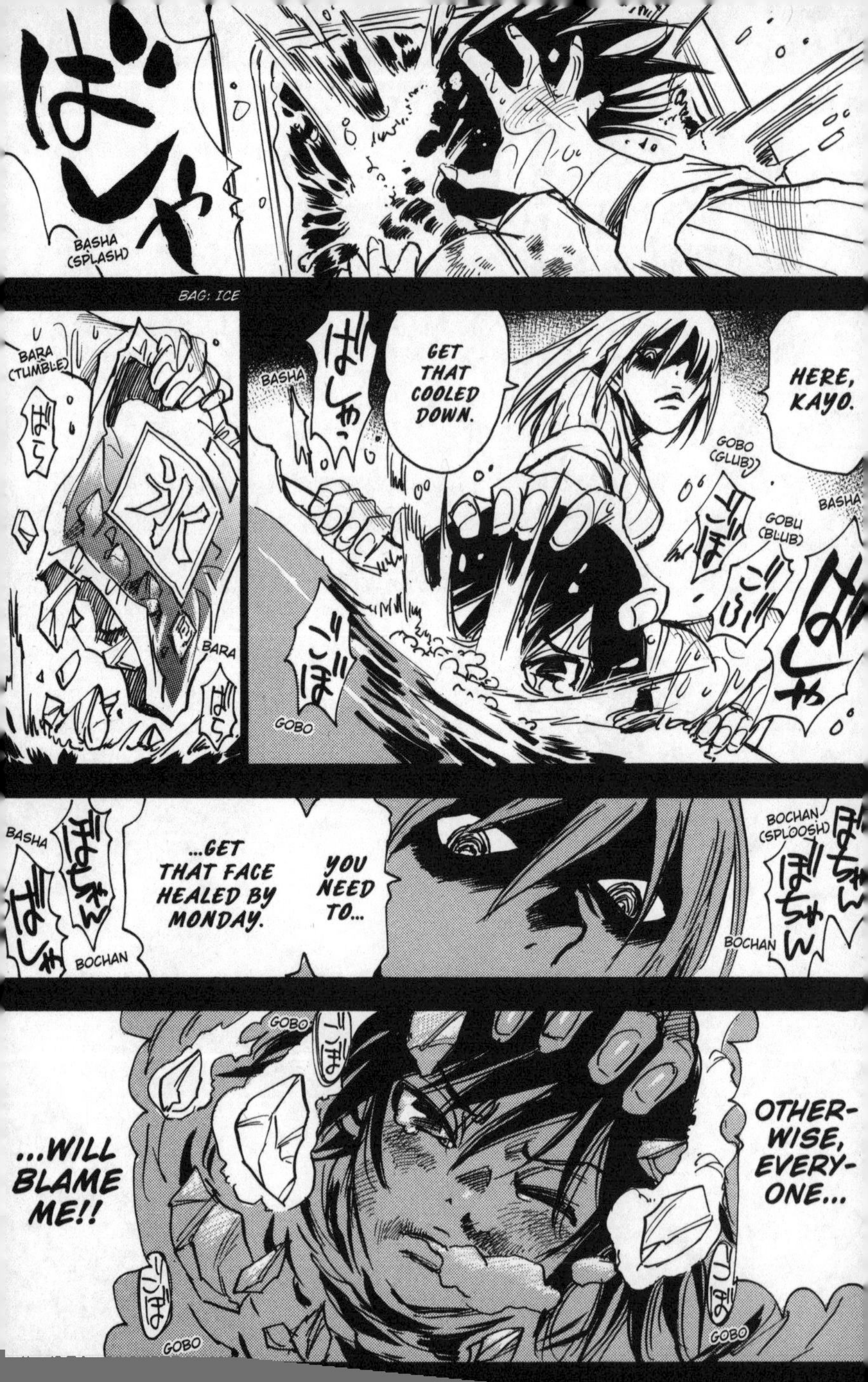
ばしゃ
BASHA (SPLASH)
HERE, KAYO.
BASHA
ばしゃっ
GOBO (GLUB)
ごぼ
GOBU (BLUB)
ごぶ
GET THAT COOLED DOWN.
BASHA
ばしゃっ
ごぼ
GOBO
BAG: ICE
氷
BARA (TUMBLE)
ばら
BARA
ばら
BOCHAN (SPLOOSH)
ぼちゃん
ぼちゃん
BOCHAN
YOU NEED TO...
...GET THAT FACE HEALED BY MONDAY.
BASHA
ばしゃ
ぼちゃん
BOCHAN
OTHER-WISE, EVERY-ONE...
...WILL BLAME ME!!
GOBO
ごぼ
ごぼ
GOBO
ごぼ
GOBO

#10: Christmas Tree, February 1988

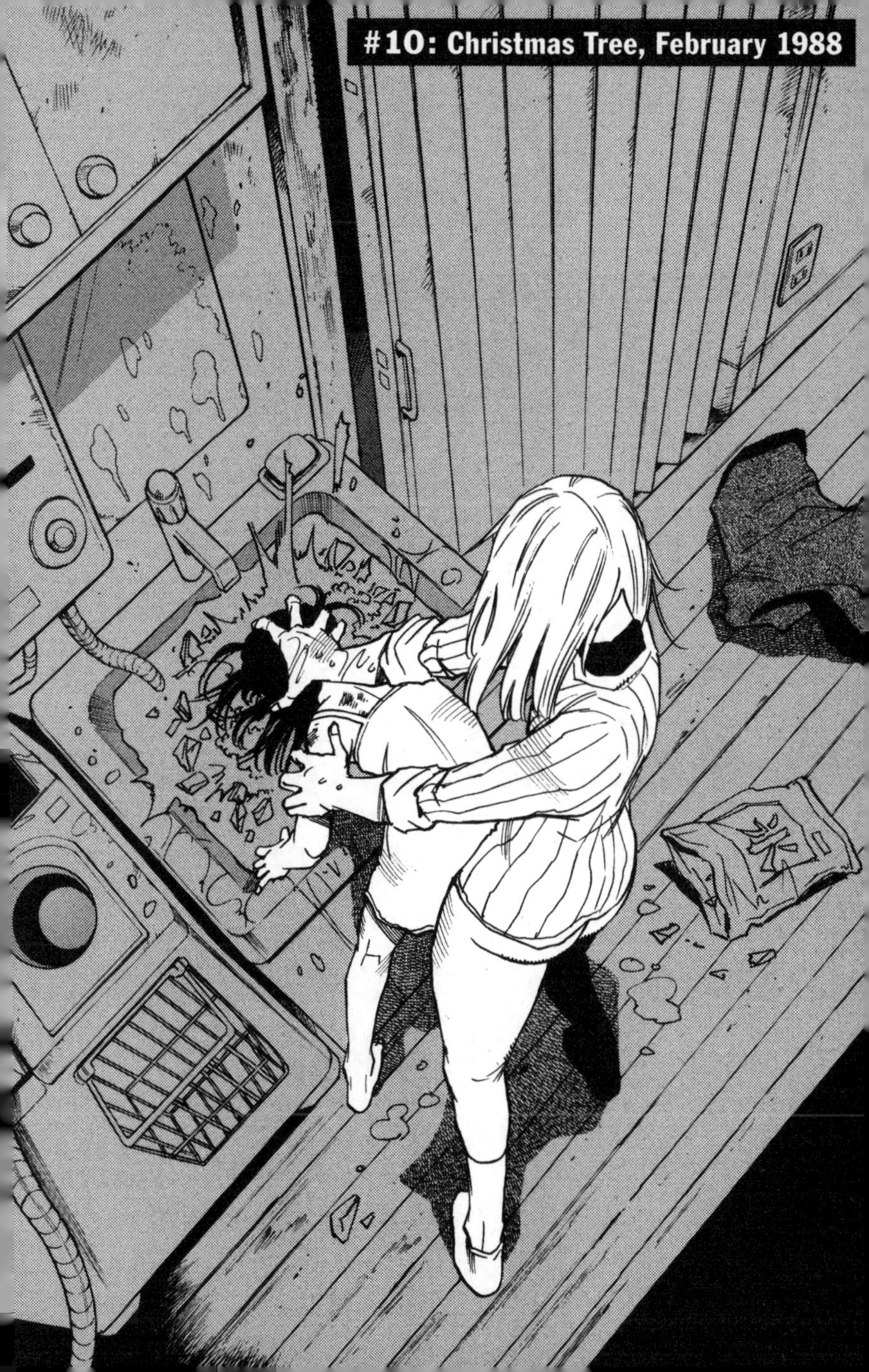

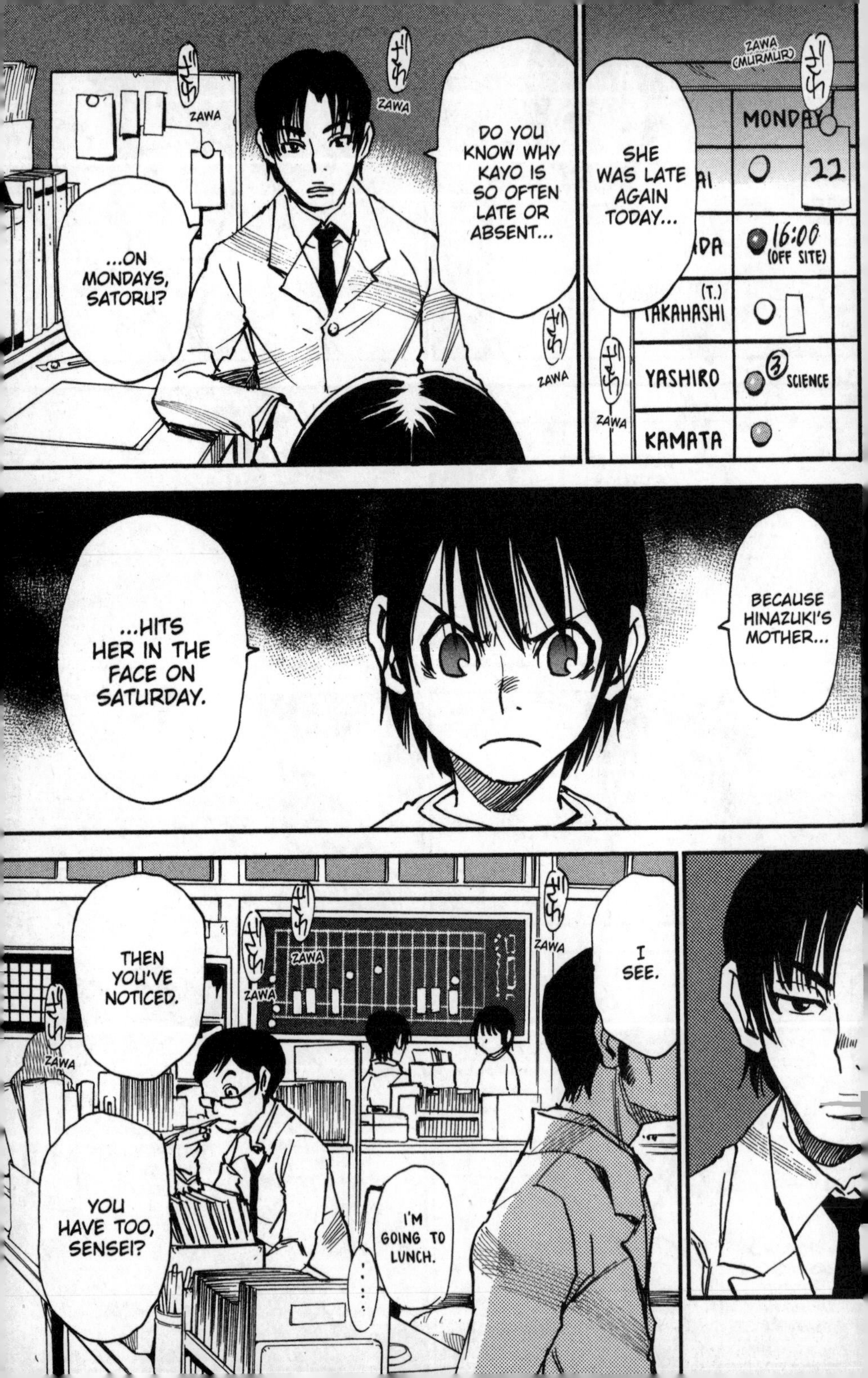
ZAWA (MURMUR)
MONDAY
22
16:00
(OFF SITE)
(T.)
YASHIRO
SCIENCE
KAMATA
SHE WAS LATE AGAIN TODAY...
ZAWA
DO YOU KNOW WHY KAYO IS SO OFTEN LATE OR ABSENT...
ZAWA
ZAWA
...ON MONDAYS, SATORU?
ZAWA
BECAUSE HINAZUKI'S MOTHER...
...HITS HER IN THE FACE ON SATURDAY.
I SEE.
ZAWA
ZAWA
THEN YOU'VE NOTICED.
ZAWA
ZAWA
I'M GOING TO LUNCH.
......
YOU HAVE TOO, SENSEI?

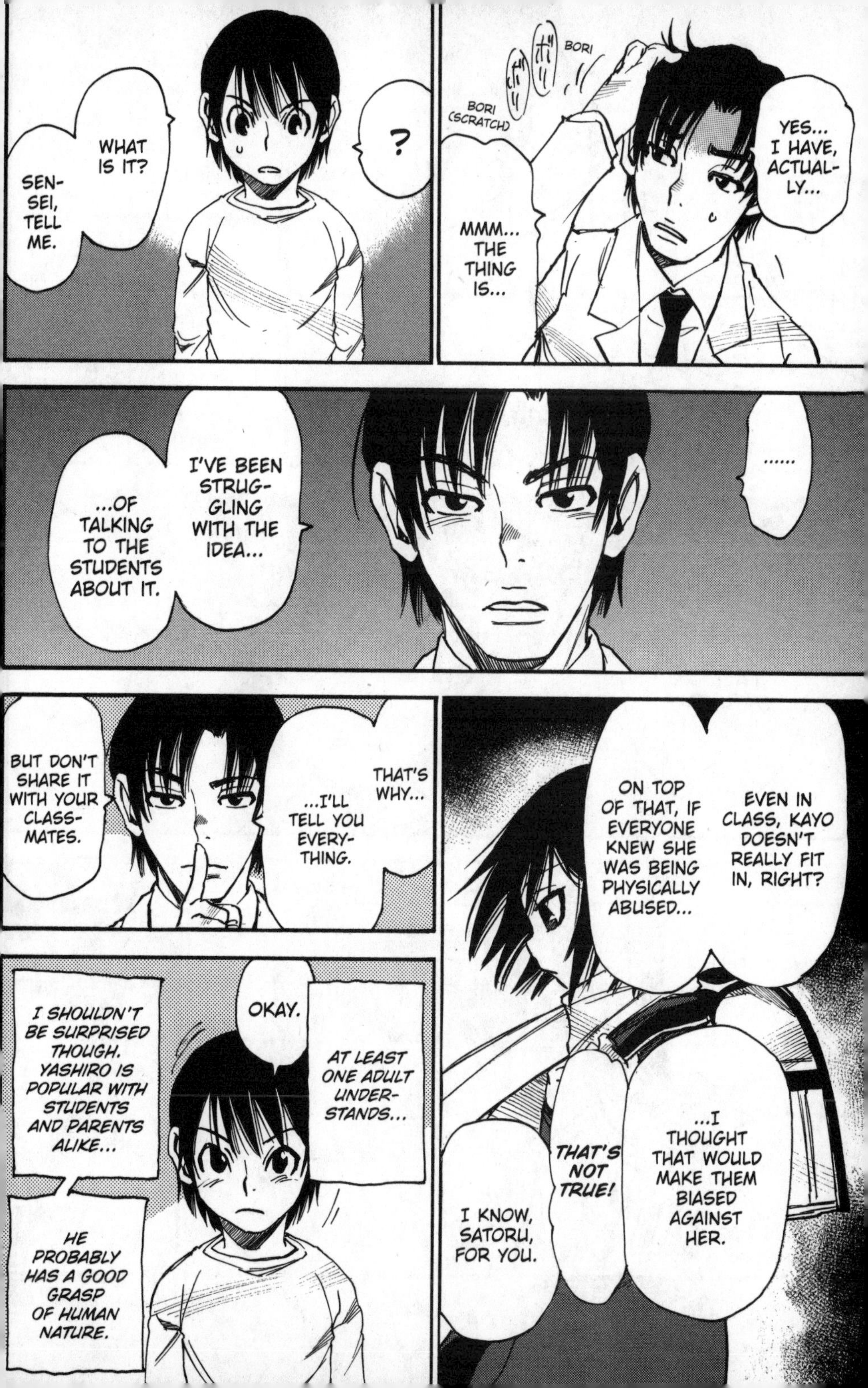
ボリ
BORI
ボリ
BORI (SCRATCH)
YES... I HAVE, ACTUALLY...
MMM... THE THING IS...
?
WHAT IS IT?
SENSEI, TELL ME.
......
I'VE BEEN STRUGGLING WITH THE IDEA...
...OF TALKING TO THE STUDENTS ABOUT IT.
EVEN IN CLASS, KAYO DOESN'T REALLY FIT IN, RIGHT?
ON TOP OF THAT, IF EVERYONE KNEW SHE WAS BEING PHYSICALLY ABUSED...
...I THOUGHT THAT WOULD MAKE THEM BIASED AGAINST HER.
THAT'S NOT TRUE!
I KNOW, SATORU, FOR YOU.
THAT'S WHY...
...I'LL TELL YOU EVERYTHING.
BUT DON'T SHARE IT WITH YOUR CLASSMATES.
OKAY.
AT LEAST ONE ADULT UNDERSTANDS...
I SHOULDN'T BE SURPRISED THOUGH. YASHIRO IS POPULAR WITH STUDENTS AND PARENTS ALIKE...
HE PROBABLY HAS A GOOD GRASP OF HUMAN NATURE.

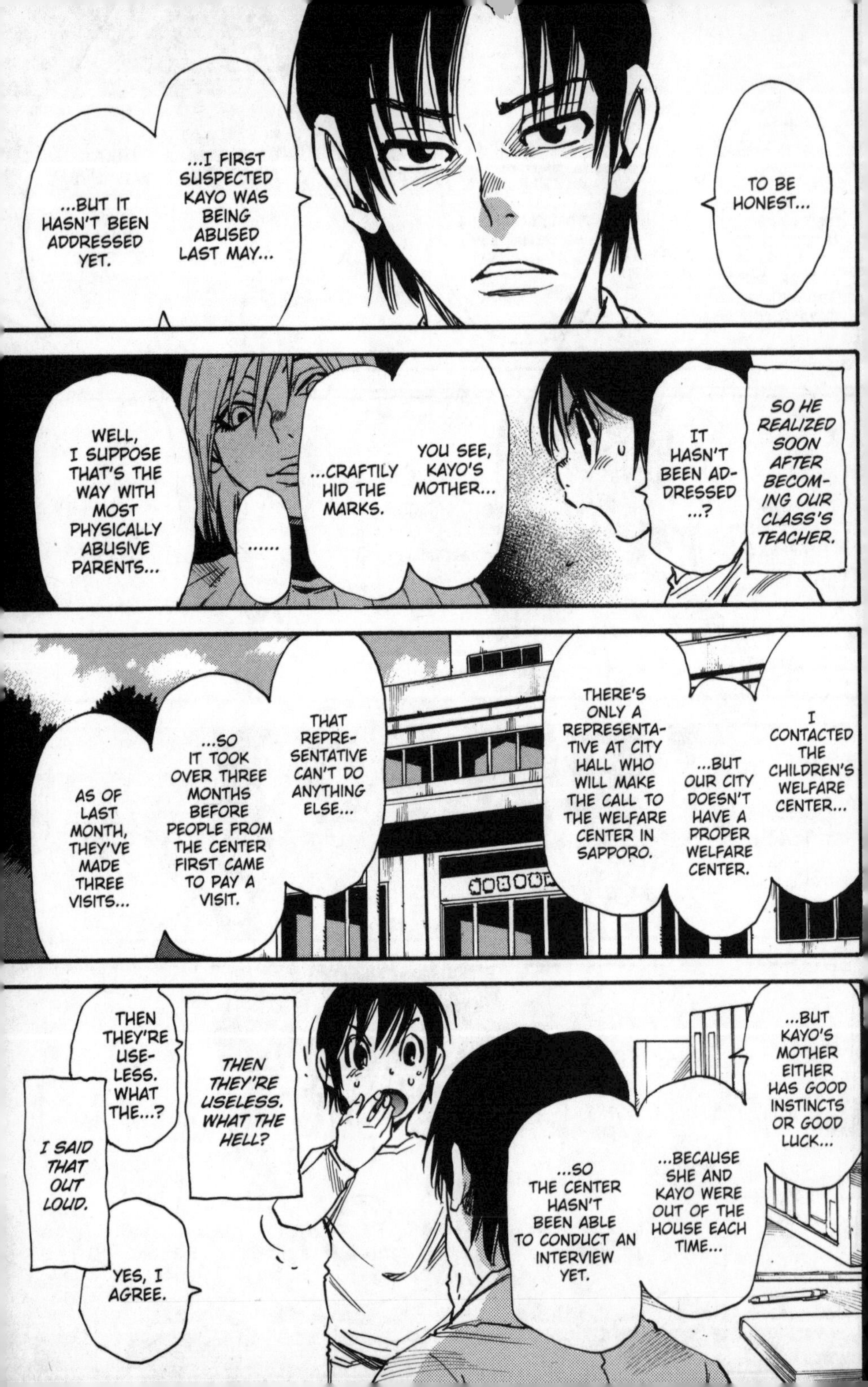
TO BE HONEST...
...I FIRST SUSPECTED KAYO WAS BEING ABUSED LAST MAY...
...BUT IT HASN'T BEEN ADDRESSED YET.
SO HE REALIZED SOON AFTER BECOMING OUR CLASS'S TEACHER.
IT HASN'T BEEN ADDRESSED ...?
YOU SEE, KAYO'S MOTHER...
...CRAFTILY HID THE MARKS.
......
WELL, I SUPPOSE THAT'S THE WAY WITH MOST PHYSICALLY ABUSIVE PARENTS...
I CONTACTED THE CHILDREN'S WELFARE CENTER...
...BUT OUR CITY DOESN'T HAVE A PROPER WELFARE CENTER.
THERE'S ONLY A REPRESENTATIVE AT CITY HALL WHO WILL MAKE THE CALL TO THE WELFARE CENTER IN SAPPORO.
THAT REPRESENTATIVE CAN'T DO ANYTHING ELSE...
...SO IT TOOK OVER THREE MONTHS BEFORE PEOPLE FROM THE CENTER FIRST CAME TO PAY A VISIT.
AS OF LAST MONTH, THEY'VE MADE THREE VISITS...
...BUT KAYO'S MOTHER EITHER HAS GOOD INSTINCTS OR GOOD LUCK...
...BECAUSE SHE AND KAYO WERE OUT OF THE HOUSE EACH TIME...
...SO THE CENTER HASN'T BEEN ABLE TO CONDUCT AN INTERVIEW YET.
THEN THEY'RE USELESS. WHAT THE HELL?
THEN THEY'RE USELESS. WHAT THE...?
I SAID THAT OUT LOUD.
YES, I AGREE.

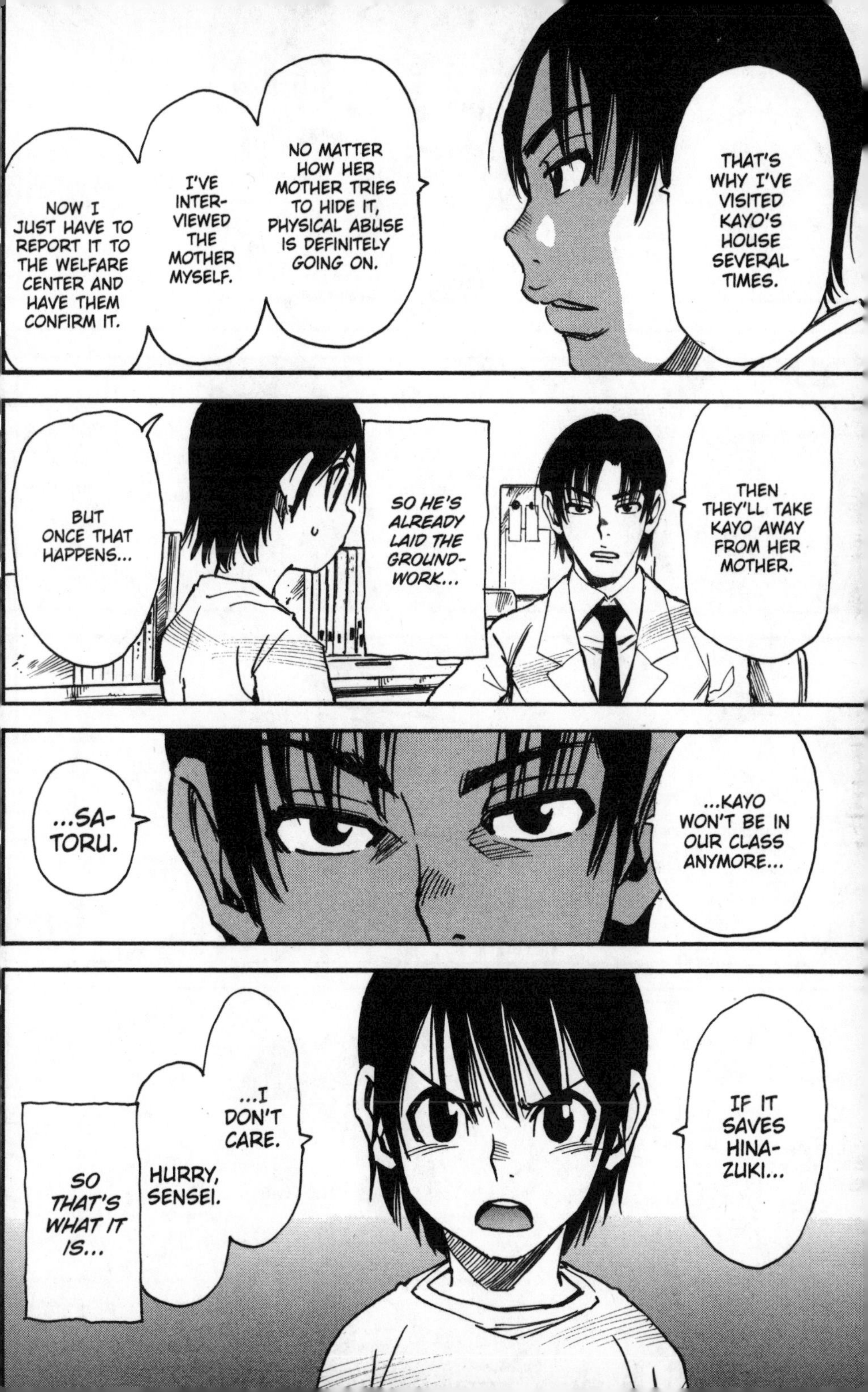
THAT'S WHY I'VE VISITED KAYO'S HOUSE SEVERAL TIMES.
NO MATTER HOW HER MOTHER TRIES TO HIDE IT, PHYSICAL ABUSE IS DEFINITELY GOING ON.
I'VE INTER-VIEWED THE MOTHER MYSELF.
NOW I JUST HAVE TO REPORT IT TO THE WELFARE CENTER AND HAVE THEM CONFIRM IT.
THEN THEY'LL TAKE KAYO AWAY FROM HER MOTHER.
SO HE'S ALREADY LAID THE GROUND-WORK...
BUT ONCE THAT HAPPENS...
...KAYO WON'T BE IN OUR CLASS ANYMORE...
...SA-TORU.
IF IT SAVES HINA-ZUKI...
...I DON'T CARE.
HURRY, SENSEI.
SO THAT'S WHAT IT IS...

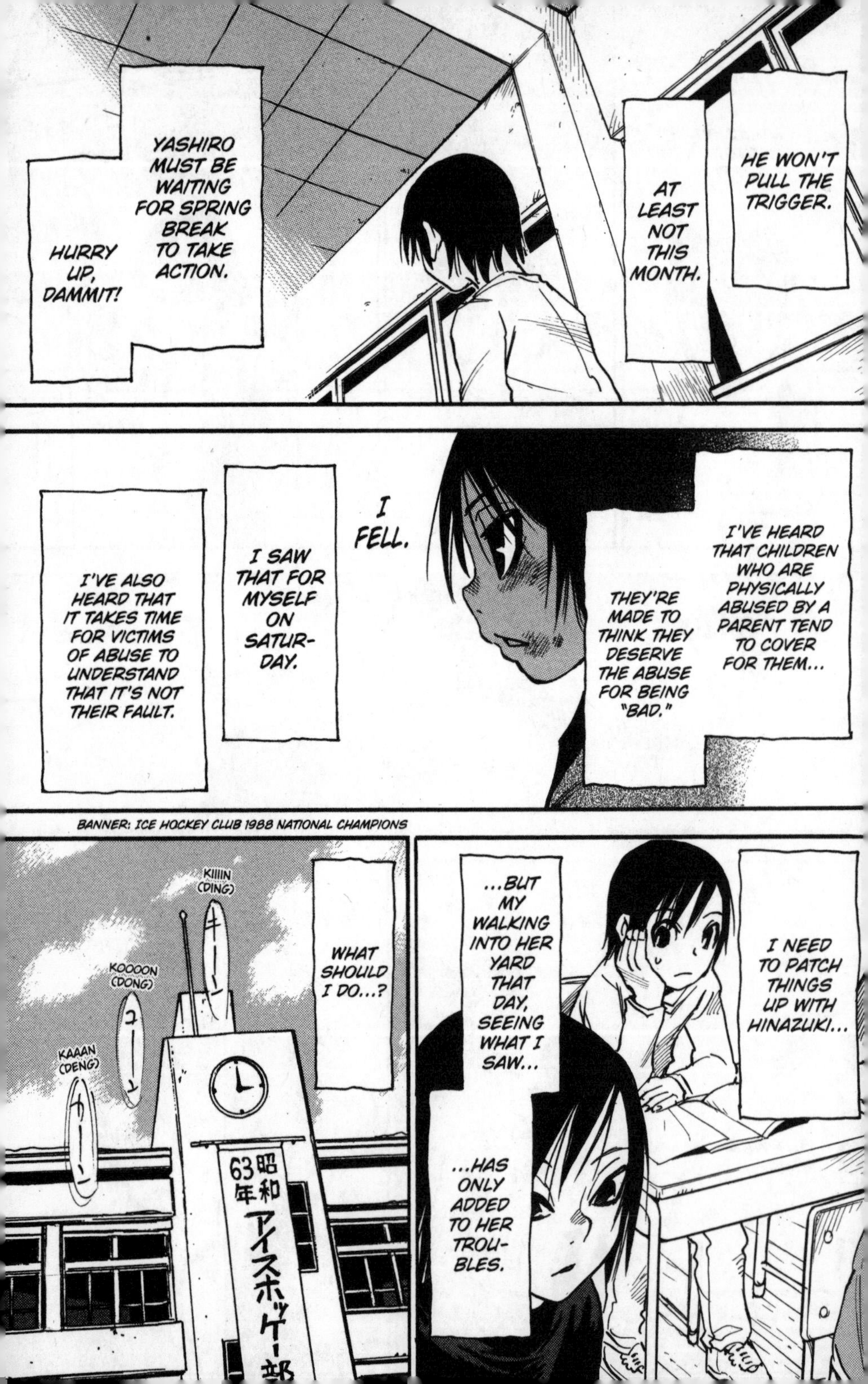
HE WON'T PULL THE TRIGGER.
AT LEAST NOT THIS MONTH.
YASHIRO MUST BE WAITING FOR SPRING BREAK TO TAKE ACTION.
HURRY UP, DAMMIT!
I'VE HEARD THAT CHILDREN WHO ARE PHYSICALLY ABUSED BY A PARENT TEND TO COVER FOR THEM...
THEY'RE MADE TO THINK THEY DESERVE THE ABUSE FOR BEING "BAD."
I FELL.
I SAW THAT FOR MYSELF ON SATUR-DAY.
I'VE ALSO HEARD THAT IT TAKES TIME FOR VICTIMS OF ABUSE TO UNDERSTAND THAT IT'S NOT THEIR FAULT.
I NEED TO PATCH THINGS UP WITH HINAZUKI...
...BUT MY WALKING INTO HER YARD THAT DAY, SEEING WHAT I SAW...
...HAS ONLY ADDED TO HER TROUBLES.
BANNER: ICE HOCKEY CLUB 1988 NATIONAL CHAMPIONS
WHAT SHOULD I DO...?
KIIIN (DING)
キーン
KOOOON (DONG)
コーン
KAAAN (DENG)
カーン
昭和63年
アイスホッケー部

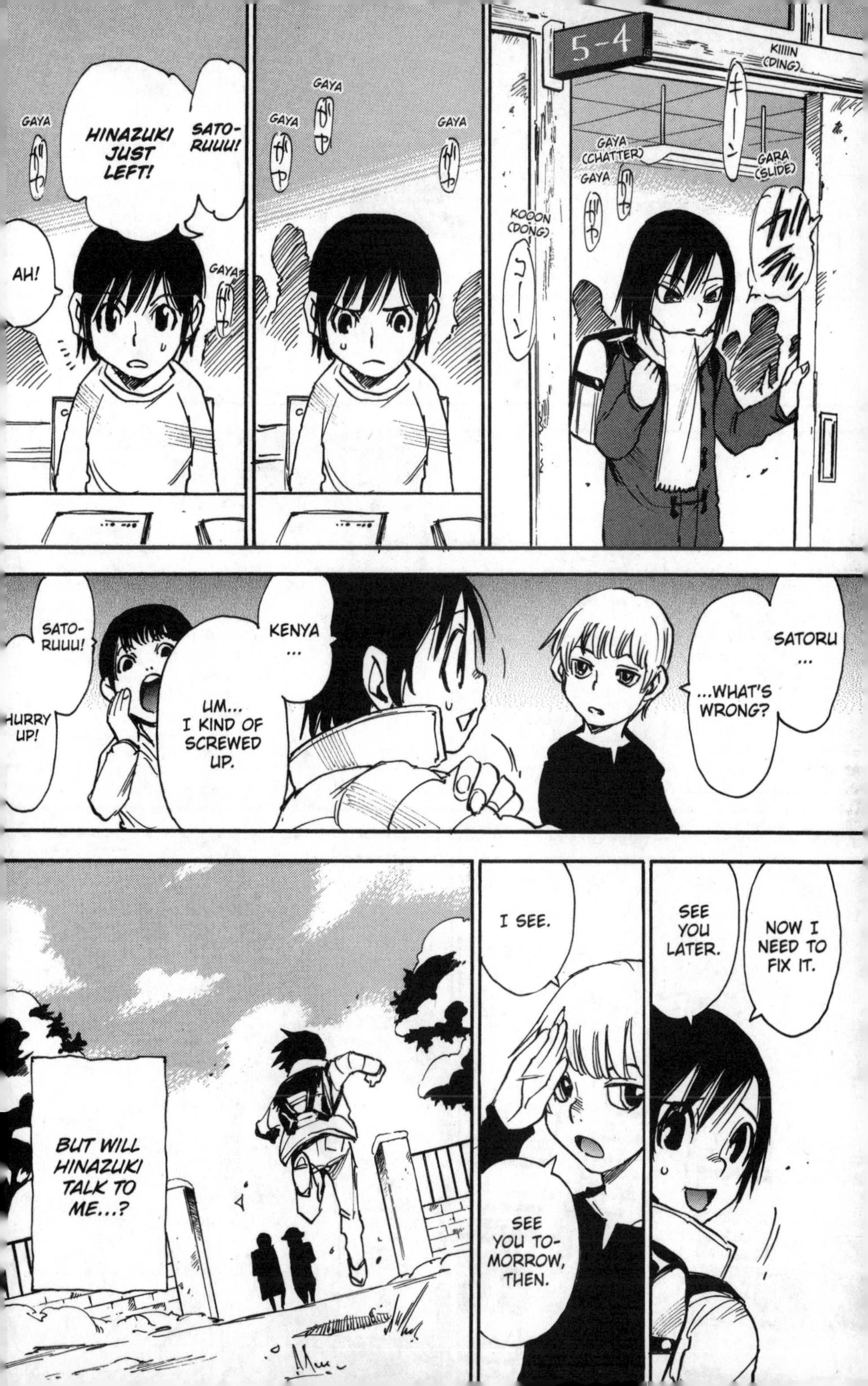
KIIIN (DING)
GAYA (CHATTER)
GAYA
GARA (SLIDE)
KOOON (DONG)
GAYA
GAYA
GAYA
SATO-RUUU!
HINAZUKI JUST LEFT!
GAYA
GAYA
AH!
SATORU ...
...WHAT'S WRONG?
KENYA ...
UM... I KIND OF SCREWED UP.
SATO-RUUU!
HURRY UP!
NOW I NEED TO FIX IT.
SEE YOU LATER.
I SEE.
SEE YOU TO-MORROW, THEN.
BUT WILL HINAZUKI TALK TO ME...?

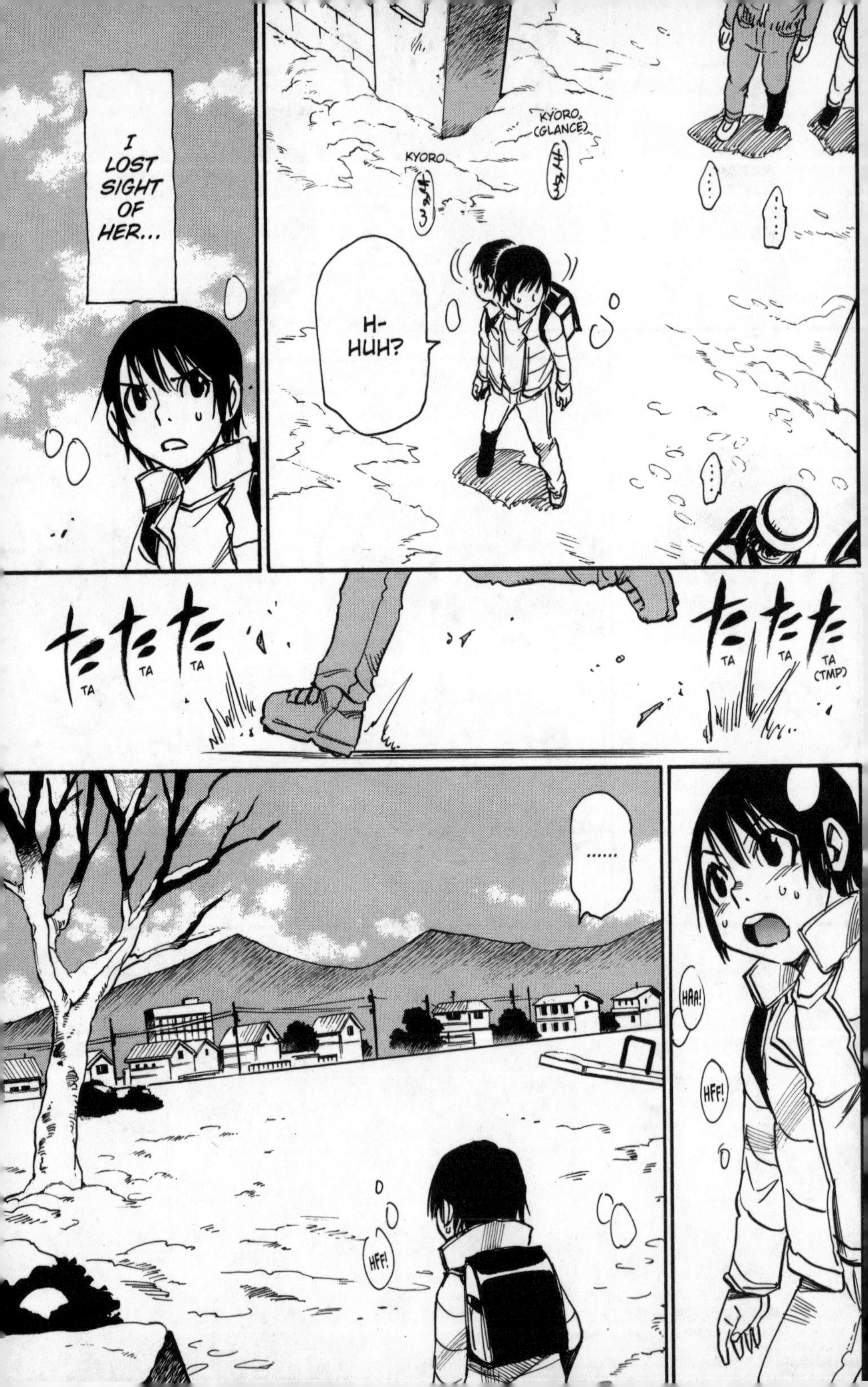
...
...
KYORO (GLANCE)
KYORO
H-HUH?
...
I LOST SIGHT OF HER...
TA TA TA (TMP)
TA TA TA
HAA!
HFF!
......
HFF!

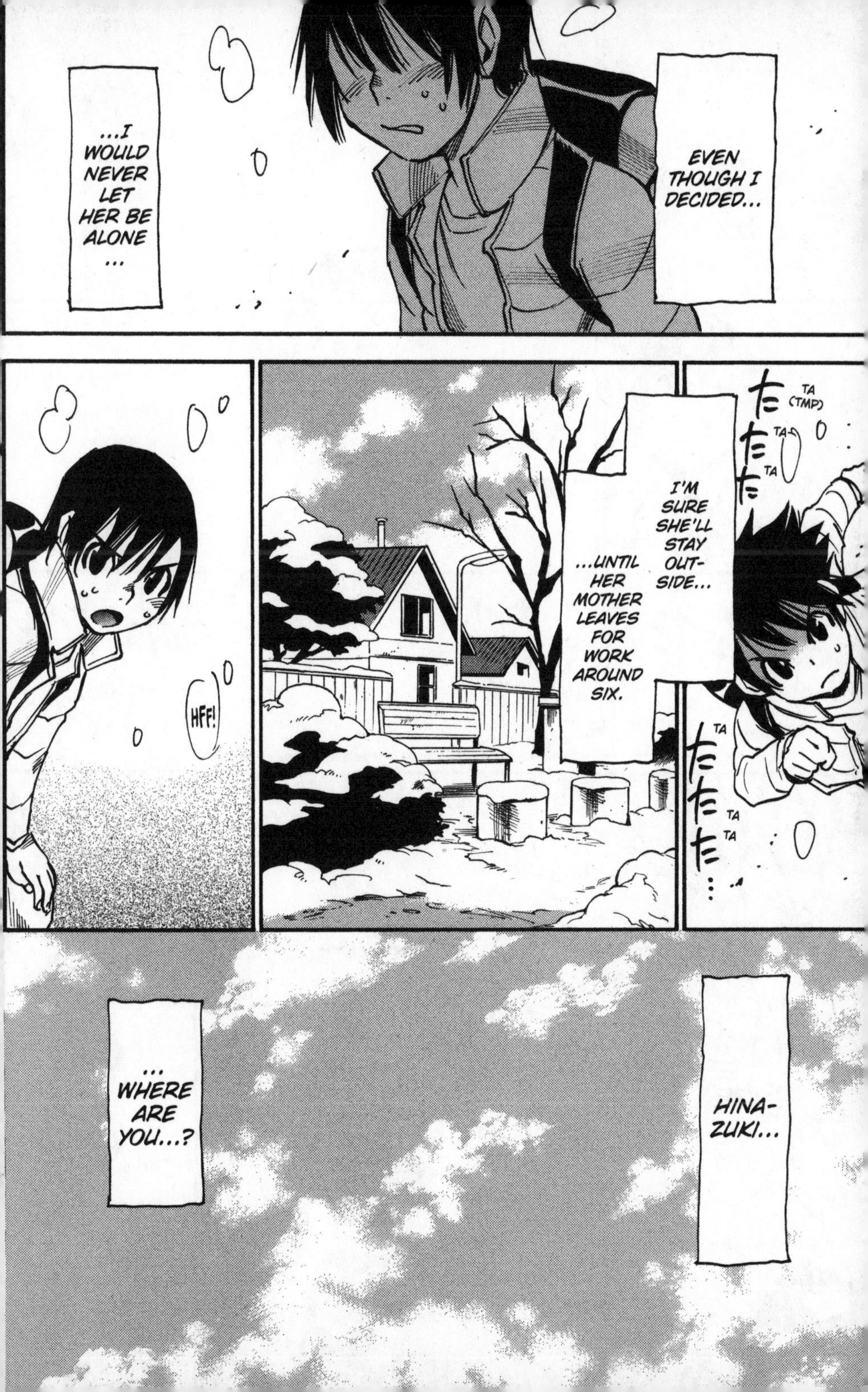
EVEN THOUGH I DECIDED...
...I WOULD NEVER LET HER BE ALONE...
たたた
TA (TMP) TA TA
I'M SURE SHE'LL STAY OUTSIDE...
...UNTIL HER MOTHER LEAVES FOR WORK AROUND SIX.
たたた...
TA TA TA
HFF!
HINAZUKI...
...WHERE ARE YOU...?

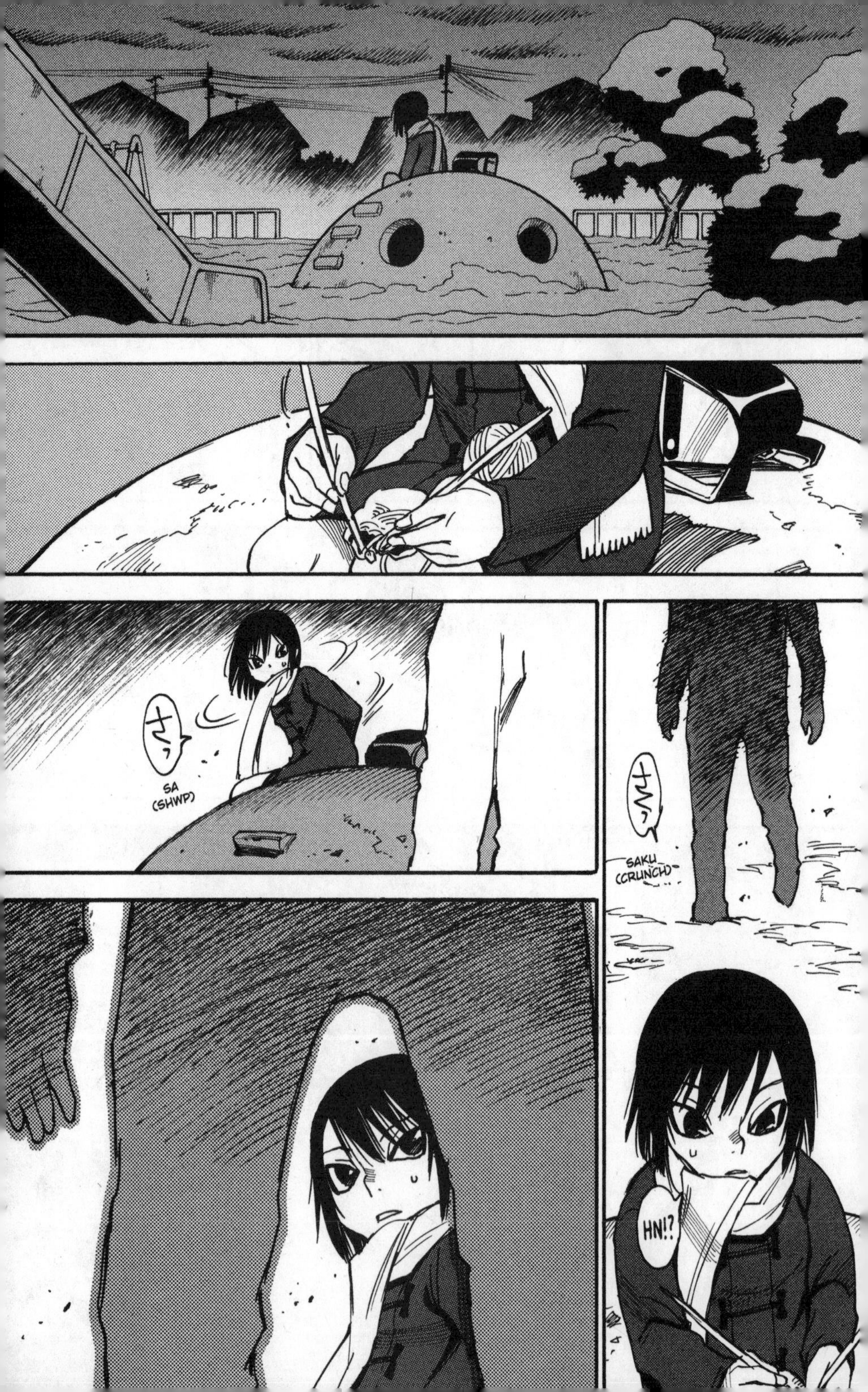

サクッ
SAKU (CRUNCH)
HN!?
さっ
SA (SHWP)

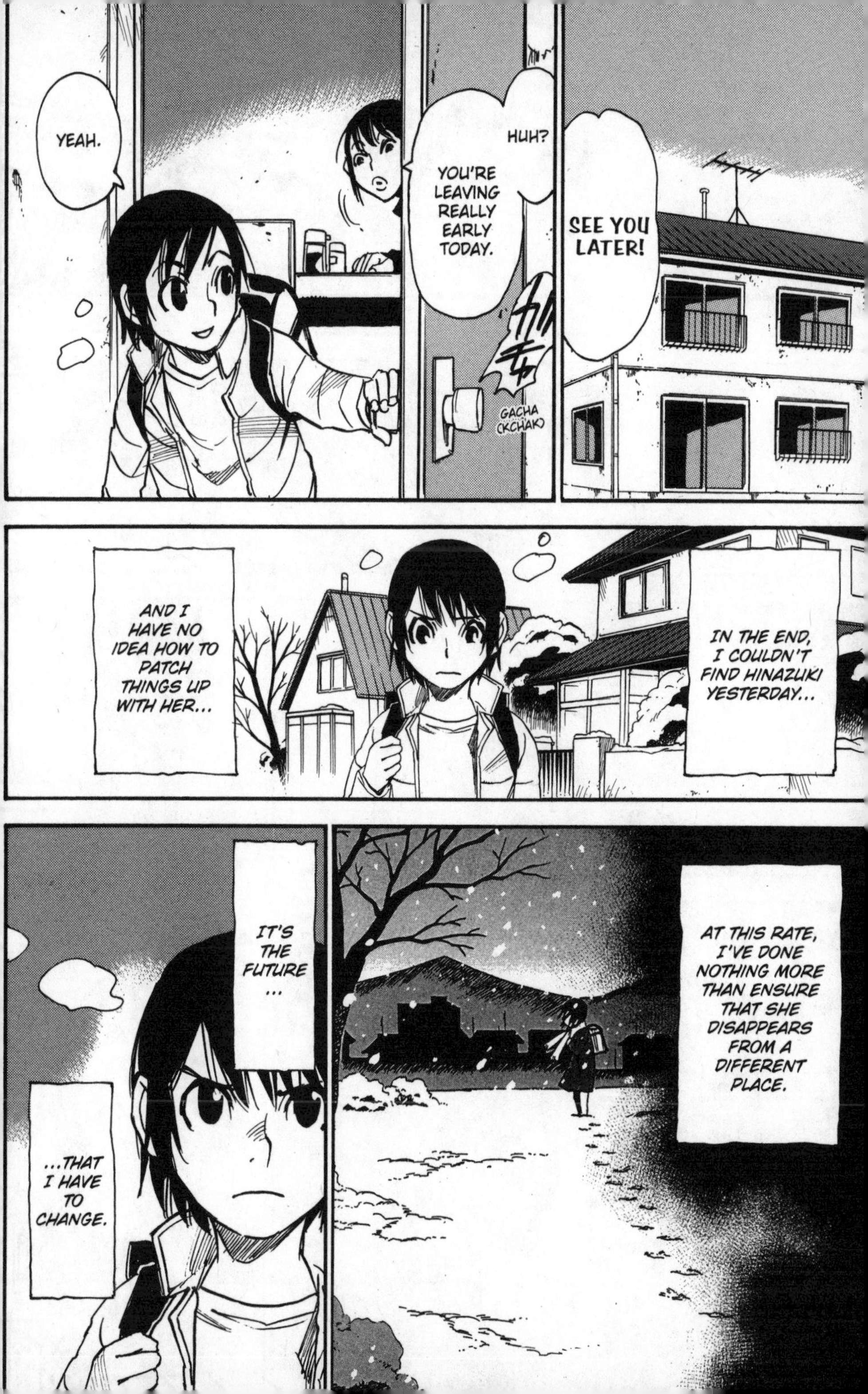
SEE YOU LATER!
HUH? YOU'RE LEAVING REALLY EARLY TODAY.
GACHA (KCHAK)
YEAH.
IN THE END, I COULDN'T FIND HINAZUKI YESTERDAY...
AND I HAVE NO IDEA HOW TO PATCH THINGS UP WITH HER...
AT THIS RATE, I'VE DONE NOTHING MORE THAN ENSURE THAT SHE DISAPPEARS FROM A DIFFERENT PLACE.
IT'S THE FUTURE ...
...THAT I HAVE TO CHANGE.

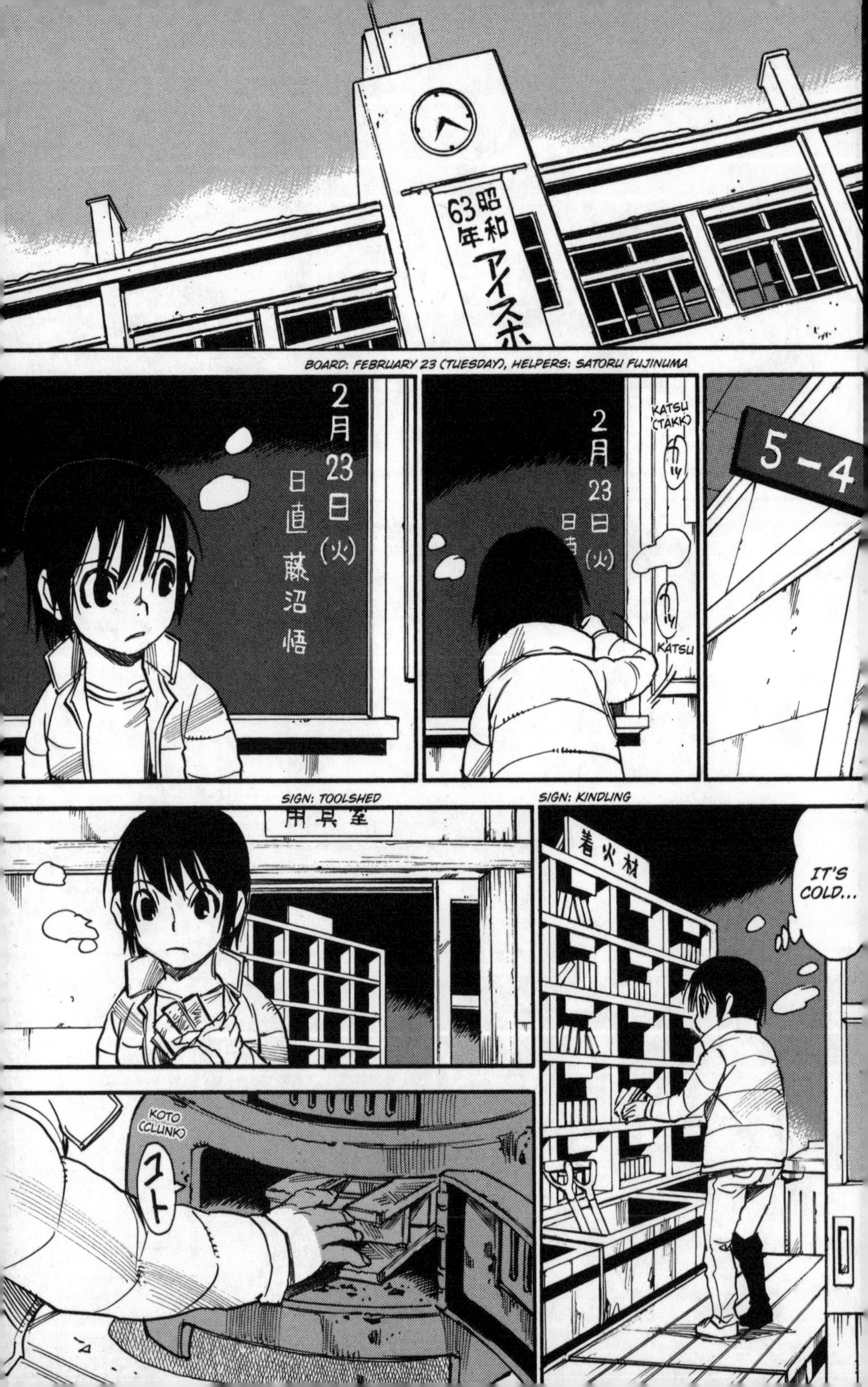
昭和63年
アイスホ
5-4
2月23日(火) 日直
カッ
KATSU (TAKK)
カッ
KATSU
BOARD: FEBRUARY 23 (TUESDAY), HELPERS: SATORU FUJINUMA
2月23日(火) 日直 藤沼悟
SIGN: KINDLING
着火材
IT'S COLD...
SIGN: TOOLSHED
用具室
コト
KOTO (CLUNK)

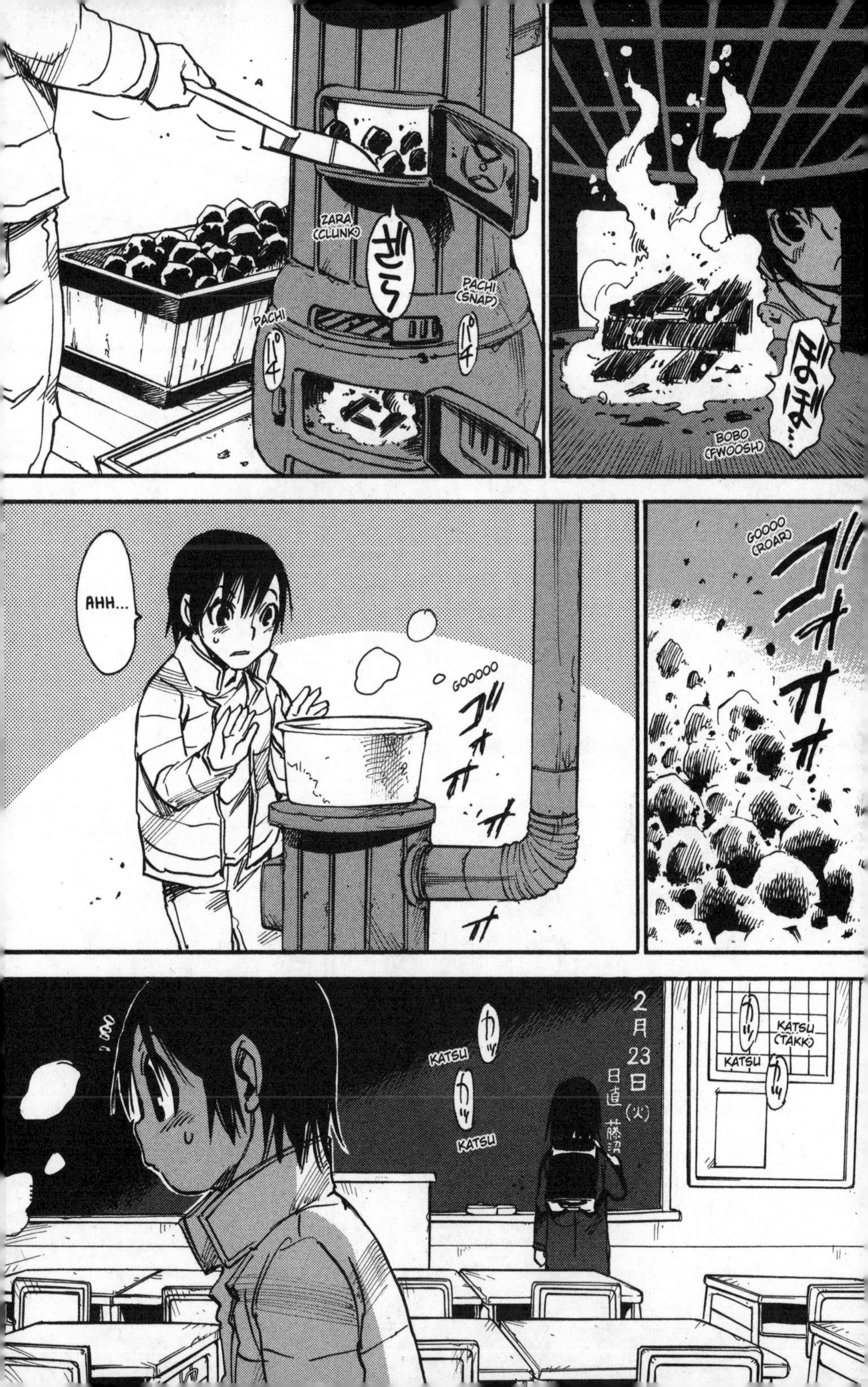
ぼぼ…
BOBO (FWOOSH)
ざら
ZARA (CLUNK)
パチ
PACHI (SNAP)
パチ
PACHI
ゴォォォ
GOOOO (ROAR)
AHH...
ゴォォォォォ
GOOOOO
カッ
KATSU (TAKK)
カッ
KATSU
2月23日(火)
日直
カッ
KATSU
カッ
KATSU

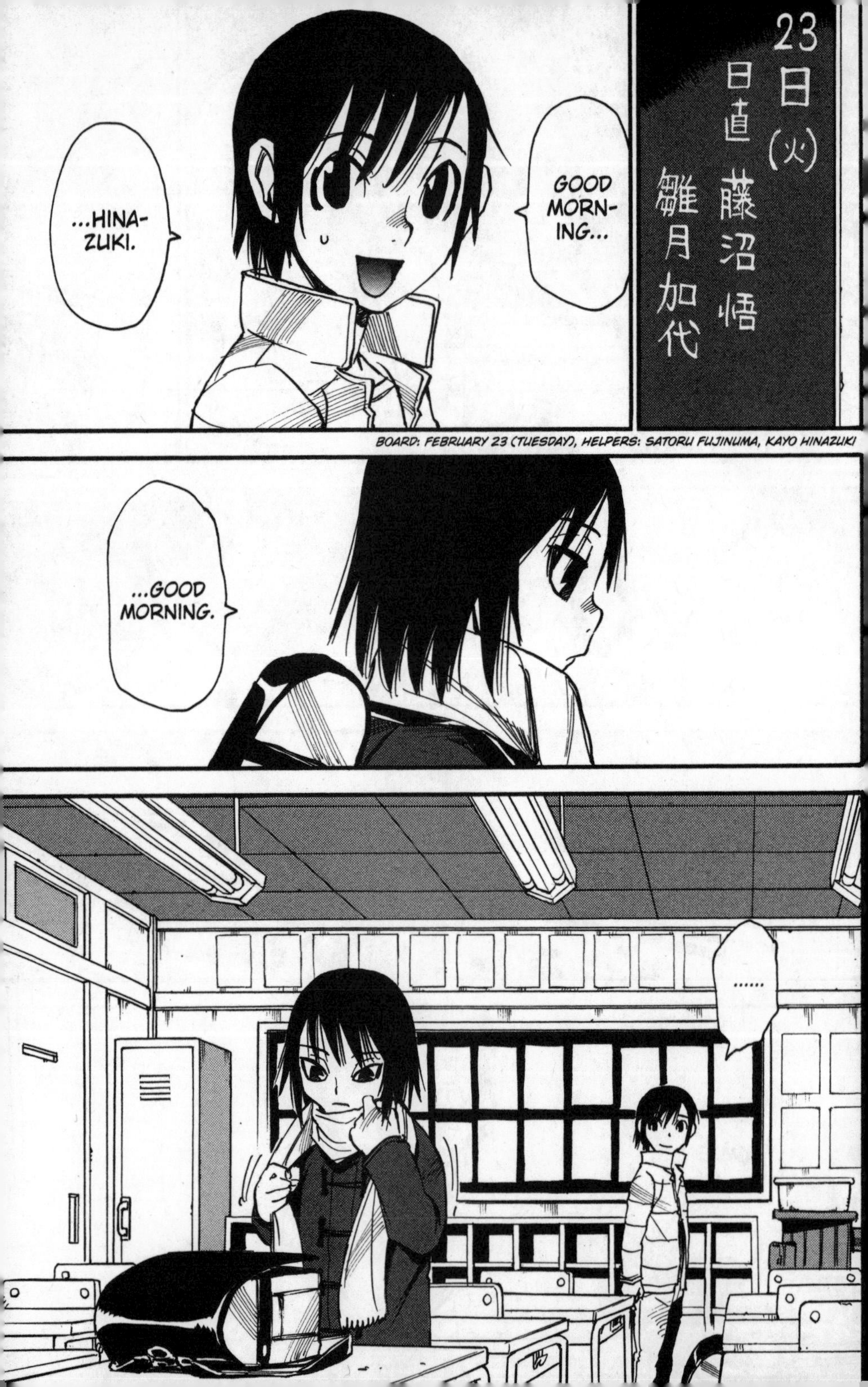
23日(火)
日直 藤沼悟
雛月加代
GOOD MORN-ING...
...HINA-ZUKI.
BOARD: FEBRUARY 23 (TUESDAY), HELPERS: SATORU FUJINUMA, KAYO HINAZUKI
...GOOD MORNING.
......

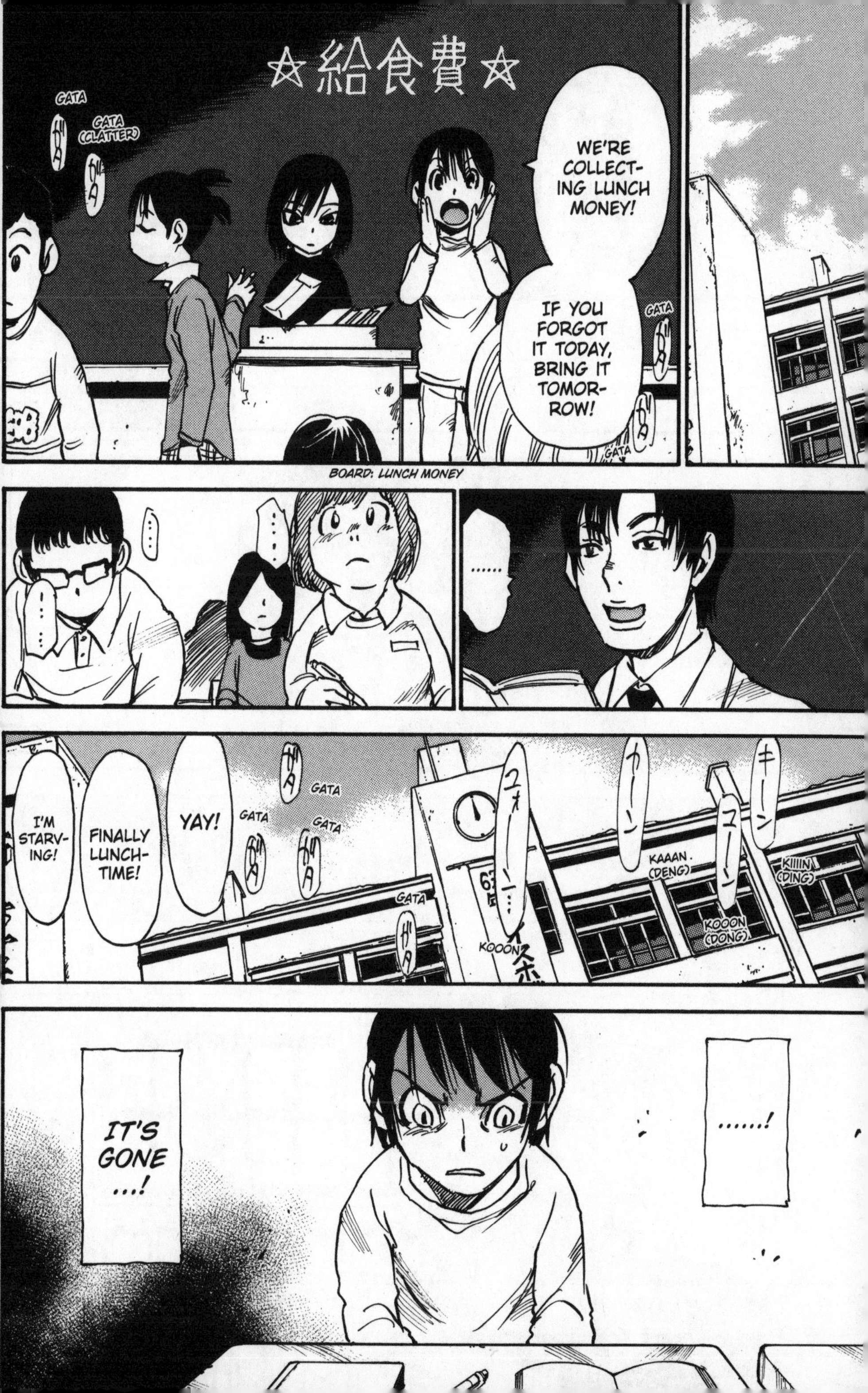
☆給食費☆
WE'RE COLLECT-ING LUNCH MONEY!
IF YOU FORGOT IT TODAY, BRING IT TOMOR-ROW!
GATA
GATA
GATA
GATA (CLATTER)
BOARD: LUNCH MONEY
......
...
...
...
KIIIN (DING)
KOOON (DONG)
KAAAN. (DENG)
KOOON
GATA
GATA
GATA
GATA
YAY!
FINALLY LUNCH-TIME!
I'M STARV-ING!
......!
IT'S GONE ...!

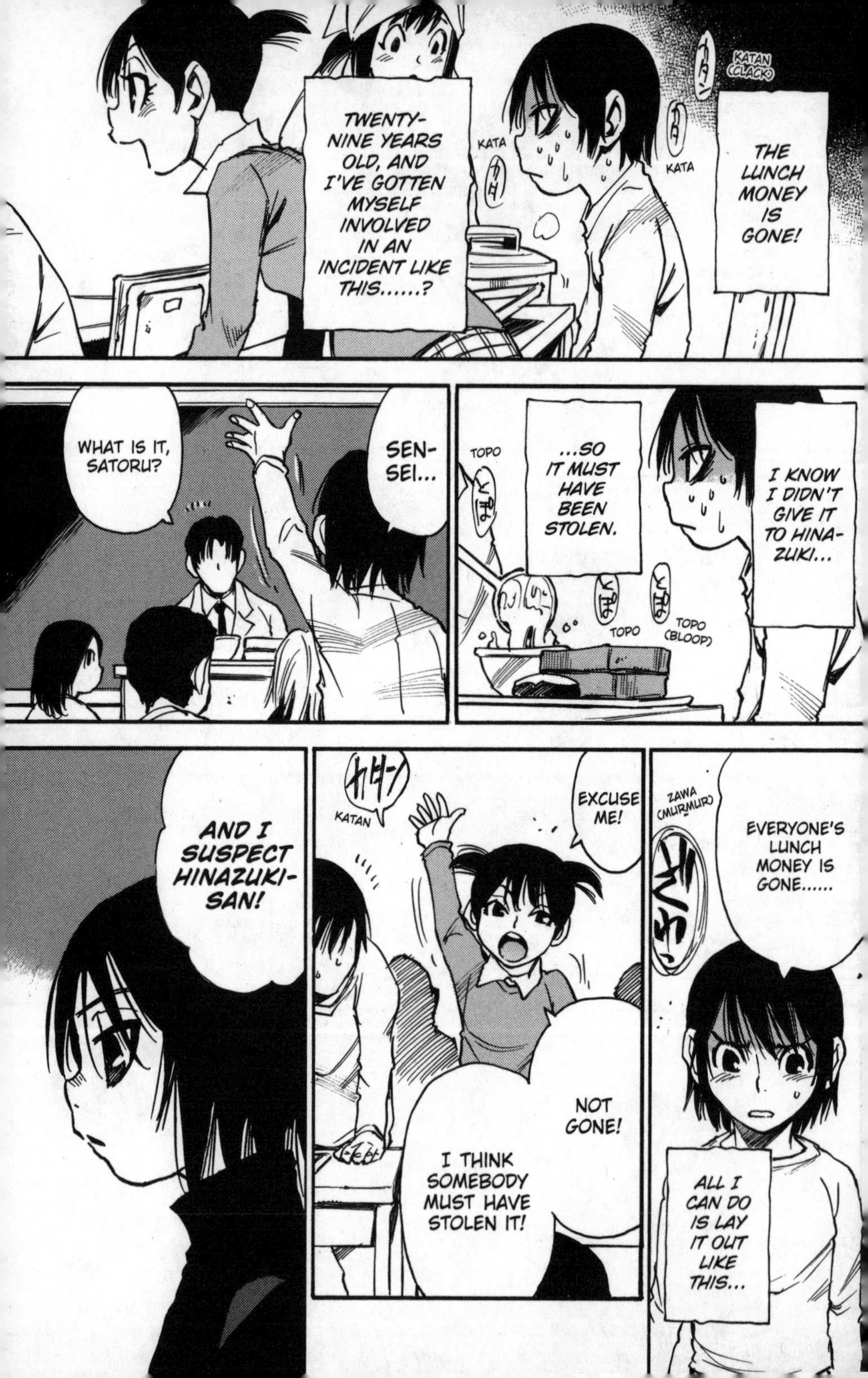
KATAN (CLACK)
THE LUNCH MONEY IS GONE!
KATA
KATA
TWENTY-NINE YEARS OLD, AND I'VE GOTTEN MYSELF INVOLVED IN AN INCIDENT LIKE THIS......?
I KNOW I DIDN'T GIVE IT TO HINA-ZUKI...
...SO IT MUST HAVE BEEN STOLEN.
TOPO
TOPO (BLOOP)
TOPO
SEN-SEI...
WHAT IS IT, SATORU?
ZAWA (MURMUR)
EVERYONE'S LUNCH MONEY IS GONE......
ALL I CAN DO IS LAY IT OUT LIKE THIS...
EXCUSE ME!
KATAN
NOT GONE!
I THINK SOMEBODY MUST HAVE STOLEN IT!
AND I SUSPECT HINAZUKI-SAN!

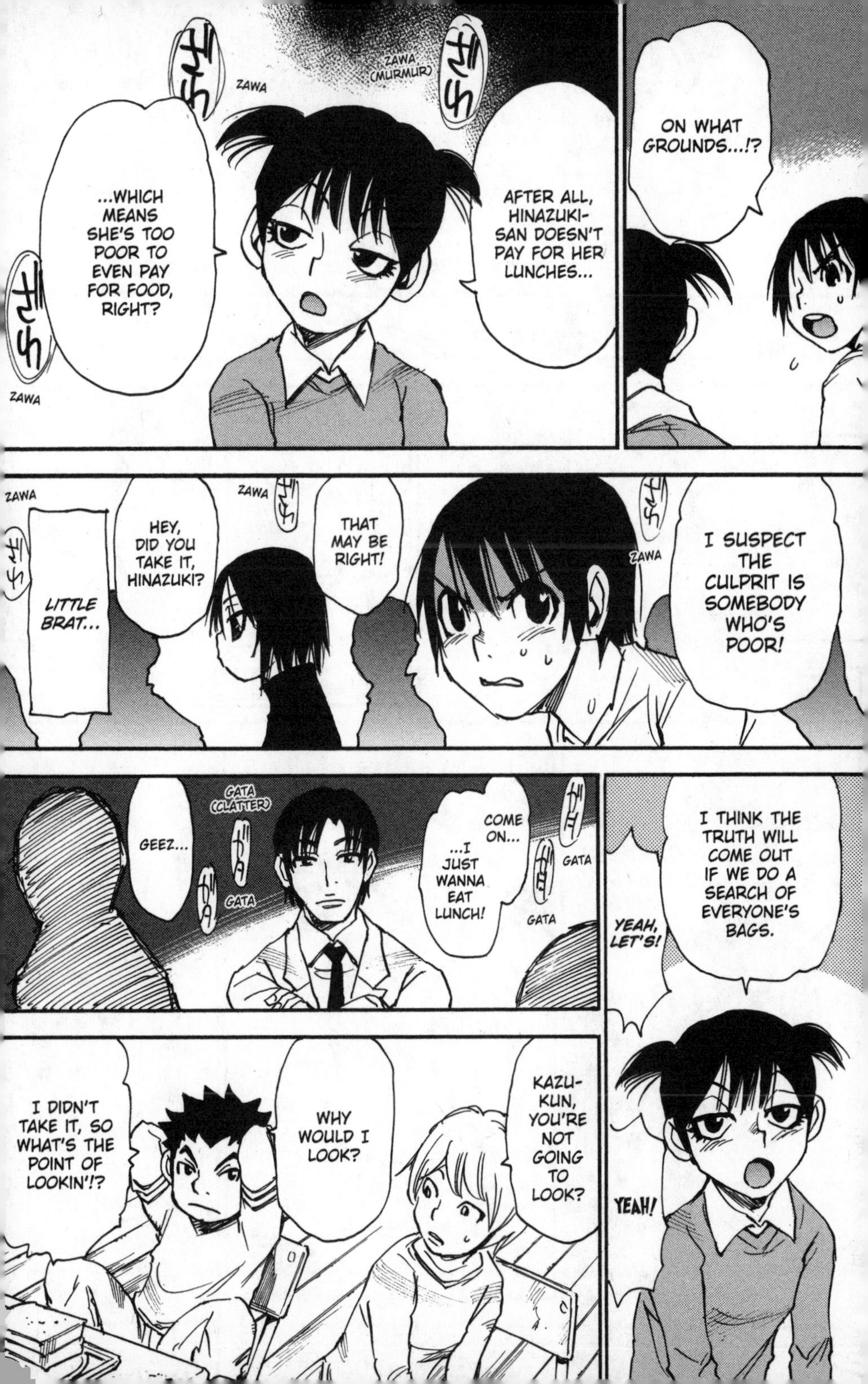
ON WHAT GROUNDS...!?
ZAWA (MURMUR)
AFTER ALL, HINAZUKI-SAN DOESN'T PAY FOR HER LUNCHES...
ZAWA
...WHICH MEANS SHE'S TOO POOR TO EVEN PAY FOR FOOD, RIGHT?
ZAWA
I SUSPECT THE CULPRIT IS SOMEBODY WHO'S POOR!
ZAWA
THAT MAY BE RIGHT!
ZAWA
HEY, DID YOU TAKE IT, HINAZUKI?
ZAWA
LITTLE BRAT...
I THINK THE TRUTH WILL COME OUT IF WE DO A SEARCH OF EVERYONE'S BAGS.
YEAH, LET'S!
YEAH!
COME ON...
...I JUST WANNA EAT LUNCH!
GATA
GATA
GATA (CLATTER)
GATA
GEEZ...
KAZU-KUN, YOU'RE NOT GOING TO LOOK?
WHY WOULD I LOOK?
I DIDN'T TAKE IT, SO WHAT'S THE POINT OF LOOKIN'!?

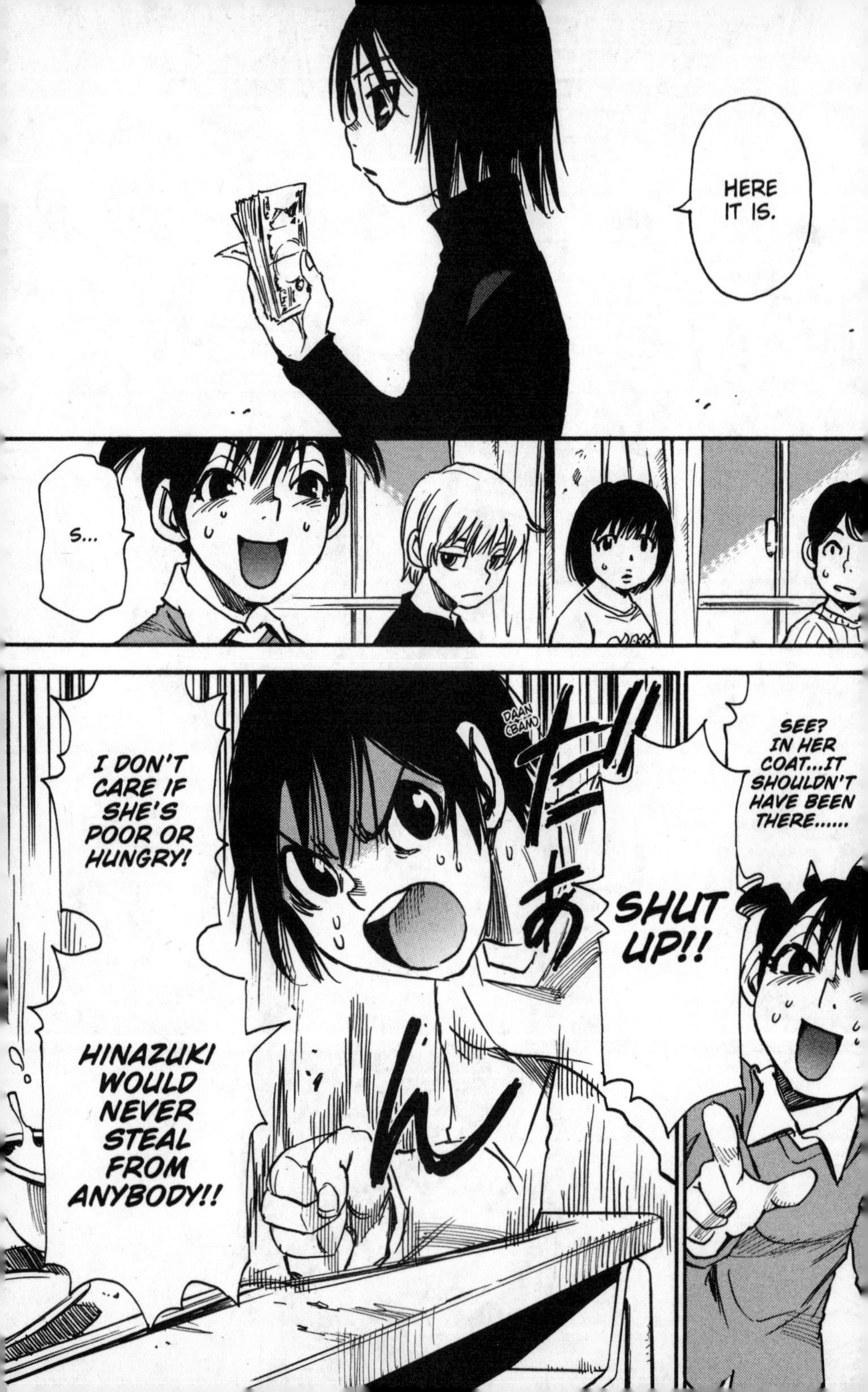
HERE IT IS.
S...
SEE? IN HER COAT...IT SHOULDN'T HAVE BEEN THERE......
DAAN (BAM)
だあん
SHUT UP!!
I DON'T CARE IF SHE'S POOR OR HUNGRY!
HINAZUKI WOULD NEVER STEAL FROM ANYBODY!!

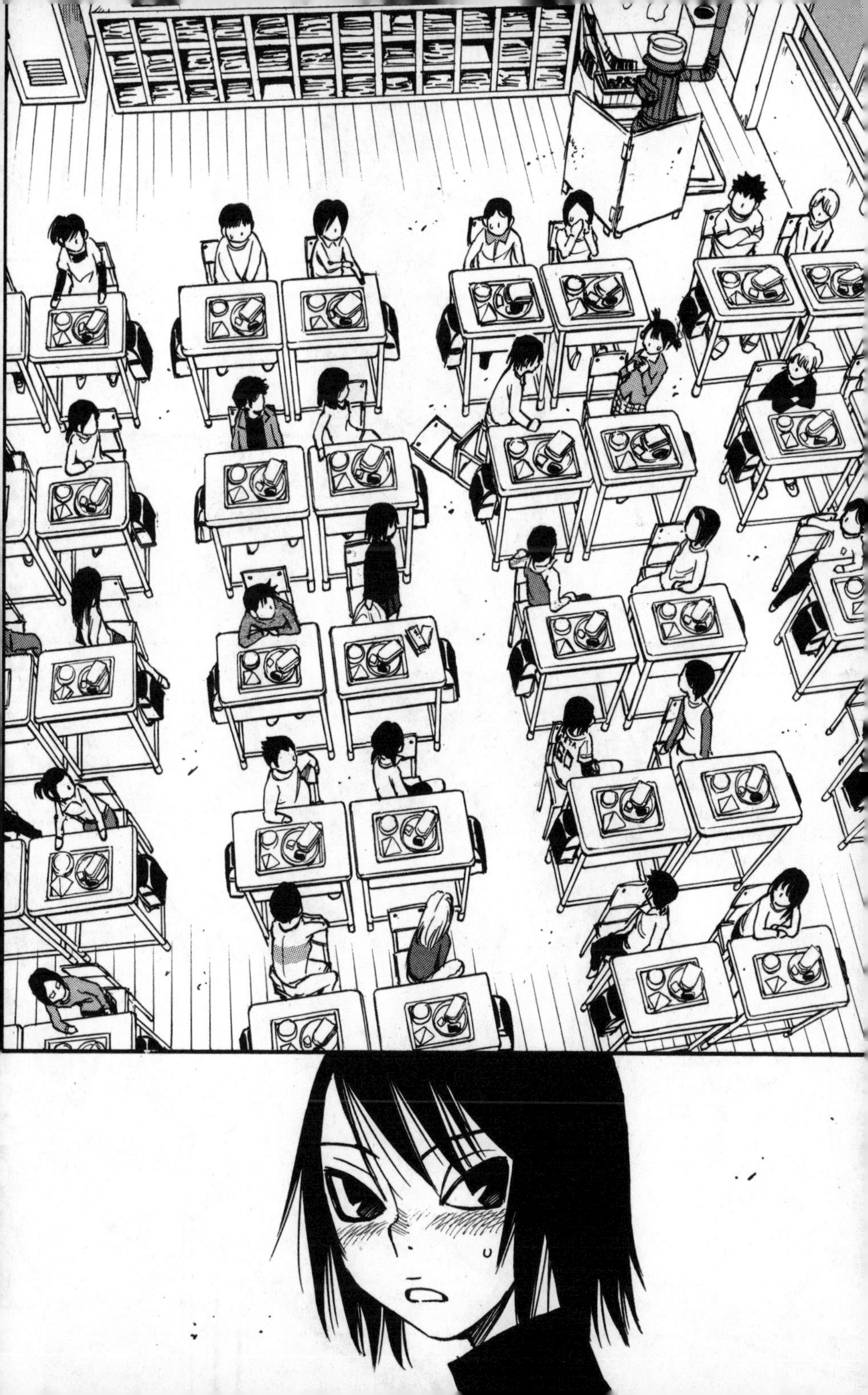

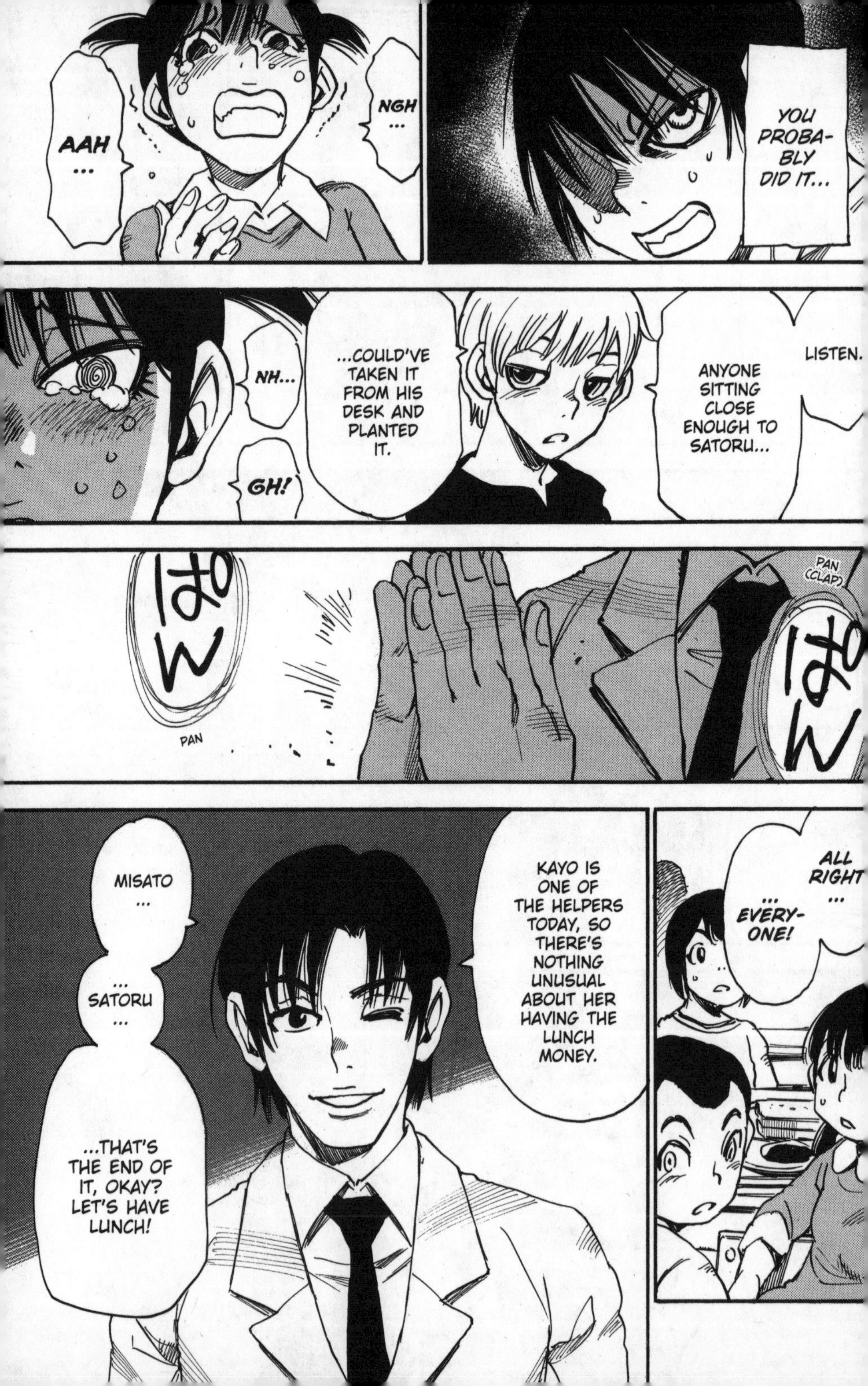
YOU PROBABLY DID IT...
NGH ...
AAH ...
LISTEN.
ANYONE SITTING CLOSE ENOUGH TO SATORU...
...COULD'VE TAKEN IT FROM HIS DESK AND PLANTED IT.
NH...
GH!
ぱん
PAN (CLAP)
ぱん
PAN
ALL RIGHT ... EVERYONE!
KAYO IS ONE OF THE HELPERS TODAY, SO THERE'S NOTHING UNUSUAL ABOUT HER HAVING THE LUNCH MONEY.
MISATO ...
... SATORU ...
...THAT'S THE END OF IT, OKAY? LET'S HAVE LUNCH!

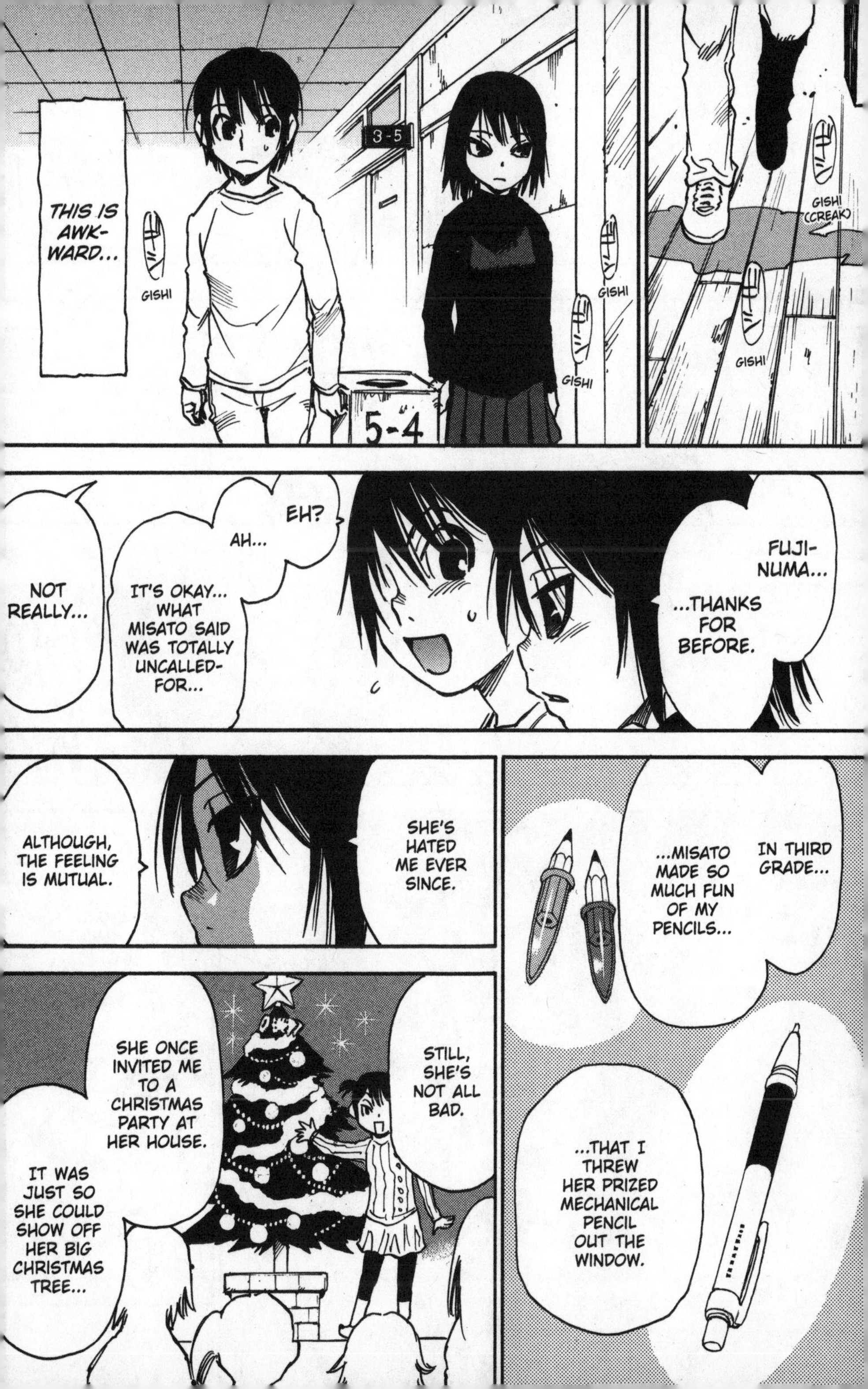
GISHI (CREAK)
GISHI
GISHI
GISHI
THIS IS AWKWARD...
GISHI
FUJI-NUMA...
...THANKS FOR BEFORE.
EH?
AH...
IT'S OKAY... WHAT MISATO SAID WAS TOTALLY UNCALLED-FOR...
NOT REALLY...
IN THIRD GRADE...
...MISATO MADE SO MUCH FUN OF MY PENCILS...
...THAT I THREW HER PRIZED MECHANICAL PENCIL OUT THE WINDOW.
SHE'S HATED ME EVER SINCE.
ALTHOUGH, THE FEELING IS MUTUAL.
STILL, SHE'S NOT ALL BAD.
SHE ONCE INVITED ME TO A CHRISTMAS PARTY AT HER HOUSE.
IT WAS JUST SO SHE COULD SHOW OFF HER BIG CHRISTMAS TREE...

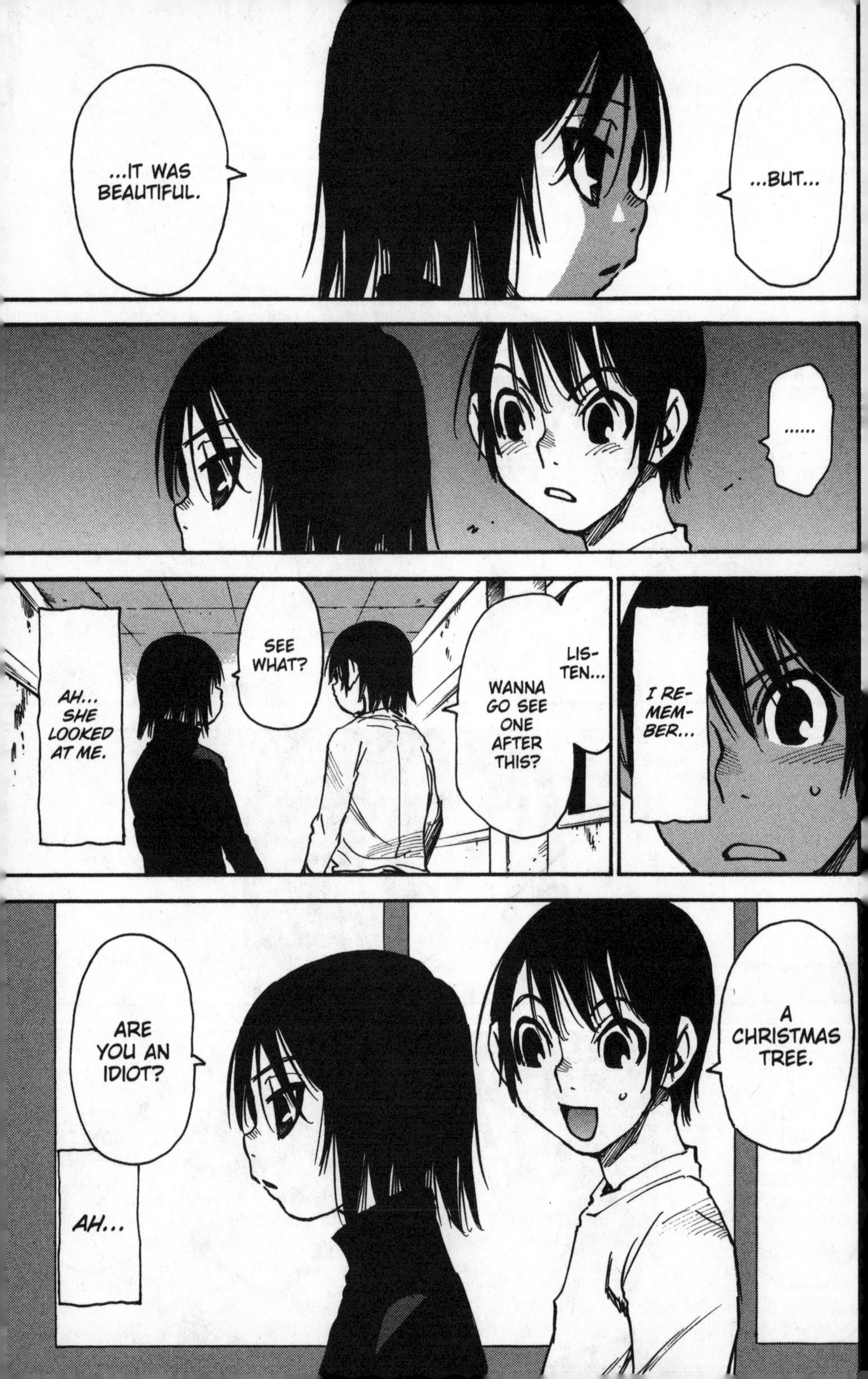

...BUT...
...IT WAS BEAUTIFUL.
......
I REMEMBER...
LISTEN... WANNA GO SEE ONE AFTER THIS?
SEE WHAT?
AH... SHE LOOKED AT ME.
A CHRISTMAS TREE.
ARE YOU AN IDIOT?
AH...

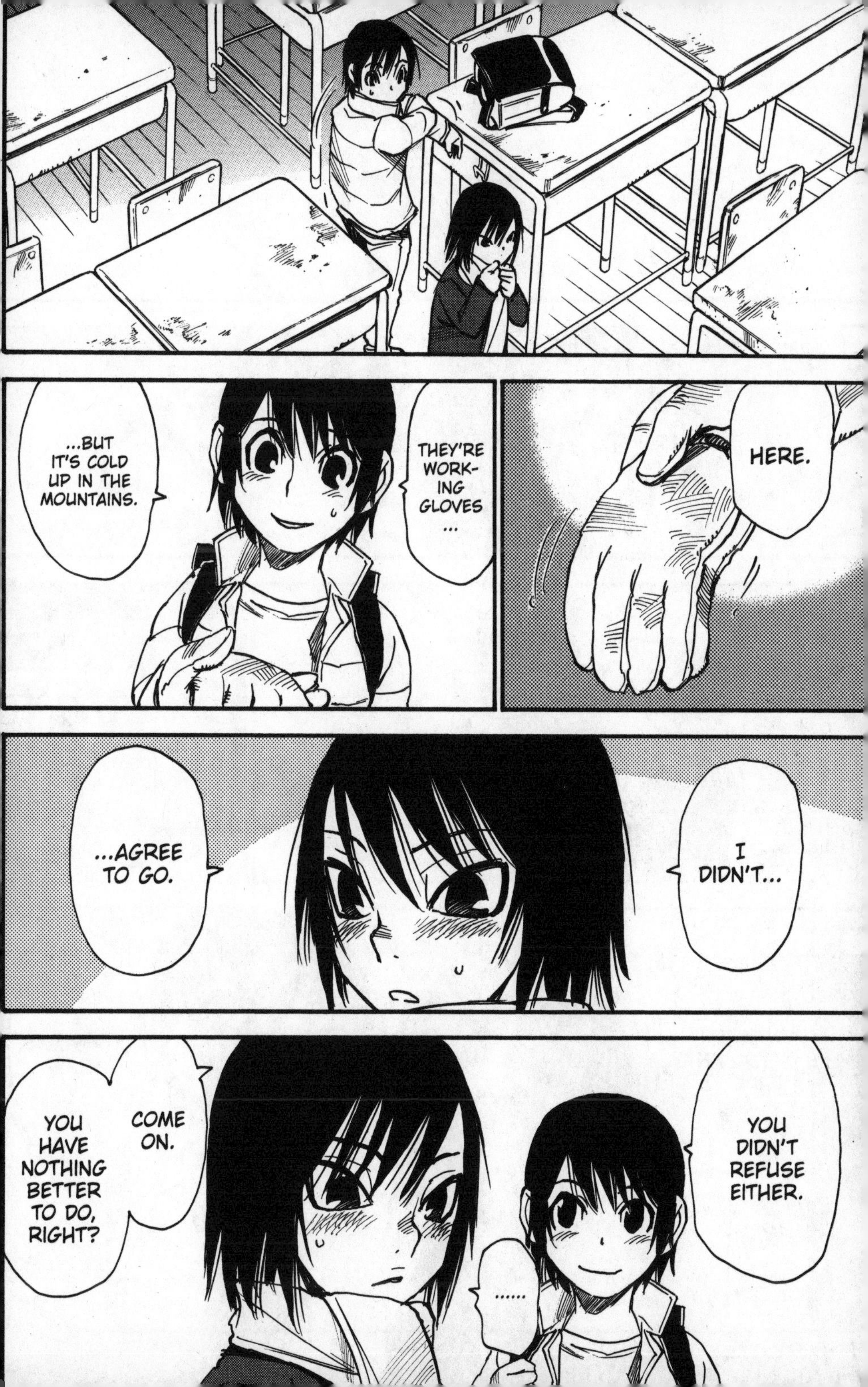
HERE.
THEY'RE WORKING-ING GLOVES...
...BUT IT'S COLD UP IN THE MOUNTAINS.
I DIDN'T...
...AGREE TO GO.
YOU DIDN'T REFUSE EITHER.
......
COME ON.
YOU HAVE NOTHING BETTER TO DO, RIGHT?

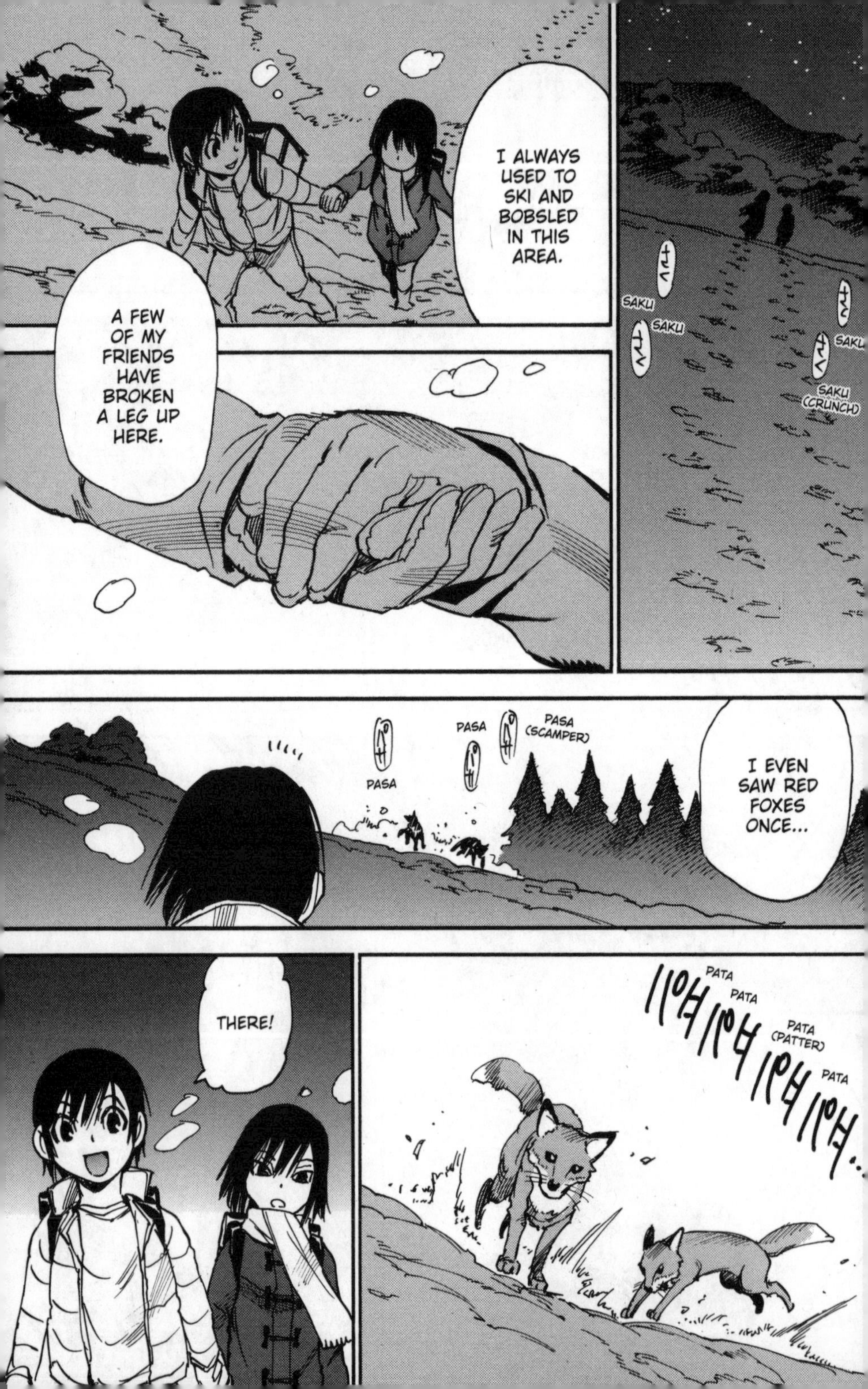
SAKU
SAKU
SAKU
SAKU (CRUNCH)
I ALWAYS USED TO SKI AND BOBSLED IN THIS AREA.
A FEW OF MY FRIENDS HAVE BROKEN A LEG UP HERE.
I EVEN SAW RED FOXES ONCE...
PASA (SCAMPER)
PASA
PASA
PATA
PATA
PATA (PATTER)
PATA
THERE!

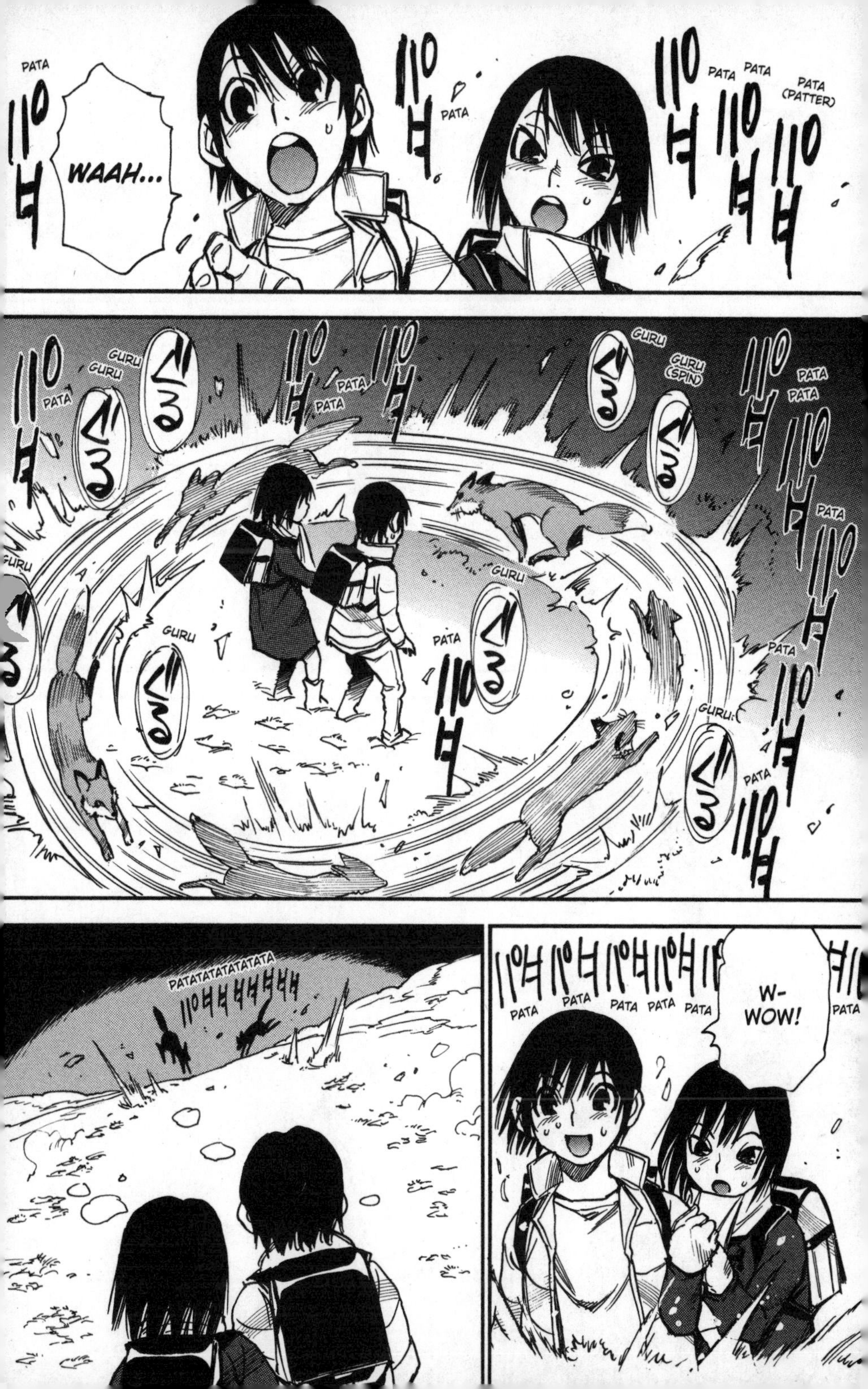

PATA (PATTER)
PATA
PATA
PATA
WAAH...
PATA
PATA
PATA
GURU
GURU (SPIN)
PATA
PATA
PATA
GURU
GURU
GURU
PATA
PATA
PATA
PATA
GURU
GURU
PATA
PATA
PATA
W- WOW!
PATA
PATA
PATA
PATA
PATA
PATATATATATATA

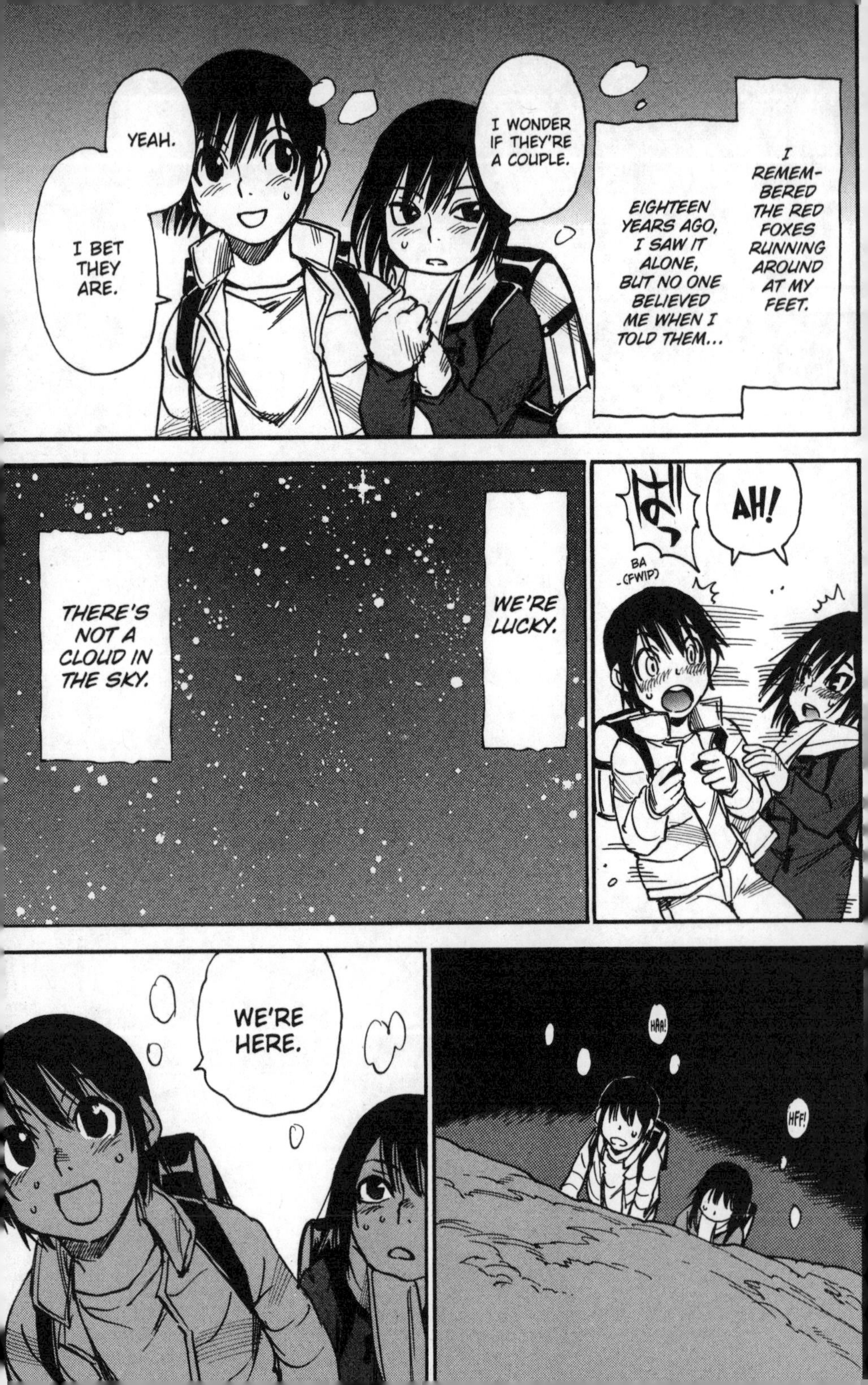
I REMEMBERED THE RED FOXES RUNNING AROUND AT MY FEET.
EIGHTEEN YEARS AGO, I SAW IT ALONE, BUT NO ONE BELIEVED ME WHEN I TOLD THEM...
I WONDER IF THEY'RE A COUPLE.
YEAH.
I BET THEY ARE.
AH!
はっ
BA -(FWIP)
WE'RE LUCKY.
THERE'S NOT A CLOUD IN THE SKY.
HAA!
HFF!
WE'RE HERE.

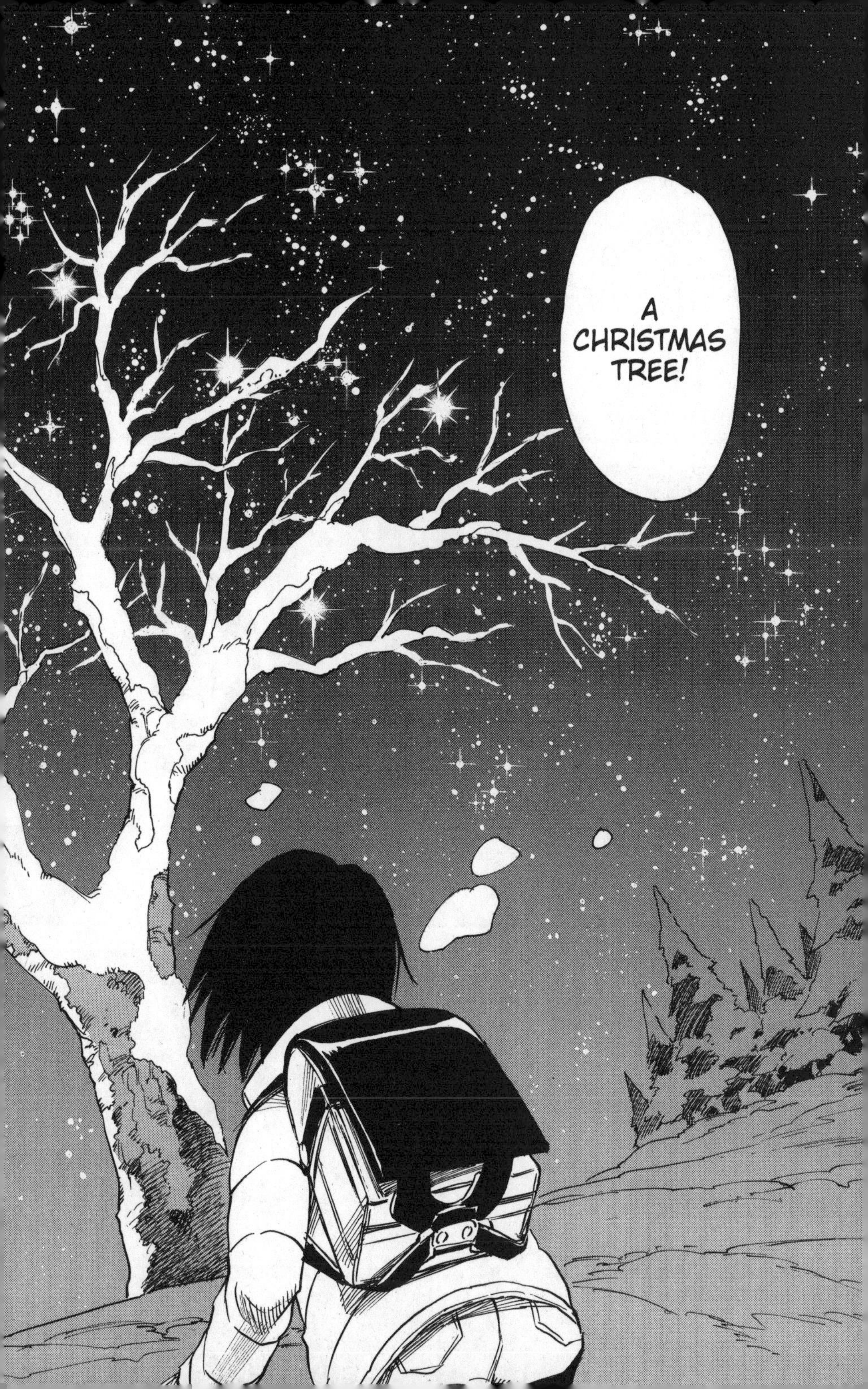
A CHRISTMAS TREE!

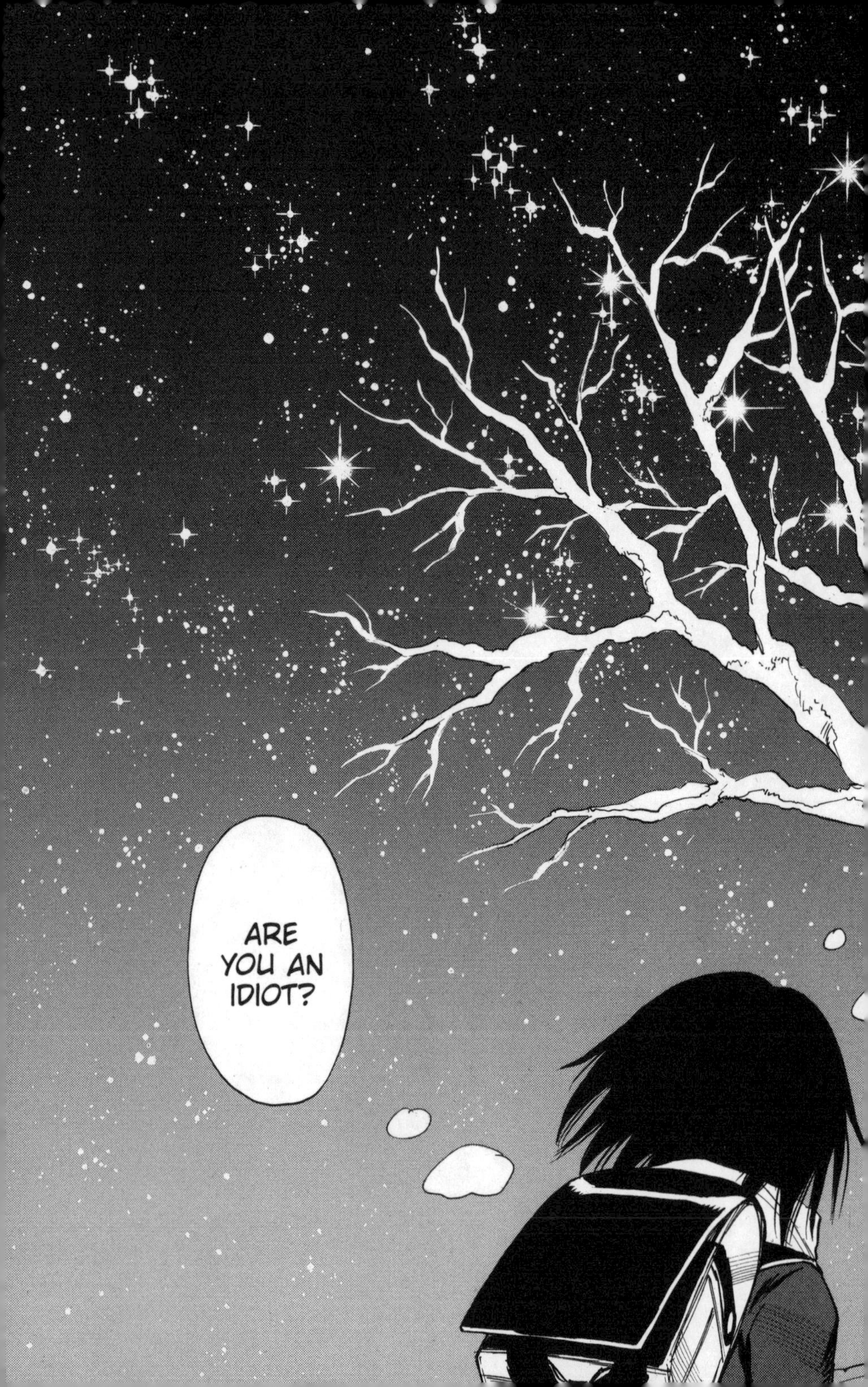
ARE YOU AN IDIOT?

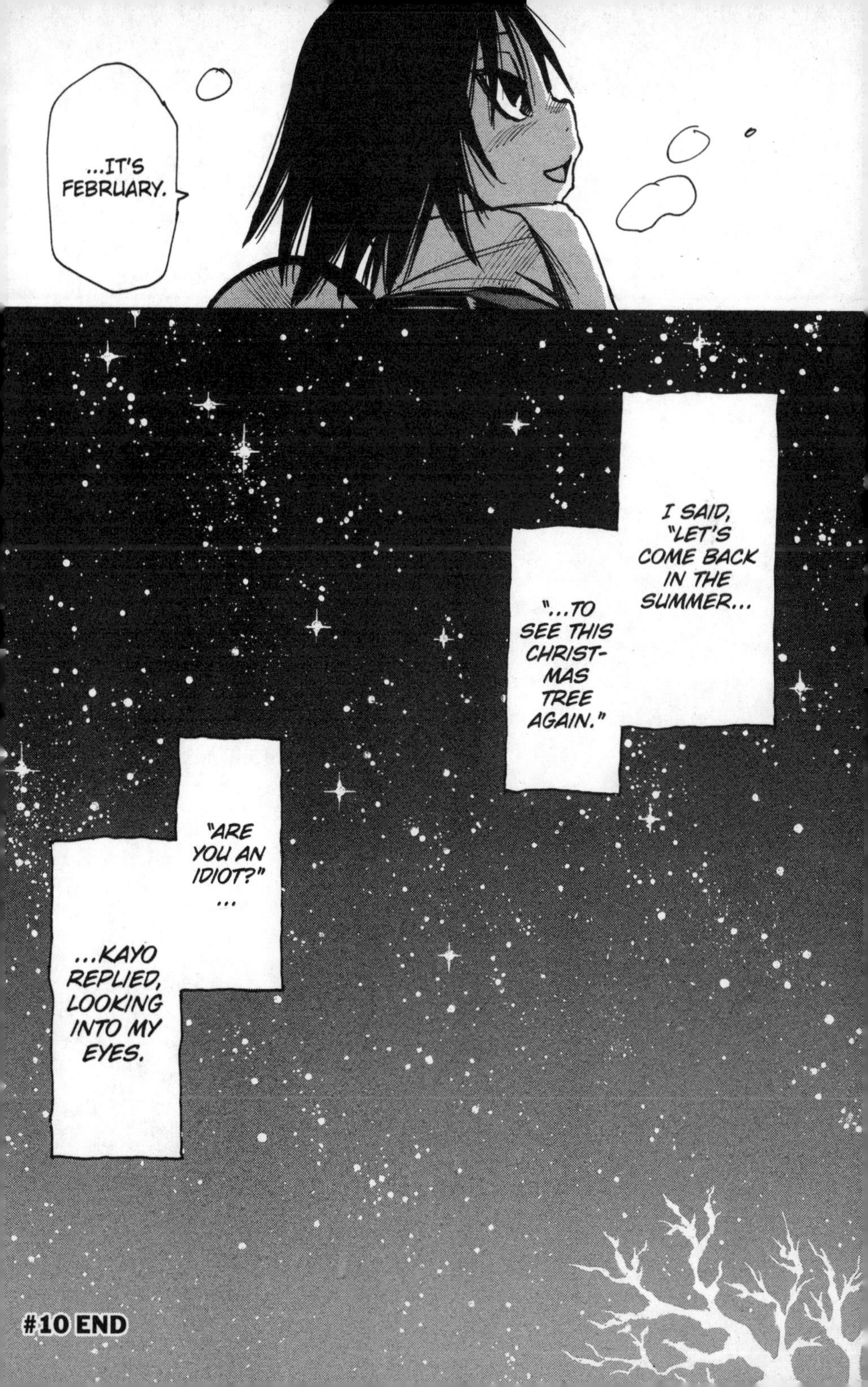
...IT'S FEBRUARY.
I SAID, "LET'S COME BACK IN THE SUMMER...
"...TO SEE THIS CHRISTMAS TREE AGAIN."
"ARE YOU AN IDIOT?" ...
...KAYO REPLIED, LOOKING INTO MY EYES.
#10 END

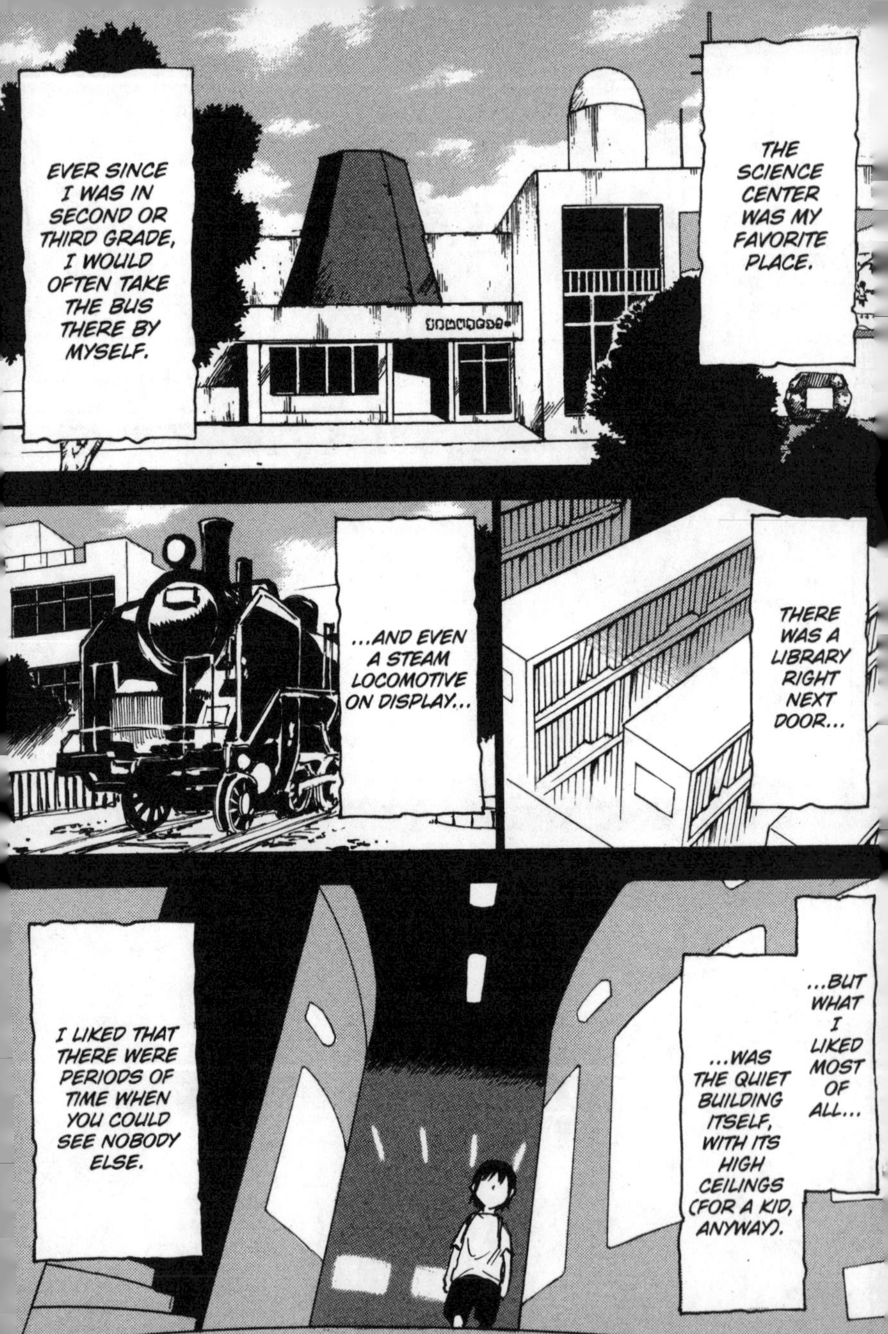
THE SCIENCE CENTER WAS MY FAVORITE PLACE.
EVER SINCE I WAS IN SECOND OR THIRD GRADE, I WOULD OFTEN TAKE THE BUS THERE BY MYSELF.
THERE WAS A LIBRARY RIGHT NEXT DOOR...
...AND EVEN A STEAM LOCOMOTIVE ON DISPLAY...
...BUT WHAT I LIKED MOST OF ALL...
...WAS THE QUIET BUILDING ITSELF, WITH ITS HIGH CEILINGS (FOR A KID, ANYWAY).
I LIKED THAT THERE WERE PERIODS OF TIME WHEN YOU COULD SEE NOBODY ELSE.

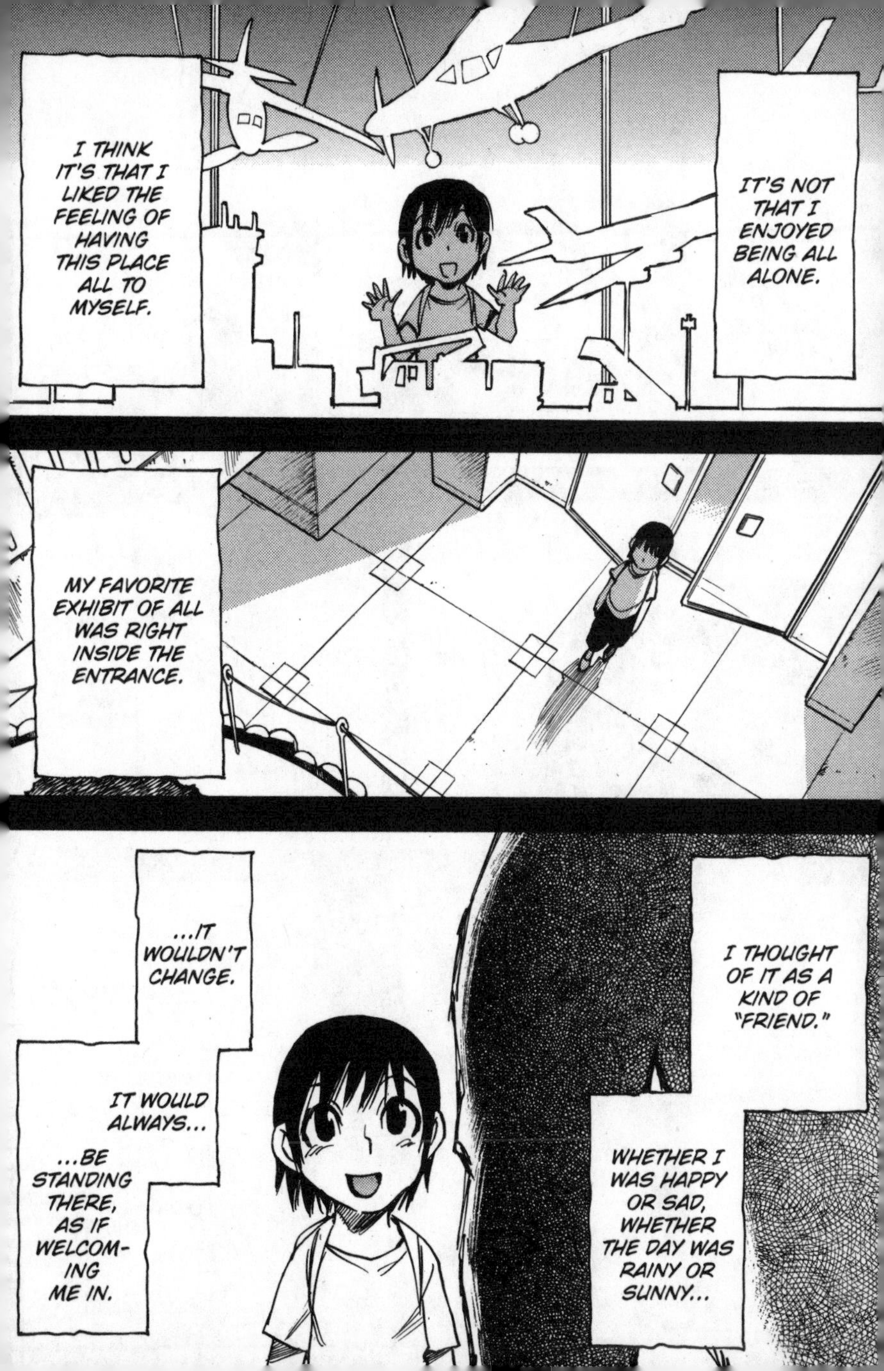
IT'S NOT THAT I ENJOYED BEING ALL ALONE.
I THINK IT'S THAT I LIKED THE FEELING OF HAVING THIS PLACE ALL TO MYSELF.
MY FAVORITE EXHIBIT OF ALL WAS RIGHT INSIDE THE ENTRANCE.
I THOUGHT OF IT AS A KIND OF "FRIEND."
WHETHER I WAS HAPPY OR SAD, WHETHER THE DAY WAS RAINY OR SUNNY...
...IT WOULDN'T CHANGE.
IT WOULD ALWAYS...
...BE STANDING THERE, AS IF WELCOM-ING ME IN.

#11: Repeated Scene, February 1988

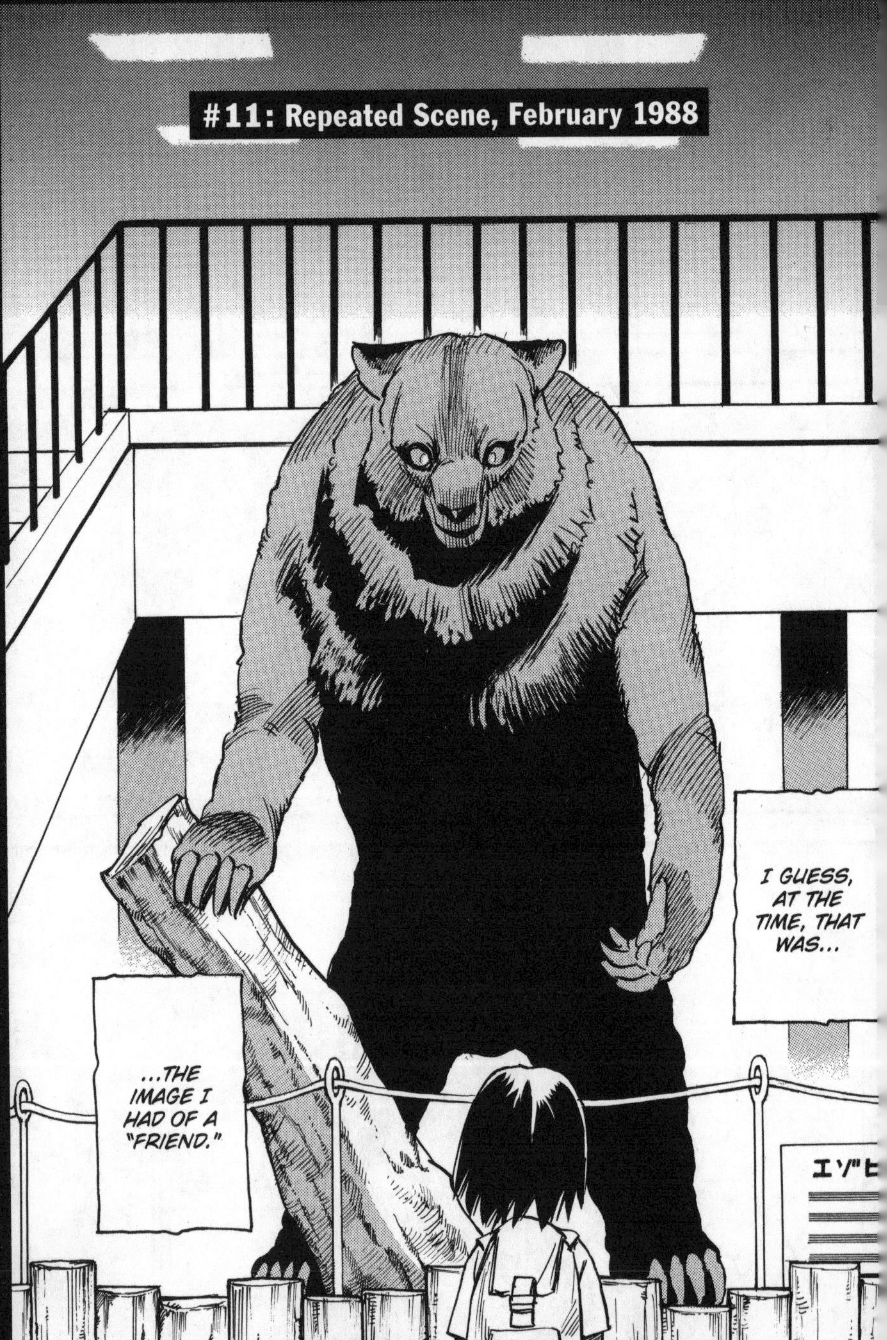

SIGN: HOKKAIDO BROWN B

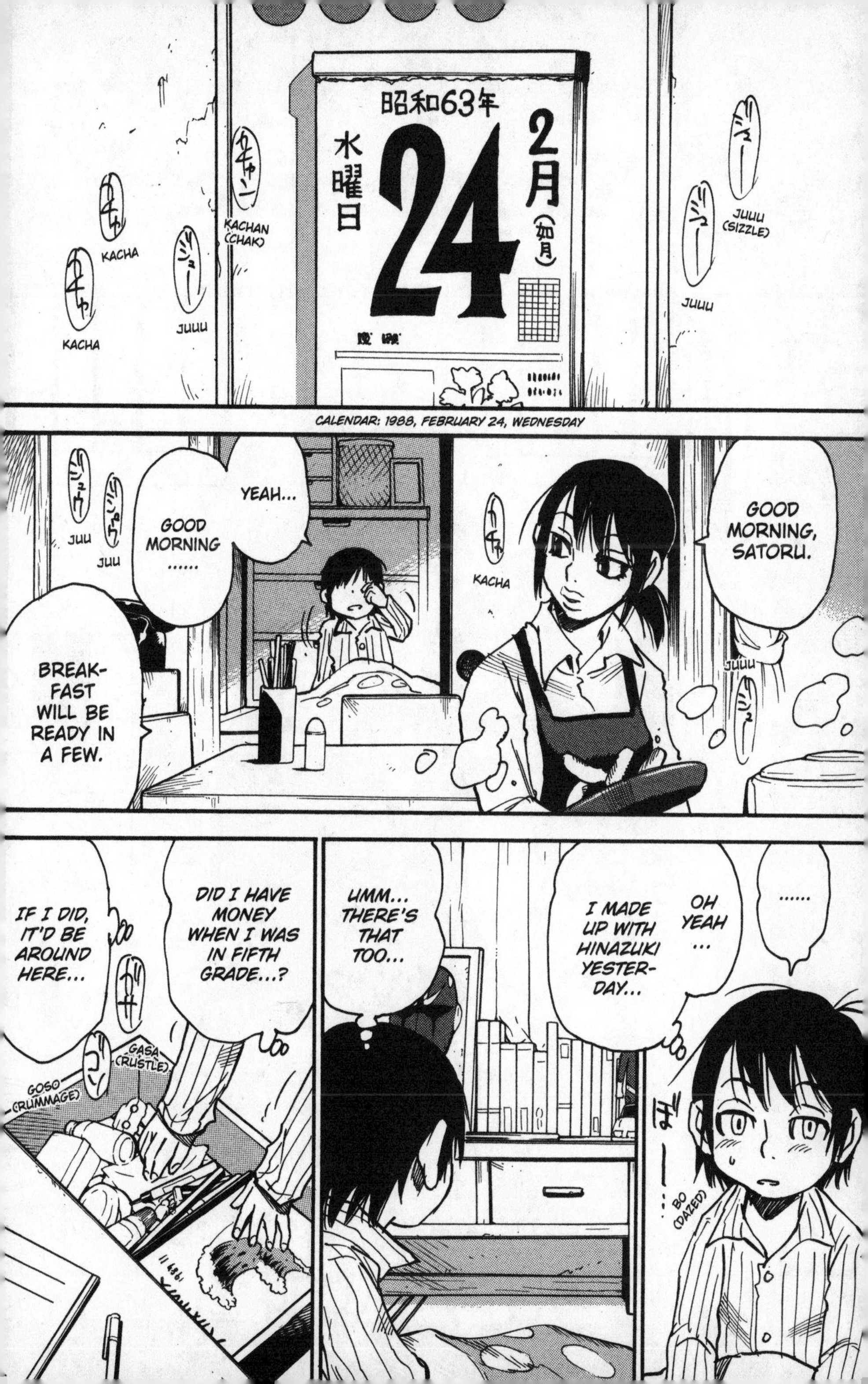
JUUU (SIZZLE)
JUUU
昭和63年
2月
(如月)
24
水曜日
KACHAN (CHAK)
JUUU
KACHA
KACHA
CALENDAR: 1988, FEBRUARY 24, WEDNESDAY
GOOD MORNING, SATORU.
JUUU
KACHA
YEAH...
GOOD MORNING ......
JUU
JUU
BREAK-FAST WILL BE READY IN A FEW.
......
OH YEAH ...
I MADE UP WITH HINAZUKI YESTER-DAY...
UMM... THERE'S THAT TOO...
BO (DAZED)
DID I HAVE MONEY WHEN I WAS IN FIFTH GRADE...?
IF I DID, IT'D BE AROUND HERE...
GASA (RUSTLE)
GOSO (RUMMAGE)

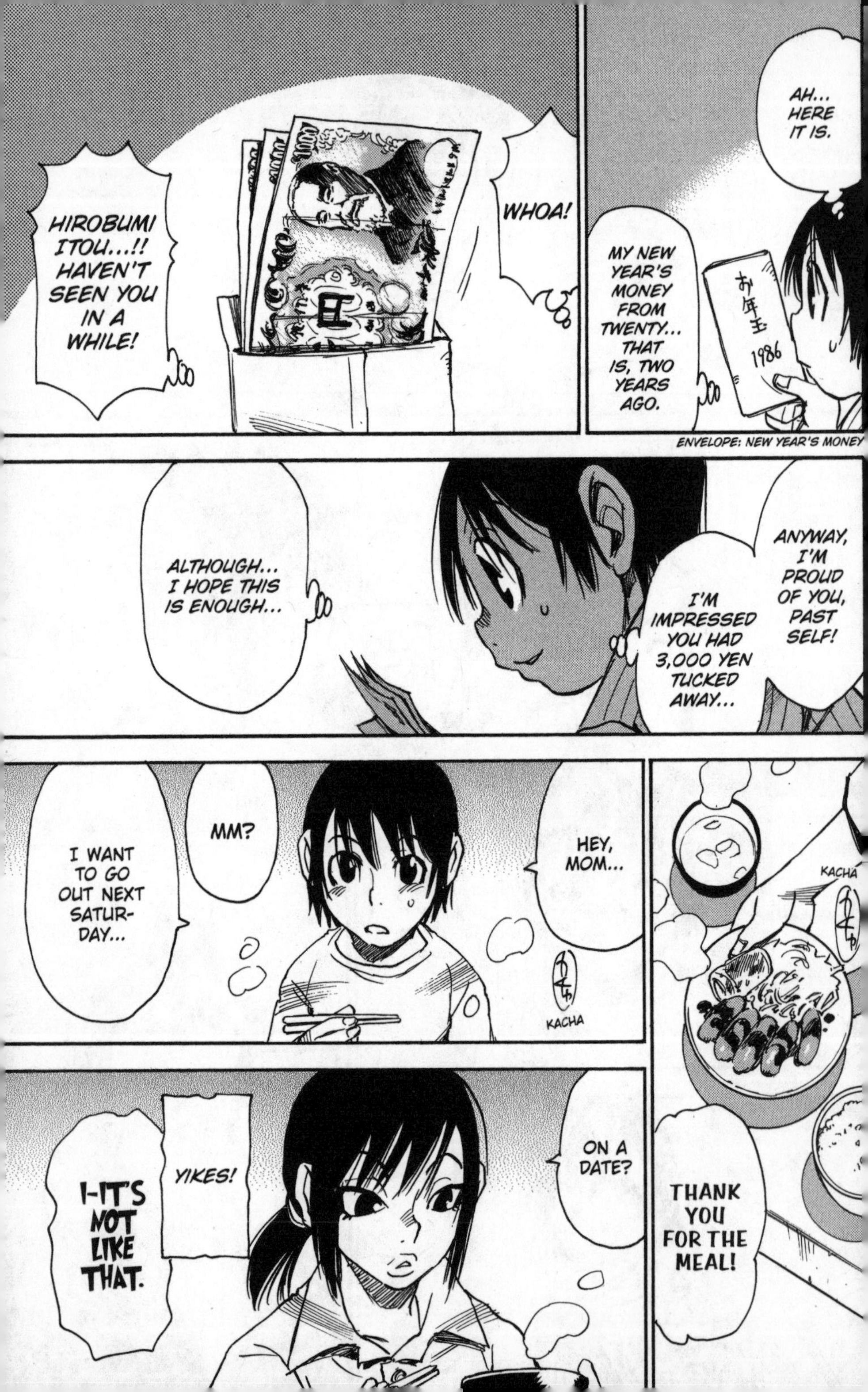
AH... HERE IT IS.
お年玉
1986
MY NEW YEAR'S MONEY FROM TWENTY... THAT IS, TWO YEARS AGO.
ENVELOPE: NEW YEAR'S MONEY
WHOA!
HIROBUMI ITOU...!! HAVEN'T SEEN YOU IN A WHILE!
ANYWAY, I'M PROUD OF YOU, PAST SELF!
I'M IMPRESSED YOU HAD 3,000 YEN TUCKED AWAY...
ALTHOUGH... I HOPE THIS IS ENOUGH...
KACHA
THANK YOU FOR THE MEAL!
HEY, MOM...
MM?
I WANT TO GO OUT NEXT SATURDAY...
KACHA
ON A DATE?
YIKES!
I-IT'S NOT LIKE THAT.

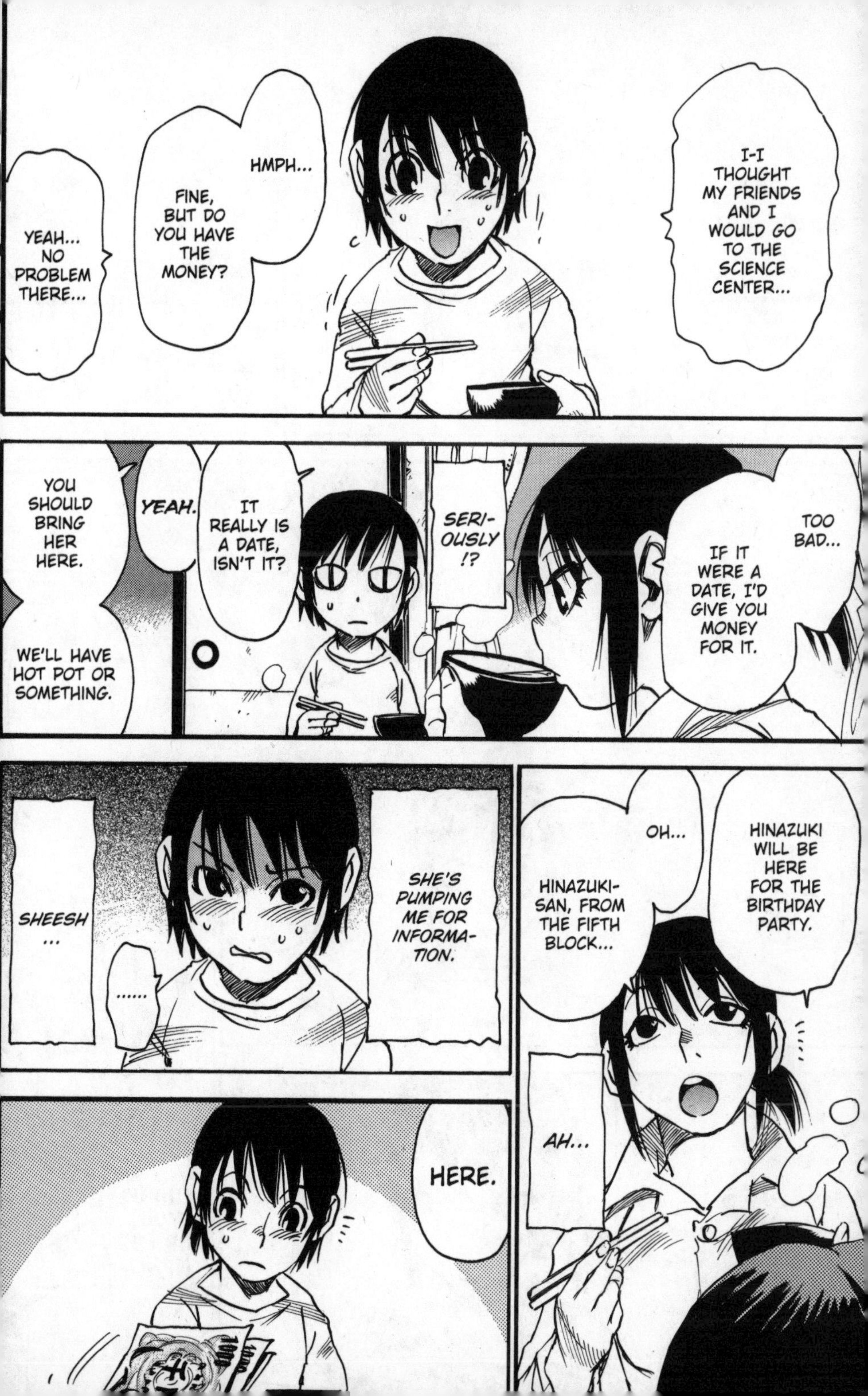
I-I THOUGHT MY FRIENDS AND I WOULD GO TO THE SCIENCE CENTER...
HMPH... FINE, BUT DO YOU HAVE THE MONEY?
YEAH... NO PROBLEM THERE...
TOO BAD... IF IT WERE A DATE, I'D GIVE YOU MONEY FOR IT.
SERI-OUSLY!?
IT REALLY IS A DATE, ISN'T IT?
YEAH.
YOU SHOULD BRING HER HERE. WE'LL HAVE HOT POT OR SOMETHING.
HINAZUKI WILL BE HERE FOR THE BIRTHDAY PARTY.
OH... HINAZUKI-SAN, FROM THE FIFTH BLOCK...
AH...
SHE'S PUMPING ME FOR INFORMATION.
SHEESH...
......
HERE.

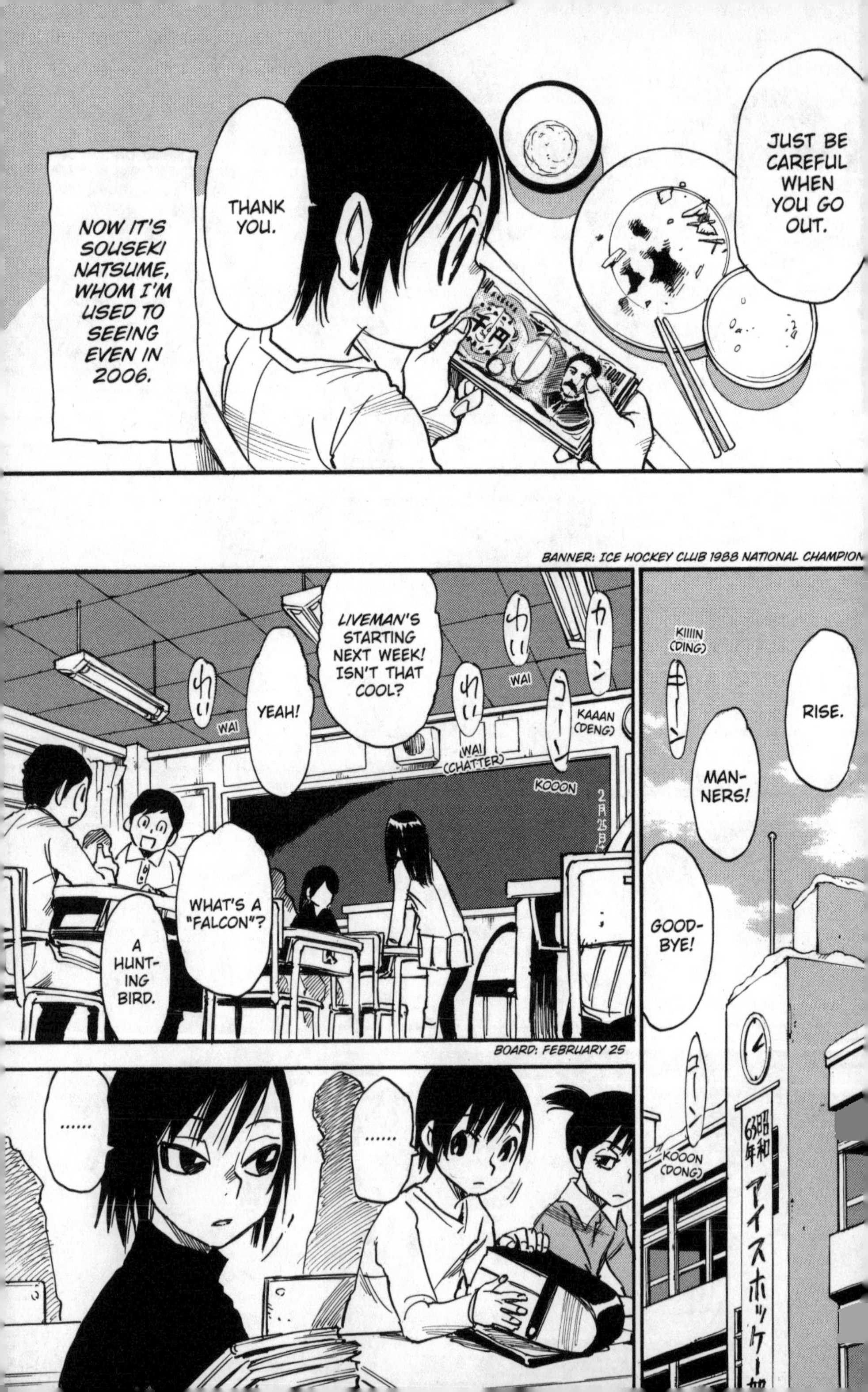
JUST BE CAREFUL WHEN YOU GO OUT.
THANK YOU.
NOW IT'S SOUSEKI NATSUME, WHOM I'M USED TO SEEING EVEN IN 2006.
BANNER: ICE HOCKEY CLUB 1988 NATIONAL CHAMPION
KIIIIN (DING)
RISE.
MAN-NERS!
GOOD-BYE!
KOOON (DONG)
KAAAN (DENG)
KOOON
LIVEMAN'S STARTING NEXT WEEK! ISN'T THAT COOL?
WAI
YEAH!
WAI
WAI (CHATTER)
WHAT'S A "FALCON"?
A HUNTING BIRD.
BOARD: FEBRUARY 25
......
......

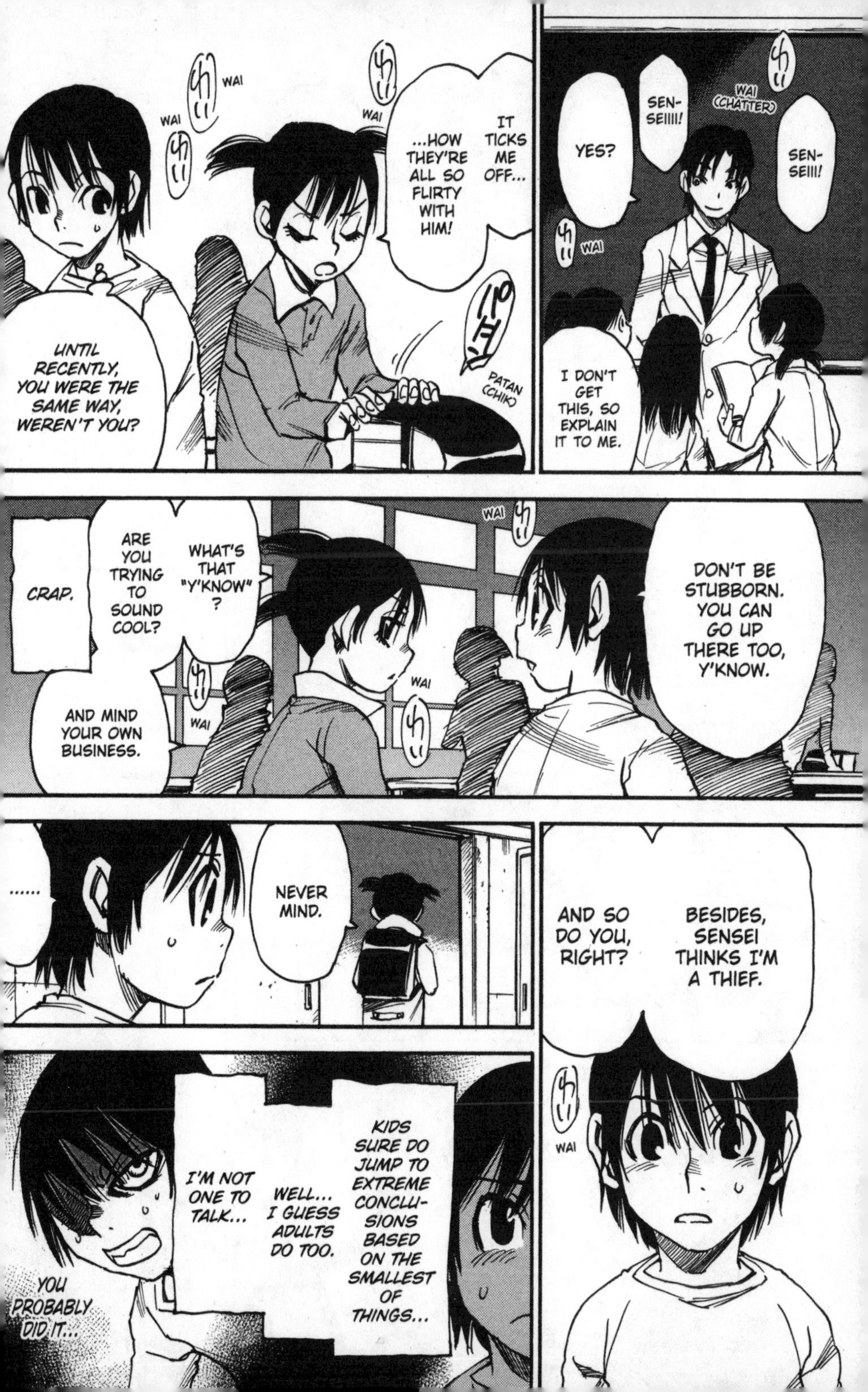
SEN-SEIII!
WAI (CHATTER)
SEN-SEIIII!
YES?
WAI
I DON'T GET THIS, SO EXPLAIN IT TO ME.
IT TICKS ME OFF...
...HOW THEY'RE ALL SO FLIRTY WITH HIM!
WAI
パタン
PATAN (CHIK)
WAI
WAI
UNTIL RECENTLY, YOU WERE THE SAME WAY, WEREN'T YOU?
DON'T BE STUBBORN. YOU CAN GO UP THERE TOO, Y'KNOW.
WAI
WAI
WHAT'S THAT "Y'KNOW"?
ARE YOU TRYING TO SOUND COOL?
WAI
CRAP.
AND MIND YOUR OWN BUSINESS.
BESIDES, SENSEI THINKS I'M A THIEF.
AND SO DO YOU, RIGHT?
WAI
NEVER MIND.
......
KIDS SURE DO JUMP TO EXTREME CONCLUSIONS BASED ON THE SMALLEST OF THINGS...
WELL... I GUESS ADULTS DO TOO.
I'M NOT ONE TO TALK...
YOU PROBABLY DID IT...

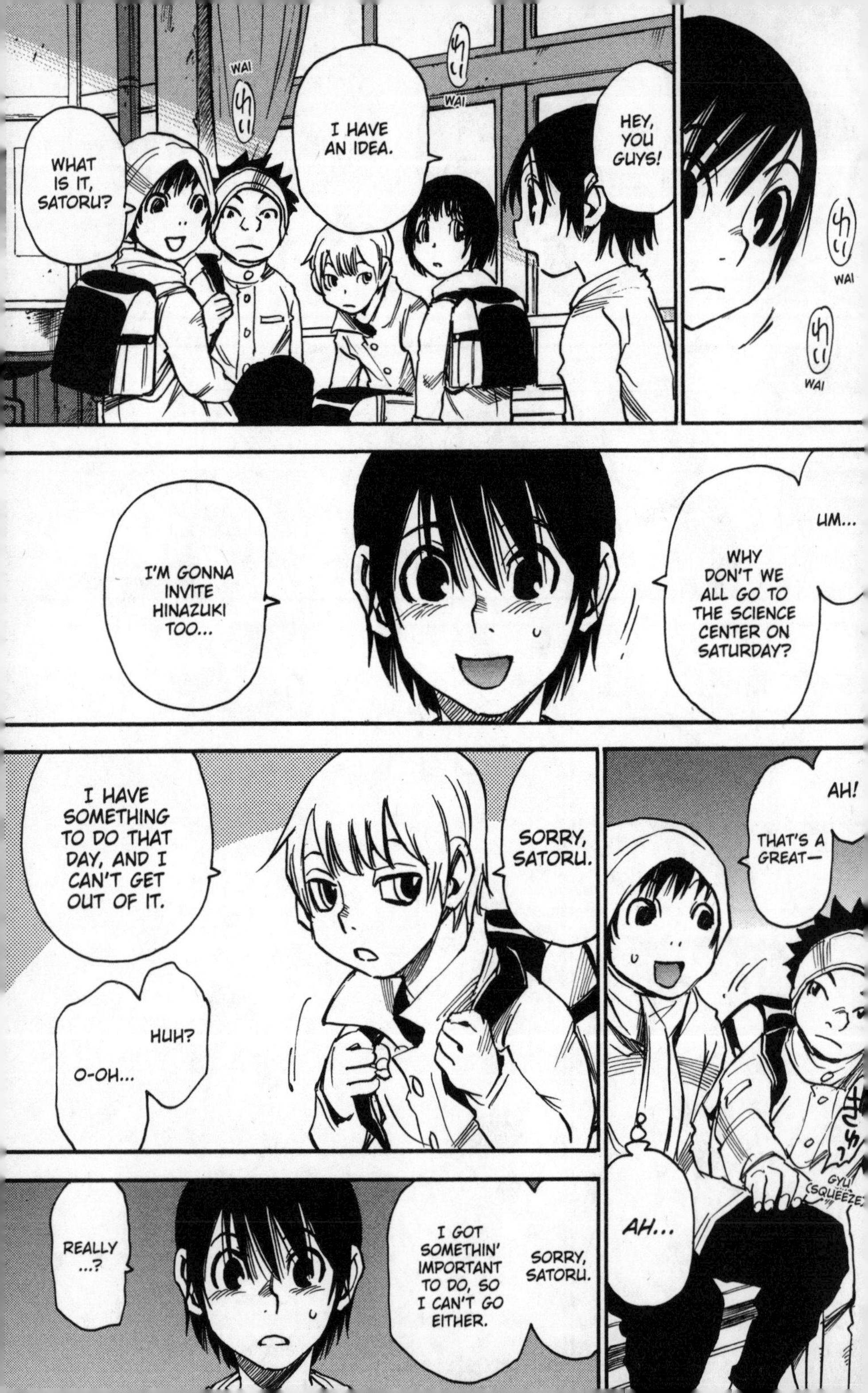
WAI
WAI
HEY, YOU GUYS!
WAI
I HAVE AN IDEA.
WAI
WHAT IS IT, SATORU?
UM...
WHY DON'T WE ALL GO TO THE SCIENCE CENTER ON SATURDAY?
I'M GONNA INVITE HINAZUKI TOO...
AH!
THAT'S A GREAT—
GYU (SQUEEZE)
AH...
SORRY, SATORU.
I HAVE SOMETHING TO DO THAT DAY, AND I CAN'T GET OUT OF IT.
HUH?
O-OH...
SORRY, SATORU.
I GOT SOMETHIN' IMPORTANT TO DO, SO I CAN'T GO EITHER.
REALLY ...?

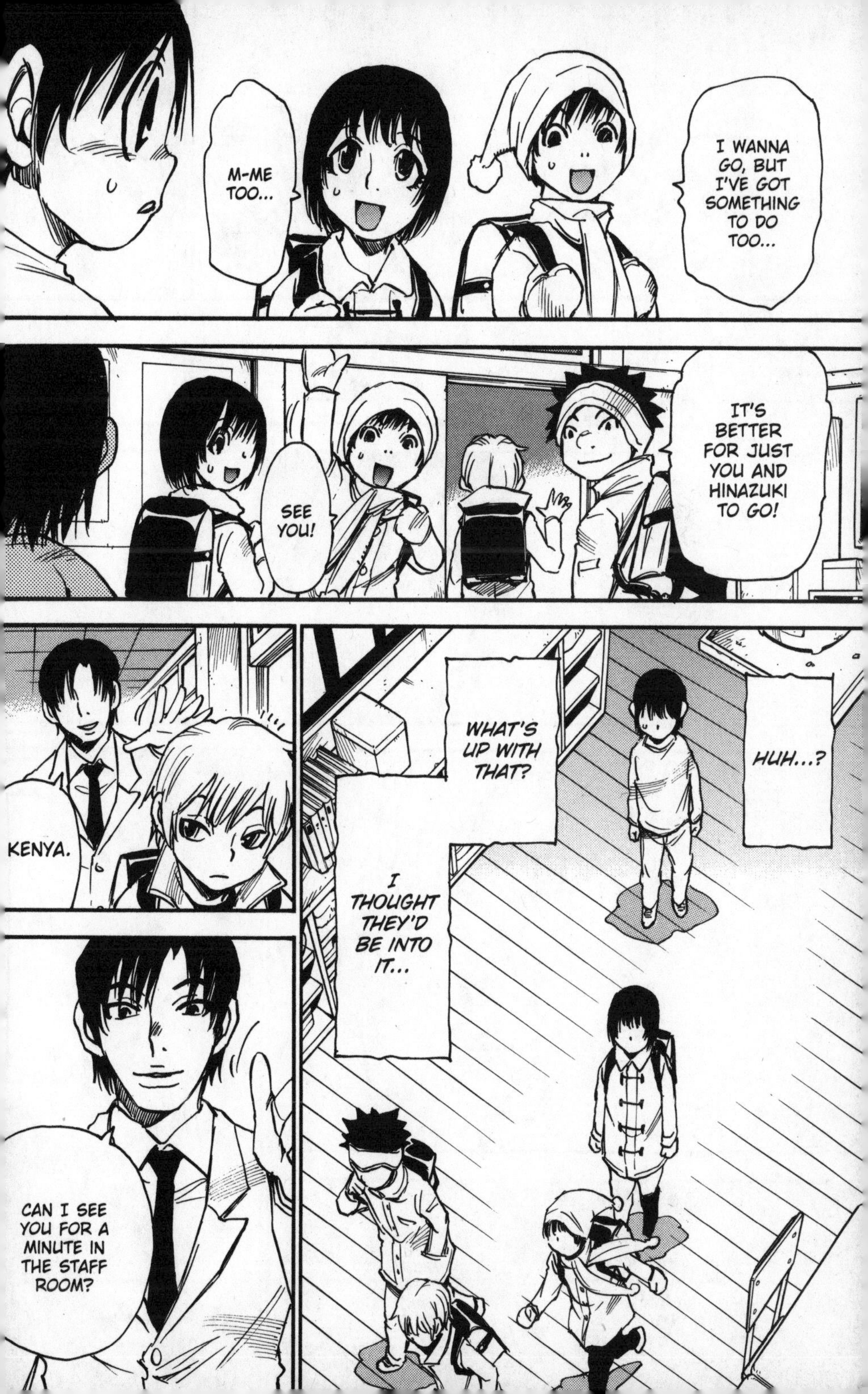
I WANNA GO, BUT I'VE GOT SOMETHING TO DO TOO...
M-ME TOO...
IT'S BETTER FOR JUST YOU AND HINAZUKI TO GO!
SEE YOU!
HUH...?
WHAT'S UP WITH THAT?
I THOUGHT THEY'D BE INTO IT...
KENYA.
CAN I SEE YOU FOR A MINUTE IN THE STAFF ROOM?

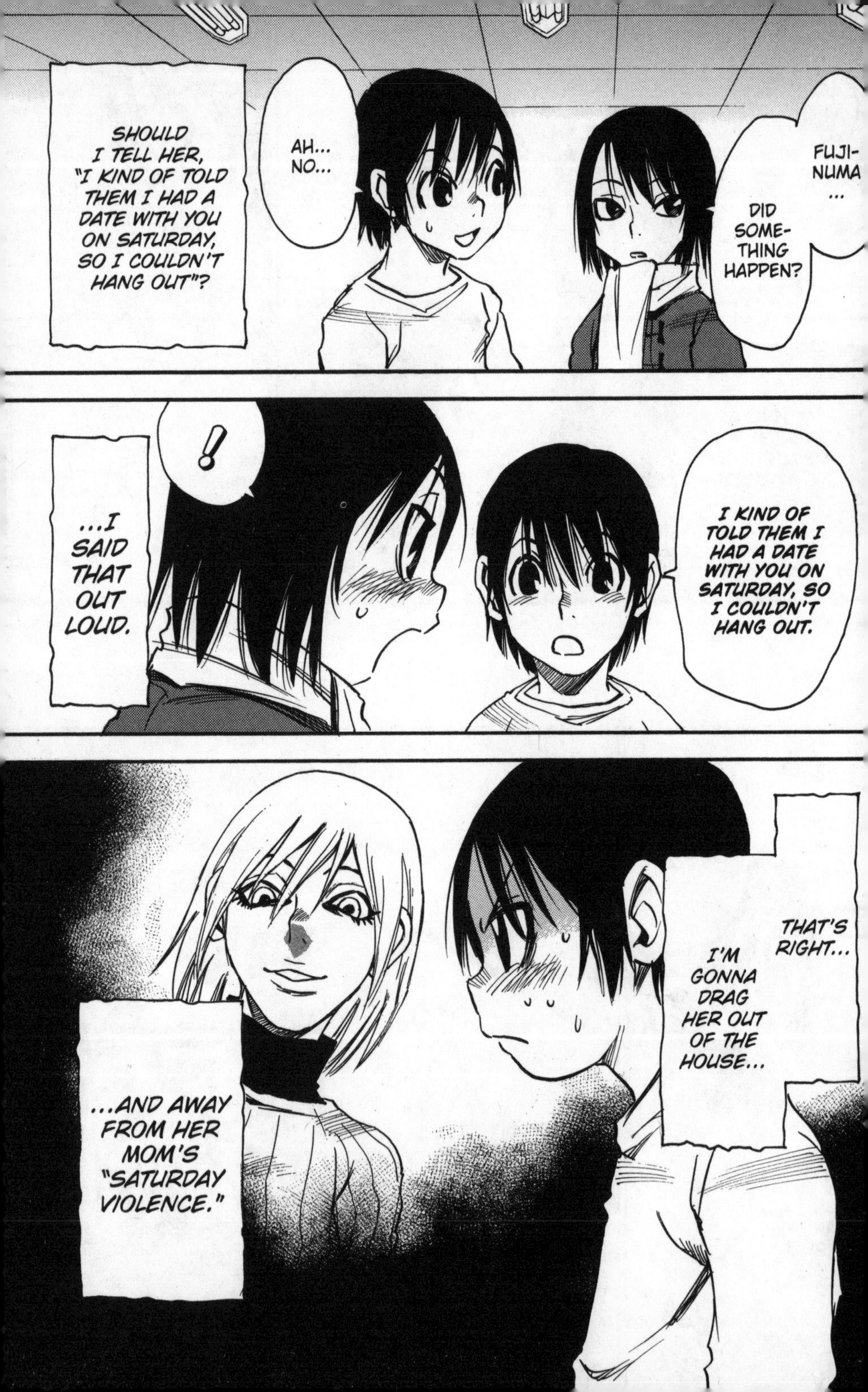
FUJI-NUMA ...
DID SOME-THING HAPPEN?
AH... NO...
SHOULD I TELL HER, "I KIND OF TOLD THEM I HAD A DATE WITH YOU ON SATURDAY, SO I COULDN'T HANG OUT"?
I KIND OF TOLD THEM I HAD A DATE WITH YOU ON SATURDAY, SO I COULDN'T HANG OUT.
!
...I SAID THAT OUT LOUD.
THAT'S RIGHT...
I'M GONNA DRAG HER OUT OF THE HOUSE...
...AND AWAY FROM HER MOM'S "SATURDAY VIOLENCE."

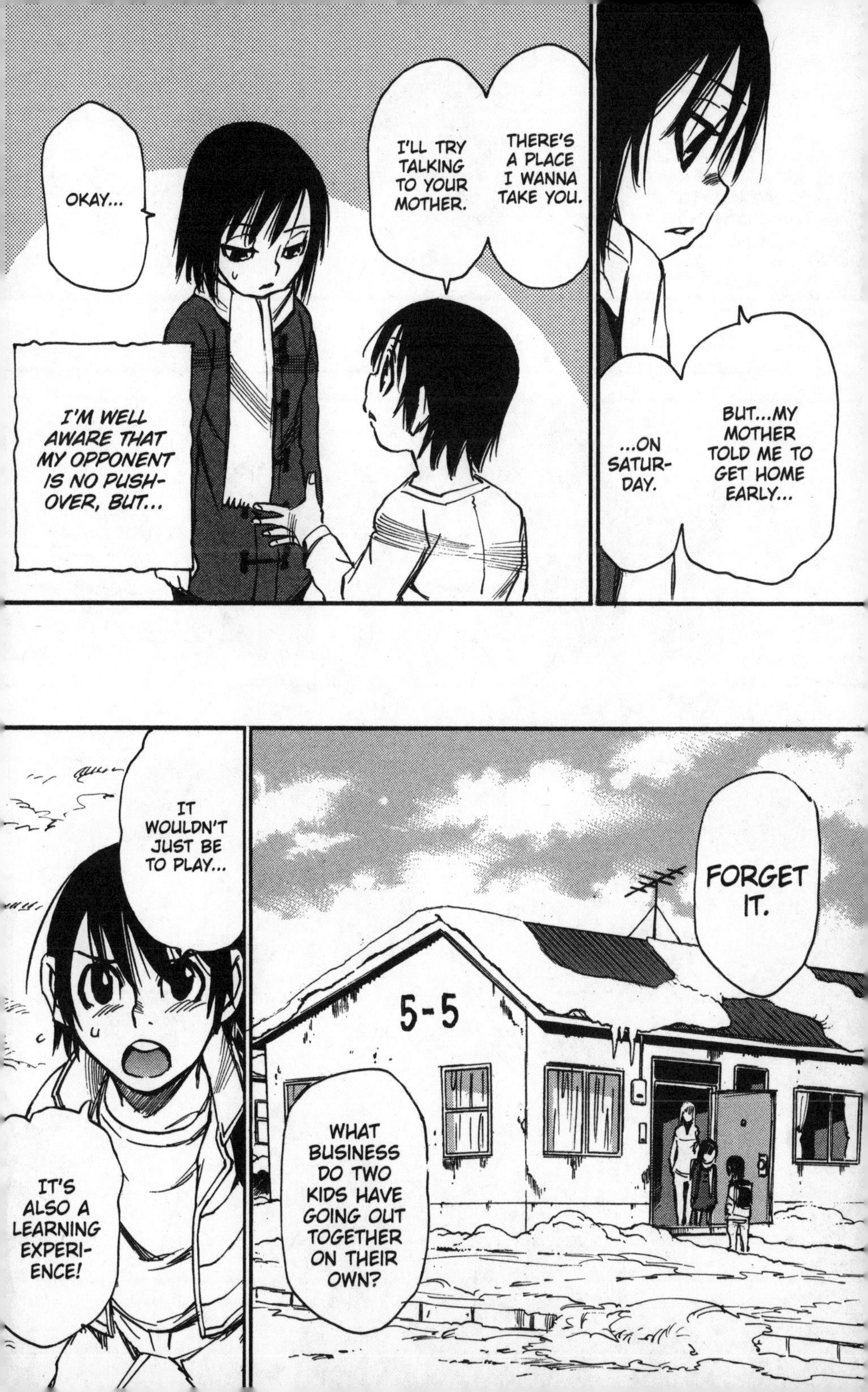
BUT...MY MOTHER TOLD ME TO GET HOME EARLY...
...ON SATURDAY.
THERE'S A PLACE I WANNA TAKE YOU.
I'LL TRY TALKING TO YOUR MOTHER.
OKAY...
I'M WELL AWARE THAT MY OPPONENT IS NO PUSHOVER, BUT...
FORGET IT.
5-5
WHAT BUSINESS DO TWO KIDS HAVE GOING OUT TOGETHER ON THEIR OWN?
IT WOULDN'T JUST BE TO PLAY...
IT'S ALSO A LEARNING EXPERIENCE!

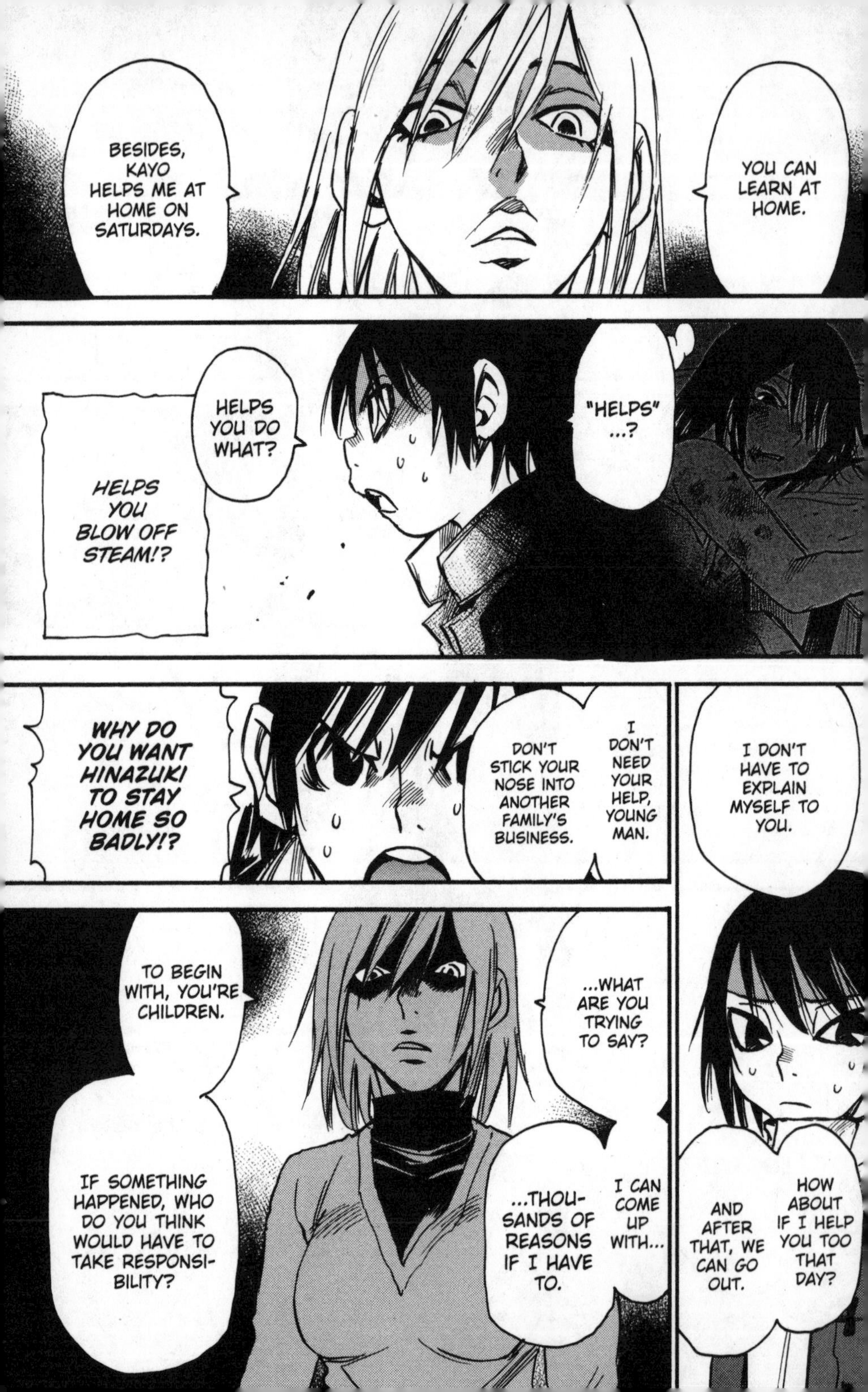
YOU CAN LEARN AT HOME.
BESIDES, KAYO HELPS ME AT HOME ON SATURDAYS.
"HELPS" ...?
HELPS YOU DO WHAT?
HELPS YOU BLOW OFF STEAM!?
I DON'T HAVE TO EXPLAIN MYSELF TO YOU.
HOW ABOUT IF I HELP YOU TOO THAT DAY?
AND AFTER THAT, WE CAN GO OUT.
I DON'T NEED YOUR HELP, YOUNG MAN.
DON'T STICK YOUR NOSE INTO ANOTHER FAMILY'S BUSINESS.
WHY DO YOU WANT HINAZUKI TO STAY HOME SO BADLY!?
...WHAT ARE YOU TRYING TO SAY?
TO BEGIN WITH, YOU'RE CHILDREN.
I CAN COME UP WITH...
...THOU-SANDS OF REASONS IF I HAVE TO.
IF SOMETHING HAPPENED, WHO DO YOU THINK WOULD HAVE TO TAKE RESPONSI-BILITY?

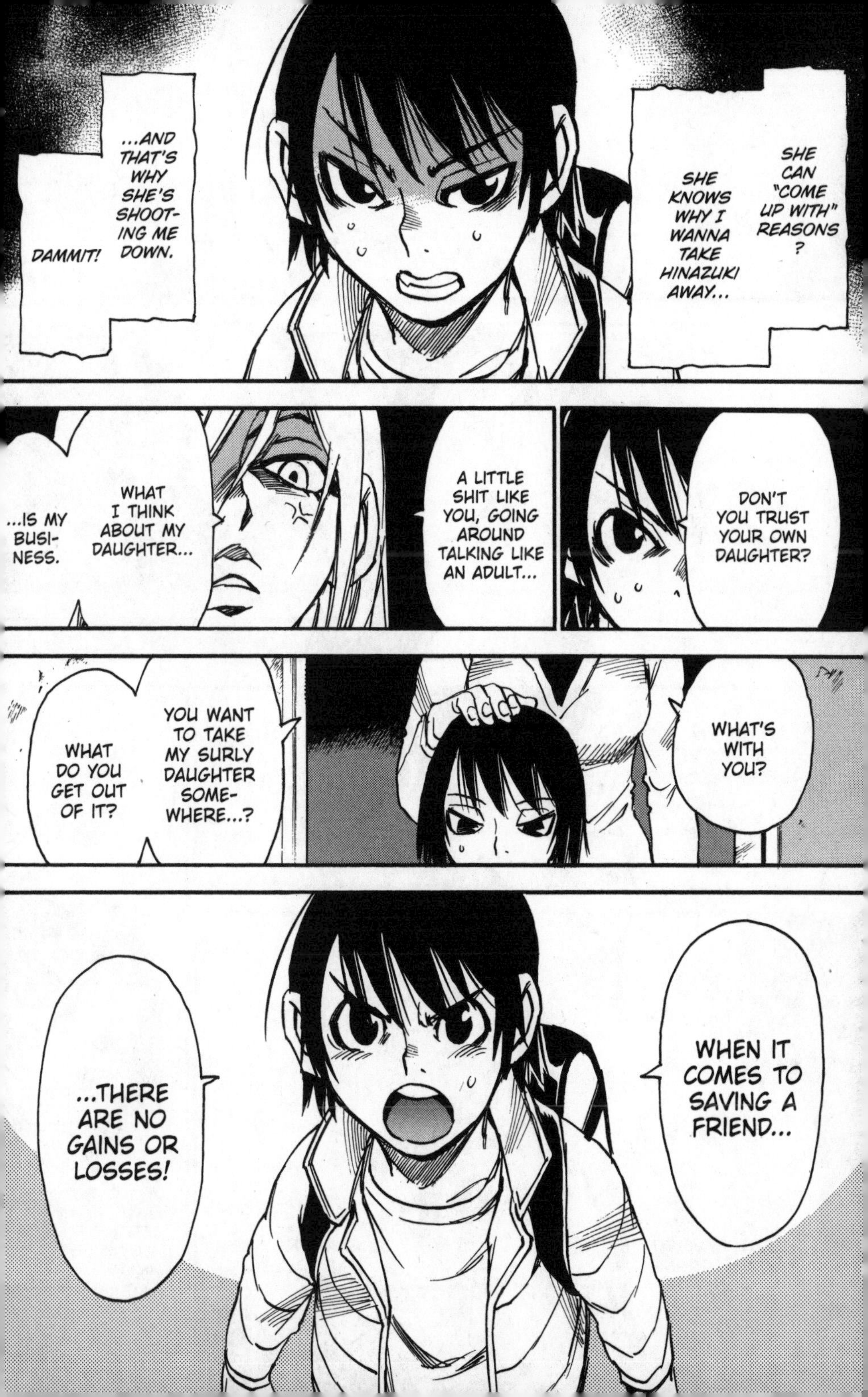
SHE CAN "COME UP WITH" REASONS?
SHE KNOWS WHY I WANNA TAKE HINAZUKI AWAY...
...AND THAT'S WHY SHE'S SHOOTING ME DOWN.
DAMMIT!
DON'T YOU TRUST YOUR OWN DAUGHTER?
A LITTLE SHIT LIKE YOU, GOING AROUND TALKING LIKE AN ADULT...
WHAT I THINK ABOUT MY DAUGHTER...
...IS MY BUSINESS.
WHAT'S WITH YOU?
YOU WANT TO TAKE MY SURLY DAUGHTER SOMEWHERE...?
WHAT DO YOU GET OUT OF IT?
WHEN IT COMES TO SAVING A FRIEND...
...THERE ARE NO GAINS OR LOSSES!

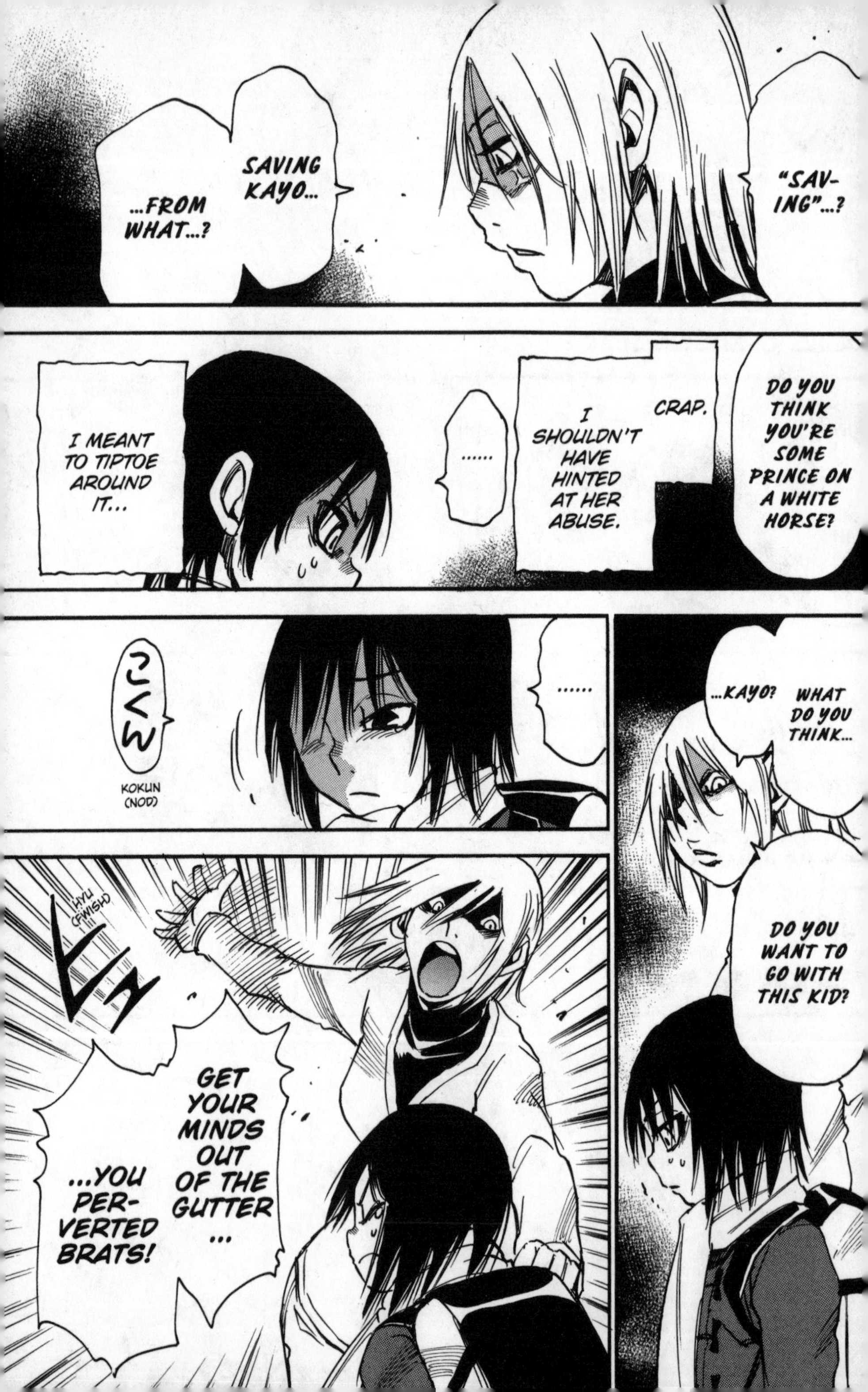
"SAV-ING"...?
SAVING KAYO...
...FROM WHAT...?
DO YOU THINK YOU'RE SOME PRINCE ON A WHITE HORSE?
CRAP.
I SHOULDN'T HAVE HINTED AT HER ABUSE.
......
I MEANT TO TIPTOE AROUND IT...
...KAYO?
WHAT DO YOU THINK...
DO YOU WANT TO GO WITH THIS KID?
......
こくん
KOKUN (NOD)
ヒュ
HYU (FWISH)
GET YOUR MINDS OUT OF THE GUTTER ...
...YOU PER-VERTED BRATS!

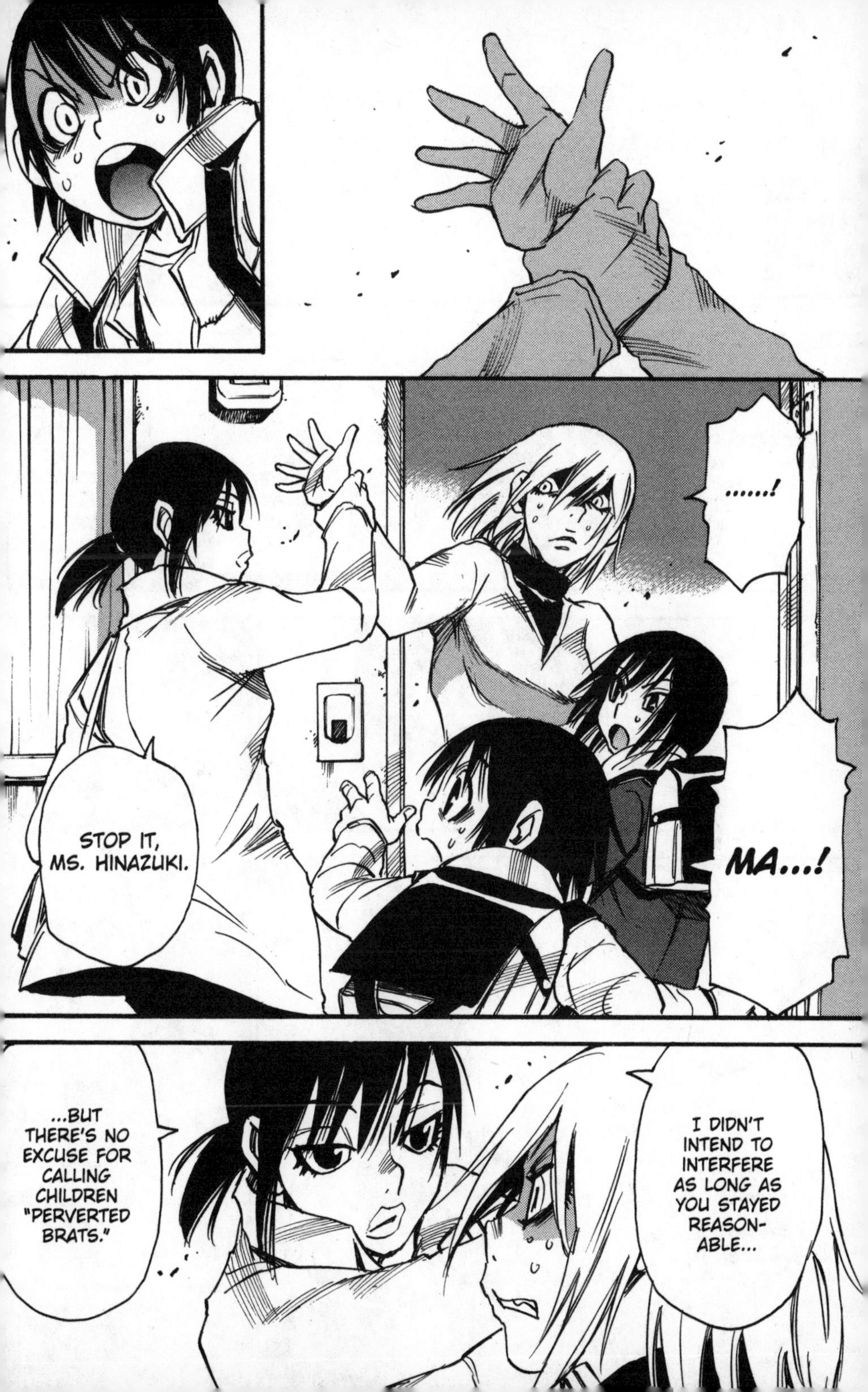
......!
MA...!
STOP IT, MS. HINAZUKI.
I DIDN'T INTEND TO INTERFERE AS LONG AS YOU STAYED REASON-ABLE...
...BUT THERE'S NO EXCUSE FOR CALLING CHILDREN "PERVERTED BRATS."

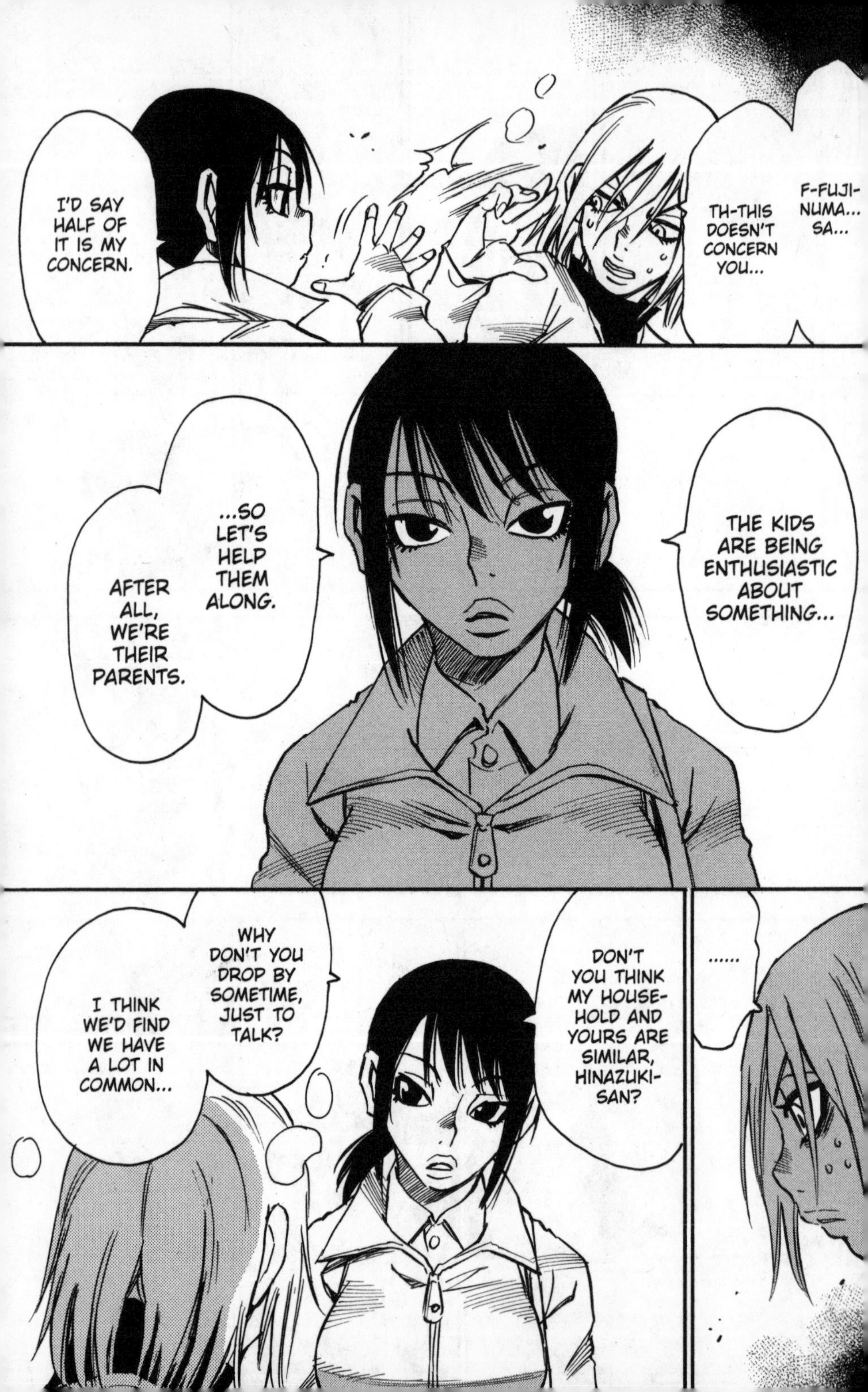
F-FUJI-NUMA... SA...
TH-THIS DOESN'T CONCERN YOU...
I'D SAY HALF OF IT IS MY CONCERN.
THE KIDS ARE BEING ENTHUSIASTIC ABOUT SOMETHING...
...SO LET'S HELP THEM ALONG.
AFTER ALL, WE'RE THEIR PARENTS.
......
DON'T YOU THINK MY HOUSE-HOLD AND YOURS ARE SIMILAR, HINAZUKI-SAN?
WHY DON'T YOU DROP BY SOMETIME, JUST TO TALK?
I THINK WE'D FIND WE HAVE A LOT IN COMMON...

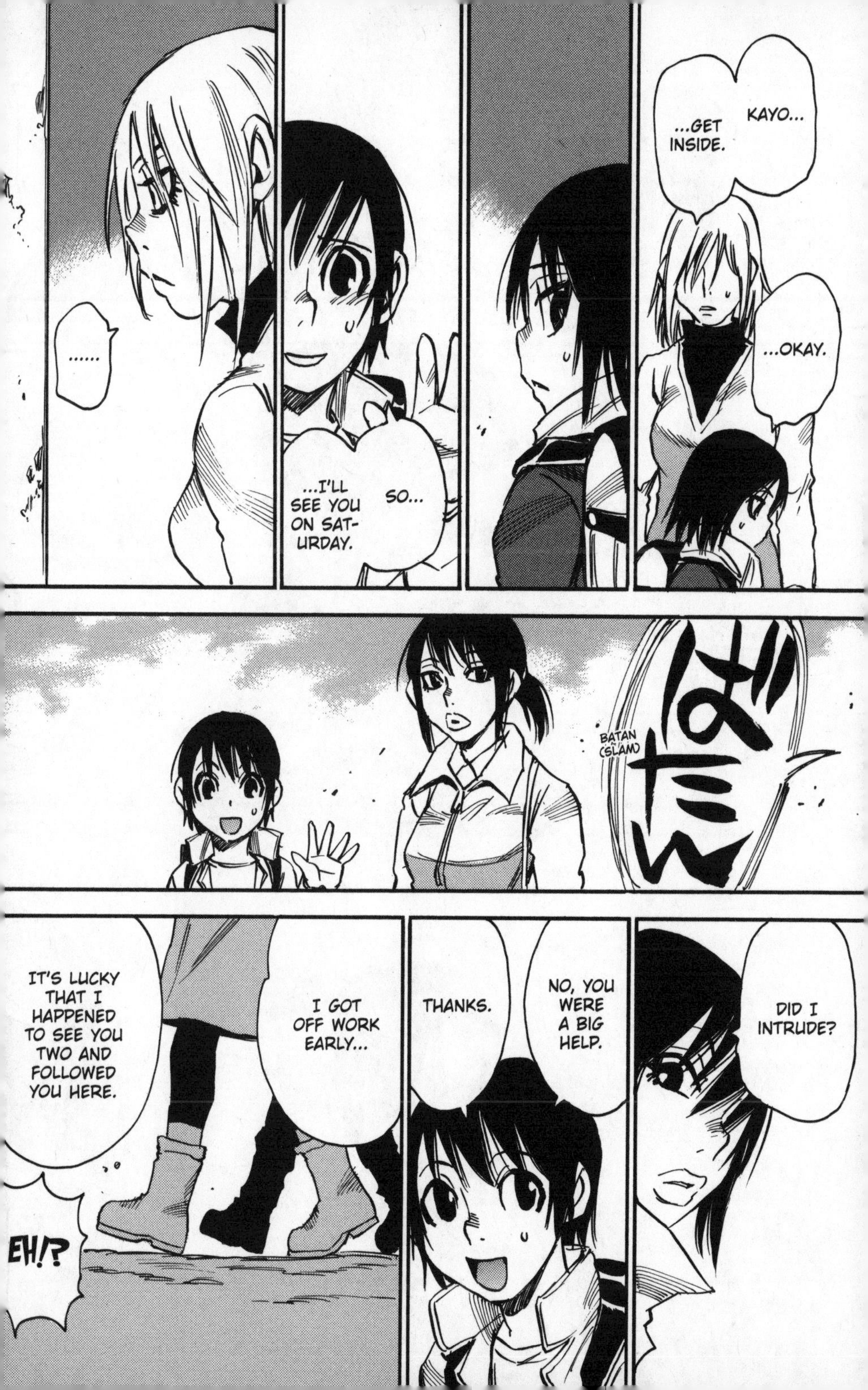
KAYO...
...GET INSIDE.
...OKAY.
SO...
...I'LL SEE YOU ON SATURDAY.
......
ばたん
BATAN (SLAM)
DID I INTRUDE?
NO, YOU WERE A BIG HELP.
THANKS.
I GOT OFF WORK EARLY...
IT'S LUCKY THAT I HAPPENED TO SEE YOU TWO AND FOLLOWED YOU HERE.
EH!?

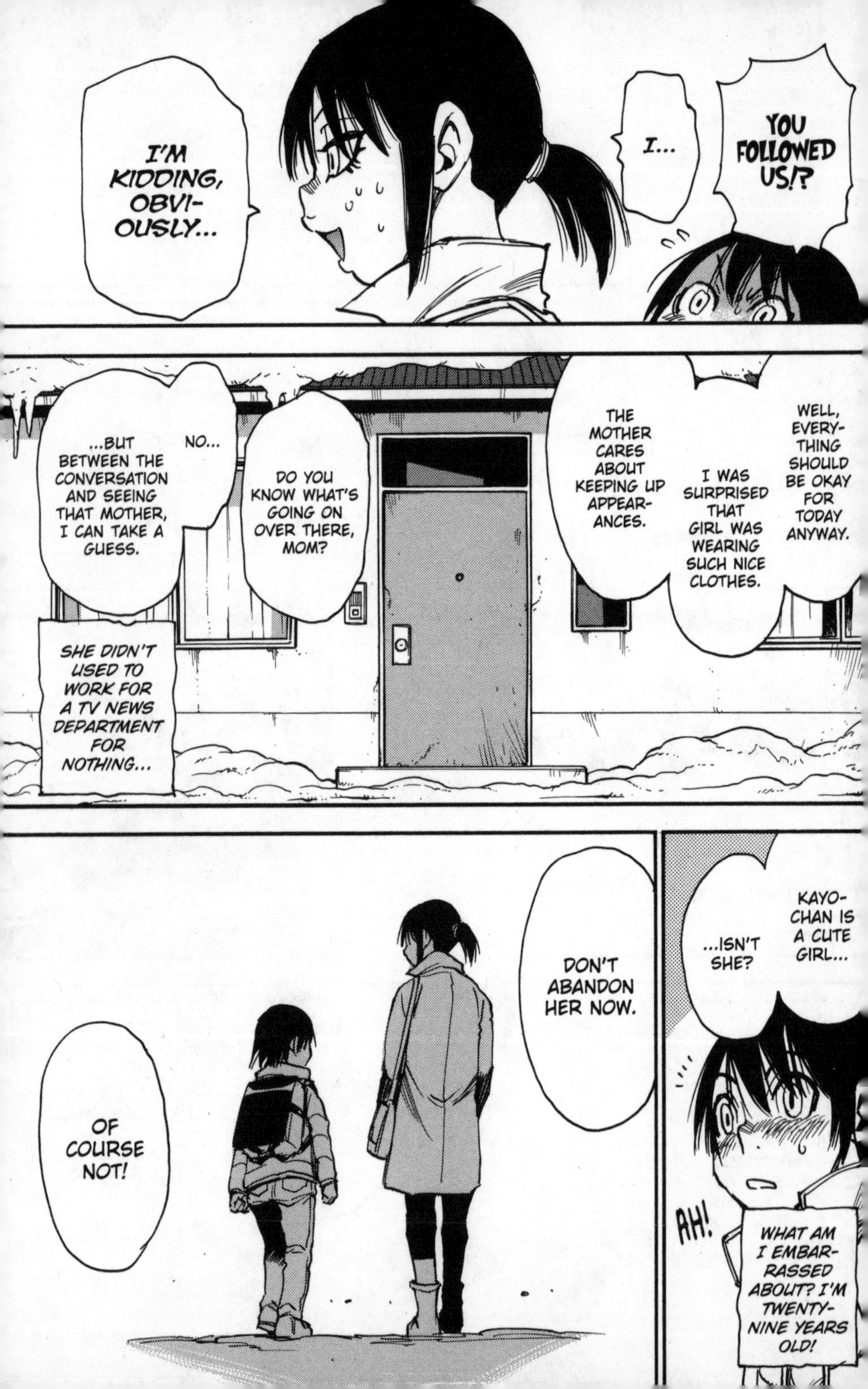
YOU FOLLOWED US!?
I...
I'M KIDDING, OBVIOUSLY...
WELL, EVERYTHING SHOULD BE OKAY FOR TODAY ANYWAY.
I WAS SURPRISED THAT GIRL WAS WEARING SUCH NICE CLOTHES.
THE MOTHER CARES ABOUT KEEPING UP APPEARANCES.
DO YOU KNOW WHAT'S GOING ON OVER THERE, MOM?
NO...
...BUT BETWEEN THE CONVERSATION AND SEEING THAT MOTHER, I CAN TAKE A GUESS.
SHE DIDN'T USED TO WORK FOR A TV NEWS DEPARTMENT FOR NOTHING...
KAYO-CHAN IS A CUTE GIRL...
...ISN'T SHE?
AH!
WHAT AM I EMBARRASSED ABOUT? I'M TWENTY-NINE YEARS OLD!
DON'T ABANDON HER NOW.
OF COURSE NOT!

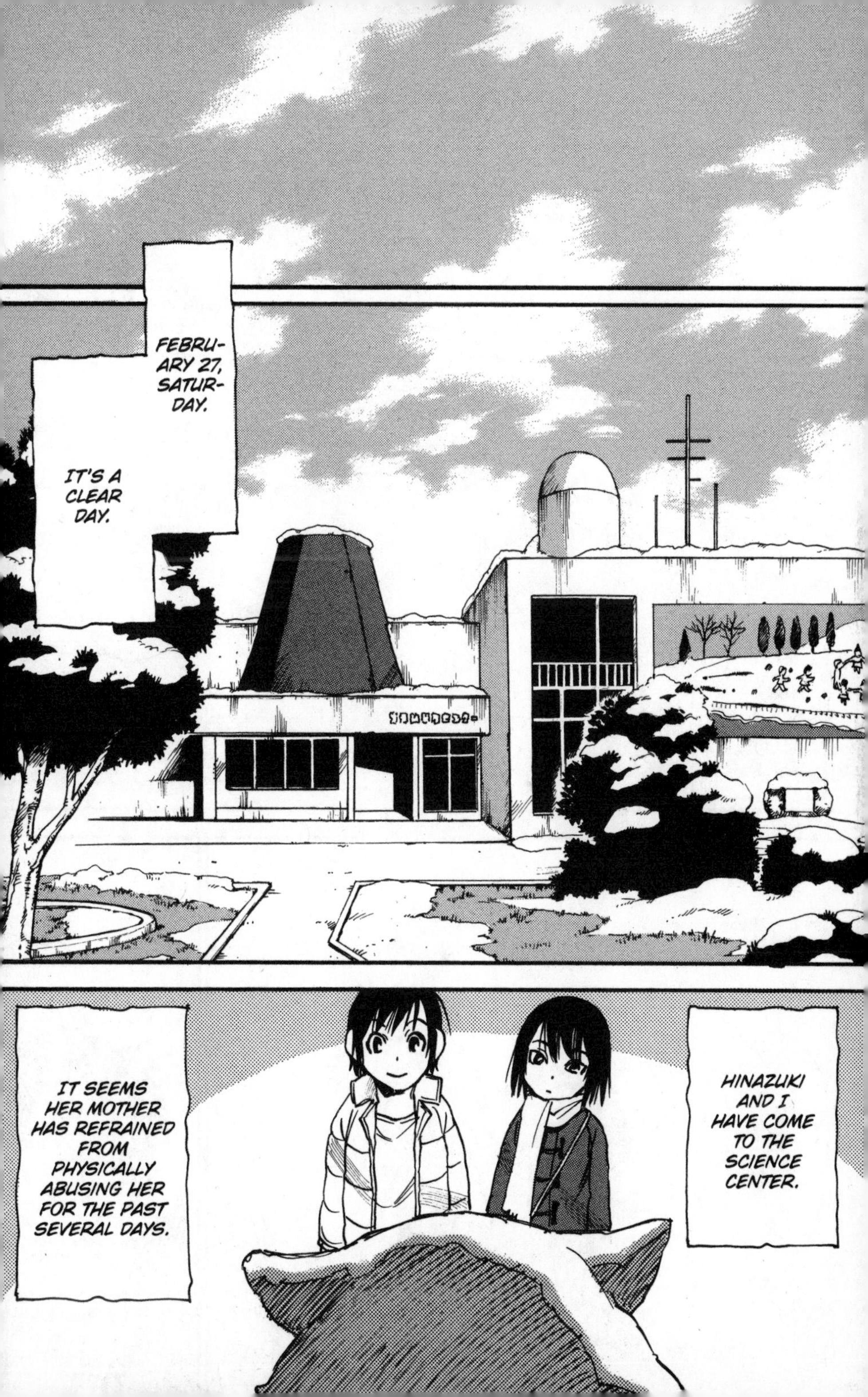
FEBRU-
ARY 27,
SATUR-
DAY.
IT'S A
CLEAR
DAY.
HINAZUKI
AND I
HAVE COME
TO THE
SCIENCE
CENTER.
IT SEEMS
HER MOTHER
HAS REFRAINED
FROM
PHYSICALLY
ABUSING HER
FOR THE PAST
SEVERAL DAYS.

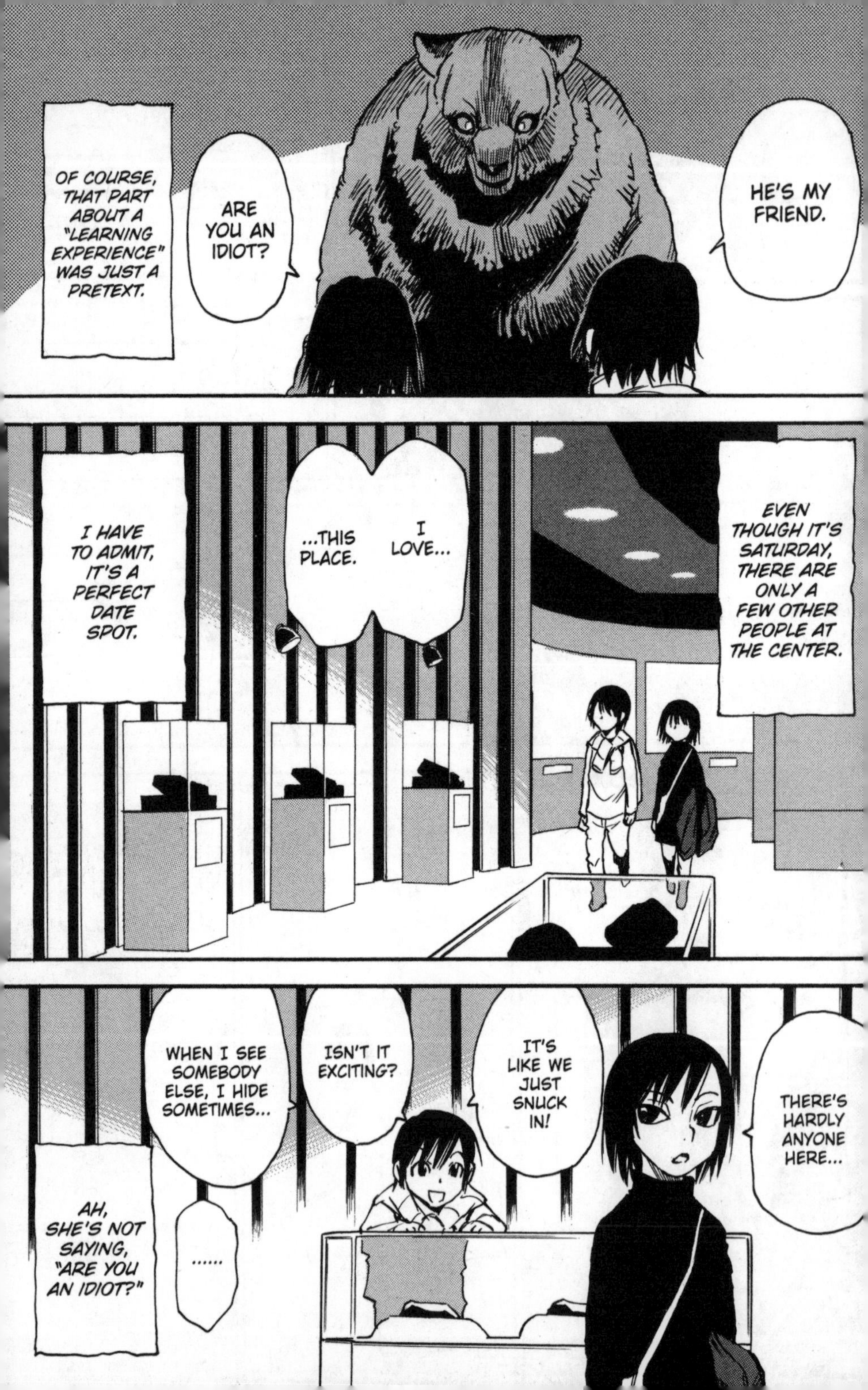
HE'S MY FRIEND.
ARE YOU AN IDIOT?
OF COURSE, THAT PART ABOUT A "LEARNING EXPERIENCE" WAS JUST A PRETEXT.
EVEN THOUGH IT'S SATURDAY, THERE ARE ONLY A FEW OTHER PEOPLE AT THE CENTER.
I LOVE...
...THIS PLACE.
I HAVE TO ADMIT, IT'S A PERFECT DATE SPOT.
THERE'S HARDLY ANYONE HERE...
IT'S LIKE WE JUST SNUCK IN!
ISN'T IT EXCITING?
WHEN I SEE SOMEBODY ELSE, I HIDE SOMETIMES...
......
AH, SHE'S NOT SAYING, "ARE YOU AN IDIOT?"

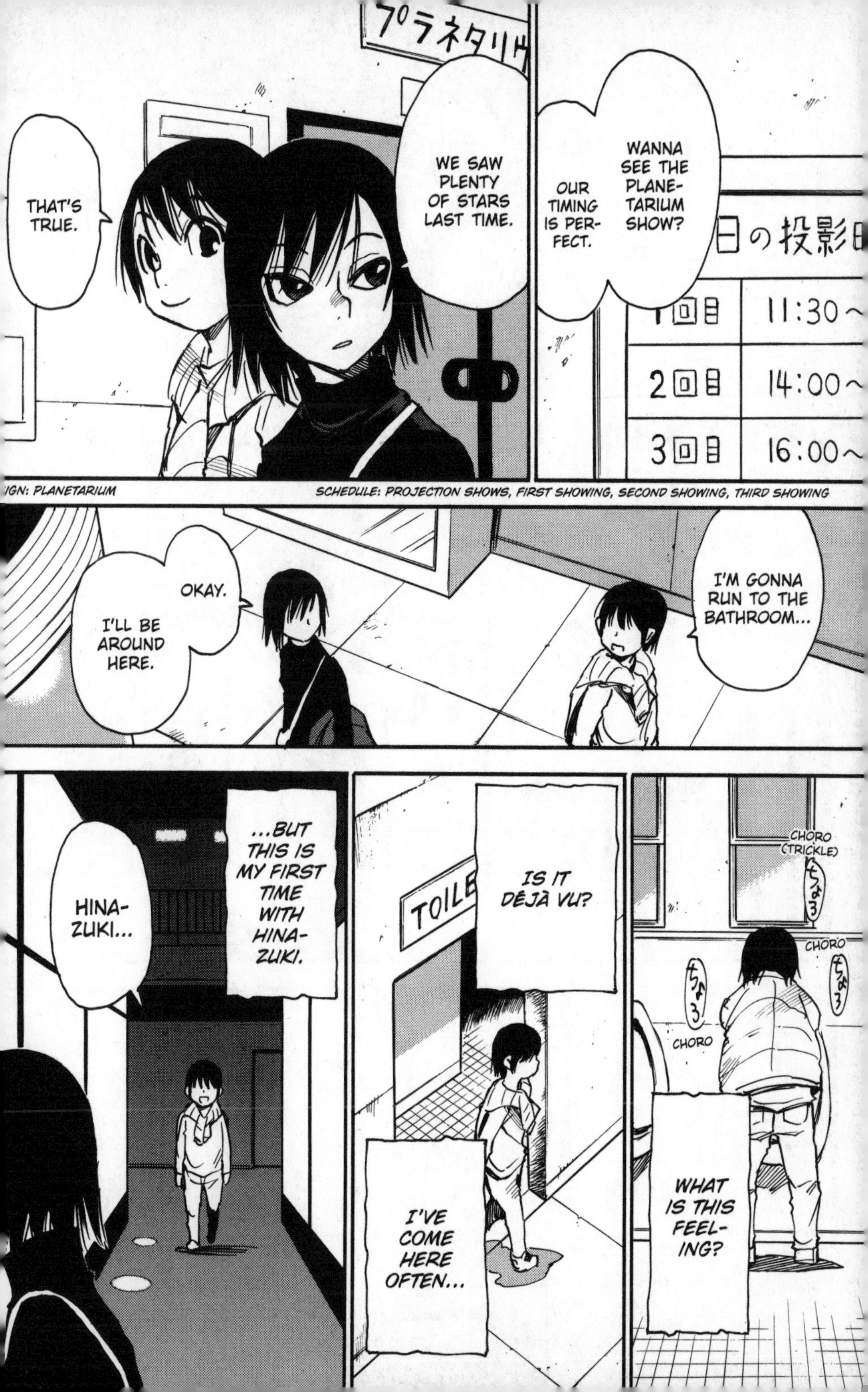
日の投影日
1回目 11:30～
2回目 14:00～
3回目 16:00～
WANNA SEE THE PLANE-TARIUM SHOW?
OUR TIMING IS PER-FECT.
プラネタリウ
WE SAW PLENTY OF STARS LAST TIME.
THAT'S TRUE.
IGN: PLANETARIUM
SCHEDULE: PROJECTION SHOWS, FIRST SHOWING, SECOND SHOWING, THIRD SHOWING
I'M GONNA RUN TO THE BATHROOM...
OKAY.
I'LL BE AROUND HERE.
CHORO (TRICKLE)
ちょろ
CHORO
ちょろ
CHORO
ちょろ
WHAT IS THIS FEEL-ING?
TOILE
IS IT DÉJÀ VU?
I'VE COME HERE OFTEN...
...BUT THIS IS MY FIRST TIME WITH HINA-ZUKI.
HINA-ZUKI...

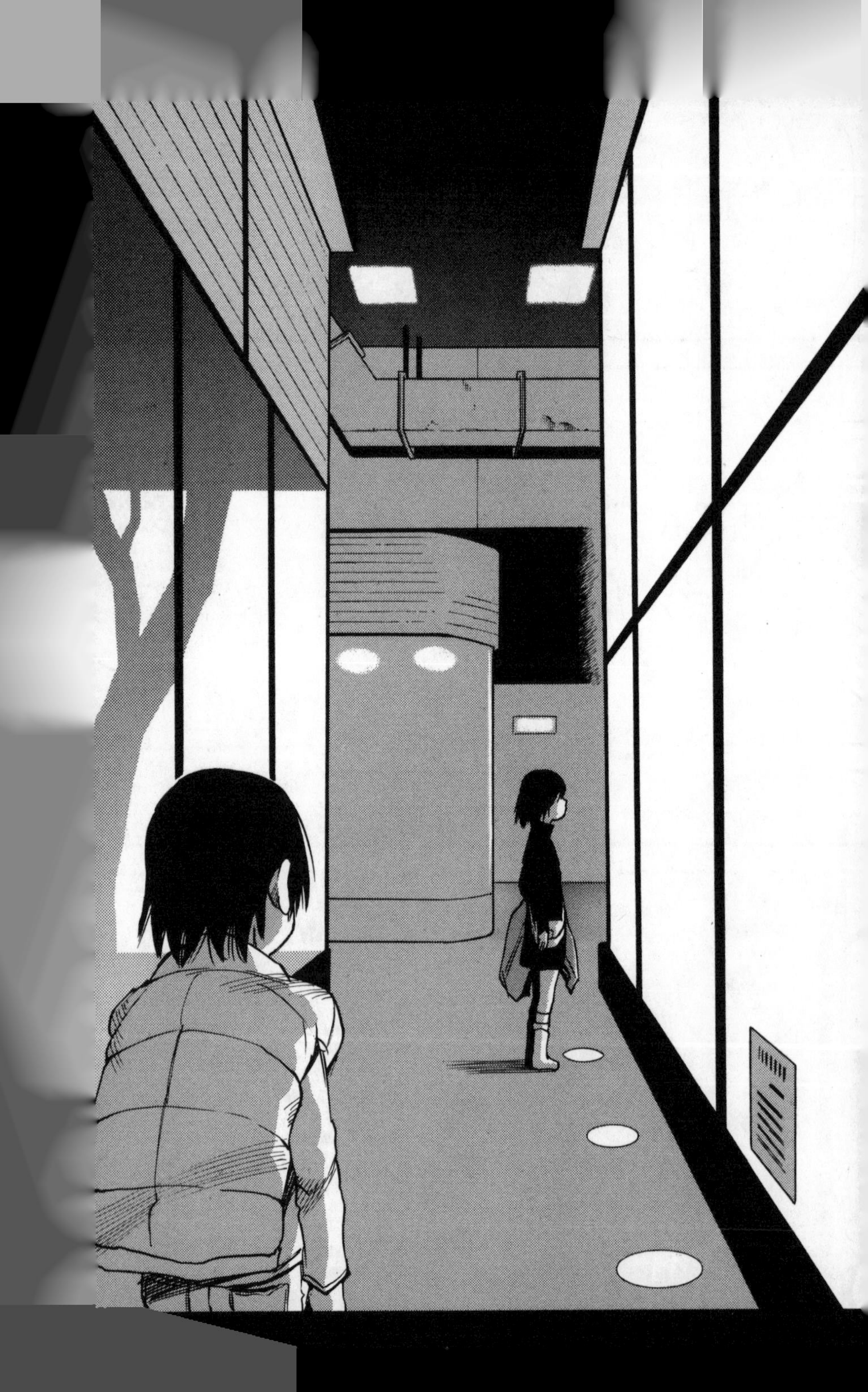

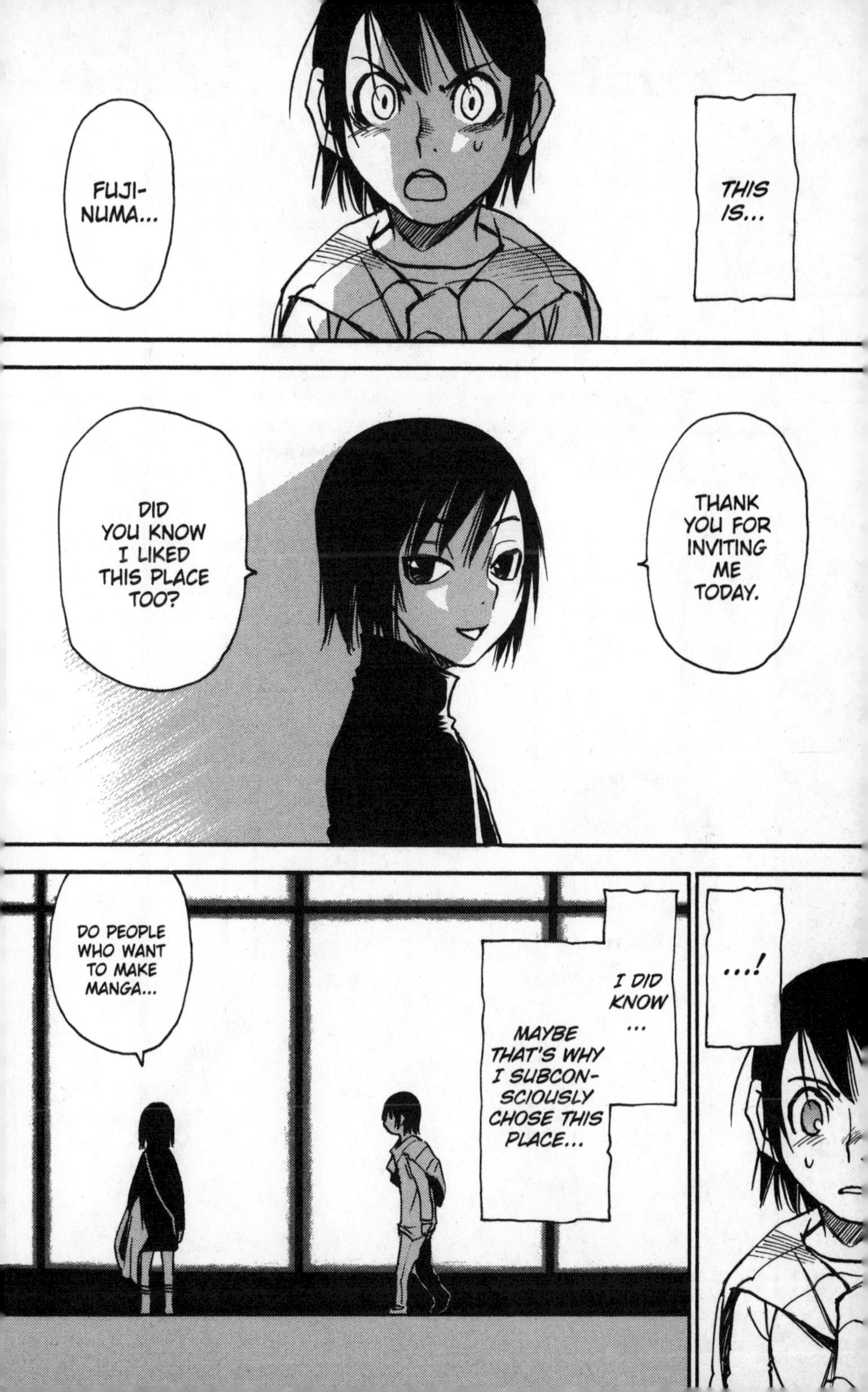
THIS IS...
FUJI-NUMA...
THANK YOU FOR INVITING ME TODAY.
DID YOU KNOW I LIKED THIS PLACE TOO?
...!
I DID KNOW ...
MAYBE THAT'S WHY I SUBCON-SCIOUSLY CHOSE THIS PLACE...
DO PEOPLE WHO WANT TO MAKE MANGA...

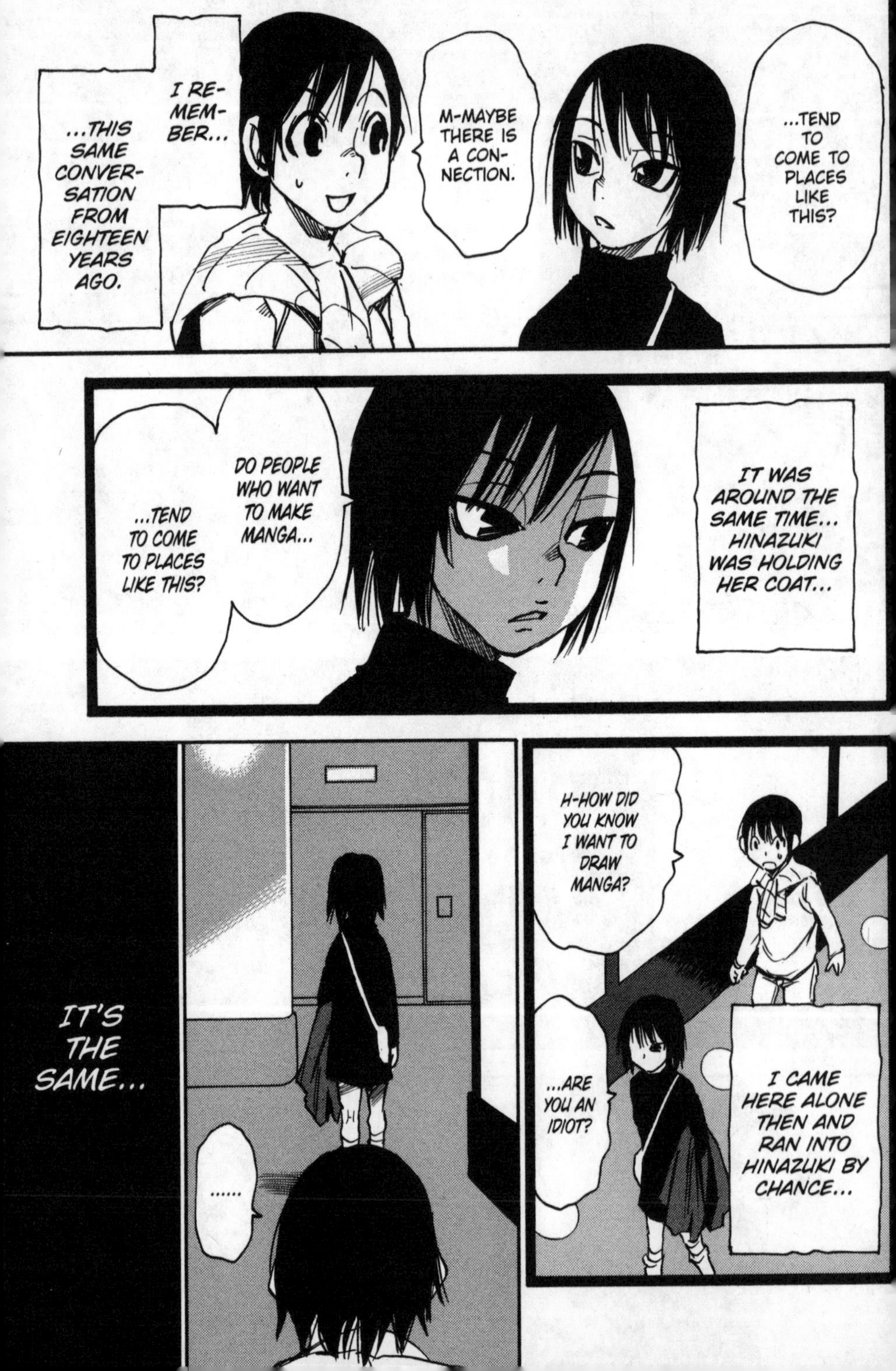
...TEND TO COME TO PLACES LIKE THIS?
M-MAYBE THERE IS A CONNECTION.
I REMEMBER...
...THIS SAME CONVERSATION FROM EIGHTEEN YEARS AGO.
IT WAS AROUND THE SAME TIME... HINAZUKI WAS HOLDING HER COAT...
DO PEOPLE WHO WANT TO MAKE MANGA...
...TEND TO COME TO PLACES LIKE THIS?
I CAME HERE ALONE THEN AND RAN INTO HINAZUKI BY CHANCE...
H-HOW DID YOU KNOW I WANT TO DRAW MANGA?
...ARE YOU AN IDIOT?
......
IT'S THE SAME...

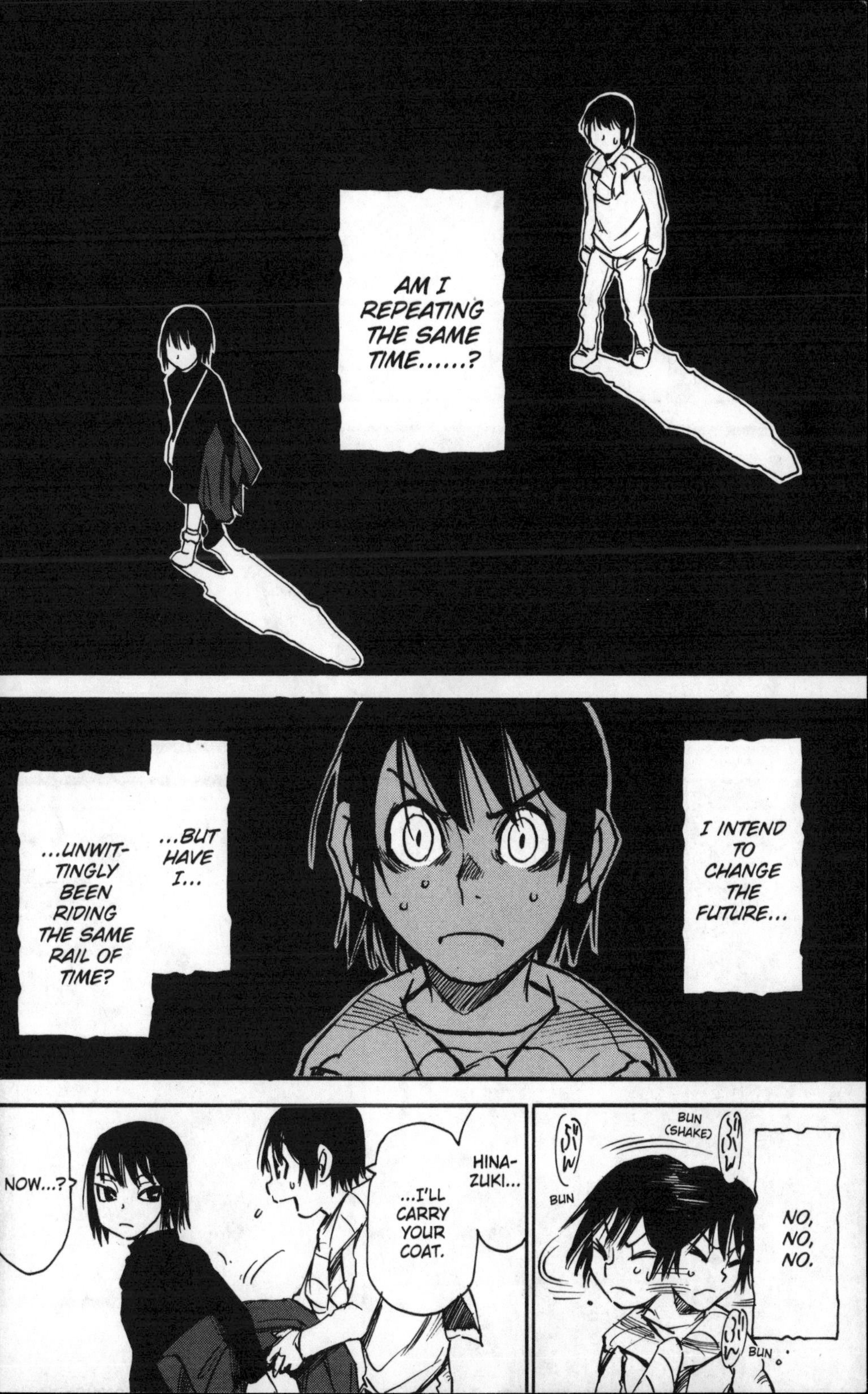
AM I REPEATING THE SAME TIME......?
I INTEND TO CHANGE THE FUTURE...
...BUT HAVE I...
...UNWITTINGLY BEEN RIDING THE SAME RAIL OF TIME?
NO, NO, NO.
BUN (SHAKE)
BUN
BUN
HINA-ZUKI...
...I'LL CARRY YOUR COAT.
NOW...?

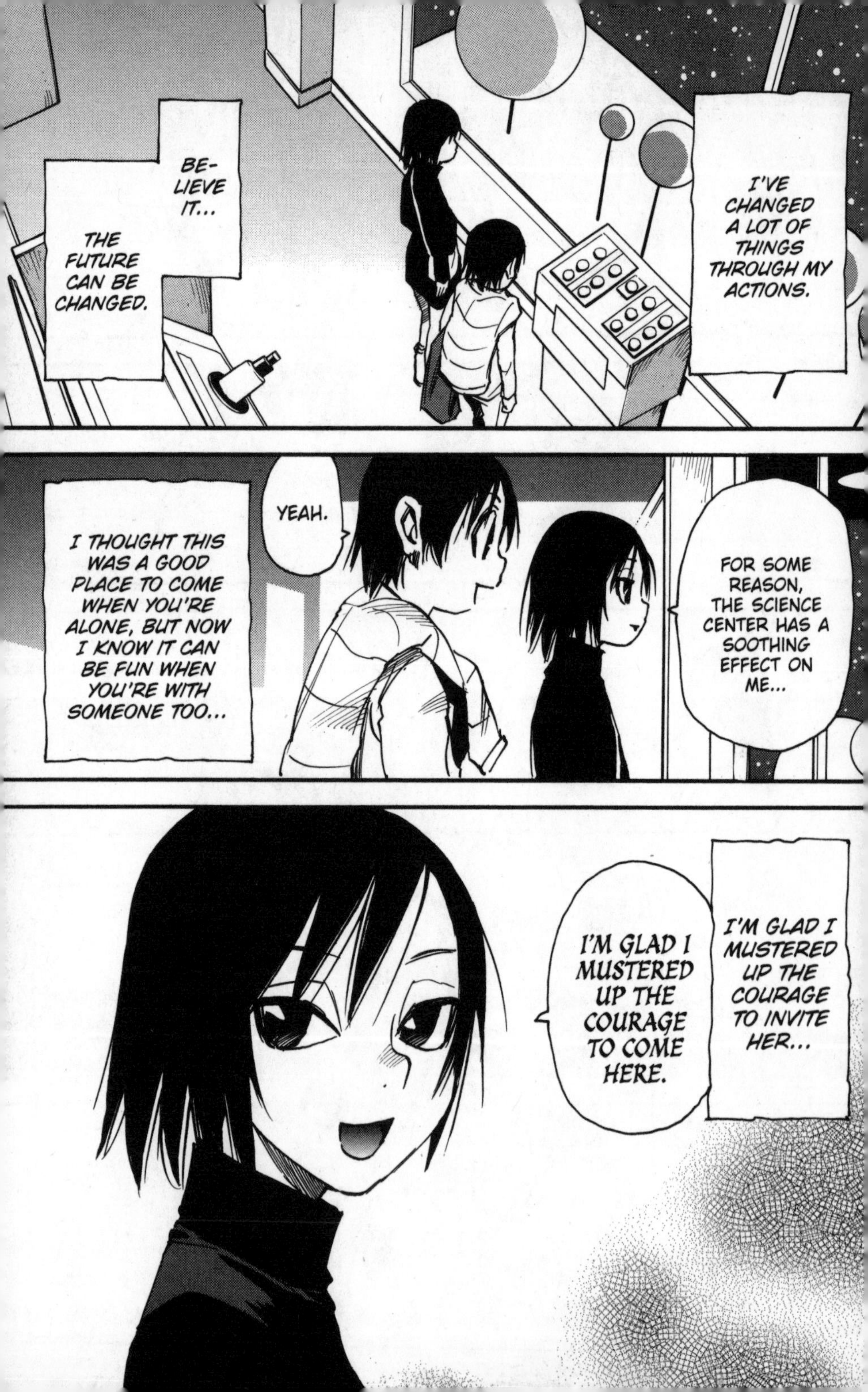
I'VE CHANGED A LOT OF THINGS THROUGH MY ACTIONS.
BE-LIEVE IT...
THE FUTURE CAN BE CHANGED.
FOR SOME REASON, THE SCIENCE CENTER HAS A SOOTHING EFFECT ON ME...
YEAH.
I THOUGHT THIS WAS A GOOD PLACE TO COME WHEN YOU'RE ALONE, BUT NOW I KNOW IT CAN BE FUN WHEN YOU'RE WITH SOMEONE TOO...
I'M GLAD I MUSTERED UP THE COURAGE TO INVITE HER...
I'M GLAD I MUSTERED UP THE COURAGE TO COME HERE.

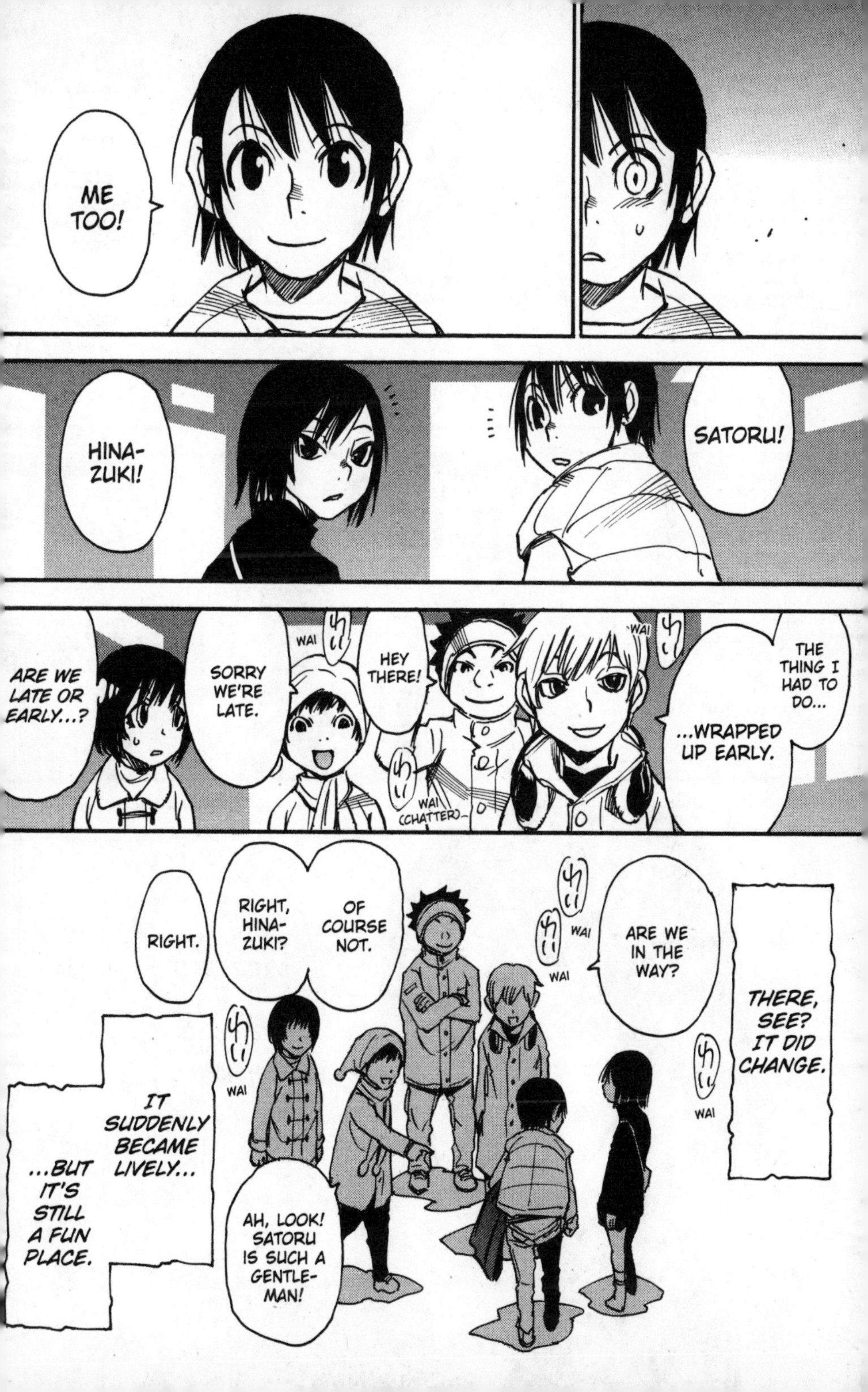
ME TOO!
SATORU!
HINA-ZUKI!
THE THING I HAD TO DO...
...WRAPPED UP EARLY.
WAI
HEY THERE!
WAI
WAI (CHATTER)
SORRY WE'RE LATE.
ARE WE LATE OR EARLY...?
THERE, SEE? IT DID CHANGE.
WAI
ARE WE IN THE WAY?
WAI
WAI
OF COURSE NOT.
RIGHT, HINA-ZUKI?
RIGHT.
WAI
AH, LOOK! SATORU IS SUCH A GENTLE-MAN!
IT SUDDENLY BECAME LIVELY...
...BUT IT'S STILL A FUN PLACE.

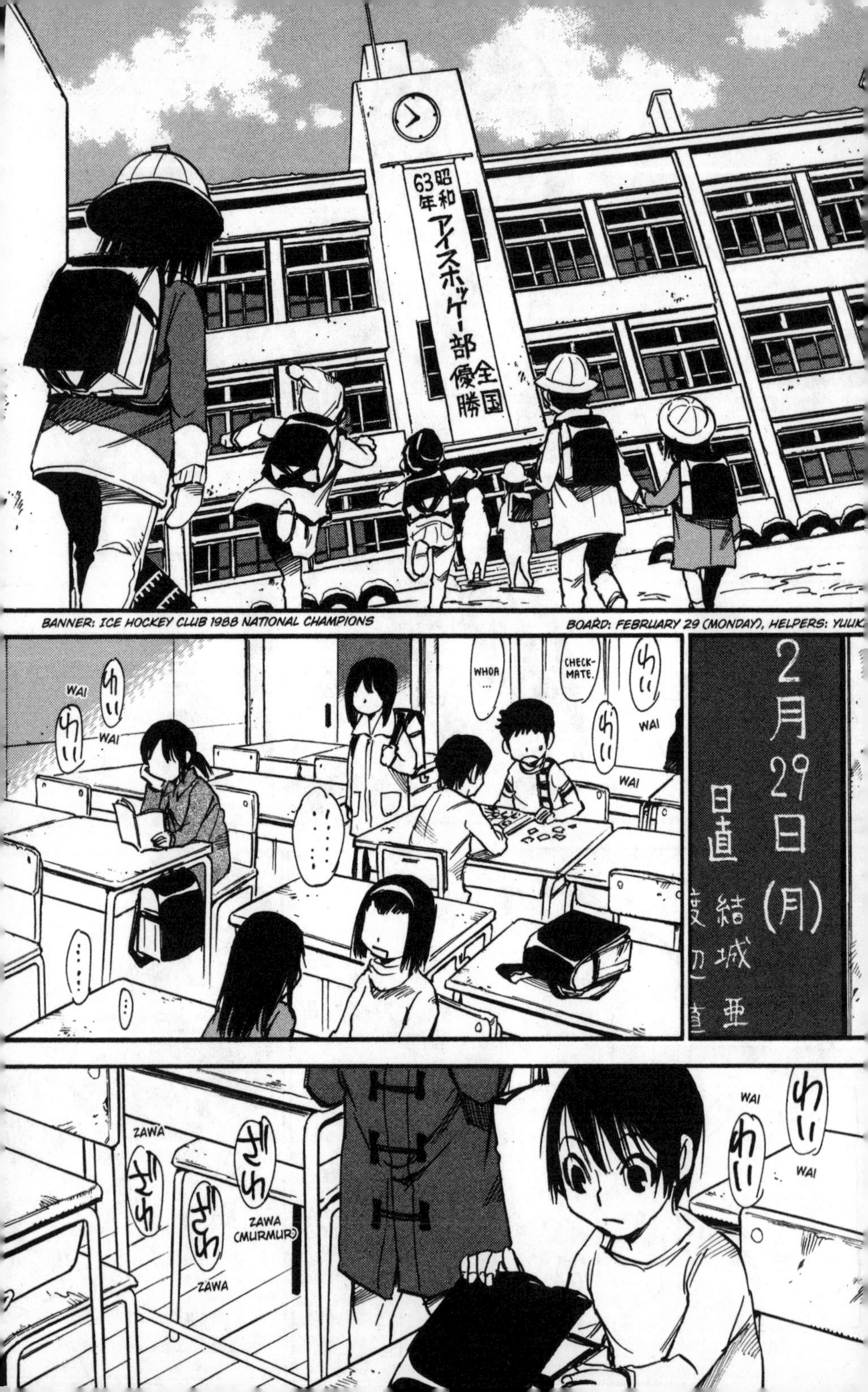
昭和63年アイスホッケー部全国優勝
BANNER: ICE HOCKEY CLUB 1988 NATIONAL CHAMPIONS
BOARD: FEBRUARY 29 (MONDAY), HELPERS: YUUK
2月29日(月)
日直
結城亜
わい
WAI
わい
WAI
CHECK-MATE.
WHOA ...
...
...
わい
WAI
わい
WAI
......
...
わい
WAI
わい
WAI
ざわ
ZAWA
ざわ
ZAWA (MURMUR)
ざわ
ZAWA

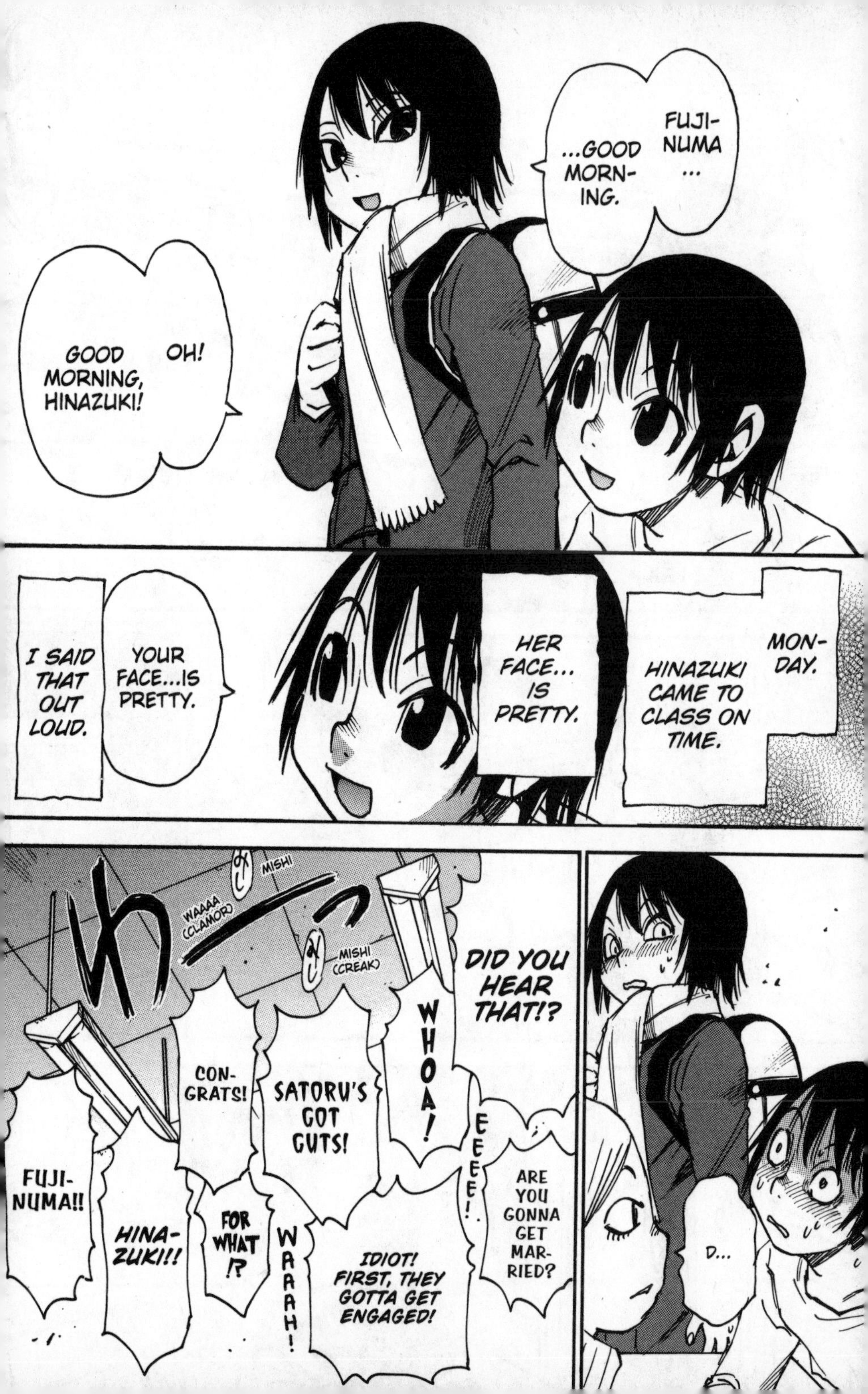
FUJI-NUMA... ...GOOD MORN-ING.
OH! GOOD MORNING, HINAZUKI!
MON-DAY. HINAZUKI CAME TO CLASS ON TIME.
HER FACE... IS PRETTY.
YOUR FACE...IS PRETTY.
I SAID THAT OUT LOUD.
D...
MISHI
WAAAA (CLAMOR)
MISHI (CREAK)
DID YOU HEAR THAT!?
ARE YOU GONNA GET MAR-RIED?
EEEE!
WHOA!
SATORU'S GOT GUTS!
CON-GRATS!
IDIOT! FIRST, THEY GOTTA GET ENGAGED!
WAAAH!
FOR WHAT!?
HINA-ZUKI!!
FUJI-NUMA!!

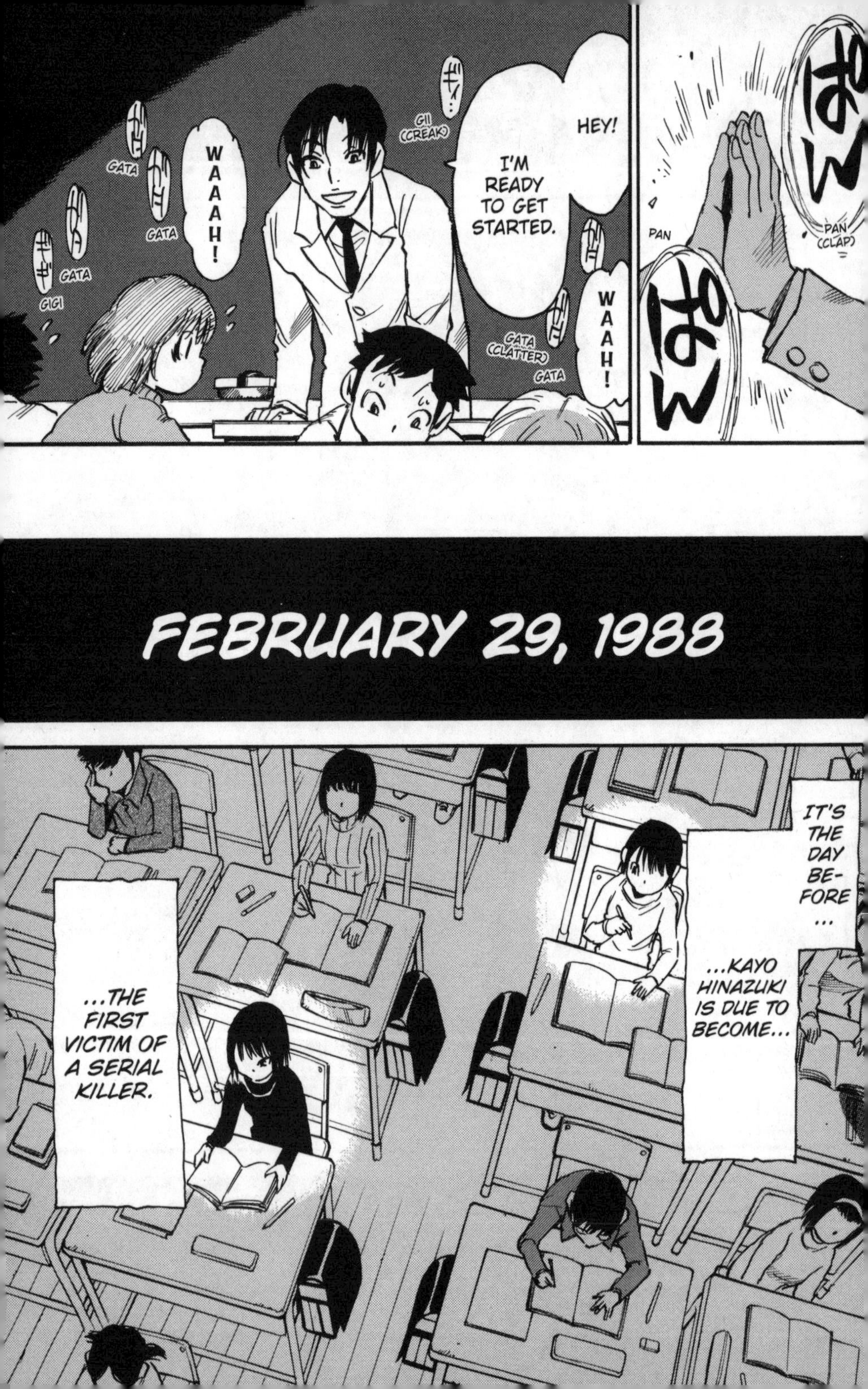

ぱん
PAN (CLAP)
ぱん
PAN
HEY!
I'M READY TO GET STARTED.
ギィ…
GII (CREAK)
WAAAH!
GATA (CLATTER)
GATA
WAAAAH!
GATA
GATA
GATA
GIGI
FEBRUARY 29, 1988
IT'S THE DAY BE-FORE…
…KAYO HINAZUKI IS DUE TO BECOME…
…THE FIRST VICTIM OF A SERIAL KILLER.

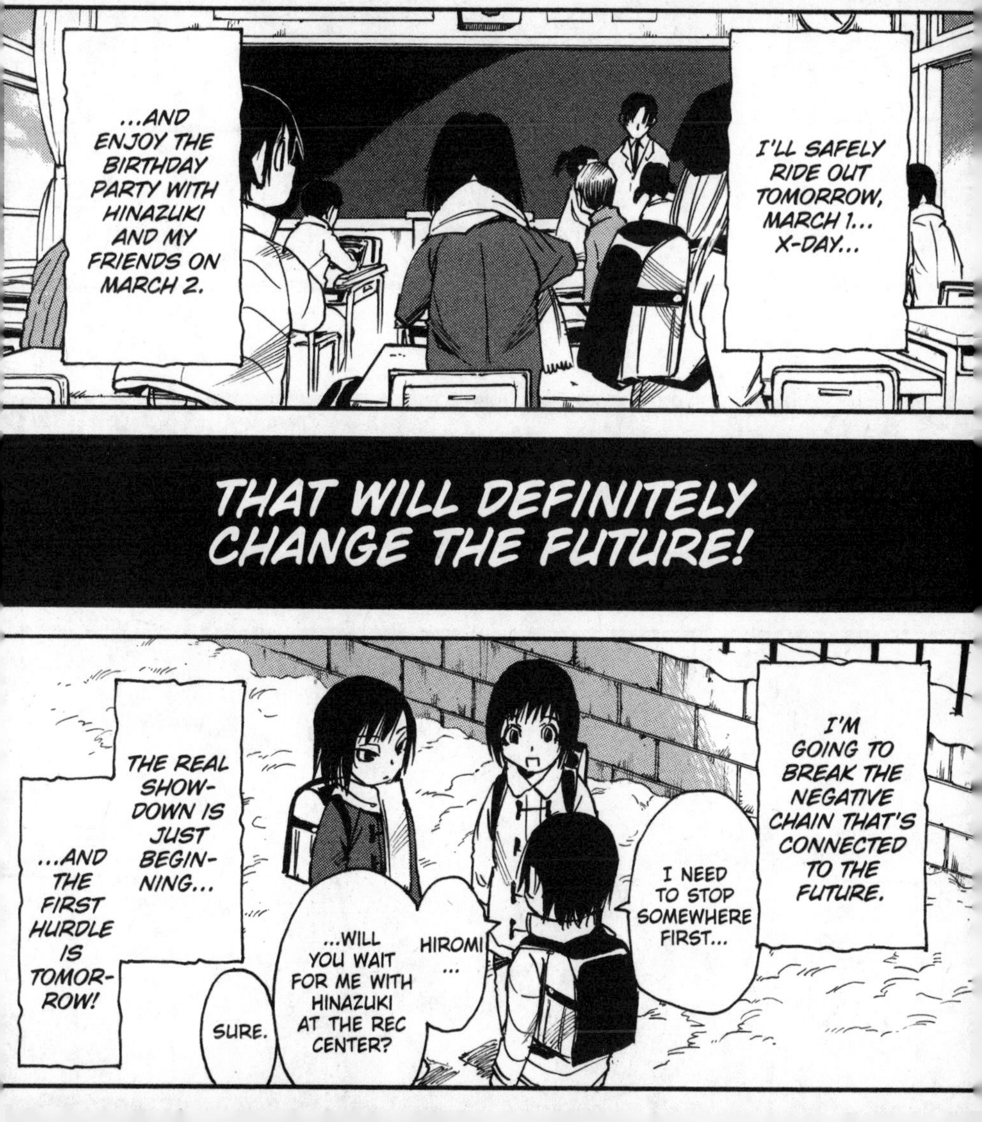
I'LL SAFELY RIDE OUT TOMORROW, MARCH 1... X-DAY...
...AND ENJOY THE BIRTHDAY PARTY WITH HINAZUKI AND MY FRIENDS ON MARCH 2.
THAT WILL DEFINITELY CHANGE THE FUTURE!
I'M GOING TO BREAK THE NEGATIVE CHAIN THAT'S CONNECTED TO THE FUTURE.
I NEED TO STOP SOMEWHERE FIRST...
HIROMI...
...WILL YOU WAIT FOR ME WITH HINAZUKI AT THE REC CENTER?
SURE.
THE REAL SHOW-DOWN IS JUST BEGIN-NING...
...AND THE FIRST HURDLE IS TOMOR-ROW!

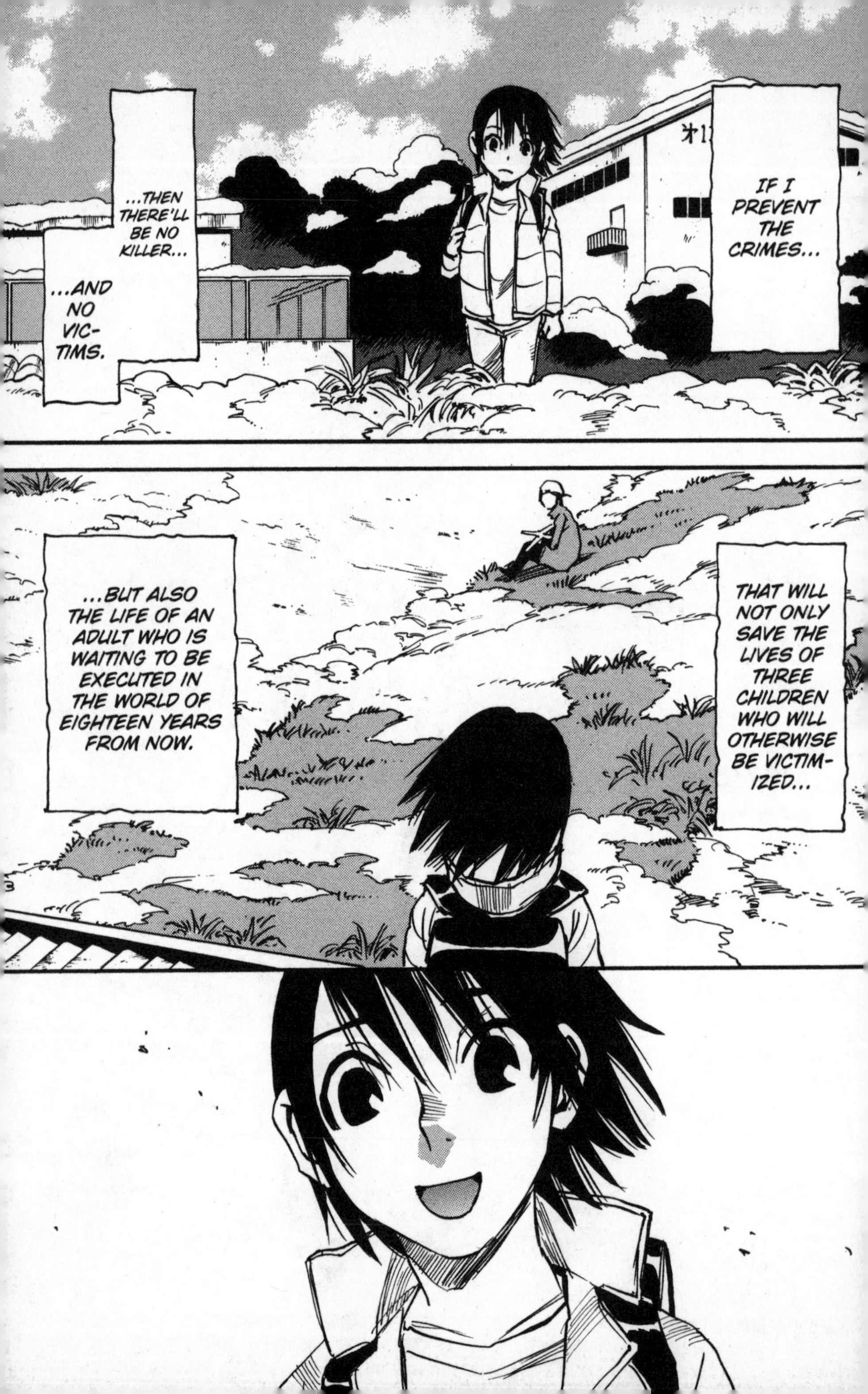
IF I PREVENT THE CRIMES...
...THEN THERE'LL BE NO KILLER...
...AND NO VIC-TIMS.
THAT WILL NOT ONLY SAVE THE LIVES OF THREE CHILDREN WHO WILL OTHERWISE BE VICTIM-IZED...
...BUT ALSO THE LIFE OF AN ADULT WHO IS WAITING TO BE EXECUTED IN THE WORLD OF EIGHTEEN YEARS FROM NOW.

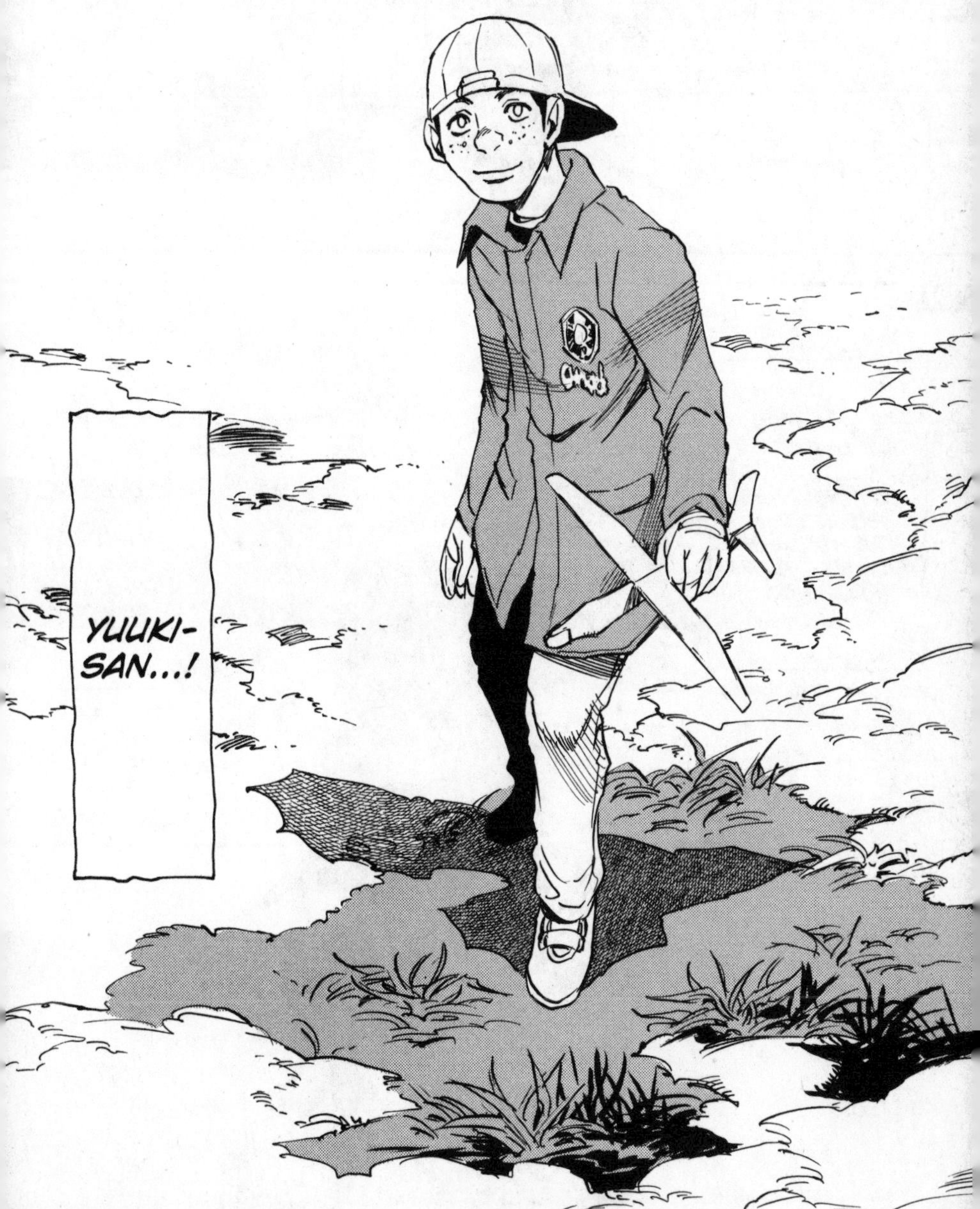
YUUKI-
SAN...!

#11 END

Jun Shiratori

Present, May 2006:
Convicted death row prisoner

Murdered two elementary school girls and one boy between March and June of 1988 in Hokkaido. Arrested September 1988. Stood trial the following year.

Has maintained his innocence since his first trial

1992: Received death penalty ruling in Sapporo courtroom. Appealed to a higher court.
1997: Appeal rejected by Sapporo appellate court.

2000: Supreme court dismisses final appeal.
Death penalty is upheld.

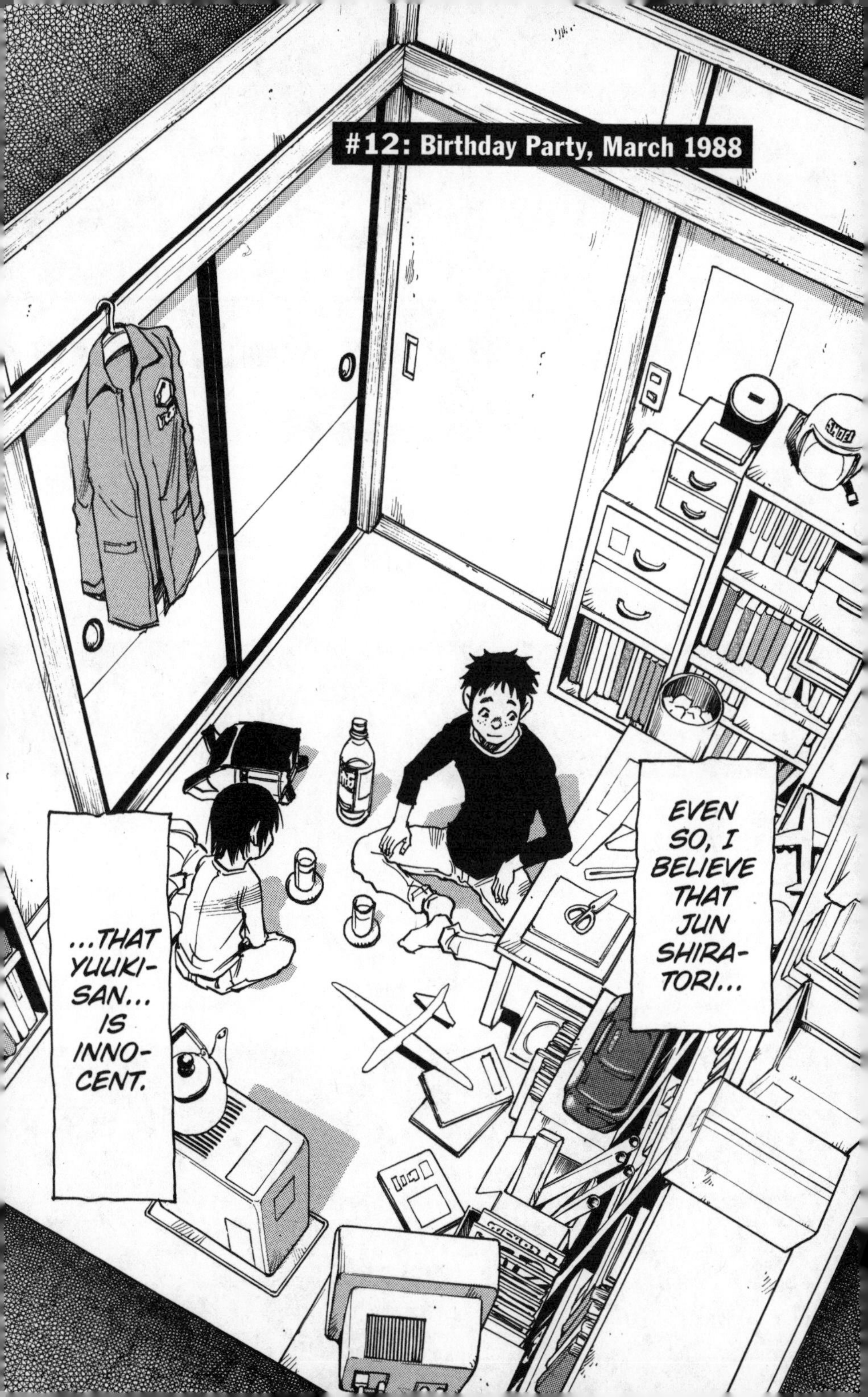
#12: Birthday Party, March 1988
EVEN SO, I BELIEVE THAT JUN SHIRATORI...
...THAT YUUKI-SAN... IS INNOCENT.

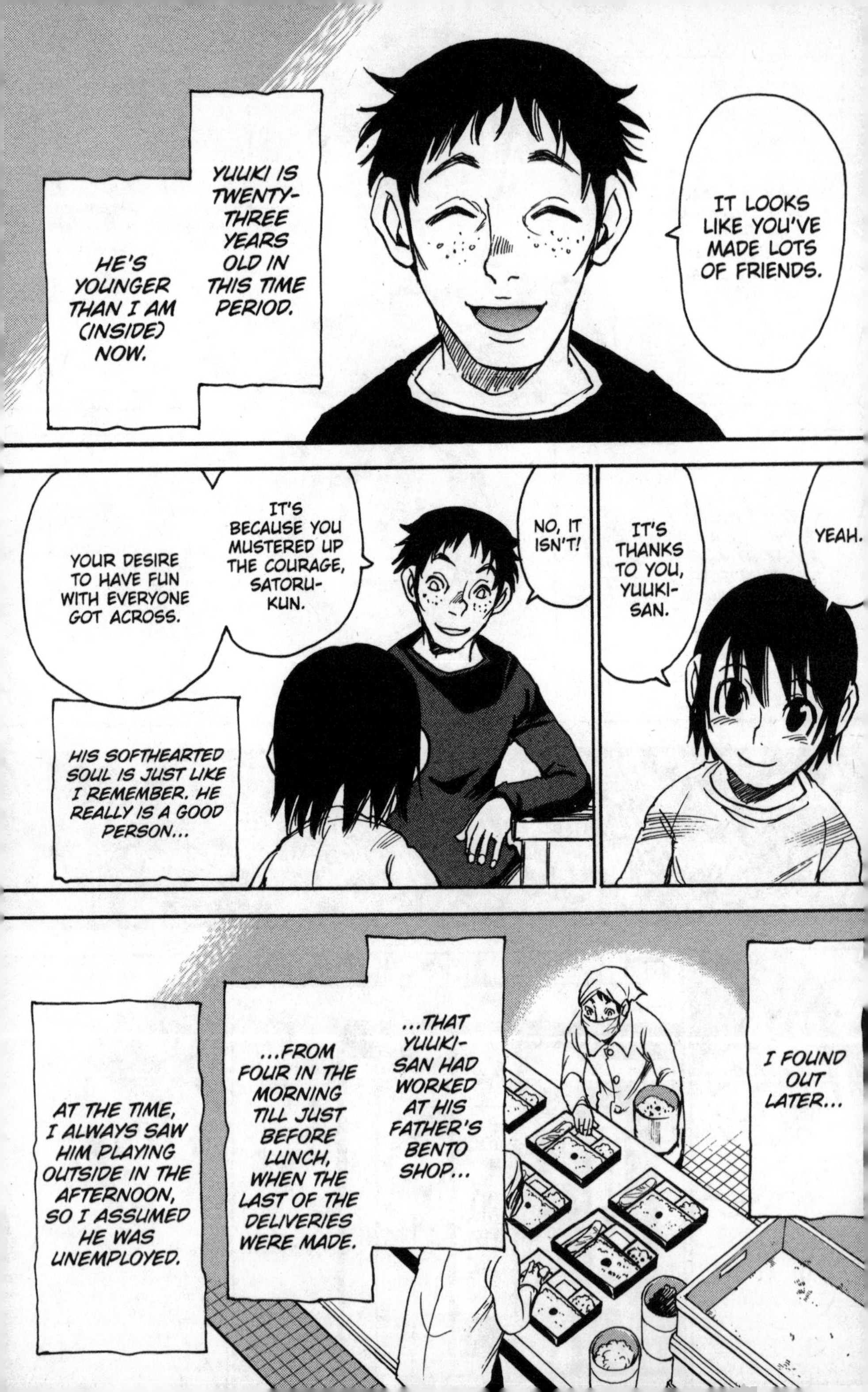
IT LOOKS LIKE YOU'VE MADE LOTS OF FRIENDS.
YUUKI IS TWENTY-THREE YEARS OLD IN THIS TIME PERIOD.
HE'S YOUNGER THAN I AM (INSIDE) NOW.
YEAH.
IT'S THANKS TO YOU, YUUKI-SAN.
NO, IT ISN'T!
IT'S BECAUSE YOU MUSTERED UP THE COURAGE, SATORU-KUN.
YOUR DESIRE TO HAVE FUN WITH EVERYONE GOT ACROSS.
HIS SOFTHEARTED SOUL IS JUST LIKE I REMEMBER. HE REALLY IS A GOOD PERSON...
I FOUND OUT LATER...
...THAT YUUKI-SAN HAD WORKED AT HIS FATHER'S BENTO SHOP...
...FROM FOUR IN THE MORNING TILL JUST BEFORE LUNCH, WHEN THE LAST OF THE DELIVERIES WERE MADE.
AT THE TIME, I ALWAYS SAW HIM PLAYING OUTSIDE IN THE AFTERNOON, SO I ASSUMED HE WAS UNEMPLOYED.

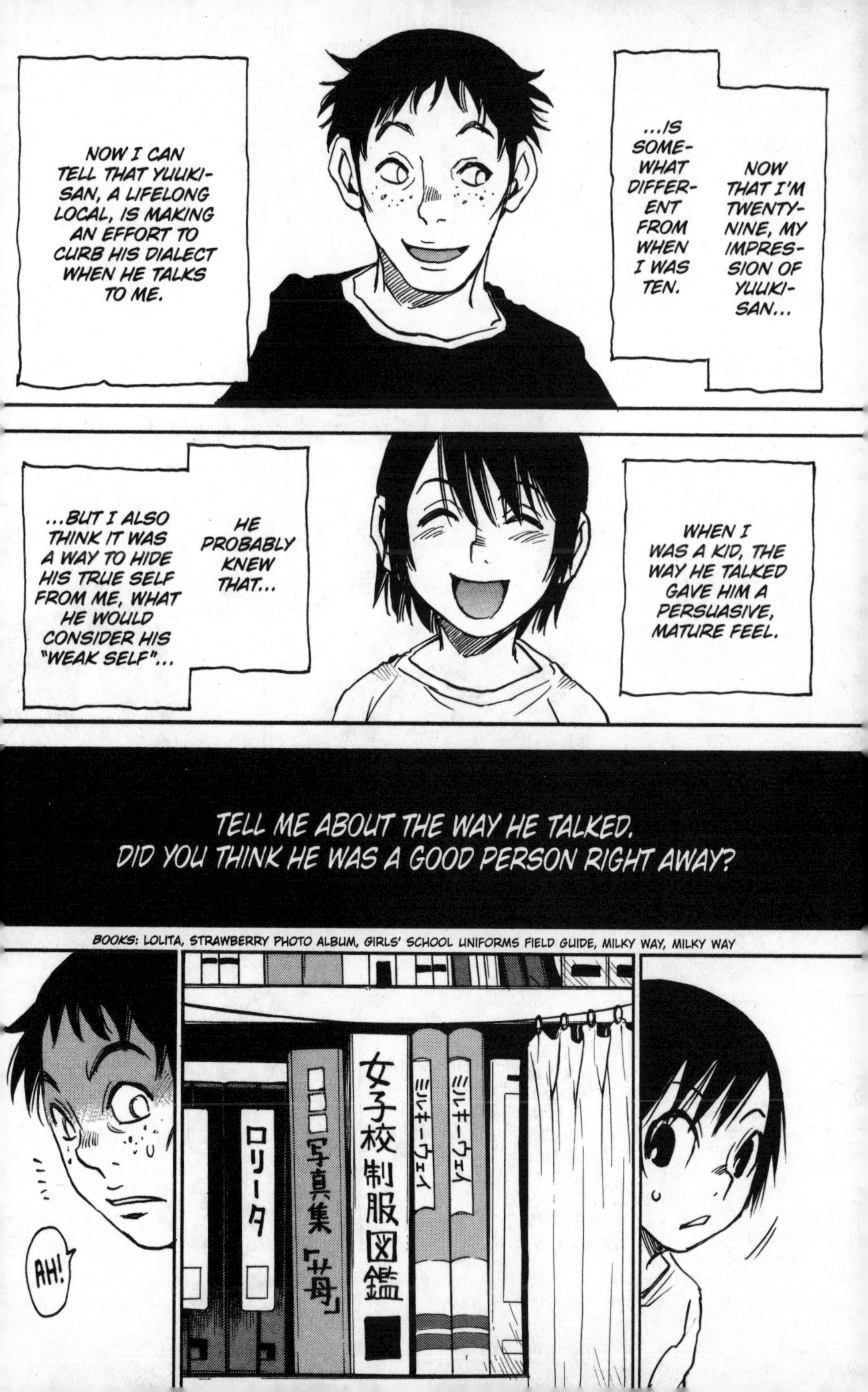
NOW THAT I'M TWENTY-NINE, MY IMPRESSION OF YUUKI-SAN...
...IS SOMEWHAT DIFFERENT FROM WHEN I WAS TEN.
NOW I CAN TELL THAT YUUKI-SAN, A LIFELONG LOCAL, IS MAKING AN EFFORT TO CURB HIS DIALECT WHEN HE TALKS TO ME.
WHEN I WAS A KID, THE WAY HE TALKED GAVE HIM A PERSUASIVE, MATURE FEEL.
HE PROBABLY KNEW THAT...
...BUT I ALSO THINK IT WAS A WAY TO HIDE HIS TRUE SELF FROM ME, WHAT HE WOULD CONSIDER HIS "WEAK SELF"...
TELL ME ABOUT THE WAY HE TALKED.
DID YOU THINK HE WAS A GOOD PERSON RIGHT AWAY?
BOOKS: LOLITA, STRAWBERRY PHOTO ALBUM, GIRLS' SCHOOL UNIFORMS FIELD GUIDE, MILKY WAY, MILKY WAY
ミルキーウェイ
ミルキーウェイ
女子校制服図鑑
写真集「苺」
ロリータ
AH!

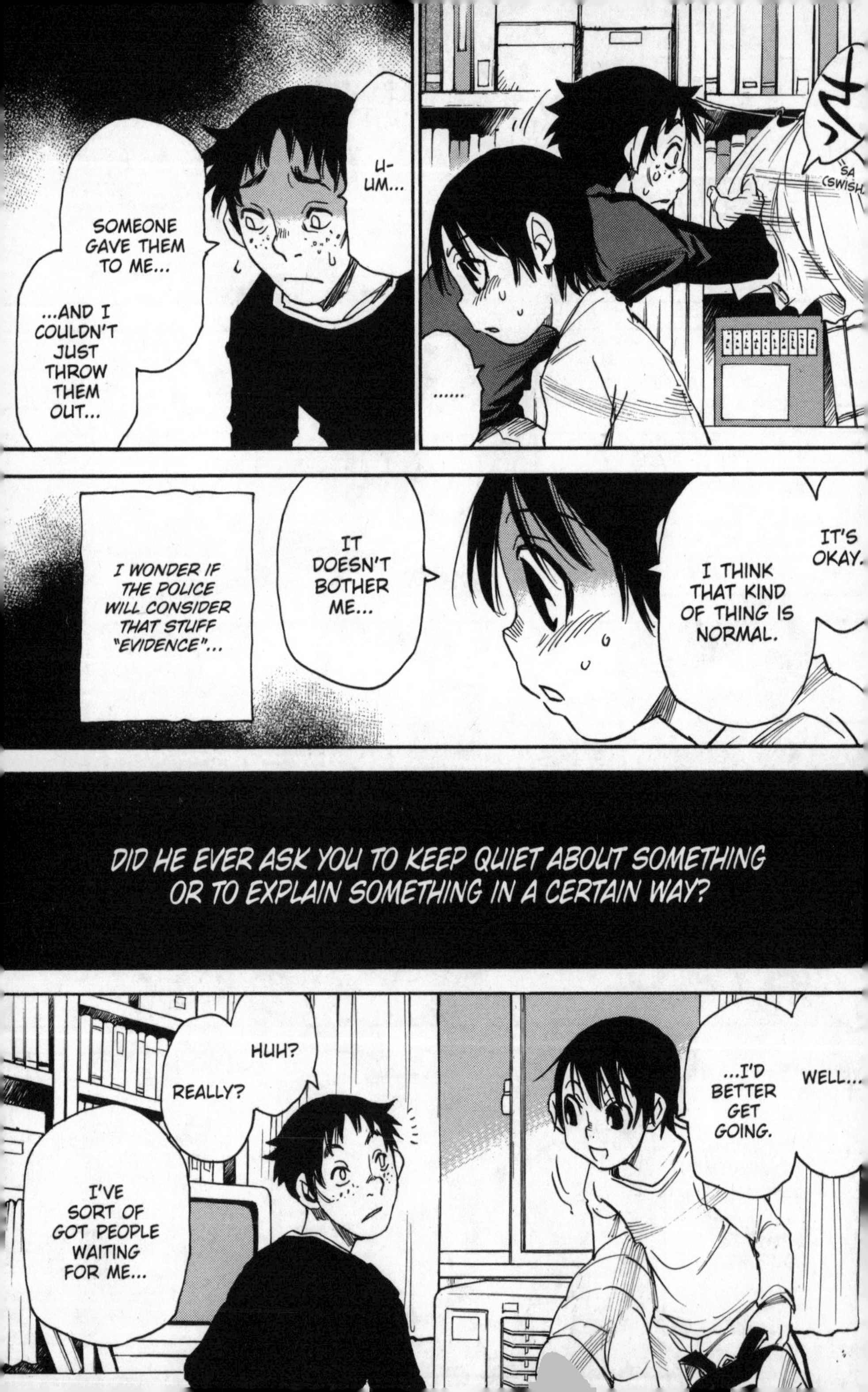
SA (SWISH)
......
U-UM...
SOMEONE GAVE THEM TO ME...
...AND I COULDN'T JUST THROW THEM OUT...
IT'S OKAY.
I THINK THAT KIND OF THING IS NORMAL.
IT DOESN'T BOTHER ME...
I WONDER IF THE POLICE WILL CONSIDER THAT STUFF "EVIDENCE"...
DID HE EVER ASK YOU TO KEEP QUIET ABOUT SOMETHING OR TO EXPLAIN SOMETHING IN A CERTAIN WAY?
WELL...
...I'D BETTER GET GOING.
HUH?
REALLY?
I'VE SORT OF GOT PEOPLE WAITING FOR ME...

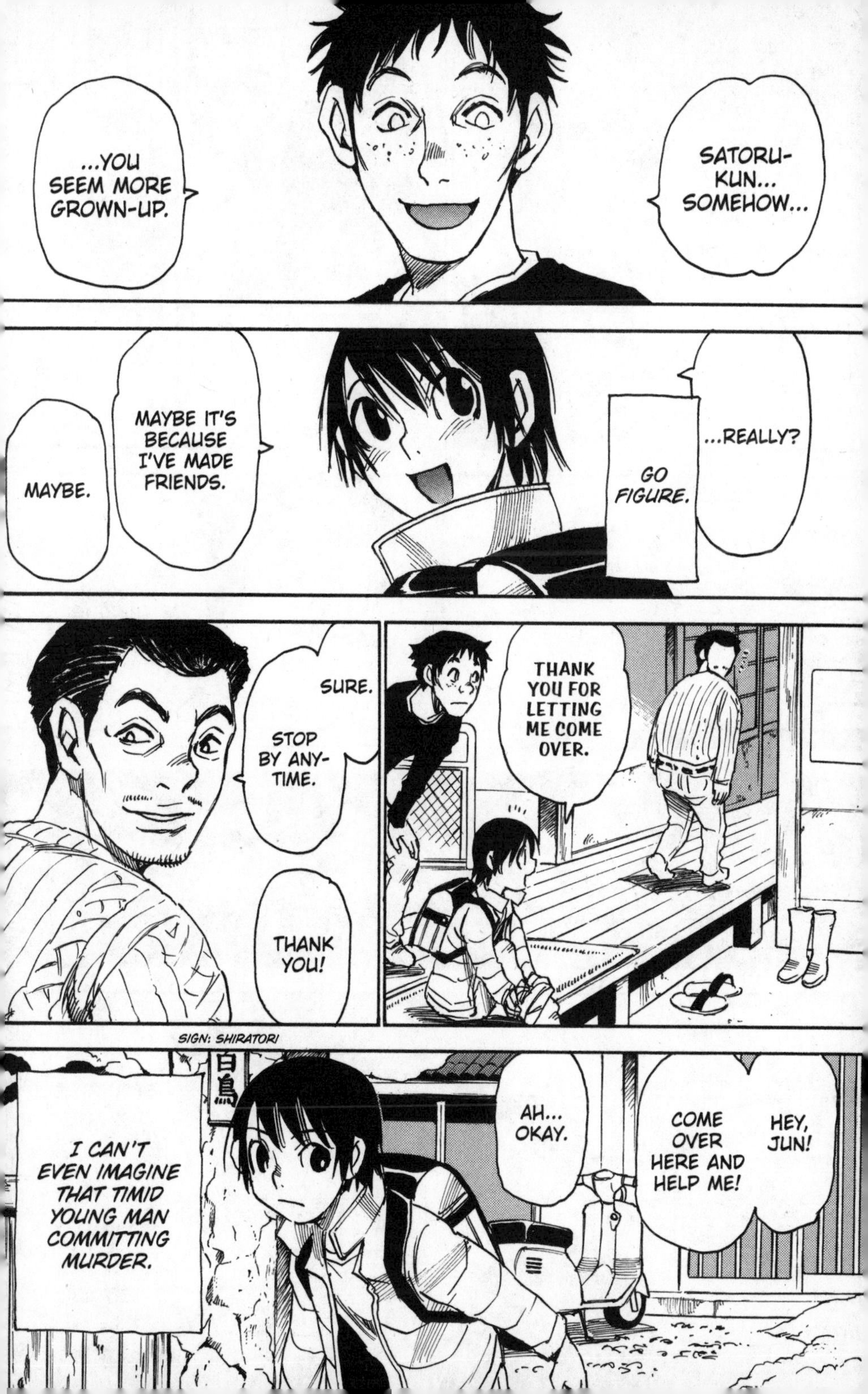
SATORU-KUN... SOMEHOW...
...YOU SEEM MORE GROWN-UP.
...REALLY?
GO FIGURE.
MAYBE IT'S BECAUSE I'VE MADE FRIENDS.
MAYBE.
THANK YOU FOR LETTING ME COME OVER.
SURE.
STOP BY ANY-TIME.
THANK YOU!
SIGN: SHIRATORI
白鳥
HEY, JUN!
COME OVER HERE AND HELP ME!
AH... OKAY.
I CAN'T EVEN IMAGINE THAT TIMID YOUNG MAN COMMITTING MURDER.

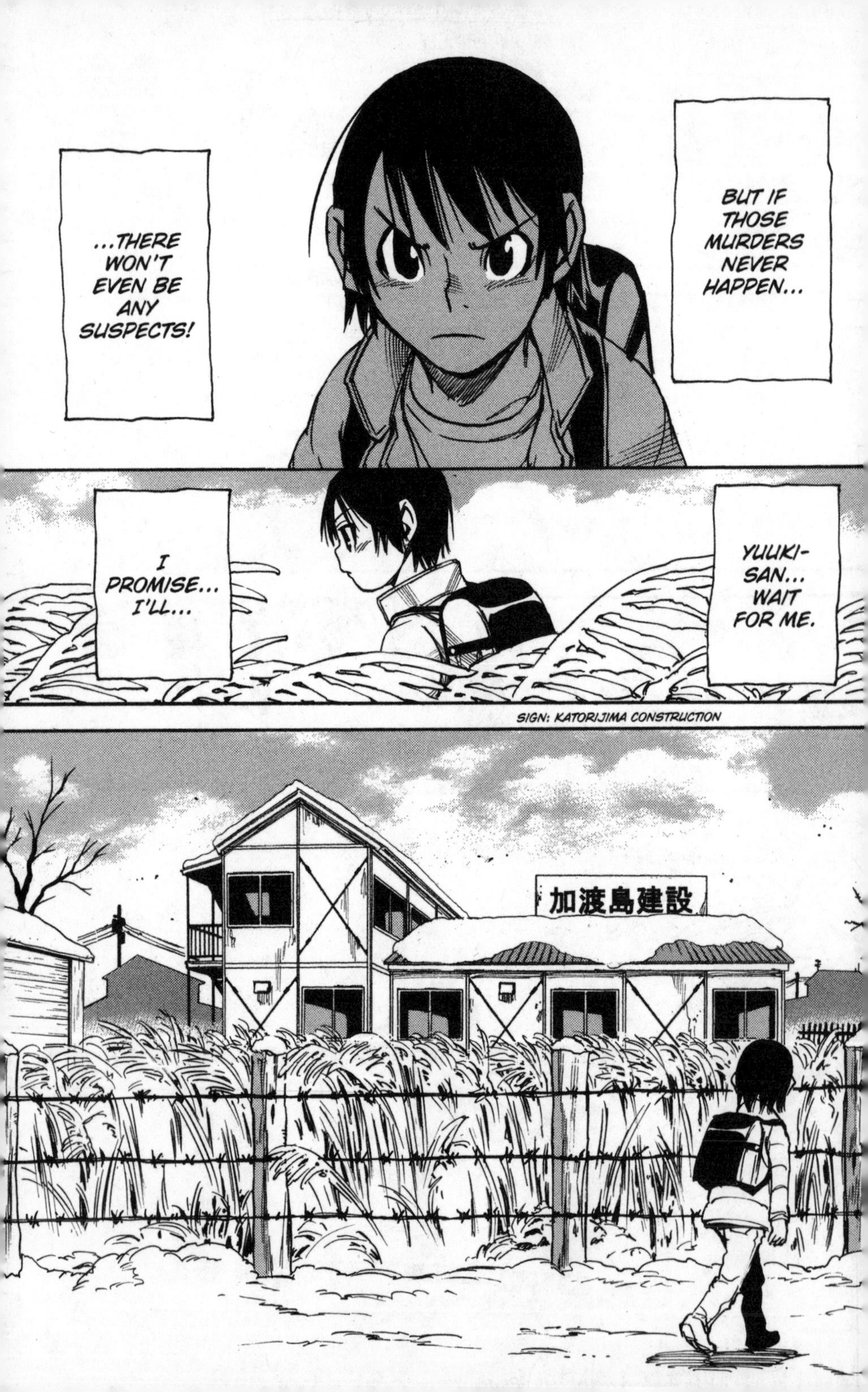
BUT IF THOSE MURDERS NEVER HAPPEN...
...THERE WON'T EVEN BE ANY SUSPECTS!
YUUKI-SAN... WAIT FOR ME.
I PROMISE... I'LL...
SIGN: KATORIJIMA CONSTRUCTION
加渡島建設

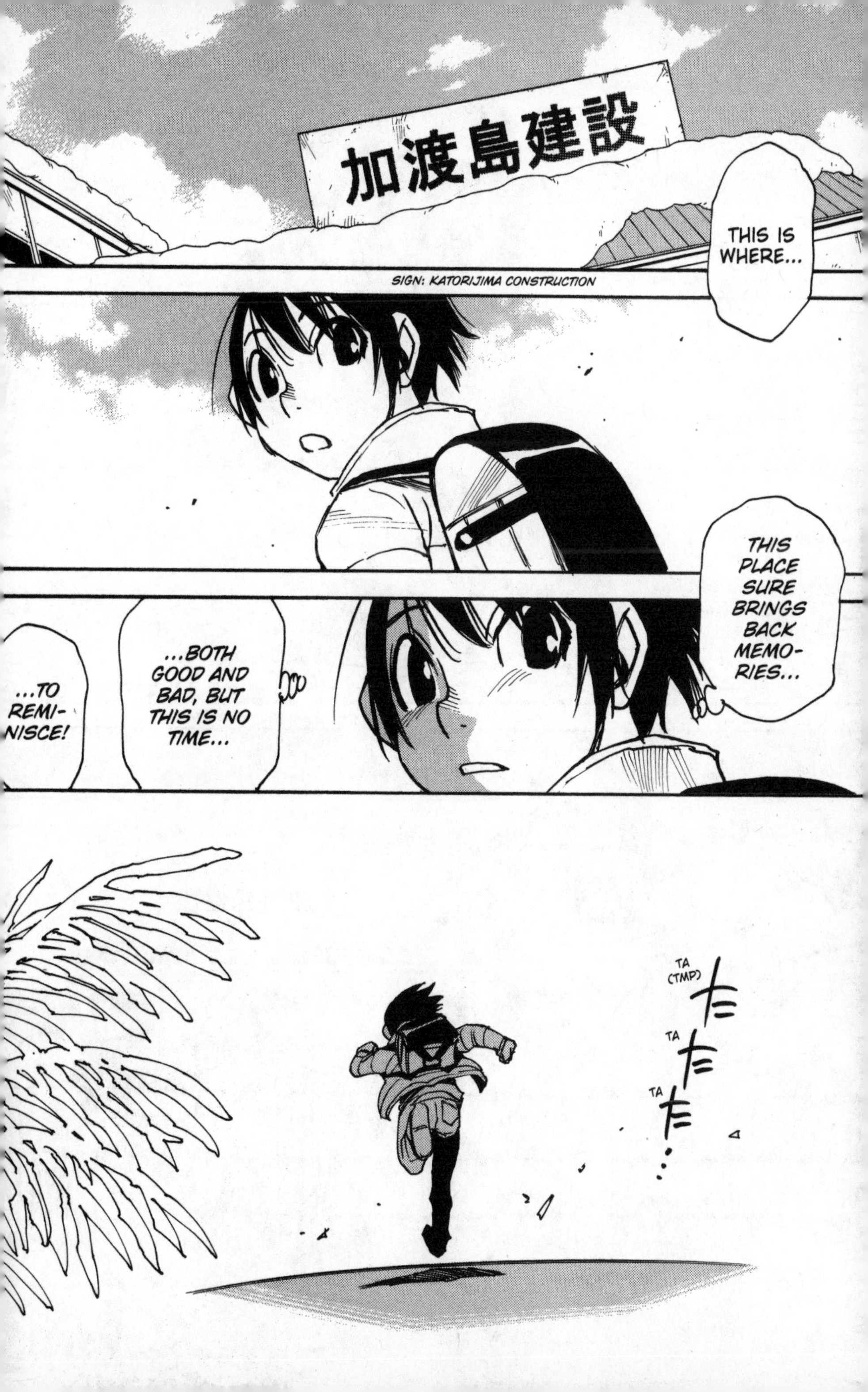
加渡島建設
THIS IS WHERE...
SIGN: KATORIJIMA CONSTRUCTION
THIS PLACE SURE BRINGS BACK MEMORIES...
...BOTH GOOD AND BAD, BUT THIS IS NO TIME...
...TO REMINISCE!
TA (TMP)
TA
TA

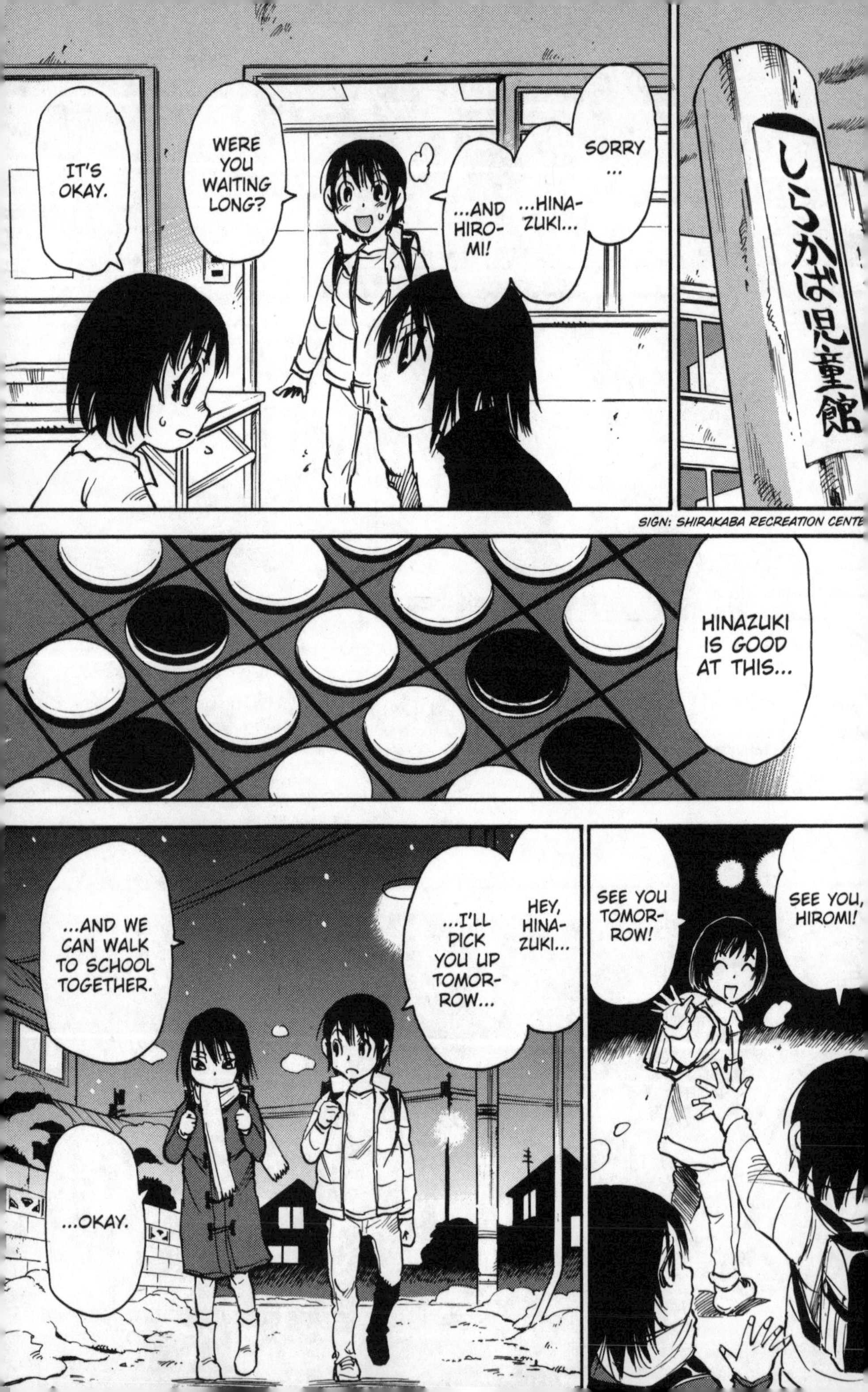
しらかば児童館
SORRY ...
...HINA-ZUKI...
...AND HIRO-MI!
WERE YOU WAITING LONG?
IT'S OKAY.
SIGN: SHIRAKABA RECREATION CENTE
HINAZUKI IS GOOD AT THIS...
SEE YOU, HIROMI!
SEE YOU TOMOR-ROW!
HEY, HINA-ZUKI...
...I'LL PICK YOU UP TOMOR-ROW...
...AND WE CAN WALK TO SCHOOL TOGETHER.
...OKAY.

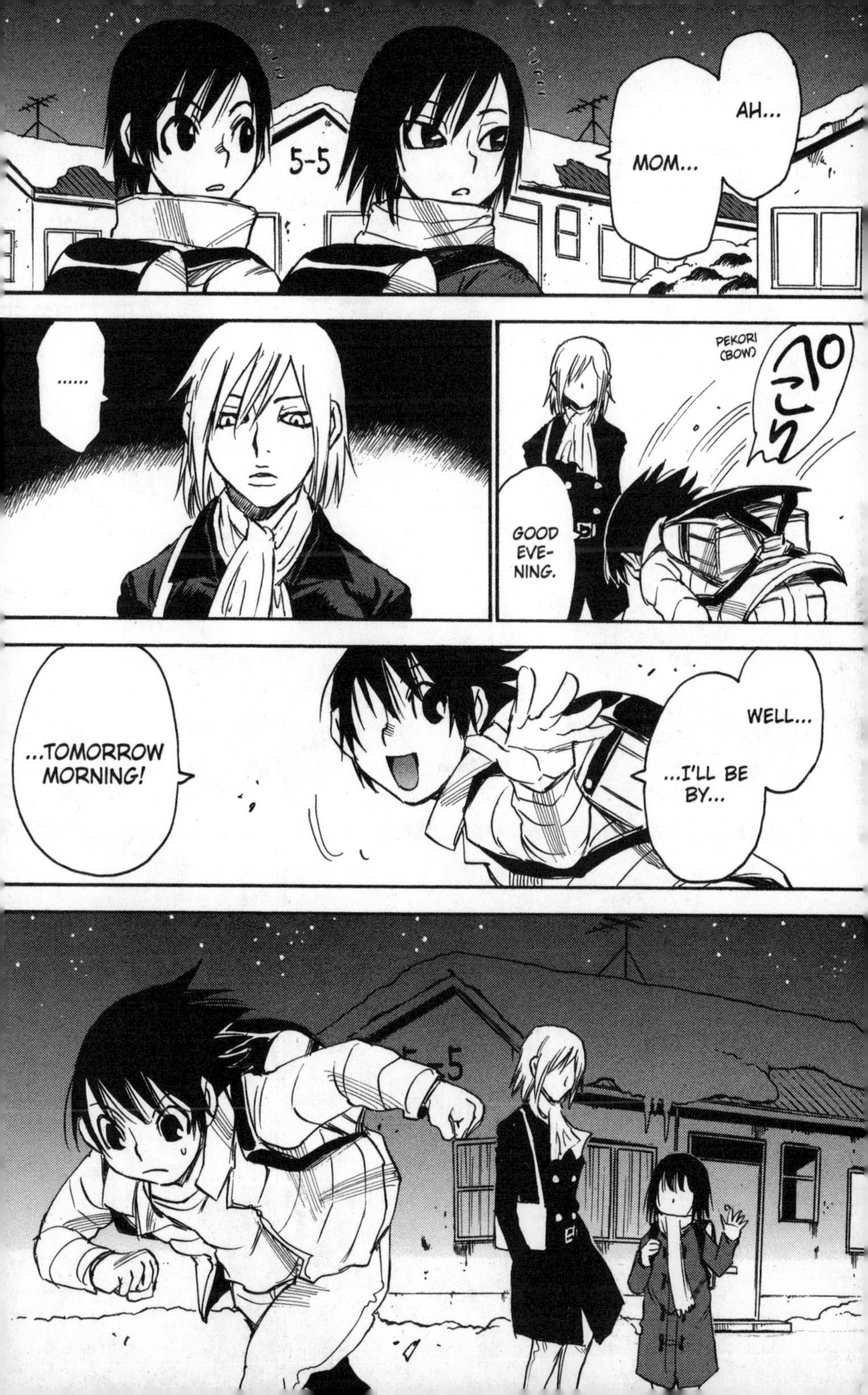

5-5
AH...
MOM...
ぺこり
PEKORI (BOW)
GOOD EVE-NING.
......
WELL...
...I'LL BE BY...
...TOMORROW MORNING!

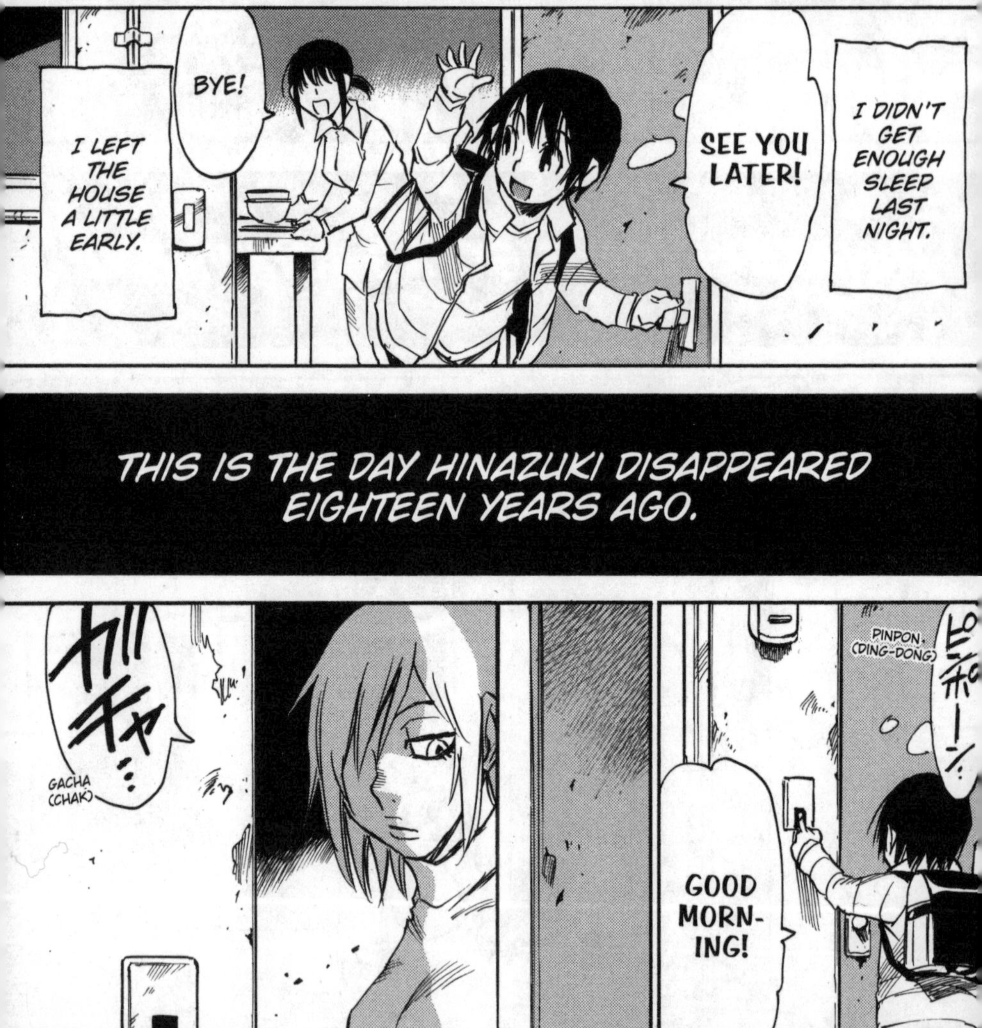
I DIDN'T GET ENOUGH SLEEP LAST NIGHT.
SEE YOU LATER!
BYE!
I LEFT THE HOUSE A LITTLE EARLY.
THIS IS THE DAY HINAZUKI DISAPPEARED EIGHTEEN YEARS AGO.
PINPON (DING-DONG)
GOOD MORNING!
GACHA (CHAK)

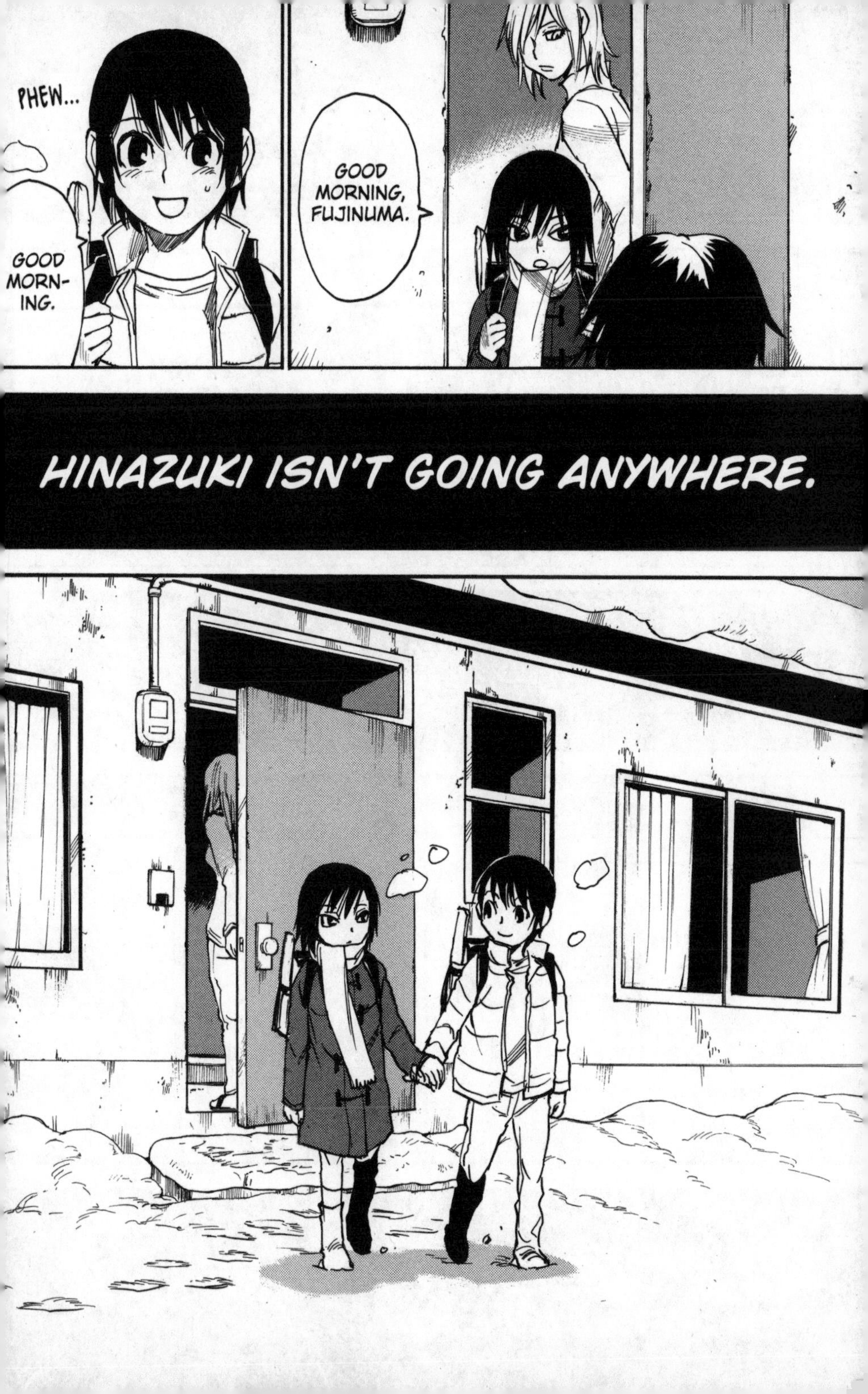
GOOD MORNING, FUJINUMA.
PHEW...
GOOD MORNING.
HINAZUKI ISN'T GOING ANYWHERE.

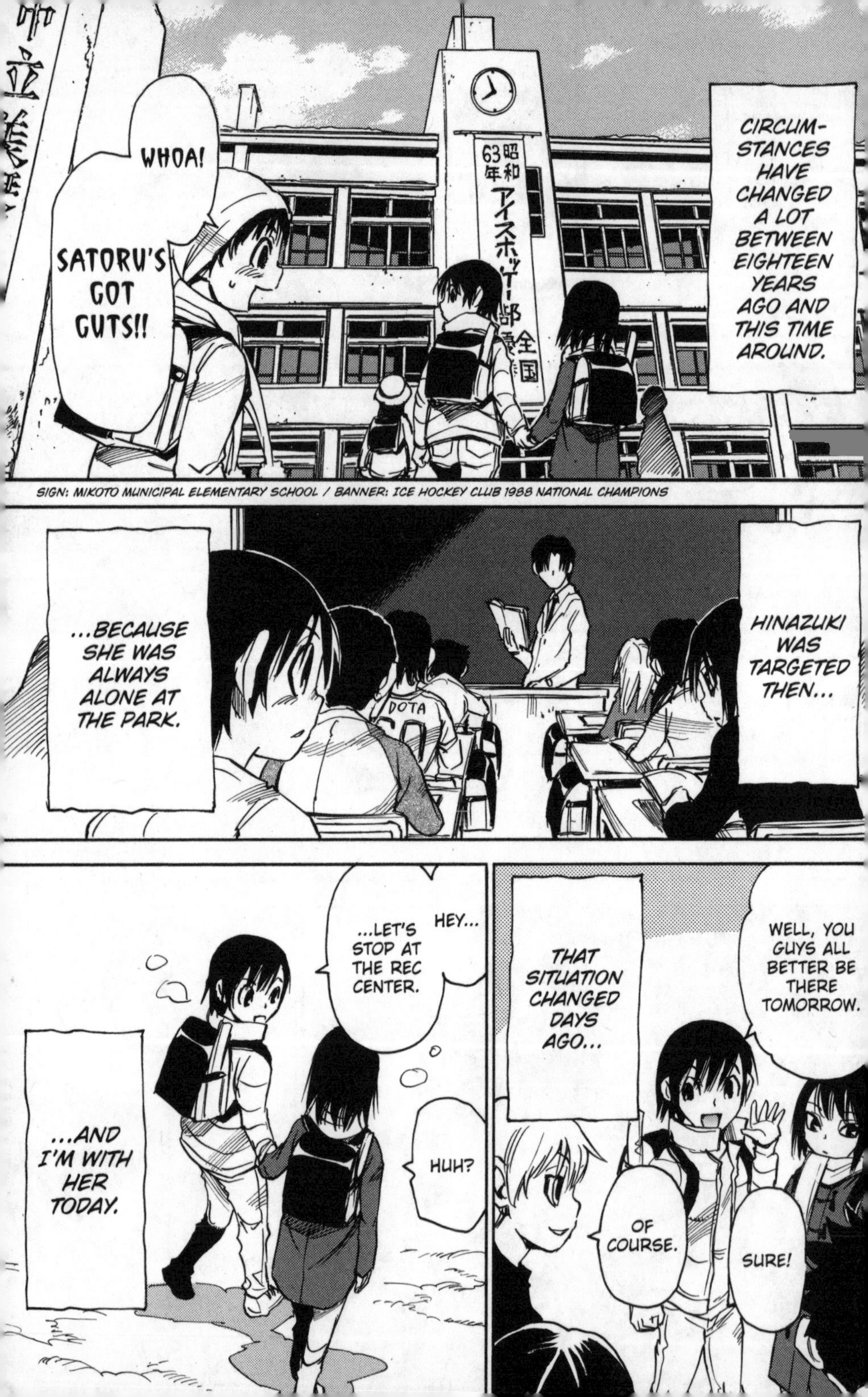
CIRCUM-STANCES HAVE CHANGED A LOT BETWEEN EIGHTEEN YEARS AGO AND THIS TIME AROUND.
WHOA!
SATORU'S GOT GUTS!!
SIGN: MIKOTO MUNICIPAL ELEMENTARY SCHOOL / BANNER: ICE HOCKEY CLUB 1988 NATIONAL CHAMPIONS
HINAZUKI WAS TARGETED THEN...
...BECAUSE SHE WAS ALWAYS ALONE AT THE PARK.
DOTA
WELL, YOU GUYS ALL BETTER BE THERE TOMORROW.
THAT SITUATION CHANGED DAYS AGO...
SURE!
OF COURSE.
HEY...
...LET'S STOP AT THE REC CENTER.
HUH?
...AND I'M WITH HER TODAY.

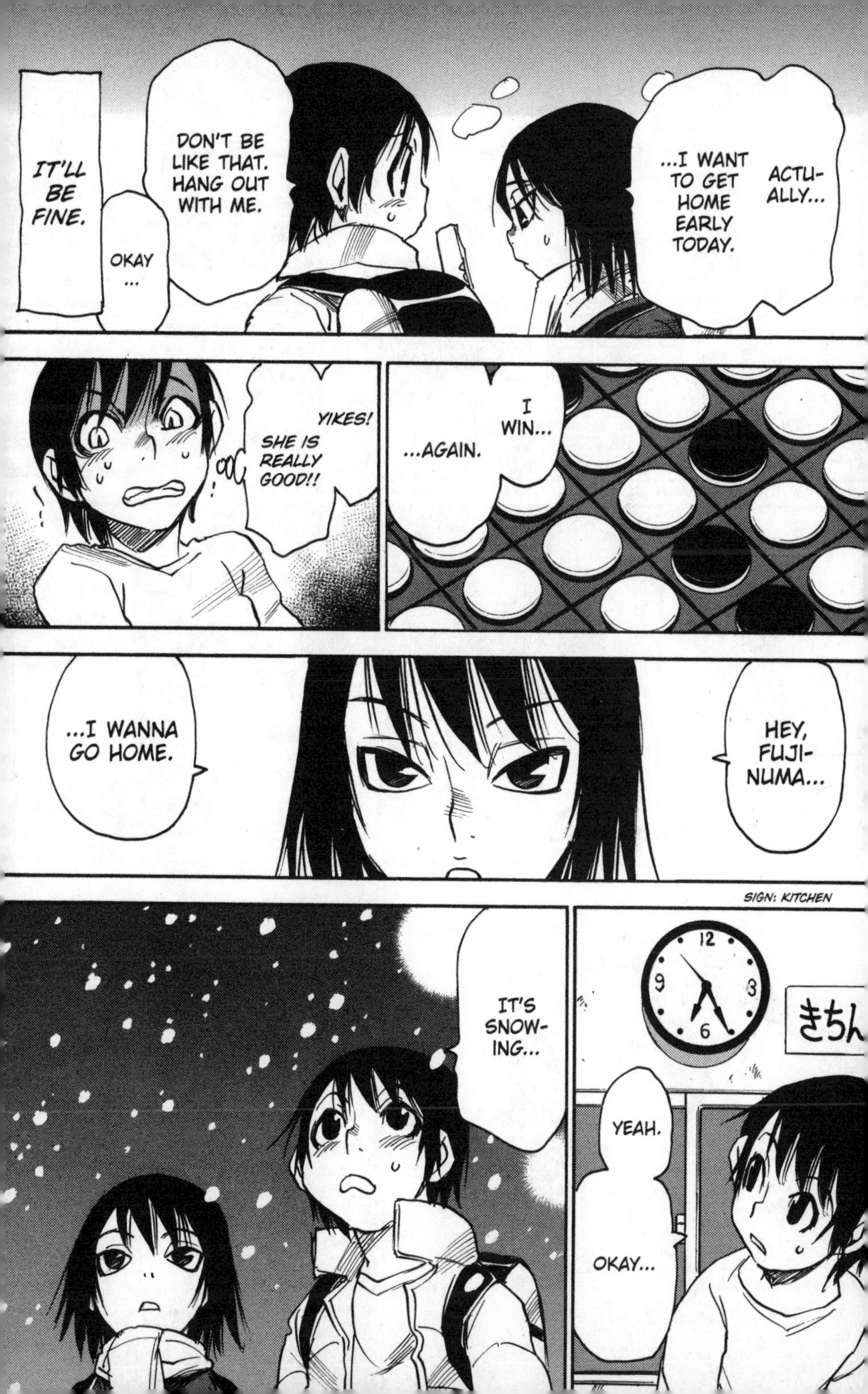
ACTU-ALLY...
...I WANT TO GET HOME EARLY TODAY.
DON'T BE LIKE THAT. HANG OUT WITH ME.
OKAY ...
IT'LL BE FINE.
I WIN...
...AGAIN.
YIKES! SHE IS REALLY GOOD!!
HEY, FUJI-NUMA...
...I WANNA GO HOME.
SIGN: KITCHEN
きちん
YEAH.
OKAY...
IT'S SNOW-ING...

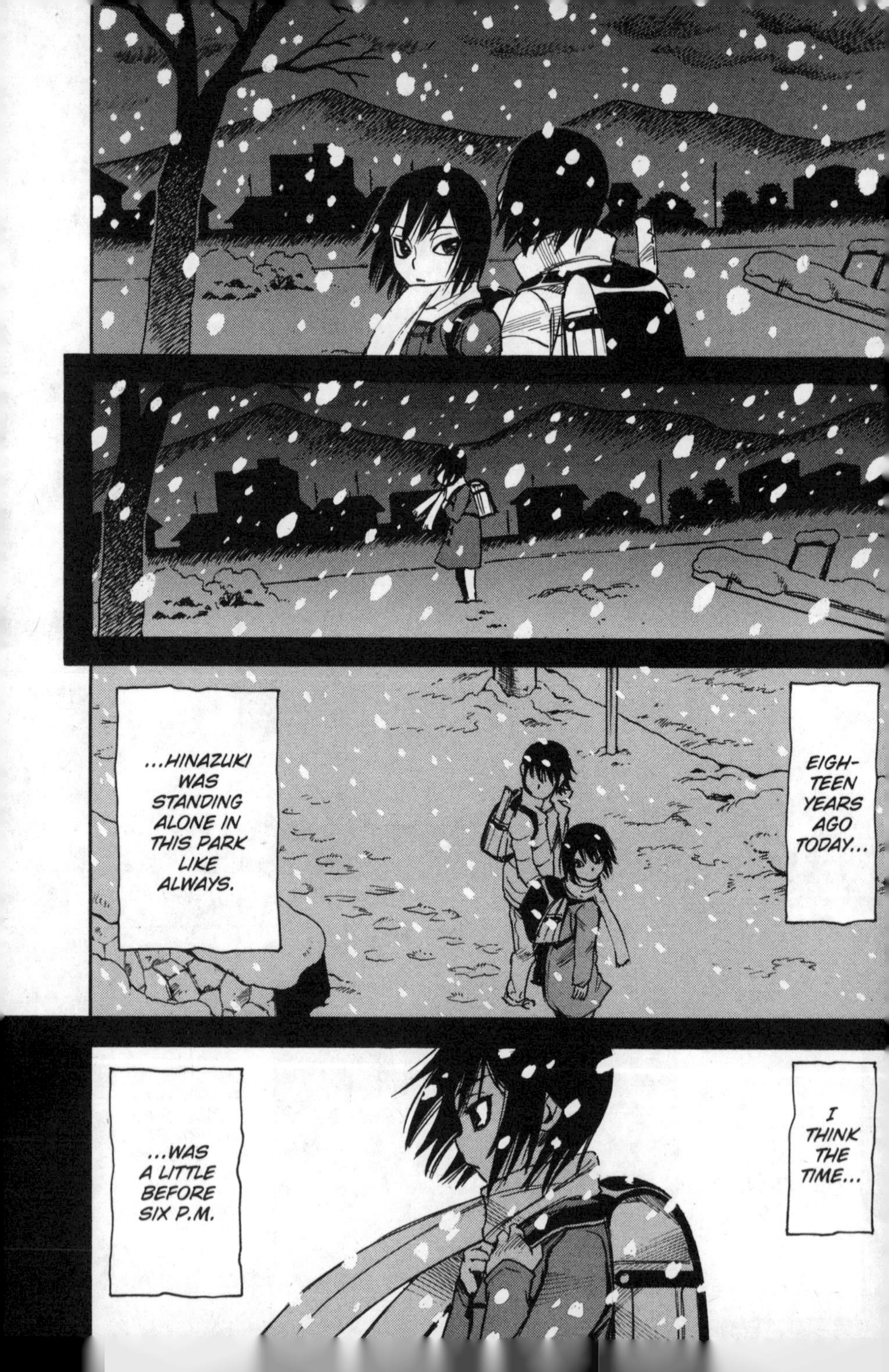
EIGH-TEEN YEARS AGO TODAY...
...HINAZUKI WAS STANDING ALONE IN THIS PARK LIKE ALWAYS.
I THINK THE TIME...
...WAS A LITTLE BEFORE SIX P.M.

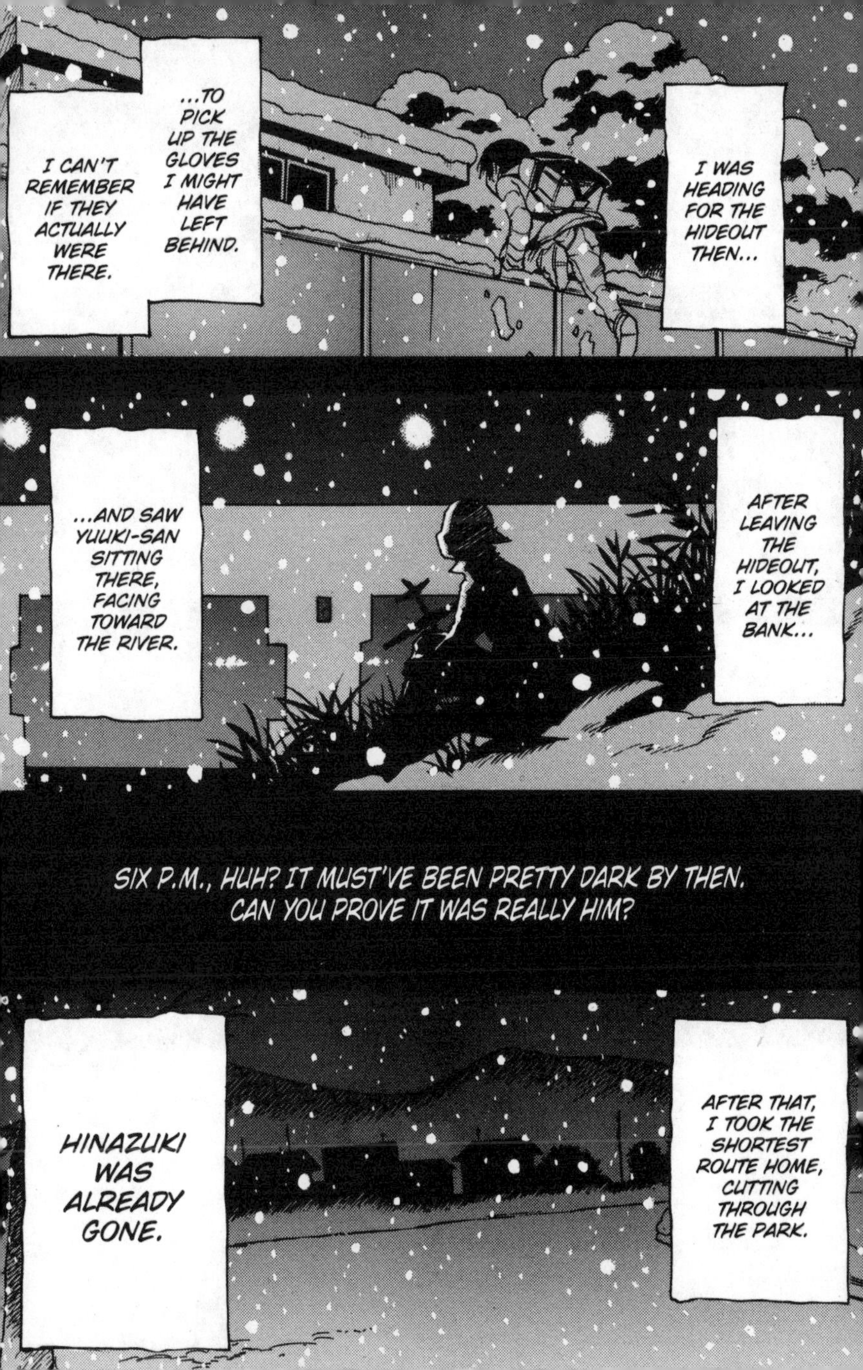
I WAS HEADING FOR THE HIDEOUT THEN...
...TO PICK UP THE GLOVES I MIGHT HAVE LEFT BEHIND.
I CAN'T REMEMBER IF THEY ACTUALLY WERE THERE.
AFTER LEAVING THE HIDEOUT, I LOOKED AT THE BANK...
...AND SAW YUUKI-SAN SITTING THERE, FACING TOWARD THE RIVER.
SIX P.M., HUH? IT MUST'VE BEEN PRETTY DARK BY THEN. CAN YOU PROVE IT WAS REALLY HIM?
AFTER THAT, I TOOK THE SHORTEST ROUTE HOME, CUTTING THROUGH THE PARK.
HINAZUKI WAS ALREADY GONE.

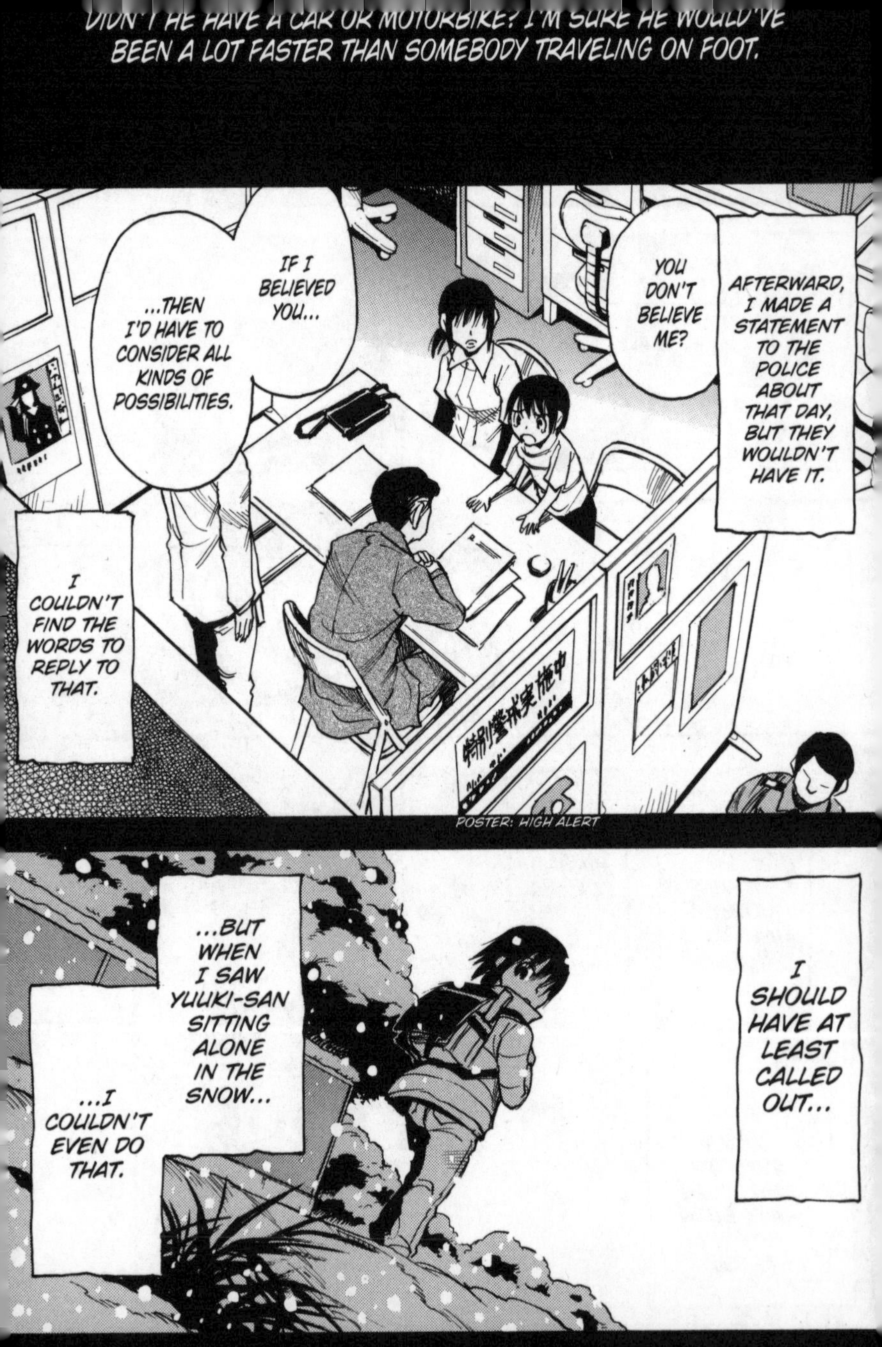
DIDN'T HE HAVE A CAR OR MOTORBIKE? I'M SURE HE WOULD'VE BEEN A LOT FASTER THAN SOMEBODY TRAVELING ON FOOT.
AFTERWARD, I MADE A STATEMENT TO THE POLICE ABOUT THAT DAY, BUT THEY WOULDN'T HAVE IT.
YOU DON'T BELIEVE ME?
IF I BELIEVED YOU...
...THEN I'D HAVE TO CONSIDER ALL KINDS OF POSSIBILITIES.
I COULDN'T FIND THE WORDS TO REPLY TO THAT.
POSTER: HIGH ALERT
I SHOULD HAVE AT LEAST CALLED OUT...
...BUT WHEN I SAW YUUKI-SAN SITTING ALONE IN THE SNOW...
...I COULDN'T EVEN DO THAT.

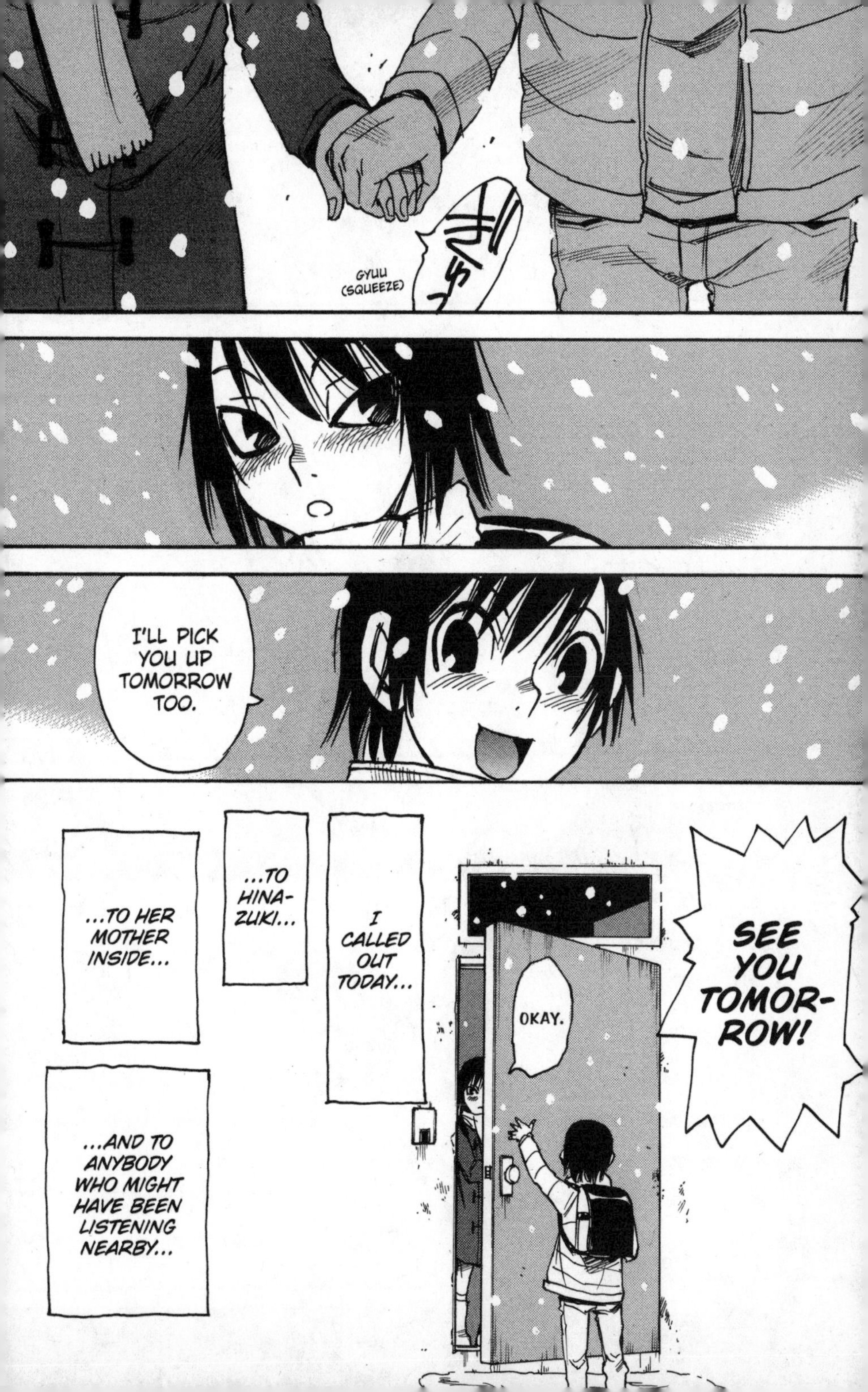
GYUU (SQUEEZE)
I'LL PICK YOU UP TOMORROW TOO.
SEE YOU TOMOR-ROW!
OKAY.
I CALLED OUT TODAY...
...TO HINA-ZUKI...
...TO HER MOTHER INSIDE...
...AND TO ANYBODY WHO MIGHT HAVE BEEN LISTENING NEARBY...

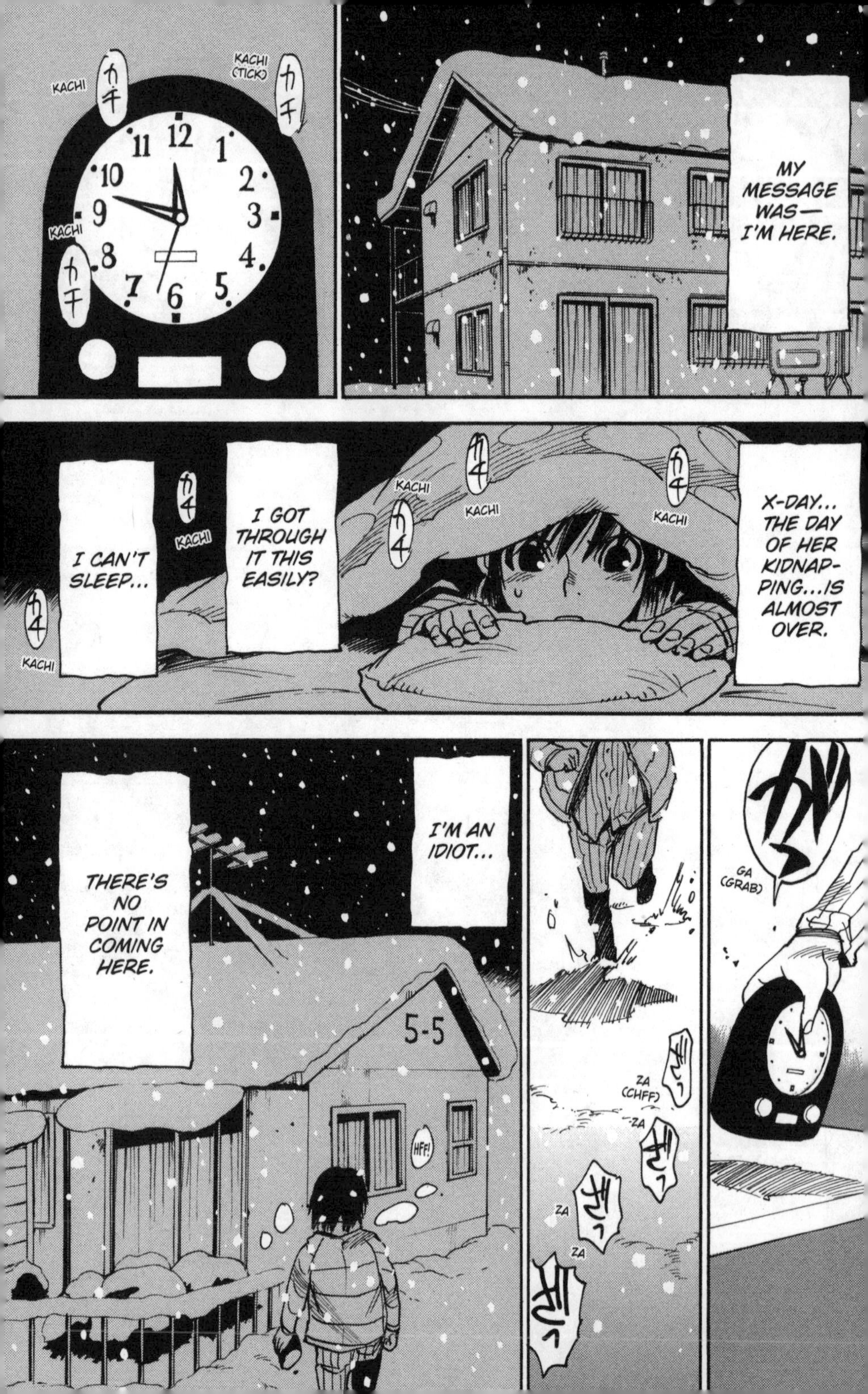
MY MESSAGE WAS— I'M HERE.
カチ
KACHI (TICK)
カチ
KACHI
カチ
KACHI
X-DAY... THE DAY OF HER KIDNAP-PING...IS ALMOST OVER.
カチ
KACHI
カチ
KACHI
カチ
KACHI
I GOT THROUGH IT THIS EASILY?
カチ
KACHI
I CAN'T SLEEP...
カチ
KACHI
GA (GRAB)
ZA (CHFF)
ZA
ZA
ZA
I'M AN IDIOT...
THERE'S NO POINT IN COMING HERE.
5-5
HFF!

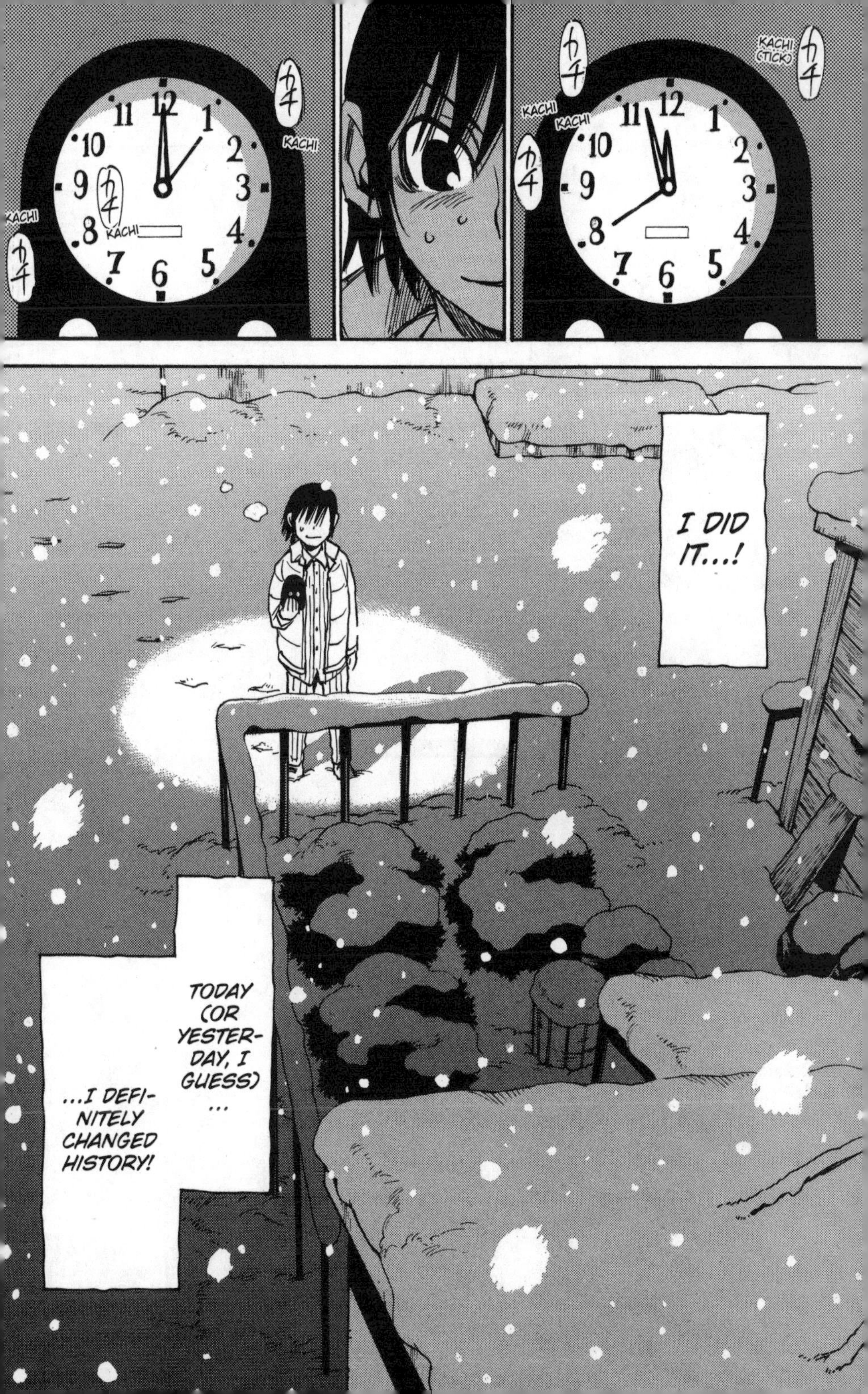カチ
KACHI (TICK)
カチ
KACHI
KACHI
カチ
KACHI
カチ
KACHI
カチ
KACHI
I DID IT...!
TODAY (OR YESTER-DAY, I GUESS)...
...I DEFI-NITELY CHANGED HISTORY!

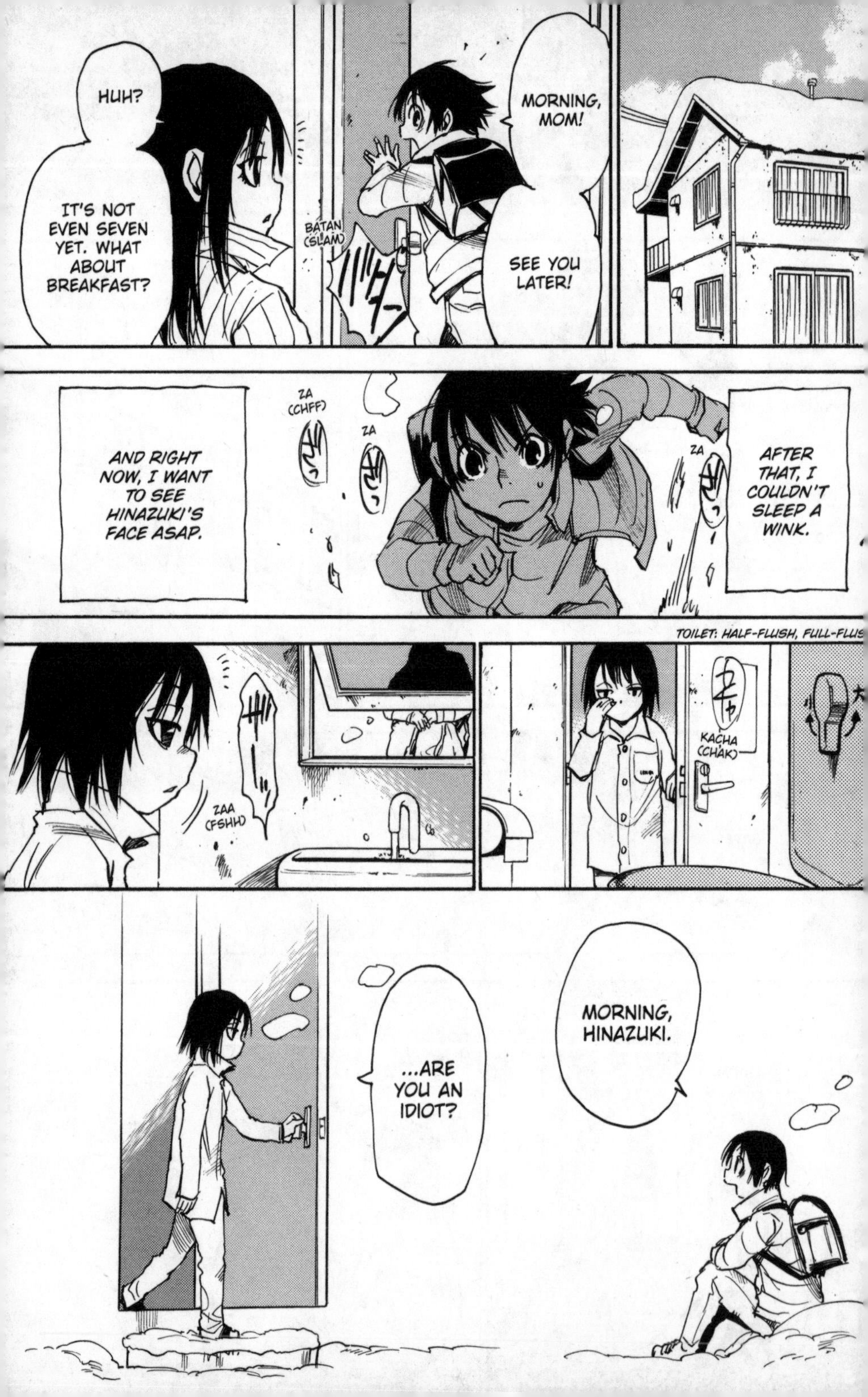
MORNING, MOM!
SEE YOU LATER!
BATAN (SLAM)
HUH?
IT'S NOT EVEN SEVEN YET. WHAT ABOUT BREAKFAST?
AFTER THAT, I COULDN'T SLEEP A WINK.
ZA
ZA (CHFF)
ZA
AND RIGHT NOW, I WANT TO SEE HINAZUKI'S FACE ASAP.
TOILET: HALF-FLUSH, FULL-FLUS
KACHA (CHAK)
ZAA (FSHH)
MORNING, HINAZUKI.
...ARE YOU AN IDIOT?

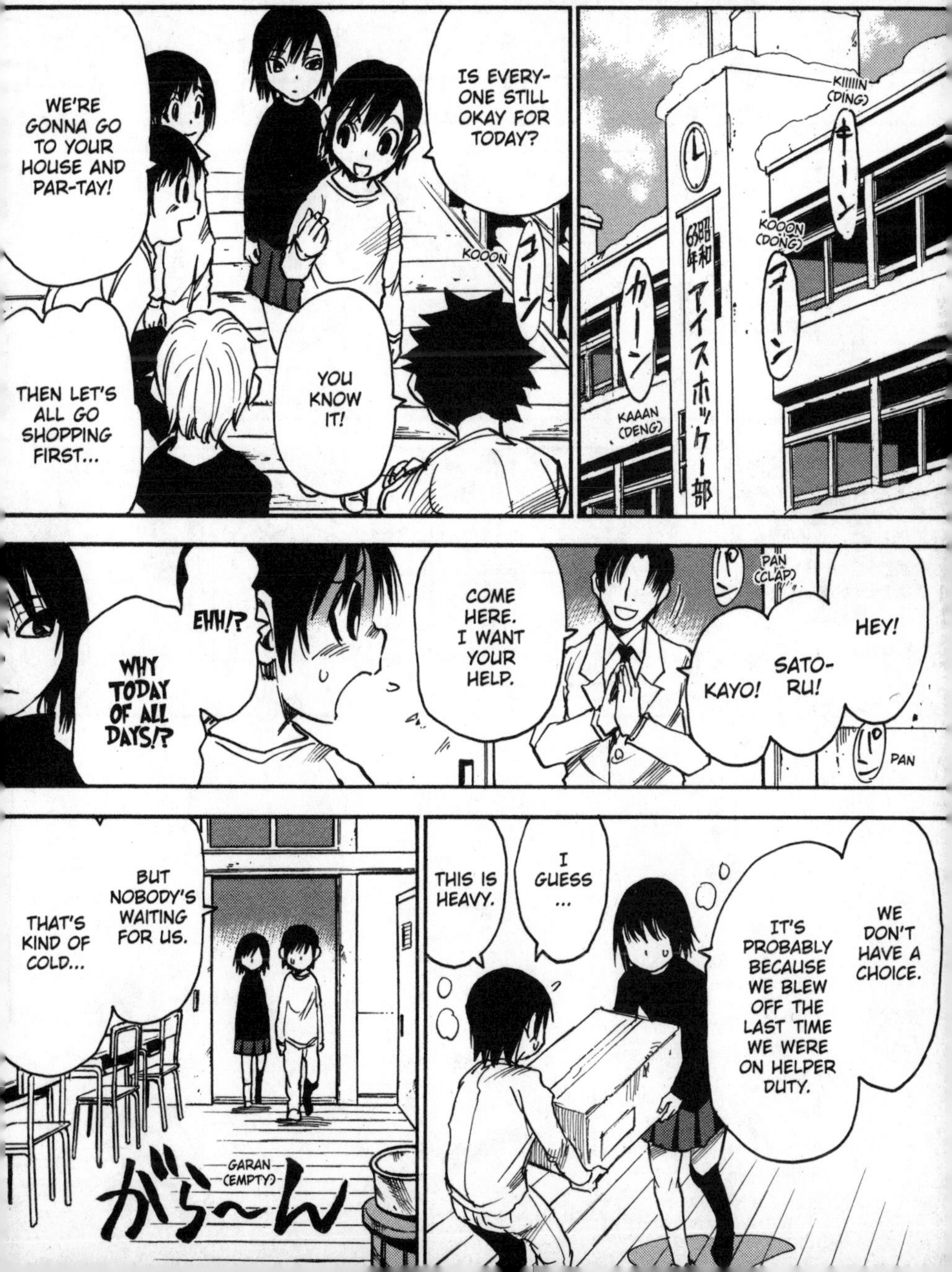
KIIIIN (DING)
キーン
KOOON (DONG)
コーン
昭和63年アイスホッケー部
カーン
KAAAN (DENG)
IS EVERY-ONE STILL OKAY FOR TODAY?
コーン
KOOON
WE'RE GONNA GO TO YOUR HOUSE AND PAR-TAY!
YOU KNOW IT!
THEN LET'S ALL GO SHOPPING FIRST...
パン
PAN (CLAP)
HEY!
SATO-RU!
KAYO!
パン
PAN
COME HERE. I WANT YOUR HELP.
EHH!?
WHY TODAY OF ALL DAYS!?
WE DON'T HAVE A CHOICE.
IT'S PROBABLY BECAUSE WE BLEW OFF THE LAST TIME WE WERE ON HELPER DUTY.
I GUESS...
THIS IS HEAVY.
BUT NOBODY'S WAITING FOR US.
THAT'S KIND OF COLD...
GARAN (EMPTY)
がら〜ん

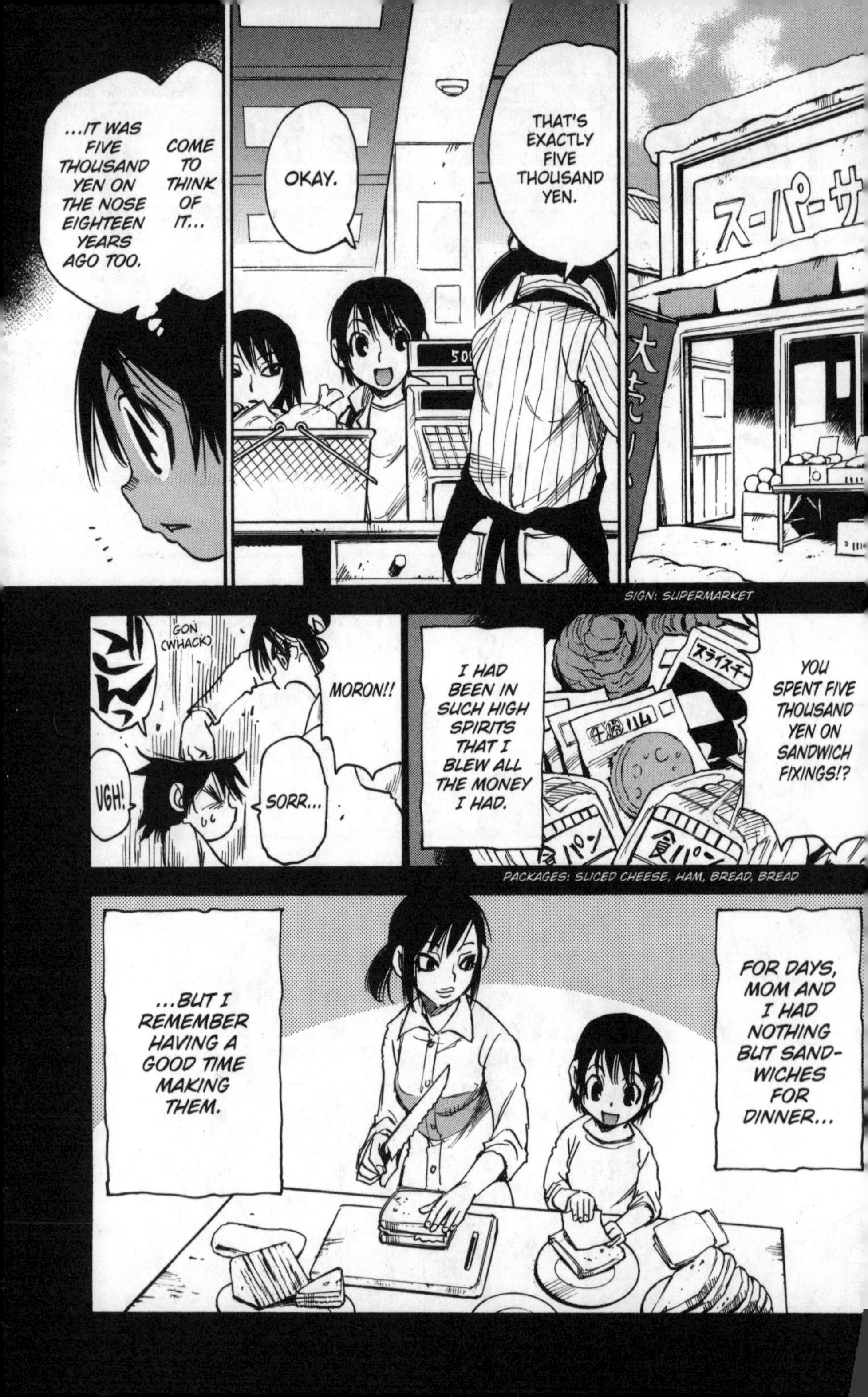
THAT'S EXACTLY FIVE THOUSAND YEN.
OKAY.
COME TO THINK OF IT...
...IT WAS FIVE THOUSAND YEN ON THE NOSE EIGHTEEN YEARS AGO TOO.
SIGN: SUPERMARKET
YOU SPENT FIVE THOUSAND YEN ON SANDWICH FIXINGS!?
I HAD BEEN IN SUCH HIGH SPIRITS THAT I BLEW ALL THE MONEY I HAD.
MORON!!
GON (WHACK)
UGH!
SORR...
PACKAGES: SLICED CHEESE, HAM, BREAD, BREAD
FOR DAYS, MOM AND I HAD NOTHING BUT SAND-WICHES FOR DINNER...
...BUT I REMEMBER HAVING A GOOD TIME MAKING THEM.

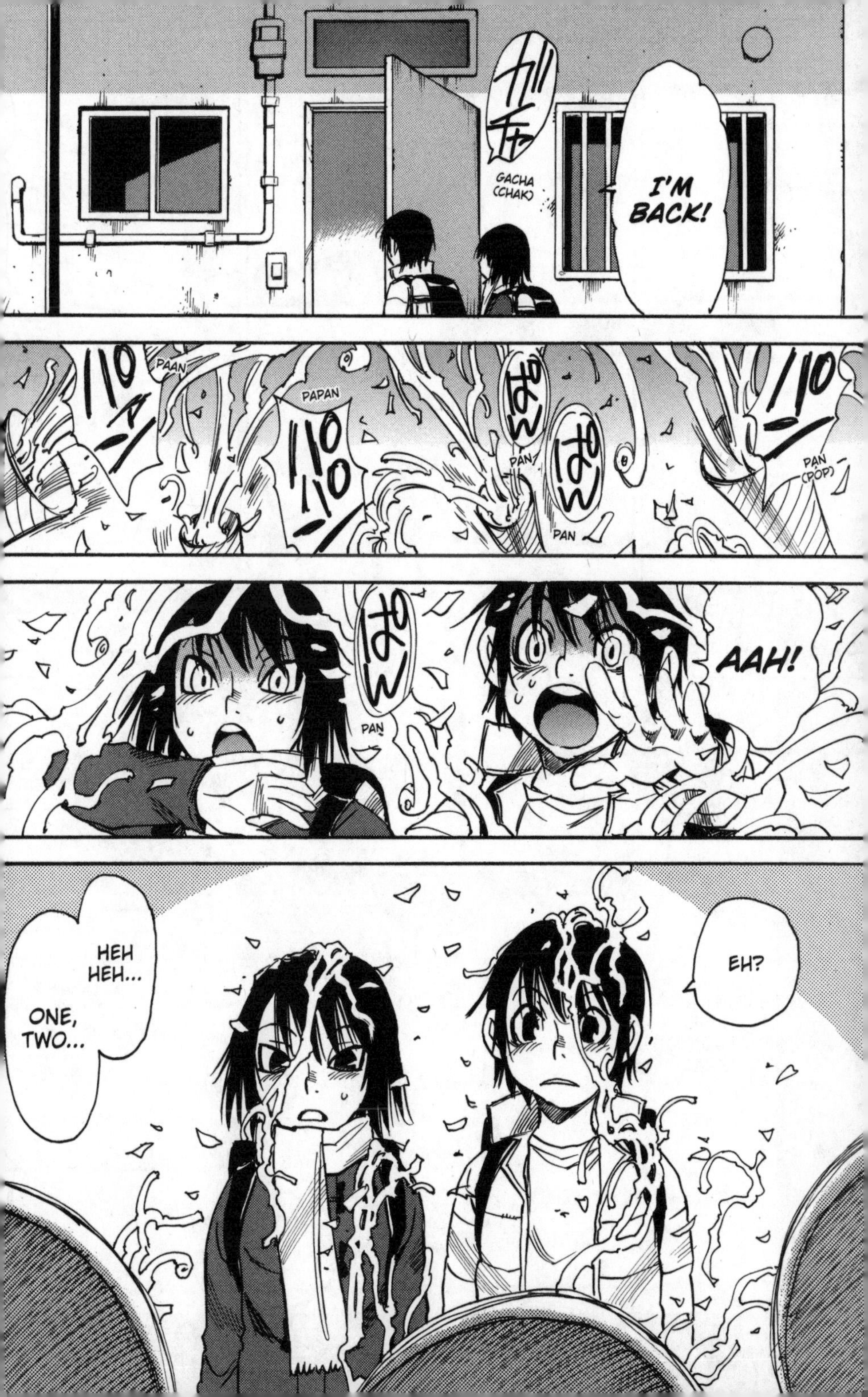

I'M BACK!
ガチャ
GACHA (CHAK)
PAN (POP)
ぱん
PAN
ぱん
PAN
PAPAN
PAAN
AAH!
ぱん
PAN
EH?
HEH HEH...
ONE, TWO...

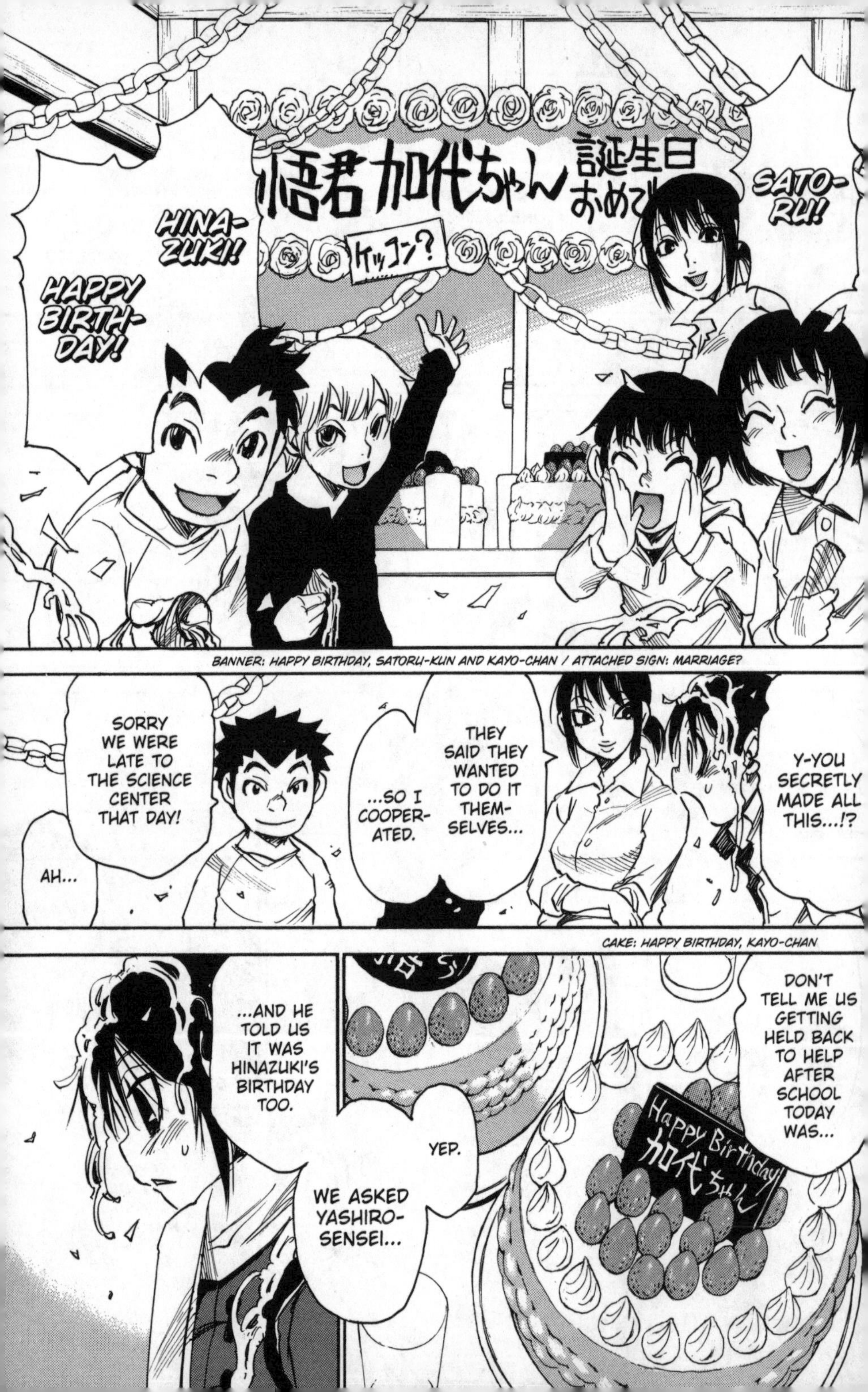
SATO-RU!
HINA-ZUKI!
HAPPY BIRTH-DAY!
ケッコン？
BANNER: HAPPY BIRTHDAY, SATORU-KUN AND KAYO-CHAN / ATTACHED SIGN: MARRIAGE?
Y-YOU SECRETLY MADE ALL THIS...!?
THEY SAID THEY WANTED TO DO IT THEM-SELVES...
...SO I COOPER-ATED.
SORRY WE WERE LATE TO THE SCIENCE CENTER THAT DAY!
AH...
CAKE: HAPPY BIRTHDAY, KAYO-CHAN
DON'T TELL ME US GETTING HELD BACK TO HELP AFTER SCHOOL TODAY WAS...
Happy Birthday 加代ちゃん
YEP.
WE ASKED YASHIRO-SENSEI...
...AND HE TOLD US IT WAS HINAZUKI'S BIRTHDAY TOO.

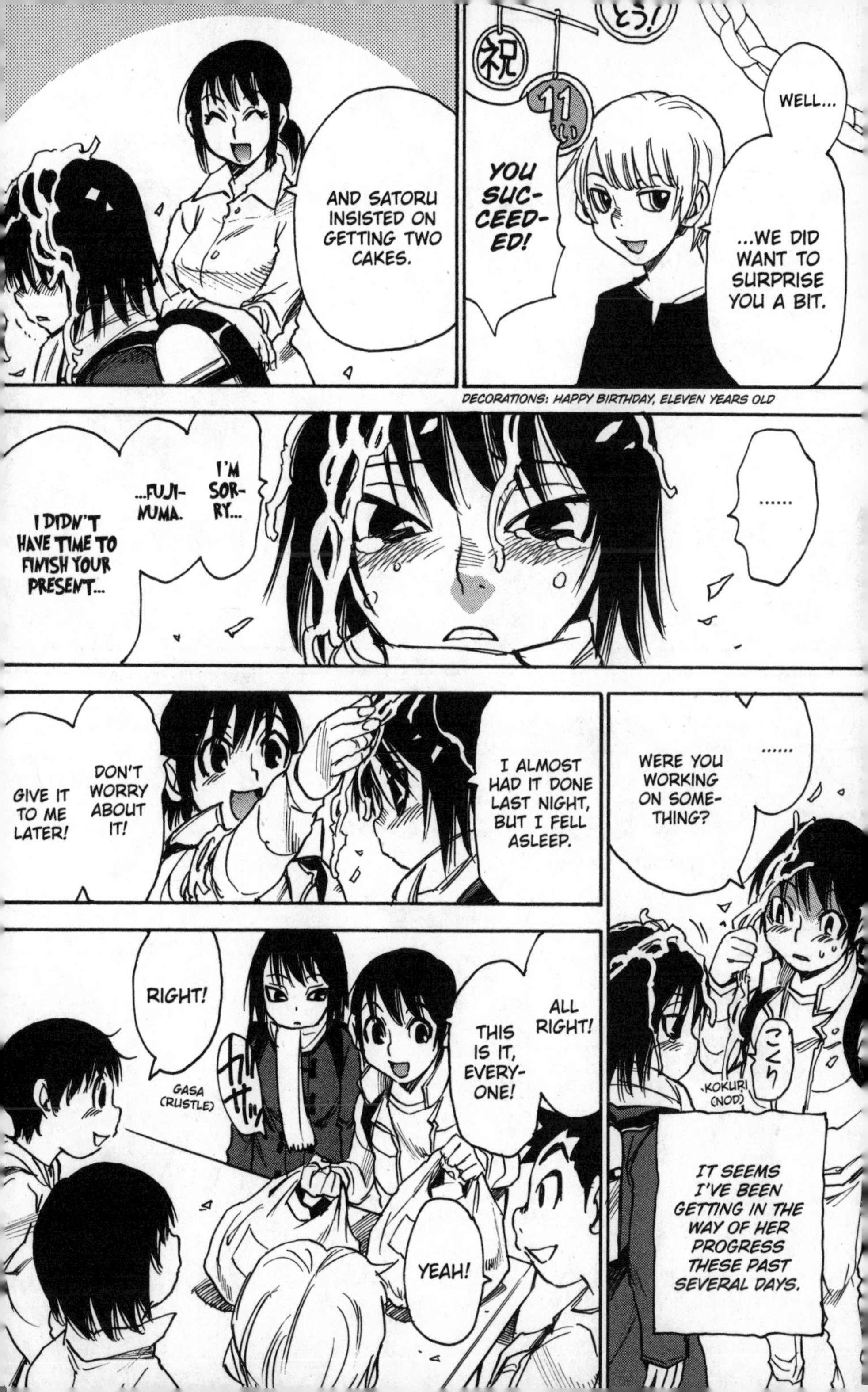
とう!
祝
11
WELL...
...WE DID WANT TO SURPRISE YOU A BIT.
YOU SUCCEEDED!
AND SATORU INSISTED ON GETTING TWO CAKES.
DECORATIONS: HAPPY BIRTHDAY, ELEVEN YEARS OLD
......
I'M SORRY...
...FUJINUMA.
I DIDN'T HAVE TIME TO FINISH YOUR PRESENT...
......
WERE YOU WORKING ON SOMETHING?
KOKURI (NOD)
IT SEEMS I'VE BEEN GETTING IN THE WAY OF HER PROGRESS THESE PAST SEVERAL DAYS.
I ALMOST HAD IT DONE LAST NIGHT, BUT I FELL ASLEEP.
DON'T WORRY ABOUT IT!
GIVE IT TO ME LATER!
ALL RIGHT!
THIS IS IT, EVERYONE!
RIGHT!
GASA (RUSTLE)
YEAH!

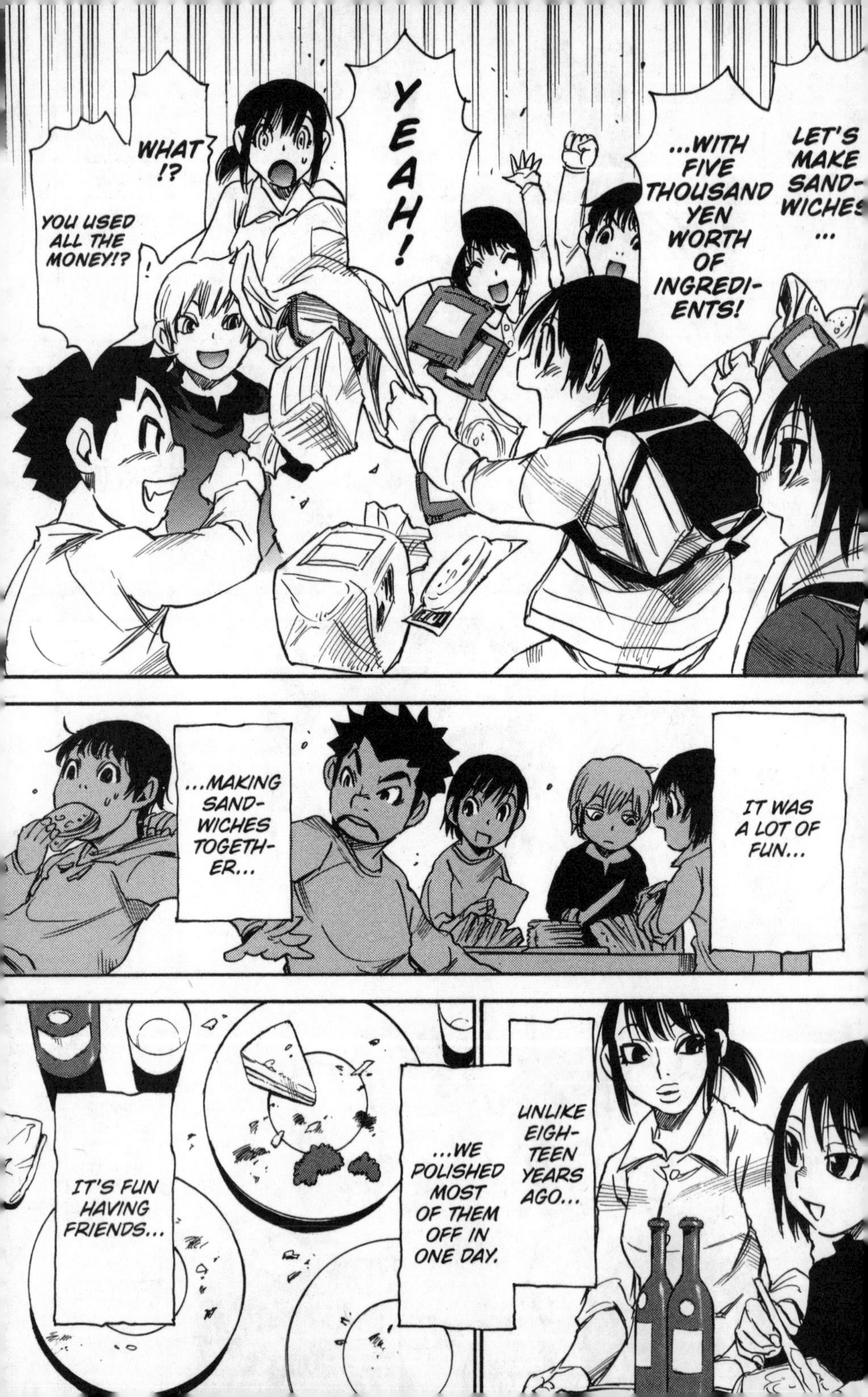
LET'S MAKE SAND-WICHES...
...WITH FIVE THOUSAND YEN WORTH OF INGREDI-ENTS!
YEAH!
WHAT!?
YOU USED ALL THE MONEY!?
IT WAS A LOT OF FUN...
...MAKING SAND-WICHES TOGETH-ER...
UNLIKE EIGH-TEEN YEARS AGO...
...WE POLISHED MOST OF THEM OFF IN ONE DAY.
IT'S FUN HAVING FRIENDS...

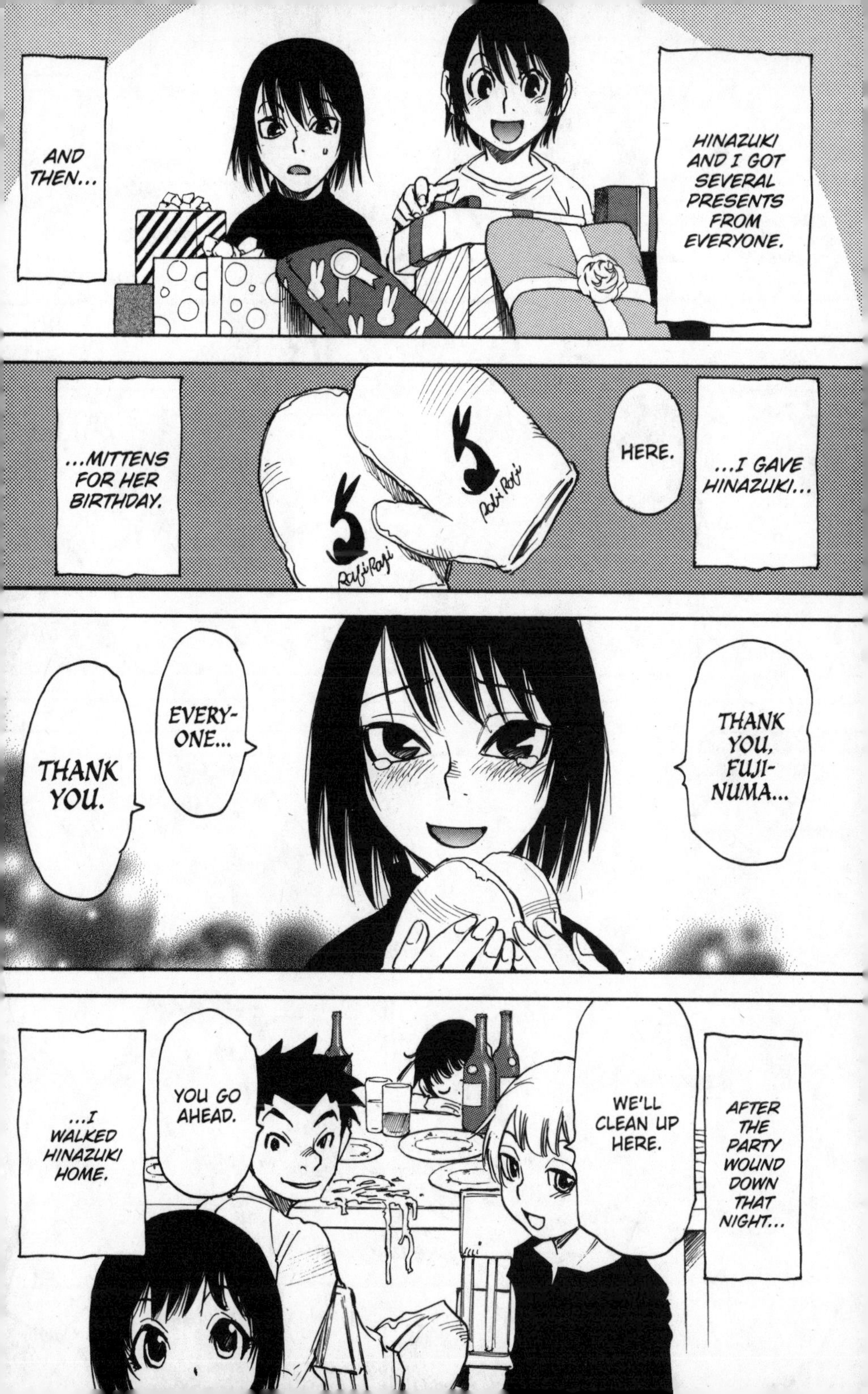
HINAZUKI AND I GOT SEVERAL PRESENTS FROM EVERYONE.
AND THEN...
...I GAVE HINAZUKI...
HERE.
Roji Roji
Roji Roji
...MITTENS FOR HER BIRTHDAY.
THANK YOU, FUJI-NUMA...
EVERY-ONE...
THANK YOU.
AFTER THE PARTY WOUND DOWN THAT NIGHT...
WE'LL CLEAN UP HERE.
YOU GO AHEAD.
...I WALKED HINAZUKI HOME.

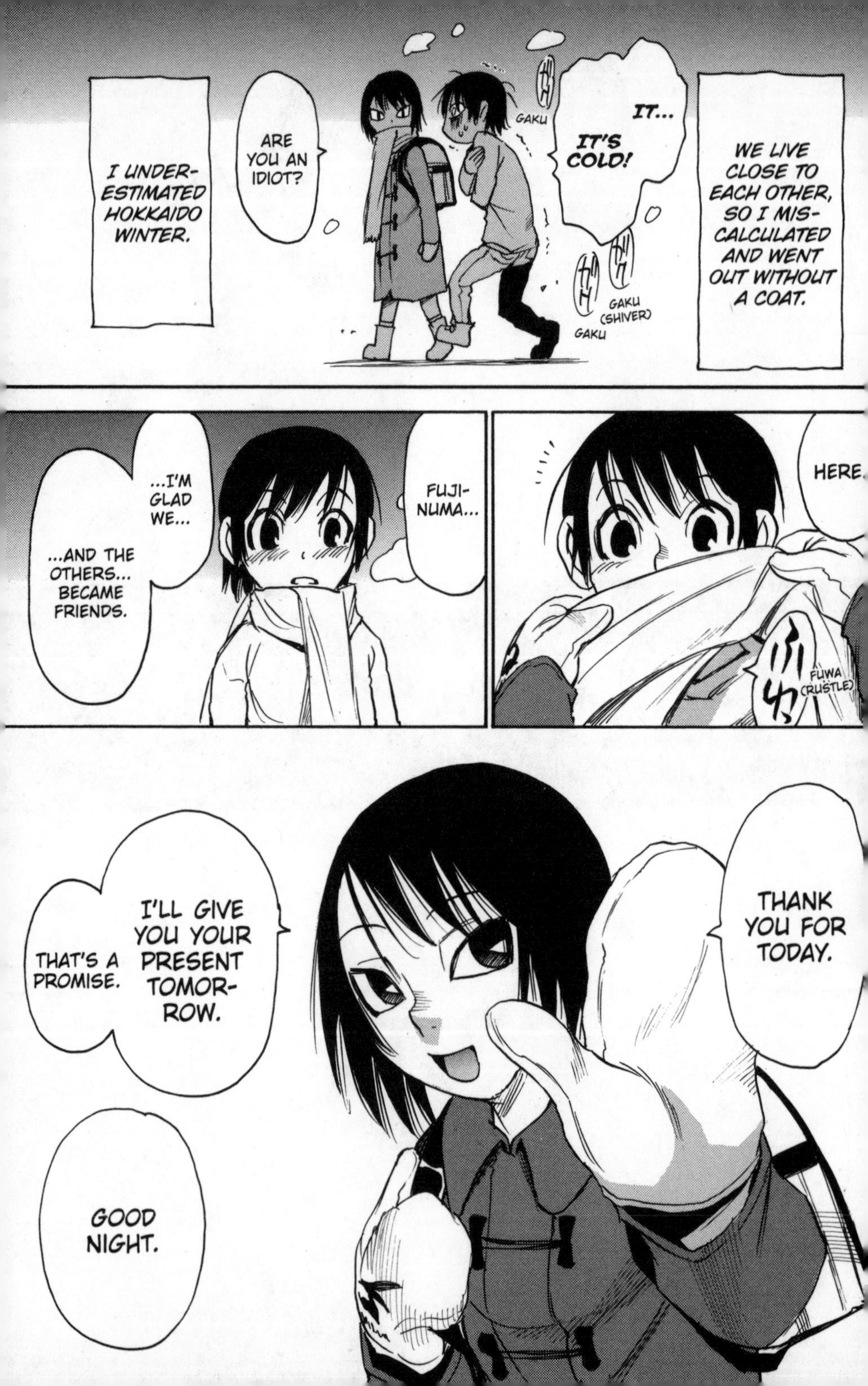
WE LIVE CLOSE TO EACH OTHER, SO I MISCALCULATED AND WENT OUT WITHOUT A COAT.
IT... IT'S COLD!
GAKU
GAKU (SHIVER)
GAKU
ARE YOU AN IDIOT?
I UNDERESTIMATED HOKKAIDO WINTER.
HERE.
FUWA (RUSTLE)
FUJINUMA...
...I'M GLAD WE...
...AND THE OTHERS... BECAME FRIENDS.
THANK YOU FOR TODAY.
I'LL GIVE YOU YOUR PRESENT TOMORROW.
THAT'S A PROMISE.
GOOD NIGHT.

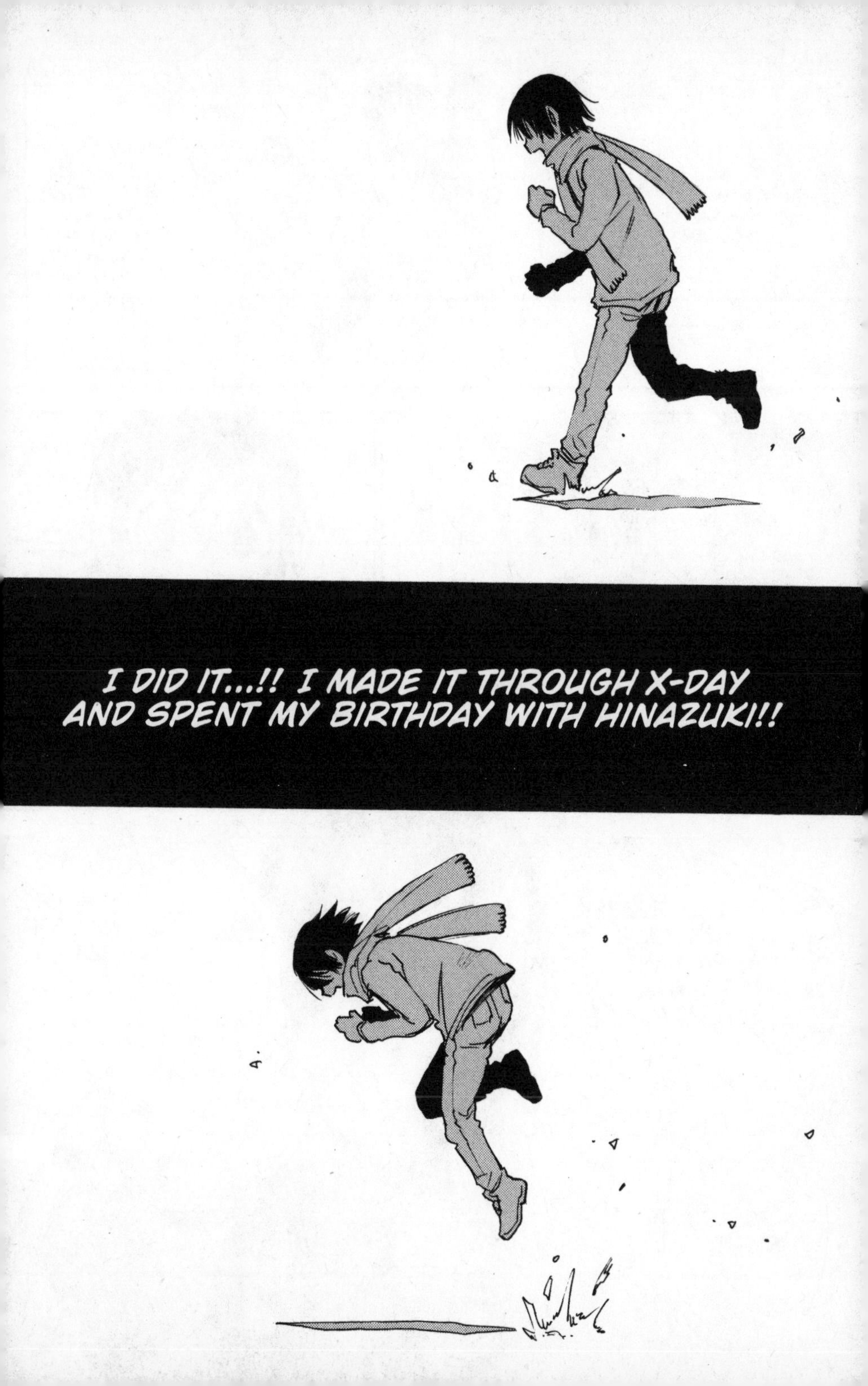
I DID IT...!! I MADE IT THROUGH X-DAY AND SPENT MY BIRTHDAY WITH HINAZUKI!!

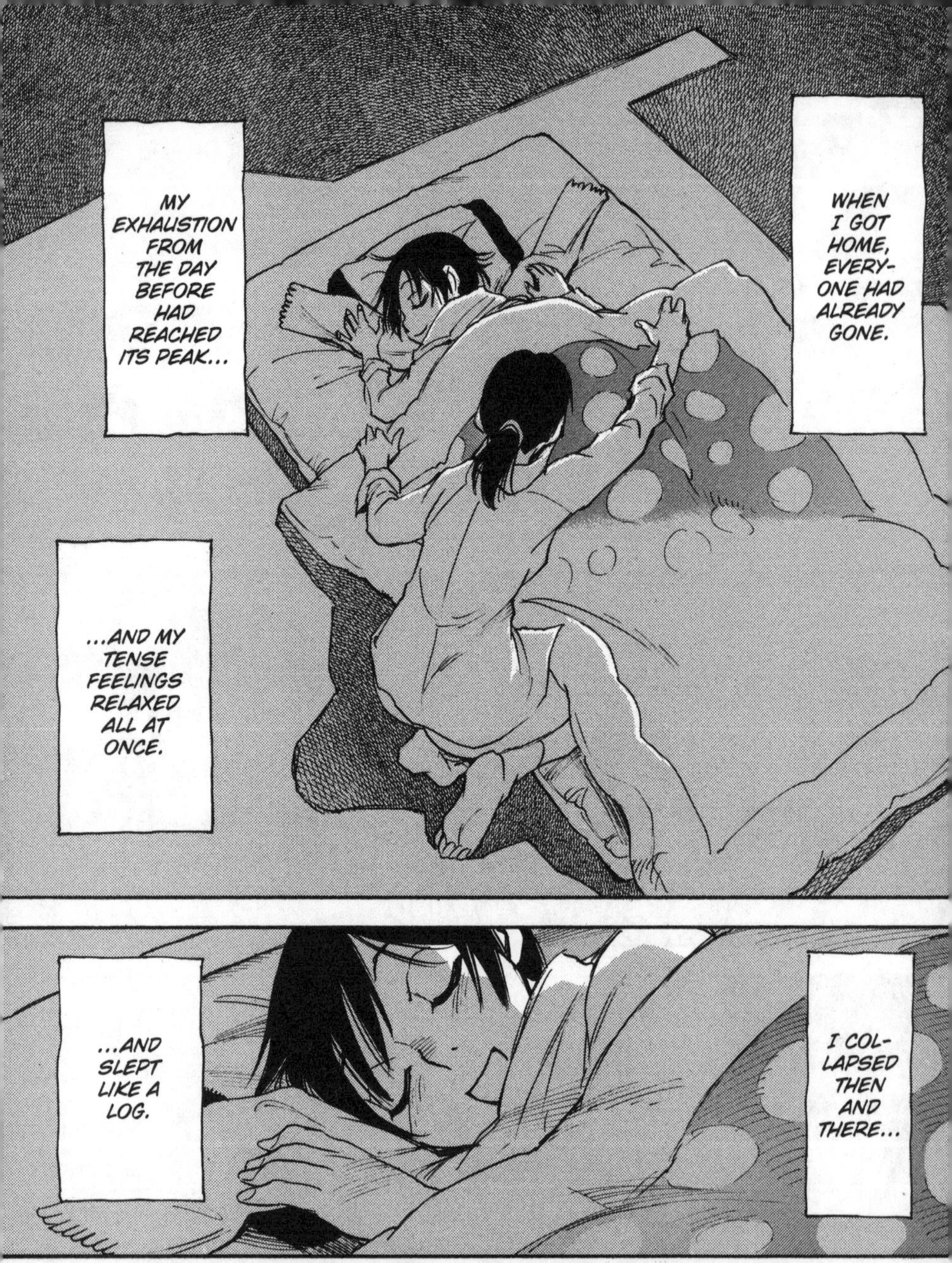
WHEN I GOT HOME, EVERY-ONE HAD ALREADY GONE.
MY EXHAUSTION FROM THE DAY BEFORE HAD REACHED ITS PEAK...
...AND MY TENSE FEELINGS RELAXED ALL AT ONCE.
I COL-LAPSED THEN AND THERE...
...AND SLEPT LIKE A LOG.

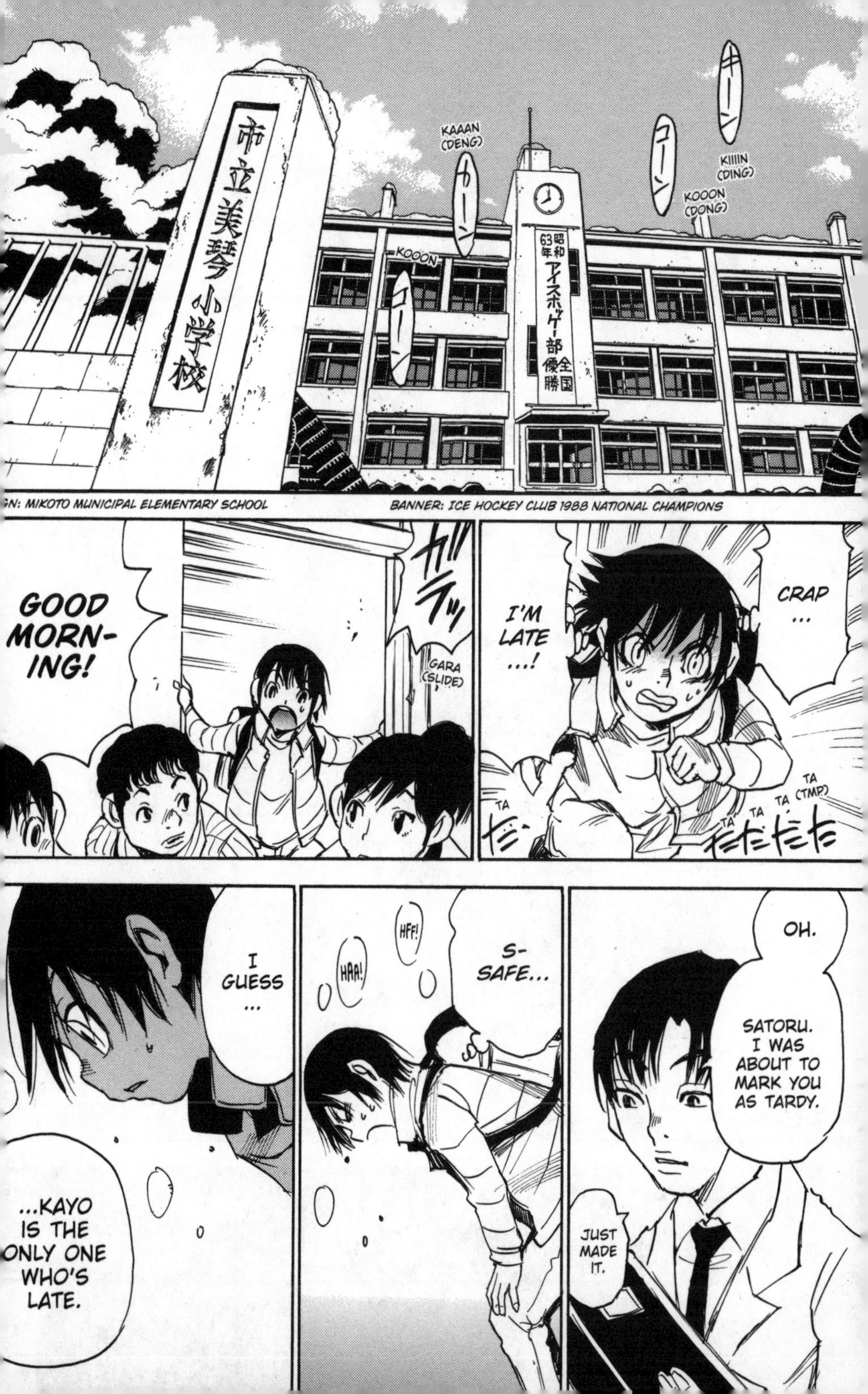
キーン
KIIIIN (DING)
コーン
KOOON (DONG)
カーン
KAAAN (DENG)
コーン
KOOON
昭和63年 アイスホッケー部 全国優勝
市立美琴小学校
BANNER: ICE HOCKEY CLUB 1988 NATIONAL CHAMPIONS
GN: MIKOTO MUNICIPAL ELEMENTARY SCHOOL
CRAP...
I'M LATE...!
TA (TMP)
TA
TA
TA
TA
ガラッ
GARA (SLIDE)
GOOD MORNING!
OH.
SATORU. I WAS ABOUT TO MARK YOU AS TARDY.
JUST MADE IT.
S-SAFE...
HFF!
HAA!
I GUESS...
...KAYO IS THE ONLY ONE WHO'S LATE.

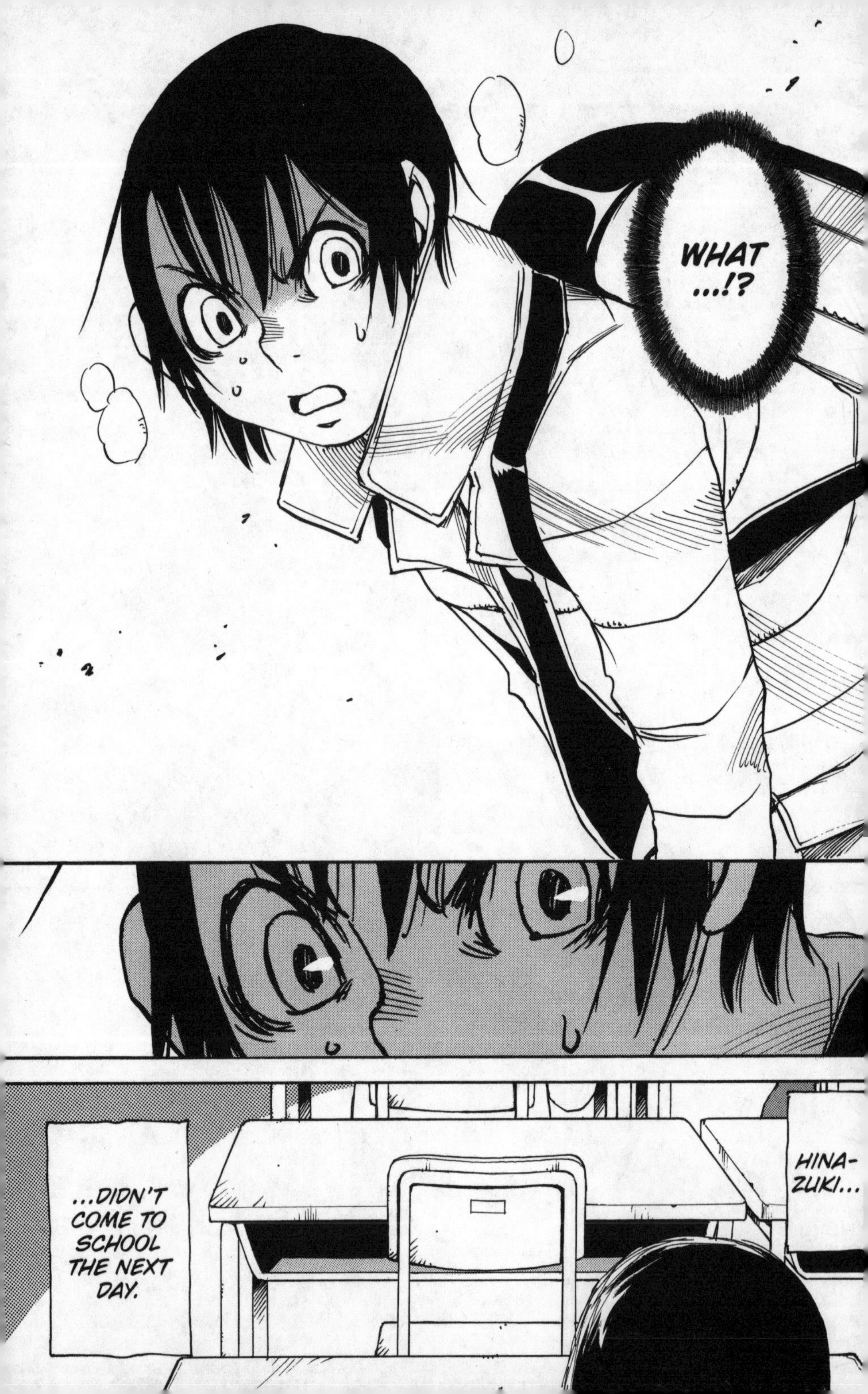
WHAT ...!?
HINA-ZUKI...
...DIDN'T COME TO SCHOOL THE NEXT DAY.

THE LAST
PROMISE
MADE
BETWEEN
ME AND
HINAZUKI...

...WAS
NEVER
FULFILLED.

STAFF

Kei Sanbe

Yoichiro Tomita
Manami 18 Sai
Shuuei Takagi
Zukku Ozaki
Koji Kikuta

Keishi Kanesada
Kunikazu Toda

SPECIAL THANKS
Hayato Yano
Soma Yano
Hinata Yano

BOOK DESIGN
Yukio Hoshino
VOLARE inc.

EDITOR
Yosuke Matsumiya

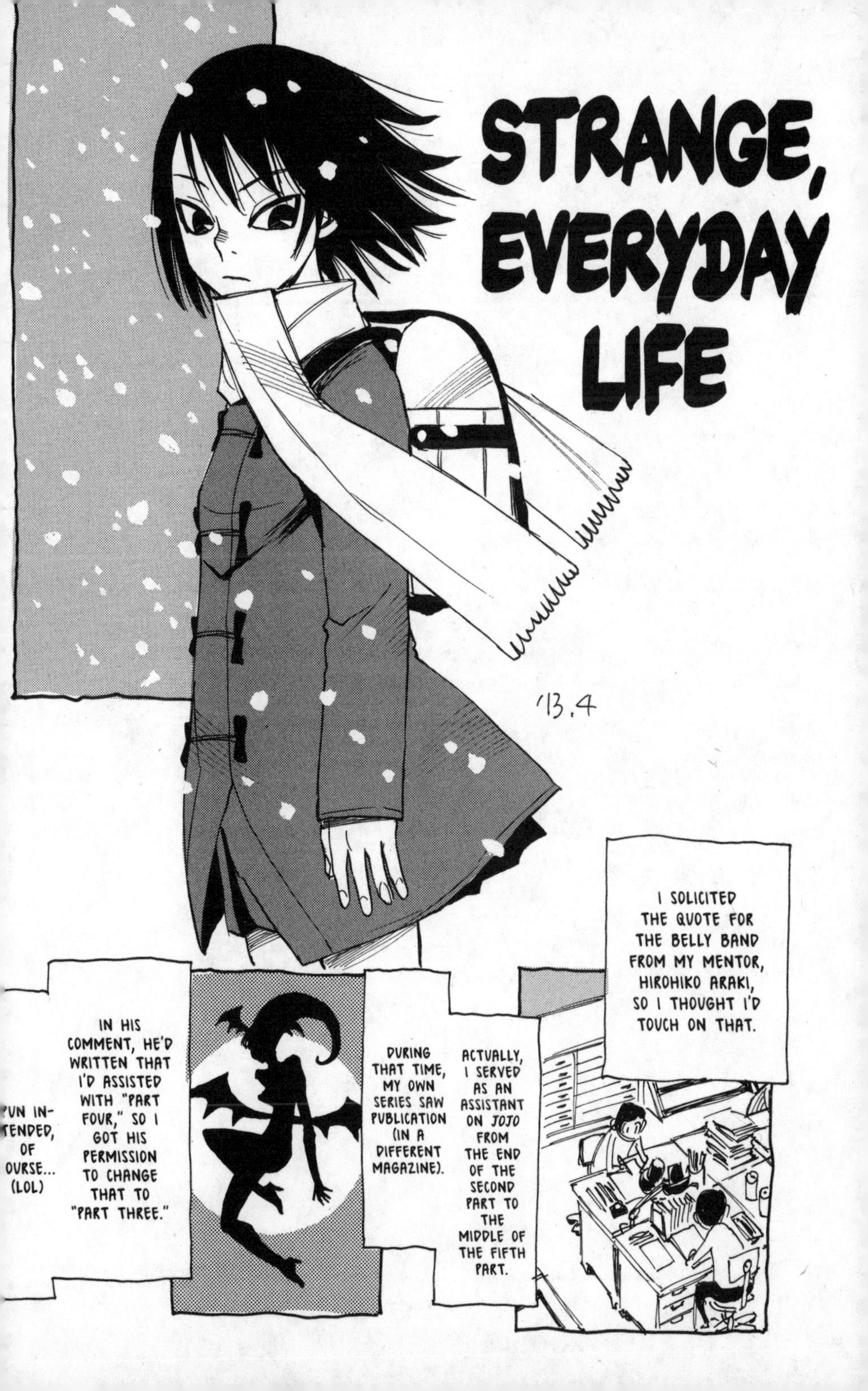
STRANGE, EVERYDAY LIFE
'13.4
I SOLICITED THE QUOTE FOR THE BELLY BAND FROM MY MENTOR, HIROHIKO ARAKI, SO I THOUGHT I'D TOUCH ON THAT.
ACTUALLY, I SERVED AS AN ASSISTANT ON *JOJO* FROM THE END OF THE SECOND PART TO THE MIDDLE OF THE FIFTH PART.
DURING THAT TIME, MY OWN SERIES SAW PUBLICATION (IN A DIFFERENT MAGAZINE).
IN HIS COMMENT, HE'D WRITTEN THAT I'D ASSISTED WITH "PART FOUR," SO I GOT HIS PERMISSION TO CHANGE THAT TO "PART THREE."
UN IN- ENDED, OF OURSE... (LOL)

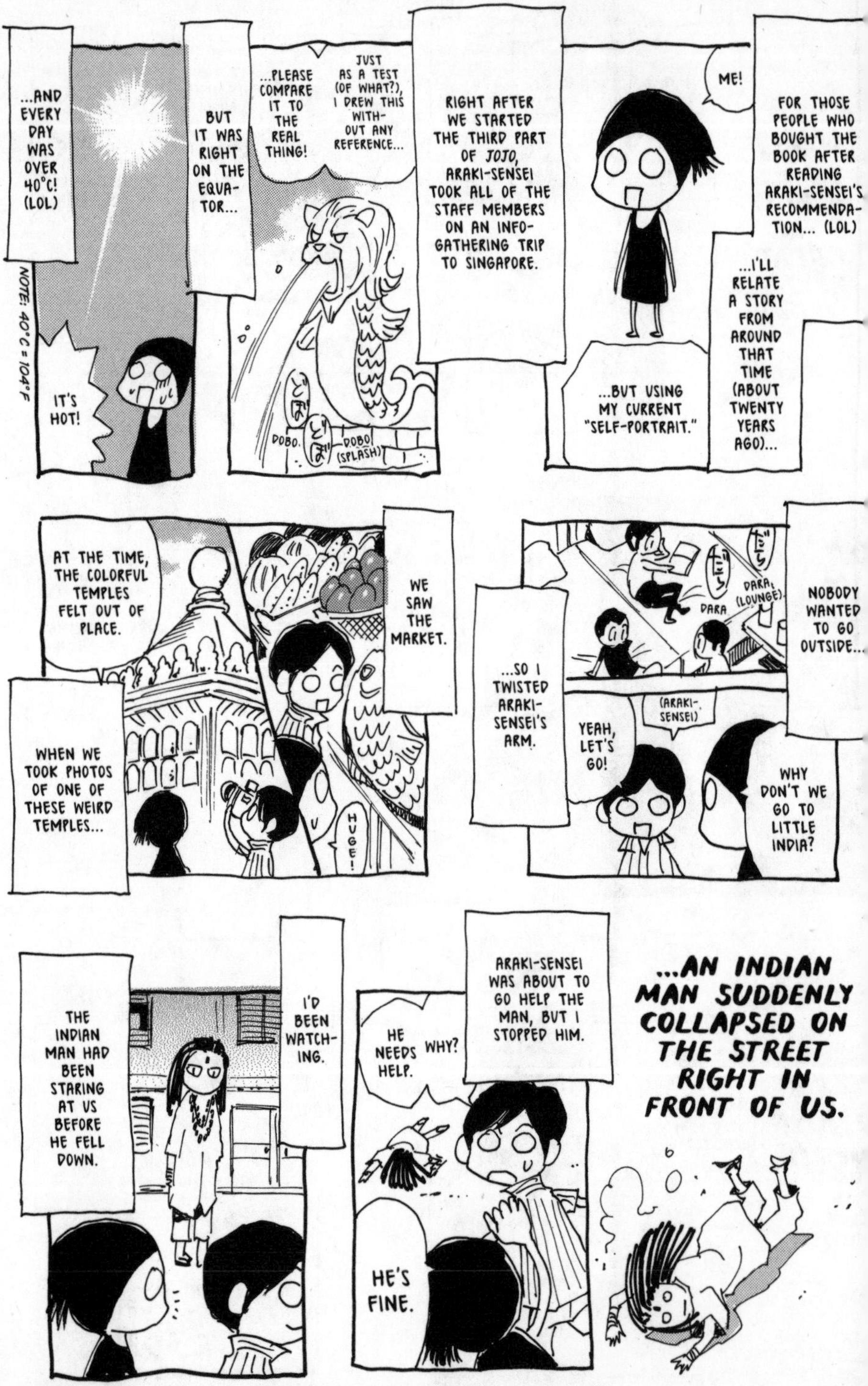
FOR THOSE PEOPLE WHO BOUGHT THE BOOK AFTER READING ARAKI-SENSEI'S RECOMMENDATION... (LOL)
...I'LL RELATE A STORY FROM AROUND THAT TIME (ABOUT TWENTY YEARS AGO)...
ME!
...BUT USING MY CURRENT "SELF-PORTRAIT."
RIGHT AFTER WE STARTED THE THIRD PART OF *JOJO*, ARAKI-SENSEI TOOK ALL OF THE STAFF MEMBERS ON AN INFO-GATHERING TRIP TO SINGAPORE.
JUST AS A TEST (OF WHAT?), I DREW THIS WITHOUT ANY REFERENCE...
...PLEASE COMPARE IT TO THE REAL THING!
DOBO DOBO (SPLASH)
BUT IT WAS RIGHT ON THE EQUATOR...
...AND EVERY DAY WAS OVER 40°C! (LOL)
IT'S HOT!
NOTE: 40°C = 104°F
NOBODY WANTED TO GO OUTSIDE...
DARA DARA (LOUNGE)
WHY DON'T WE GO TO LITTLE INDIA?
(ARAKI-SENSEI)
YEAH, LET'S GO!
...SO I TWISTED ARAKI-SENSEI'S ARM.
WE SAW THE MARKET.
HUGE!
AT THE TIME, THE COLORFUL TEMPLES FELT OUT OF PLACE.
WHEN WE TOOK PHOTOS OF ONE OF THESE WEIRD TEMPLES...
...AN INDIAN MAN SUDDENLY COLLAPSED ON THE STREET RIGHT IN FRONT OF US.
ARAKI-SENSEI WAS ABOUT TO GO HELP THE MAN, BUT I STOPPED HIM.
WHY?
HE NEEDS HELP.
HE'S FINE.
I'D BEEN WATCHING.
THE INDIAN MAN HAD BEEN STARING AT US BEFORE HE FELL DOWN.

ARAKI-SENSEI COMMENTS: "IT SEEMS I'M NOT A VERY ATTENTIVE PERSON. (LOL)"

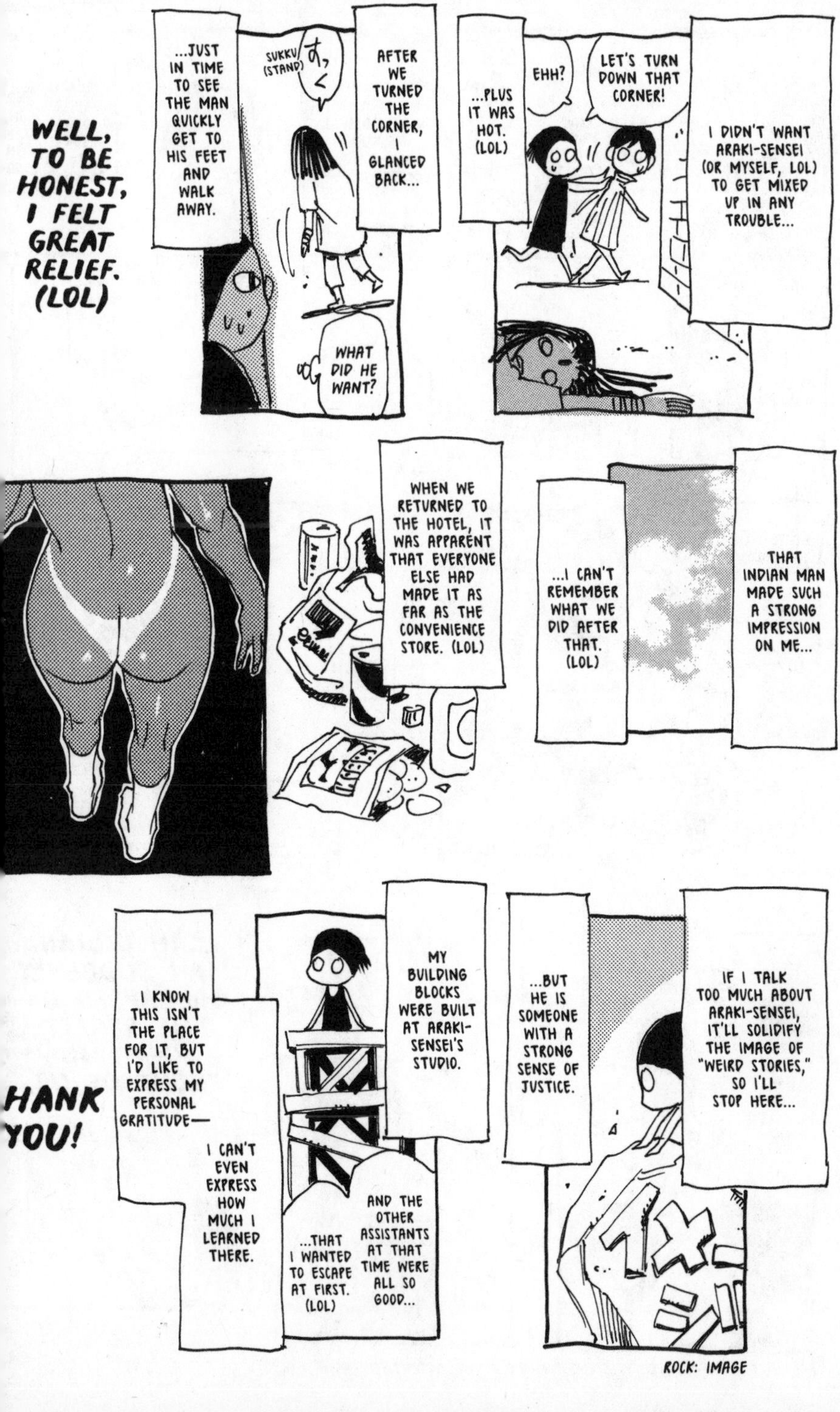
I DIDN'T WANT ARAKI-SENSEI (OR MYSELF, LOL) TO GET MIXED UP IN ANY TROUBLE...
LET'S TURN DOWN THAT CORNER!
EHH?
...PLUS IT WAS HOT. (LOL)
AFTER WE TURNED THE CORNER, I GLANCED BACK...
SUKKU (STAND)
すっく
...JUST IN TIME TO SEE THE MAN QUICKLY GET TO HIS FEET AND WALK AWAY.
WHAT DID HE WANT?
WELL, TO BE HONEST, I FELT GREAT RELIEF. (LOL)
THAT INDIAN MAN MADE SUCH A STRONG IMPRESSION ON ME...
...I CAN'T REMEMBER WHAT WE DID AFTER THAT. (LOL)
WHEN WE RETURNED TO THE HOTEL, IT WAS APPARENT THAT EVERYONE ELSE HAD MADE IT AS FAR AS THE CONVENIENCE STORE. (LOL)
IF I TALK TOO MUCH ABOUT ARAKI-SENSEI, IT'LL SOLIDIFY THE IMAGE OF "WEIRD STORIES," SO I'LL STOP HERE...
...BUT HE IS SOMEONE WITH A STRONG SENSE OF JUSTICE.
MY BUILDING BLOCKS WERE BUILT AT ARAKI-SENSEI'S STUDIO.
AND THE OTHER ASSISTANTS AT THAT TIME WERE ALL SO GOOD...
...THAT I WANTED TO ESCAPE AT FIRST. (LOL)
I KNOW THIS ISN'T THE PLACE FOR IT, BUT I'D LIKE TO EXPRESS MY PERSONAL GRATITUDE—
I CAN'T EVEN EXPRESS HOW MUCH I LEARNED THERE.
HANK YOU!
ROCK: IMAGE

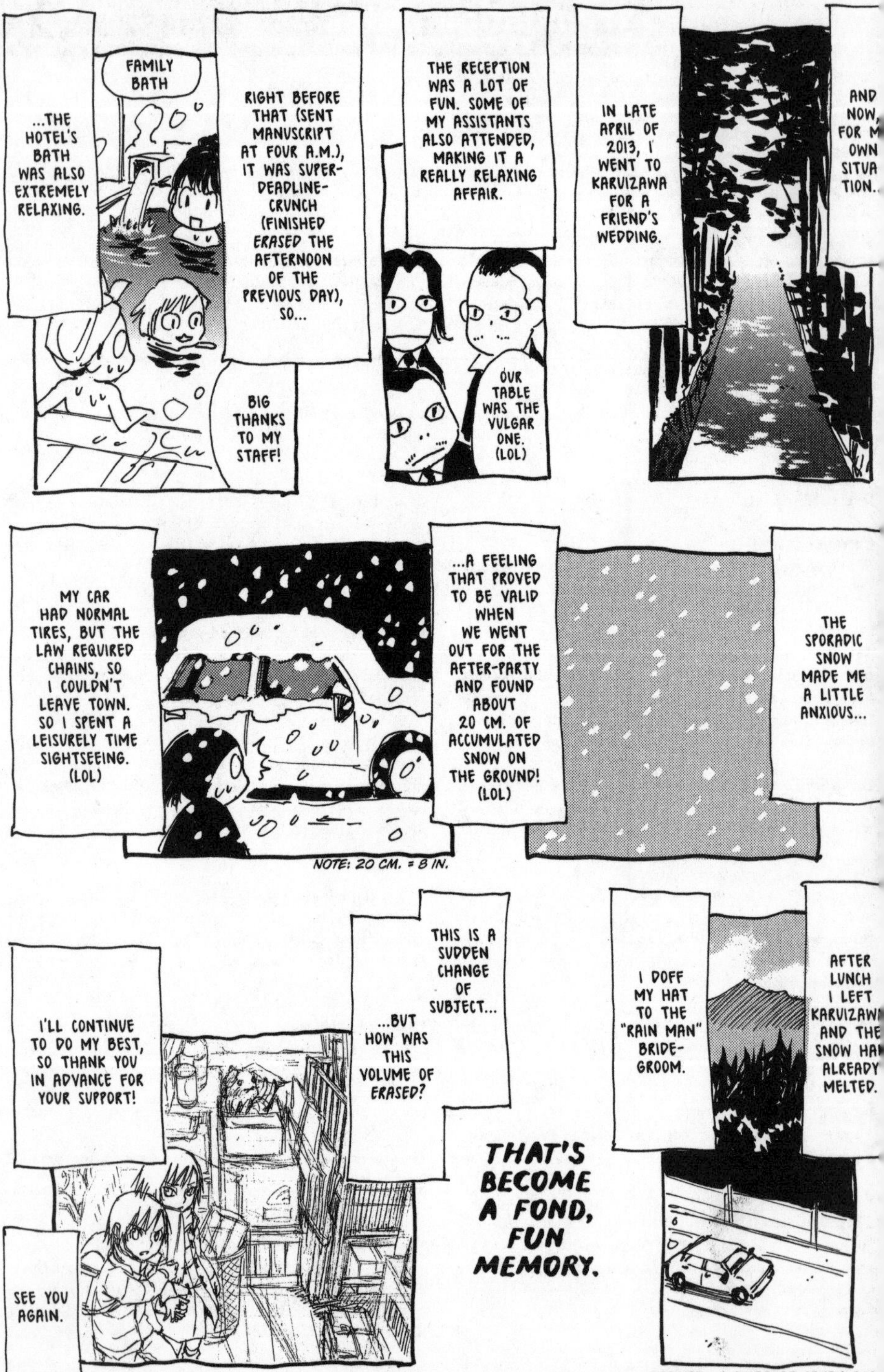
AND NOW, FOR M OWN SITUA TION...
IN LATE APRIL OF 2013, I WENT TO KARUIZAWA FOR A FRIEND'S WEDDING.
THE RECEPTION WAS A LOT OF FUN. SOME OF MY ASSISTANTS ALSO ATTENDED, MAKING IT A REALLY RELAXING AFFAIR.
OUR TABLE WAS THE VULGAR ONE. (LOL)
RIGHT BEFORE THAT (SENT MANUSCRIPT AT FOUR A.M.), IT WAS SUPER-DEADLINE-CRUNCH (FINISHED ERASED THE AFTERNOON OF THE PREVIOUS DAY), SO...
...THE HOTEL'S BATH WAS ALSO EXTREMELY RELAXING.
FAMILY BATH
BIG THANKS TO MY STAFF!
THE SPORADIC SNOW MADE ME A LITTLE ANXIOUS...
...A FEELING THAT PROVED TO BE VALID WHEN WE WENT OUT FOR THE AFTER-PARTY AND FOUND ABOUT 20 CM. OF ACCUMULATED SNOW ON THE GROUND! (LOL)
MY CAR HAD NORMAL TIRES, BUT THE LAW REQUIRED CHAINS, SO I COULDN'T LEAVE TOWN. SO I SPENT A LEISURELY TIME SIGHTSEEING. (LOL)
NOTE: 20 CM. = 8 IN.
AFTER LUNCH I LEFT KARUIZAW AND THE SNOW HA ALREADY MELTED.
I DOFF MY HAT TO THE "RAIN MAN" BRIDE-GROOM.
ARRIVED IN CHIBA AT SEVEN P.M.
THAT'S BECOME A FOND, FUN MEMORY.
THIS IS A SUDDEN CHANGE OF SUBJECT...
...BUT HOW WAS THIS VOLUME OF ERASED?
I'LL CONTINUE TO DO MY BEST, SO THANK YOU IN ADVANCE FOR YOUR SUPPORT!
SEE YOU AGAIN.

Translation notes

Common Honorifics

no honorific: Indicates familiarity or closeness; if used without permission or reason, addressing someone in this manner would constitute an insult.

-san: The Japanese equivalent of Mr./Mrs./Miss. If a situation calls for politeness, this is the fail-safe honorific.

-sama: Conveys great respect; may also indicate the social status of the speaker is lower than that of the addressee.

-kun: Used most often when referring to boys, this indicates affection or familiarity. Occasionally used by older men among their peers, but it may also be used by anyone referring to a person of lower standing.

-chan: An affectionate honorific indicating familiarity used mostly in reference to girls; also used in reference to cute persons or animals of either gender.

-sensei: A respectful term for teachers, artists, or high-level professionals.

Currency Conversion

While conversion rates fluctuate daily, an easy estimate for Japanese yen conversion is ¥100 to 1 USD.

Page 64

Youkai: A term that encompasses all types of Japanese folk creatures, ghosts, and other supernatural entities. Satoru doesn't reference a specific *youkai* here but implies (sarcastically) that his mother's ageless appearance is because she's some sort of supernatural being.

Hakuhou: Shou Hakuhou, a professional sumo wrestler from Mongolia. Hakuhou made his debut in 2001 and was elevated to the highest sumo rank, yokozuna, in 2007.

Ozeki rank: Second-highest sumo ranking, just under yokozuna. To attain this status, a sekiwake-ranked wrestler (third-highest tier) must generally win thirty-three matches over three consecutive tournaments; winning a tournament, defeating higher-ranked wrestlers, and other factors may also contribute to promotion.

Miyabiyama: Tetsushi Miyabiyama, a sumo wrestler who debuted in 1998, attained the rank of ozeki and retired in 2013.

Page 70

Yuuki: *"Yuuki"* means "courage," a trait Jun Shiratori espoused so much that Satoru made it into his nickname.

Page 74

Tokusatsu: Literally "special filming," this term generally applies to live-action, special effects-oriented TV shows and movies, particularly *kaiju* (giant monster) movies and superhero TV serials such as *Kamen Rider* and *Super Sentai* (*Power Rangers*).

Page 123

Narashino: Small city in Western Chiba, less than twenty miles from Tokyo.

Page 127

Bicycle safety law: Although it's fairly common to see two people riding a single-seater bike with one person sitting sidesaddle on the bag rack, it is illegal and carries a potential fine of ¥20,000.

Page 140

Takoyaki: Popular "street snack" that originated in Osaka. Essentially a small fried ball of wheat-flour batter with a piece of boiled octopus inside.

Page 142

"Good work!": It's customary to "compliment" workers upon their return to the place of business after being out on the job. This also applies when an employee is leaving work before their coworkers.

Page 146

Era names: The Showa period lasted from 1926-1989, and the Heisei period began on January 8, 1989, the day after Emperor Hirohito's death. His son, Akihito, then ascended the throne as emperor.

Page 150

Statute of limitations: The statute of limitations for murder was an astonishing fifteen years in 2006, the setting of this story's "present" time period, but was abolished altogether in 2010.

Page 161

"This isn't Hokkaido!": This reaction is based on the assumptions of country vs. city living; in a rural area like Hokkaido, it might be presumed safe enough to leave one's front door unlocked.

Page 201

Classroom helpers: In many Japanese schools students take turns assisting with various classroom duties, such as trash removal, cleaning blackboards, collecting printouts, collecting lunch money, and so on.

Page 215

Hamburg steak: A fried steak patty formed from ground beef or pork and breadcrumbs.

Page 302

School lunch: Rather than eating lunch in a common cafeteria, in many elementary schools, student helpers are responsible for collecting the school lunch from the kitchens, bringing it back to their classrooms, and serving lunch to their classmates.